Brasil! Brasil!

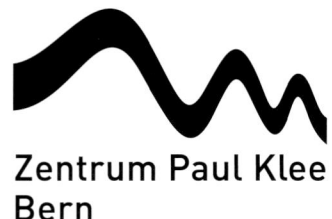

Zentrum Paul Klee
Bern

RA Royal
Academy
of Arts

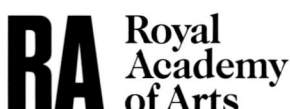

snoeck

Brasil! Brasil!

The Birth
of Modernism

Foreword

Nina Zimmer
Director Kunstmuseum Bern –
Zentrum Paul Klee

The exhibition *Brasil! Brasil! The Birth of Modernism* originated in an earlier project. For the team at the Zentrum Paul Klee, engaging with Brazilian modernism began in 2019 with the major Paul Klee retrospective *Equilíbrio Instável* (Unstable Equilibrium) that we realized at three venues in São Paulo, Rio de Janeiro, and Belo Horizonte, Brazil. The public's overwhelming interest in Paul Klee and his significance for the development of modernism there opened our eyes to the dynamic and diverse Brazilian art scene that is still relatively unknown in this country due to our deeply entrenched Eurocentric view of art history.

For some time, there has been a growing interest in questions related to the phenomenon of global modernism. At the Zentrum Paul Klee, we have also endeavoured to shift the focus to modernism outside Europe with exhibitions such as *Bauhaus Imaginista, Etel Adnan*, and *Hamed Abdalla*. We continue to expand this horizon with the exhibition *Brasil! Brasil! The Birth of Modernism*, and, for the first time in Switzerland, provide a comprehensive overview of modern Brazilian art. The current show offers the unique opportunity to discover the work of ten Brazilian artists active in the first half of the twentieth century who are only occasionally represented in European exhibitions and collections. In Brazil itself, the view of Brazilian modernism has broadened in recent years, and artists who were long ignored in art history are now receiving attention. The main exhibition at this year's Venice Biennale, the 60th International Art Exhibition, was likewise dedicated to expanding the canon. In this respect, the appointment of the Brazilian curator Adriano Pedrosa and the great international attention drawn by his concept *Foreigners Everywhere* – which encompassed some of the artists in our exhibition – was a fortunate coincidence.

Brasil! Brasil!

My sincere thanks go to the curators who initiated and realized this project together: Fabienne Eggelhöfer, chief curator of the Zentrum Paul Klee, Bern, and Roberta Saraiva Coutinho, Director of the Museu da Língua Portuguesa, São Paulo. Their collaboration began with the extremely successful Klee exhibition in Brazil, and after it proved successful, they seamlessly transitioned to the preparation for the Brazilian exhibition in Bern. With great passion and perseverance, they led a continual transatlantic Swiss-Brazilian dialogue with their respective teams to conceive, research, and ultimately realize this exhibition.

I would also like to thank our partner, the Royal Academy of Arts, London, where the exhibition will be on view from January 28 to April 21, 2025. I am grateful to Secretary and Chief Executive Axel Rüger, Director of Exhibitions Andrea Tarsia, and Chief Curator Adrian Locke for the enjoyable collaboration and the wonderful opportunity to present the exhibition to a wider British public.

Special thanks go to Her Excellency Cláudia Fonseca Buzzi, Ambassador of Brazil to Switzerland and Liechtenstein, for her accompanying support in the preparation of the exhibition.

For the financial support of this exhibition, which is ambitious in every respect, we thank the Canton of Bern, the Federal Office of Culture (BAK), Swisslos, the Museumsstiftung für Kunst der Burgergemeinde Bern, the Ruth & Arthur Scherbarth Foundation, the Ursula Wirz Foundation and Banco Itaú Suisse SA.

Foreword

Foreword

Rebecca Salter PRA
President, Royal Academy of Arts

In November 1944 the Royal Academy hosted the first – and still the largest – exhibition of modern Brazilian paintings to have taken place in Britain. *The Daily Telegraph* remarked that it brought "an exotic richness to the walls of Burlington House". A diplomatic initiative, the show comprised 168 paintings and works on paper donated by Brazilian artists for sale in aid of the Royal Air Force Benevolent Fund. Alongside, in adjacent galleries, *Brazil Builds*, a separate photographic exhibition focusing on the history of architecture in Brazil, had been transferred to the Royal Academy from the Museum of Modern Art in New York where it had been shown the previous year. It feels extremely apposite that *Brasil! Brasil! The Birth of Modernism*, which explores the emergence of modern art in Brazil through the work of ten artists, should be hosted by the Royal Academy in 2025, and that it should include four paintings by three artists who originally showed work at Burlington House just over eighty years ago.

The exhibition is the initiative of the Zentrum Paul Klee in Bern, and we thank Nina Zimmer, its Director, for facilitating this partnership with the Royal Academy. *Brasil! Brasil! The Birth of Modernism* has been skilfully curated by Fabienne Eggelhöfer, Chief Curator of the Zentrum Paul Klee, and Roberta Saraiva Coutinho, Director of the Museu da Língua Portuguesa, São Paulo, with the assistance of Registrar Svenja Eckell and Curatorial Assistant Myriam Dössegger in Bern and Registrar Patrícia Betti Queiroz in São Paulo. We thank them and all their colleagues at the Zentrum Paul Klee and in Brazil. We are extremely grateful to all our public and private lenders in Brazil and Switzerland, not least because a significant number of their loans have never been seen outside Brazil before. We acknowledge all the contributors to this elegant catalogue, which has been assembled by Snoeck Verlagsgesellschaft.

At the Royal Academy, Adrian Locke, Chief Curator, has added some additional works to reflect the holdings of British public collections and to capture the essence of the 1944 exhibition; two works in particular (p. 127 and 105) were purchased by the British Council from the exhibition and presented to the National Galleries of Scotland in 1945 and the Mercer Art Gallery, Harrogate, in 1946. To deliver this project, Adrian Locke has worked alongside Rebecca Bray, Assistant Curator; Natasha Fyffe, Genesis Future Curator; Idoya Beitia, Head of Exhibitions; Flora Fricker, Senior Exhibitions Manager; Helena Cooper, Assistant Exhibitions Manager; Giulia Ariete, Rights and Repro Manager; the Royal Academy's art handlers, led by Max Holder; and the AV team under Benji Fox. We thank Tate, the National Galleries of Scotland, the Royal Academy of Arts, the Mercer Art Gallery, Harrogate, Museum & Art Swindon, the Swiss National Library, Bern, the Kirkland Collection, the Fundação Edson Queiroz, Fortaleza and those private collectors who wish to remain anonymous, for their support through the additional loans in London. Furthermore, we acknowledge the help and support of Axel Rüger, Secretary and Chief Executive, Andrea Tarsia, Director of Exhibitions, and Stephen Chambers RA, Chair of the Royal Academy's Exhibitions Committee. The exhibition has been designed by Carla Juaçaba with graphic design by Marina Willer and Cleber de Campos of Pentagram, and lighting design by David Atkinson Lighting Design Ltd.

We thank His Excellency Antonio de Aguiar Patriota, Ambassador of Brazil to the United Kingdom of Great Britain and Northern Ireland, and Secretary Ana Flavia Jacintho Bonzanini, Head of the Cultural Section at the Embassy of Brazil in London, for their enthusiastic support of the project. In addition, we express our gratitude to Hayle Gadelha, previous Head of the Cultural Section, and author of *Public Diplomacy on the Front Line: The Exhibition of Modern Brazilian Paintings*, a comprehensive study of the 1944 exhibition, for his help and guidance. Finally, we thank our friends and supporters who have worked alongside us to realise this exhibition.

Foreword

Acknowledgements

The exhibition would not have been possible without the generosity of numerous individuals and private and public institutions. We extend our warmest thanks to the following private collectors and institutions, in Fortaleza: Edson Queiroz Neto, Igor Queiroz, Lenise Queiroz Rocha, President of the Fundação Edson Queiroz, in Maceió: Maria Fernanda Vilela, in Rio de Janeiro: Carlos Alberto Gouvêa Chateaubriand, Conrado Mesquita and Camila Guarita, Hecilda and Marta Fadel, Leonel Kaz, Luciana and Luis Antonio de Almeida Braga, Luís Paulo Montenegro, Luiz Carlos Ritter, Max Perlingeiro, Ronaldo Cezar Coelho, Victor Adler, in São Paulo: Alfredo und Daniela Villela, Ana Eliza und Paulo Setúbal, Carlos Dale Jr. und Antônio Almeida, Directors of the Almeida & Dale Galeria de Arte, Carol and Flavio Veitzman, Eduardo Monteiro, Director of the Fundação Maria Luisa e Oscar Americano, Eduardo Saron, President of the Fundação Itaú, Fabiana and Lenora de Barros as well as Michel Favre, Fábio Faisal, Mauris Ilia Klabin Warchavchik, Orandi Momesso, Paulo Segall, Sofia Fan, Head of Visual Arts and Archives, Itaú Cultural, and several anonymous private collectors.

Our profound gratitude is likewise extended to the following public institutions and their staff: Rodolfo Ernani Beltrão Silva, Director, Centro Cultural São Paulo; Monica Dantas, Director and Bianca Dettino, Collection Manager, Instituto de Estudos Brasileiros da Universidade de São Paulo; Fernanda Celidonio, Director and Laura Rodríguez, Head of Collection and Archive, Museu de Arte Brasileira, São Paulo; Adriano Pedrosa, Director and Regina Teixeira de Barros, Chief Curator, Museu de Arte de São Paulo; Paulo Vieira, President of the Board and Pablo Lafuente, Artistic Director, Museu de Arte Moderna, Rio de Janeiro; Marcelo Monzani, previous Director and Paulo Lima, current Director, Museu Lasar Segall, São Paulo; Daniela Matera Lins, Director, Museu Nacional de Belas Artes, IBRAM, Rio de Janeiro; Jochen Volz, Director, Pinacoteca, São Paulo; Damian Elsig, Director, Swiss National Library, Bern; Fabien Dubosson and Vincent Yersin, Swiss Literature Archive, Bern.

In addition, the Royal Academy extends its thanks to the following private collectors and institutions for their support of its presentation in London: Maria Balshaw, Catherine Wood, Tobias Ostrander, Carol Burnier, and Martha Greenhough, Tate, London; Adam Waterton, Edwina Mulvany, Martha Graves, and Jennifer Camilleri, Royal Academy of Arts, London; Anne Lyden, Patrick Elliott, and Jacqui Austin, National Galleries Scotland, Edinburgh; Katie Ackrill, Museum & Art Swindon; Karen Southworth, Mercer Art Gallery, Harrogate; and Jack Kirkland and Flor Souto of The Kirkland Collection as well as lenders who want to remain anonymous. The Royal Academy would also like to acknowledge the help and support of the following individuals: Paulo Kuczynski, Escritório de Arte, São Paulo; Cecilia Brunson, Cecilia Brunson Projects, London; Alex Sainsbury and Oliver Williams, Raven Row, London; Eduardo Brigagão and Peter Sawbridge.

In our search for the works, we received the extraordinary steadfast support from Max Perlingeiro of Pinakotheke Cultural in Rio de Janeiro. We are grateful for his generous support locating and managing loans from collections in different cities across the country. We also thank Erica Schmatz and Paul Jenkins from Almeida & Dale Galeria de Arte in São Paulo as well as Fabiana de Barros and Michel Favre of the Geraldo de Barros Estate in Geneva. For the organization of the loans we thank Patrícia Betti Queiroz, loan coordinator in Brazil, Svenja Eckell from the Zentrum Paul Klee in Bern and Idoya Beitia, Flora Fricker, Helena Cooper, and Giulia Ariete at the Royal Academy in London as well as Bruna Araújo from Pinakotheke Cultural in Rio de Janeiro.

Over the past four years, a great number of individuals and institutions offered support and enthusiasm that contributed meaningfully to our efforts. We wish to thank: Aracy Amaral, Flávia Toni, Jorge Schwartz, Marcelo Mattos Araujo, Raphael Fonseca, Valeria Piccoli.

As an important record of the project and a lasting scholarly resource, the catalog features the insightful contributions of outstanding Brazilian scholars: Alecsandra Matias de Oliveira, Ana Paula Cavalcanti Simioni, Cacá Machado, Eduardo Jorge de Oliveira, Genêse Andrade, Giancarlo Hannud, Guilherme Wisnik, Jacob Klintowitz, Maria Alice Milliet. Special thanks also to Myriam Dössegger for the coordination of this highly complex editorial project and to Eduardo Jorge de Oliveira for the thorough copy editing of the essays. We are indebted to the expert translations by Adriana Francisco and Sarah McGavran, the meticulous and thoughtful proof reading of Susie Hondl, and the exciting design of Flávia Nalon and Fábio Prata. We are particularly grafteful to Andrea Bolanho for organizing the images and clearing the copyright. We commend the Snoeck Verlagsgesellschaft, specifically Andreas Balze, for their enthusiastic commitment to bringing forward the results of this study in a quality, scholarly publication.

We thank the entire staff at the Zentrum Paul Klee and the Royal Academy for the unwavering support and their contribution to the successful realization of this project.

Nina Zimmer, Director Kunstmuseum Bern – Zentrum Paul Klee
Axel Rüger, Secretary and Chief Executive Royal Academy of Arts
Fabienne Eggelhöfer, Chief Curator Zentrum Paul Klee
Roberta Saraiva Coutinho, co-curator
Adrian Locke, Chief Curator Royal Academy of Arts

9   # Acknowledgements

Table of Contents

Brasil! Brasil!

Brasil! Brasil!
The Birth of Modernism

Fabienne Eggelhöfer
Roberta Saraiva Coutinho

Le Brésil est un Grand Etat Moderne en formation. Plus que n'importe quel autre Etat, il a besoin de se faire connaître.
Blaise Cendrars, 1924[1]

Exactly one hundred years ago, the Swiss writer Blaise Cendrars sketched out a plan for a propaganda film about Brazil. His aim was to make Brazil, which was becoming a modern state, known around the world. Modern Brazilian art, which played a decisive role in the country's development, is relatively unknown in Europe today. With the exhibition *Brasil! Brasil! The Birth of Modernism*, we aim to help the European public gain a greater understanding of this art and the context in which it was created.

As Cendrars noted, at the beginning of the twentieth century, Brazil was a young nation in the process of forging its own identity. In 1822, Brazil became independent from Portugal. Only seventy-seven years later, in 1889, it became a republic with the city of Rio de Janeiro as its capital. The population consisted mostly of Indigenous groups; formerly enslaved people, most of whom had roots in West Africa; Portuguese colonisers; and migrants from all over Europe. And soon immigrants would come to Brazil from Japan as well. In view of the heterogenous population with its diverse cultures, the construction of an independent national identity would prove to be an exceptional challenge.

In the early twentieth century, Brazil profited from having all but a monopoly on the worldwide coffee trade. The coffee was shipped from the city of Santos in the state of São Paulo, drawing immigrants from other parts of the country and leading to the city's rapid expansion. Rubber extraction in the Amazon and sugarcane production in the northeast had declined. Slavery was banned in Brazil in 1888 – relatively late compared to other countries in the Americas. Many of the formerly enslaved people and exploited workers then migrated to São Paulo to take advantage of the economic boom there.

In 1922, one of the most influential oligarchs, the coffee magnate Paulo Prado, financed a week of cultural events, the so-called *Semana de Arte Moderna* (Modern Art Week), to transform the economic centre of São Paulo into the capital of modern artistic movements as well. Until then, Rio de Janeiro had been the political and cultural capital. The significance of the two cities – Rio de Janeiro and São Paulo – for the development of modern art remains fiercely debated in Brazil to this day. As scholars reassess this history, motivated in part by the recent centennial of the *Semana de Arte Moderna*, many now emphasise that there were artistic efforts to develop contemporary forms and subject matter throughout Brazil.

At the outset of the twentieth century, artists realised that the style imposed by the Portuguese colonisers was in keeping neither with the times nor the young Brazilian nation. As in Europe, they wanted to overcome the nineteenth-century canon of classical, academic art, which was highly institutionalised. It is, therefore, hardly surprising that they sought dialogue with their European contemporaries. As a result of World War I and World War II, many Europeans immigrated to Brazil. The Lithuanian artist Lasar Segall, who lived in Germany until 1923, is one example featured in our exhibition. Some artists, who came from wealthy families in Brazil or who received travel fellowships, were able to afford longer stays in European cities. Anita Malfatti, for instance, spent time in Berlin while Tarsila do Amaral, Candido Portinari, Vicente do Rego Monteiro, and Geraldo de Barros lived in Paris. Their exploration of European avant-garde art, especially Expressionism, Futurism, and Cubism, made its mark on their work. Back in Brazil, however, all of them strove to create a modern Brazilian art. The aforementioned Blaise Cendrars provided one impetus for turning away from Europe and toward their own past and present. In the 1920s, Paulo Prado invited him to Brazil three times. Together with the artist Tarsila do Amaral and her husband, the writer Oswald de Andrade, and others, he travelled through Brazil in 1924, and was completely overcome by the Afro-Brazilian culture in Rio de Janeiro and the Baroque in Minas Gerais. In lectures, Cendrars impressed Brazilian audiences by praising the engagement with African cultures in European avant-garde circles. This was also the source of his fascination with Afro-Brazilian traditions, including samba and carnival, which his Brazilian companions dismissed as mere popular culture. Cendrars was critical to furthering a new understanding of these forms of expression as cultural touchstones.

Shortly thereafter, in 1924, Oswald de Andrade published a poetic manifesto in the newspaper *Correio da Manhã*. The title, *Pau-Brasil* means Brazilian wood and refers to one of Brazil's most important export goods from the colonial period. To counter the import of European artistic ideas, he advocated for the export of Brazilian poetry to Europe. In his poetry, he combined high and popular culture, incorporating elements from everyday life and spoken language, and thereby gave a voice to living Brazilian culture. Four years later, his *Manifesto Antropófago* (Anthropophagic Manifesto, 1928) was inspired by conversations with

Brasil! Brasil!

Tarsila do Amaral and by her painting *Abaporu* (fig. 1, p. 66), also of the same year. The title means "man, who eats man" in the language of the Indigenous Tupi-Guarani people. In the *Manifesto Antropófago* he calls for the consumption of foreign European culture, for it to be digested in a sense, so that it could be transformed into an independent Brazilian art. The manifesto was de Andrade's response to the *Semana de Arte Moderna*, which he considered, from a distance, to be a manifestation of ideas imported from Europe.

The Brazilian avant-garde then appropriated motifs from Indigenous and Afro-Brazilian cultures. Unlike the Europeans, however, they were not motivated by the idea of breaking with prevailing artistic traditions and searching for a supposedly original, universal visual language. In Brazil, the engagement with Indigenous cultures was much rather about going back to the roots and appreciating the country's cultural history before European colonisation. Thus, the *Manifesto Antropófago* is primarily to be understood as a "subversive act (...), as a revolt of the colonised against the colonisers."[2]

As in Europe, those who initially adopted these forms of Indigenous visual expression and Afro-Brazilian rituals were from the upper classes who exploited these peoples for profit. From today's perspective, this is seen as problematic, as in the more recent art historical research on Tarsila do Amaral. Indeed, through this cultural lens, the Indigenous and Afro-Brazilian populations of Brazil are presented as idealised objects while their difficult life circumstances are ignored. A second generation of modern artists shown in our exhibition, who descended from Indigenous or enslaved African peoples and came from more modest backgrounds, such as Djanira da Motta e Silva and Rubem Valentim, drew upon personal experience to articulate social inequalities.

In 1929, the stock market crash led to a collapse in coffee prices, which contributed significantly to the Revolution of 1930. The people rebelled against the oligarchical system of the wealthy few, and the military installed the populist Getúlio Vargas as president; he established a dictatorship in 1937. His concept of the Estado Novo, borrowed from Portuguese Salazarism, was defined by nationalism, authoritarianism, centralism, and a certain social reformism. Many artists, including Candido Portinari and Tarsila do Amaral, responded by turning to social themes rendered in a more realistic style. When both the dictatorship and World War II ended in 1945, the country began to open up again. Artists once more cultivated a lively exchange with other countries, and the first museums for modern art in Brazil were opened.

By the 1950s, a national consciousness seems to have emerged. It is reflected in varied movements, such as the second generation of modern artists, who addressed themes characteristic of the Brazilian context, including race, religion, and work. Later, it was also expressed in Concrete and Neo-Concrete art and the *Tropicália* movement, as well as in architecture and music. Modern Brazilian architecture reached its apex with the construction of the new capital Brasília, designed by Lúcio Costa and Oscar Niemeyer, between 1956 and 1960. In music, bossa nova, an international export of *brasilidade*, became a hit. The military coup of 1964 established a violent nationalist and anti-communist dictatorship. A new era began in Brazil, during which artists addressed political and social oppression.

Within this complex, and, as in Europe, economically and politically unstable context, the development of modernism in Brazil is a particularly compelling example of global modernism. The exhibition explores ten artists who emerged in the first half of the twentieth century and reveal different facets of Brazilian modernism: Anita Malfatti (1889–1964), Vicente do Rego Monteiro (1899–1970), Tarsila do Amaral (1886–1973), Lasar Segall (1889–1957), Candido Portinari (1903–1962), Flávio de Carvalho (1899–1973), Alfredo Volpi (1896–1988), Djanira da Motta e Silva (1914–1979), Rubem Valentim (1922–1991), and Geraldo de Barros (1923–1998). This focus was important to us, because it allowed us to present several works by each artist, thus revealing their artistic trajectories.[3] The public should have the opportunity to immerse themselves in each artist's oeuvre and to understand what they contributed to the diversity of Brazilian modernism. This multiplicity is also reflected by the fact that in Brazil today, one speaks of "Modernismos" – or modernisms in plural. These diverse artistic perspectives are intended to demonstrate just how varied the search for a Brazilian culture was in a place where plurality is understood to be part of its DNA. This also meant foregoing artists who already belong to the canon or those whose significance was first highlighted by researchers in more recent years.

Anita Malfatti, Vicente do Rego Monteiro, Tarsila do Amaral, Lasar Segall, and Candido Portinari have long been established as part of the Brazilian modernist canon. They also cultivated connections with the European avant-garde and, to a certain extent, discovered aspects of Brazilian culture from the outside perspective of European intellectuals. For example, Tarsila do Amaral only began to appropriate motifs from Afro-Brazilian cultures after the Swiss writer Blaise Cendrars visited Brazil. Anita Malfatti and Vicente do Rego Monteiro both exhibited works in the aforementioned *Semana de Arte Moderna* in 1922, which has long been regarded as the beginning of Brazilian modernism. Whereas Malfatti's visual language was shaped by European Expressionism and thus provoked fierce resistance at her first exhibition in Brazil in 1917, Rego Monteiro was interested in Indigenous cultures quite early on, which he encountered indirectly in books and museums. Upon his immigration, Lasar Segall was struck by the Indigenous and Afro-Brazilian peoples and the lush nature, as were many of his European predecessors.

We have also selected five artists who did not belong to the canon: Flávio de Carvalho, Alfredo Volpi, Djanira da Motta e Silva, Rubem Valentim, and Geraldo de Barros. Since they were not classically trained, their work was long regarded as "primitive" or "popular". Volpi and Djanira found their subject matter in traditional customs, such as village festivals and rituals. Similarly, Valentim integrated symbols including the arrow, triangle, circle, and axe, which are anchored in the rituals of Candomblé, an Afro-Brazilian religion. Unlike the other artists, however, they were not mere observers but members of these cultures. De Carvalho moved between the visual arts, architecture, design, and performance, making his work difficult to categorise. His actions (*Experiências*), which called social norms into question, elicited strong reactions. He also painted expressionist-style portraits of women in provocative, self-confident poses, which likewise were met with a great deal of incomprehension. Like de Carvalho, Geraldo de Barros embraced furniture design and architecture, making it difficult to categorise him neatly within the art historical canon as well.

De Barros represents a transition to Concrete art, which shaped Brazilian culture from the 1950s onward. Like Rubem Valentim, he became interested in Paul Klee early on and visited Klee exhibitions at the Kunstmuseum Bern during his sojourns in Switzerland. This connection to Klee, which is also shared by Lasar Segall, who lived in Germany before his immigration to Brazil, did not inform our selection of the ten artists. Rather, our aim was to choose a variety of approaches to demonstrate that, as in other countries, the development of art in Brazil was neither linear nor isolated. This is in keeping with the multi-layered processes of cultural transfer that took place between Brazil and Europe as well as among different cultures within Brazil.

1 "Brazil is a great modern state in formation. More than any other state, it must make itself known." In: Blaise Cendrars, *Suggestions pour la réalisation d'un grand film de propagande brésilien*, 1924, Archives littéraires suisses (ALS). Fonds Blaise Cendrars, Inv. Nr. P41

2 Sperling 2011, p. 190

3 Andrade 2022b

Anita Malfatti

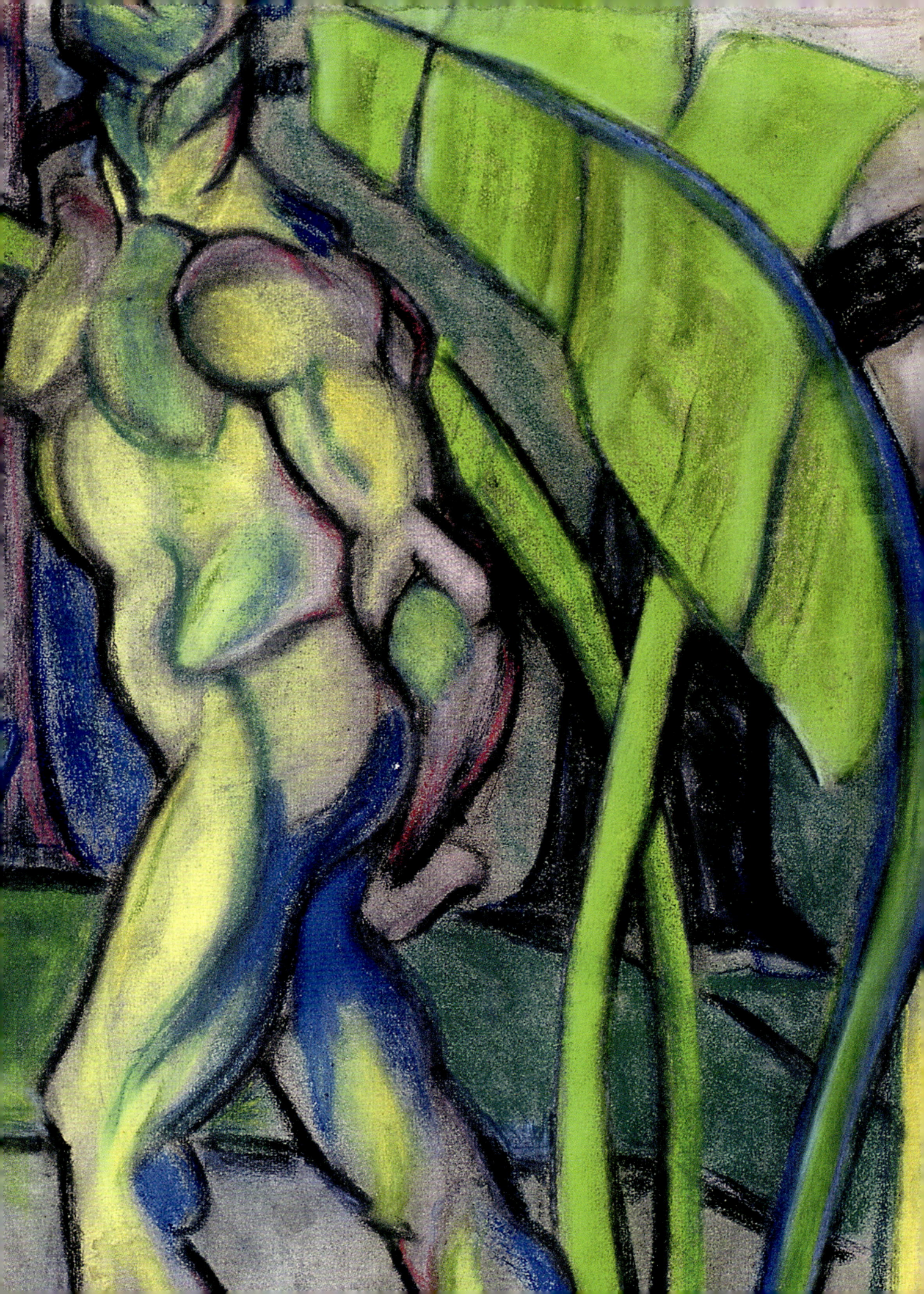

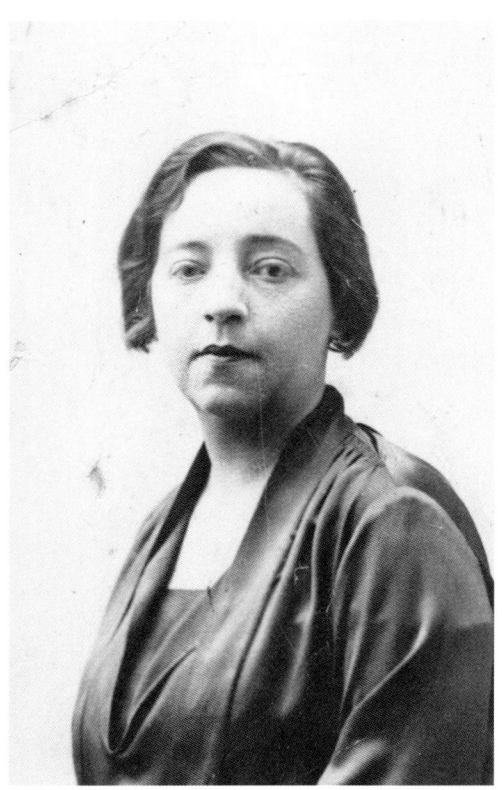

Anita Malfatti
1889, São Paulo, Brazil –
1964, São Paulo, Brazil

Born into a middle-class family of the burgeoning immigrant community that Brazil, particularly the city of São Paulo, saw flourish in the last years of the nineteenth and early decades of the twentieth century, Anita Malfatti was the end-result of the intertwining of diverse heritages: on her father's side Catholic and Italian and on her mother's Protestant and German American. Malfatti, the couple's second child, was born on 2 December 1889, a few weeks after the coup that deposed the emperor Dom Pedro II and instituted the French-inspired First Republic. With the death of her father in 1901, the Malfatti family knew a steep decline in fortune. They moved into Malfatti's grandparents' house, and her mother was forced to teach language classes and painting to make a living. Her mother was Malfatti's first teacher, her earliest surviving artistic experiences dating to around 1909. However, her first opportunity to seriously study painting came along when the Shalders, friends of the family, decided to move to Germany to pursue musical studies. Financed by her maternal uncle Jorge Krug, who after the death of her father played a central role in her education, she moved with them to Berlin in 1910, where she would remain until 1914. On the occasion of her departure, her uncle reportedly told her to "never accept the mediocre."[1]

In Berlin Malfatti at first attended classes at the Königliches Kunstgewerbemuseum but would soon abandon them to study drawing with Fritz Burger. She would eventually seek Lovis Corinth's counsel in painting, becoming his pupil in around 1912. She was treated kindly by Corinth, by all accounts a teacher of mercurial temperament. She would also train with Ernst Bischoff-Kulm. The Sonderbund exhibition held in Cologne in 1912 was yet another formative experience for Malfatti. In it the young artist encountered over 600 paintings and one hundred sculptures from the likes of Vincent Van Gogh, Paul Cézanne, Paul Gauguin, Maurice Denis, Pierre Bonnard, Henri Matisse, Kees van Dongen, Egon Schiele, Oscar Kokoshka, Emil Nolde and Edvard Munch, to name but a few. The effect of such an immersion into what was then taking place in the wider European context was profoundly impactful, especially if we consider that these were artists whose names were practically unknown in Brazil, and that closer contact with their production was nigh impossible in her home country. As she would later say: "I saw painting for the first time only when I arrived in Europe. When I visited the museums, I was made dizzy by what I saw."[2] Her work of this period betrays wide-ranging influences. Not entirely

Modernist, but rather Post-Impressionistic, it revels in strong and opposing colours, quick brushwork, and a penchant for distortions of the figure.

With the clouds of war gathering over Europe, Malfatti decided to return home in early 1914. Back in Brazil she found herself in a rather backward environment, a place where her experiments created dumbfounded responses. Her family, for instance, found her German output technically crude, even if strong in expression. Nevertheless, she managed to exhibit her work in a solo show, in which she presented paintings, etchings and drawings produced during her Berlin years. The show had a modicum of critical reception. Her colouristic abilities and vigour of expression were amply noted, but she still felt she had more to learn. With the doors of Europe closed to her, Malfatti decided to move to the United States, arriving there in late 1914. In early 1915 we find her enrolled as a student at the Art Students League in New York. She spent the summer of that year on the island of Monhegan in Maine, where she produced a great many seascapes (figs pp. 32 and 33), the first properly mature works of her career where we can see her interest in colour and deformation being allied to a sense of synthetisation of nature in an Expressionistic idiom. Upon her return to New York she continued her experiments, turning out works of great vigour and energy, particularly in her life drawings. In these angled, elongated studies of mostly male nudes one can sense her mirth in the distortion of form for the achievement of expressive effects. Mounds of geometricized muscles are vigourously drawn in thick marks of charcoal with a mastery of effect quite notable for an artist just twenty-six years of age (fig. 1). Her use of colour and interest in its effects can also be clearly perceived in other works, for example, in *Primeiro nu cubista* ou *O pequeno nu* (fig. p. 30). In the paintings of the same period, we see Malfatti already master of her talent, beautifully allying her taste for expressive forms and colours to the modelling of the figure, examples being *O japonês* and *O homem amarelo* (figs pp. 29 and 27). We do not know what reason prompted Malfatti to return to Brazil in August 1916, but it is safe to say that the São Paulo of 1916 would not have been a place able to offer the adequate milieu for the flourishing of her work, something she would soon find out.

In 1916 São Paulo counted something like 300,000 inhabitants, but despite these not insignificant numbers it housed only one museum, where a few paintings, none of which were even remotely Modernist, could be seen, and no art galleries; most exhibitions were held in improvised locations such as hotel lobbies, meeting rooms of newspaper offices and department stores. The whole scene smelt of well-behaved hesitation. It is thus no surprise that Malfatti's work, violent in its forms and exuberant in colours, conceding very little to the prevalent bourgeois taste, would be received with surprise and incomprehension. The canvases she brought in her trunk were against everything that polite society expected of well-brought up young ladies of the middle classes. Her uncle and protector Jorge Krug stated: "This is not painting, these are Dantesque things!"[3] So offended was he that he prohibited the paintings from entering his house. Naturally shy, withdrawn, and sweet-natured, her family's criticism took its toll on her. But

Anita Malfatti

she continued to paint, producing one of her most famous works, *Tropical* (fig.2), soon after. In it Malfatti allies the Expressionist idiom of her work to a typically Brazilian subject, a mixed-race fruit vendor. A common theme during the nineteenth century, a great many academic painters depicting similar scenes, it was the first time that a Modernist formal vocabulary was utilised to depict a distinctly Brazilian theme. She would eventually show work from her American period alongside more recent paintings in a solo show that opened in December 1917, the *Exposição de pintura moderna Anita Malfatti*, its title making clear her ambition to be not only a Modernist artist, but one who identified as such. The first reactions to the show, which was heavily visited during the month in which it was open were, if not all positive, at least well intentioned, most critics trying to understand the paintings in their own terms. She even managed to sell some of the paintings.

However, on 20 December 1917, the writer Monteiro Lobato published a review that would go on to become one of the most famous attacks an artist Brazil had yet seen. In it Lobato decried the danger of the introduction of Modern art to Brazil, defending a naturalistic approach to representation. He defined Malfatti as someone who saw the world in an abnormal fashion, in the light of "ephemeral theories" and under the "diplopic influence of rebellious schools", "pustules of excessive culture"[4]. It was a farce, a caricature of colour and form. The esteem in which Lobato was held implied that many who had if not celebrated the exhibition at least considered it seriously, were made to revise their opinions, creating a polemic of violent words, making Malfatti the palm-bearer and proto-martyr of what would eventually become the São Paulo based branch of the Modernist movement in Brazil. It may be said that Malfatti's exhibition was the first of its kind to openly propose a Modern approach to art in Brazil, as well as the first event in which one saw the conscious digging up of trenches of artistic discussion, opposing two fields of thought, ones for Modernism, whatever that may have meant, and the proponents of a more academic approach to the production of art. Malfatti was deeply disturbed by the brutality of the attacks, and withdrew almost entirely from the scene after the closing of the show. As she would later say: "Then the weight of ostracism began. All my work was cut – students, painting sales, and fights started in the newspapers."[5]

Fig. 1
Anita Malfatti, *Academia VIII*, c.1916, charcoal on paper, 62 × 47,5 cm, Collection Gilberto Chateaubriand, Museu de Arte Moderna, Rio de Janeiro

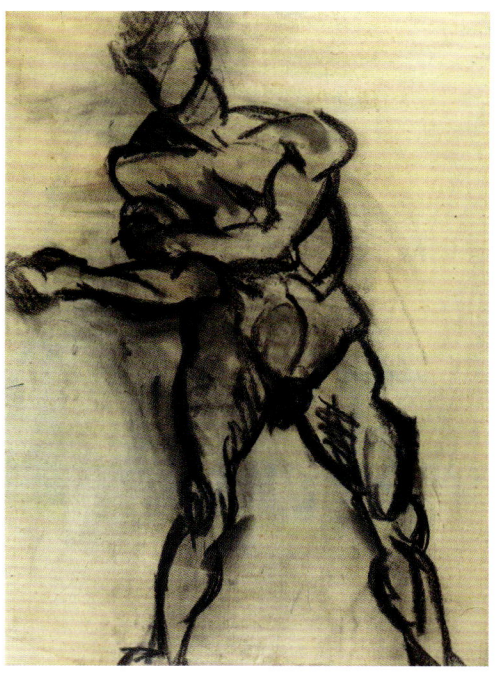

Brasil! Brasil!

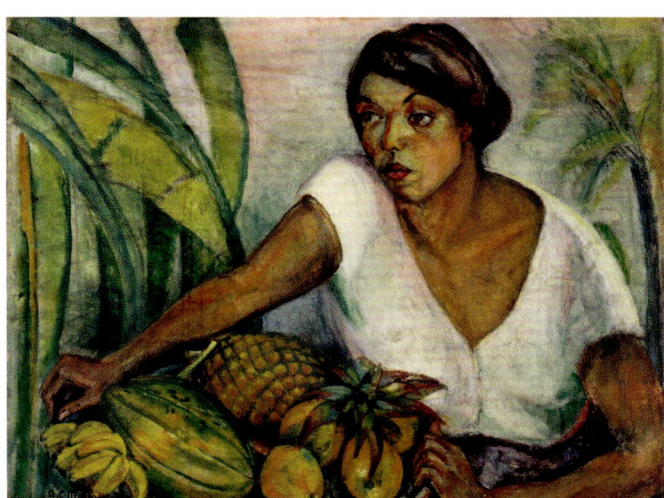

Fig. 2
Anita Malfatti, *Tropical*,
1913, oil on canvas,
77 × 102 cm, Pinacoteca de
São Paulo

During the next couple of years Malfatti backed down from the more progressive elements of her work, living a life of relative isolation, and stuck to a more palatable style for the likes of local society, exhibiting her new work in 1920, which did not attract defences nor harsh criticisms. That was also the moment in which she started her rapprochement with the emerging Modernist movement that had at its center the duo comprised of the poet, journalist and pantagruelian intellectual Oswald de Andrade and the poet, critic, folklorist and musicologist Mário de Andrade, both of whom Malfatti would portray in paintings of great expression and depth (figs pp. 36 and 37). If Mário de Andrade was one of the most important names of the Brazilian Modernist movement, as well as a fundamental interlocutor for many of its artists, Oswald was its enfant terrible, offending the old order and ridiculing its members whenever possible, whilst providing a playful, innovative conceptual framework for its development. These were the characters that would congregate alongside a number of other artists, musicians, poets and intellectuals, for the forging of a movement of which the *Semana de Arte Moderna* (Modern Art Week) of 1922, an arts festival held at the São Paulo Municipal Theatre in February 1922 in which conferences, lectures, concerts, reading of poems and an art exhibition were presented to the public, was one of its crowning achievements. It must be said that at its time the *Semana* knew few, if any, reverberations. A fascinating event, no doubt, but one which would only later become the aborning date for the introduction of Modernism in Brazil. If the *Semana* was at its time a mere ripple, with the passing of the years and the prominent positions many of its participants would come to occupy, it would grow into a monumental wave, for better or worse, swallowing parallel movements of artistic renovation and monopolizing the narrative of the introduction of Modernist styles of art to Brazil. The exhibition itself, held at the entrance hall of the theatre, banded together the work of 12 participants. Anita Malfatti, held as the great forerunner of the movement, presented a reduced version of her 1917 exhibition, including the more flagrantly radical *Homem de sete cores* (fig. p. 31), one of the most impressive of the achievements of her American period. Her work, yet again, was the recipient of violent critiques. However, no longer isolated in her proposals of renovation, she took them in much better light than before.

Anita Malfatti

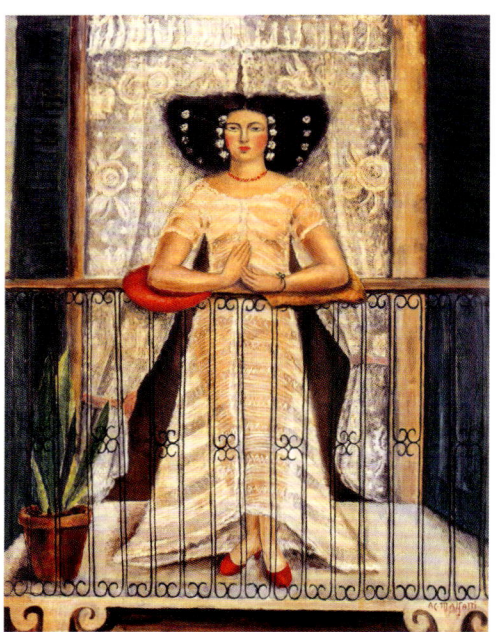

Fig. 3
Anita Malfatti, *Mulher do Pará*
(Woman from Pará), 1927
oil on canvas, 80 × 65 cm,
Private collection

Still eager to continue her studies, Malfatti managed to obtain in 1923, when she counted thirty-three years of age, the scholarship of the Pensionato Artístico Paulista, a scholarship financed by the state of São Paulo destined to young artists desirous of finishing off their studies in Europe, something Malfatti, a fully-fledged talent in ample possession of her powers with two spells of studies outside of Brazil behind her, was far from being. Despite that, in August 1923 she crossed the Atlantic as the recipient of the scholarship to pursue studies in the French capital. She would remain there until 1928. In Paris she set up house and studio in Montparnasse, leading the life of a student in search of a new style. She sought counsel with French painter Maurice Denis, in particular as regards religious painting, for Malfatti was a profoundly devout woman. In the work she produced during her stay we can sense a return to Classicism, following the steps of many post-war artists, but also a quest for new expressive possibilities, one in which she was influenced by the contemporaneous works of Henri Matisse. The truth is that just as she had done in Germany, and in the USA, Malfatti sought out the most progressive styles and movements, engaging deeply with these innovative artistic tendencies. Perhaps the best example of her Parisian period is the painting *Mulher do Pará* (fig. 3), a Matissean image of a woman standing on a balcony, most likely a prostitute, eyes facing us, wearing a transparent white negligée, sandals, and a heavily bouffant hairdo decorated with little white flowers. Exhibited in the Salon d'Automne of 1927 it was particularly well received by French critics.

Upon her return to São Paulo Malfatti found a much-changed city. Modernist circles had expanded, and new artists had emerged, as well as architects and designers. Even if the Modernist dream pursued by these people was far from becoming a reality, they were no longer seen as the destructive threat they once had been. The solo show she would open upon arrival showcased her recent French production, and sign of the changing times, was not met with vicious offensives nor unanimous applause. Most commentators were baffled by the wide variety of styles pursued by the artist, and their analysis focused on making sense of such diversity. The truth is that she found herself in the uncomfortable position of being an already fundamental character in the narratives of Brazilian Modernist art that were slowly being constructed, but one which found very little space for the commercialisation of her work, a fact that impelled her to start teaching painting and art history to make ends meet. With little time to work on her painting, the production of the years following her return is remarkably uneven.

During the following decades she would remain active in the local art scene, showing in salons and taking part in Modernist congregations. Her work, in turn, would wander from the heavy influence of the Early Renaissance to eventually find itself immersed in the universe of Brazilian popular art. This part of her output was unpopular amongst critics, mostly all of them agreeing that the artist had fallen from the heights of her first Expressionist endeavours into a land of doubtful inspiration. Abandoned by her former defenders, who did not openly criticise her but nonetheless never praised it, she gradually isolated herself. Her interest in popular art during the last two decades of her life fits in perfectly with what was happening in the Brazilian art scene of the 1950s, showing once more how attuned she was to contemporary artistic developments. While it may not be particularly inspired, a certain hesitancy always present in her efforts, they nevertheless show us a picture of an artist deeply in tune with her times. What she did paint was consigned to religious subjects, some of which are of high quality and inventiveness, and scenes of popular celebrations, religious processions, carnivals, sambas, and such, in a style of utter simplicity and directness reminiscent of the North American painter Grandma Moses. After years of ill-health Anita Malfatti died on 6 November 1964, one year after being honoured in the VII Bienal de São Paulo with a retrospective, and seven months after the coup d'état that initiated a military dictatorship in Brazil, her place as the historic facilitator of Modernism in Brazil safely assured.

Giancarlo Hannud

1   Malfatti 1951, p. 23

2   Malfatti 1951, p. 23

3   Malfatti 1951, p. 29

4   Lobato 1917

5   Rio de Janeiro 1952

O homen amarelo
(Yellow Man), 1915–1916

Brasil! Brasil!

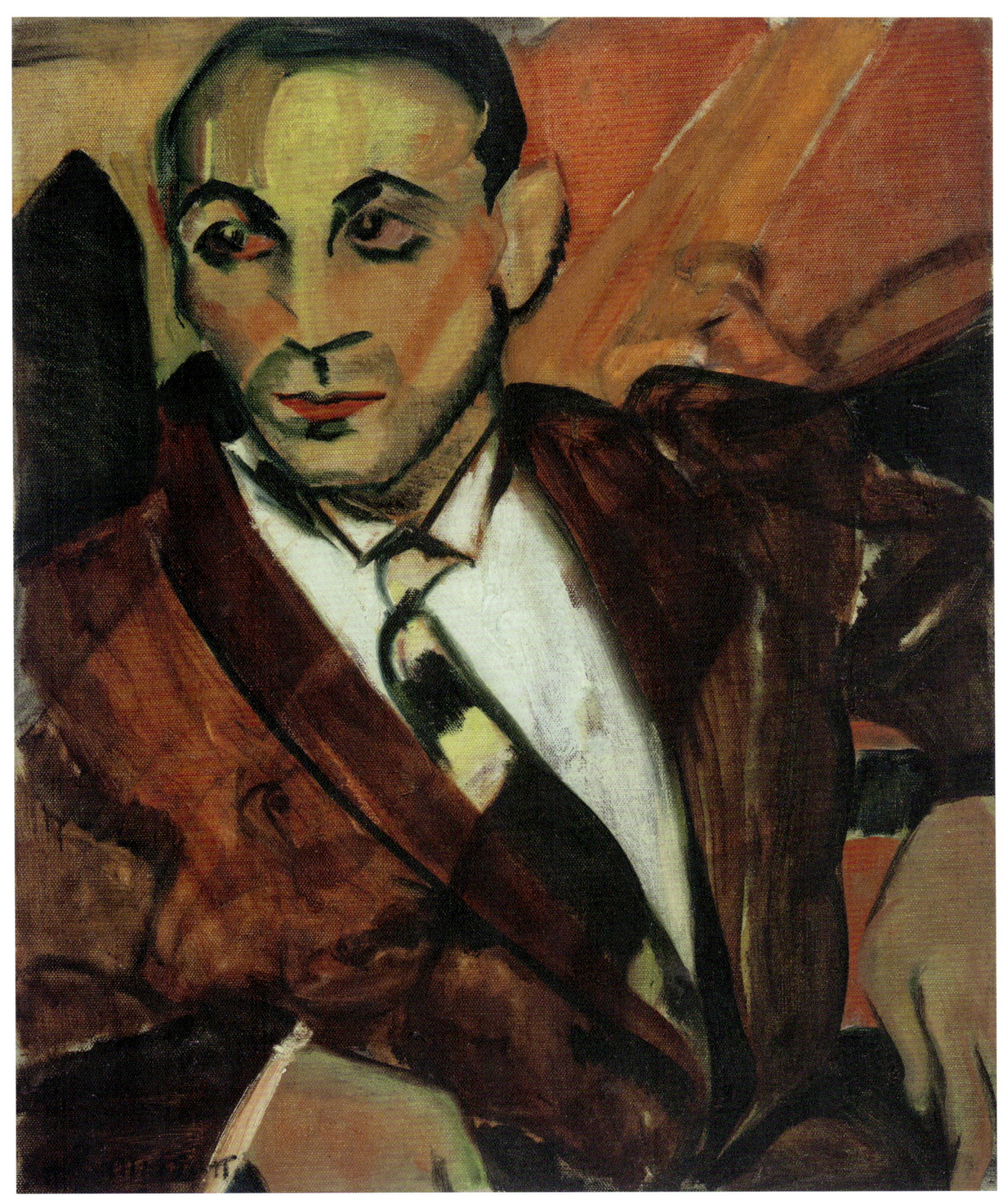

Anita Malfatti

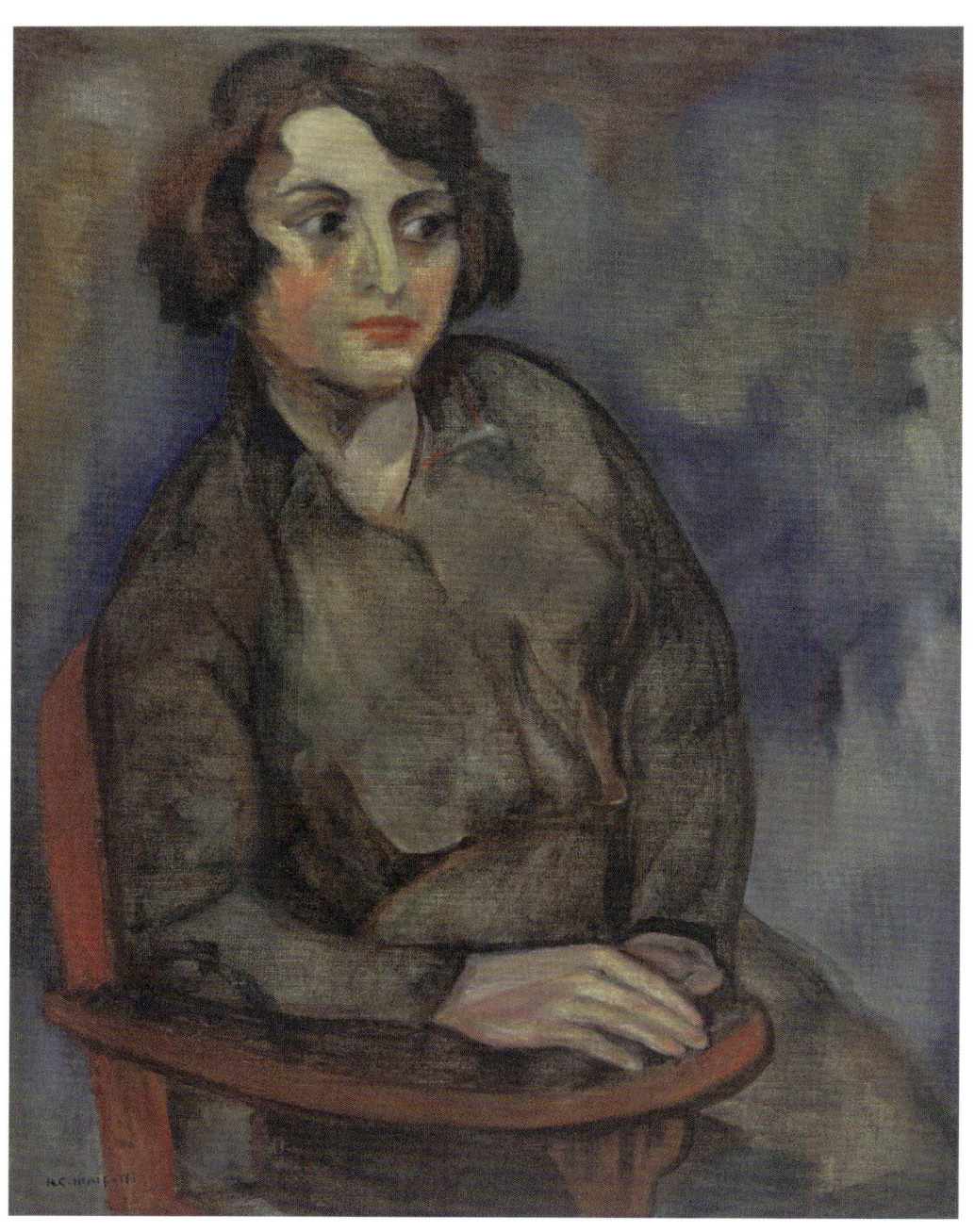

A estudante russa
(**Russian Student**), c. 1915

O japonês (Japanese Man), 1915–1916

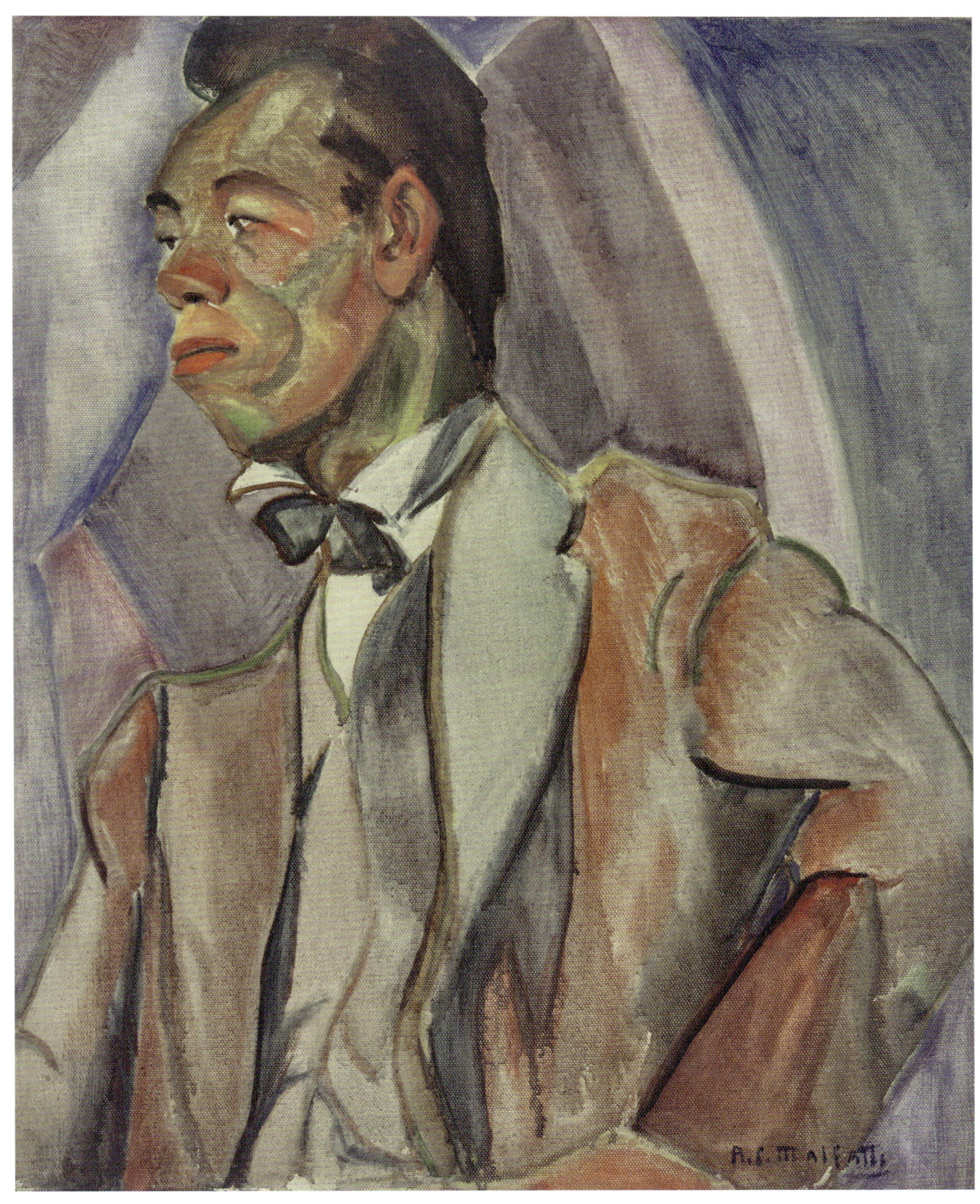

29   **Anita Malfatti**

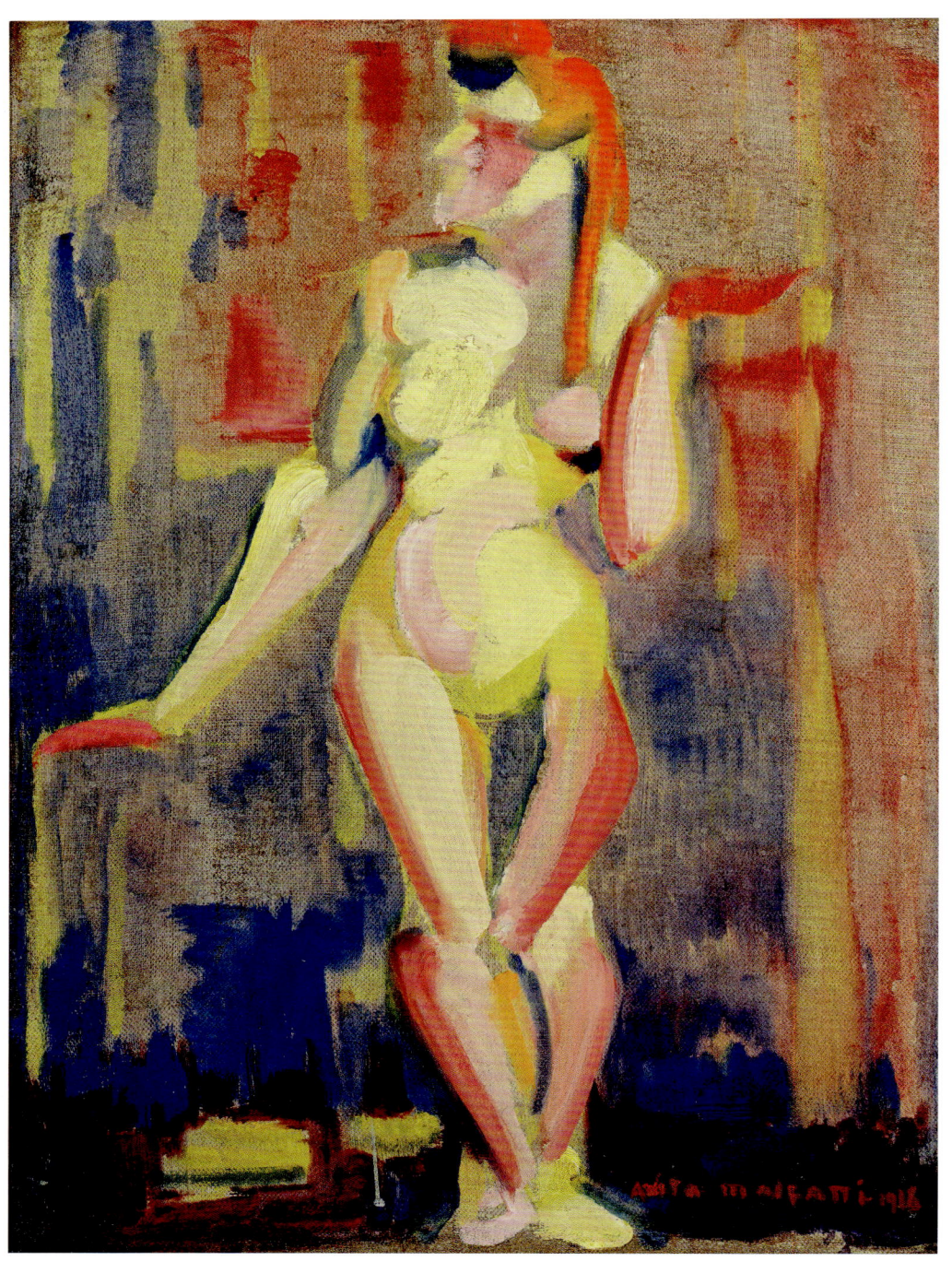

Primeiro nu cubista ou
O pequeno nu (First Cubist
Nude or Little Nude), 1916

Homem de sete cores (Man
of Seven Colours), 1915–1916

Brasil! Brasil!

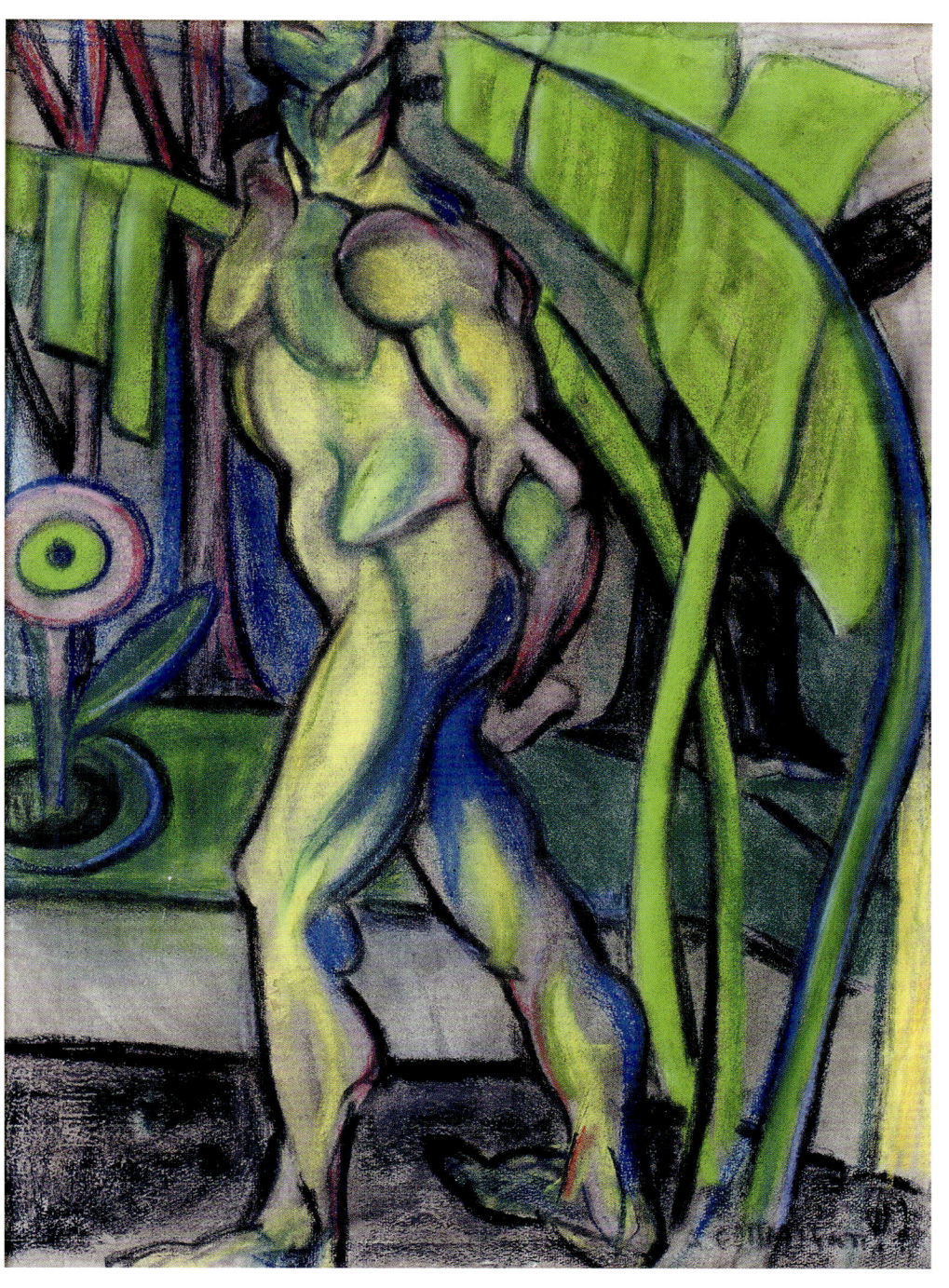

31　　　　**Anita Malfatti**

Marinha (Penhascos)
(Seascape, Cliffs), 1915–1917

Marinha, Monhegan
(Seascape, Monhegan), 1915

A onda (Wave), c. 1915–1917

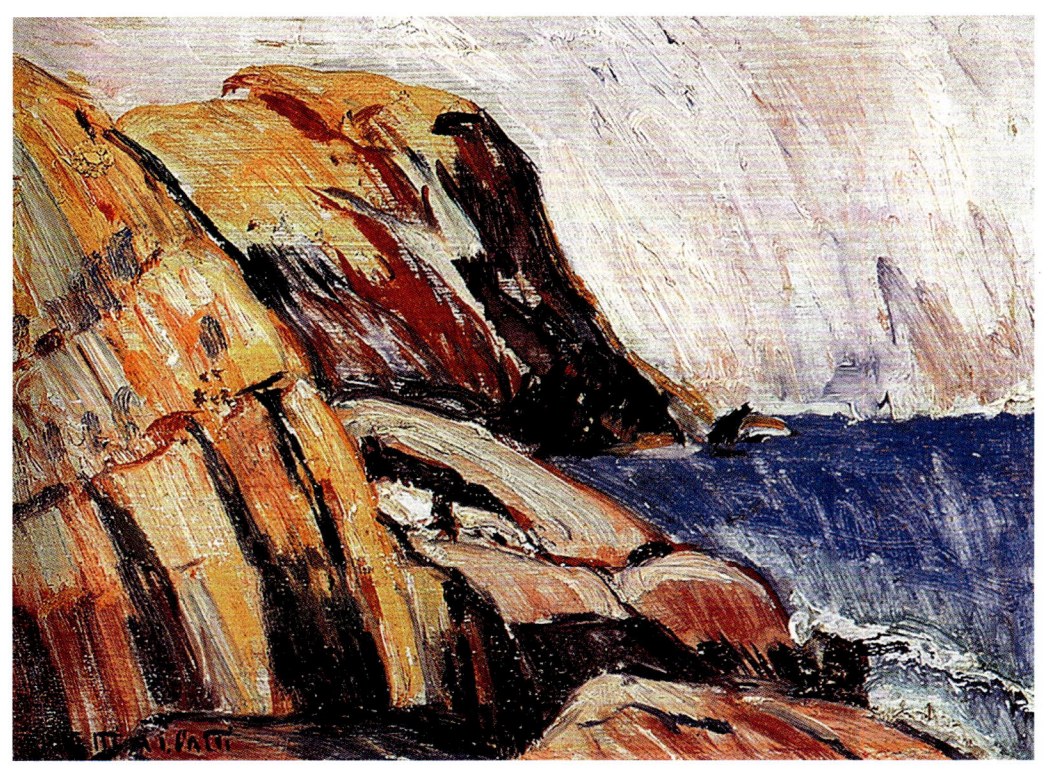

Brasil! Brasil!

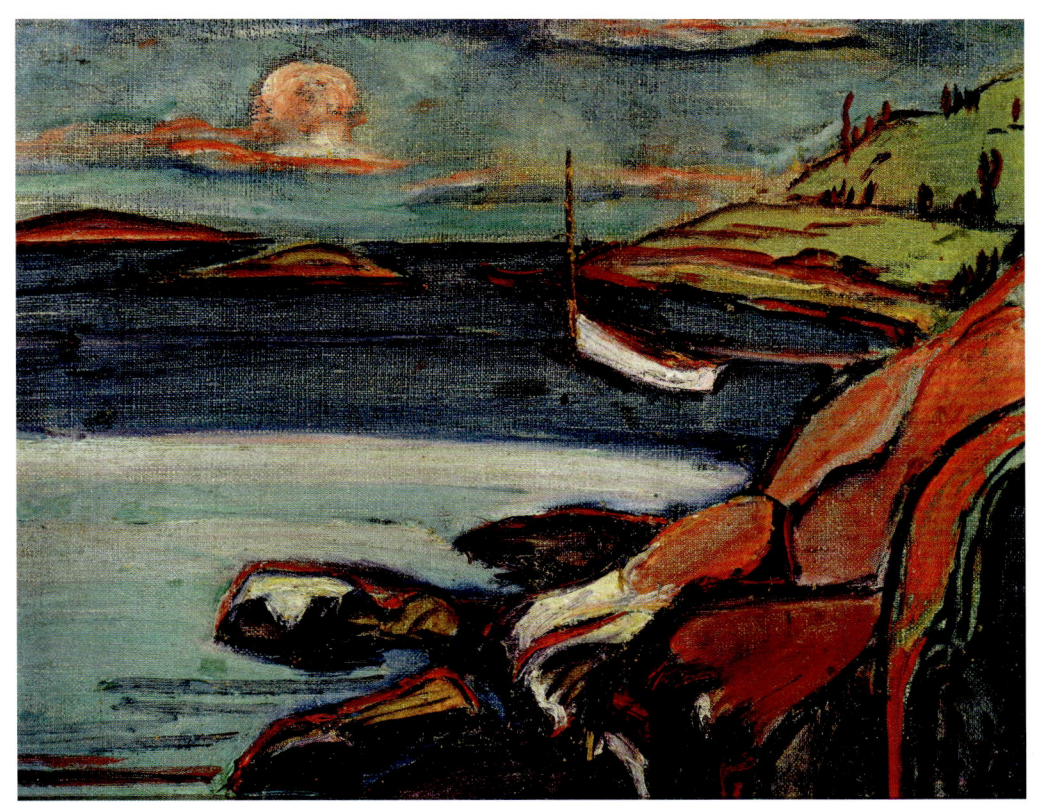

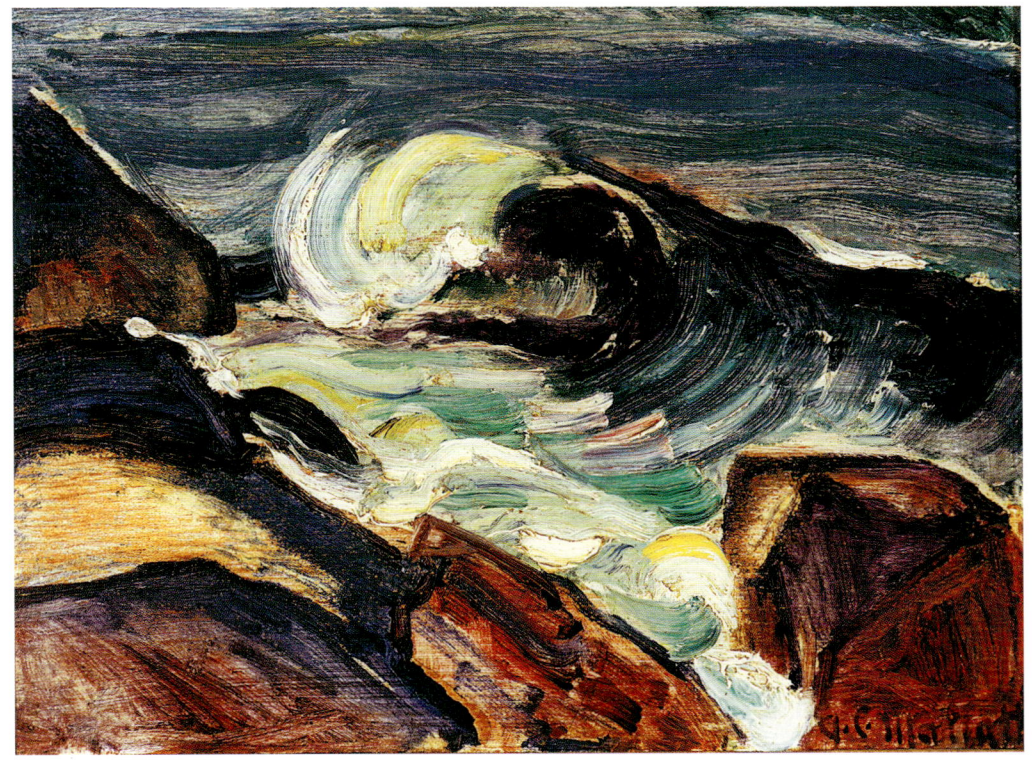

33   **Anita Malfatti**

O farol (Lighthouse), 1915

A chinesa (Chinese Woman), c. 1922

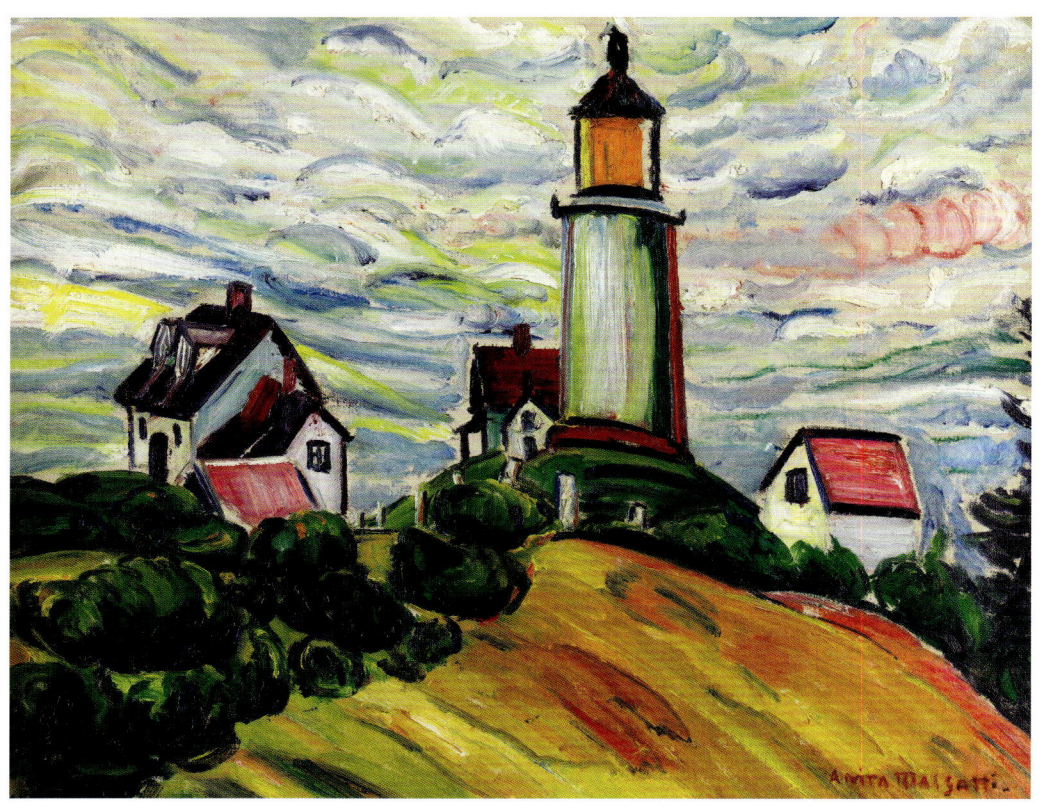

Brasil! Brasil!

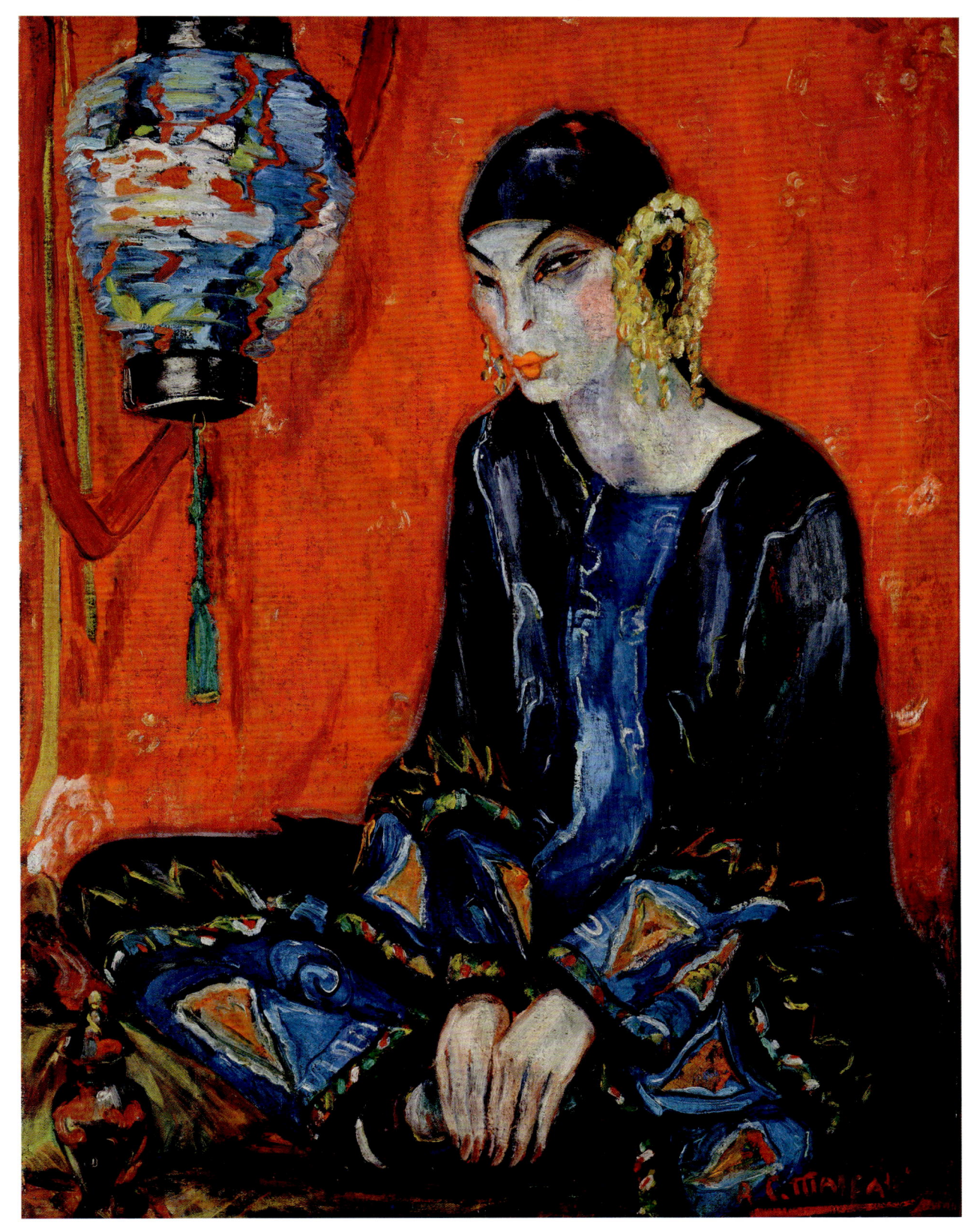

Anita Malfatti

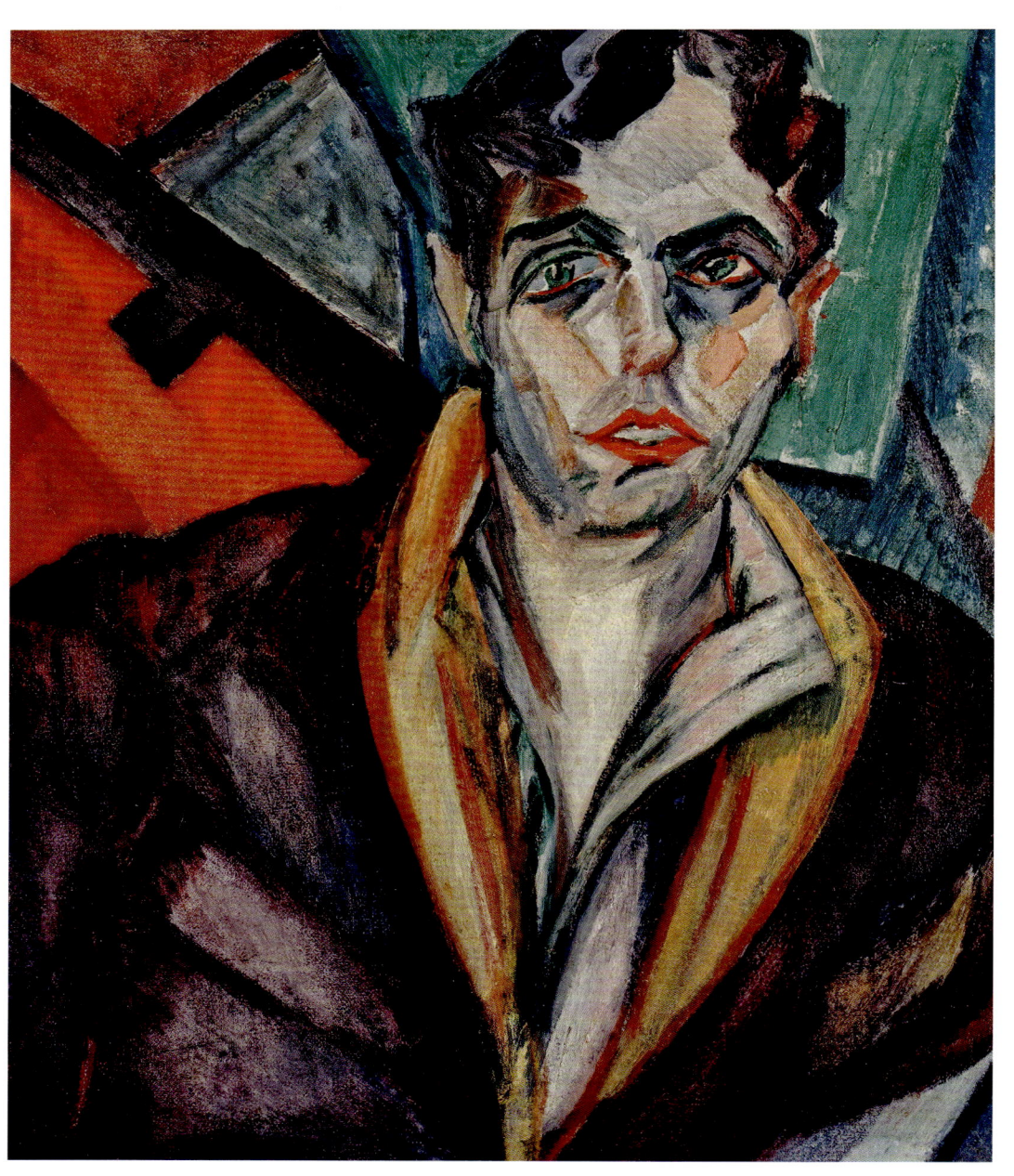

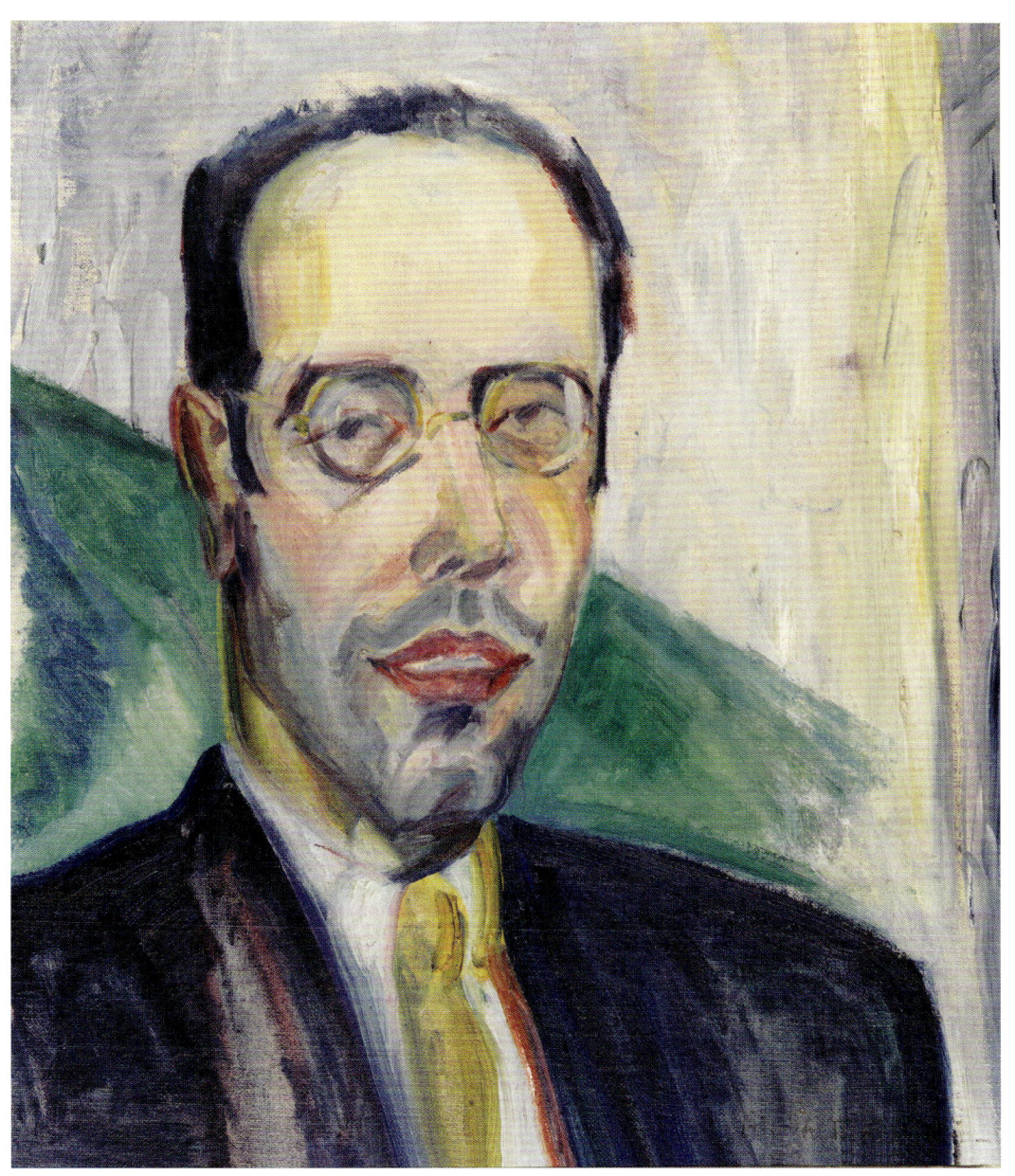

**Retrato de Oswald
(Portrait of Oswald)**, 1925

**Retrato de Mário de
Andrade (Portrait of Mário
de Andrade)**, c. 1923

Anita Malfatti

Vicente do Rego Monteiro

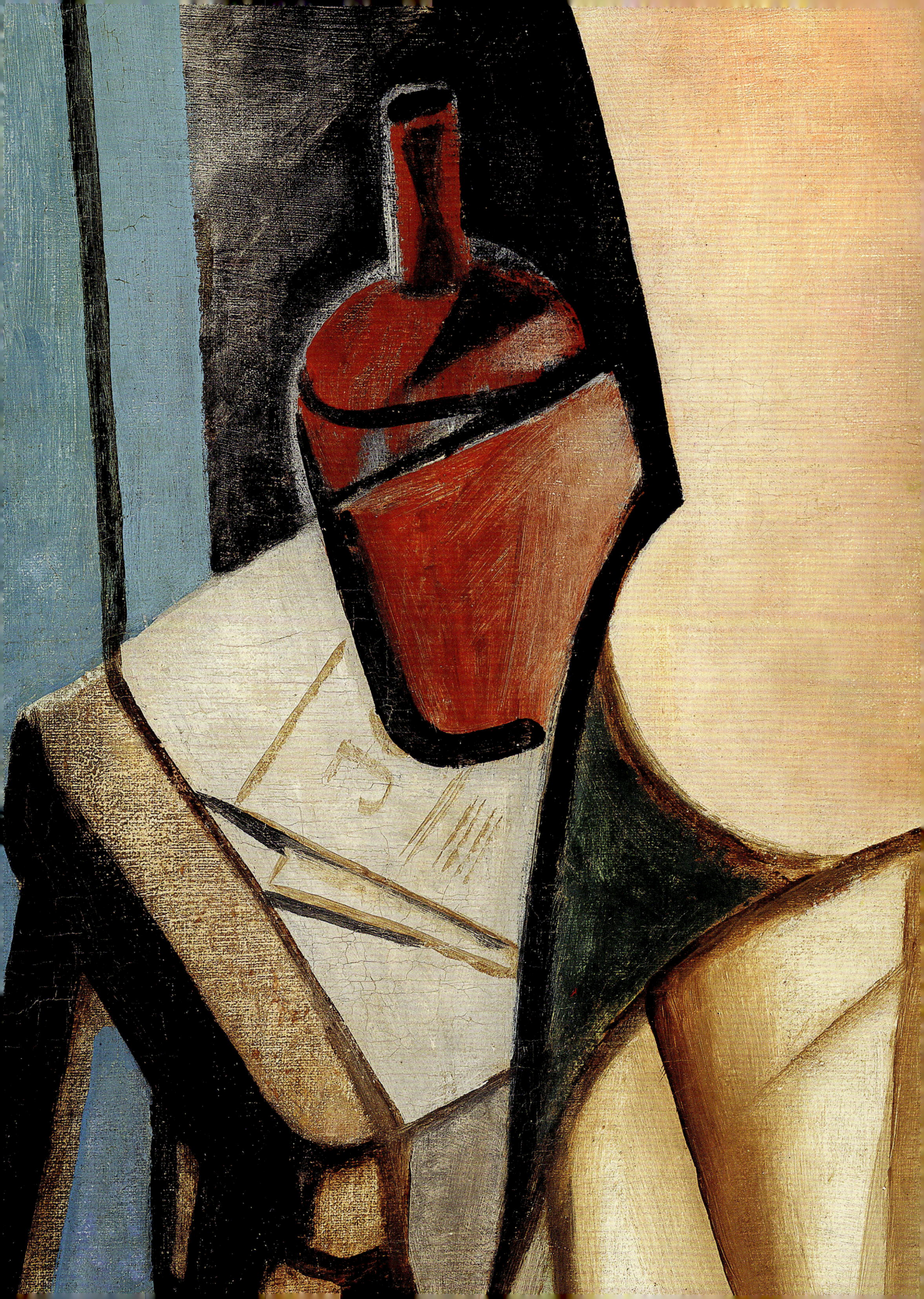

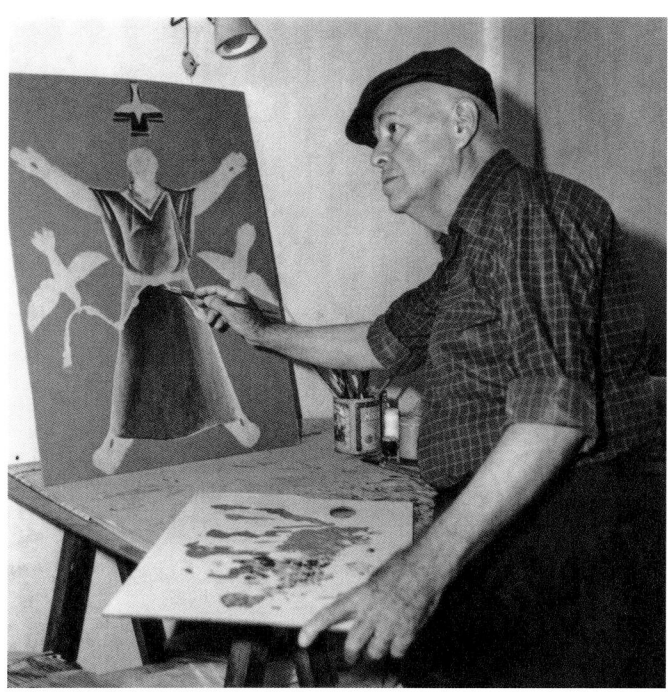

Vicente do Rego Monteiro
1899, Recife, Brazil –
1970, Recife, Brazil

One of the outstanding artists of his generation and a pre-eminent poet both in the French and Portuguese languages, Vicente do Rego Monteiro was in addition a journalist of note, intrepid editor, and original typographer. His is a particularly interesting case of an artist who spent nearly as much time in his home country as in France, where he intensely engaged with the local artistic and poetic milieus, leaving behind a solid poetical legacy. He is, in a sense, as much part of French as of Brazilian culture. As he said, "I'm a citizen of nowhere, but I love Paris above all"[1]. In spite of the preference, Vicente do Rego Monteiro was born in the capital city of the north-eastern state of Pernambuco, Recife, on 19 December 1899. The Brazilian Venice, as the city is known, is a central place in the historical development of Brazil, the seat of a proud, aristocratic local culture, as distant from the industrial dispositions of São Paulo as from the cosmopolitan proclivities of the then capital Rio de Janeiro. His family was one of pronounced artistic sensibilities, as well as deep religious piety, a particularity that would shape some of Monteiro's output, as one of his brothers, Joaquim, was a talented artist in his own right. It was, however, with his elder sister Fédora that Monteiro initiated his artistic studies whilst still a child.

In 1908 the Monteiro family relocated to Rio de Janeiro. There his sister enrolled at the Escola Nacional de Belas Artes, the Republican heir to the Academia Imperial de Belas Artes, Brazil's most ancient, as well as most traditional, institution for the training of artists. Monteiro attended the classes at the Escola informally in the company of his sister. The family's time in Rio was short-lived, for they moved a second time in 1911, this time to Paris, where Monteiro continued his studies, concentrating in drawing and sculpture at the Académie Moderne, the Académie Julian, the Académie Colarossi, and the Académie de La Grande Chaumière. During his first Parisian residence Monteiro travelled widely around Europe, visiting Britain, Belgium, Germany, Italy and Switzerland, places where he came in contact with the European canon of art, and more importantly for the development of his tastes, with the art of the Ancient Near East and of Classical Antiquity. More noteworthy than these contacts was the inclusion, when he was only fourteen years old, of one of his paintings and a sculpture

Brasil! Brasil!

in the Salon des Indépendants of 1913, where he showed alongside artists such as Robert Delaunay, Albert Gleizes, Piet Mondrian, and Francis Picabia. No works have been preserved from this period, so we can only imagine what their qualities were, if any. It was also during this time that his lifelong fascination with dance and the moving body began, as he was indeed an accomplished dancer.

With the outbreak of World War I, the family returned to Brazil, settling at first in Rio de Janeiro. We know little of the first few years following his return other than that he concentrated his artistic efforts in the field of sculpture. With his interest in dance ignited by Sergei Diaghilev's Ballets Russes in Paris and by a performance by Ana Pavlova in Recife, he started planning a ballet based on the tales and legends of Brazilian Indigenous peoples, an idea that would follow him for years, but which unfortunately never got off the ground. He showed his first truly mature works in a solo show in Recife in 1919, one that was quickly followed by a more ambitious one in São Paulo in May 1920, which would later travel to Rio and Recife, comprised of drawings and watercolours in which we can see his newly found interest in the legends and myths of the Indigenous peoples of the Amazon. These works breathe a heavy symbolist atmosphere, and if they are not exactly modernist, they at least betray a certain restlessness of form in their eclecticism, not to mention a search for new expressive possibilities. The exhibition also had the merit of being the instigator for the introduction of Monteiro to the group of young artists, poets, and intellectuals that was taking shape in São Paulo, and would eventually converge in the *Semana de Arte Moderna* (Modern Art Week) of 1922. It was whilst the exhibition was on show in Rio that Monteiro encountered the Museu Nacional's collections of ceramics of the Marajoara people, an ancient pre-Columbian civilisation that flourished on the Marajó island at the mouth of the Amazon River in northern Brazil. He diligently drew their remarkable decorative compositions of geometric forms and abstractions with the intention of utilizing their motifs in his own work.

A third solo show followed in Rio de Janeiro in June 1921 where Monteiro showed drawings and watercolours, all of which were once again dedicated to Indigenous themes (fig. 1). Their heavy air of symbolist decadence fashion proved an interesting, even if problematic, stylistic paradox with their subject matter. The works received an enthusiastic response from important local critics such as the poet and diplomat Ronald de Carvalho, a character that would play an important role in Monteiro's inclusion *in absentia* in the *Semana de Arte Moderna*. As the only north-eastern artist to be included in the *Semana*, which says a good deal about the politics of power and geography at play during these years, Monteiro showed a group of watercolours and oil paintings which he had left with Ronald de Carvalho before leaving for Paris. A stylistically incoherent selection of works, pointing to different directions and styles, they prefigure the work he would do upon his arrival in Paris, such as the masterful *Mulher diante do espelho* (fig. p. 45) of 1922, a work in which we see Monteiro's soaking up of some of the more formalistically palatable elements of the European avant-gardes.

Arriving in a much-changed Paris, where he would remain until 1933 with occasional visits to Brazil from 1930 onwards, and where innumerous expat artists congregated in the so-called École de Paris, Monteiro took part in the artistic developments of the French capital, engaging vividly with the local art scene, befriending artists and poets. One of the long-lasting friendships he made during this period was with the critic and poet Géo-Charles, who would write of his work, which he particularly enjoyed due to its highly elaborate technique and use of historical references: "He does not paint decorative vapidities, spiritless abstractions, or small still lifes and photographed flowers, but canvases vast in subject and volume, material and soul."[2]. He also exhibited regularly at the Salon des Indépendants, from 1923 to 1929, as well as at the Salon d'Automne of 1925, and the Salon des Tuileries, in 1923 and 1925, and would be one of the co-founders of the Salon des Surindépendants in 1930. His work quickly evolved during this period, integrating Indigenous formal elements mostly taken from Marajoara culture to the decorative synthetisations of the Art Deco style, notable examples of this modus operandi being the entirely abstract geometrisations of the *Composição indígena* (figs pp. 46 and 47). The first abstract compositions produced by a Brazilian artist, they had no influence over the development of his country's art, and were not shown publicly in Brazil for many years to come. But he would return to figuration, forging an entirely personal language of vast, archaic monumentality characterised by formal concision, indifference to colouristic effects, and symmetrical, straightforward compositions, nearly banal in their simplicity. The same language was used to depict both his more typically Brazilian subjects, such as *Menino nu e tartaruga* (fig. p. 55) and in 1923 in the monumental, mural-like canvas *A caçada* (fig. 2), one of the chief achievements of this period, which would be acquired by the French State in 1959, as well as contemporary Parisian street scenes of proletarian workers, the best example of this being *Os calceteiros* (1924). His continuing interest in sculpture can also be felt in works of the time such as *Crucifixão* (fig. p. 51), one of the many religious subjects he worked on during the 1920s.

Fig. 1
Vicente do Rego Monteiro,
A cobra grande manda para sua filha a noz de Tucunã (Big Snake Sends Her Daughter the Tucunã Nut), 1921, watercolour on paper, 28 × 23,7 cm, Museu de Arte Moderna, Rio de Janeiro

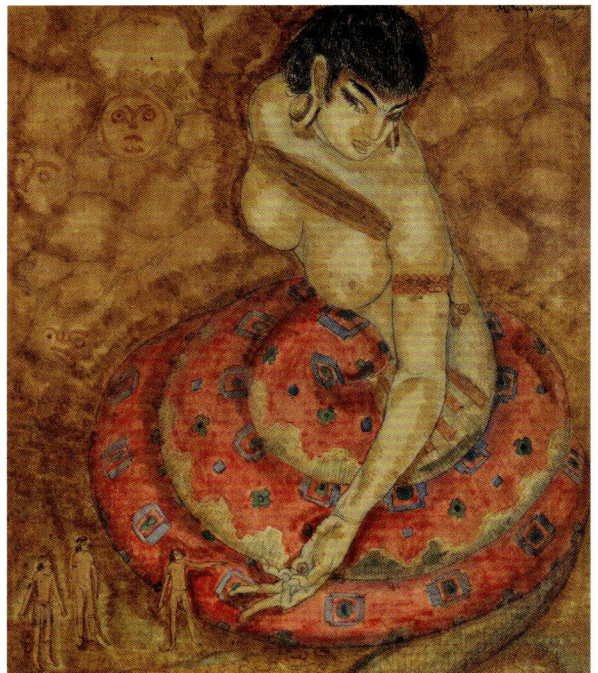

Brasil! Brasil!

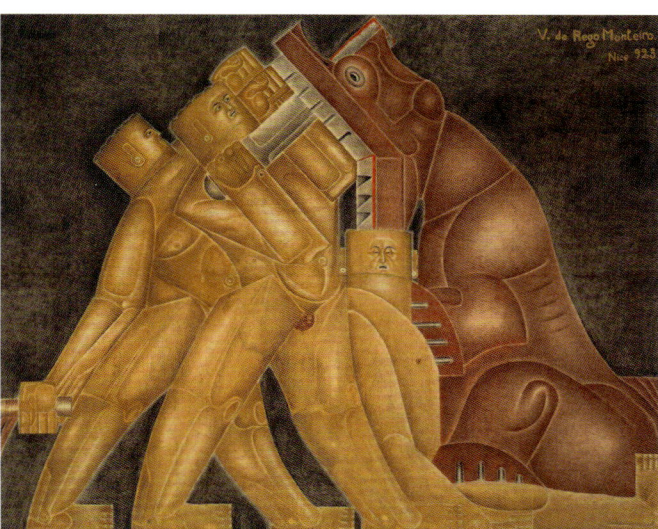

Fig. 2
Vicente do Rego Monteiro,
A caçada (The Hunt), 1923,
oil on canvas, 202 × 259,2 cm,
Musée National d'Art
Moderne, Centre Georges
Pompidou, Paris

It was in Paris that his involvement with poetry and the publishing world gained momentum, activities which would eventually take precedence over his artistic endeavours. In 1923 he illustrated the book *Légendes, croyances et talismans des Indiens de l'Amazone*. As its title makes clear the book explores the legends, beliefs, and talismans of Amazonian natives, and was illustrated by the artist in a language akin to that of *Composição indígena*, its fascinating vignettes reworking some of his earlier Amazonian inspired drawings. Two years later, in 1925, he published Quelques visages de Paris, a book dealing with the poetical and satirical possibilities of the contrasting of European and Amerindian cultures in the context of Modernism. In it a fictional Indigenous chieftain, supposedly visited by Monteiro in the Amazon, visits Paris incognito, leaving behind his impressions of *la ville lumière*. His musings are fixed in ten poems accompanied by stylised illustrations mimicking formal aspects of Indigenous visual culture, a fascinating document, which playfully explores the inversion of roles of who it is that determines impressions of the other and otherness. His interest in sports and athletics was also kindled during this time, particular in the second half of the decade, following his marriage to Marcelle Louis Villard in 1925. Monteiro depicted lithe tennis players (fig. p. 53), burly wrestlers, and dexterous boxers, producing images of notable suppleness and novel elegance.

Having grown tired of his practice as a painter, Monteiro returned to Brazil in 1933. He established himself at the Engenho Várzea Grande, a vast rural property on the outskirts of the city of Gravatá in Pernambuco. There he began a project producing high-quality cachaça, a distilled spirit made from fermented sugar cane juice. Infamous for its rarity and the quality of its labelling, designed by Monteiro himself, it soon went bankrupt. He practically did not paint during these years. He did, however, produce a number of drawings, some of which would be used as illustrations later on. He would return briefly to Paris in 1937 to take part in the *Exposition Internationale des Arts et Techniques dans la Vie Moderne*, for which he produced a monumental canvas depicting Our Lady of Lourdes with Saint Bernadette at her feet. With the ongoing menace of war in Europe, Monteiro returned to Brazil in 1938, where he was appointed director of the Imprensa Oficial do Estado and started teaching drawing

Vicente do Rego Monteiro

at the Ginásio Pernambuco. He was very active in the cultural milieu of Recife, establishing a magazine, *Renovação*, in which he worked as illustrator, poet and author, which he sometimes even printed by hand in a press he built himself. Remarkable for its unique layout and the quality of its articles and illustrations, the magazine openly declared its allegiance to the Estado Novo, the dictatorial regime established by Getúlio Vargas in 1937. Despite criticizing the burgeoning fascist dictatorships of Europe, Monteiro celebrated Vargas's totalitarian and populist regime, one which persecuted a great many intellectuals and artists. A fact that did not give him many sympathisers; a tendency towards more conservative leaning ideals was a crime not easily forgiven by the cultural intelligentsia of Brazil. He was one of the organisers of the *Primeiro Congresso de Poesia do Recife* in 1941 and published a couple of books of poems in the following years before eventually going back to painting, producing serene still lifes characterised by their lens-like distortions, uncannily spectral images of everyday objects that have yet to be properly studied. Despite his distance from Paris he closely accompanied the plight of occupied France, working actively in favour of the Resistance by writing articles, making drawings, and writing poems in its defense that are testimonies to his deep love of France, where he returned to in 1946, remaining there for the next eleven years.

On his third sojourn in the city, he concentrated his efforts on the publication of the work of young French poets with little access to the traditional world of publishing. The few works produced by Monteiro during this period show us a return to the style of the 1920s, which if technically apt betray a certain ennui. He did, however, experiment with black-and-white monotypes from 1954 onwards, creating dark, abstract constructions of geometric forms and liquid effects that indicate his interest in the contemporary developments of painting. He suffered a heart attack in 1955 and during his period of convalescence wrote thirty-five poems which would be published in book form as *Broussais-La Charité*, for which he was awarded the Prix Guillaume Apollinaire. In 1957 Monteiro returned to Recife. During the last stretch of his life, he dedicated himself more and more to painting, leaving poetry behind him. In order to make ends meet he worked as an art teacher. He also produced new versions of works from the 1920s, sought after by collectors. He even backdated some of them to pass them off as 1920s originals. As he would say in a letter to his wife Marcelle, "people do not like anything other than my old canvases, they are not easy to make and this takes up a good deal of time"[3]. In 1969, Monteiro suffered another heart attack and died in Recife on 5 June 1970.

Giancarlo Hannud

1 Apud Zanini 1997, p. 20

2 Géo-Charles 1944, p. 47

3 Apud Zanini 1997, p. 346

Brasil! Brasil!

Mulher diante do espelho
(Woman in Front of the Mirror), 1922

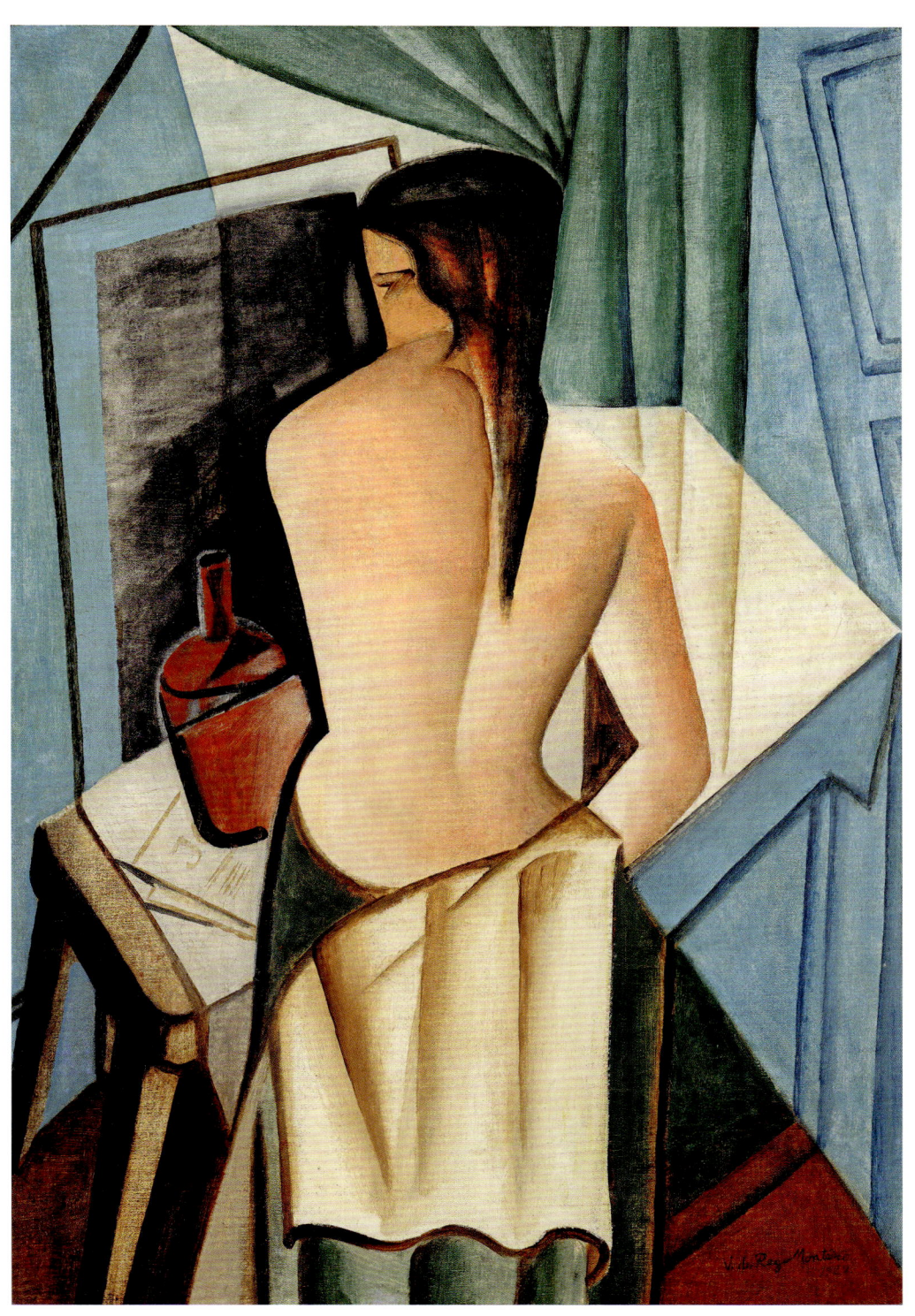

Vicente do Rego Monteiro

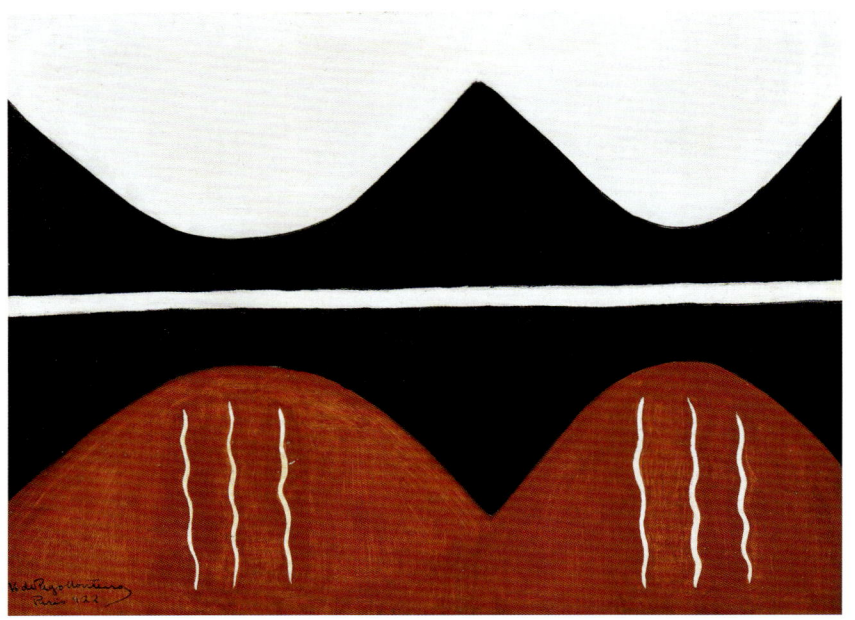

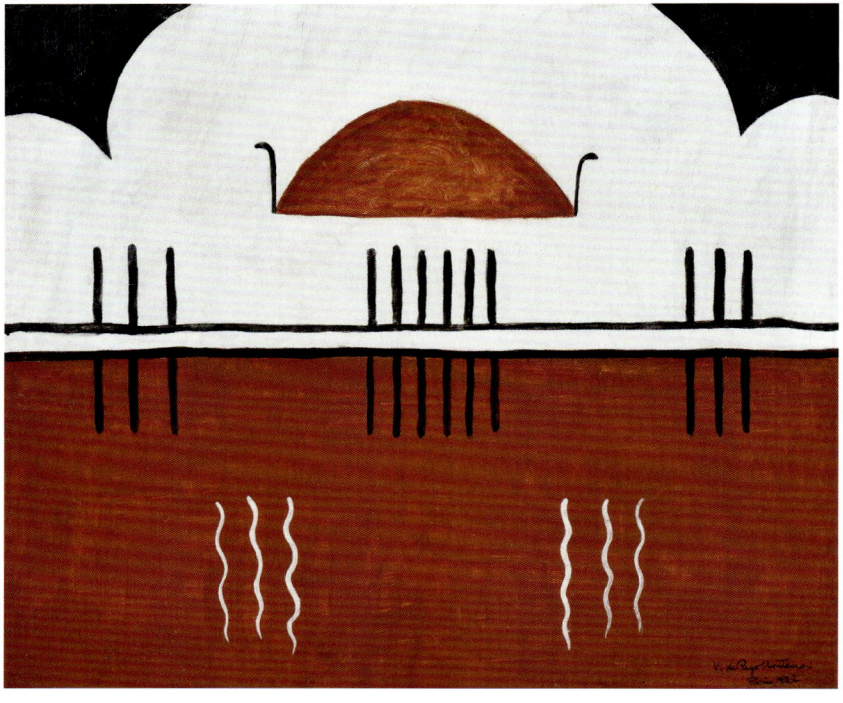

Composição indígena
(Indigenous Composition), 1922

Composição indígena
(Indigenous Composition), 1922

Composição indígena
(Indigenous Composition), 1922

Brasil! Brasil!

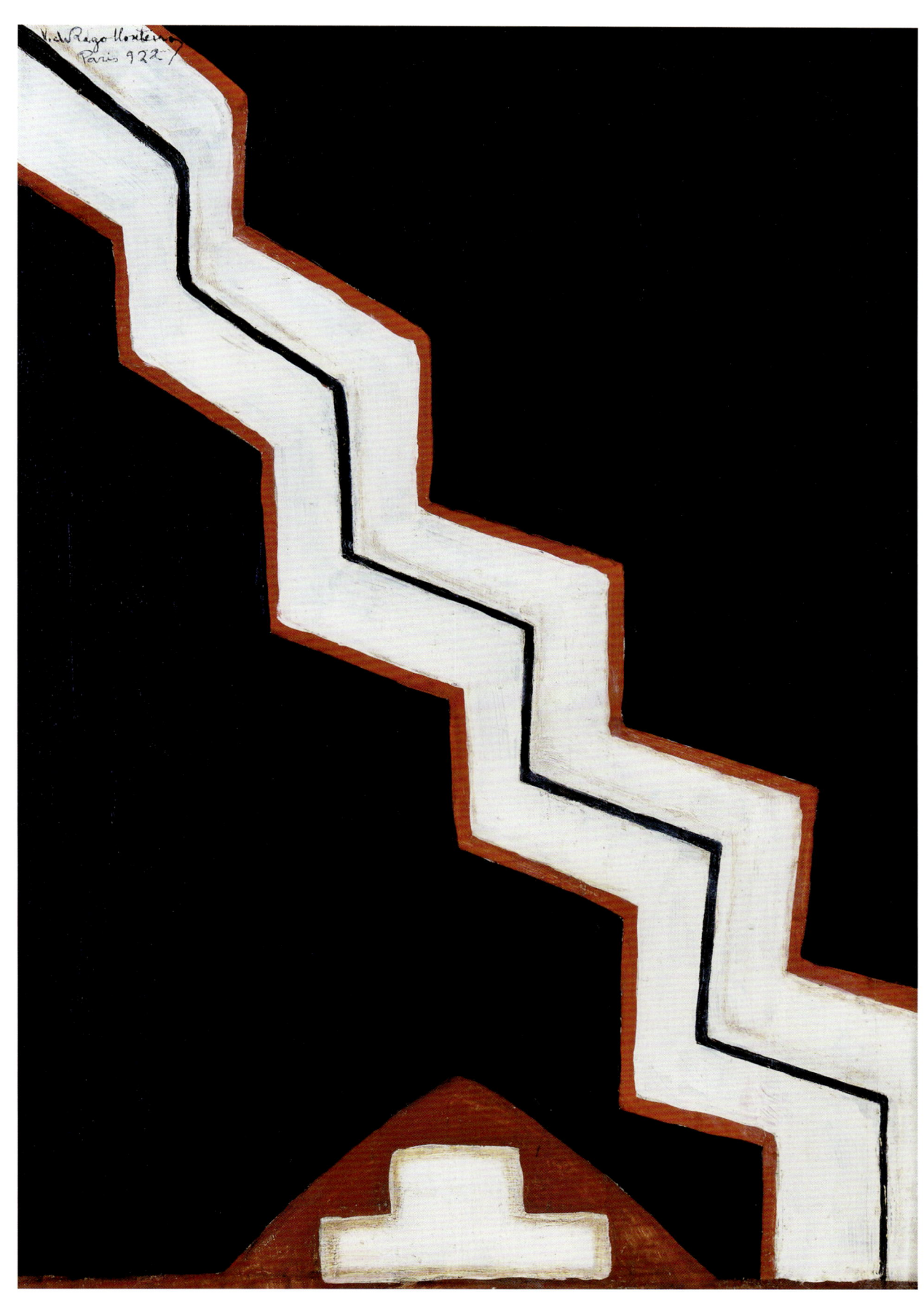

47   **Vicente do Rego Monteiro**

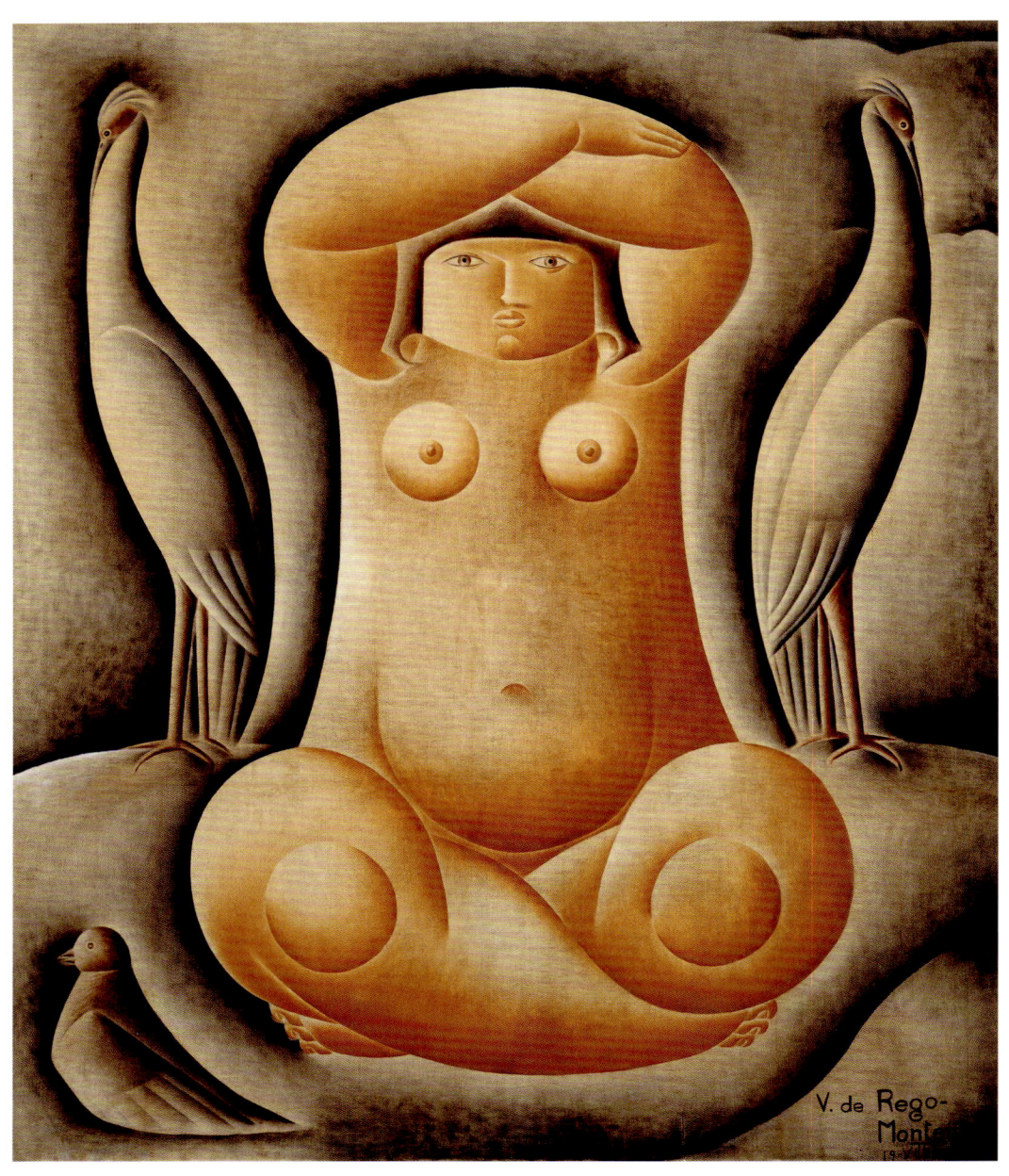

Mulher sentada
(Seated Woman), 1924

Baigneuses
(Bathers), 1924

Brasil! Brasil!

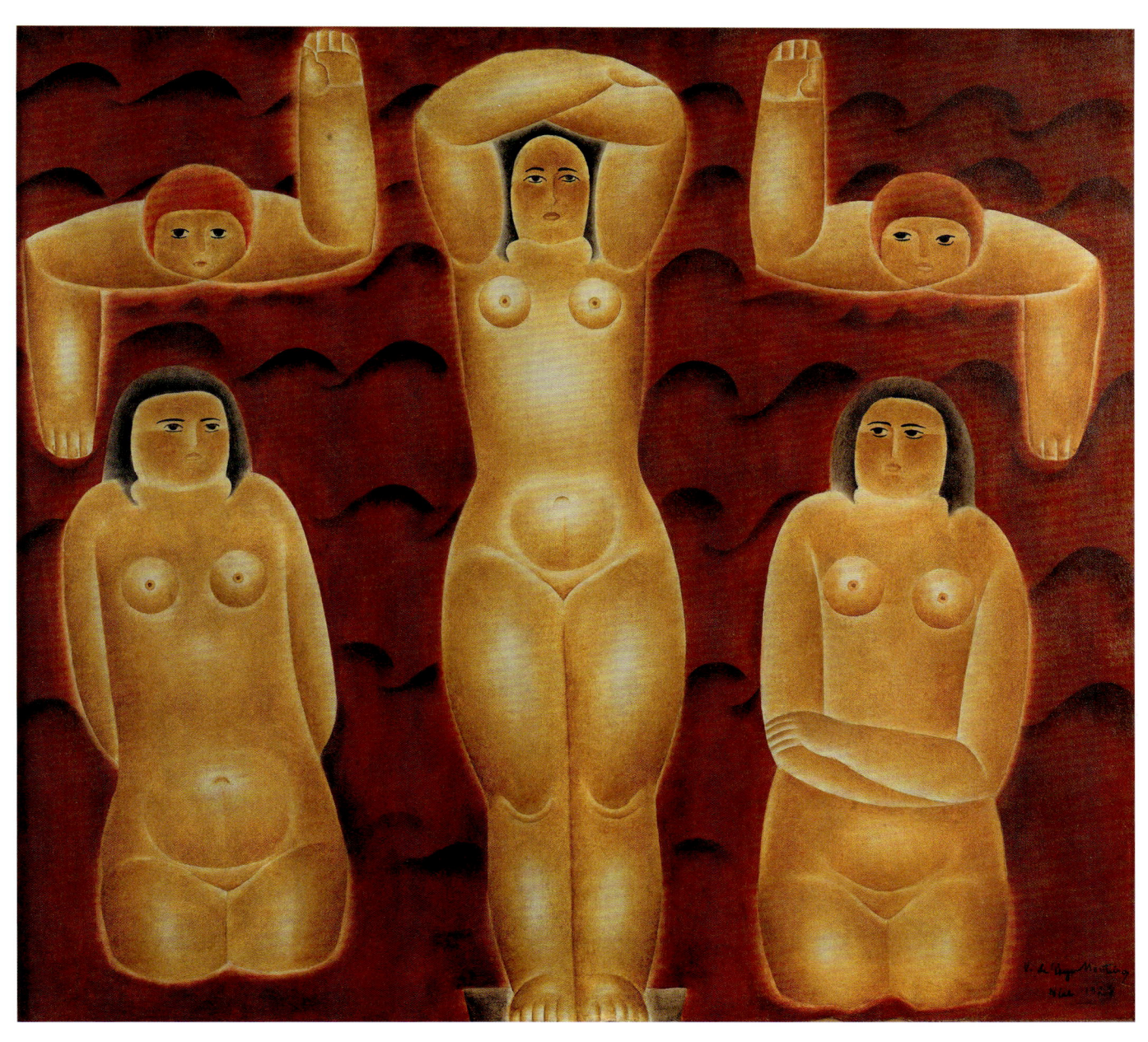

49   **Vicente do Rego Monteiro**

O atirador de arco
(Archer), 1925

Crucifixão
(Crucifixion), 1922

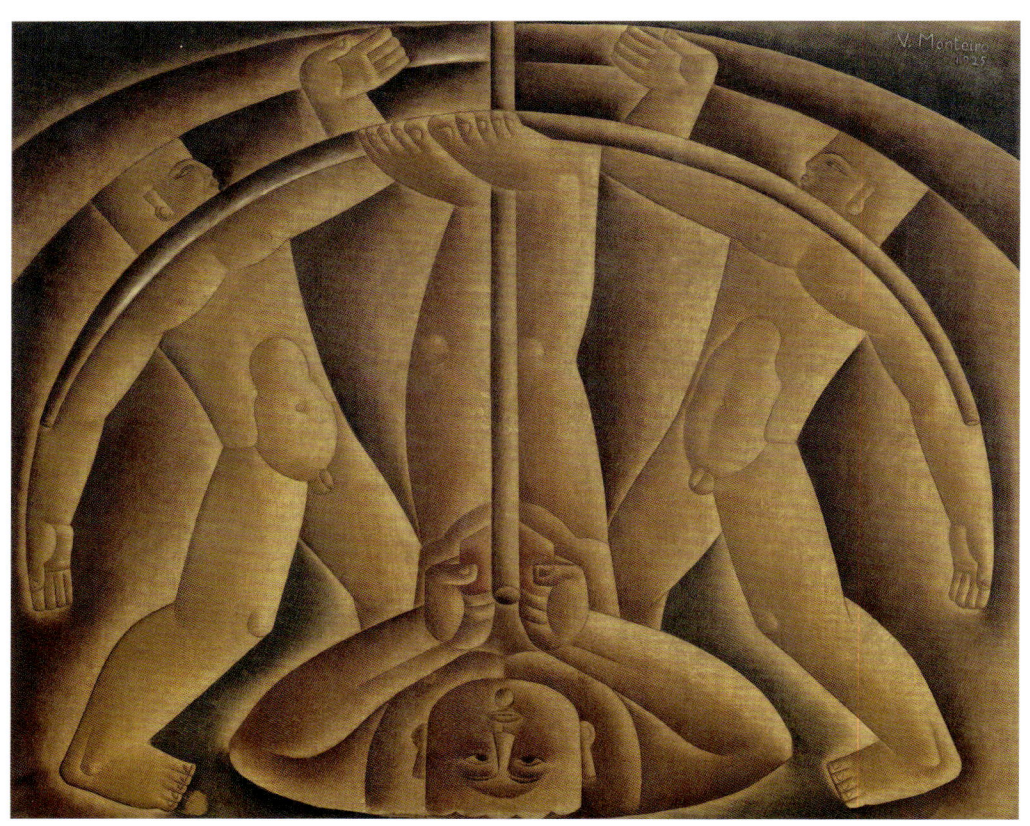

Brasil! Brasil!

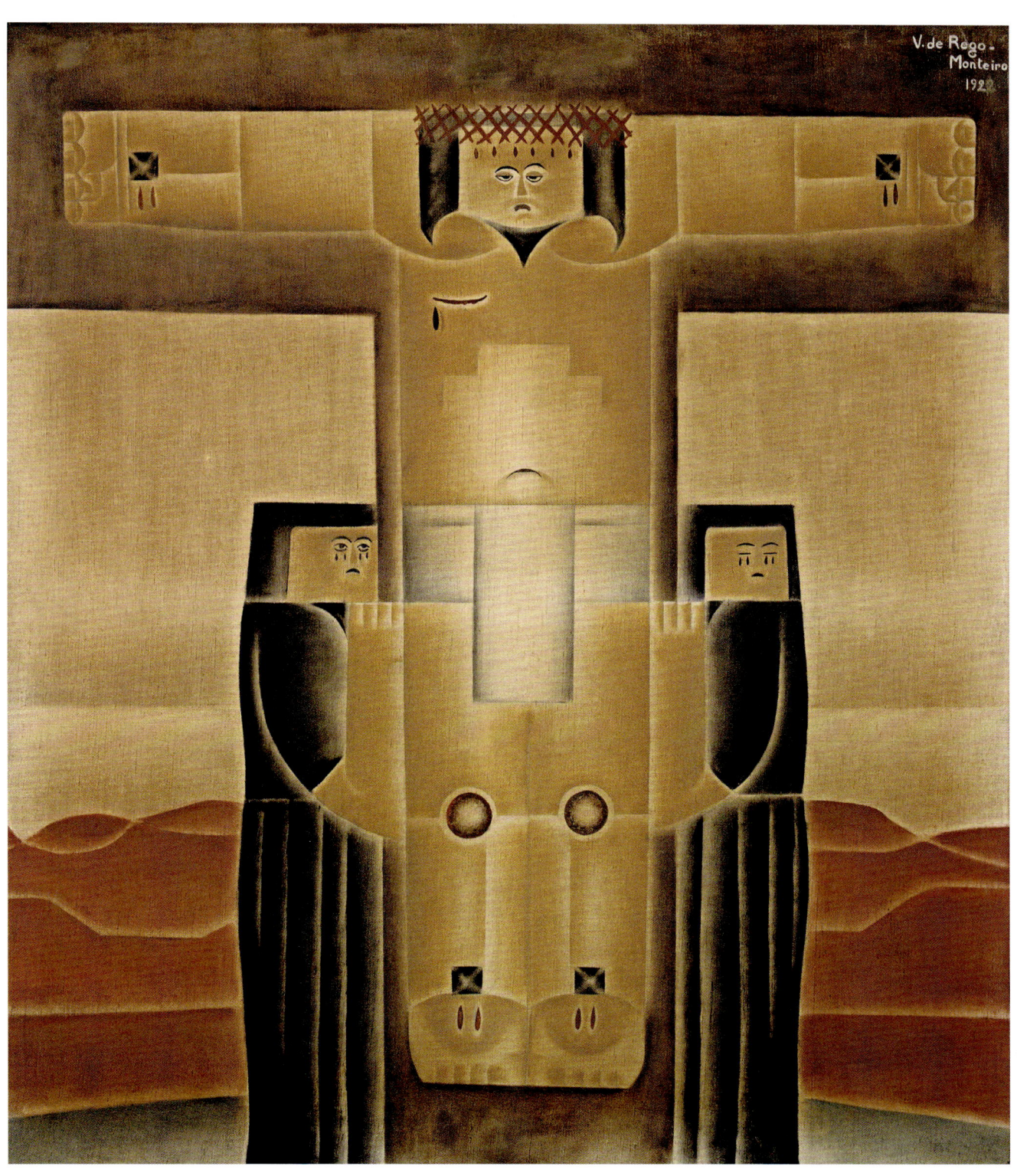

51   **Vicente do Rego Monteiro**

Tênis (Tennis), 1928

Brasil! Brasil!

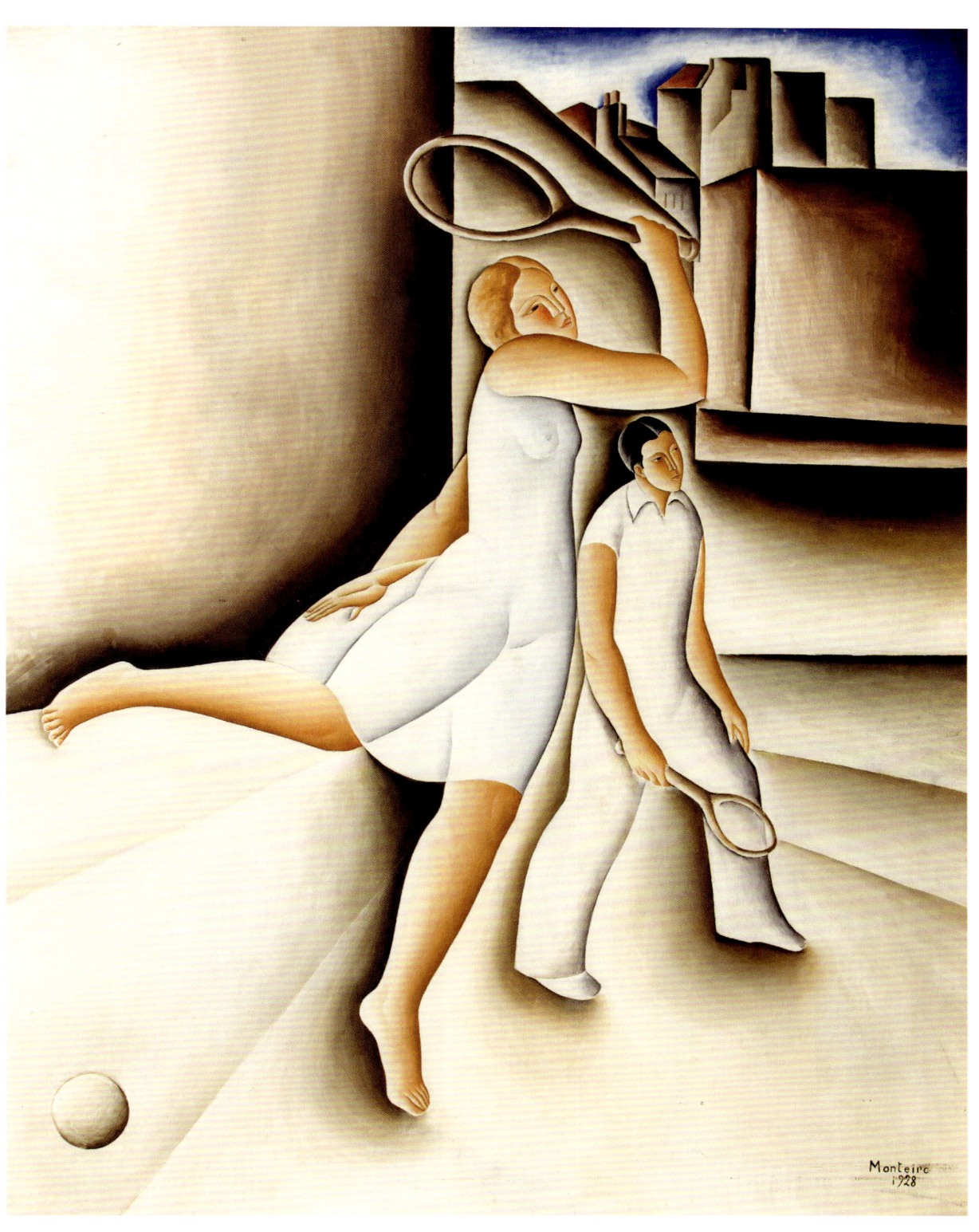

53 **Vicente do Rego Monteiro**

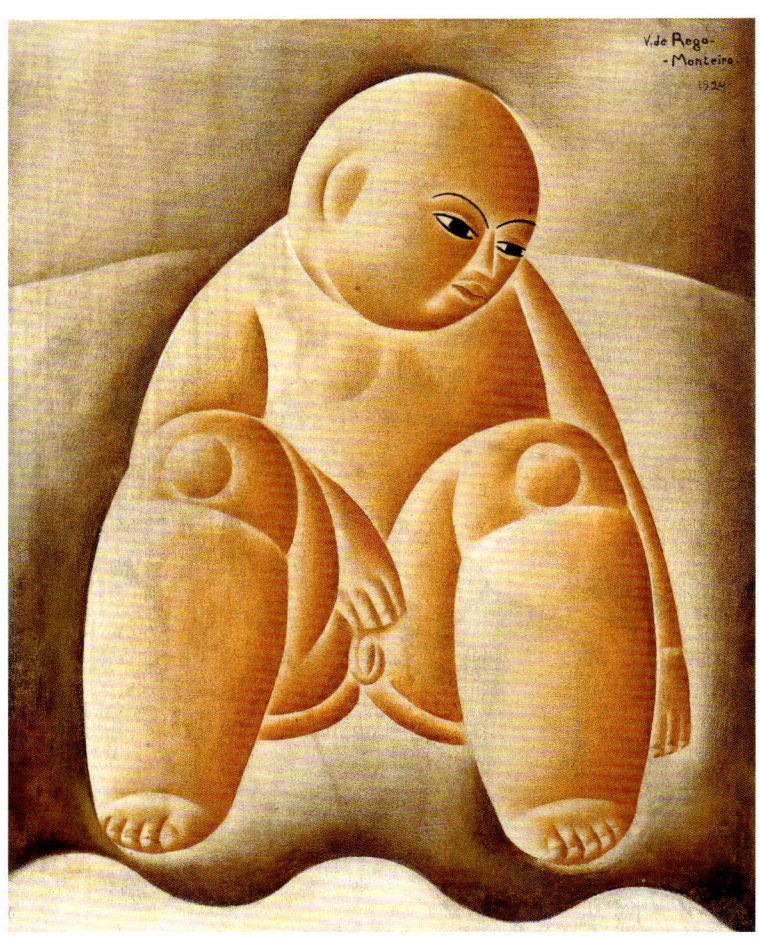

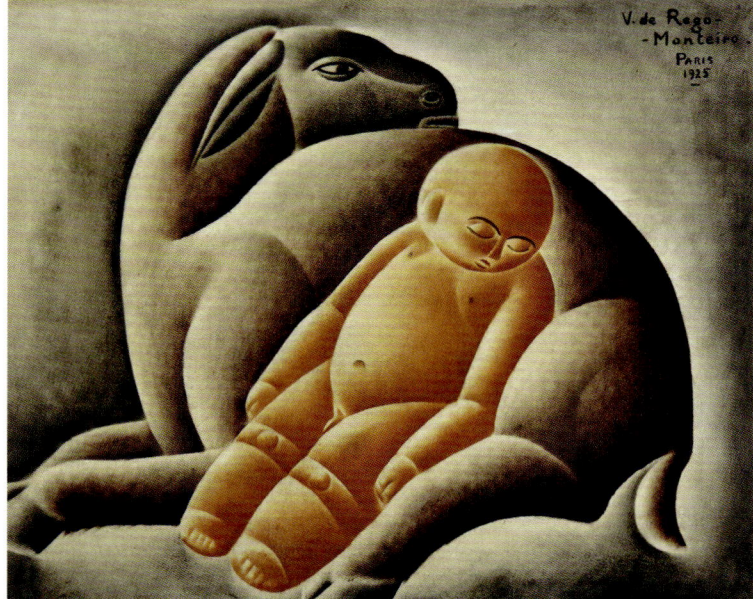

Brasil! Brasil!

Untitled, 1924

**Menino e ovelha
(Boy and Ewe)**, 1925

**Menino nu e tartaruga
(Nude Boy and Turtle)**, 1923

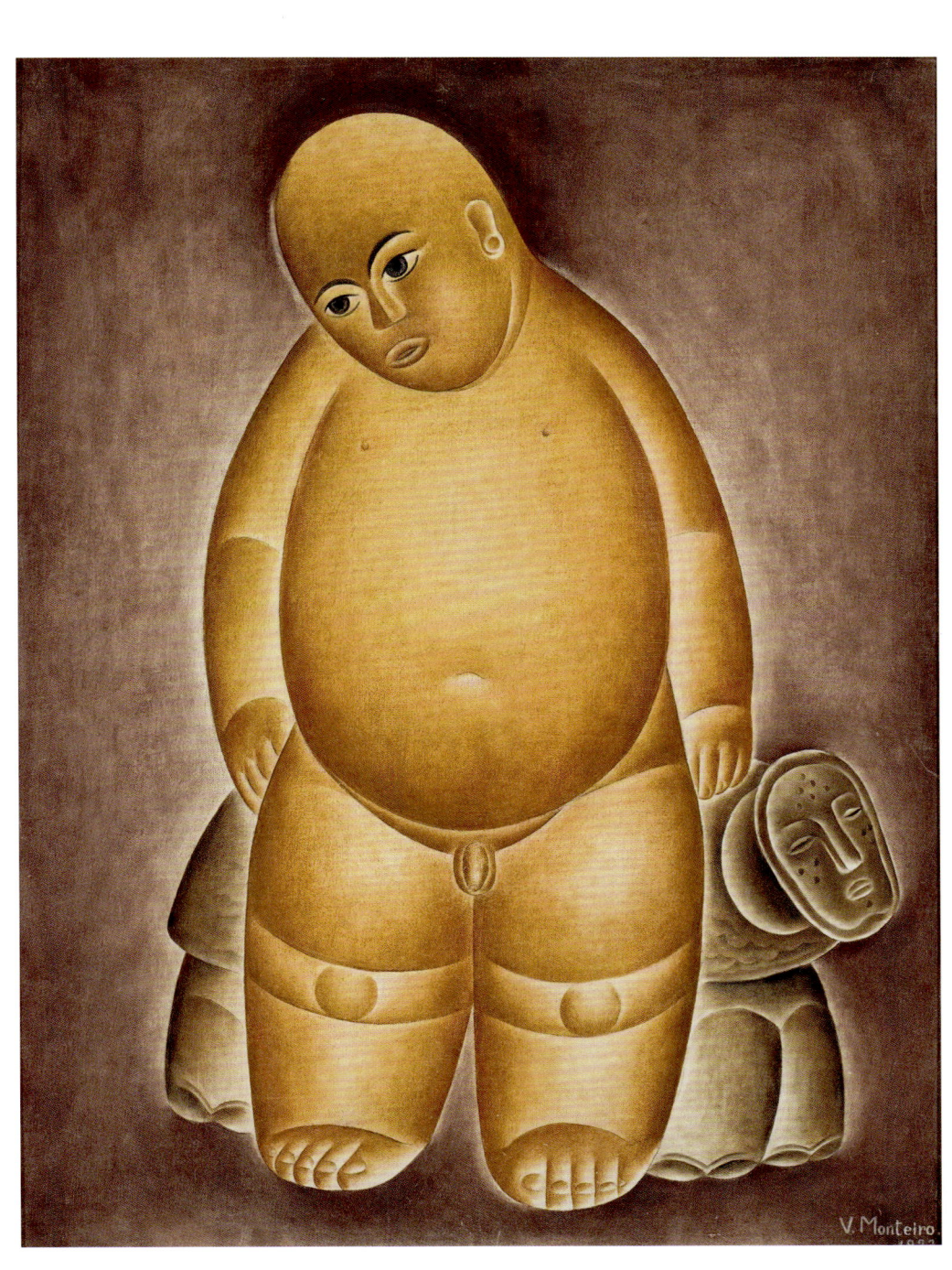

55   **Vicente do Rego Monteiro**

Literature

The Head of Mário de Andrade: Spectres of *Macunaíma* in Brazilian Culture

Eduardo Jorge de Oliveira

In 2018, the Indigenous artist Denilson Baniwa depicted what could be considered the head of Mário de Andrade in a basket (fig. 1). Black, with closed eyes and an open mouth, the head rests beside an edition of *Macunaíma*, Andrade's masterpiece published in 1928. The novel is widely regarded as one of the most significant achievements of São Paulo modernism and has become an indispensable work of twentieth-century Brazilian literature. In Baniwa's painting, a note placed in the same basket reads "here lies the simulacrum Macunaíma". Baniwa criticises the modern ideal of a Brazilian people as well as the *Manifesto Antropófago* (Anthropophagic Manifesto, see pp. 14–15), which was published not by Mário but by Oswald de Andrade in the same year as *Macunaíma*. Could this be the head of Mário, of Macunaíma, or of a figure as hybrid and ghostly as Macunaímário? On the one hand, Baniwa's gesture can be seen as a desacralisation of the anthropophagic canon, or at best, as an Amerindian re-appropriation of the characterless hero[1]. On the other hand, it can be understood as an accomplishment that would have delighted Mário de Andrade himself, especially when considering the verses of *Lira paulistana* (Lyre from São Paulo), a poem in his eponymous book published in 1945, shortly after the poet's death. Mário was extremely deliberate about the division of his own body after death, even requesting that his heart ("a living heart and a dead one") be buried in the São Paulo city centre, at Pátio do Colégio, and his ears be left at the Telegraphs ("I want to know about other people's lives"). "Bury my feet on Rua Aurora, / Leave my sex in Paissandu, / On Lopes Chaves, my head, / Forget about it." Irony did not fail to produce a metaphor: Mário's head ended up in a museum, as Baniwa's painting is part of the collection of the Pinacoteca de São Paulo. This is certainly not an end but rather a new beginning. The supposed head of Mário de Andrade remains in São Paulo, associated with the "simulacrum Macunaíma". Denilson Baniwa aptly captured the ghostly dimension of Macunaíma, a character so controversial that, since 1928, he has circulated within Brazilian literature and culture under the epithet of *the hero with no character*.

In 2019, a small book titled *Makunaimã – O mito através do tempo* (Makunaimã: The Myth Through Time) was published. This theatrical and polyphonic work features Mário de Andrade as one of the characters and is set on Lopes Chaves Street, where the author of *Macunaíma* once

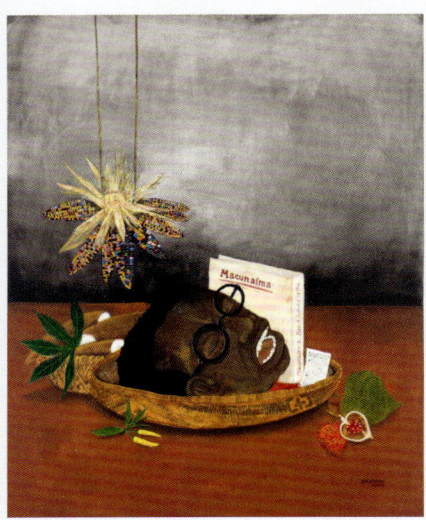

Fig. 1
Denilson Baniwa, *Re-Antropofagia*,
2018, mixed media, 120 × 100 cm,
Artist's collection, on loan at
Pinacoteca de São Paulo

lived. Adapted into book format, the text is complemented by paintings by Indigenous artist Jaider Esbell. The myth of Makunaimã, collected by the German ethnographer Theodor Koch-Grünberg, is depicted in a photograph: Akuli Taurepang, in the role of an Indigenous informant, recounts the myth to a visitor who diligently transcribes it with notebook and pen. Their position in the photo resembles a "writing lesson", to borrow an expression from Claude Lévi-Strauss in *Tristes tropiques*[2]. "Makunaima" is a myth featured in *Vom Roraima zum Orinoco*, a book that served as one of the primary sources for Mário de Andrade, who identified himself as the character, stating: "I came across Macunaíma at the German Koch-Grünberg. And Macunaíma was a hero surprisingly lacking in character. (I was thrilled.) I lived his cycle of exploits up close."[3] This lively and unsettling source deals with various layers of traditions and translations. One aspect pertains to the myth's circulation among the Taurepang, Macuxi, and Wapichana peoples, while another involves the direct translation of the narrative into German before the myth

began to circulate, in literary form, in Brazil through Mário de Andrade. With this singularity, Mário helped solidify a new sensibility following the early years of modernism. The reason is well known: adjusting the hands on the clock of modernity did not simply entail imitating what was being produced in Europe. This also applies to Futurism, which was often misunderstood in Brazil. Corresponding changes were reflected in the course of the 1920s in Brazilian modernism, where technical achievements were combined with popular culture. Thus, in the cultural sphere, Mário de Andrade played an effective, passionate, and compelling role, as his actions were pivotal for both establishing cultural institutions[4] and preparing for the *Semana de Arte Moderna* (Modern Art Week) in 1922.

In 1921, when reckoning with Parnassianism by writing a lengthy study titled *Mestres do Passado* (Masters of the Past), Mário de Andrade buried the extravagances of this literary style, which was devoted to formal perfection, far removed from the country's reality. Mário da Silva Brito is the first to take up Andrade's distancing from the Parnassian and symbolistically charged atmosphere in the period before the *Semana de Arte Moderna*. At the same time, he refers to the confusion that followed in the search for a new artistic language between Futurism and Primitivism. The blending of Futurism and Primitivism took place in all artistic fields, where technical, civilisational, and political issues were constantly being discussed anew against the backdrop of the zeitgeist. Thus, as Silva Brito writes, "Brazil begins the conquest of the twentieth century and its benefits by leveraging the means and resources that can provide it with well-being and mechanics."[5] In the same work, he recounts that the biggest name in Parnassian poetry, Olavo Bilac, took his first ride in an automobile in Brazil alongside the abolitionist José do Patrocínio. The poet was involved in the first car accident in Brazil, crashing into a tree. The anecdote seems to encapsulate the incompatibility between Parnassianism and Futurism, a term that has undergone various personal interpretations and misunderstandings.

One notable dispute arose between Oswald de Andrade and Mário de Andrade when the former wrote a contentious article about the latter titled *Meu poeta futurista* (My Futurist Poet) in 1921. Regardless of the influence of the manifesto by Italian artist Filippo Marinetti, mechanisation represented a sort of harbinger of the ages to come.

At the turn of the twentieth century, amid technological aspirations and the dream of literally taking flight, with balloons, airships, and his 14-bis airplane, the Brazilian inventor and aviator Alberto Santos-Dumont epitomised the desire for technical mastery (fig. 2). Under his father's orders, he heeded the advice: "Go to Paris, the most dangerous place for a young man. Let's see if you can make a man of yourself; I'd rather you didn't become a doctor; in Paris, with the help of our cousins, you will look for a specialist in Physics, Chemistry, Mechanics, Electricity, etc., study these subjects and don't forget that the world's future lies in Mechanics...".[6] In addition to the case of Santos-Dumont, the

Fig. 2
Santos-Dumont circling the Eiffel Tower, 1901.

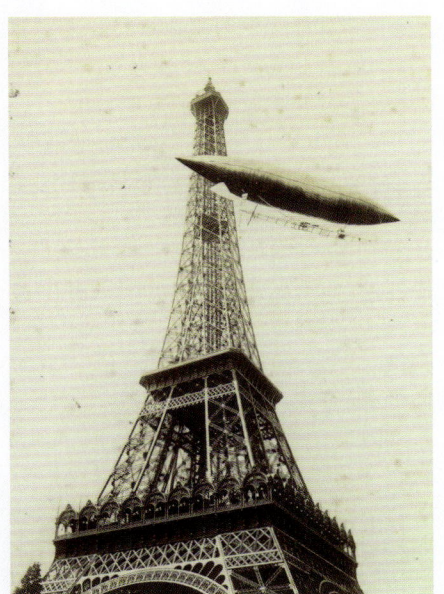

faith in mechanics, belief in fluids, and hope for steam were consistently intertwined with tropical elements such as vegetation and fruits. This amalgamation reflected a burgeoning poetics seen in works like Mário de Andrade's *Pauliceia desvairada* (Hallucinated City, 1922) and Oswald de Andrade's *Manifesto da Poesia Pau-Brasil* (1924) and his anthropophagic *Manifesto Antropófago* (1928), as well as the image of the "technicised barbarian" in *Revista de Antropofagia*, which adopted a more radical tone than the *Semana*. In Mário's *Pauliceia*, the poem *O domador* (The Tamer) vividly captures this urban environment amid the advent of technology:

Heights of the Avenue. Tram 3.
Asphalt. Vast, high streams of dust
under the harlequin of a
gold-pink-green sky...
The ensnarled filth of urban planning.
Manueline fillets. Bald spots of Pennsylvania.
Gothic cries.
Ahead, the irrigation tram
where a bewitched sun disperses
in a Persian triumph of emeralds,
topazes, and rubies...
Languid Boticellis reading Henry Bordeaux
in the dragonless cloisters of the turrets...

Mário, pay the two hundred réis.
There are five at the bank: one white,
one night, one gold,
one grey from consumption and Mário...
Solicitudes! Solicitudes!

But... behold, oh my nostalgic eyes of yesterdays,
this enchanted Avenue spectacle!
Revive, oh gauchos from São Paulo, ancestrally!
And oh, horses of bloodthirsty cholera!
Chinese orange, Chinese orange, Chinese orange!
Avocado, cambucá and tangerine!
Watch out! To the applause
of the exuberant clown,
heroic successor of the rugged
race of bandeirantes,
a son of immigrant passes by proudly,
blondly taming an automobile![7]

It is already a broken Mário who speaks in 1922. The city is a fragmented whole. São Paulo is a mosaic of architectural styles and traditions. The poem criticises architecture, which proliferates in different styles and grows uncontrollably, blending fruit names, vendors' cries, a fading past, and transformed migration. The automobile symbolises not only progress but also fusion, as depicted in *Macunaíma*, where the puma, Palauá, consumes petrol, loses its scent, and acquires car-like characteristics: "She roams all around with wheels on her paws, a motor in her belly, castor oil in her gullet, water in her nostrils, gasoline in her derriere, those two great big fireflies in her mouth, with that banana leaf cape on top, holy moly! ready to take off like a shot".[8] Here, the Brazilian language operates in the transformation of the becoming of speech itself, with traces of orality contaminating technical progress with mythopoetic thought. In addition to addressing cultural hybridity, the quote evokes the figure of Macunaíma as a national spectre, one that haunts any attempt to create a literature that is legitimately Brazilian. The hero's lack of character suggests ambiguous and border-crossing origins, as Eduardo Sterzi points out, noting that the character's birthplace lies on the border between the Brazilian state of Roraima and Venezuela: "Macunaíma is as Brazilian as he is Venezuelan", with a destiny that extends beyond national borders and into "song and constellation".[9] The forest disregards borders and expands through various forms of knowledge conveyed by myths. The current issue around Macunaíma concerns political-national impurities and mytho-cosmological purities that the novel accentuates through the perspective of a character with a collective voice – the Brazilian "people" – particularly focusing on Indigenous and African voices that become "whitened" in the urban landscape. In this context, the metropolis itself, exemplified here by São Paulo, shares a *characterless* dimension, its transformation intertwined with the assimilation of *Tristes tropiques* by Caetano Veloso, who said, "here everything seems like it is still in construction and already in ruin". However, in Mário de Andrade's poem, this condition has yet to fully materialise. Mário de Andrade greets a new Brazilian generation that is nationally as impure as Macunaíma. In this light, it is noteworthy to consider Sterzi's interpretation of *Macunaíma*, which posits that the notion of an "allegory of national formation" does not align with the "hero with no character" in the subtitle of the book. According to Sterzi, "at the time of its making and publication, 1926–1928, Brazilian modernism was already undergoing a major internal crisis".[10]

Modernism thrives on crises, ambiguities, and criticism but also on irony, humour, and even sarcasm. Antonio Candido keenly observed this aspect, noting the influence of the 1922 *Semana de Arte Moderna*, which even extended to educational practices: "In literature, what may have seemed like a joke gradually became recognised as the norm of the new era, infiltrating even the guarded confines of education".[11] The *Manifesto Antropófago* and *Macunaíma*[12] not only grapple with the clash of civilisations and the historical violence stemming from the endless process of colonisation but also embody a literary principle that revisits legends, myths, and rituals across various document variations. Paradoxically, by delving into this repertoire, they distanced themselves from a European anthropological and scientific tradition, thus foreshadowing a later moment, as early as the 1930s, in relation to the depictions of the Brazilian people and the effervescence of popular culture. According to Bosi, this would lead to a resurgence of these works – Oswald's manifesto and Mário's rhapsodic novel – with *tropicalismo* in the 1960s, when, amid a countercultural atmosphere, Joaquim Pedro de Andrade brought the novel to cinema screens, creating a visual representation that immortalised the performance of actor Grande Otelo, who embodied Macunaíma's impertinence.

Denilson Baniwa's painting shares this impertinent, ironic, and humorous atmosphere. It not only evokes the modernist spirit but also the countercultural ethos, grappling with the spectres of Macunaíma throughout the decades. The painting is also part of a gallery of portraits of Mário de Andrade produced by artists such as Anita Malfatti, from 1923, Lasar Segall, from 1927, Candido Portinari, from 1935, and Flávio de Carvalho, from 1939 (figs pp. 37, 126, 96, 141). Each painting transports Mário de Andrade's face to a different place. The figurative struggles in depicting Mário expose divergent readings and visual interpretations not only in relation to the subject himself but also to the impact of his work on Brazilian culture. In this way, Baniwa's painting draws nearer to the multiple renderings of *Macunaíma*, embracing its morphological essence as suggested by Haroldo de Campos, and, even, as described by Alexandre Nodari, its metamorphological essence, capturing the myriad transformations that take place within the novel: "I did not come into the world to be a stone" but rather celestial: Macunaíma aspires to become a constellation; his future is ancestral, among the stars.[13] In this sense, following Nodari's argument, Macunaíma emerges as a narrative that seeks to transform bad encounters into good ones: "Brazil will only break free from inertia when it succeeds in transforming (turning) bad encounters into opportunities for good ones that surpass us, when it ceases to fragment the history of colonisation at its core, when it proliferates".[14]

　　These depictions of *Macunaíma* carry underlying themes that resonate with the importance of revisiting the novel, which gains new relevance for each new era, as evidenced in Oswald de Andrade's *Manifesto Antropófago*. It is evident now that *anthropophagy* has once again experienced a resurgence, this time through the works of Indigenous artists such as Denilson Baniwa, who are radically inviting a re-examination of their presence in Brazilian art and literature.

1　The re-appropriation of anthropophagy is the subject of a lengthy debate that examines the incorporation of Afro-Indigenous elements in the works of modernist authors and artists, as well as how the movement resulted in the absence of the very cultural actors who were the subjects of their representation. This theme has dominated discussions surrounding the centenary of the Modern Art Week of 1922.

2　Lévi-Strauss and Mário de Andrade had a friendly relationship that was also shared by the French anthropologist's partner, Dina Lévi-Strauss, who worked with Mário during their time in Brazil. See: Valentini 2013. It was with Mário de Andrade that the young professor from USP conducted ethnographic studies during weekends in the outskirts of São Paulo. A striking photograph capturing Mário in action, diligently taking notes, was taken by Claude Lévi-Strauss.

3　Andrade 2017, p. 212, translated by Katrina Dodson, published 2023, p. 217

4　See, for example, the case of the Preliminary Project for the Preservation of National Artistic Heritage, drafted by Mário de Andrade in 1936, which guided the institutionalisation of the National Historic and Artistic Heritage Service (SPHAN). In this regard, see: Torelly 2015, pp. 11–15

5　Brito 1974, p. 26

6　Santos-Dumont 1956, p. 17

7　Andrade 2013

8　Andrade 2017, p. 161, translated by Katrina Dodson, published 2023, p. 166

9　Sterzi 2017, p. 222

10　Sterzi 2017, pp. 220–221

11　Candido 2022 (1971), p. 10

12　In *Dialética da colonização* (The Dialectics of Colonisation, 1992), Alfredo Bosi highlights the *mythopoetic* essence of modernism centred in São Paulo and the Tupi sensibility that emerged from historical documents later reinterpreted in the *Manifesto Antropófago* and *Macunaíma*.

13　Nodari 2020, pp. 41–67

14　Nodari 2020, p. 45

Tarsila do Amaral

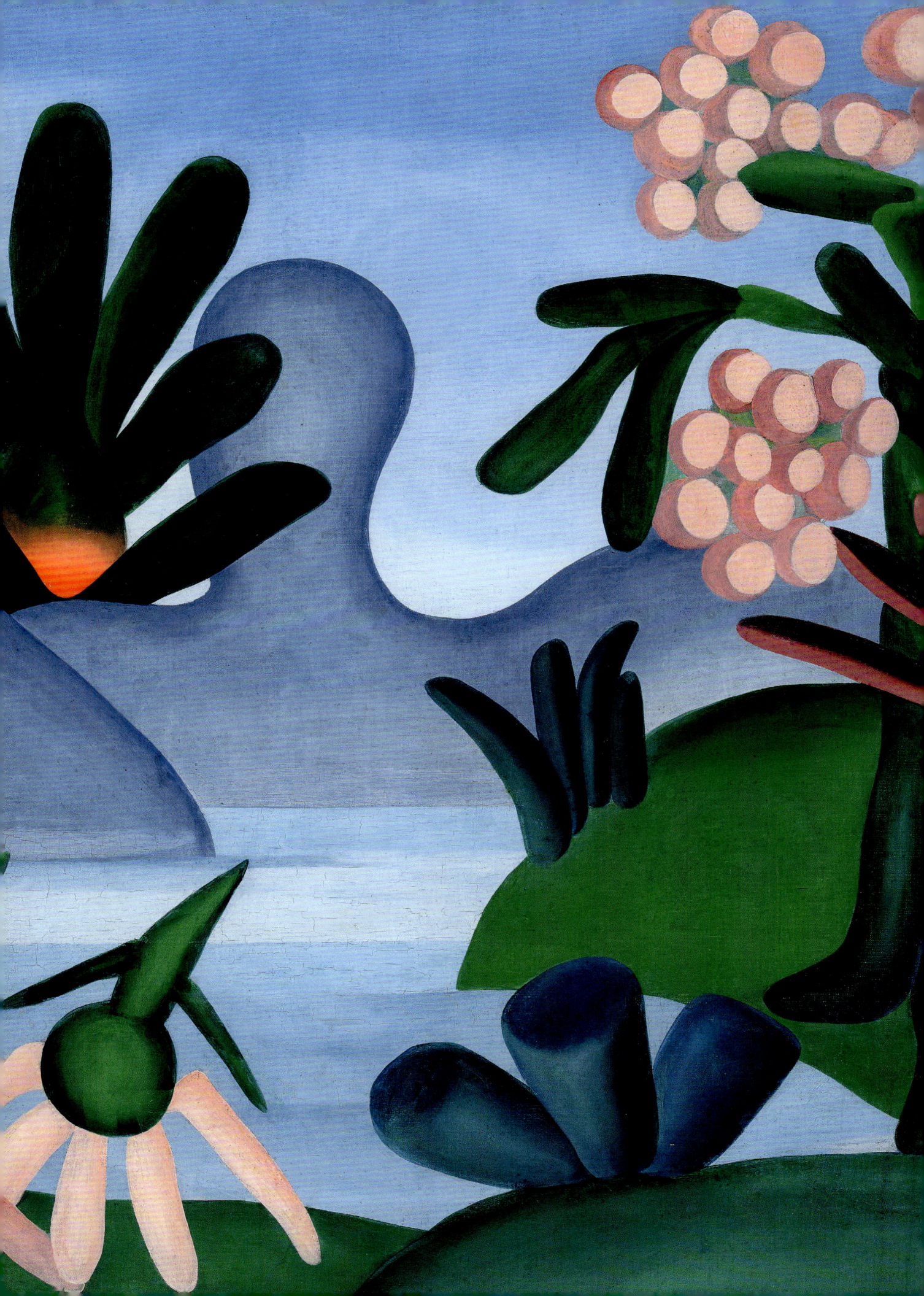

Tarsila do Amaral was born in Capivari, in the state of São Paulo, on 1 September 1886, two years before the abolishment of slavery in Brazil. She was the daughter of high ranking members of the rural coffee aristocracy of the state that had grown scandalously rich with the increasing worldwide demand for this commodity. Her childhood was spent mainly on her father's farms, where she experienced the rich *caipira*[1] culture of rural Brazil, living a relatively free existence among the lawns and earthen enclosures adjacent to the farm's main house. She played with rag dolls under the watchful eyes of formerly enslaved women, employees of the farm, who told her capricious stories of fantastical beings and otherworldly animals, immersing herself in the folklore and popular traditions of her country. At the same time, she was engrossed in European, particularly French, culture, as was then the custom amongst the Brazilian elite. She was taught her first letters by a Belgian nanny, played French music on the house's grand piano, and read French literature whilst lounging on the French furniture upholstered in French textiles that adorned its interiors. In 1902, after a stint of studies in São Paulo, she travelled with her family to Europe, enrolling with one of her sisters at a boarding school in Barcelona, where she would stay until 1904. On her return to Brazil she was quickly married off, as was to be expected of a lady of her rank. However, with her separation from her first husband, a scandalous affair at the time, (divorce would only be officially recognised in Brazil in 1977), and her move to São Paulo in 1913, her life story took a vertiginous spin as she started to seriously entertain the idea of becoming an artist.

In the coming years do Amaral studied with the sculptor William Zadig and the local master Pedro Alexandrino, as she said, "an old-fashioned painter. He spent 20 years in France and knew classical painting, the French painting of the time"[2]. Under his guidance she had a skylit, high-ceilinged studio purposely built for her, the first of its kind in São Paulo. In it Alexandrino gave lessons, and amongst his pupils was Anita Malfatti. Following the scandal of her 1917 exhibition, Malfatti had gone in search of a more traditional orientation for her work. Do Amaral and her soon became close friends. She would also study with Georg Fischer Elpons, a painter of Dutch Golden Age inspired still-lives. In 1920 do Amaral travelled with her daughter Dulce (from her first marriage) to London, where she left her in a boarding school, soon thereafter settling in Paris, where she attended the life drawing classes of the Académie Julian. She would also study drawing with Émile Renard. The work she produced during this stint of Parisian

Tarsila do Amaral
1886, Capivari, Brazil –
1973, São Paulo, Brazil

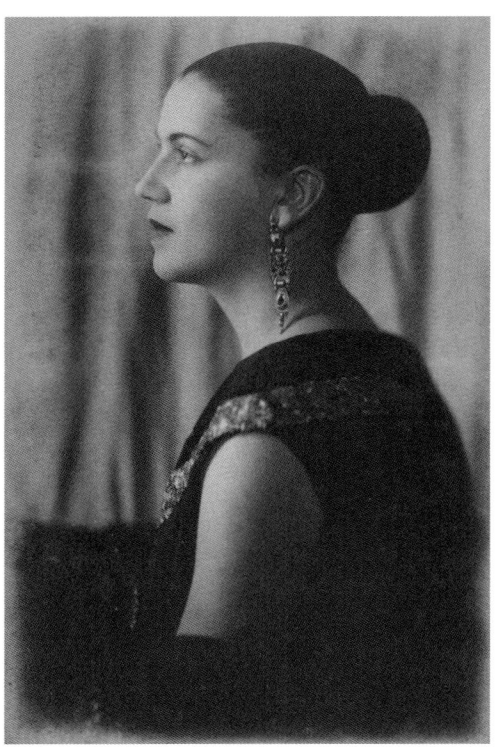

Brasil! Brasil!

studies is unremarkable, showing us a diligent student eager to master the more technical aspects of her craft, as becomes patent on examination of her self-portrait of 1921 (fig. p. 70). Back in Brazil in June 1922, four months after the *Semana de Arte Moderna* (Modern Art Week), she came in touch, thanks to her friendship with Anita Malfatti, with Mário de Andrade, Oswald de Andrade, both of whom she would portray in the same year in fluent, Post-Impressionistic portraits, and the poet Menotti Del Picchia. The five would call themselves the *Grupo dos Cinco*, driving around the city in Oswald's green Cadillac, whilst engaging in momentous discussions on the future paths of Modernism. A fruitful intellectual and romantic relationship soon flourished between Tarsila and Oswald, and they moved to Paris in the same year. By March 1923, Oswald would write to Mário de Andrade saying that he and Tarsila were already "shacked up".[3]

Back in Paris, do Amaral this time chose to study with more artistically progressive figures, such as André Lhote, Albert Gleizes and Fernand Léger. She deeply absorbed their works and Cubist aesthetics, as can be observed in *O modelo,* of 1923 (fig. p. 73). At the same time, she started amassing an important collection of Modernist art, one which would eventually include works by Pablo Picasso, Giorgio De Chirico, Marie Laurencin, André Lhote, Joan Miró, Robert Delaunay, Fernand Léger, and Constantin Brancusi. She also forged bonds of friendship with not only several Brazilian intellectuals and artists resident in Paris at the time, such as the writer, essayist, art critic and translator of Michel Montaigne into Portuguese, Sérgio Milliet, whom she also portrayed (fig. p. 71), but also French intellectuals, among them Jean Cocteau. More importantly she became close to the Swiss poet Blaise Cendrars, who would become a constant companion of the Tarsila/Oswald couple, nicknamed "Tarsiwaldo" by Mário de Andrade. The most influential work she produced during this time is undoubtedly *A negra* (fig. 6, p. 264), where for the first time in her oeuvre she manages to portray characters and memories from her childhood in the language of post-Cubist, modernist European painting. Several preparatory drawings for the painting have been preserved, and in them we see the many stages of development of this composition depicting a heavy, voluptuously monumental afro-Brazilian central figure with drooping, thick-set lips and a single bulky breast hanging heavily towards the ground (fig. p. 74). Do Amaral would declare that the hanging breast was a reference to a story she was told as a child that amongst the older enslaved women it had been a custom to tie a stone to their nipples in order to elongate them. Thus, it would have been possible for them to throw the extended breast over their shoulders, where their infants, tied to their backs, could be nursed whilst they worked the fields[4]. Behind this mother figure we find a geometric progression of colour fields, the obvious result of her apprenticeship with Léger, a semi-curved diagonal, a geometricised banana leaf, on the righthand side of the canvas breaking the hieraticism of the composition. A deep feeling for her home country and childhood memories is here allied with the desire for a contemporary Brazilian art in close contact with the formal developments of the European avant-gardes.

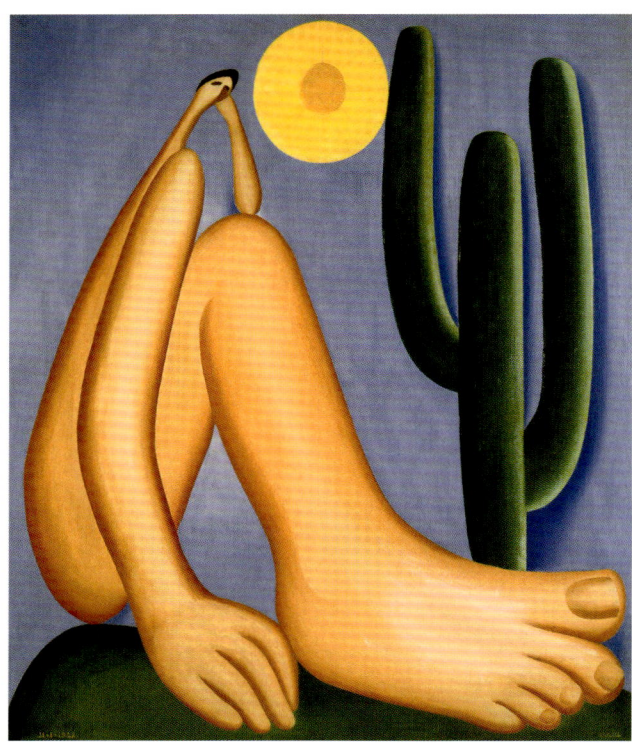

Fig. 1
Tarsila do Amaral, *Abaporu*,
1928, oil on canvas,
85 × 73 cm, Museo de
Arte Latinoamericano de
Buenos Aires – Fundación
Costantini, Buenos Aires

As she would write to her family:
"I feel more and more Brazilian:
I want to be the painter of my
homeland. How grateful I am to
have spent my entire childhood
on the farm."[5]

Do Amaral returned
to Brazil in early 1924, and for the
rest of the decade would alternate
periods in São Paulo with stays
in Paris. Soon after her return,
Blaise Cendrars arrived in Brazil
and, together with her, Oswald de
Andrade, Mário de Andrade, and
others, took part in the journey that
became known as the "Rediscovery
of Brazil", passing through Rio de
Janeiro during Carnival, and Minas
Gerais during Holy Week. The trip
exerted a powerful influence over
do Amaral, who made beautiful line
drawings of the places she visited
which would serve as starting points
for the illustrations she produced for
Blaise Cendrar's book of poems
Feuilles de route (figs pp. 78 and 79).
The artist would later declare: "It
was on occasion of Blaise Cendrars'
visit to our land that I, without the
slightest premeditation, or desire to
found anything like a school, produced the painting they dubbed Pau-Brasil.
(...) I, recently returned from Europe, felt a certain wonder before the folksy
decor of the housing in São João del-Rei, Tiradentes, Mariana, Congonhas
do Campo, Sabará, Ouro Preto and other little towns throughout Minas, all
full of grassroots poetry. So I turned back to tradition, to simplicity."[6] This
phase of her painting is characterised by her adaptation of Cubist formal
devices to the realities of her country's forms and colours, the ones she had
known and loved in her childhood. In *Morro da favela* and *A feira II* (figs
pp. 75 and 77) we see how successful do Amaral was in the development
of a highly original language, characterised by flatly blunt compositions of
Brazilian themes netted in pale pinks, blues and greens. It is interesting and
by no means fortuitous that Oswald de Andrade published his *Manifesto
da Poesia Pau-Brasil* in the same year. In it, he defended the principles of
what should be the aims of Modernist Brazilian poetry: primitive, naive, and
in tune with the proposals of the European avant-gardes. A year later he
would publish in Paris the book of poems *Pau-Brasil*, in which a dialogue
with do Amaral's paintings of the period is evident, the painter influencing

Brasil! Brasil!

the poet and vice versa. Do Amaral both illustrated the book and designed its cover, a stylised Brazilian flag. As Oswald would declare years later: "She (do Amaral) created *Pau-Brasil* painting. If we, the Modernists of 22, announced an export-grade poetry, it was she who illustrated that phase of material presentation."[7]

Her first solo exhibition was held in Paris, at Galerie Percier, in June 1926. She exhibited a collection of drawings and watercolours and paintings dating from 1923 to 1926, including *Lagoa Santa* (fig. p. 81), a diluted semi-urban landscape of discarnate forms. Eager to wed Oswald, a flamboyant, albeit deeply religious man at the time, do Amaral sought the annulment of her first marriage and wed him in a private oratory in São Paulo in 1926. They settled in São Paulo in an imposing mansion where do Amaral displayed part of her significant collection of Modernist art. There she also entertained intellectuals and artists whilst acting as a sort of luminary muse, her elegantly tailored beauty and sophisticated persona doing much to establish her as the leading lady of the movement.

The second phase of her painting, known as *Antropofágica*, began in 1928. The story goes that do Amaral gave as a birthday gift to Oswald the painting that would come to be known as *Abaporu* (fig. 1). Fascinated by it, Oswald invited one of his friends, the poet Raul Bopp, to see it. Deeply impressed by the telluric strength of the yet unnamed canvas depicting a monstrous central figure flanked by a gigantic cactus on its right and lit by an oppressively hot, sun shaped like a slice of an orange, they picked a Tupi[8] dictionary in search of a possible title. They eventually came up with the title *Abaporu*, a name composed of two different words, *aba*, meaning man, and *poru*, meaning who eats. The man who eats. The painting would inspire Oswald's writing of the *Manifesto Antropófago*, where we find the famous phrase "Tupi, or not tupi, that is the question"[9]. In it he proposed a vision of Brazilian culture in which its greatest strength was the ability to cannibalise other cultures, forging something new out of the digestion. Anthropophagy, a deeply set sacred custom of most Amerindian peoples prior to the colonisation of Brazil, was thus a symbolic escape from foreign cultural domination, and a means to proudly assert Brazil's heterogeneous culture. The movement that arose around Oswald's writings would in turn lead Tarsila to produce in 1929 another emblematic painting, *Antropofagia* (fig. 2), one in which formal elements derived from *A negra* are blended with others from *Abaporu*. Together these cannibalised formal snippets form a new monstrous figure, placed against a background also made up of elements from both paintings, such as the sun, the cactus, now fully occupying

Fig. 2
Tarsila do Amaral, *Antropofagia*, 1929, oil on canvas, 126 × 142 cm, Fundação José e Paulina Nemirovsky, São Paulo

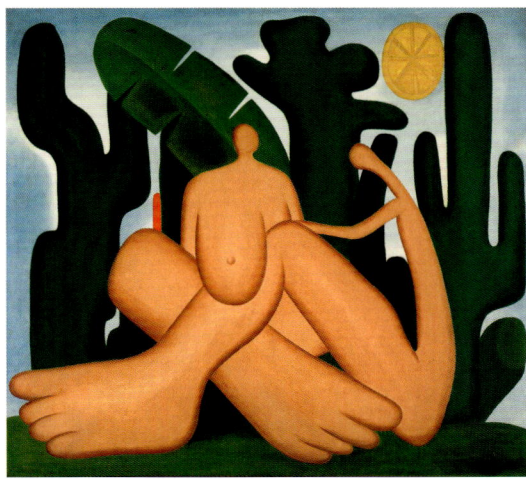

Tarsila do Amaral

the scenery against a pale blue sky, and the diagonal banana leaf. *O lago* (fig. p. 83), a still, metaphysical landscape of nocturnal silence inhabited by quasi-human cacti and other anthropomorphic flora, is another example of this phase of her painting.

With the crash of the New York Stock Exchange in 1929, the Tarsilwaldo couple and Brazil experienced dramatic changes. After the collapse of coffee prices on the international market do Amaral suffered serious financial setbacks. The artist was forced to give up the luxurious lifestyle she had known until then. Getúlio Vargas seized power and deposed President Washington Luís, Tarsila's best man at her wedding to Oswald, upturning the previous order. As Mário de Andrade would recall years later: "Nineteen thirty... It was all going to pieces – politics, families, artist couples, aesthetics, deep friendships. The destructive and festive drive of the Modernist movement had lost its reason for being, having fulfilled its legitimate destiny. In the streets, the people revolted, chanting: 'Getúlio! Getúlio!...".[10] Oswald de Andrade, in turn, started a romantic relationship with Patrícia Galvão, known as Pagu, "a schoolgirl that Tarsila and Oswald decided to transform into a doll. They dressed her, put shoes on her, and brushed her hair",[11] as Flávio de Carvalho described her. Because of this betrayal, do Amaral decided to separate from him.

Separated from Oswald, Tarsila became romantically involved in 1931 with the Marxist psychiatrist Osório César. She travelled with him to the USSR, where she held an exhibition of her work in Moscow. To finance the trip, do Amaral sold part of her collection of Modernist art. Returning to Brazil, she illustrated Osório César's book *Onde o proletariado dirige* (Where the proletariat leads), the result of his experiences in Soviet territory. She was shortly imprisoned in 1932 as a result of her visit to the Communist country. The following year, she gave a lecture on Soviet poster art and produced two socially engaged works, *Operários* (fig. 3) and *Segunda classe* (fig. p. 85). Sérgio Milliet, her friend of many years, described this phase of her work. "A third phase in Tarsila's painting would have the same impact on the Brazilian artistic scene: her social, or socialising, phase. (...) Tarsila would reach this new socially aware phase more through feeling than ideology, which is why she couldn't resist the appeal to return to her previous sensitivity for very long. She would soon return to her country landscapes, the innocent figures."[12] In the same year, no longer attached to Osório

Fig. 3
Tarsila do Amaral,
Operários (Workers), 1933,
oil on canvas, 150 × 205 cm,
Acervo Artístico-Cultural
dos Palácios do Governo do
Estado de São Paulo

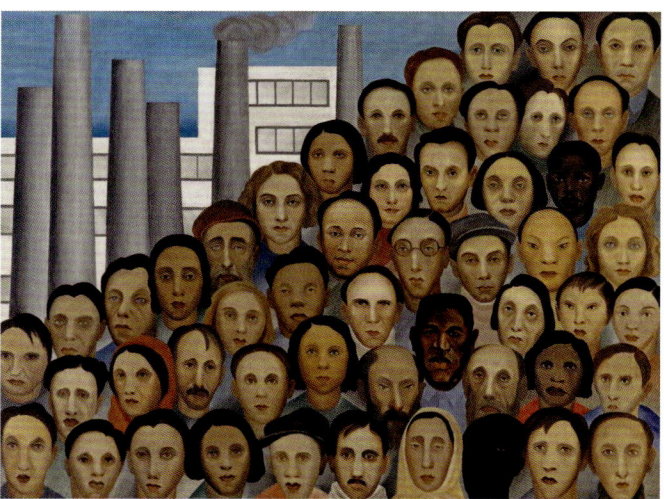

César, she organised an exhibition at the Palace Hotel in Rio de Janeiro, and met Luis Martins, a writer twenty years her junior with whom she would live until 1951.

During the 1930s and 1940s do Amaral would experiment with a series of different styles and formal possibilities, producing portraits, scenes of workers, and landscapes of varying degrees of quality. It must be said that her production suffered a considerable decline from then onwards. During the 1950s she would return to her style of the 1920s, remodeling subject matter and themes treated previously, such as in *Povoação I* (fig. p. 80). In 1950, an extensive retrospective of do Amaral's work, organised by her old friend Sérgio Milliet, was inaugurated at the Museu de Arte Moderna in São Paulo. After a period of relative neglect, her work began to be revisited by Brazilian critics. Nonetheless, her paintings would not be included in the inaugural edition of the Bienal de São Paulo in 1951. Three years later, in 1953, the monograph *Tarsila*, with an essay by Sérgio Milliet, was published, and her work once again began to be celebrated by commentators, her place in the history of Brazilian art thus reaffirmed. In 1969 the most important and extensive exhibition of her work was opened to the public, *Tarsila: 50 anos de pintura*, consolidating the unique place occupied by do Amaral's work in the Brazilian artistic panorama. At that moment she had been confined to a wheelchair for quite some time, suffering from ill health. On the morning of 17 January 1973, she died in São Paulo.

Giancarlo Hannud

1   The Portuguese term *caipira* has at its origin a series of Tupi words that originally referred to the inhabitants of the countryside. It designates the inhabitants of rural, remote areas of some Brazilian states, usually devoid of formal education, and their rich, miscegenetic culture.

2   São Paulo 1975a, p. 52

3   Apud Casarin 2022, p. 66

4   For a discussion of Tarsila's problematic appropriation of Afro-Brazilian and Indigenous subjects see the essays of Alecsandra Matias de Oliveira and Ana Paula Cavalcanti Simioni included in this catalogue.

5   Amaral 2003, p. 37

6   Amaral 1939, n. p.

7   Andrade 1991, p. 125

8   Tupi was the language spoken by many of the Indigenous inhabitants of the coastal regions of Brazil, belonging to the Tupi-Guarani language family. It was the *lingua franca* of Brazil during good part of the colonial period and played a significant role in the colonisation of the country and the forced conversion of its original inhabitants.

9   Andrade 2005a, p. 227

10   Andrade 2005b, p. 244

11   Apud Casarin 2022, p. 229

12   Milliet 1969

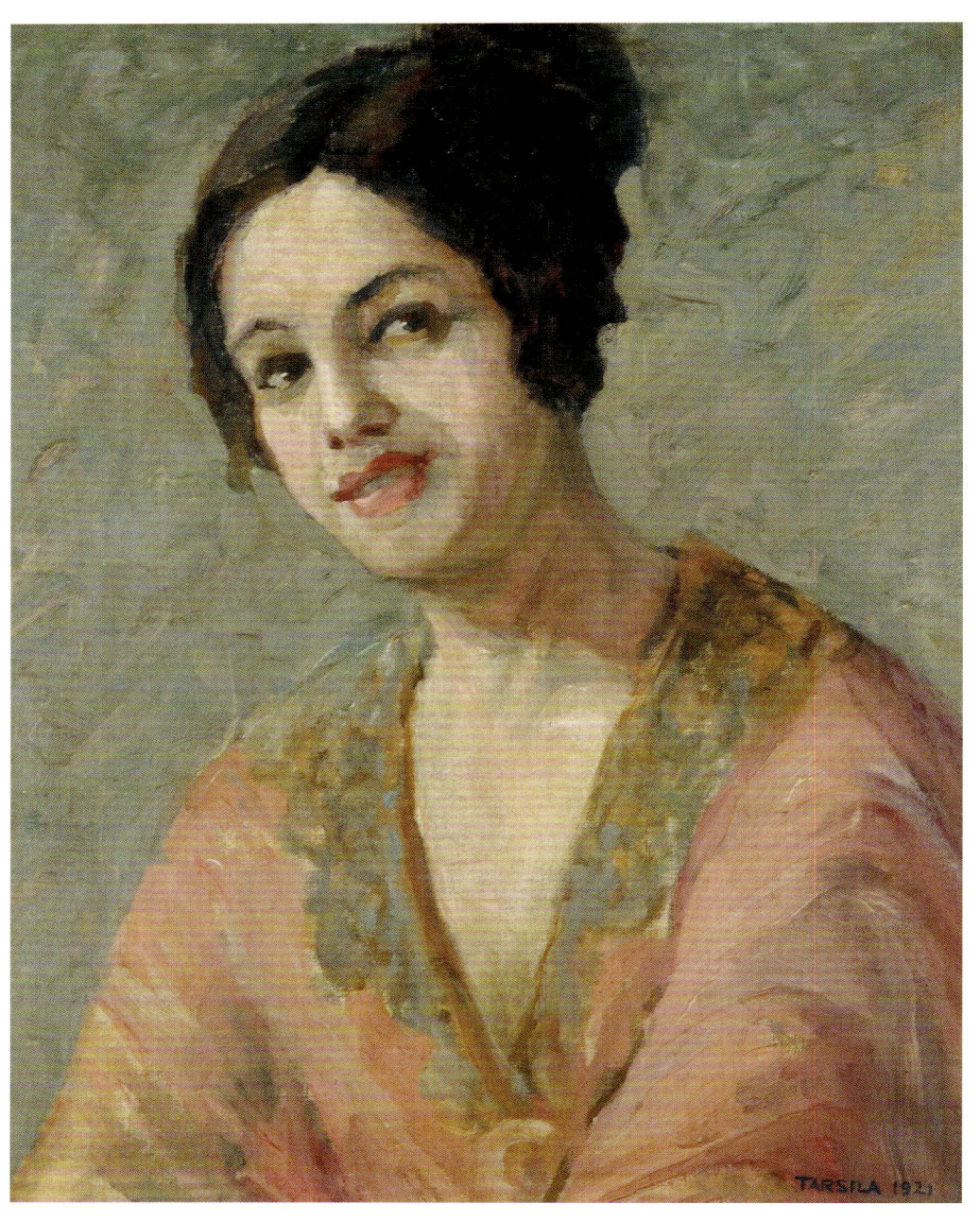

Autorretrato com vestido
laranja (Self-Portrait
with Orange Dress), 1921

Retrato azul (Sérgio
Milliet) (Blue Portrait,
Sérgio Milliet), 1923

Brasil! Brasil!

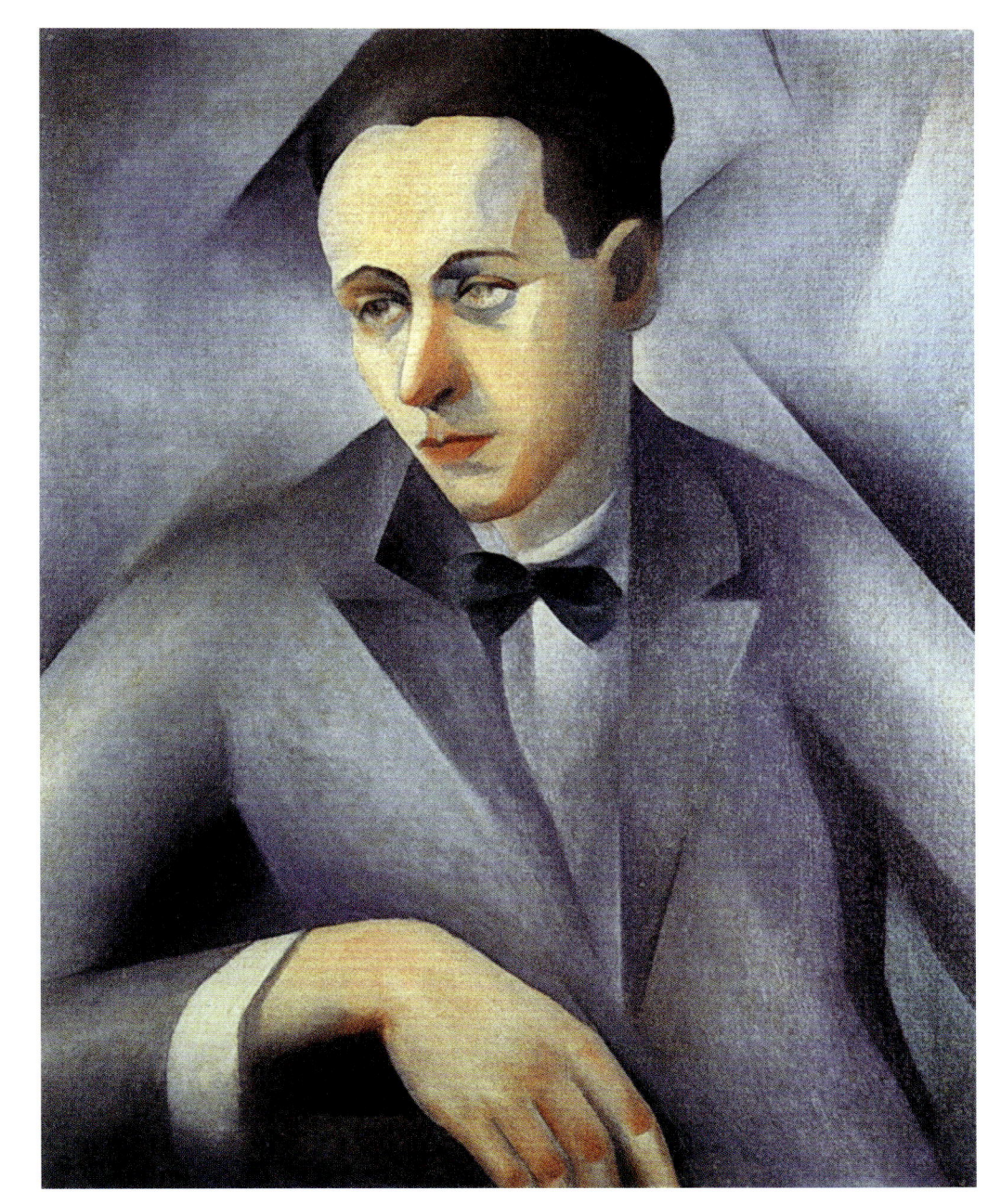

71   **Tarsila do Amaral**

O modelo (Model), 1923

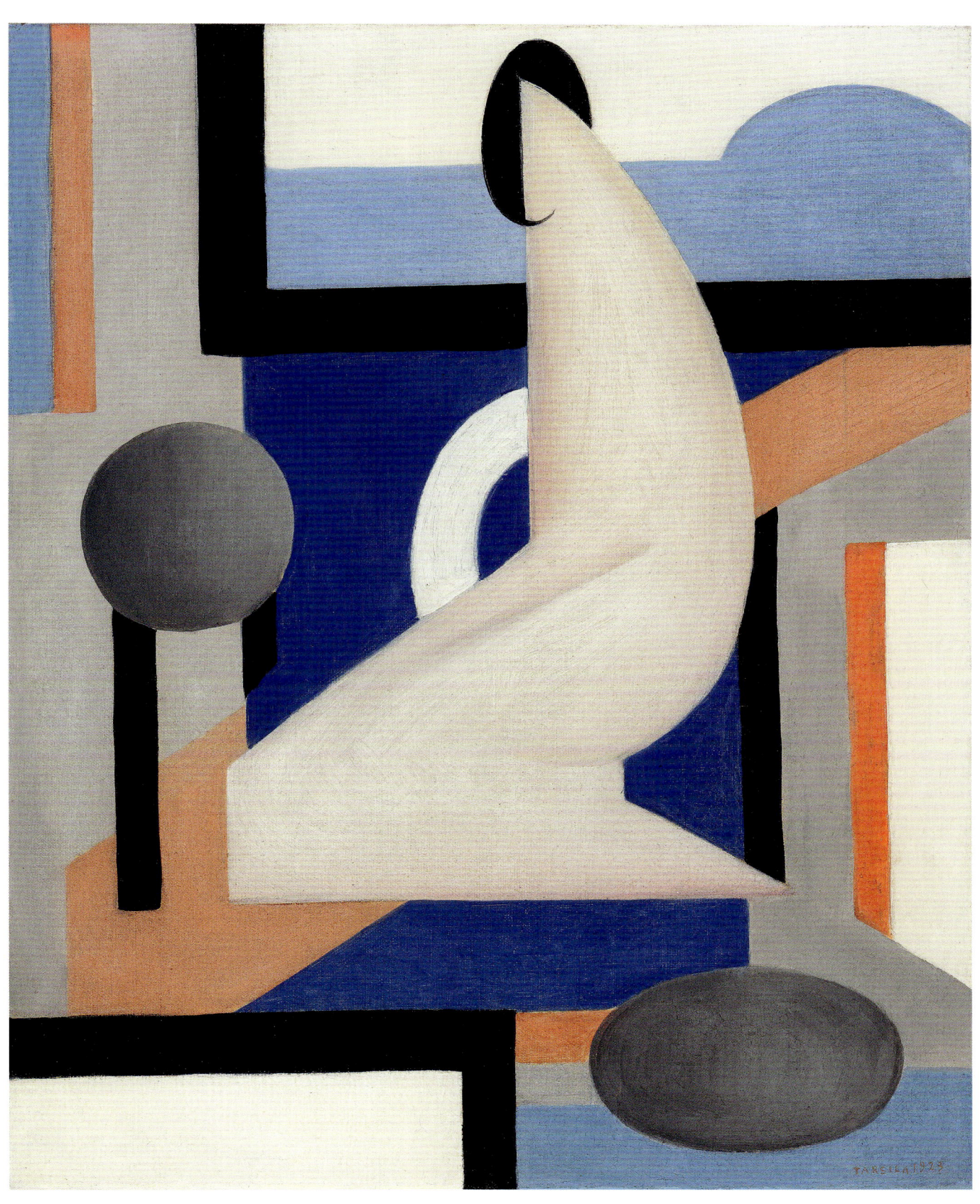

73   **Tarsila do Amaral**

Esboço para *A negra* (Sketch for *Black Woman*), 1923

Morro da favela (Favela Hill), 1924

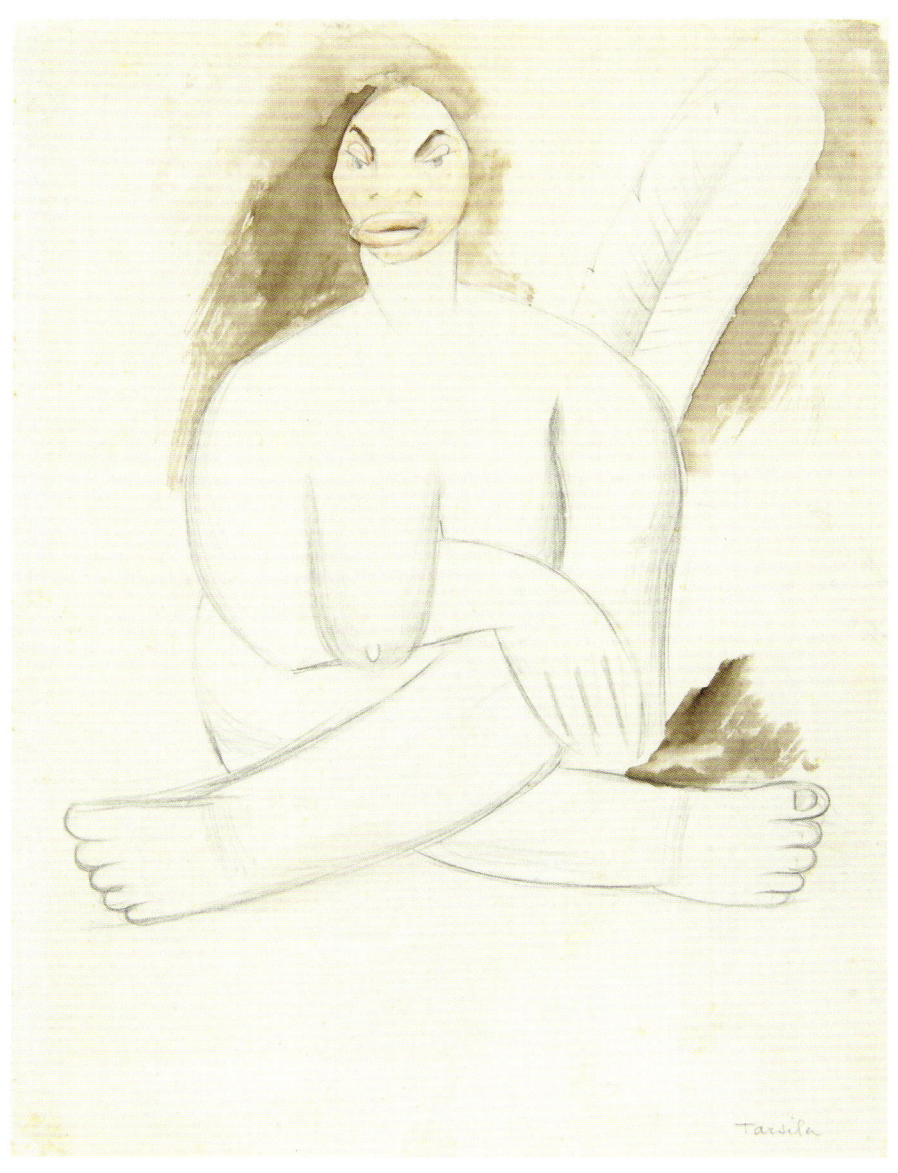

Brasil! Brasil!

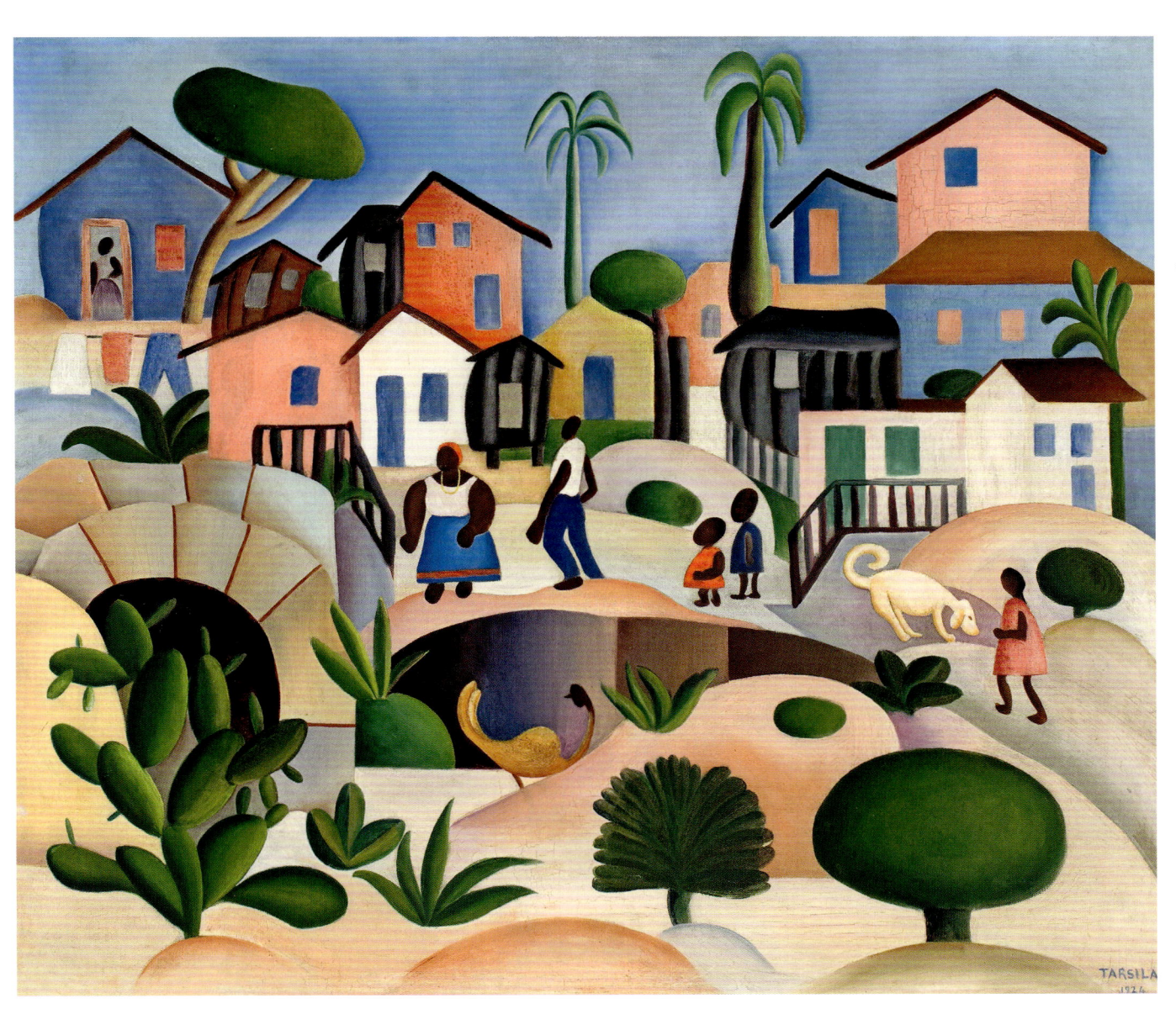

Tarsila do Amaral

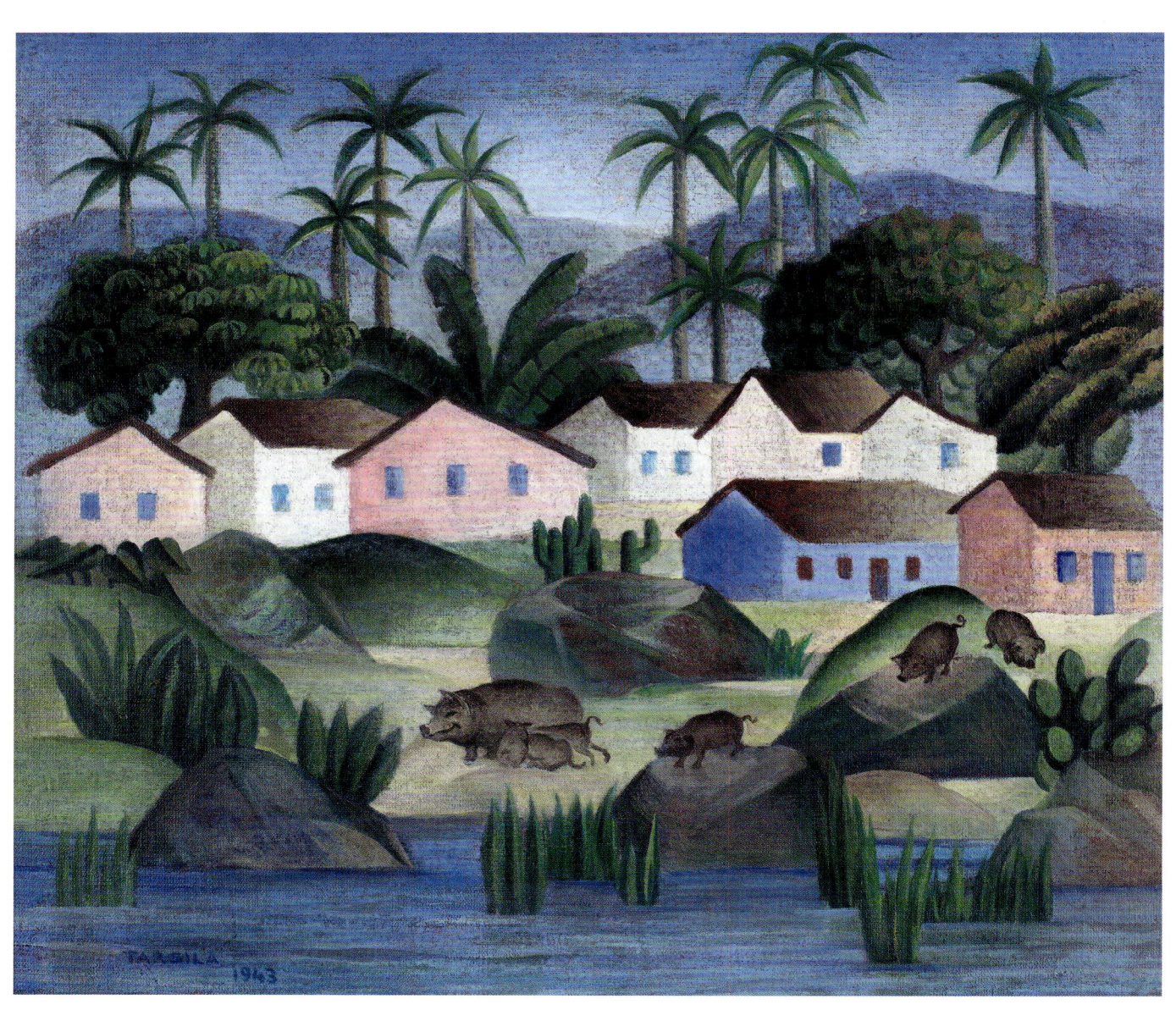

Brasil! Brasil!

Fazenda com sete porquinhos
(Farm with Seven Piglets), 1943

A feira II (Market II), 1925

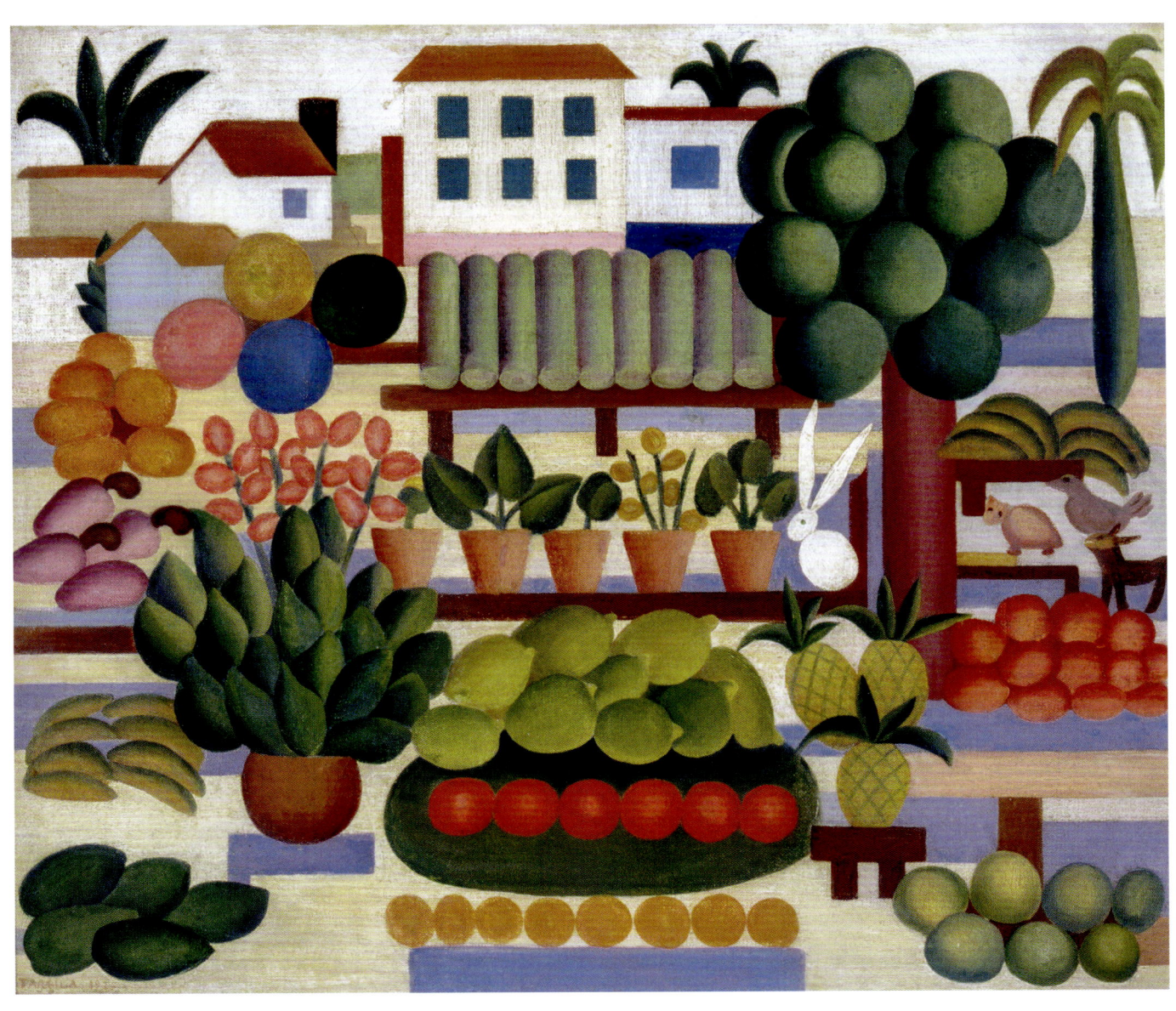

Tarsila do Amaral

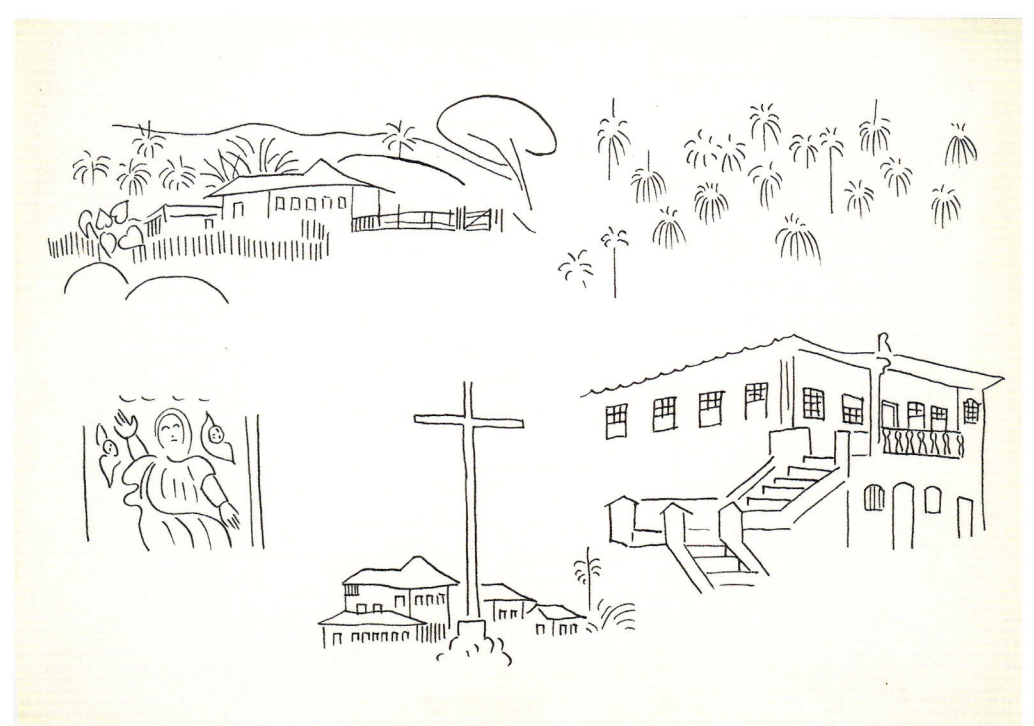

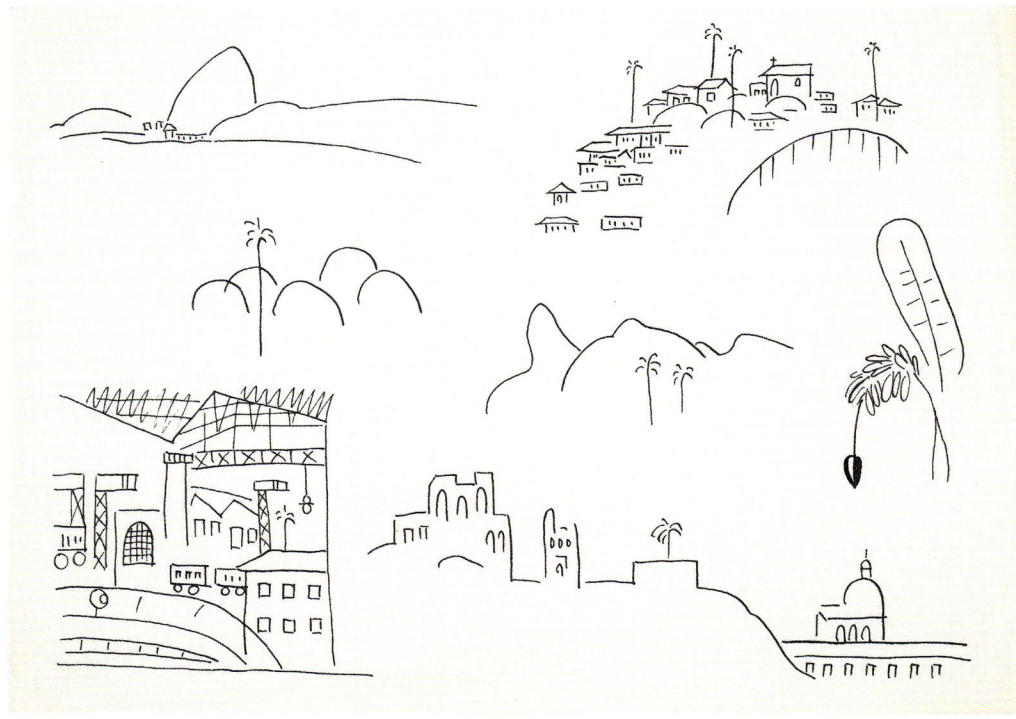

Brasil! Brasil!

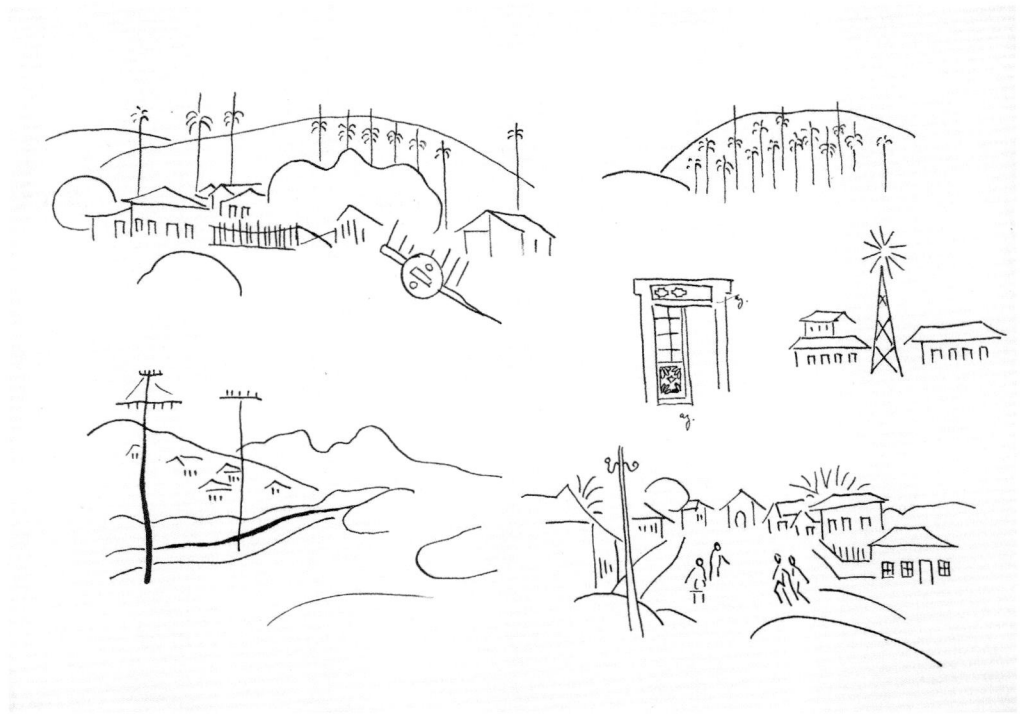

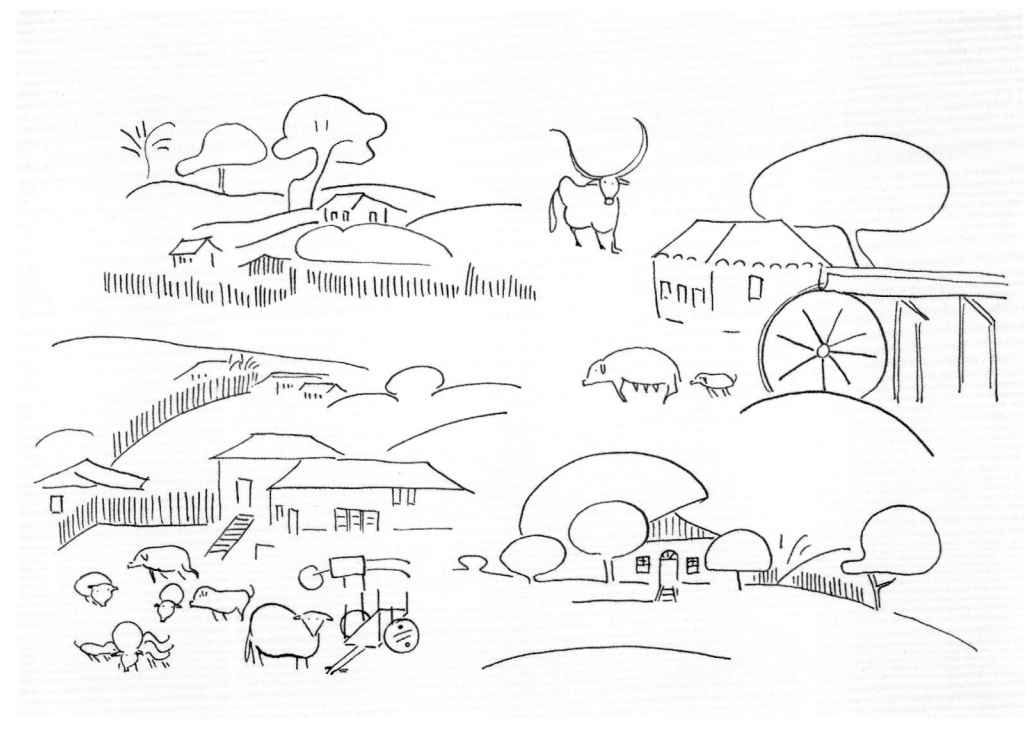

Tarsila do Amaral

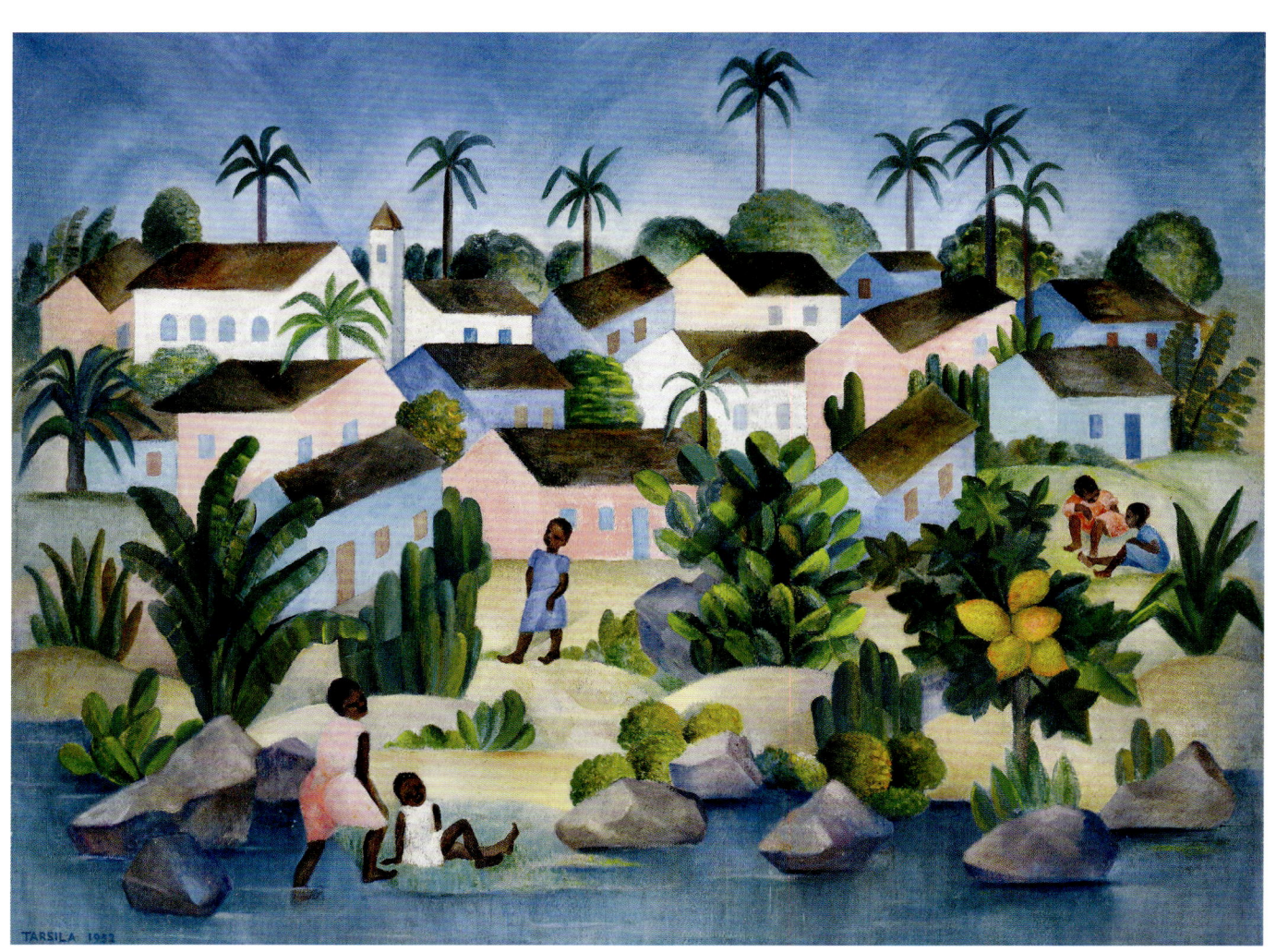

Povoação I
(Settlement I), 1952

Lagoa Santa, 1925

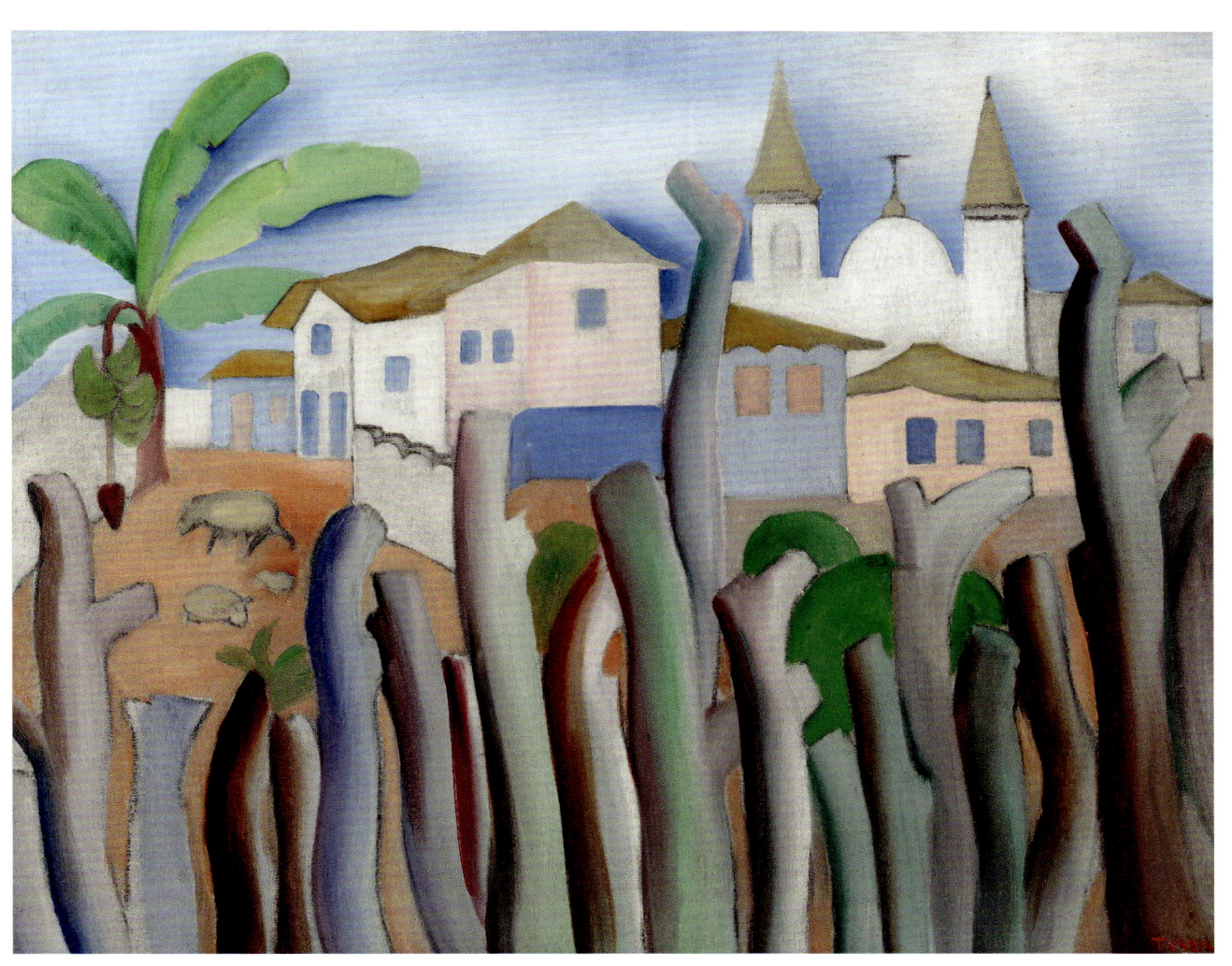

81   **Tarsila do Amaral**

Paisagem com ponte
(Landscape with Bridge), 1931

O lago (Lake), 1928

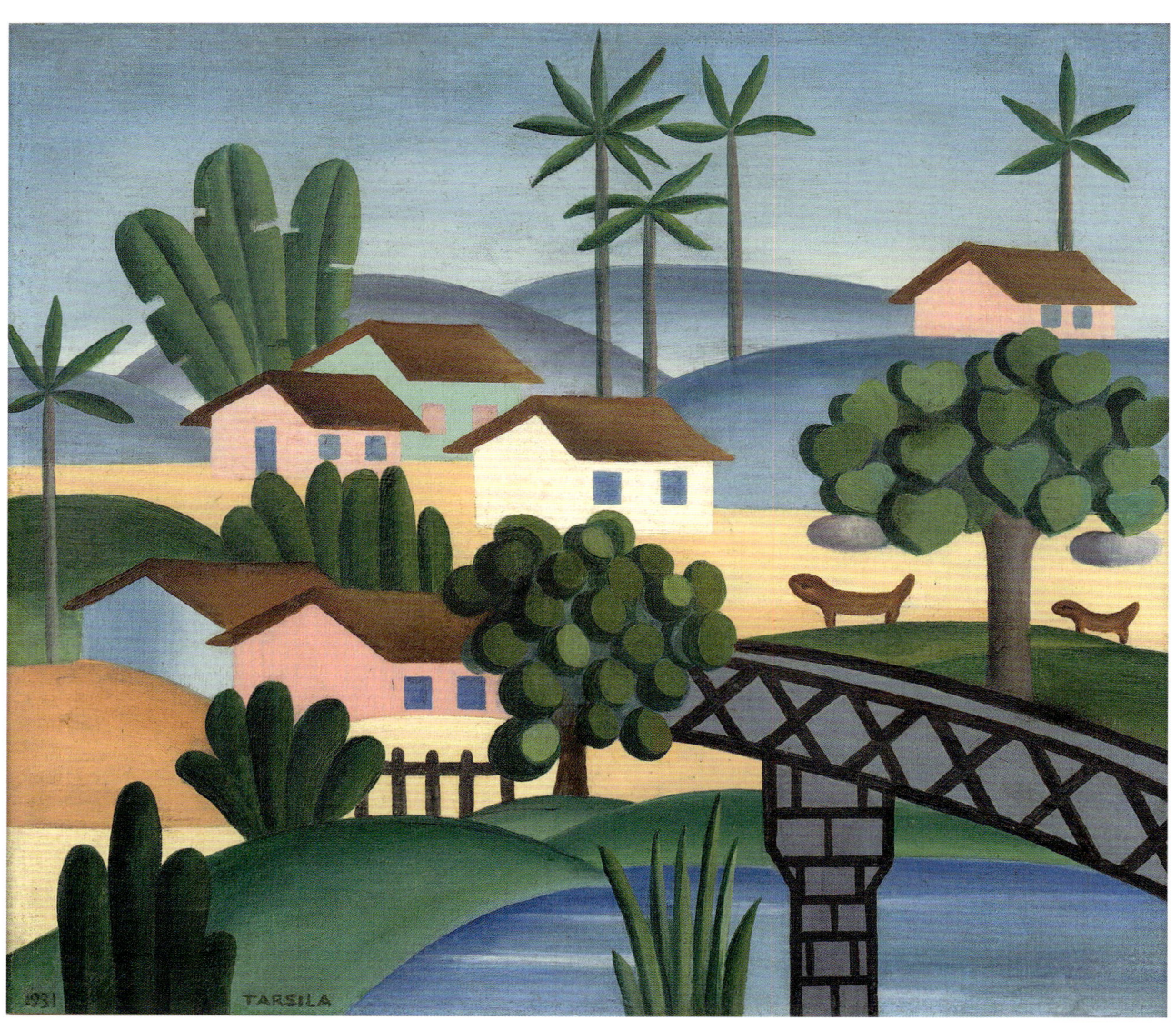

Brasil! Brasil!

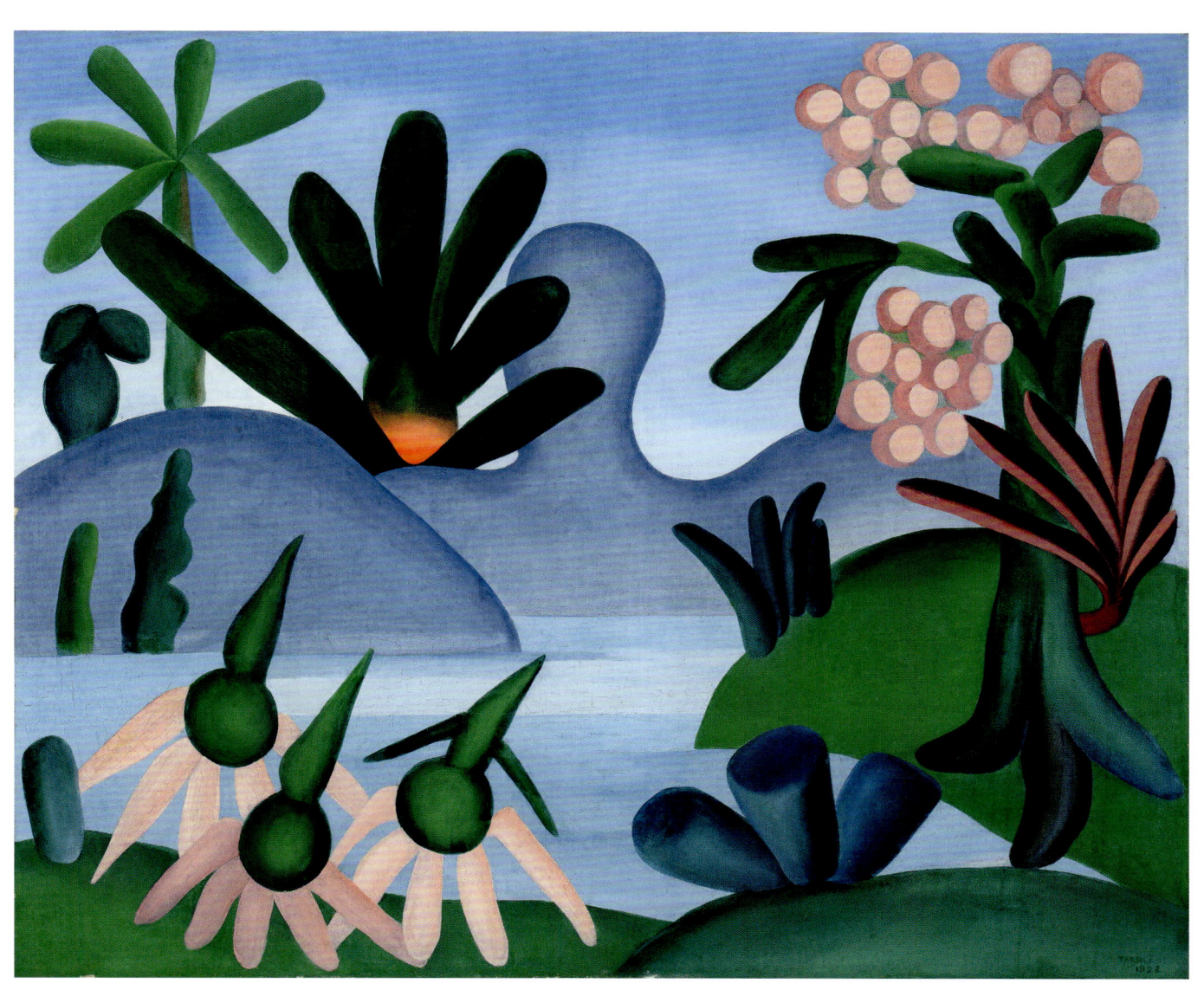

83   **Tarsila do Amaral**

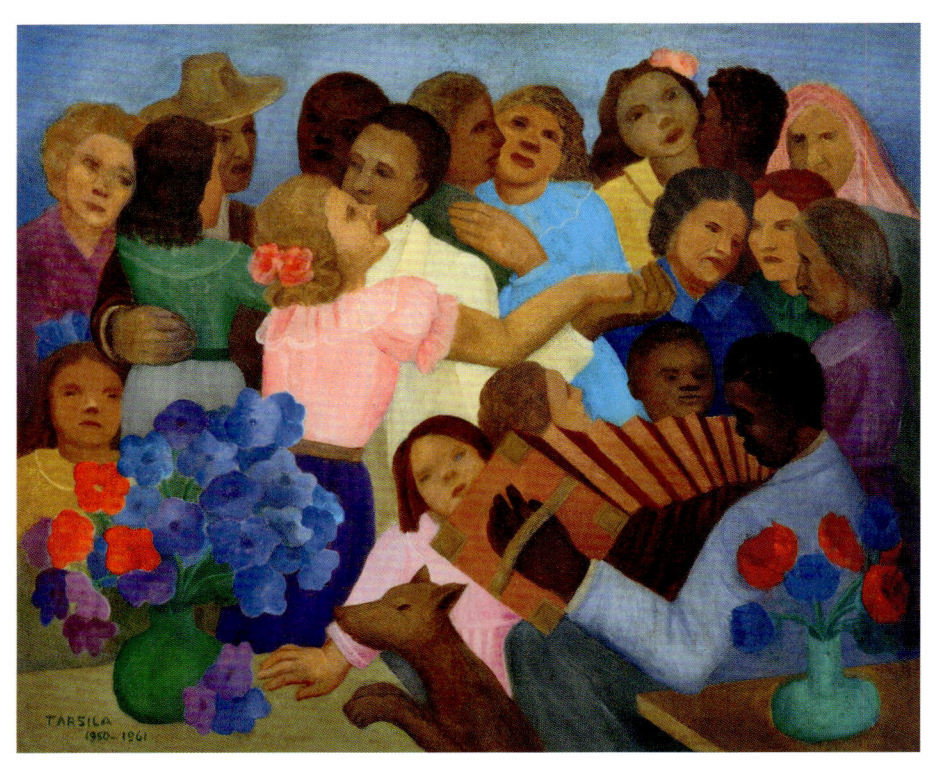

Brasil! Brasil!

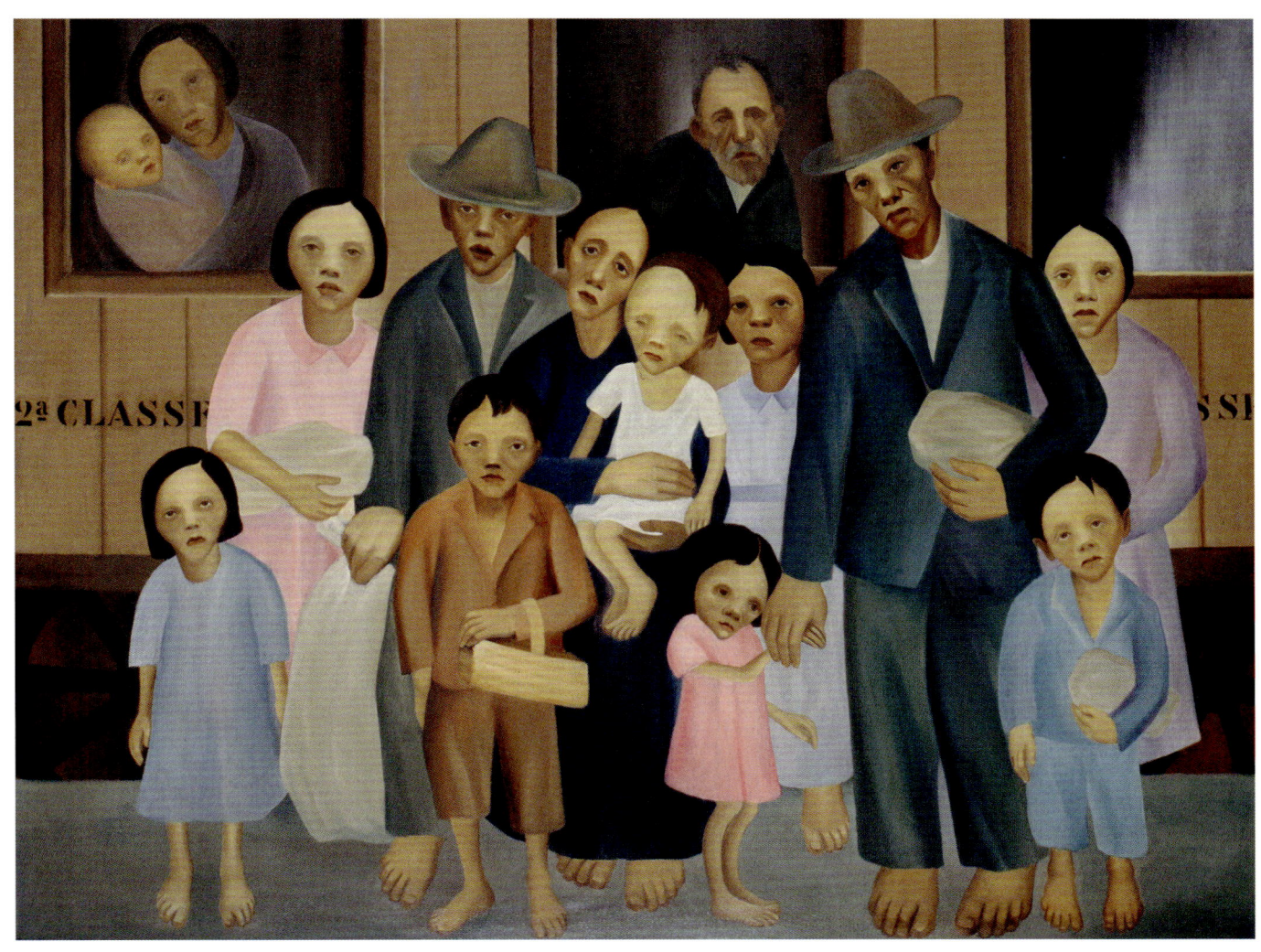

85 **Tarsila do Amaral**

Candido Portinari

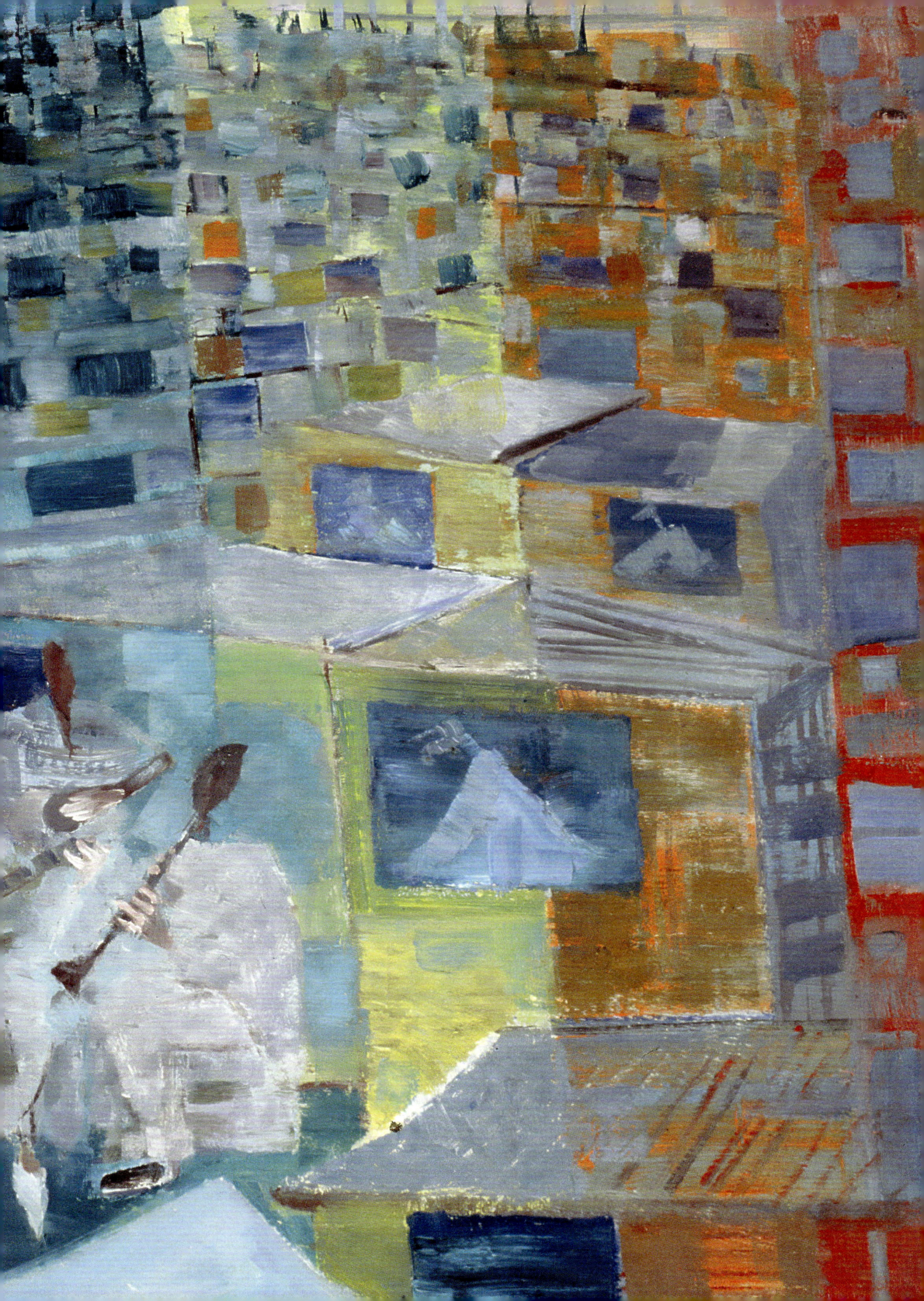

Memorial Fragments of Perceived Beauty. It is surprising that the artist who created so many extraordinary murals – works that required extensive studies, planning, time, assistants, and spacious studios – held such affection for the everyday world that surrounded him, or witnessed his growth. Animals, landscapes, family members, domestic objects, childhood friends, scarecrows, funeral processions, and children's games. In each of these encounters or memories, Portinari always seemed to perceive the hidden essence within the ordinary surface, something that dignified and made it unique. Not the appearance, but rather the soul that lay beneath or beyond banality. Each time, the solemnity and depth of his paintings impose themselves. This is a description of art, not a conventional understanding. Candido Portinari painted the Brazilian odyssey – memorial fragments of perceived beauty.

Candido Portinari was born on 29 December 1903 and died on 6 February 1962, at the age of fifty-eight. During his life, he became the most important religious painter in Brazil, the country's leading muralist, and the "revealer" of Brazilian people's ethnicity. He gave form to our memory and became an epic figure. He researched the sacred nature of Carajá art throughout his journey. His Carajá dancers are part of our history of recovering the culture of Indigenous peoples – not by merely copying their geometry, but by recognising their sacred and totemic rites. Through his work with churches and the Nonna's Chapel, he captured the sacred, the religious, the totemic, and the recording of our myths, thereby rendering permanent the affirmation of our modernism.

Candido Portinari is a visionary, a builder of reality from fragments.

Candido Portinari is the archetypal reference of Brazilian art. The affirmation of modernism.

Candido Portinari is a paradigm. He brings us a dream of what is to come. He is an artist immersed in our humanity, embodying both Brazilian and universal qualities. At the same time, he is a monument of the psyche, a milestone in our consciousness, a being who gave himself entirely, a slave to talent, a "miracle worker" who created a language that seems impossible for someone so physically fragile, and who died prematurely. Through his work, he shows us that it is possible. By giving himself, by putting himself at the disposal of his talent, Portinari did not empty himself but became a child of adventure, a man on his journey, in dialogue with history.

Candido Portinari
1903, Brodowski, Brazil –
1962, Rio de Janeiro, Brazil

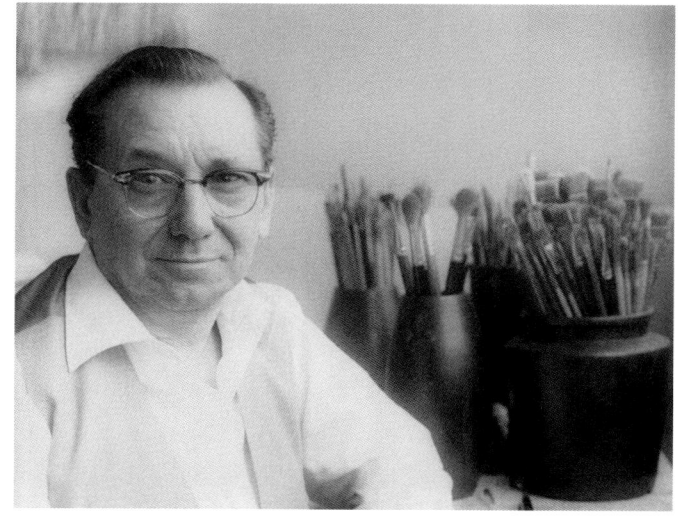

Brasil! Brasil!

"It was through you that we achieved our most universal expression, not only because of your work's resonance but also because of the very nature of your creative genius, which, even if ignored or denied, would still save us for the future" Letter from Carlos Drummond de Andrade, one of Brazil's foremost poets, to Portinari in 1946.

I consider Portinari the definitive marker of our modernism, one of the greatest Brazilian artists of all time, a national artistic symbol, and the creator of a monumental body of work with few equivalents worldwide. He authored an odyssey about Brazilian life and people. Furthermore, Portinari's aesthetic quality, the grandeur of his themes, the boldness of his interpretations, and his courage in choosing subjects with immense challenges characterise him as one of the great artists of the twentieth century. Portinari is the narrator of myths, our Homer. In his work, we find the stillness of tragedy, the timelessness of symbols, and the absence of the turbulence of simple drama. Portinari is the fabric that organises and forms the foundation of Brazilian art, the mark of our maturity, the alpha point from which we can contemplate our panorama.

Candido Portinari. No círculo de luz. Na asa do sol – this is the title of my book[1], which, with a slight modification, was taken from a poem dated 1 November 1961 by Portinari, shortly before his death. This poem is extraordinary, perhaps the best Portinari wrote, and, in my opinion, the most revealing. Portinari narrates his frustration at not being able to see Grünewald's Christ in Colmar, France. As the museum was about to close, he saw the Christ only briefly through a door that was slightly ajar. He speaks of his love for the artist and reflects on his impending death, framing the encounter as a poignant farewell. As he recounts his contemplation, dialogue with the artist, and the artwork he glimpsed, he unveils his own perception and unwavering spirit in the face of adversity. Through bidding farewell to the symbolic work, he reveals his way of perceiving the world. Without explicitly intending to, he shows us how the artist Portinari relates to the essence and light of the world. He describes seeing the monumental work through a sliver of light, as if on the wing of the sun, luminous. This title serves as a portrait of the enigmatic Portinari.

Candido Portinari was born on 29 December 1903. He would be 121 years old now, which seems of special significance to us. As we reflect on the trajectory of his work – because that is our focus now – we marvel at how it has been accepted, denied, and recognised, and how its aesthetic and historical importance has grown each time, presenting itself as a major reference, like a poetic gesture that expands the meaning of reality. In a speculative scenario, if Portinari had never existed, our understanding of humanity would be diminished.

The song of love and pain that accompanies Candido Portinari's farewell from life also highlights his enchantment with the beauty of the world. His poem Grünewald is a hymn of praise to the delightful enigma of existence.

In the cadence of words, with their marked and striking rhythm, the artist reflects on his journey on this planet, the grandeur of art, and

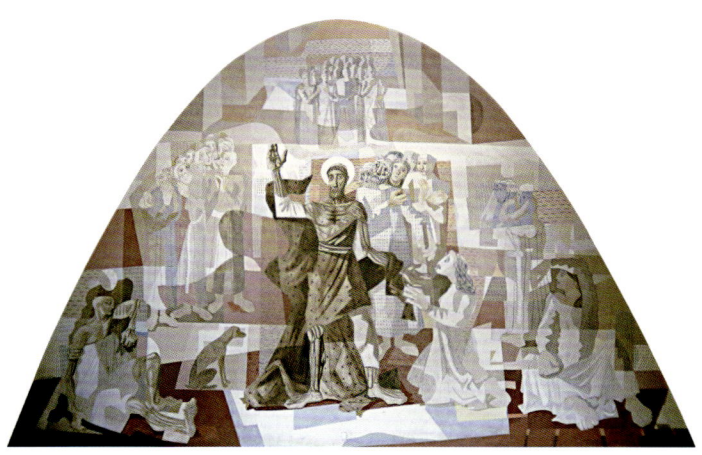

Fig. 1
Candido Portinari, fresco
depicting Saint Francis,
Igreja São Francisco de Assis,
Pampulha

on creation, and language as profoundly moving human contributions. He leaves us not only with a creed in favour of life but also with the concealed script of his creative ritual – his impetus and the paths of his personal movements. The tale of a lifetime: fifty-eight years, an existence so brief for a love so profound.

As I reflect on Candido Portinari, it strikes me that his tender sentiments explain his tireless documentation and interpretation of things in this world. Alongside the remarkable poem *Grünewald*, there exists another poem – an essay in the form of a prayer, written close to his death, dedicated to his granddaughter Denise, the eldest daughter of João Candido Portinari. It is dated "Paris, 6 Nov 1961". In this poem, Portinari assumes the role of a loving grandfather crafting a prayer, like a mantra, wishing a path of happiness for his beloved granddaughter.

In 1941, already a world-renowned artist, Candido Portinari transformed a room in his family home into a chapel, creating a place for prayer and meditation. He painted Saint John the Baptist, Saint Lucy, Saint Peter, the Visitation of the Virgin Mary to Saint Elizabeth, the Holy Family, Jesus Christ, Saint Francis of Assisi, and Saint Anthony of Padua.

His paternal grandmother, Pellegrina, elderly and bedridden, cried because she could no longer attend Mass as regularly as before. Candinho, as she affectionately called him, comforted her: "Nonna, don't cry, I'll paint a little chapel for you." Known as Nonna's Chapel, it stands as a unique testament to pictorial quality, sacred sentiment, and familial love.

In the case of Candido Portinari, painting sacred themes is not simply a technical and detached representation of traditional motifs. Instead, it is the interpretation and recreation of the loving sentiment of spiritual life, a rediscovery of religious significance – the "re-ligare", the merging of celestial and earthly realms, retying the knot that binds heaven and earth. It is a celebration of the primordial covenant between the creature and the Creator, a manifestation of the ecstatic joy of existence.

In truth, we are continuously debating the nature of art, social issues, and most vehemently, our identity. These are the doubts and assertions of those of us living in the new world, coexisting with our colonial heritage and the historic struggles for political independence, forged from a rich blend of many peoples. Even the fundamental concept of belonging to Western civilisation faces ongoing internal and external questioning and restrictions.

The significance of Candido Portinari's work, within the ongoing process of self-analysis, affirmation, and negation of national identity, lies in his role as the artist who visually defined and "invented" the Brazilian odyssey. He is our foremost muralist, our greatest historical painter, the creator of the country's most moving and profound sacred works, the most expressive portraitist, and ultimately, the artist who presents the most complete depiction of Brazil ever created. Portinari's work is so influential that it contributes to the understanding of Brazilian social reality, economic development, and political history. It provides an anthropological view of the Brazilian people, it also records customs, offers an aesthetic reinterpretation of Indigenous heritage, expresses the religious sentiments of the population, and affirms the aesthetics of national art while engaging in the debates around avant-garde art and languages. His work is not only a reference point in discussions around national identity but also fundamental in the cultural identification process of Brazilians.

The painter and theorist Israel Pedrosa, a former student of Portinari, offered a fresh perspective to his friend Antonio Bento, author of *Portinari, O pintor do terceiro mundo* (Portinari, the Painter of the Third World), by saying that Candido Portinari is the painter of the New World. He drew on the historical European fascination with the discovery of new continents and the imaginary promises of a revived Paradise. For Pedrosa, the author of the monumental *Da cor à cor inexistente* (From Colour to Non-existent Colour), the "painter of the new world" was a nickname that heralded the future. "No other painter has painted their country as extensively as Portinari has", said painter and theorist Israel Pedrosa in a statement to the Portinari Project in 2003. With such breadth, multiplicity of themes, gargantuan ambition, and capacity for achievement, I know of no other example.

Portinari created a truly monumental body of work, considering the scale of his production, its quality, and the various media and techniques he employed. Portinari is the greatest muralist in our history, with his work displayed in major buildings such as the Ministry of Education and Health in Rio de Janeiro, a cornerstone of our modernist architecture; the Church of Pampulha in Belo Horizonte (fig. 1), located in the modern Pampulha neighbourhood, a precursor to the future capital Brasília; the Library of Congress in Washington; and the United Nations headquarters in New

Fig. 2
Candido Portinari, *Guerra e Paz* (War and Peace), lobby of the United Nations headquarters, New York

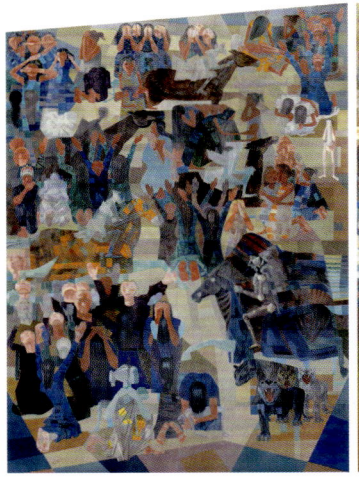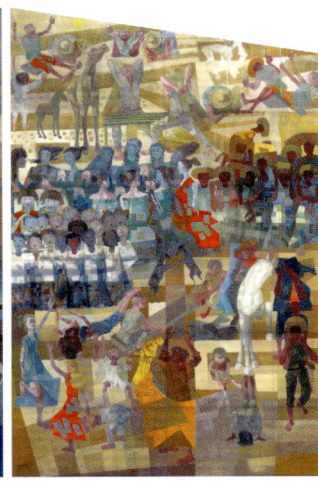

Candido Portinari

York (fig. 2). Furthermore, his work tackled the most significant issues in the country – from childhood to rural life, from the social woes of north-eastern migrants to the historical saga of national formation. In each of these areas, the artist's contributions have become indispensable references.

Since the late 1930s, Portinari has established himself as a prominent artist through his representations and interpretations of Brazilian social reality, notably in the series *Os retirantes* (fig. p. 103). In 1936, he began creating frescoes and tile panels for the Ministry of Education and Health building. In 1956, upon the inauguration of the *War and Peace* murals at the United Nations (fig. 2), he received the Guggenheim Internaltional Award and in 1957 the Hallmark Art Award. Notable exhibitions he participated in include the Salão Nacional de Belas Artes in Rio de Janeiro in 1922 and 1931; a solo exhibition at the Museum of Modern Art in New York in 1940; the Venice Biennale in 1950 and 1954; the Bienal de São Paulo in various editions from 1951 to 1985; the Guggenheim Museum in New York in 1957; and at Wildenstein Gallery in New York in 1959.

On 6 February 1962, at the age of fifty-eight, the painter Candido Portinari died from poisoning resulting from his use of oil paint, especially white paint containing heavy metals. His dedication and tireless work allowed him to create a remarkable body of work, an unparalleled portrayal of Brazil. Perhaps the artist foresaw a brief life for such profound passion.

Jakob Klintowitz
This text was written at the suggestion of
Prof. João Candido Portinari.

1   Candido Portinari. *No círculo de luz. Na asa do sol.* (In the circle of light. On the wing of the sun) is the title of the exhibition curated by Jacob Klintowitz on the occasion of Candido Portinari's 120th birthday, which took place in 2023 at the Galeria Frente in São Paulo, as well as the title of the exhibition catalogue.

Brasil! Brasil!

Baiana (Woman from Bahia), 1947

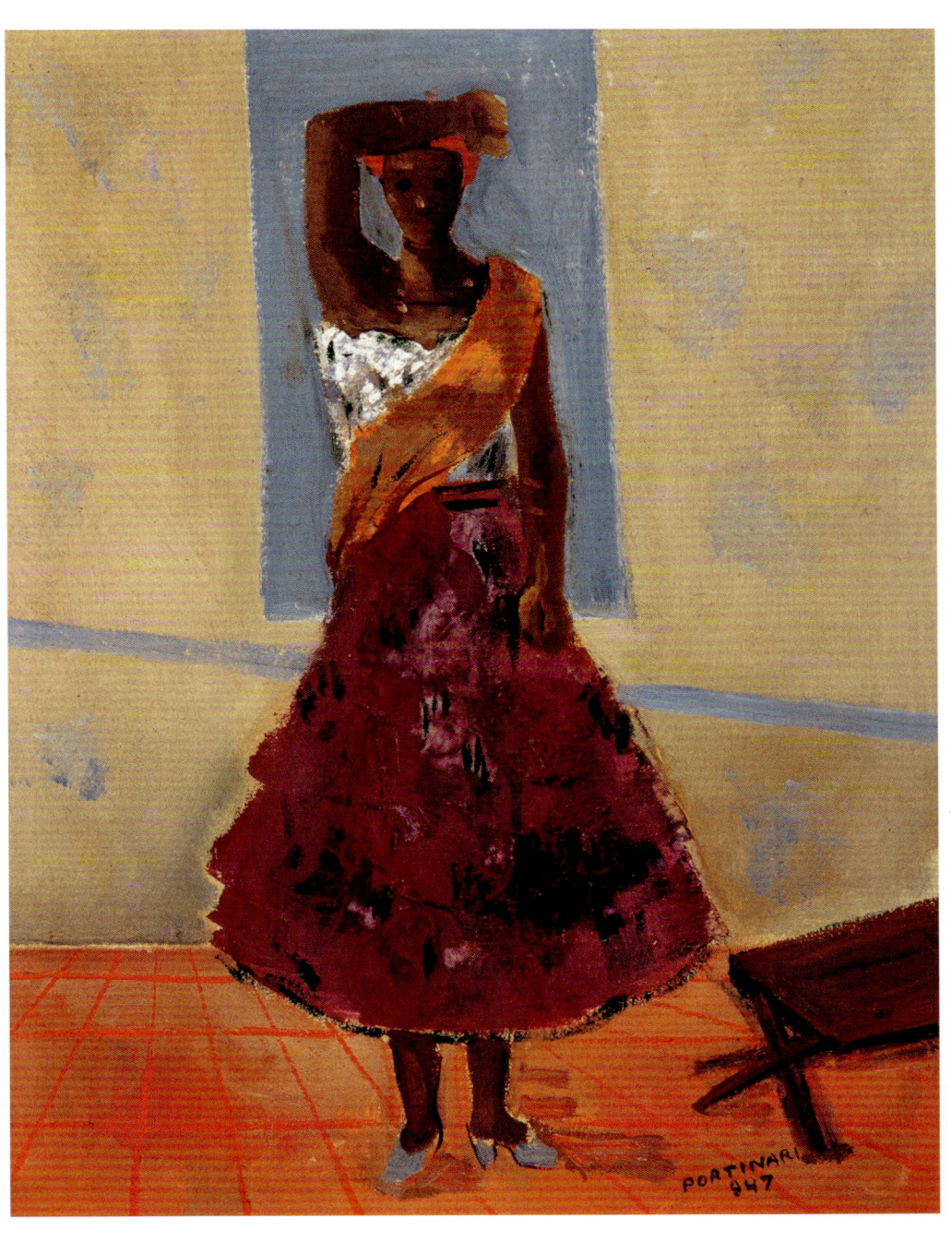

Candido Portinari

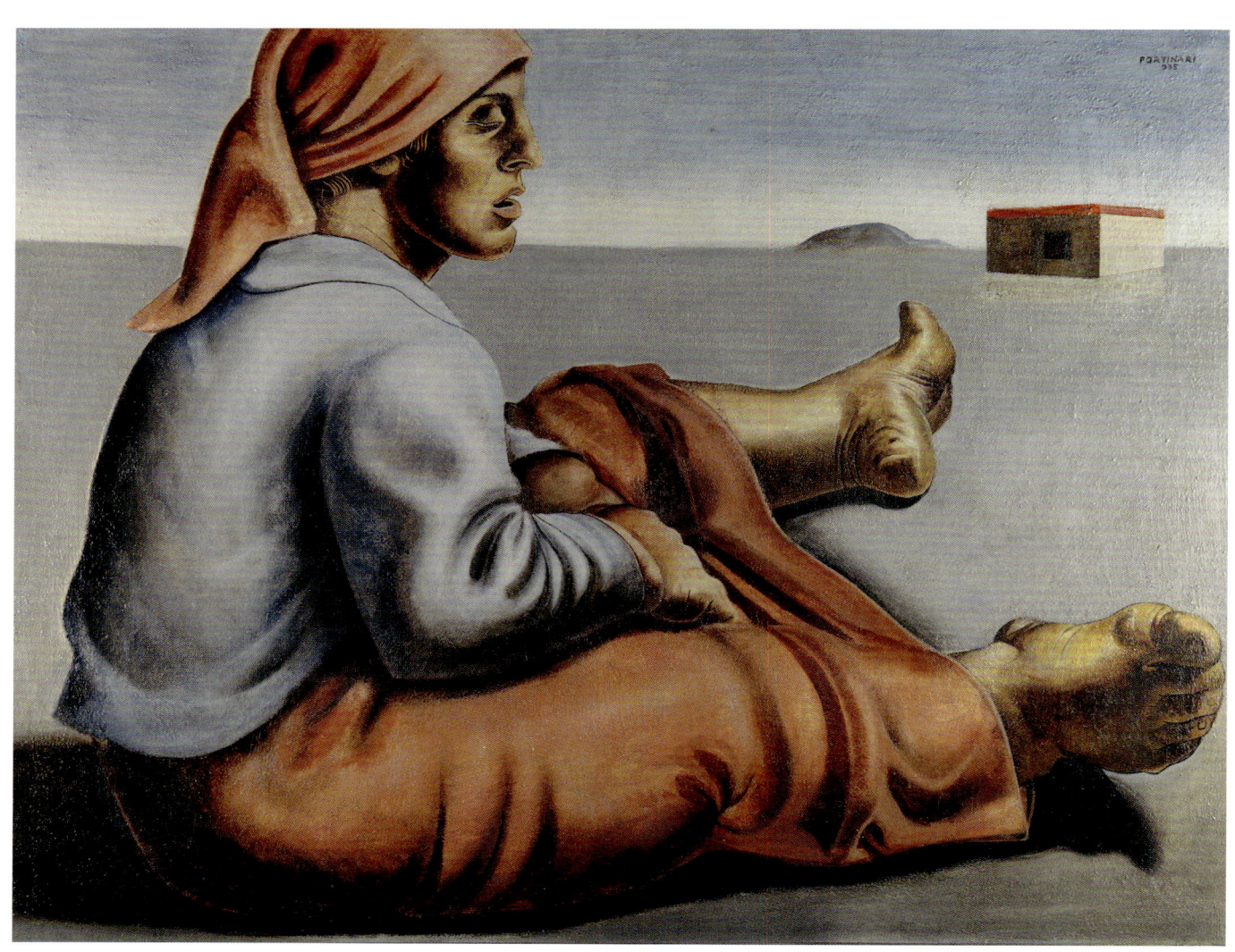

A colona (Settler), 1935

O lavrador de café (Coffee Agricultural Worker), 1934

Brasil! Brasil!

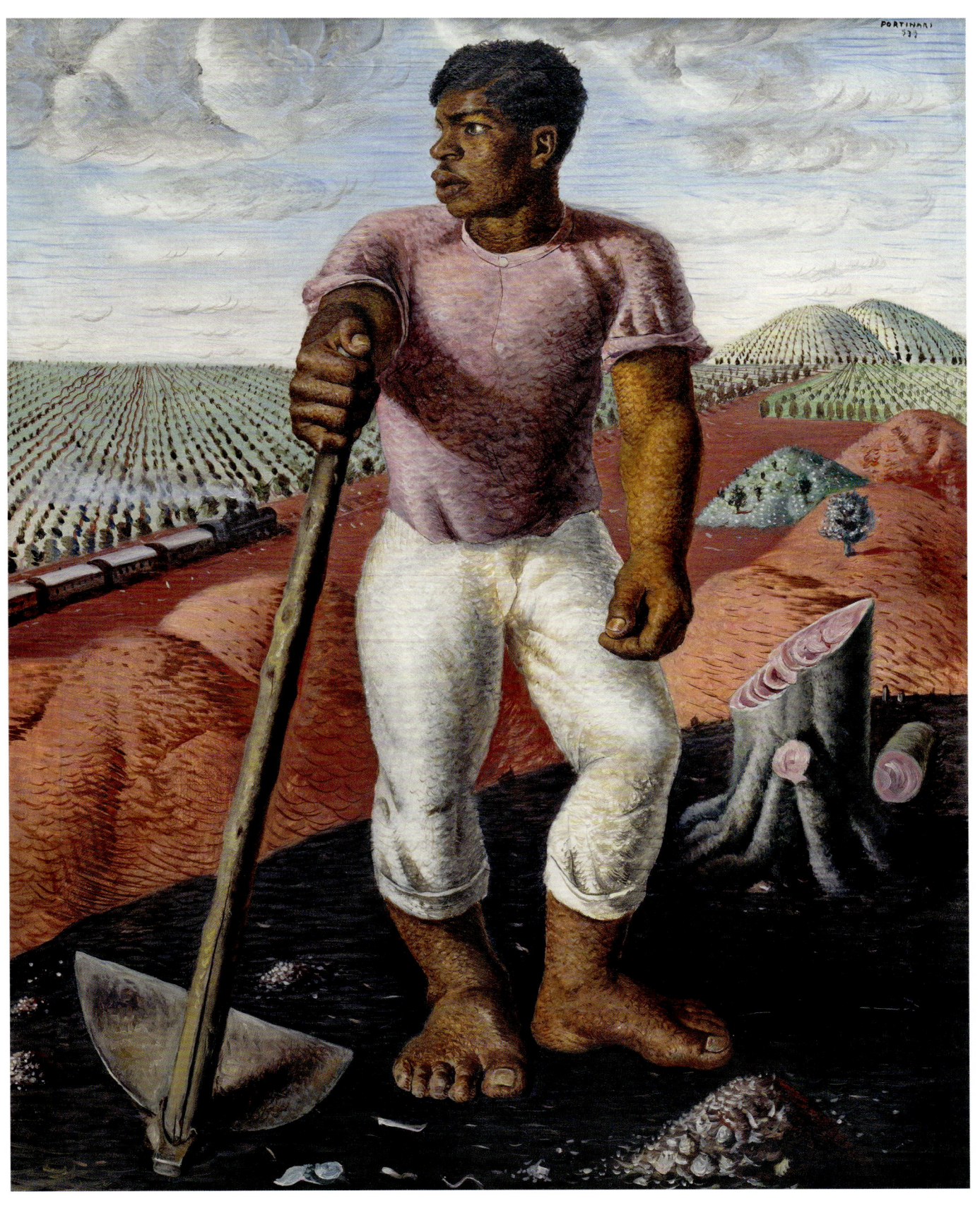

95 **Candido Portinari**

Retrato de Mário de Andrade (Portrait of Mário de Andrade), 1935

Mestiça (Mixed-Race Woman), 1934

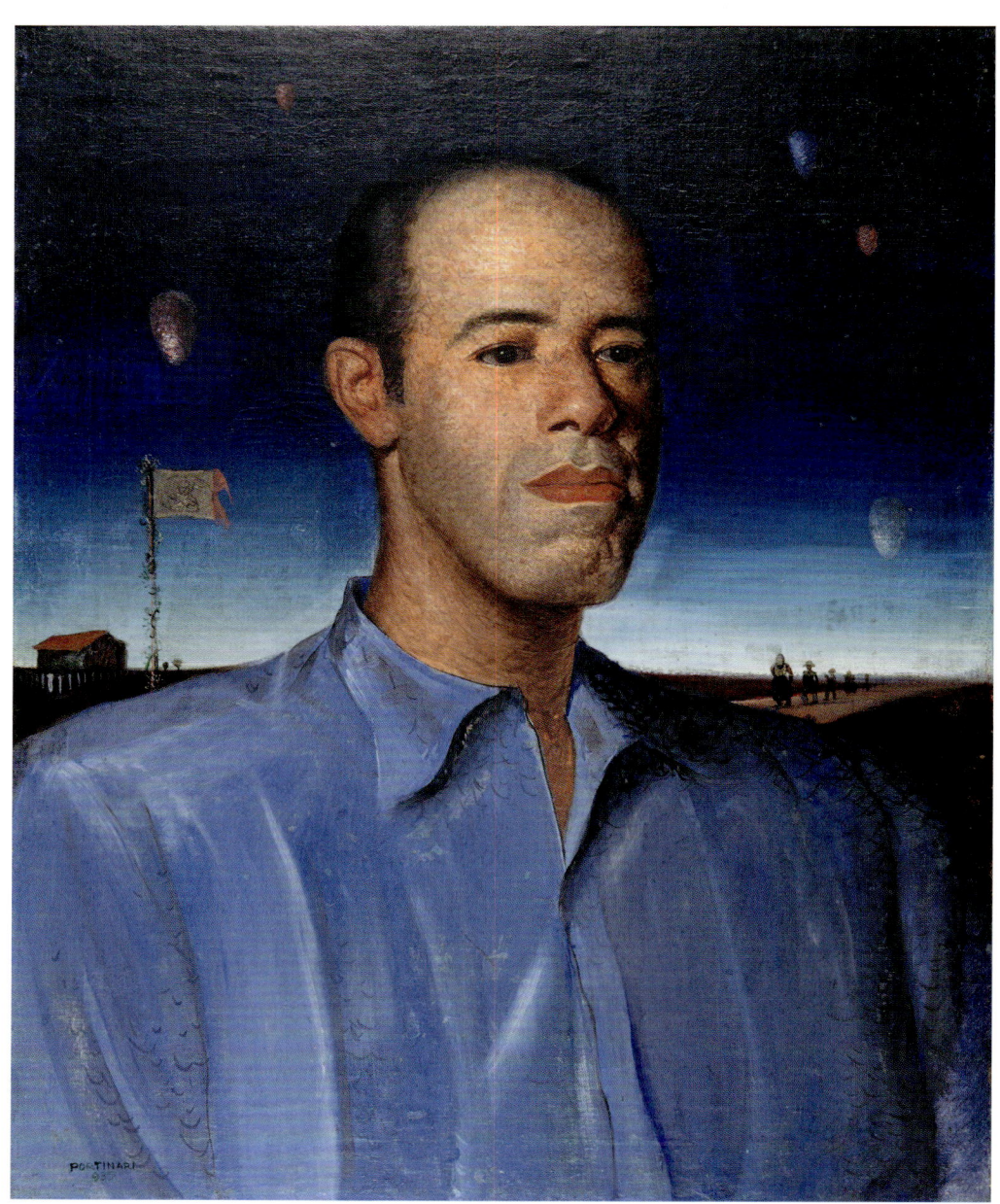

Brasil! Brasil!

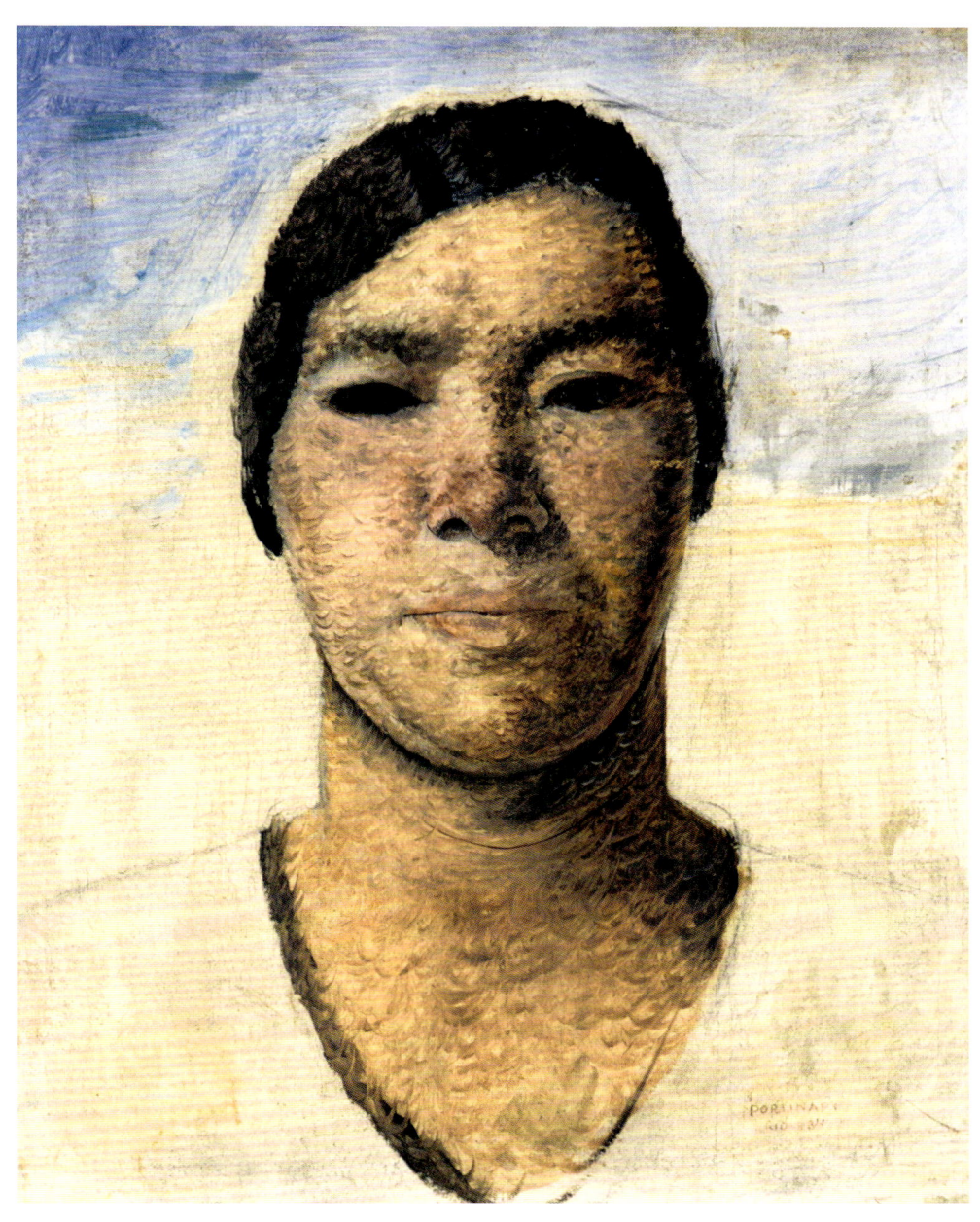

97   **Candido Portinari**

Menino com carneiro
(Boy with Ram), 1941

Brasil! Brasil!

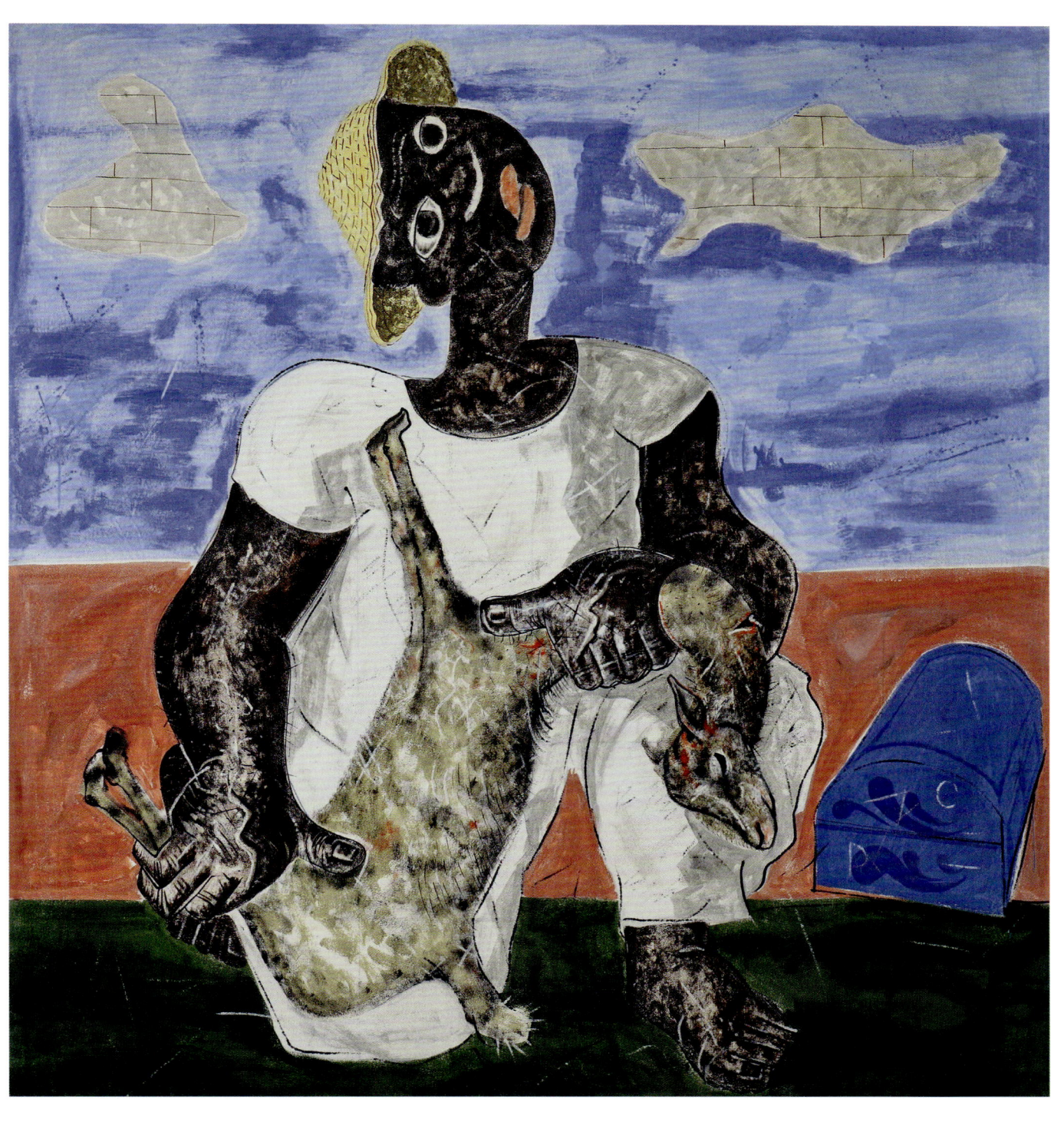

99   **Candido Portinari**

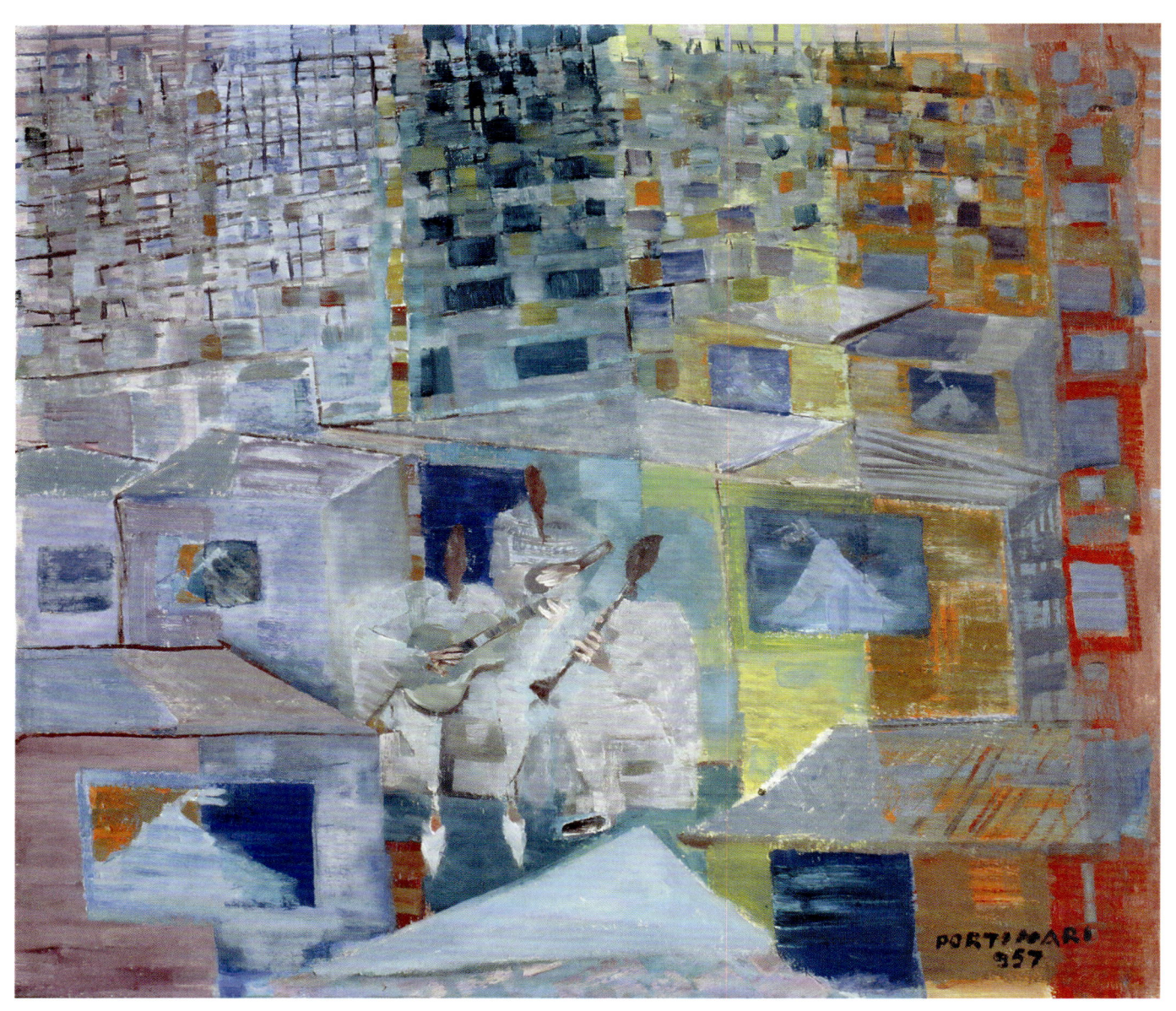

100   **Brasil! Brasil!**

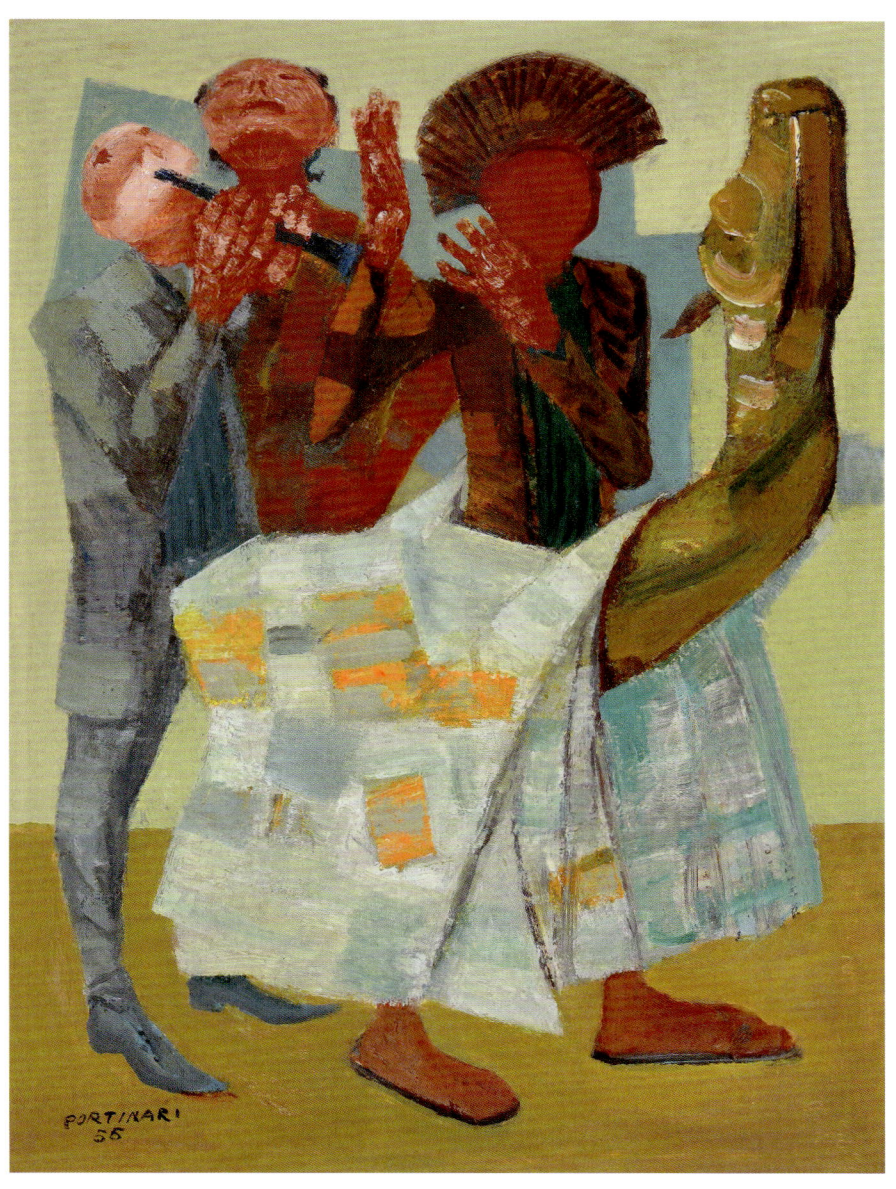

Favela com músicos
(Favela with Musicians), 1957

Bumba meu boi, 1956

101   Candido Portinari

Retirantes (Migrants), 1944

Brasil! Brasil!

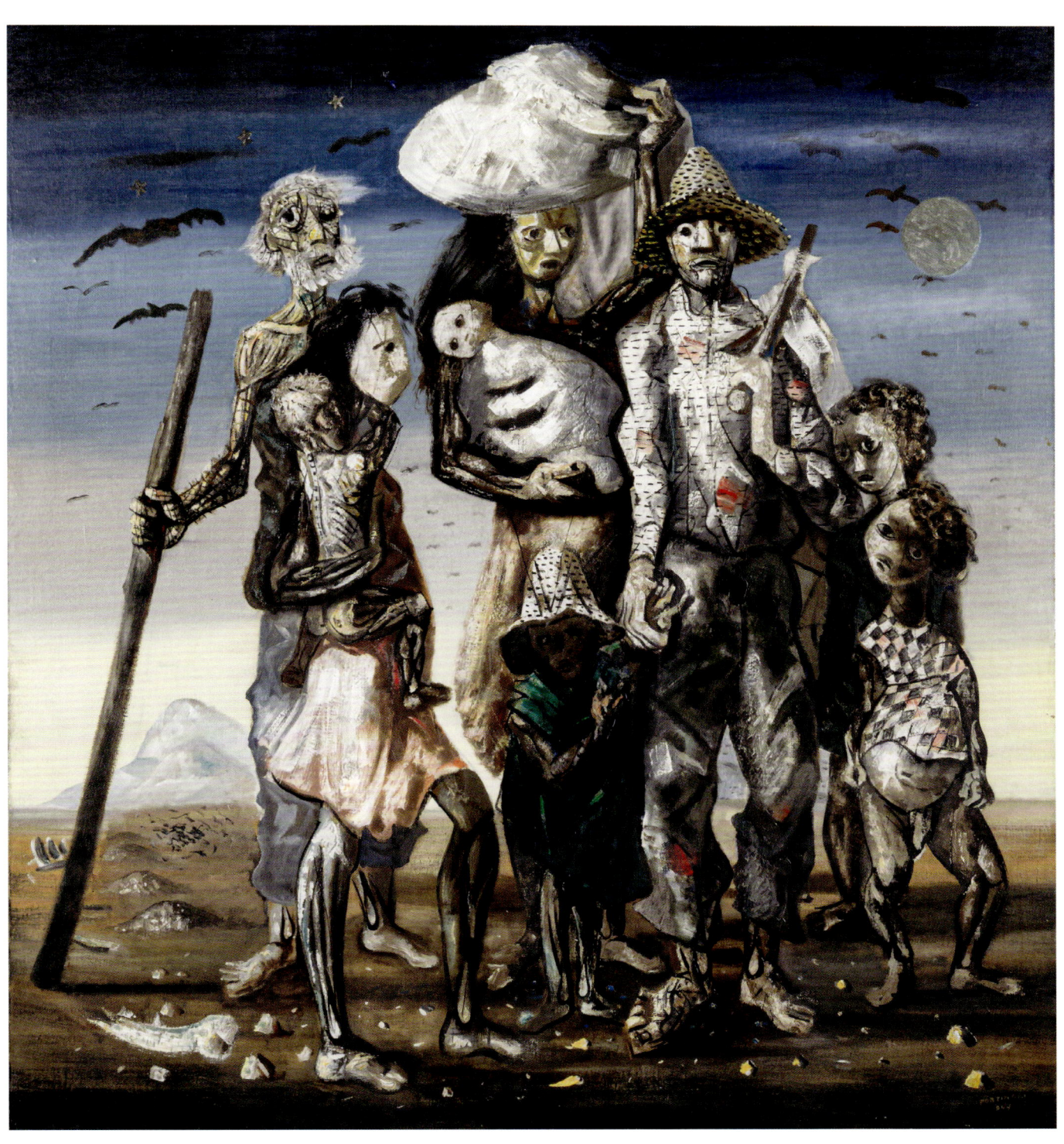

Candido Portinari

**Mulher e crianças
(Woman and Children)**, 1940

Espantalho (Scarecrow), 1940

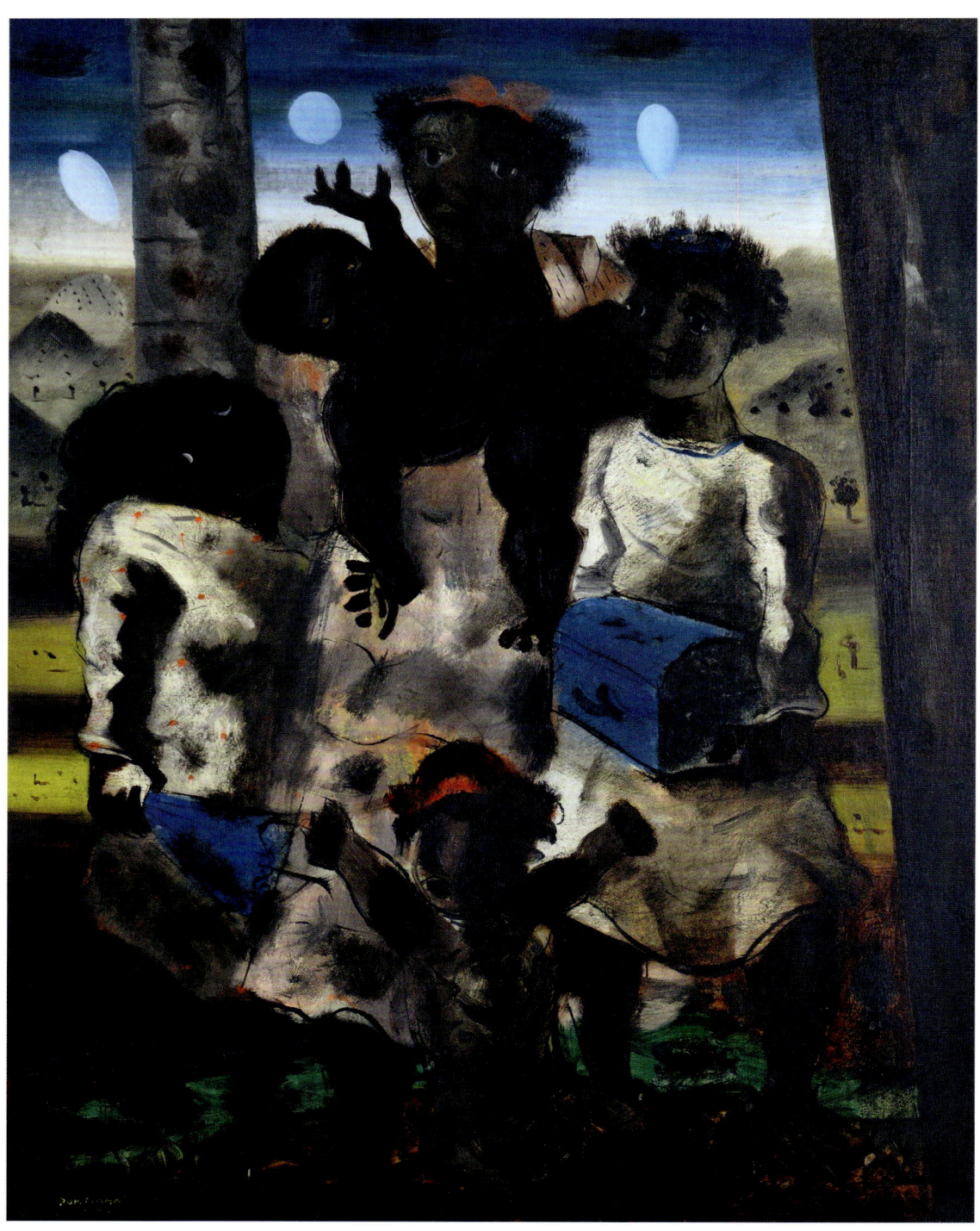

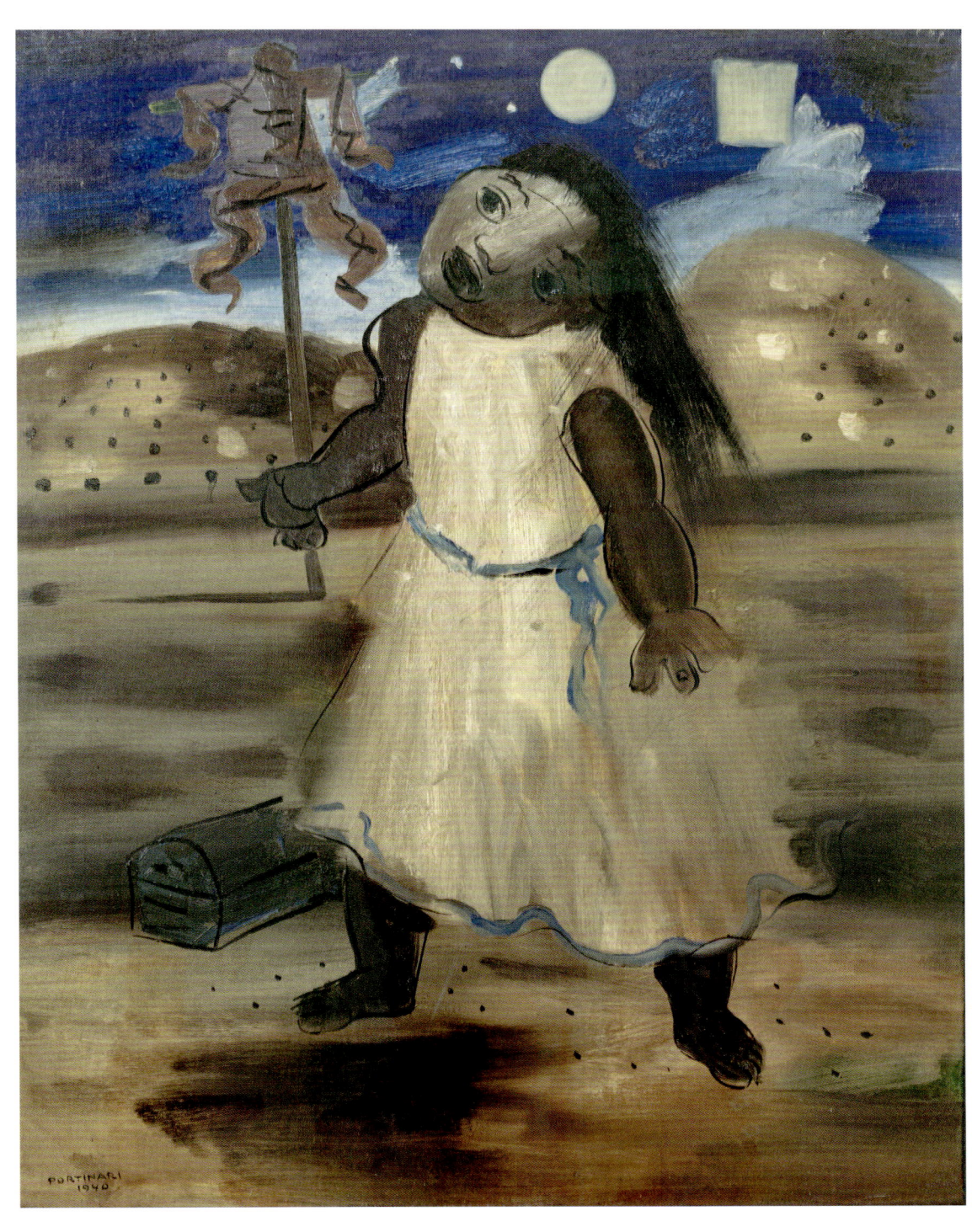

Candido Portinari

MUSIC

Brazilian Modernisms: Rhythms of Exception

Cacá Machado

During a diplomatic mission to Brazil in 1917, the French composer Darius Milhaud (fig. 1) noted the following impression of the music being played in the city of Rio de Janeiro:

The rhythms of this popular music intrigued and fascinated me. There was an imperceptible suspension in the syncopation, a casual breath, a small pause that was very difficult for me to grasp. So, I bought a lot of maxixes and tangos and set about playing them, with their syncopations passing from one hand to the other. My efforts were rewarded, and I was finally able to express and analyse this typically Brazilian "little nothing".[1]

The European classical musician had to reconcile what he heard with what he saw, as the "imperceptible suspension" of the syncopation in Rio's maxixes was not notated to match what he had heard in street performances. For popular musicians, sheet music was merely a reference, if they could read it at all, as music was mainly transmitted orally and physically. For Milhaud, a composer trained in the abstract principles of European musical theory, the score represented a framework set in stone, with musical practice necessarily following the theoretical process of notation where body and mind were divided into subject and object. This is why the Frenchman bought sheet music. Yet, what intrigued and fascinated him most was precisely what, in his culture, was considered an exception: syncopation.

In music theory, "syncopation" is the term for a shift in rhythmic emphasis that goes against the metric norm. Recognising the exception as the norm meant appreciating what was typical of the place, in this case, the New World: a Brazilian "little nothing".

In my view, this fragment of Darius Milhaud's recollection encapsulates three issues of varying significance: 1) the foreign gaze coloured by exoticism; 2) local singularity as a marker of national modernities; and 3) the contrast between visual perception (cultivated European experience) and auditory experience (popular American experience), hinting at what could be termed an "acoustic turn"[2] in narratives of modernity.

Starting at the end, when Milhaud returned to France, he premiered his symphonic suite *Le boeuf sur le toi* (The Ox on the Roof, 1919) in 1920, with a stage script by Jean Cocteau, securing him a prominent place in French avant-garde artistic circles. The compositional techniques that later cemented his reputation with the "group of six" were all already present: polytonality, timbral spatialisation, and poly-rhythm. *Le boeuf sur le toi* is a sort of collage drawn from an anthology of popular music themes from Rio de Janeiro, composed by figures such as Marcelo Tupinambá, Ernesto Nazareth, Chiquinha Gonzaga, Catulo da Paixão Cearense, Sinhô, Eduardo Souto, Álvaro Sandin, and others. There are also nods to Brazilian classical composers, including Alexandre Levy and Alberto

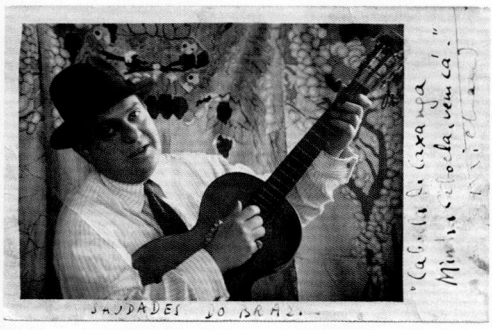

Fig. 1
Postcard sent by Darius Milhaud to his Brazilian friends after his return to France in 1919.

Nepomuceno. The title comes from the hit song of the 1918 carnival, *O boi no telhado* (The Ox on the Roof), by Zé Boiadeiro, a pseudonym of José Monteiro[3].

In the early twentieth century, Rio de Janeiro boasted a well-established integration of authorship, musical works, and audiences within its popular music scene, which functioned as a consolidated system, as outlined by Antonio Candido[4]. Whether through Chiquinha Gonzaga's maxixe-like polkas for musical theatre, Ernesto Nazareth's Brazilian tangos filling cinema halls, or Sinhô's emerging carnival tunes, popular music served as a cultural bridge across all social classes in the city. Despite authors catering to specific audiences, their works circulated transversally, facilitated by the sale of sheet music, particularly to the cultured elite – young ladies entertaining their hosts with piano performances in mansion parlours – as well as through oral and physical transmission of spontaneous musical practices, especially in impoverished neighbourhoods like Cidade Nova.

Darius Milhaud encountered this vibrant and exuberant system of popular music in an exotic urban setting surrounded by forests. In the subsequent decades, particularly in the 1920s and 1930s, this system gained momentum with the creation of popular songs centred around carnival and the emergence of radio and records, notably samba. The subsequent evolution, extending until the 1960s, underscores the pivotal role that commercial popular music came to play in Brazilian culture. This influence manifested itself not only in artistic "movements" like bossa nova and tropicalismo but also in a "network of messages"[5] internally embedded within the system – author, work, and audience – accommodating various external aesthetic influences, from high literary culture (Tom Jobim/ Vinícius de Moraes) to avant-garde post-tonal music (Rogério Duprat/ tropicalistas) and political engagement (Musical *Opinião* by Nara Leão, Zé Keti, and João do Vale).

In this context, it is important to acknowledge that the modernities at play here diverge from the narratives primarily centred around Mário de Andrade, who, in his exploration of music, literature, and emerging ethnology, defined and shaped a significant portion of the conceptual frameworks of Brazilian modernism. Amidst the various strands, paths, and deviations, a recurring demand for a point of harmonisation of national experiences persisted throughout the long period of modernism. From a certain perspective, it seems there was a desire to "choralise" Brazil, that is, to envision the nation as a vast choral ensemble capable of uniting all its differences, contradictions, and paradoxes – encompassing both its liberating and normative forces. Indeed, it was in the 1920s and 1930s that this desire for the "choralisation" found two tangible examples: Mário de Andrade's theoretical formulations, particularly in his *Ensaio sobre a música brasileira* (Essay on Brazilian Music, 1928), and the introduction of *Canto Orfeônico* (Orpheonic Chant, 1931), by composer Heitor Villa-Lobos (fig. 2), into the secondary school curriculum. Later, these efforts would become part of the broader reform of the Organic Law of Education, led by Gustavo Capanema and Anísio Teixeira during the Getúlio Vargas era.

The wider context here pertains to the condition of a nation that was formed within a European colonialist framework and that sought, and continues to seek, its self-recognition and autonomy in a permanent tension with the other. Hence, Brazilian modernism should be viewed in plural terms, as "Brazilian modernisms"[6]. In this context, the traditional European distinctions between "erudite", "popular", or "mass" culture intertwine, giving rise to a unique space within our local experience.

If, on the one hand, we must recognise the importance of popular culture in Brazilian modernism at this moment of critical assessment of the centenary of its institutional milestone – the *Semana de Arte Moderna* (Modern Art Week) of 1922, on the other hand, the two-way street between Europe, particularly France, and Brazil is another important dimension for characterising the experiences of Brazilian modernism. Let us take a closer look.

On 13 December 1927, French writer Lucie Delarue-Mardrus reviewed a concert featuring works by Villa-Lobos, partly conducted by the composer himself, in Paris, for the newspaper *L'intransigeant*. In this remarkable text, titled *L'aventure d'un compositeur: musique cannibale* (The Adventure of a Composer: Cannibal Music), Delarue-Mardrus recounts the adventures of our "gentleman Indian", commenting on the unusual originality of his "cannibal" music. The article unintentionally or intentionally raises some of the central issues for understanding the cultural relations between France and Brazil, and Brazil and France, around the 1920s. Far from suggesting a direct relationship between, for example, Delarue-Mardrus's 1927 article and Oswald de Andrade's *Manifesto Antropófago*, published a year later in 1928, or Mário de Andrade's book *Macunaíma*, also published in 1928, the proximity of dates indicates, at the very least, that themes surrounding "primitivism", "exoticism", and by extension, "cannibalism" and "anthropophagy", formed the basis of a certain interchange and sociability between French and Brazilian artists. The poets Paul Claudel and Blaise Cendrars and the composer Darius Milhaud spent time in Brazil between 1917 and 1924. Our young modernists Oswald de Andrade, Tarsila do Amaral, Victor Brecheret, Emiliano Di Cavalcanti, Sérgio Milliet, Anita Malfatti, and Villa-Lobos were in Paris in 1923. The exchange of perspectives between Brazilians and the French left a profound impact on the experiences of modernism in both countries.

Returning to the article, the writer narrates a tale that Villa-Lobos would later become notorious for: his adventures in the Brazilian jungles, the episode of his capture by Indigenous tribes, and his composure in the face of the imminent threat of becoming the main course in a "cannibal ritual", all the while recording the melodies and rhythms of the music that animated the celebration. In Brazil, the Rio de Janeiro press was more concerned with the "negative" portrayal of the country's image associated with the savage cannibalism of its Indigenous peoples than with the accuracy of the narrative itself. Villa-Lobos's biographer, Vasco Mariz, recounts that Delarue-Mardrus became friends with the composer and one day saw at his house the book *Duas viagens ao Brasil* (Two Journeys to Brazil, 1557), written by the sixteenth-century German traveller and merchant Hans Staden.[8] The writer took the book with her. It is likely that the subject and narrative originated from there, as the similarities go far beyond mere coincidences. As is known, Staden was captured by the Tupinambá people in 1554 and remained imprisoned for nine months, according to his account, constantly on the brink of becoming a meal.

Fig. 2
Heitor Villa-Lobos with Reco-Reco, 1957

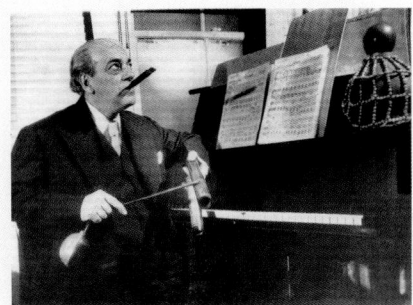

As noted by researcher Anaïs Flechet[9], a double symbolism between Staden/Villa-Lobos emerges here, evoking the concepts of the "noble savage" and the "adventurer". In essence, French critics from the 1920s agreed that Villa-Lobos and his music epitomised the noble savage, characterised by authenticity, purity, and seriousness, as he, akin to French ethnologists, engaged directly with first-nation Americans.

Following the captivating narrative of Villa-Lobos's adventures, Delarue-Mardrus provides insights into his music:

Villa-Lobos's compositions are brimming with new life. His use of choirs, the power, youthfulness, and sincerity of his discoveries, along with the introduction of unfamiliar instruments amidst the drums, which play a significant role in his orchestra – this mesmerising music exudes a sense of savagery, eliciting shock and even admiration, while modern audiences, from Darius Milhaud to Poulenc and others, are literally accustomed to everything.

Fig. 3
Score cover of *O boi no telhado*

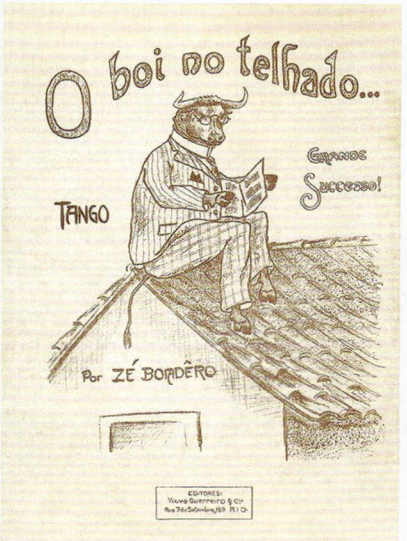

The extravagances of contemporary harmony, often reminiscent of the Loges Party or the Neuilly Fair, find here a rhythmic framework that prompts involuntary shoulder movements upon hearing it, the beginning of a dance, and perhaps even a sort of cannibalism, leading one to a sonic explosion despite oneself.[10]

From Delarue-Mardrus's viewpoint, figures like Darius Milhaud and others (including Claude Debussy, Erik Satie, Edgar Varès, and Francis Poulenc) paved the way for the "modern audience" to embrace contemporary music. Once again, Villa-Lobos's music is characterised by an image of "savagery", evoking both shock and admiration. The critic Florent Schmitt made a similar observation about the premiere of *Choros VIII* in 1927 in Paris:

The orchestra roars and rages, swept up in a jazzium tremens. And just when it appears the bounds of an almost superhuman dynamism have been reached, suddenly, four lumberjack arms spring into action, twenty fingers equivalent to a hundred set two formidable drums of fifteen octaves vibrating, which, against this tumultuous backdrop, erupt with the thunder of an earthquake in hell.[11]

Both Delarue-Mardrus and other French critics recognise rhythm and dynamics (from *pianissimo* to *fortissimo*) as elements that transform the modern listening experience. The explicit or implicit savagery is still present. However, in the excerpt from Delarue-Mardrus's article, the involuntary shoulder movements, which suggest, in addition to dancing, a movement that is "perhaps even a sort of cannibalism", promotes an inversion of meaning: the threat of cannibalism from the savage world takes on an expansive positive connotation that leads the listener to a sonic explosion. All the elements converge here: popular music (rhythm and dynamics); primitivism; exoticism; and, finally, the distinction between cannibalism and anthropophagy.

There is a common notion which suggests that recognition, whether personal or collective, is influenced by distancing oneself from one's place of origin. That is, the process of distancing oneself from one's origins contributes to self-awareness. This may hold true in some cases. However, even though a certain critical tradition[12] corroborates this idea in the context of the relations between France and Brazil in the 1920s, using as an example the "discovery" of Brazil by Brazilian modernists in Paris in 1923, the emphasis on distance might be less relevant than the interaction across a two-way street. Mário de Andrade, for instance, never left Brazil, yet he still "discovered" his country. Overemphasising abstract discussions of identity and nationality may be the biggest mistake in this line of interpretation.[13] Instead, the consideration of the transatlantic journeys of Villa-Lobos and Darius Milhaud suggests a different narrative. The validation from Paris's cultured artistic scene – the "navel of the world" – was as vital for Villa-Lobos as the endorsement from the Brazilian popular cultural sphere was for Milhaud. What varies are the approaches. France, operating under a colonialist modus operandi, naturally viewed Brazil through the prism of "exoticism" and "primitivism". Conversely, Brazil incorporated and challenged the French model of civilisation, as seen in Milhaud's fascination with Brazilian maxixes and tangos. The myth of the "Ox on the Roof" was created and reinforced through multiple perspectives across different transatlantic territories.

In the Paris of 1923, the concept of anthropophagy was taking root and revealing itself even before its manifesto. Oswald de Andrade encapsulated and projected the future with a *boutade*: "we write what we hear – never what there was".[14]

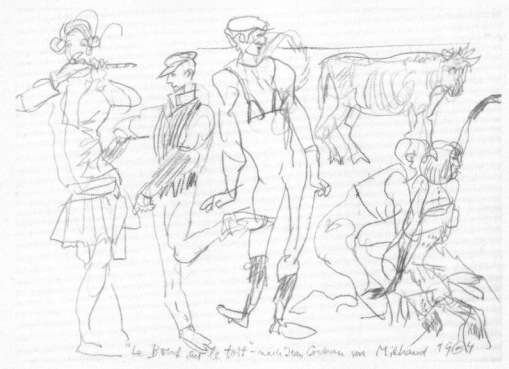

Fig. 4
Hanny Fries, *Le Bœuf sur le toit*, 1964, illustration for *Vom Stadttheater zum Opernhaus*, pencil on paper, 26,5 × 36,4 cm, Graphische Sammlung, ZB Zürich

1   Milhaud 1949, pp. 80–81

2   The literary critic Julio Ramos offers an original take on this perspective concerning the saturation of the "optical schema" in his essay *Descarga acústica* (Acoustic Discharge). According to Ramos: "Let us say, in conclusion, that debates surrounding the supremacy of the optical schema (and the love for writing) lead us today to acknowledge the heavy and sometimes saturated influence of the acoustic order within soundscapes. Such orders are clearly irreducible to the issue of pre-literate "orality". Instead, they represent mixed orders, traversed by the complexities of capitalist history, by technological shifts, as well as the incarnate and raw struggles of bodies breaking free from inherited schemas of sensory programming." Ramos 2010, pp. 76–77

3   Cf. Lago 2012

4   Cf. Candido 2000

5   Cf. Wisnik 2004, pp. 213–240

6   Cf. Simioni 2013b; Coelho 2012; Cardoso 2022b

7   The researcher Pedro Rodrigues extensively explores the various versions of Villa-Lobos's "formative" journeys in his doctoral thesis. See Rodrigues 2019, pp. 45–65

8   Cf. Mariz 2004, pp. 56–58

9   Cf. Flechet 2004

10   Delarue-Mardrus 1927, p. 1

11   Apud Beaufils 1982, p. 88

12   Cf. Guérios 2003, pp. 81–108

13   The publication organised by Filipe Ceppas and João Camillo Penna extensively explores the theme from a perspective that opposes identity and nationalist discussions. Cf. Ceppas and Penna 2021

14   Andrade 2022f

Lasar Segall

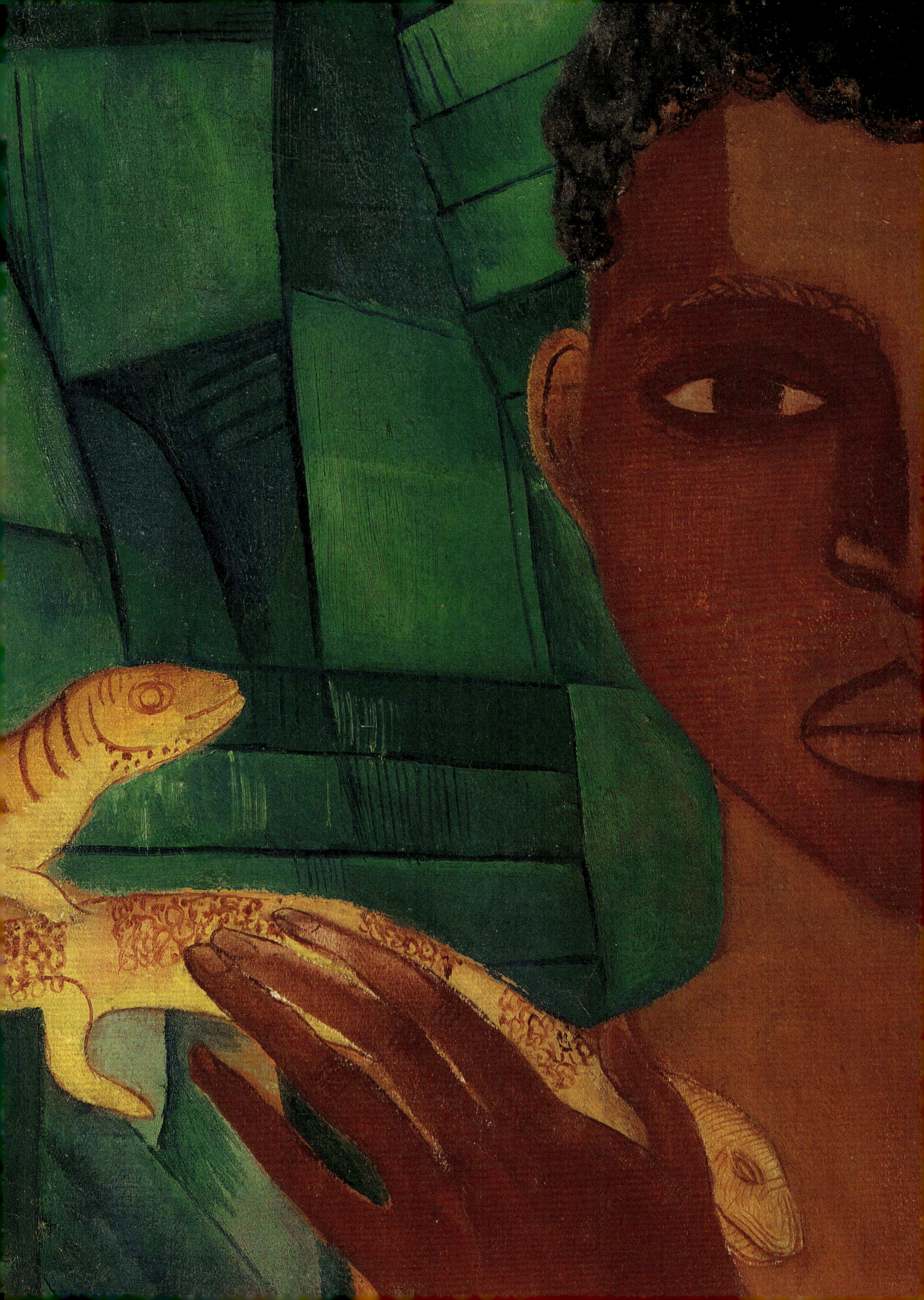

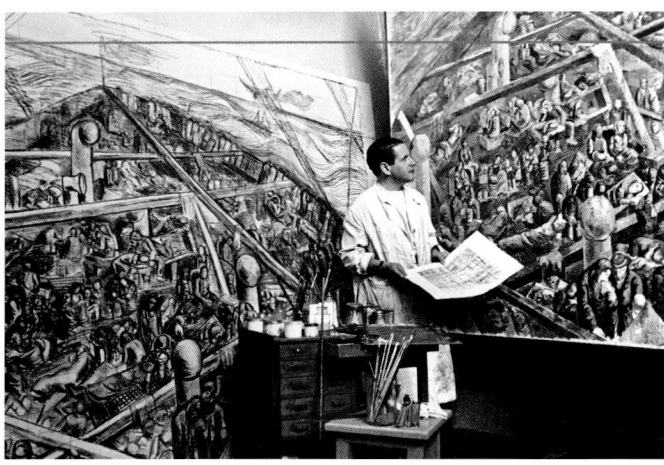

Lasar Segall
1889, Vilnius, Lithuania –
1957, São Paulo, Brazil

An artist of the frontiers, Lasar Segall was born in Vilnius, current capital of the Republic of Lithuania, on 21 July 1889, the sixth of eight children his parents had. Aside from a successful merchant his father was also a sofer, a scribe of the Torah. From his childhood, his early years of training in Germany, up until his artistic maturity in Brazil, Segall would consistently find himself in the uncomfortable position of the other, of the stranger and the foreigner. In consequence, he took the visual experience of things as the starting point for understanding of the world around him. To do so, Segall kept "his eyes wide open"[1], to quote his own words. To translate them, Segall focused his concern on the basic issues of artistic craft, diligently shaping his technical virtuosity to attain what he defined as art, "the truth fashioned into forms"[2]. Though acclaimed by critics and the recipient of official accolades in Brazil, Segall would be the victim, in the country he chose as his own, of attacks in which his foreignness was rigorously pointed out, a peculiar situation in a country whose population was composed mainly of immigrants such as himself. The seldom-disguised anti-Semitism of such attacks was furthered by the xenophobic narrow-mindedness of many of his peers.

Segall's experience in Vilnius, amidst its faiths, languages and peoples, would be a constant in his life. It was there that Segall began his artistic studies, training at the local drawing school. To continue his studies, he emigrated for the first time at the age of seventeen, arriving in Berlin in 1906, capital of the German Empire, where he studied at the Kunstgewerbemuseum for six months. He would eventually be accepted to the Königliche Akademische Hochschule für die Bildenden Künste where he studied for a three-year period. Segall's training provided him with an enviable virtuosity, one which he constantly resorted to. Though he himself claimed that technique was a means, not an end in itself, it is worth bearing in mind that he also said that "without technique, without knowledge of the method, artists do not speak, but stutter".[3] Unhappy with the Berlin Academy, Segall moved to Dresden in 1910, where he studied at the Hochschule für Bildende Künste Dresden. It was in the second half of 1912 that Segall set off on a long journey, one which would take him to the country that subsequently became his home. He chose as his destination São Paulo, where his older sister Luba had settled sometime previously, opening an exhibition that would also travel to the neighbouring

Brasil! Brasil!

city of Campinas. In these shows Segall exhibited beautifully fluent post-Impressionistic works, some of which are remarkably modernist in their aspirations, such as *Desfiando fumo* (fig. 1). They were curiously well-received by critics, a favour that would not be bestowed on Anita Malfatti a few years later, probably because not only was he a male artist showing in a male-dominated environment, but also a European one, trained in highly regarded European institutions.

Back in Europe in November 1913, Segall continued his studies in Dresden with the omnipresent menace of war in the background. Born in Vilnius during the Czarist occupation of the region, he was, accordingly, a Russian citizen, and consequently an enemy of Germany, subject as such to several restrictions. With the help of influential friends they would soon be lifted. It was during this time that he strengthened his relationship with the actress Margarete Quack, his first wife, whom he would marry in 1919. During the years of the war his work saw a dramatic expressive shift, one in which distortions of form and violently aggressive chromatic solutions were ubiquitous. He joined avant-garde movements such as the Neue Kreis in 1917 and was a co-founder of the Dresdner Sezession 1919, becoming one of the leading characters of the Dresden Expressionist movement. His participation in these circles becomes evident if we remember that, in 1920, *Die ewigen Wanderer* (fig. 2), one of the best examples of his Expressionist period and a deeply moving, ghostly painting of fragmented wandering figures in deep purples and greys, was acquired by the Modern Art Department of the Dresden City Museum. In 1920 Segall opened his first solo exhibition in Germany at the Museum Folkwang. He showed a collection of paintings, drawings and prints, some of which would be acquired by state museums, all of which, in turn, would be confiscated by the Nazi regime years later, being dubbed degenerate and included in the infamous exhibitions of the same name.

The subjects explored by the artist during this period establish the themes with which he would engage in later years. Throughout his career Segall was profoundly coherent when it comes to the choice of his subject matter. He addressed oppression, the helpless, violence, and the drama of immigration, as well as motherly love and the beauty of nature and its vast landscapes, with an ever-present sensitive and empathic outlook on the elements of the world. Segall's perspective on these issues is first and foremost empathetic and solidary, rather than accusatory, as sometimes is the case in the work of his fellow Expressionists. He is both the artist of those who live on the margins, of the forgotten, persecuted, and undefended,

Fig. 1
Lasar Segall, *Desfiando fumo* (Shredding tobacco), 1910, oil on cardboard, 44.5 × 34 cm, Private collection

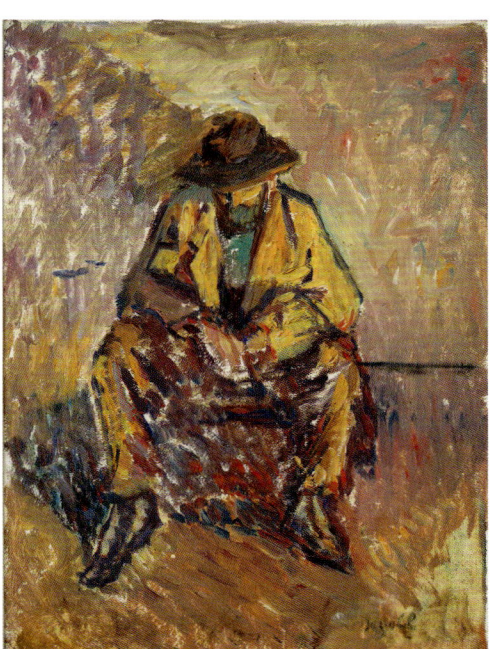

Lasar Segall

of the favelas and tenements, and the artist of scenes of motherly kindness, of the silent and intimate poetry of domestic life, of forests and lyrical rural landscapes.

Having moved with his wife Margarete to Berlin in 1921 Segall continued to produce works of great force, such as the powerful album of drypoints *Erinnerung an Wilna* (fig. 3), a recording of his impressions while visiting his hometown in 1917. The desolate landscape of the city deeply moved the artist, who produced several drawings based on the experience which would serve as the source for these prints. As he recorded: "The people of Vilnius, especially the Jews, have been through several horrors in the past, including bloody pogroms and calamities, which have been paled out by everything that has befallen upon it. It is difficult, practically impossible to describe these things in detail, for there are no adequate words for this situation, and it takes seeing it in person, to experience, in its terrible reality, the immense suffering that threatens the lives of thousands of condemned souls...".[4] Suffocated by the Weimar Republic's precarious economic situation, shaken by inflation, Segall left the country in late 1923 accompanied by his wife with the intention of settling in Brazil, where he arrived in December of the same year. In a letter to his brother, Oscar Siegel, Segall wrote: "On the one hand, of course there is the chasing after better financial conditions; however, on the other, and far more important, is the wish for a country where the aspiration for art is stronger than that of now-depleted Europe... I often long for purer air, away from the filth that surrounds me"[5]. The couple established themselves in São Paulo but did not live together for long. Unable to adapt to life in what could only be seen by her as a fundamentally provincial city, unlike himself, who was quickly adopted by the Modernist circles of the city, Margarete decided to return to Germany in late 1924, at which point they separated.

Immediately welcomed by the group of modernist artists, poets and writers that had congregated for the putting together of the *Semana de Arte Moderna* of 1922, and feted as a paragon of artistic Modernism, Segall was the subject of a series of laudatory articles on the local press, 1924 marking the beginning of what Mário de Andrade, whom he portrayed in a stunningly revealing portrait of 1927 (fig. p. 126), referred to as the artist's Brazilian phase. This chapter of his production, the best known of his periods and one which would earn him the admiration of local intellectuals such as de Andrade,

Fig. 2
Lasar Segall, *Die ewigen Wanderer* (Eternal Wanderers), 1919, oil on canvas, 138 × 184 cm, Acervo Museu Lasar Segall – IBRAM/ Ministério do Turismo

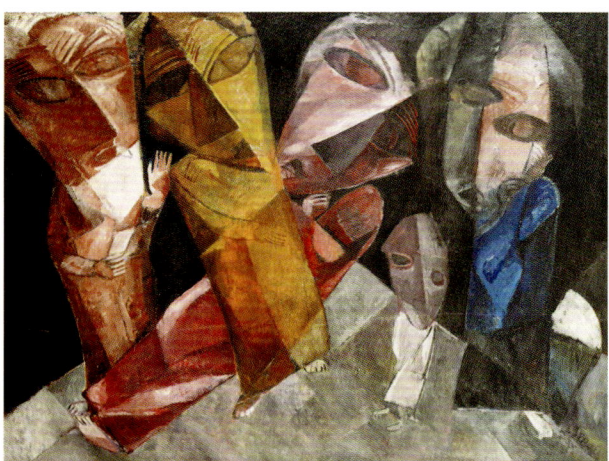

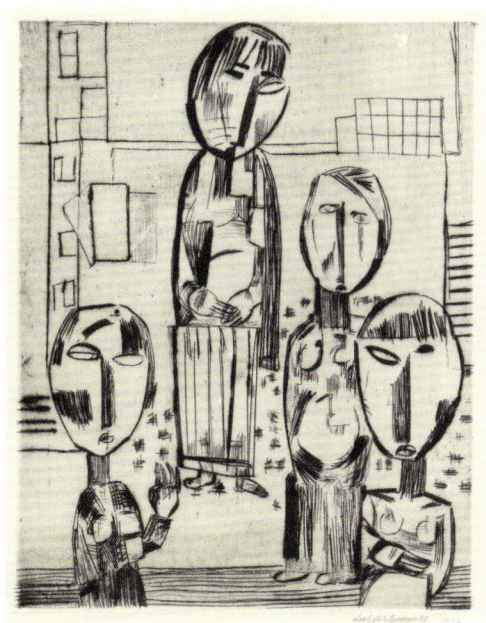

Fig. 3
Lasar Segall, *Erinnerung an Wilna* (Memories of Vilnius), 1917, engraving, 27.9 × 21.7 cm

would last until 1928. During this time, he revelled in the colouristic and formal possibilities that Brazil had opened up to him, with hitherto unknown hues he found in the tropical landscape coming into his work. The paintings he produced are a fascinating testimony to the remarkable synthesis Segall was able to create of a modernist formal language in a foreign, "exotic" land, and its varied, newly found motifs. As he himself was a stranger among foreigners, having the outcasts of society as his equals, Segall sought to formally transcribe such conditions in his work. The racial drama he found in Brazil, its many forms of violence, inequalities, and deep perversity, further contributed to his prior concerns, giving rise to a set of works, which, to this day, speak loudly to our hearts. A good example of this is the painting *Bananal* (fig. p. 122), in which we see, amidst the deep and multivarious tints of green of a banana plantation the angled head of an Afro-Brazilian man, akin in form to the African masks that had so influenced the work of his fellow expressionists back in Germany. Based on drawings by Segall in 1925 of Olegário, a former enslaved man, his face shows us no immediate expression. He is a mere mask, lamentably uprooted from the other side of the Atlantic to involuntarily work the land of a country not his own. This would be the first modernist painting to be purchased by a Brazilian public collection, having been acquired by the Pinacoteca de São Paulo in 1928. It is noteworthy, to say the least, that it took a foreign-born artist for the art of Modernism to gain the official recognition of the nation.

Despite the high regard in which he was held in São Paulo, Segall's financial situation was not entirely satisfactory, a state of affairs that would be resolved by his marriage to Jenny Klabin on 2 June 1925. Daughter of Maurício Freeman Klabin and Berta Klabin, and heiress to a vast real estate fortune, she was, in addition to this, one of the foremost intellectuals of her generation. Her translation of Goethe's *Faust* is to this day the preferred edition of the Mephistophelian play's Brazilian readers. The couple's first son Mauricio was born in Berlin in April 1926. Their second son, Oscar, was born in Paris in 1930 during the family's stay in the French capital. Having lost his mother in his teen years and left the stability of family life at a very young age, the domestic warmth he experienced with his wife and two children became a central axis of Segall's interests. One which can be observed in the canvas *Mulata com criança* (fig. p. 120) in which a mixed race figure, this time a mother holding her infant, is portrayed against the backdrop of a favela. During the four years he spent in Paris, from 1928 to 1932, Segall's output took new and surprising

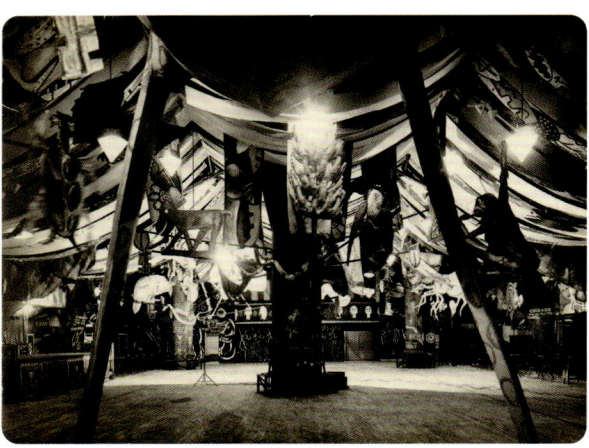

Fig. 4
Wall decoration for carnival
ball "Matas Virgens de
Spamolândia", 6 February
1934, Museu Lasar Segall

paths influenced by the artistic developments taking shape in the French capital. Concentrating on a synthetisation of form and a shrinking of the voluptuous excesses of his colouristic experiences from the Brazilian period, the works he there produced are noteworthy for their emotional restraint and formal concision. The mixing of sand to his paints betrays a newly found interest in the three-dimensional, and it is no surprise that during this time he intensely experimented with sculpture.

Back in Brazil in 1932, one year before the rise to power of Adolf Hitler in Germany, whose government would successfully seek to erase Segall's role in the development of German art, he found a deeply changed country. One in which Getúlio Vargas, after assuming the leadership of the country in a coup in 1930 and severely restricting personal freedoms, was paving the way for the establishment of his dictatorial, pseudo-fascist Estado Novo. He established himself with his family in the São Paulo district of Vila Mariana in a house designed by his brother-in-law Gregori Warchavchik, one of the introducers of modernist architecture to Brazil. He initially became deeply involved in the local art scene and, in 1932, alongside Anita Malfatti, Mário de Andrade, Tarsila do Amaral, his wife Jenny, and his in-laws the Warchavchiks, he became one of the founders of the Sociedade Pró-Arte Moderna – SPAM, whose principal aim was to promote modern art and disseminate its ideas. To raise funds for its activities, SPAM held Carnival balls for two consecutive years, the organisation of its decorations being delegated to Segall, a task he carried out with great gusto. For the second of its balls he conceived a ghostly forest inhabited by huge prehistoric animals and otherworldly figures in a strikingly rough-hewn style (fig. 4). Despite raising considerable funds for the society's activities, the ball was viciously attacked in the local press for its boisterous revelries, Segall being the object of vicious Antisemitic and xenophobic attacks. Following this traumatic episode, Segall withdrew from the more public of his activities, concentrating almost exclusively in his artistic work. His output of the late 1930s and early 1940s shows his deep, angst-ridden concern with the horrors that were slowly unfolding in the old continent. *Pogrom* (fig. p. 131, 1937) is one of its best examples. Amidst the sad ruins of what might have been a synagogue, or the melancholy remains of a shtetl, from which springs the dry twigs of a ghostly tree, we see a

Brasil! Brasil!

collection of piled up corpses in dejected shades of ochre, grey, and purple. A small pot with the incipient branches of a newly formed plant hangs on its left, whilst on the upper part of the canvas a solitary fluttering dove watches over the scene of destruction.

During the last years of his life Segall concentrated on the creation of a series of deeply moving works depicting forests and favelas. In the favelas we see his virtuosity in full bloom, their geometric constructions of superimposed shacks and downhearted shadows of men and women willingly concealing much of the richness of the colouring behind the more obvious shades of greys and blacks of their foreground. In the forests Segall restricted himself to a limited set of formal possibilities, vertical rich stripes of subtle chromatic modulations depicting the darkened depths and recesses of the woods he encountered in the mountainous region of Campos do Jordão. A site where he spent increasingly more time in the last two decades of his life. In their longing for what may lie beyond, on the other side, they depict the existentialist examinations of a master of his craft, one who is actively absorbing himself in the timings of his own mortality. Suffering from a debilitating heart condition Segall died on 2 August 1957, at his home in Vila Mariana, his house subsequently being turned into a museum dedicated to his life and work.

Giancarlo Hannud

1   Rio de Janeiro 1944, p. 49

2   Segall 1993, p. 31

3   Rio de Janeiro 1944, p. 49

4   Hannud and Monzani 2019, p. 68

5   Hannud and Monzani 2019, p. 72

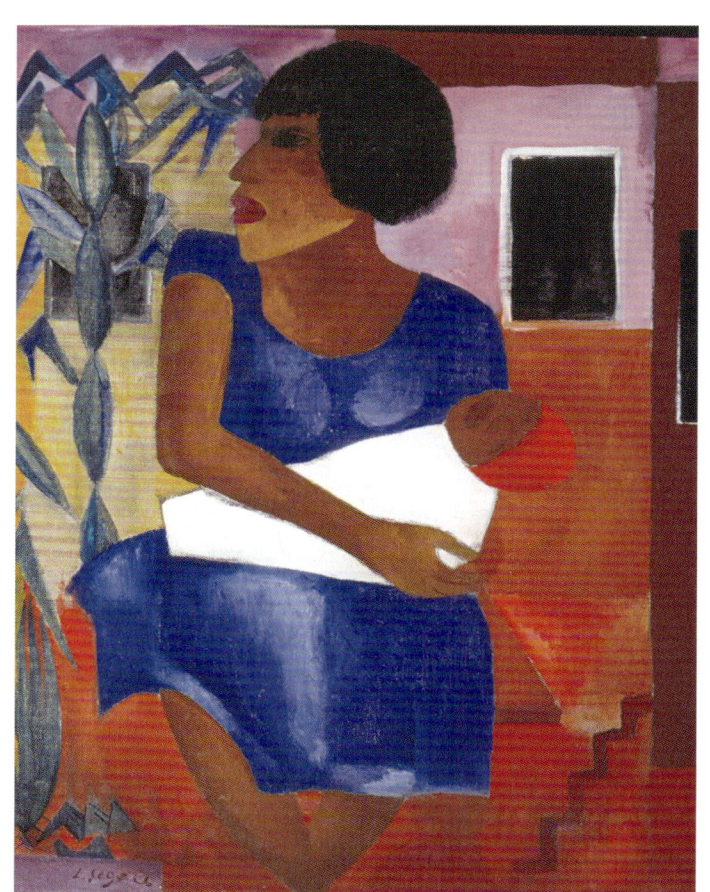 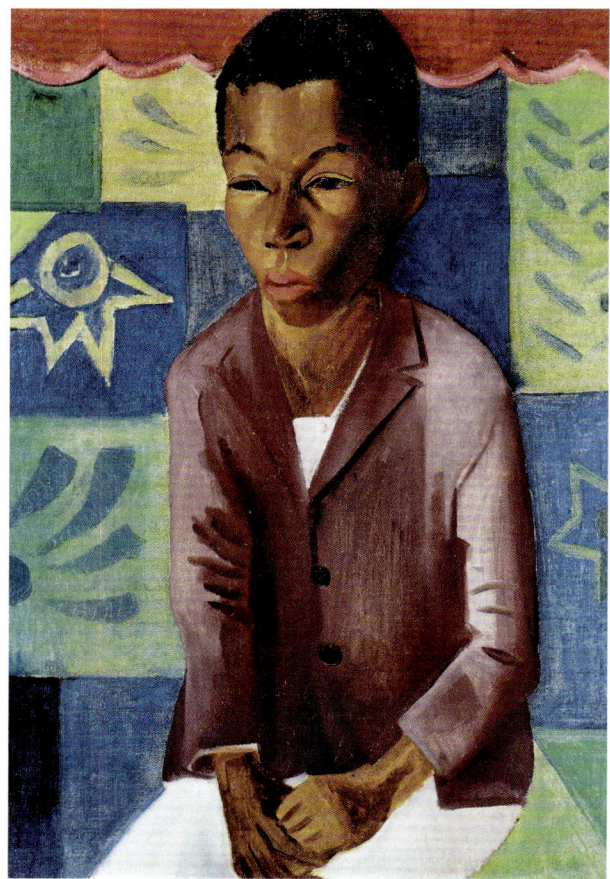

**Mulata com criança
(Mixed-Race Woman
with Child)**, 1924

**Mulato II (Mixed-Race
Boy II)**, c. 1924

**Paisagem brasileira
(Brazilian Landscape)**, 1925

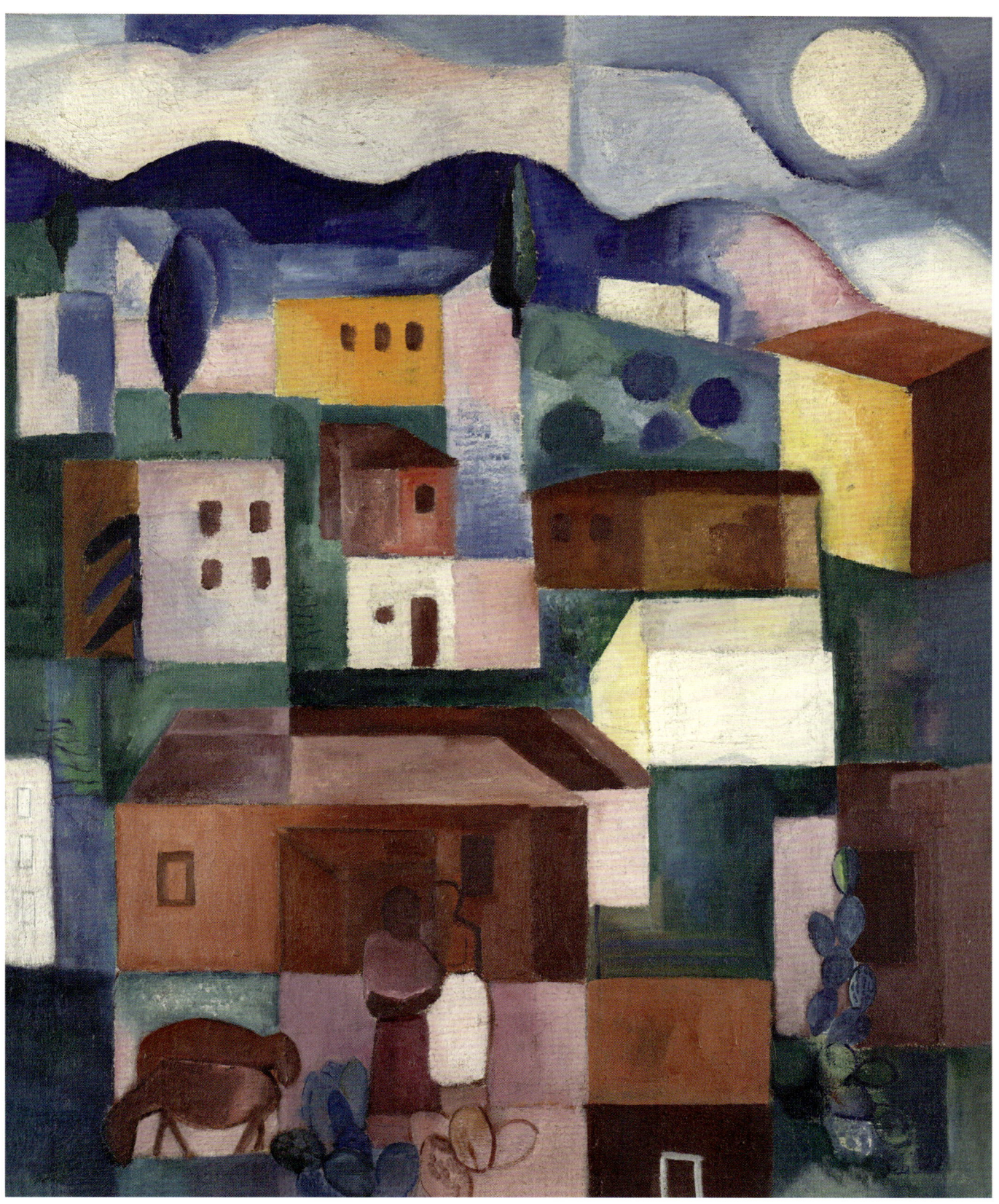

121   **Lasar Segall**

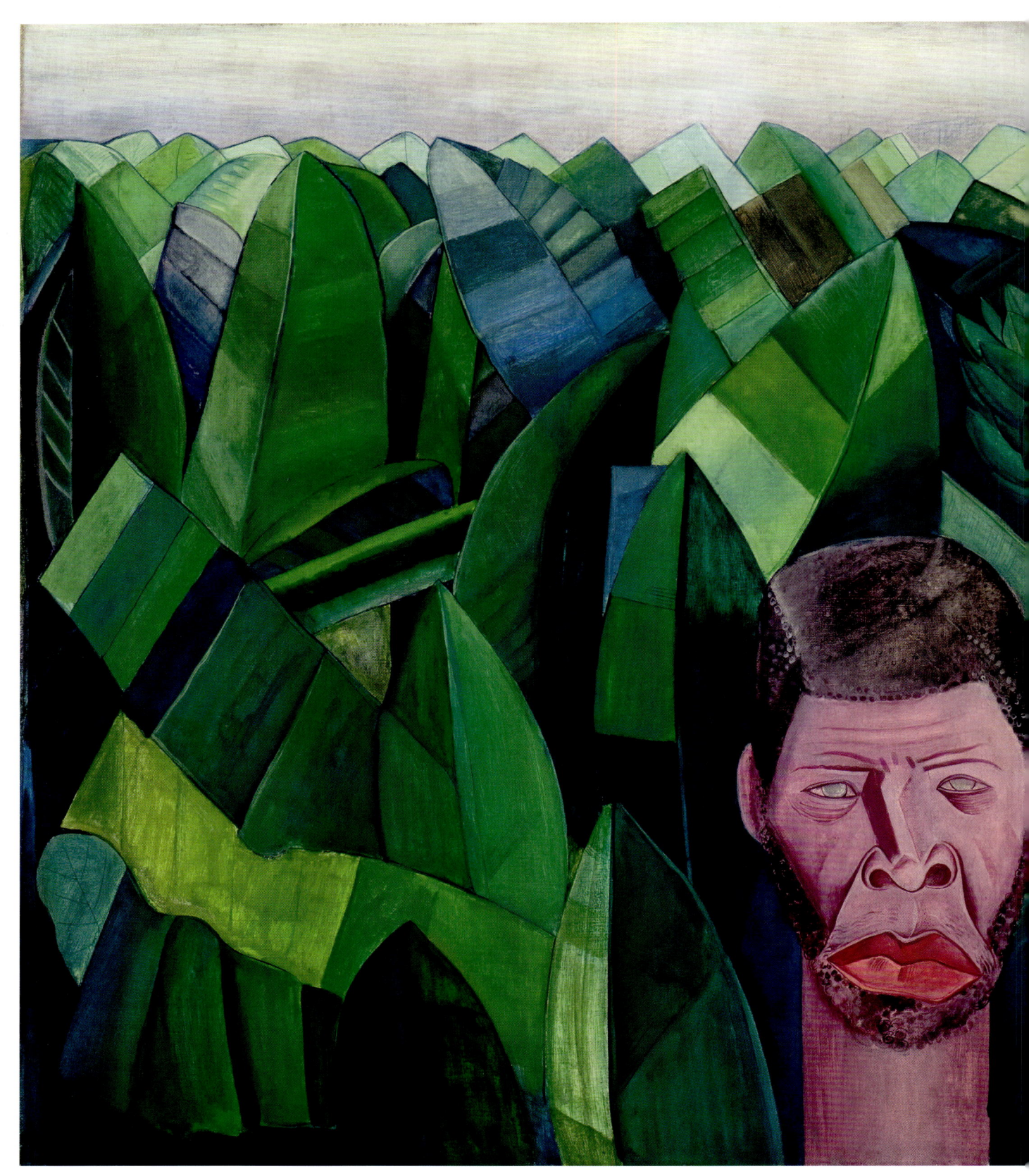

Brasil! Brasil!

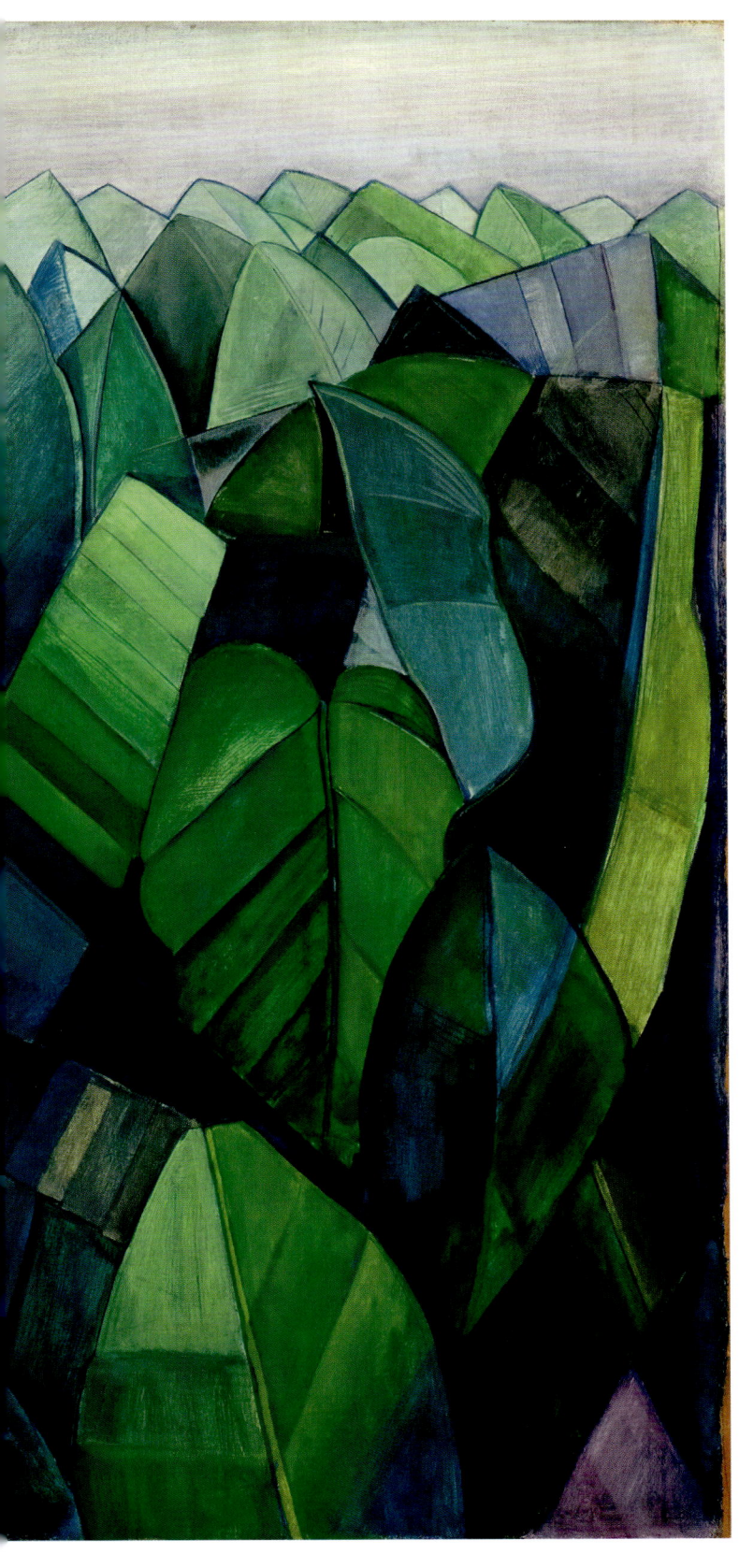

Bananal
(Banana Grove), 1927

Lasar Segall

Menino com lagartixas
(Boy with Geckos), 1924

Brasil! Brasil!

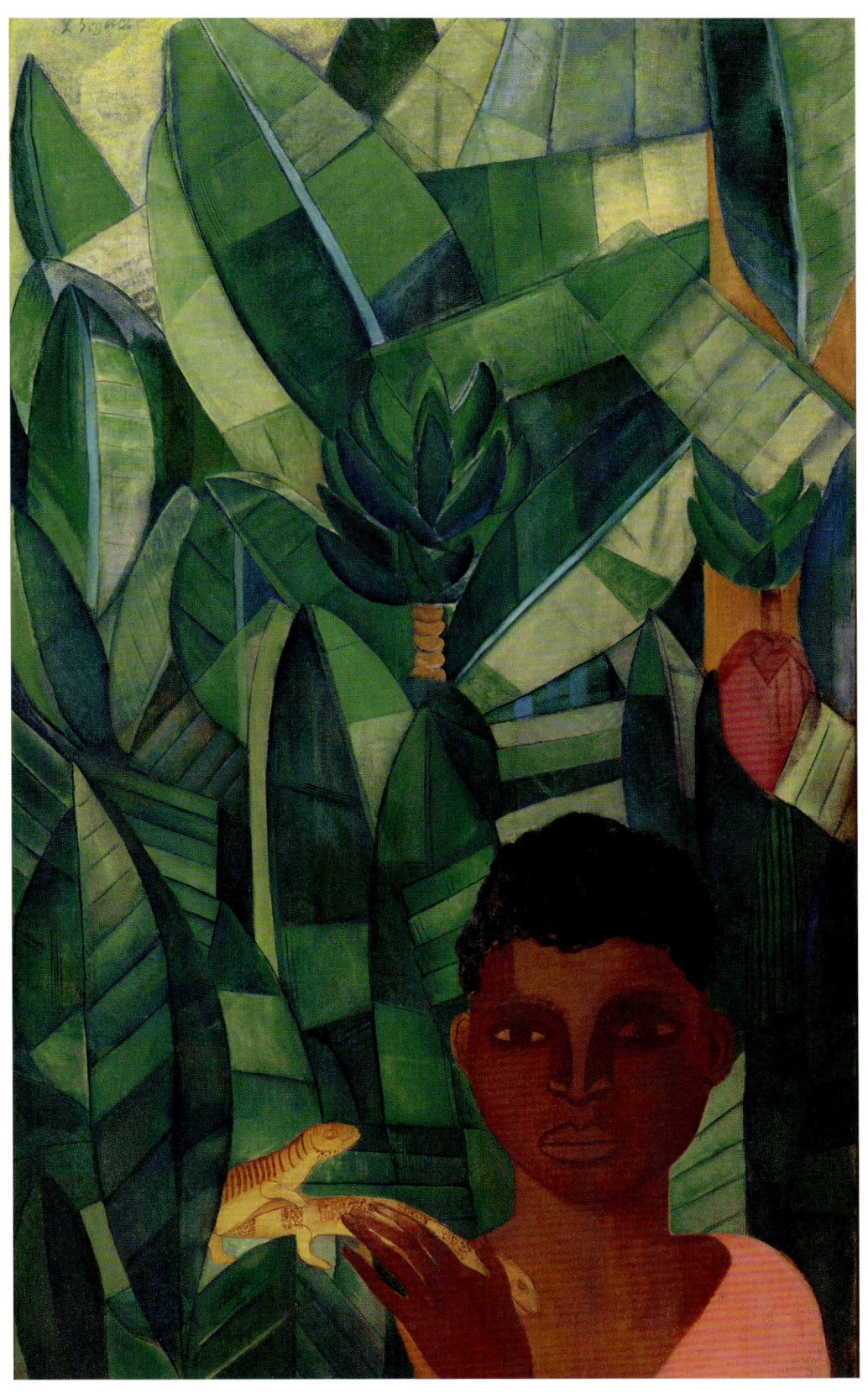

125   **Lasar Segall**

Retrato de Mário de Andrade (Portrait of Mário de Andrade), 1927

Lucy com flor (Lucy with Flower), 1939– 1942

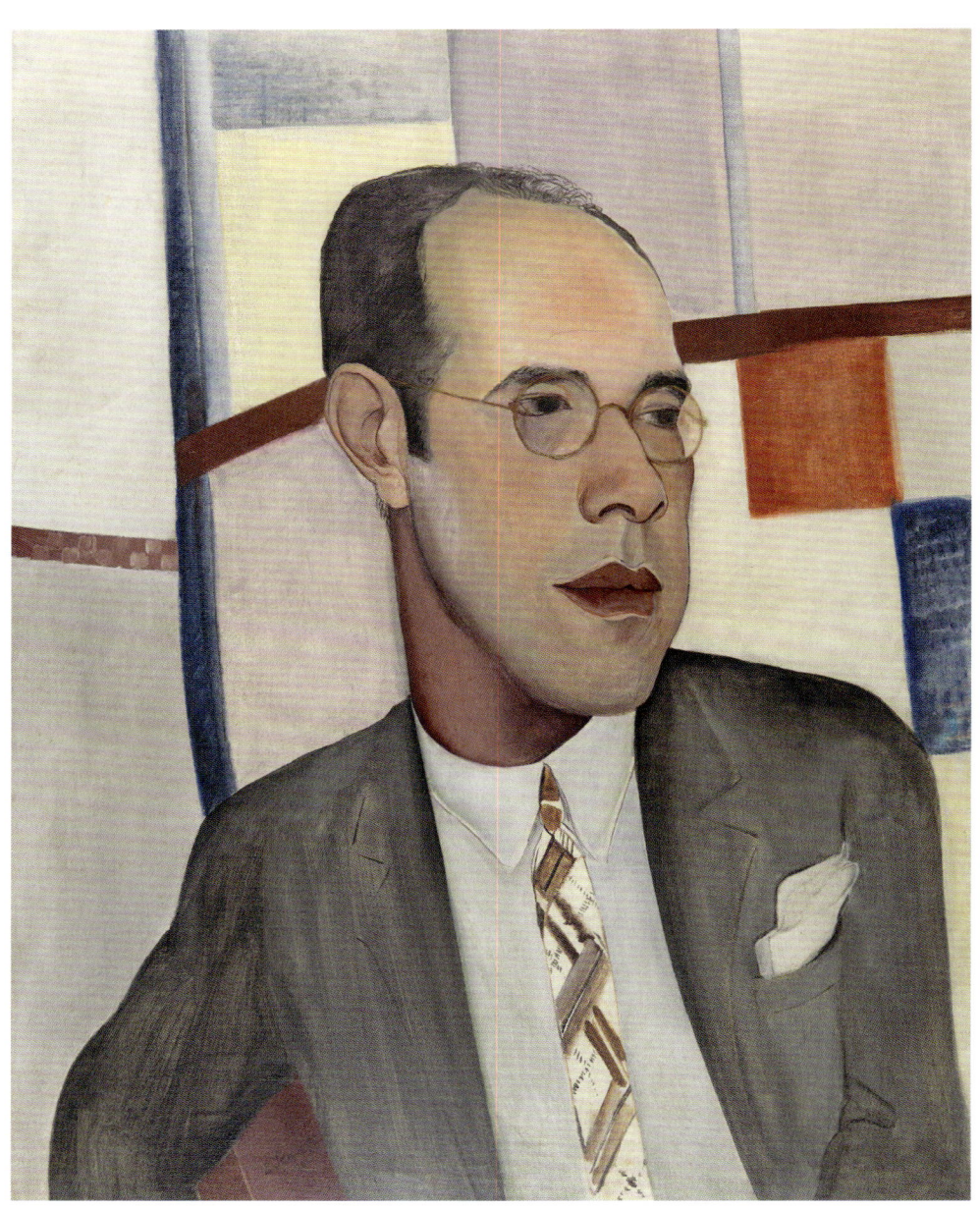

Brasil! Brasil!

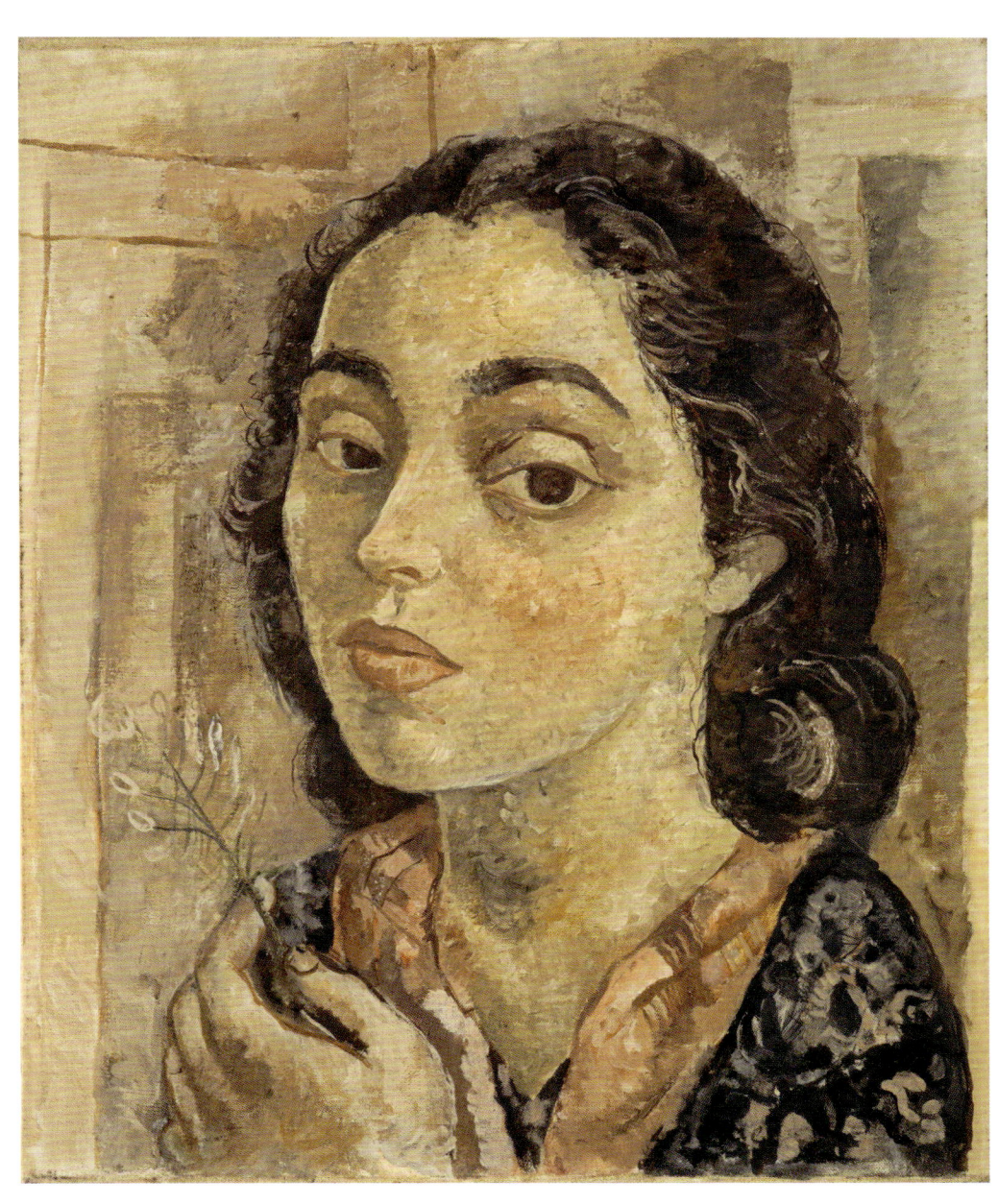

127   **Lasar Segall**

Luz na floresta (Light Reflecting in the Forest), 1954

Floresta fechada (Dense Forest), 1954

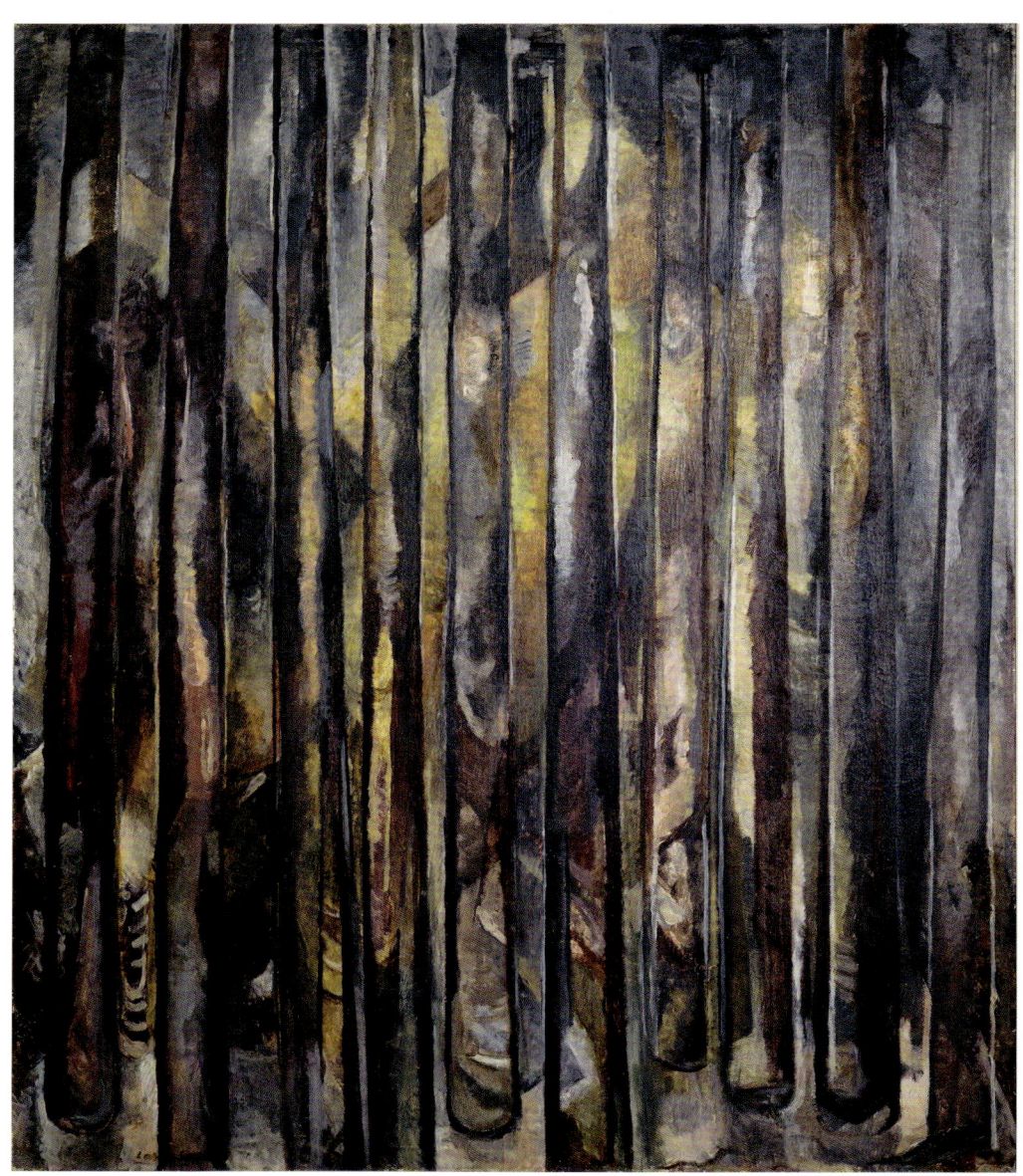

Brasil! Brasil!

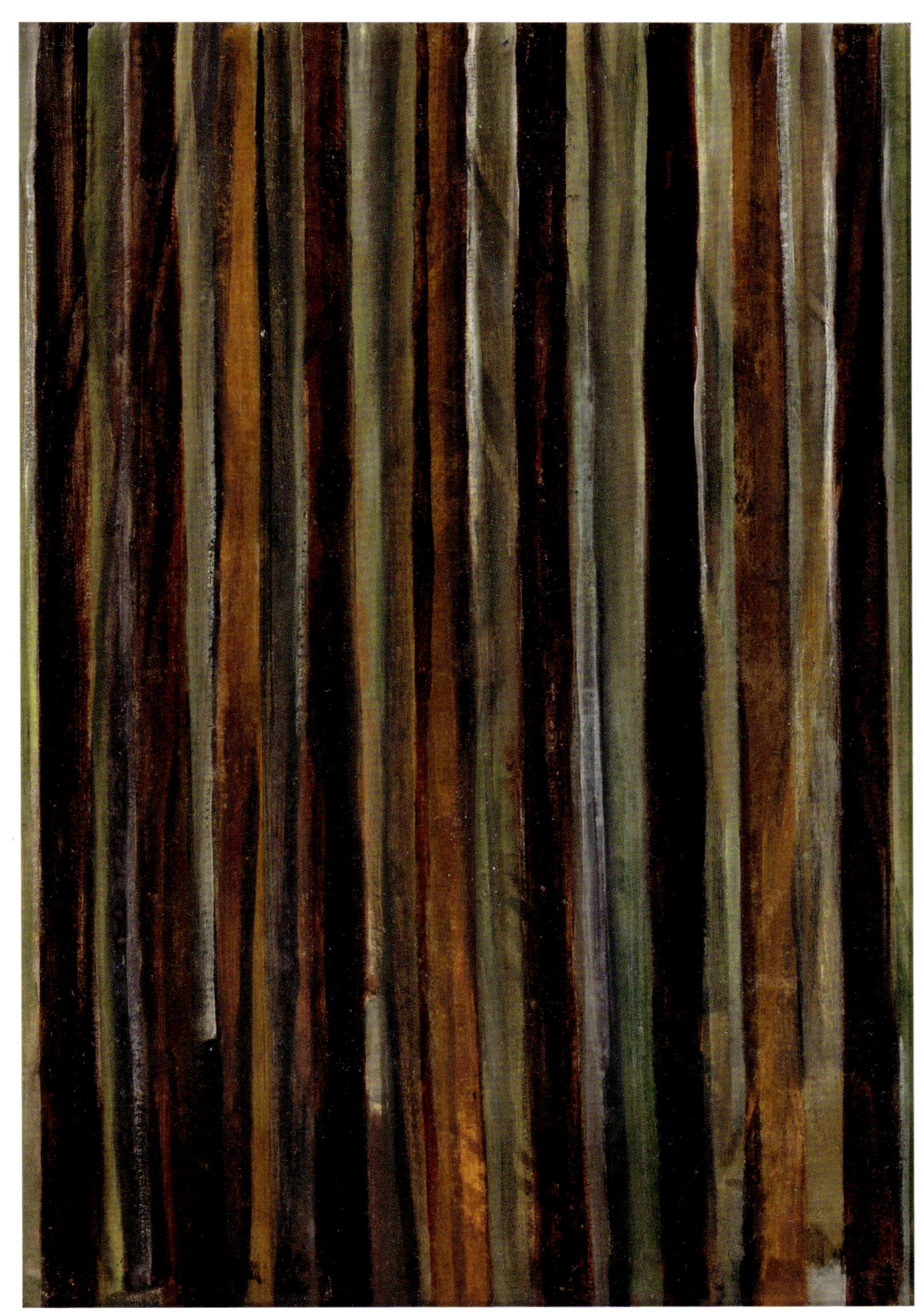

129   **Lasar Segall**

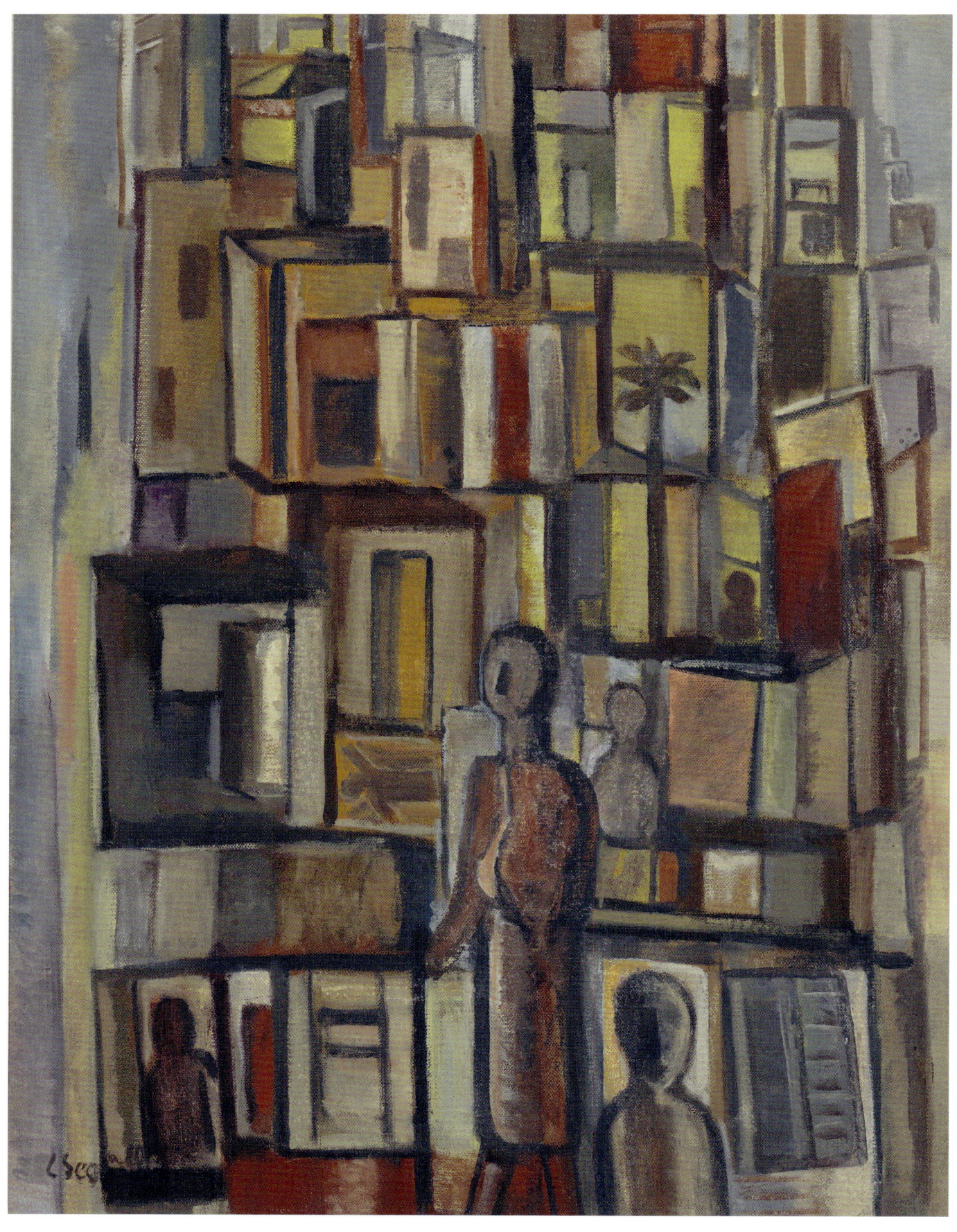

130   **Brasil! Brasil!**

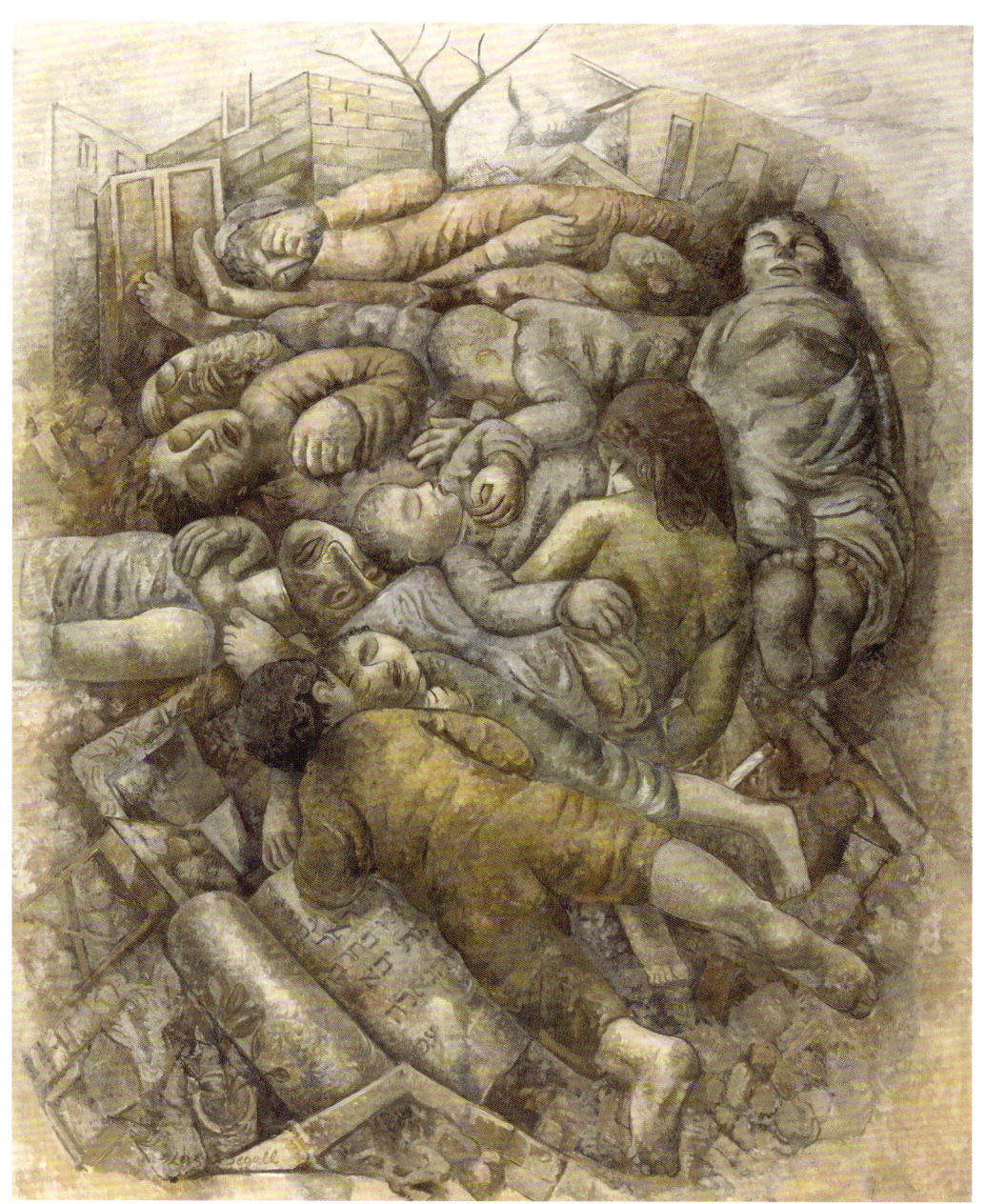

Favela, 1954–1955

Pogrom, 1937

131　　　　**Lasar Segall**

Flávio de Carvalho

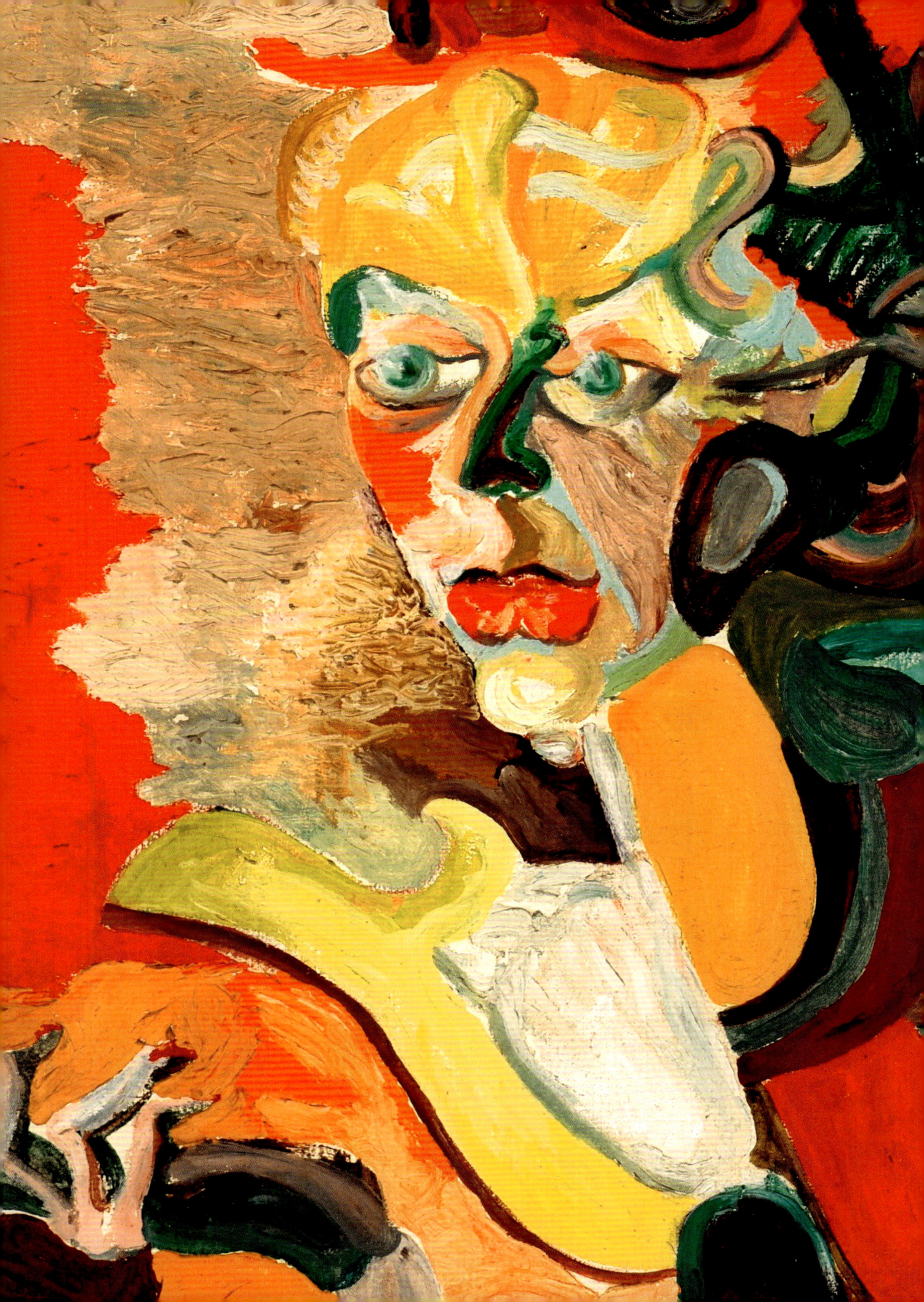

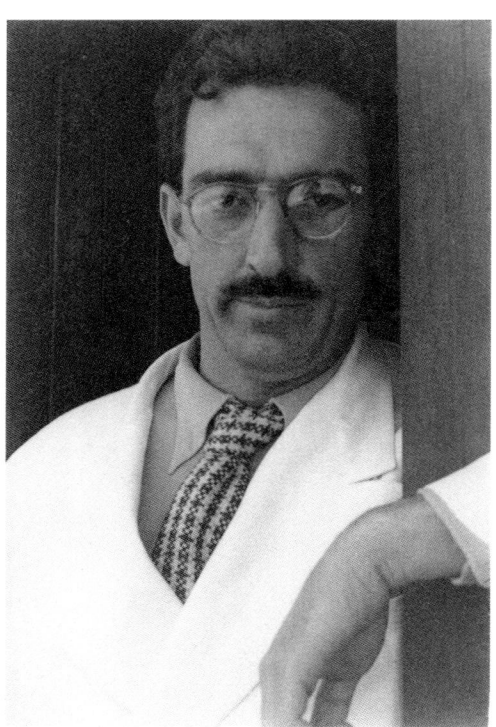

Flávio de Carvalho
1899, Barra Mansa, Brazil –
1973, Valinhos, Brazil

The artistic trajectory of polymath Flávio de Rezende Carvalho who, besides being a painter of great inventiveness and idiosyncratic draughtsman, was also an engineer, architect, sculptor, journalist, and playwright, constitutes one of the most interesting and multifaceted episodes of Brazilian Modernism. He was born on 10 August 1899, in Barra Mansa, into an aristocratic family whose wealth came from growing coffee on the farms that dot the border region between the states of Rio de Janeiro and São Paulo. When he was a toddler his family moved to São Paulo, taking him along to the city, and in 1911, when he was no more than twelve years old, moved to France to continue his education at the Lycée Janson in Paris. On holiday in England at the time of the outbreak of the Great War in 1914, he was forced to remain there for the duration of the conflict, eventually enrolling at the Jesuit Stonyhurst College, whose motto, *Quant je puis*, meaning "As much as I can", is an apt maxim for his own life and work, in which the creative possibilities of the human species and its enmeshment with life itself were explored in an entirely novel, unfettered way. With his primary education completed, de Carvalho went on to study civil engineering at Durham University, attending evening drawing classes at the King Edward VII School of Fine Arts, the only formal artistic training he would ever receive.

Back in Brazil in the second half of 1922, a few months after the *Semana de Arte Moderna* (Modern Art Week), with a more than reputable engineering diploma on his back, de Carvalho acquainted himself with the local circle of modernist artists and intellectuals, producing some illustrations for local newspapers. He would also be employed, in 1924, as an engineer in the most established architectural firm of São Paulo, the Escritório Técnico Ramos de Azevedo. Named after its founder, the influential architect-engineer Ramos de Azevedo, it concentrated all the most important building projects of the city, running a near monopoly on its stylistic development. He would work with the grand old man of *paulista* architecture until 1926, when he opened his own practice.

De Carvalho's work in architecture began with his participation in a competition for the design of the city's new State Palace in 1927 (fig. 1). Submitted under the pseudonym Eficácia, it was intensely discussed in the local press for its modernist characteristics as well as the fact that it seemed unrealisable. Of mammoth dimensions and monumental volumetry, it included platforms for the landing of airplanes, anti-aircraft cannons, immense spotlights for the lighting of São Paulo's night-skies, a lighthouse and observatories, as well as immense ballrooms with panoramic views of the city, two hanging gardens teeming with birds and specimens of local flora, and the traditional residential areas for the governor and his family. A mix of fortress, Mayan pyramid and modernist rational ideals, the project was way beyond what was technically feasible for its place and time, but its ambition and lack of concern for the material conceivability of its execution inspired many a discussion on what architecture was able to achieve in a country such as Brazil. Mário de Andrade, despite having reservations would nevertheless declare it to be the only project that honoured the state with its daring propositions. De Carvalho would eventually paint an illuminatively rugged portrait of Mário in 1939 (fig. p.141), about which the writer would say: "When I confront the portrait Flávio did of me I feel scared, because I see in it the dark side of myself, the side that I hide from others."[1] In it the writer's face becomes a tangled net of nervously dashed brushstrokes, his visage merely hinted at.

In the years following the State Palace competition de Carvalho would propose several other projects for national and international competitions, none of which were built. It was during the 1930 Pan-American Congress of Architects, held in the Brazilian cities of Rio de Janeiro and Belo Horizonte, that he had the opportunity to present his ideas on architecture to a knowledgeable public. He presented his conference *A cidade do homem nu* (City of the Naked Man), proposing a fresh approach to the building of cities. It was time to start anew, unencumbered by religious dogmatisms, taking the body, a feeling, thinking, living body, as its guiding centre, one that blended in equal parts elements of the erotic (a fundamental aspect of his thought), the visual and the aesthetic in its conceptualisation. The whole city was to be the naked man's house, where he would find in organised form all that was necessary for his existence. He concluded the conference by inviting the American representatives of the Congress to doff their "masks of civilization and show off their anthropophagous inclinations repressed by colonial conquest."[2] He would also dabble with the theatre at this time, writing an experimental play dealing with the provocative story of the birth and death of a god, *Bailado do Deus Morto*, in 1933, for which he also designed the sets and costumes. The scenography was of the utmost simplicity, composed as it was of an aluminium column and a long chain hanging over the stage, lighting effects taking the central role. The costumes were also simple, long white blouses, and the actors, nearly all of whom were Afro-Brazilian, wore aluminium masks (fig. 2). It caused a stir in the city, some conservative journalists demanding police action after its opening night. The play would eventually be censored following its second performance.

Soon after the Pan-American Congress de Carvalho gave start to the building of the couple of projects authored by him that ever saw transposition from the land of ideas to concrete realisation. The first is a group of rental modernist houses built between 1936 and 1938 (fig. 3), and the second the main house of de Carvalho's farm, the Fazenda Capuava, of

Flávio de Carvalho

1938. Both have come down to us in very bad condition, not to say utterly deformed in their original intentS. In the group of modernist houses, his main concern was with the comfort of its inhabitants, not only physical, but also psychological, in which the colours employed in its interiors played a decisive role. The interior distribution of the houses was particularly novel, abolishing corridors and having bedrooms open directly to the double-height living room. As could be expected, they were not received by their neighbours in a positive light, police having to intervene to stop the constant throwing of oranges and bananas at the construction site. But de Carvalho did not have the present as his preferred audience, thinking of the future as his real, interested public: "In the rental houses I built I chose to look forward, building them for men more civilised than the ones of today."[3] If on the one hand the modernist rental houses were meant for people other than himself, his outlook having necessarily to take into account at least a few of the more quotidian worries of a middle class family, with the Fazenda Capuava, on the other, he did not have to think about anything other than his own unconventional tastes. An immense central block, close in spirit to a pyramid or ancient mausoleum, holds the main living space of the structure, eight meters tall and flanked by balconies that spring, wing-like, from the concrete structure. Directly in front we find the swimming pool, once again immense, and a place where de Carvalho held rowdy pool parties to which guests were invited to partake naked. The interiors were just as exuberant, a fireplace in the central living space having compartments for the placing of water, which when in contact with the fire would vaporise, creating a mysterious mistiness to the space.

De Carvalho's training as an engineer and his wish to engage with concrete interventions upon reality rather than merely formal or theoretical ones becomes evident when we investigate his *Experiências*, an early form of performance art that exemplify his desire to act upon the social lattices of reality. There is a total of four distinct *Experiências*. The first one is still a motive of dispute among scholars, some claiming it never actually occurred. The fact is that we do have a good deal of information of the second, or perhaps first, who knows, *Experiência*. Dated to 1931 it consisted in de Carvalho's own actions upon actuality. During a Corpus Christi procession in downtown São Paulo, a serious affair in those days, he walked opposite the flow of the religiously inclined throng, refusing, whilst doing so, to remove a green velvet cap from his schoolboy days in Britain.

Fig. 1
Flávio de Carvalho alias Efficácia, design of the city's new State Palace, 1927

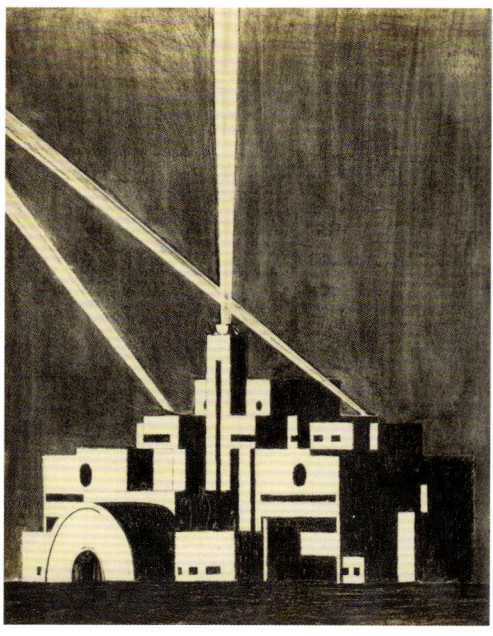

Brasil! Brasil!

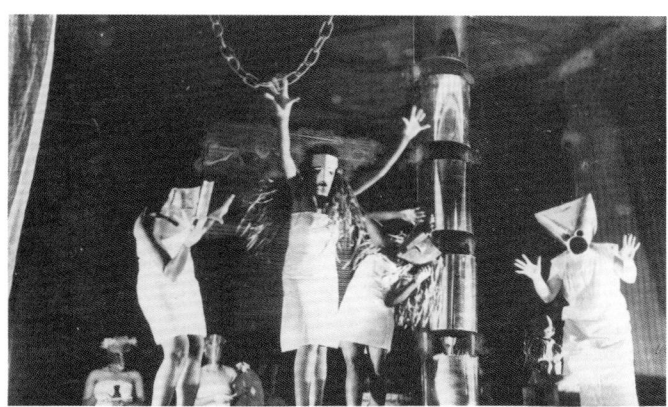

Fig. 2
Scene of Flávio de
Carvalho's *Bailado do
Deus Morto* (Dance of
the Dead God), 1933

The members of the procession, in an outburst of collective fury, called for his lynching in turn for his disrespect, and he was forced to escape the loud, angry mob, being escorted by policemen to a station where he was kept at a safe distance from them. Some months after the experience, de Carvalho published a book explaining his actions, the *Experiência N.2*, a dramatic, fun and monstrous tome, as described in the ads promoting it, illustrated by the artist himself. In it he narrates the event whilst attempting to explain the psychology at play behind the fury of a mob so intimately offended in its spiritual beliefs.

The third *Experiência*, and probably the best known of them, was the *New Look*, of 1956 (fig. 3, p. 201). It consisted of the designing of a new outfit – hygienic, breathable, clean, affordable – appropriate for the peoples of the Tropics. It was composed of a skirt, vertical-striped blouse, fishnet stockings and leather sandals. De Carvalho himself wore the new outfit on October 18, 1956, parading around the city of São Paulo. Obviously, this provoked an unheard-of scandal; an imposing man, de Carvalho being of above than average height, wearing a skirt proved highly offensive to local society. This highly innovative fashion show-turned-parade was the culmination of a concerted effort on de Carvalho's part to discuss fashion, its history and norms in a weekly newspaper column of his, where he published nearly forty articles dealing with the subject from March to October of that year. Fashion to him was a means to free the human spirit of centuries of sartorial oppression. Forbidden to breathe, to show itself, to exist in liberty, the time had come for bodies to be liberated from the traditional shackles of tie, suit, bouffant dresses, and petticoats. The final of his experiences was an expedition to the northernmost region of the Rio Negro in the Amazon in 1958. The expedition's aim was to register the space and the peoples of the region, documenting their mores and the specificities of the landscape in film. From the start it was plagued by troubles. Forced to turn back, it ended in absolute frustration. As he would write, "And thus it was, the most important epic of my life, one in which I nearly lost my life."[4]

Despite his concrete interventions upon reality, de Carvalho also pursued more traditional forms of artmaking. He painted and drew constantly during his career. In his canvases we are confronted with an otherworldly universe, entirely individual, of forms and colours, one in

Flávio de Carvalho

which their process is just as relevant as their materiality. They seem to be making themselves as we look at them, revealing their temporal layers through the dense archaeology of their brushstrokes of mixed-up colours. The oils *Ascensão definitiva de Cristo* and *A inferioridade de Deus* (figs pp. 143 and 142), were produced following his *Experiência N.2*. Their titles, particularly outrageous for the place for which they were produced, make this kinship even more evident. Their formal elements – stairwells, columns, little flags, ameboid forms and geometric inventions – give rise to a world of surreal vagueness and ambiguity, nothing being what it seems in these remarkably prickly compositions. Unique in their fashioning, they are formal hybrids, elements from Surrealism, Expressionism, and Cubism here converging to create something new, more barbarous, and less polished than its European counterparts. Despite the high inventiveness of his paintings, it must be said that de Carvalho never entirely espoused, nor truly understood abstract art, as with so many other Brazilian artists of his generation, even though we find several nearly abstract compositions in his body of work, such as *Nossa Senhora do Desejo* and *Composição paisagem interna*, both from 1955 (figs pp. 151 and 150). He would go so far as declaring in the late 1940s that "abstract painting is painting without a 'soul'. Its rational nature, into which it recedes, serves all sorts of mental blackmail. (...) The greatest justification one could give abstract art is the invocation of the artist's creative liberty, to say that the artist has the right to manifest and express himself just as he pleases."[5]

De Carvalho would remain active in the Brazilian artistic scene throughout the last two decades of his life. Not only did he produce one of the most poignant series of drawings of Brazilian art history, *Série trágica*, of 1947 (fig. 4), in which he documents, from life, in lightly nervous strokes the slow death of his mother, but also a series of portraits of the most varied characters of Brazilian life. After having seen his works refused by the IV Bienal de São Paulo in 1957, a moment in which his constantly turbulent relations with institutional spaces of art was at its most pronounced, he would eventually be given a retrospective at the VII Bienal de São Paulo in 1963, and yet another one at the eleventh edition of the event in 1971, solidifying his position as one of the most important Brazilian artists

Fig. 3
Flávio de Carvalho, Row of houses on Lorena Street, São Paulo, 1936

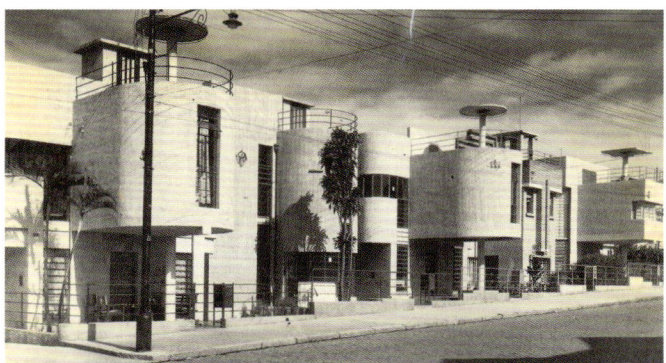

Brasil! Brasil!

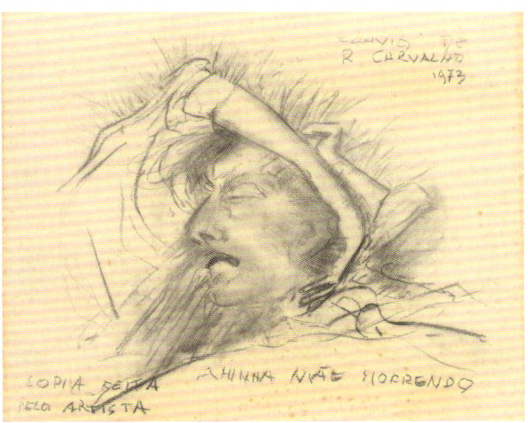

Fig. 4
Flávio de Carvalho,
Copy of *Série trágica*,
1947/1973, UNICAMP

of his generation. His last large scale work was a whimsically profound monument honouring the poet Federico Garcia Lorca. One year after its installation in 1968 it was vandalised by defenders of morality. Being the work of a communist, Flávio de Carvalho, and a homosexual, Garcia Lorca, it had no place in the city of São Paulo. It would lead a peripatetic existence in the following years, moving from place to place, until reinstalled in its place of origin in 1979. Flávio de Carvalho died in his house at the Fazenda Capuava on June 4, 1973, being true to the end to his words "abnormal art is the only good art"[6].

Giancarlo Hannud

1   Barros 2005, p. 238

2   Maia and Rezende 2015, p. 41

3   Apud Leite 2008, p. 42

4   Maia and Rezende 2015, p. 251

5   Ferreira 2013, pp. 132–133

6   Carvalho 1936

Mário de Andrade, 1939

Brasil! Brasil!

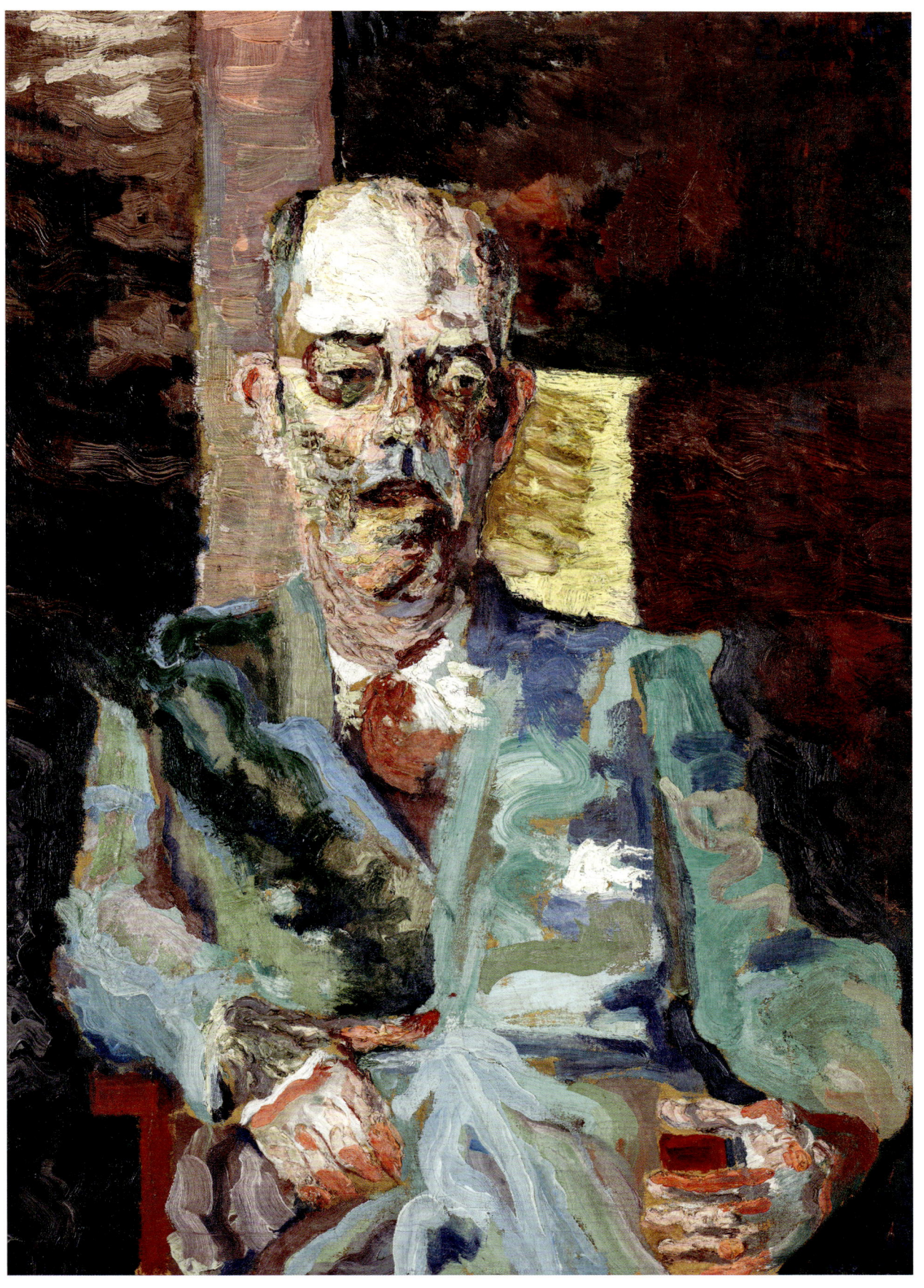

141   **Flávio de Carvalho**

A inferioridade de Deus
(Inferiority of God), 1931

Ascensão definitiva de Cristo
(Christ's Final Ascension), 1932

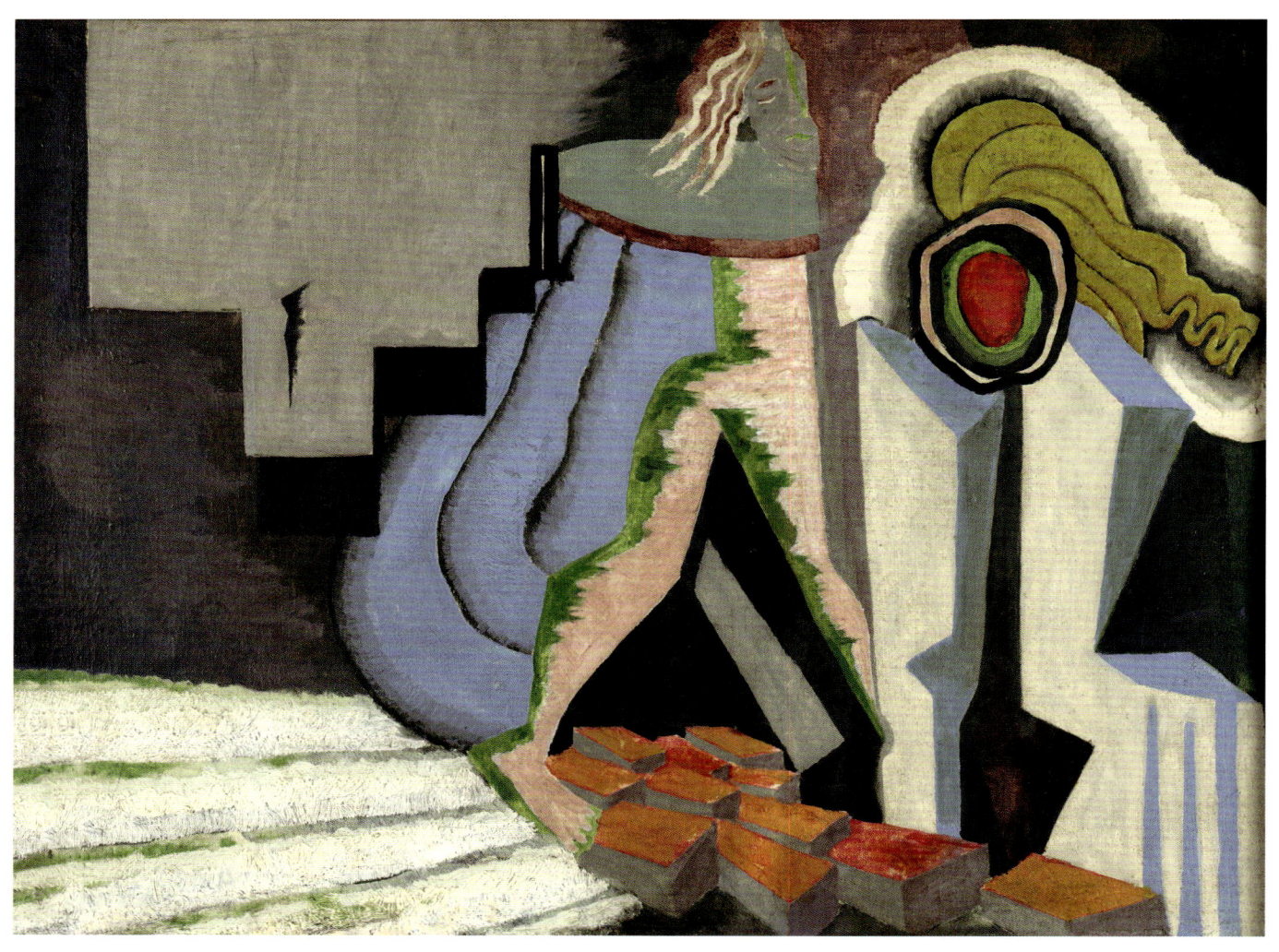

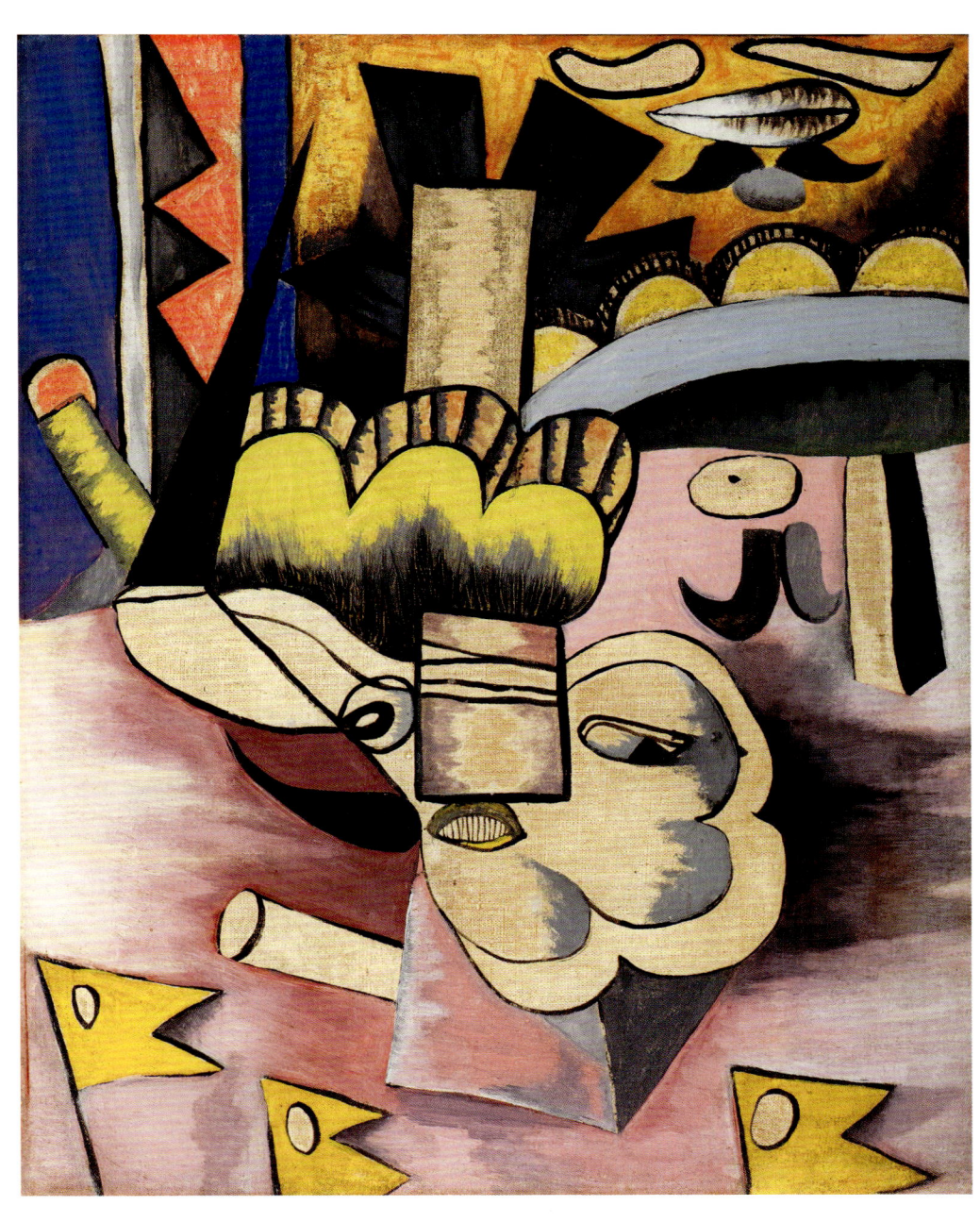

143   **Flávio de Carvalho**

Retrato ancestral
(Ancestral Portrait), 1932

Brasil! Brasil!

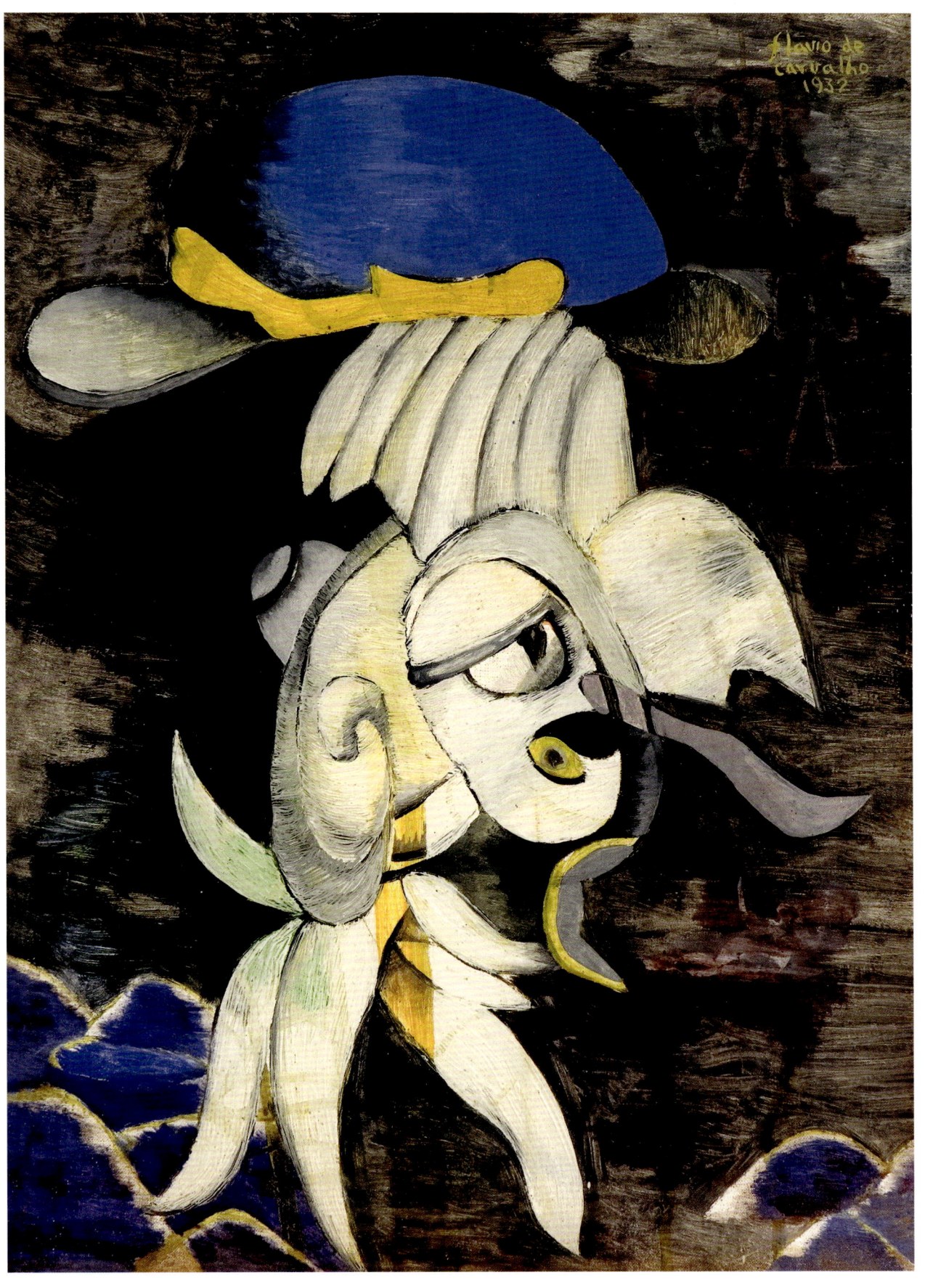

145   **Flávio de Carvalho**

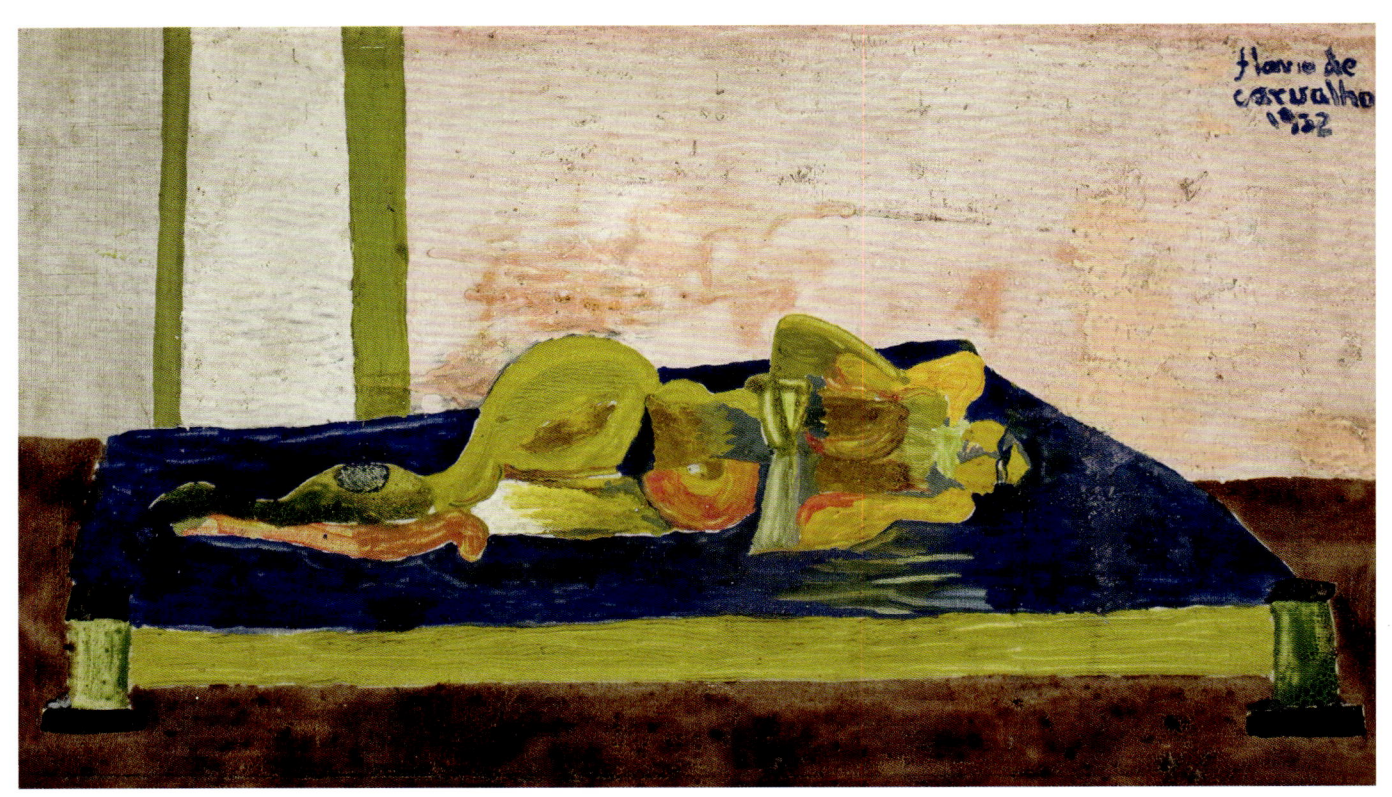

**Nu feminino deitado
(Reclined Female Nude)**, 1932

Casal (Couple), 1932

Brasil! Brasil!

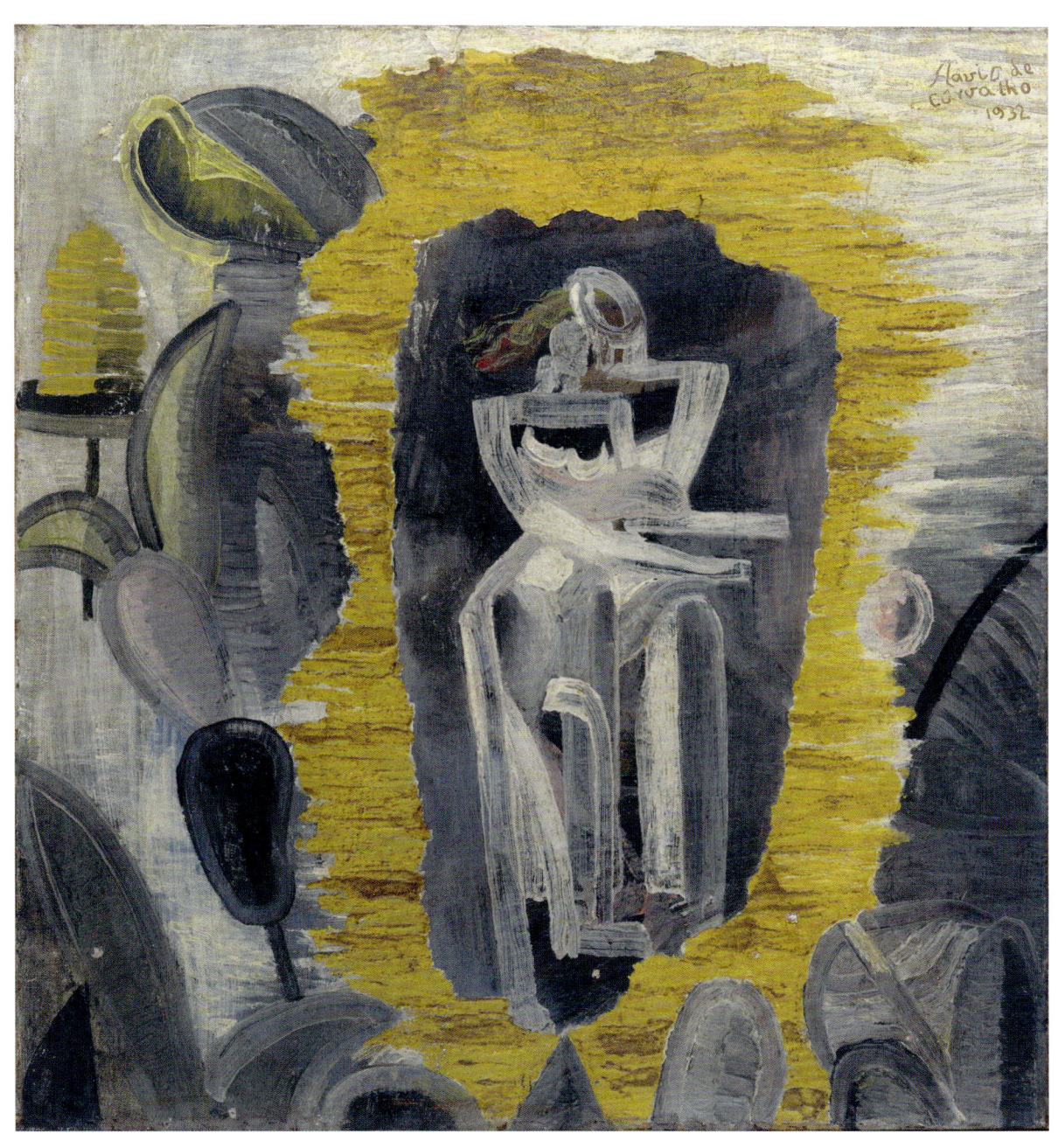

147   **Flávio de Carvalho**

Anteprojeto para Miss Brasil
(Study for Miss Brazil), 1931

Retrato de Ivone Levi
(Portrait of Ivone Levi), 1951

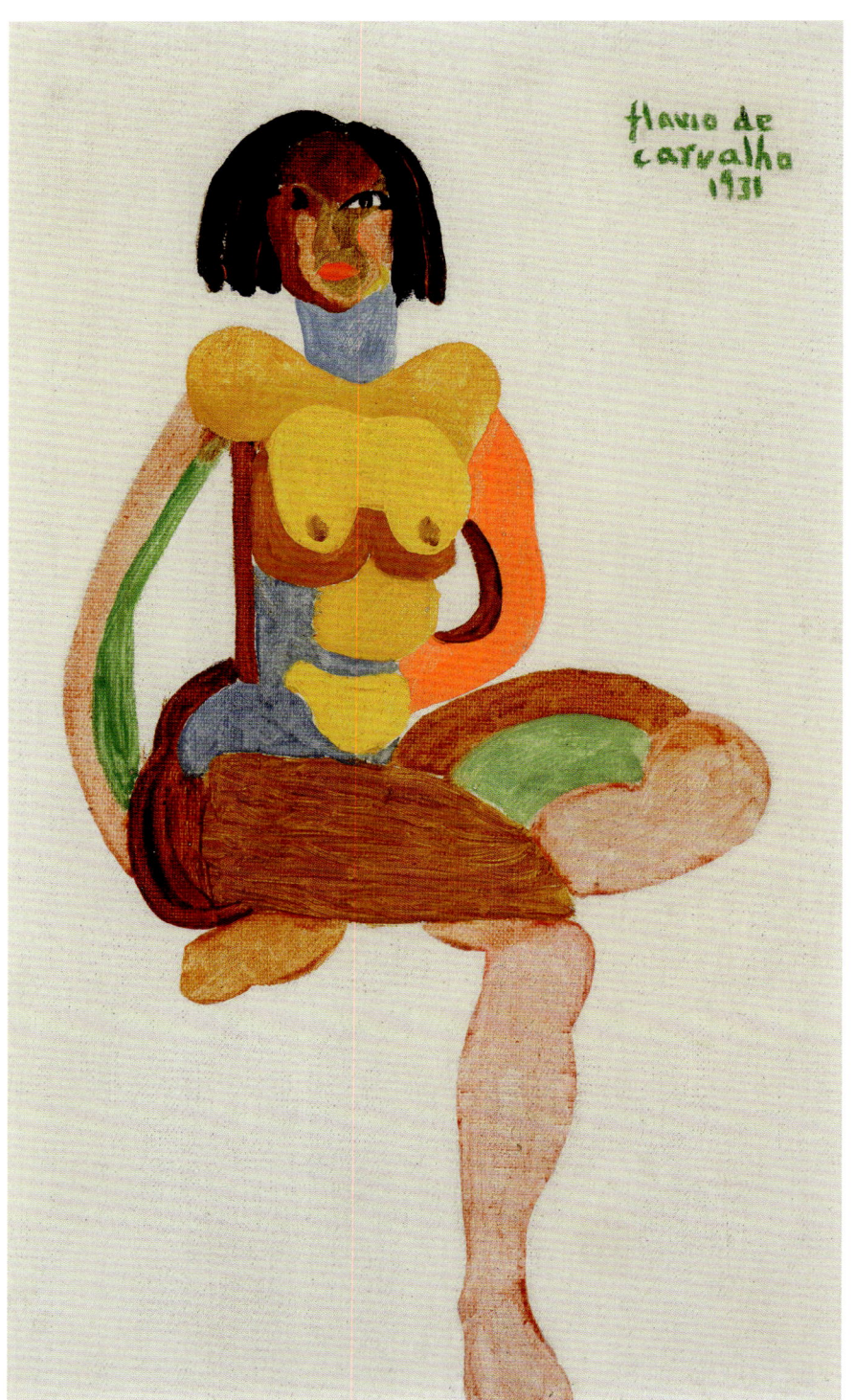

Brasil! Brasil!

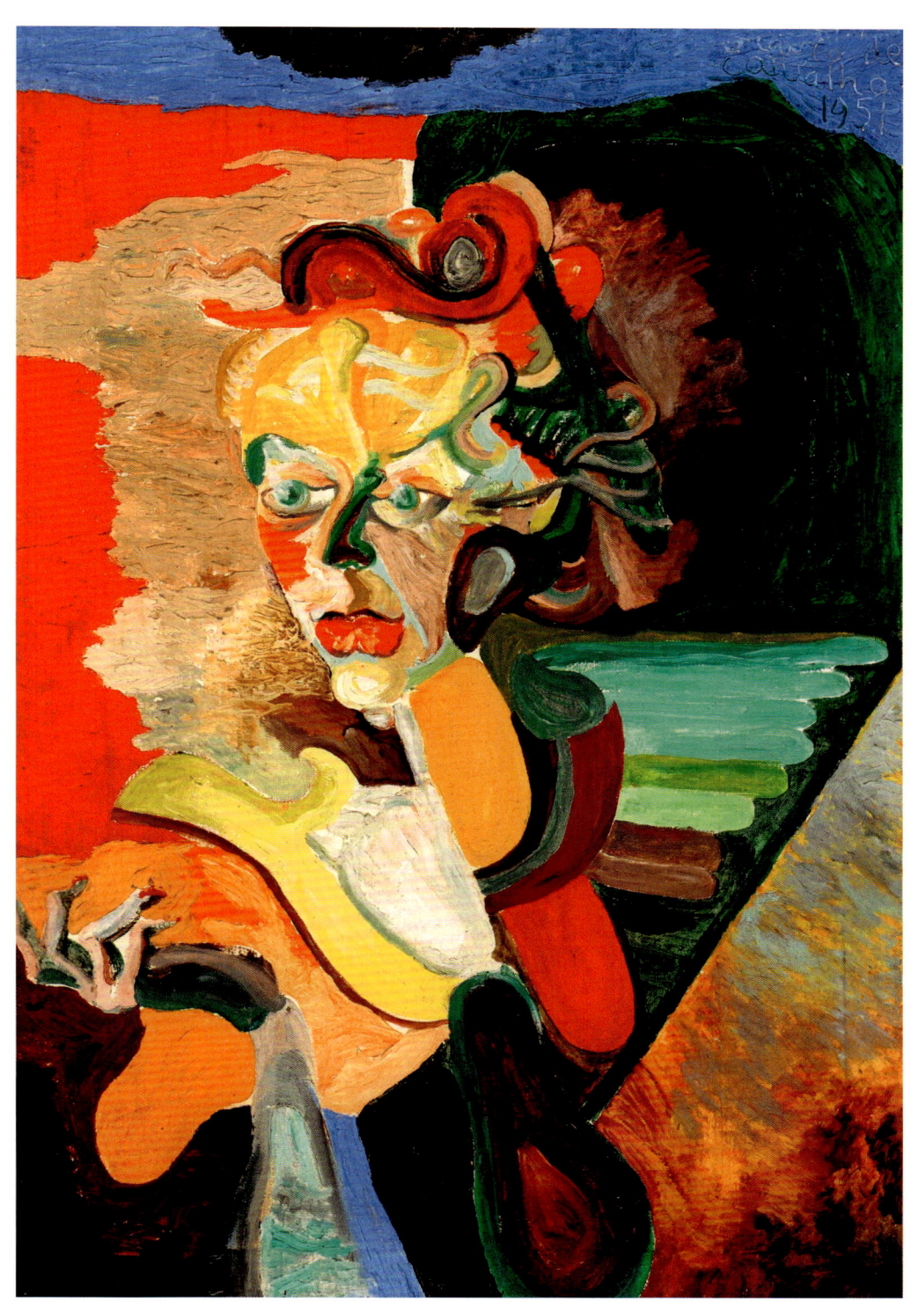

149 **Flávio de Carvalho**

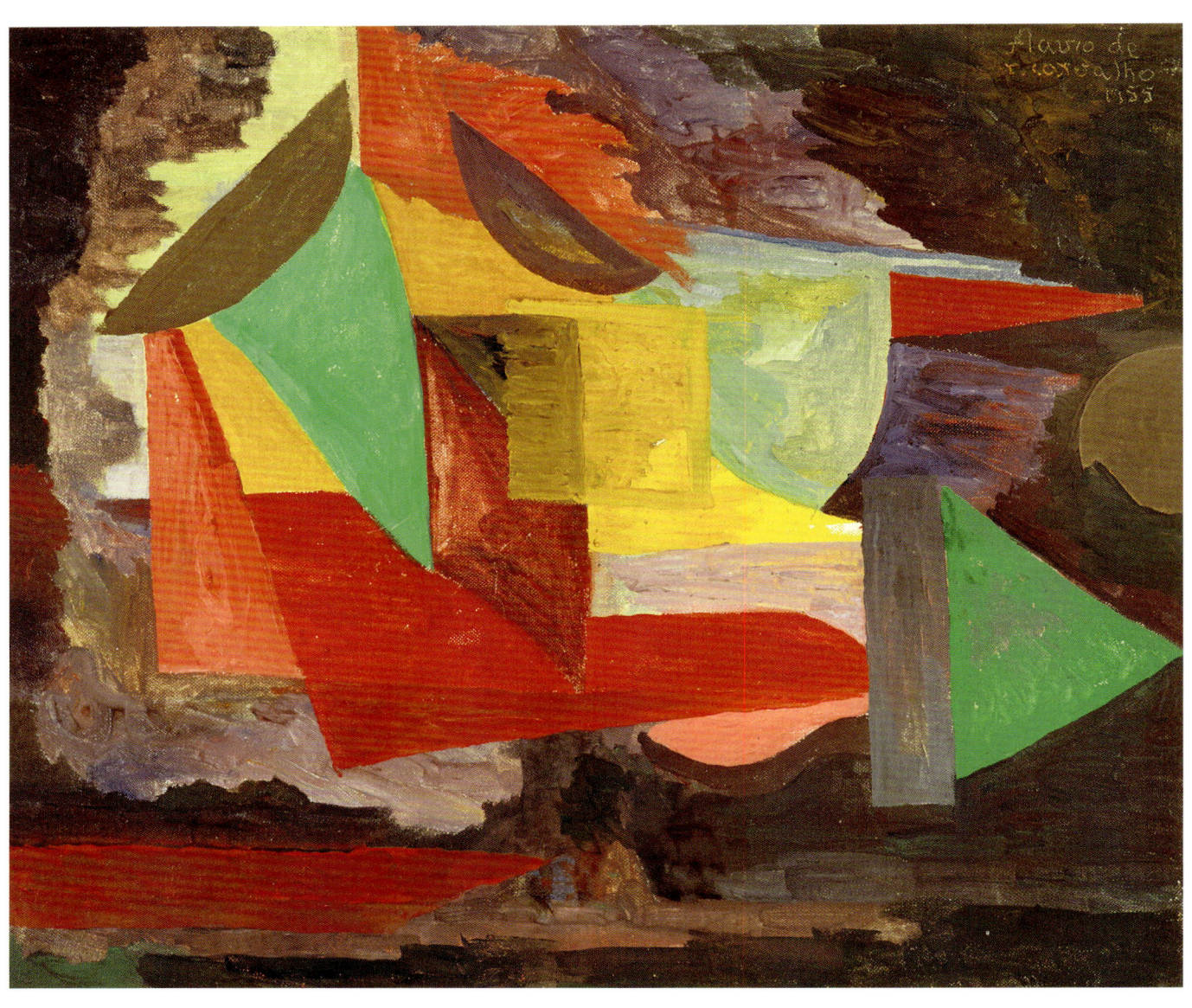

**Composição paisagem
interna (Interior Landscape
Composition)**, 1955

**Nossa Senhora do Desejo
(Our Lady of Desire)**, 1955

**Retrato de Niomar Moniz
Sodré Bittencourt (Portrait
of Niomar Moniz Sodré
Bittencourt)**, 1955

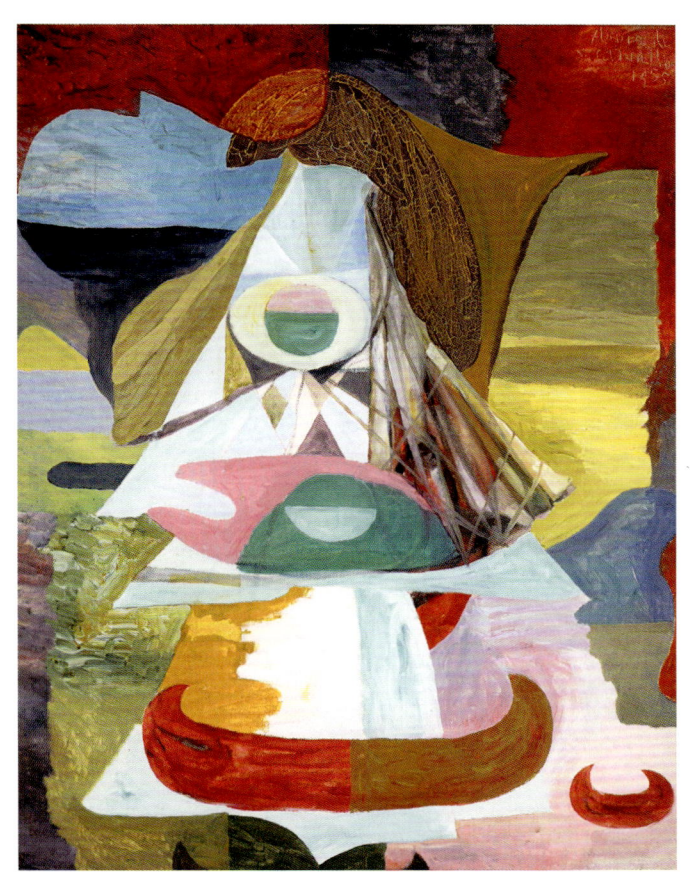 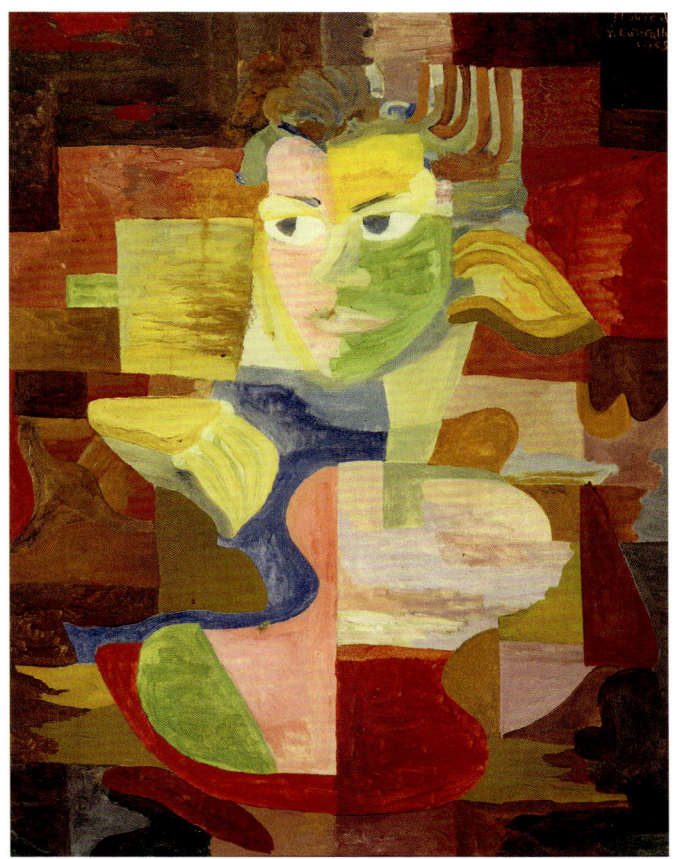

151   **Flávio de Carvalho**

Architecture

Overcoming National Identity: The Role of Architecture in Brazilian Modernism

Guilherme Wisnik

In 1961, German semiotician Max Bense, a professor at the Ulm School of Design, visited the newly inaugurated city of Brasília, accompanied by modernist poet João Cabral de Melo Neto. Fascinated by the city's rational clarity and the country's remarkable organisational skill to build it in such a short time, he regarded the new capital as the quintessential symbol of "Brazilian Cartesian intelligence". In his view, at that historical juncture, Brazil emerged as a prominent stronghold of the Western rationalist Enlightenment. According to Bense, Brasília represented "the first visible manifestation of Cartesianism in the form of design". In other words, it embodied "a total design akin to the concept of a total work of art, serving as a vast repository of both technical and artistic ingenuity – a deliberate and essential representation of these synthetic forces within a forward-looking space of civilisation".[1]

Today, over sixty years later, as we witness Brazilian cities engulfed in chaos and informality, and the social and political landscape resurrecting obscurantist and anti-modern values, it is difficult to believe that respected figures like Max Bense – and he was not alone in this – harboured such illusions about Brazilian rationalism. Indeed, we must ask: was that era merely an episodic spasm of rationality amidst a history dominated by endemic violence, structural inequality, and the ongoing sacrifice of public values in the name of private interests? Surely, it could be argued that the adoption of modern rationality in Brazil, seen from the perspective of an industrialising nation, was an attempt to address its economic backwardness and the social barriers linked to inequality, which reinforce the aspects associated with barbarism and irrationalism present in Brazil's history.

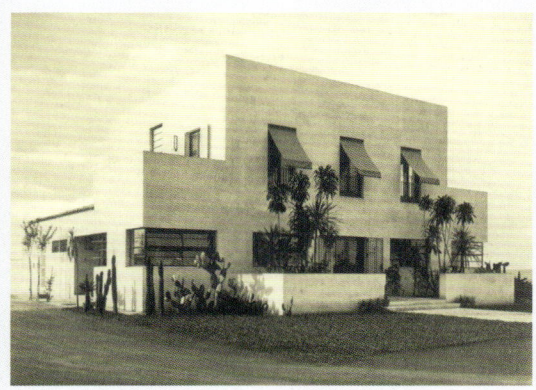

Fig. 1
Gregori Warchavchik, Casa Modernista,
Santa Cruz Street, São Paulo, 1928

There is a historical arc that comprises this significant attempt to instil social rationality in Brazil through the means of culture, spanning the period from the 1920s to the first half of the 1960s. More precisely, it extends from the *Semana de Arte Moderna* (Modern Art Week) in 1922 to the civil-military coup that launched a dictatorial regime in 1964, marking the end of a historical period characterised by hopes for transformation and social emancipation through the ideals of modernism. Moreover, this historical arc can be understood in two distinct phases: initially, a period dominated by literature and the visual arts, where modern influences intertwined with efforts to shape and define a national identity; and subsequently, a phase led by architecture, accompanied by significant advancements in the visual arts and poetry, reinforcing the dimensions of abstraction and internationalism.[2] This latter phase owes much to the constructivist ethos of the avant-gardes, commonly referred to in Brazil as Concretism.

In fact, architecture had minimal involvement in the *Semana de Arte Moderna*, an event held in February 1922 at the São Paulo Municipal Theatre. While literature, painting, and music showcased distinctly modern works that opposed prevailing academicism, Brazilian architecture had yet to see any modern expressions.

The only architects participating in the event were proponents of the neocolonial movement.[3]

The infiltration of neocolonial architects into a modernist movement may seem odd. However, to understand this occurrence, we must consider at least two factors. The first is the inherent inertia of architecture compared to other arts. Architects often encounter greater obstacles in effecting swift historical changes due to the high costs of construction and the significant influence of conservative client preferences. The second factor is the importance of "national identity" for Brazilian modernists, which sets Latin American modernism apart from its European roots. While European modernist avant-gardes advocated for a clean slate approach to history and the promotion of universalism to combat belligerent nationalism (in the context of World War I), modernism in Latin America emerged at a time when young nations needed to craft a self-image while confronting their colonial and slaveholding pasts. The task, therefore, was to create a modernism that did not negate the Brazilian past or nationality but, on the contrary, affirmed them in a new and decisive way.[4] From this perspective, the proximity to the neocolonial movement is not surprising.

The main solution to this contradiction between national identity and modernism was proposed by writers, notably Oswald de Andrade, in his *Manifesto Antropófago* of 1928. According to him, the essence of Brazilian modernism lies in the act of devouring the modernity imported from abroad, thereby assimilating its strength from a unique, inherently wild perspective.

An avid and enthusiastic reader of the magazine *L'Ésprit nouveau*, edited by Le Corbusier and Amédée Ozenfant, the poet and novelist Mário de Andrade was already discussing the emergence of architectural rationalism in Belgium, the Netherlands, and Austria as early as the 1920s.[5] Interested in the subject, he wrote newspaper articles advocating for a true modern architecture in Brazil, while also considering the importance of imbuing it with some local flavour that could mark it out as distinctly Brazilian. This notion was shared by many other modern artists and thinkers in Brazil during the 1920s and 1930s.

This perspective was vital in the later evolution of Brazilian modern architecture, especially through a nativist trend led by Lúcio Costa. This approach aimed to integrate the vocabulary of international modern architecture, including pilotis, brise-soleils, and expansive glass panels, with traditional Brazilian construction elements such as wooden trellises, ceramic block lattices (*cobogós*), and tile panels (*azulejos*). Costa's residential complex Parque Guinle (1943–1952) in Rio de Janeiro is a prime example of this synthesis.

However, the emergence of modern architecture in the country can be traced back to the late 1920s, and it was led by two significant figures in São Paulo: Flávio de Carvalho and Gregori Warchavchik. Carvalho, a prominent Brazilian artist from the local elite, studied in France and England, graduating as an engineer. A versatile artist and one of Brazil's pioneers of performance art, he was a vanguardist in

Fig. 2
Ministério da Educação e Saúde Pública, Rio de Janeiro, 1937–1945

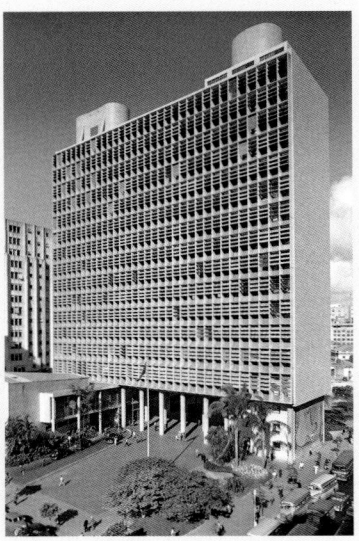

many different areas, contributing to the design of rationalist buildings in São Paulo. In turn, Warchavchik, a Ukrainian immigrant educated in Rome, arrived in São Paulo's capital in 1923, publishing a manifesto advocating for modern architecture two years later.[6] As a member of the International Congresses of Modern Architecture (CIAM), he had close ties to Walter Gropius.[7] Married to Mina Klabin, an artist and landscape architect from a progressive industrialist family, Warchavchik established himself within São Paulo's intellectual and affluent circles, erecting houses that became known as the country's first modernist architectural works.

Constructed with straight lines, reinforced concrete structures, smooth white walls, and concealed roofs behind upstands to give the impression of flat roofs, the houses designed and built by Carvalho and Warchavchik evoke the concept of the "machine for living in", as proposed by Le Corbusier. In the late 1920s in São Paulo and the subsequent decade, their works emerged as provocative anomalies, akin to unidentified flying objects – dubbed "futurists" by the local press – suddenly landing amidst the ornate palaces of eclectic styles that dominated the landscape of São Paulo's elite neighbourhoods.

1928, Warchavchik designed the first modernist house for himself (fig. 1), and in 1930 the second Casa Modernista was inaugurated on Itápolis Street. Open to public visitation under the title *Exposição de uma casa modernista* (Exhibition of a Modernist House), it featured works by Tarsila do Amaral, Anita Malfatti, Victor Brecheret, Di Cavalcanti, Regina Gomide, and the Swiss artist John Graz, among others. As a sort of "total work of art", the house allowed the public to immerse themselves in the still unfamiliar realm of modern art. This completed a cycle of "fight against academic relics"[8], according to Oswald de Andrade, which had begun eight years earlier with the *Semana de Arte Moderna*. While a painting or sculpture may have a fleeting and discreet presence in society, a building imposes itself on the cityscape, becoming a permanent and unavoidable reference point. From that moment on, although sporadic and in isolated cases, modernism would also begin to shape the face of Brazilian cities. However, it did so by embracing international abstract art without yet yielding to local or national influences.

It is not possible to summarise here all the facts and works that define the ascent of Brazilian modern architecture after Le Corbusier's second visit to Rio de Janeiro in 1936. It is important to mention, however, a key landmark in this history: the construction of the Ministry of Education and Health (1936–1945), also known as the Gustavo Capanema Palace (fig. 2). Initially designed by Le Corbusier, it was developed by a team of young Brazilians led by Lúcio Costa, with significant input from Oscar Niemeyer. The Ministry building embodies many defining qualities of modernism in a single work. It is a monumental public building whose construction affirmed the State's adoption of the new architectural language. Occupying an entire block in the city centre, the architects used pilotis to structure the ground floor, creating a public plaza that accommodated the flow of pedestrians and redefined the urban experience. Additionally, with its main tower oriented north–south, one façade featured full glazing, while another was shielded by adjustable brise-soleils, forming a geometric grid that allowed for pleasant variations.

Fig. 3
Oscar Niemeyer, National Congress, Brasília, 1958

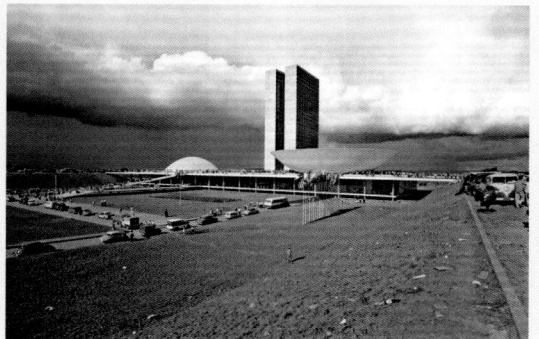

There are many significant works from this period, such as the Brazilian Pavilion at the New York World's Fair (1938–1939), designed by Lúcio Costa and Oscar Niemeyer, and the Pampulha Complex (1940–1943) in Belo Horizonte, which was designed solely by Niemeyer. Alongside the Ministry building and a noteworthy collection of new works, these projects were prominently featured in the major architecture magazines worldwide during the 1940s and 50s, as well as at the *Brazil Builds* exhibition at the Museum of Modern Art in New York in 1943.[9] Niemeyer was the architect of numerous public buildings in Brasília, the new capital built from 1956 to 1960 (fig. 3).

Here, unlike the more abstract and impersonal architecture of Warchavchik, distinctly Brazilian elements began to emerge, notably in the use of tiles, sun protection systems, and the incorporation of tropical plant species in Roberto Burle Marx's gardens. Also notable were the sensual curves of Niemeyer's reinforced concrete structures – but not limited to him – which, in a sense, modernised the plasticity of our baroque tradition dating back to the works of Aleijadinho in Minas Gerais during the eighteenth and nineteenth centuries.[10] This plastic baroque style proved to be a source of irritation for Max Bill during his visits to Brazil in the early 1950s.[11] Niemeyer designed numerous public buildings in the new capital, Brasília, which were built between 1956 and 1960 (fig. 3).

Also worth mentioning here is the case of Lina Bo Bardi. Having moved to Brazil from Italy in 1946 with her husband Pietro Maria Bardi, she brought with her Milanese rationalism, which she translated into her first work, the Casa de Vidro (Glass House, 1951) in São Paulo. Her engagement with the culture of north-eastern Brazil from the late 1950s, with its distinct Indigenous and African influences, significantly altered her perception of Brazil and architecture as a whole, leading her to seek a fusion of rationalism and the north-eastern vernacular. This is evident in notable examples such as the staircase of Solar do Unhão in Salvador (1959, fig. 4) and her *Cadeira de beira de estrada* (Roadside Chair, 1967).

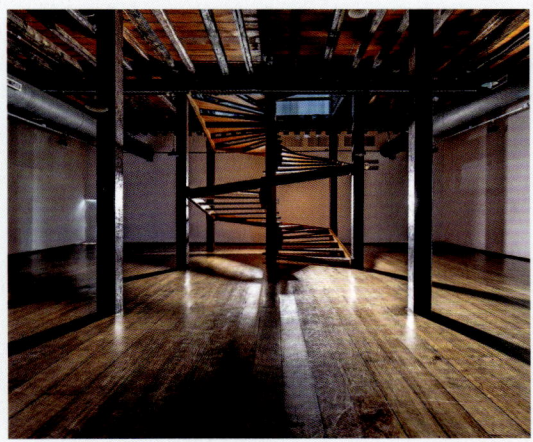

Fig. 4
Lina Bo Bardi, Staircase in Solar do
Unhão, Salvador da Bahia, 1959

Nonetheless, despite some foreign critics using the term "Brazilian style" to describe Brazil's modern architecture[12], there has never been any doubt that this architecture was a legitimate manifestation of the avant-garde spirit, hence its broad international recognition. Engaged early on in what he termed the "battle for abstraction" in Brazilian art, critic Mário Pedrosa not only developed an interest in architecture but also advanced the idea that architecture in Brazil was the art form leading aesthetic constructivism. He believed that its widespread critical recognition would help shift the tone of visual arts production, promoting a departure from a mimetic naturalism rooted in nationalist and social themes in favour of the true abstraction of Concretism.

Hence, he argued that the true leaders of Brazil's artistic modernisation were the architects of the so-called "Carioca School", rather than the painters, musicians, and writers labelled as modernists. Pedrosa contended that free from the "primitivism" of the literary and musical figures, or the "nationalism" of political writers and painters, Brazilian architects did not engage in the same "discovery or rediscovery of the country" as their counterparts did, opting instead to focus solely on its "geographical

and physical reality".[13] This approach allowed them to align swiftly and accurately with the core of the European architectural avant-garde while asserting their local uniqueness, thus quickly assuming a prominent role internationally.

There was, as we can see, a clear departure from the ideological nationalism of painters like Portinari, Di Cavalcanti, and Tarsila do Amaral, which seemed outdated when juxtaposed with the bold formalism of architects such as Oscar Niemeyer, Affonso Eduardo Reidy, and many others. It was an architecture made of broad gestures, seemingly free from Portuguese reserve or the complex of a colonised nation – structural residues that have marked Brazilian art history, resulting in a perpetual struggle with its "difficulty of form", as noted by critic Rodrigo Naves.[14] It was also an architecture that, from the outset, embraced the dimensions of a modern world, pioneering its legibility by leveraging a somewhat undefined artisanal malleability – the plasticity of reinforced concrete – capable of etching the still tentative gestures of a nascent culture directly onto the canvas of technical modernity.

1 Bense 2009, p. 32

2 See Arantes 1997, pp. 113–133

3 Georg Przyrembel, from Poland, and Antonio Garcia Moya, from Spain

4 See Candido 1965

5 See Grembecki 1969

6 Warchavchik 1925

7 See Warchavchik 1969, pp. 9–16

8 Andrade 1930

9 See Tinem 2002

10 See Costa 1995, p. 199

11 See Bill 1954

12 See Banham 1962

13 Pedrosa 2015, p. 62

14 See Naves 1996

Alfredo Volpi

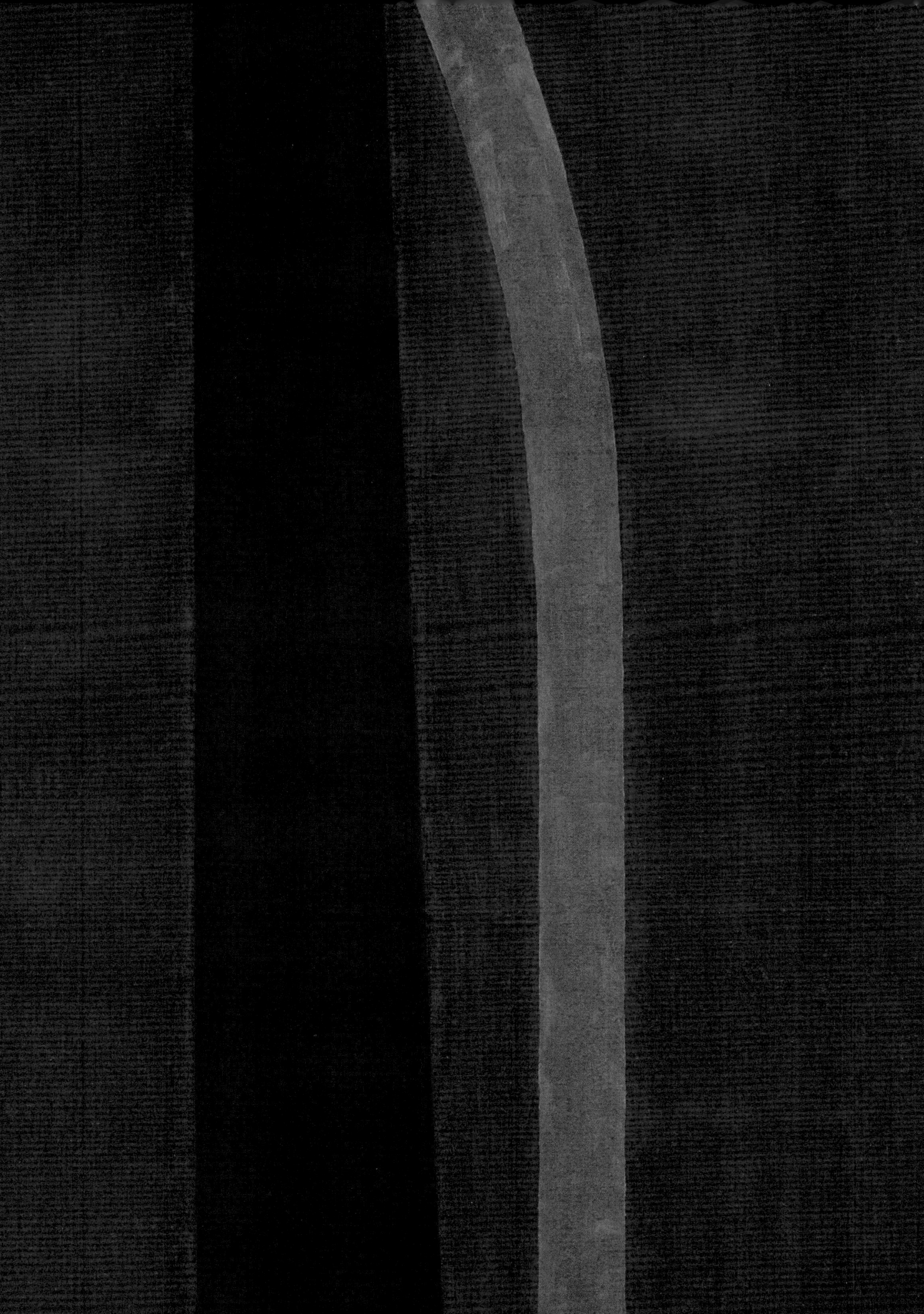

Born in Lucca, Italy, on 14 April 1896, Alfredo Volpi was only two years old when his family left Europe for Brazil in October 1898, part of the 1.4 million Italians who emigrated to the country from 1870 to 1920. He never naturalized himself, speaking Portuguese in a heavy Italian accent up to the end of his life. A working-class artist, his father owned a tiny corner shop in the São Paulo neighborhood of Ipiranga, selling wine and cheese to the Italian workers established in the area. He studied his first letters in a local Italian school, abandoning formal studies when he was twelve, at which point he worked in several occupations – woodworker, bookbinder, typographer, and painter-decorator – to help support his family. His long and remarkably coherent career, one in which we witness the slow development of an entirely personal and original style of painting, spanned over seven decades, and it is in the totality of his oeuvre, rather than in individual works, that we see his highly lyrical development from figuration into abstraction. He would keep himself at a safe distance from the many movements, theories of art-making and artistic consortiums that Brazil saw flourish far and near from the 1940s onwards, allowing his style to slowly mature in the relative isolation of a frugal studio in the neighborhood of Cambuci, termed by the critic Mário Pedrosa, one of the most influential art critics of his generation, as "the insular from Cambuci"[1]. That does not mean he was unaware of the artistic developments taking place around him, picking from them whatever he found useful for his own work, but never more. His career constitutes an instance of the workman-artist: he made his own paints, constructed his own stretchers, and primed his own canvases, treating his paintings as visual problems to be solved by intuition alone, unaided by theories or art-making primers. As he said: "You put the first colour in. Then you look. Then you put the second one in. Then you look again. If it's right, you see it. If it's not, you also see it, and then you clear it and start over."[2]

Alfredo Volpi
1896, Lucca, Italy –
1988, São Paulo, Brazil

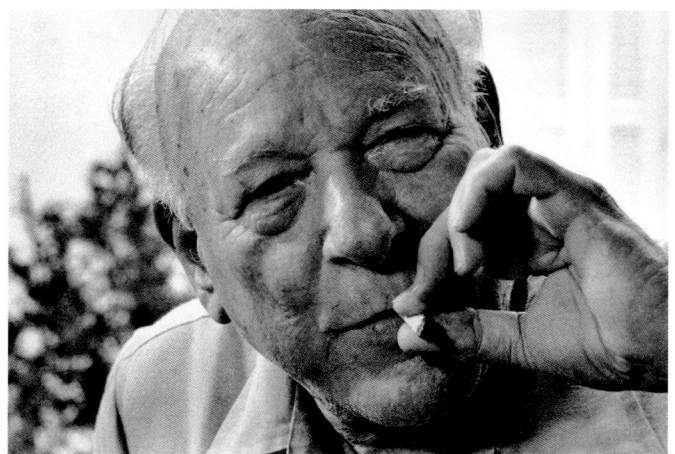

It must be said that Volpi was an entirely self-taught artist, never having pursued formal studies in institutions or in the studios of other artists. As such, he gave start to his artistic activities in around 1911 as a painter decorator. With the money earned in these projects he was able to buy painting materials for his own work and have free time to paint what he wanted to. Despite inhabiting a world socially distant from the artistic circles of the city, he did keep himself in tune with its innovations, having visited Anita Malfatti's infamous 1917 exhibition, even if he did not visit, nor was aware, of the *Semana de Arte Moderna* of 1922,

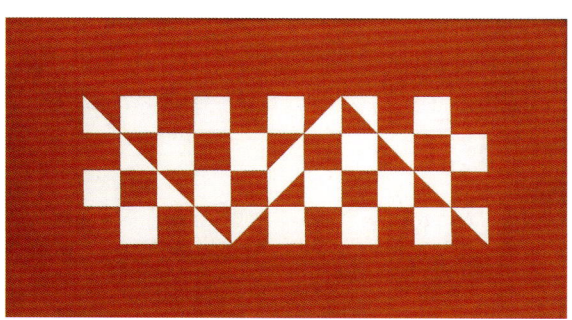

Fig. 1
Alfredo Volpi, Untitled (Red and
White Concrete Composition),
1956, tempera on canvas,
54 × 100 cm, Private collection

an indication of how circumscribed to the local elite the modernist event was. His work of the 1920s shows us a very conventional painter heavily influenced by the Italian macchiaioli, evidently eager to master the more technical aspects of his craft. His first insertion into the artistic circle of the city was the inclusion of one of his paintings, in the 1925 *Exposição Geral de Belas Artes*, an event organised by a committee composed of the exhibiting artists themselves. The painting was well enough received, so much so that he sold it, apparently the first sale of his career. Paintings of the period such as *Baiana* and *Rua de Ouro Preto* (figs pp. 167 and 166) show us the direction his work was taking in these years. Still painting in oils, which he would abandon entirely in favour of egg tempera in the late 1940s, a particularly appropriate technique for his gossamer sensibilities, he creates pulsating images of rarefied, dampened colours, nearly transparent in their materiality, in which the subject matter rarely makes itself felt, the material aspects of painting taking centre stage.

In 1934, Volpi came in contact with a group of largely self-taught artists and similar backgrounds, immigrant and working-class, such as Francisco Rebolo, Mário Zanini, Manoel Martins, Aldo Bonadei, and Fulvio Pennacchi. Having to work other jobs to make a living and being unable to life off their work as artists they joined forces to pay for models from which they would draw, and rented rooms that functioned as studios at Praça da Sé's, São Paulo's main square, Palacete Santa Helena. The group would eventually be named the Grupo Santa Helena, and their work is characterised by a traditionalist approach to art making, concentrating on the more technical aspects of painting whilst depicting genre scenes and plein-air landscapes of utter simplicity and thin colours. Despite their camaraderie, their differences were bigger than their similarities, Volpi declaring years later: "A group didn't really exist. It would only be invented much later."³ In spite of that they were fundamental in the forging of a certain community where ideas and critiques could be exchanged. Working beyond the gaze of the public and established critics, they were isolated from the official or elite-oriented circles of modernist art. In the late 1930s Volpi started to paint street scenes of Mogi das Cruzes, a small town located sixty kilometres from São Paulo that kept much of its vernacular colonial heritage intact. Doorways, windows, terracotta roof tiles, church façades, latices and balustrades are depicted in these paintings by means of superimposed fields of transparent colours, his evident relish in the colouristic effects made possible by this method making itself felt in works such as *Capelinha* (fig. p. 168). It was at this

Alfredo Volpi

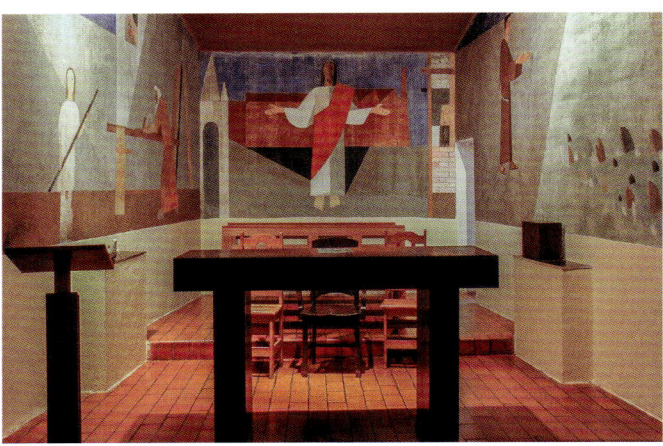

Fig. 2
Alfredo Volpi, frescos in the Capela
Cristo Operário, 1951, Sociedade
Impulsionadora da Instrução da
Ordem dos Dominicanos, São Paulo

time that several critics, including Mário de Andrade, who was awestruck by Volpi's work, started to take note of a group of artists of working-class origins that included some of the members of the Santa Helena group, including Volpi, who called themselves the Família Artística Paulista. De Andrade would be responsible for several articles about them, and despite reservations, in particular their lack of formal audacity or individual expression, they were instrumental in the dissemination of Volpi's work.

In 1936 Volpi met Benedita da Conceição, known as Judite, a mixed-race woman with whom he would maintain a lifelong relationship, marrying her in 1942. Diagnosed in 1939 with an illness that demanded her relocation to a coastal location, she moved to the seaside town of Itanhaém, Volpi visiting her there regularly. Not only did he find there the same colonial vernacular architecture that had enchanted him in Mogi das Cruzes, but he also encountered the work of Emídio de Souza, a popular artist whose flattened forms and schematic compositions would influence the next phase of Volpi's artistic development, one in which we see a gradual magnification of the architectural details with which he had been working. His palette was also affected during this time, his colours, now flattened and cleaned-up, assuming the guiding role of his compositions, which would be reduced to their most basic elements in the following years. 1944 would see the opening of his first solo exhibition, the artist then counting forty-eight years of age. It was a resounding success, the sense of discovery of a mature artist hitherto unknown toning much of the excitement. All the paintings shown were sold, one of them to Mário de Andrade, and reviews were full of praise. Volpi at last found due recognition after so many years of arduous, silent labor. From then on, he would never lack buyers for his paintings, nor critics to praise it, so much so that a group of collectors funded his only journey to Europe in 1950, the year in which his work was included in the Venice Biennale. He visited Paris, Venice, Rome, Naples, and Sicily, but it was in Padua that he had his most profound European artistic encounter, visiting Giotto's Capella Scrovegni no less than eighteen times. The Italian master had a profound impact on Volpi's work, which upon his return would become more and more synthetic in form and colour.

It was in the first half of the 1950s that Volpi's work became increasingly abstract, his landscapes, street scenes, and architectural façades being transmuted into pure form and colour. Their suggestion, nevertheless, remains firmly in place (such as in fig. p. 171). It was with works like this that Volpi was awarded the prize for best national painter at the II Bienal de São Paulo in 1953. The story goes that the awardee of the prize had been previously agreed upon by the panel of judges, all of them concurring that it should go to the carioca Modernist Emiliano Di Cavalcanti, a painter of voluptuous scenes of Rio de Janeiro's bohemian life and one of the characters behind the planning of the *Semana de Arte Moderna*. However, with the arrival of the international judges, the British art historian Herbert Read being one of them, things took an unexpected turn. After seeing the exhibition Read declared that if any painter deserved the award, that painter was Volpi. In a typically Brazilian compromise of perfect cordiality, it was decided that the prize should be divided, *ex aequo*, between them. Unsurprisingly, the division of the prize caused great discomfort to Di Cavalcanti, at that time engaged in a violent attack on abstraction. He would later declare that "an artist is not one who *makes* a work of art, but one who *creates* them. Volpi paints banderoles, banderoles, banderoles."[4] The banderoles to which he alludes are an omnipresent formal element explored by Volpi from the 1950s onwards. Referencing typical decorations used to adorn *Festas juninas*, annual Brazilian celebrations held around the day of St. John's Nativity, June 24, that besides the hanging of colourful banderoles include maypoles, square dancing and the lighting of immense bonfires, they appear in Volpi's work at times as straight recognisable banderoles, at others as pure geometric form, suffering at his hand all manner of constructive manipulations (figs pp. 165 and 173). The artist, in a revealing 1971 interview, tells the story of their inception. "I was alone, waiting for the train early in the morning. I went for a walk and then I had this impact, I saw those banderoles. (...) So, I composed the façades with the banderoles. Later I managed to solve it (the painting) just with banderoles."[5]

Volpi's natural and steady progression towards abstraction, and an autochthonous form of it at that, with its many reminiscences of vernacular colonial architecture, popular celebrations and themes, endeared him in the 1950s to a group of artists then experimenting with Concrete Art in both São Paulo and Rio de Janeiro. He befriended them, happy to see the high regard in which he was held and took part in group exhibitions with them. He even adapted some of their painterly methods, reducing his compositions to the bare minimum. He also eliminated all trace of his trademark brushstrokes, beautifully fluid and precise, creating opaque fields of colour. The result was a series of works in which we see him as if refreshed by the

Fig. 3
Alfredo Volpi, *O sonho de Dom Bosco* (Dom Bosco's Dream), 1966, fresco, Palácio Itamaraty, Brasília

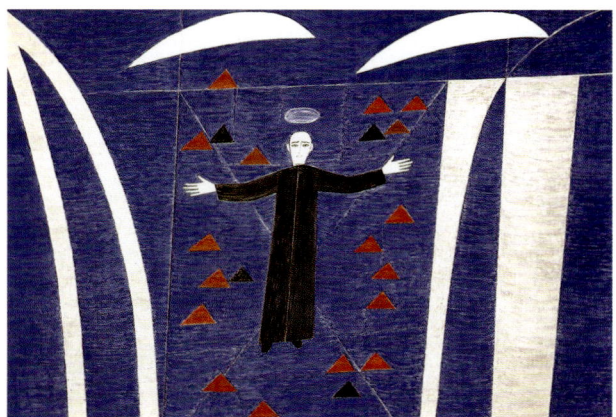

Alfredo Volpi

contact (fig. p. 177), He produced simple investigations of form, squares broken down into triangles and fugue-like diagonal suggestions of shapes in an innovatively starry-eyed interpretation of Concrete rationales, such as in the white and red composition from 1956 (fig. 1), one of the outstanding achievements of the time. Volpi's own intuitive method was entirely at odds with his younger counterparts' *modus operandi*, interested as they were in rational explanations, and a method for art-making that precluded intuition or emotion. He did not keep to this pseudo-Concrete style for very long, returning to his free-flowing designs of shapes and colours. Speaking in 1975 he said, "I never think about what I'm doing. I just think about the problem of line, shape, colour. Just that. (…) The problem is just painting."[6] Volpi, and in this he was markedly individual and sagacious, treated his paintings as problems to be solved by the eye's wisdom alone.

Particularly interesting are Volpi's experiments in the 1950s and 1960s with mural painting. He had, as a painter-decorator, previously worked with architecture as a support, painting decorative friezes in his earlier years, all of which were traditional in style and understanding of space. The first noteworthy instance of his activities in the field was with the Capela do Cristo Operário in 1951, a small chapel constructed by the Dominican order in the then outskirts of the city of São Paulo. For it Volpi painted charming, geometricised murals in its chancel depicting Jesus, Saint Joseph, and Saint Anthony (fig. 2), as well as four stained-glass windows depicting the Evangelists for its sacristy. He would also work in Brasília in 1966, producing the *O sonho de Dom Bosco* (fig. 3) for the Palácio Itamaraty, the headquarters of the Ministry of Foreign Affairs, a scintillating depiction in blue of the nineteenth century Italian clergyman's prophetic vision of Brasília's construction that shows us the force of his work when done in close symmetry with its architectural support. The 1960s and 1970s saw the natural progression of his investigations of the previous decades. Absolute master of his trade, diligently working to resolve his canvases, he playfully manipulated a personal lexicon of shapes and forms that constantly bring into play the tension between abstraction and figuration. Developing his colouristic virtuosity further and further, he managed to achieve an unparalleled level of depuration and sophistication in his canvases. The last decade of his life, however, was marked by ill-health and a steep decline in the quality of his painting. Honored with two vast retrospectives in São Paulo in 1986, at which point his artistic legacy was firmly rooted into Brazilian artistic canons – as Mário Pedrosa wrote, "In Brazil, no other master surpasses him"[7] – he died, aged 92, on 28 May 1988.

Giancarlo Hannud

1   Mário Pedrosa, "Volpi 1924–1957", in Rio de Janeiro 1957, p. 10

2   In Olívio Tavares de Araújo, in São Paulo 2006, p. 32

3   Araújo 1976, p. 128

4   Araújo 1976, p. 127

5   São Paulo 2022, p. 229

6   São Paulo 1975b

7   Pedrosa and Amaral 1981, p. 61

Fachada (Façade), 1963

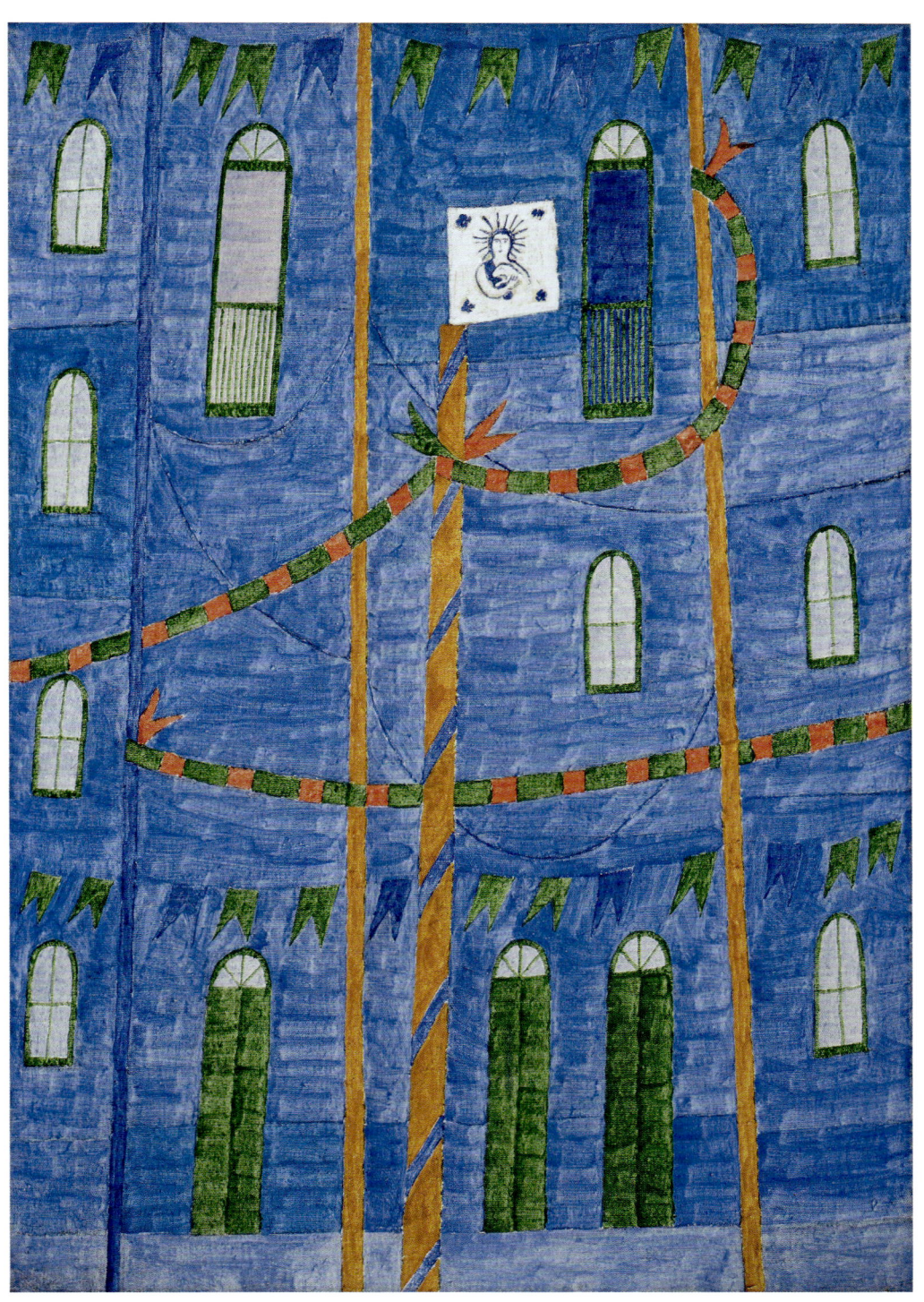

Alfredo Volpi

Rua de Ouro Preto (Street in Ouro Preto), c. 1935

Baiana (Woman from Bahia), 1930

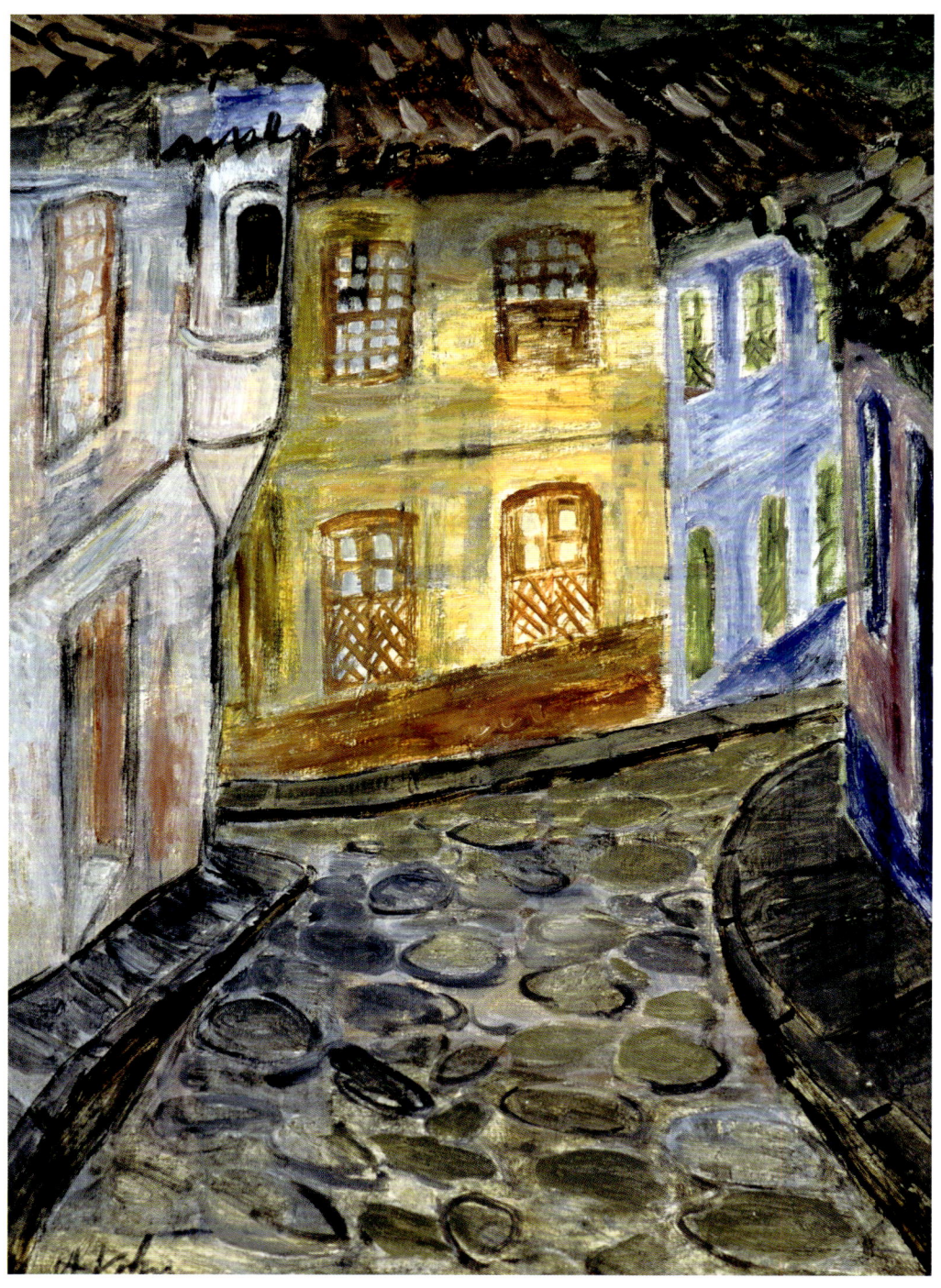

Brasil! Brasil!

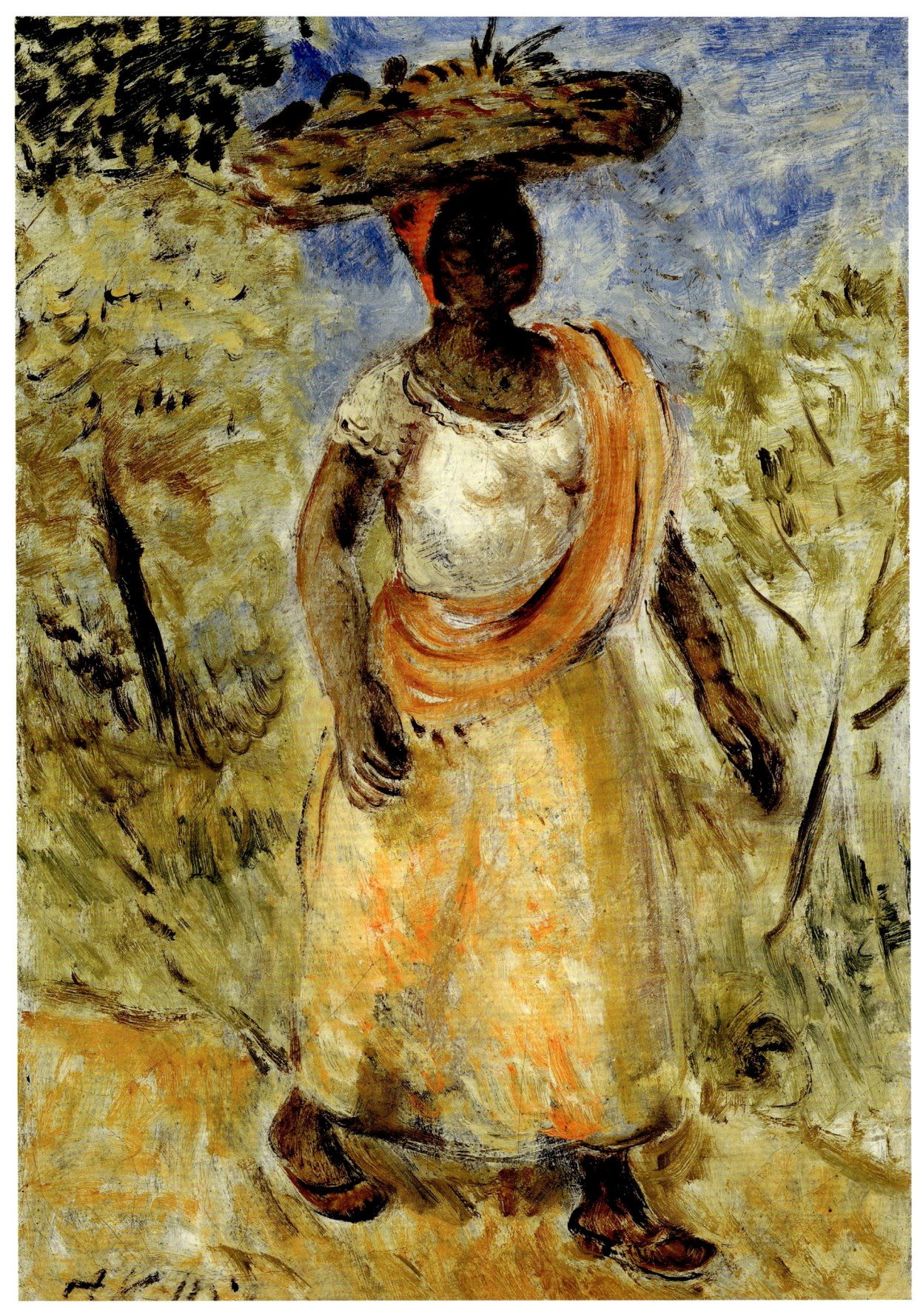

167　　　**Alfredo Volpi**

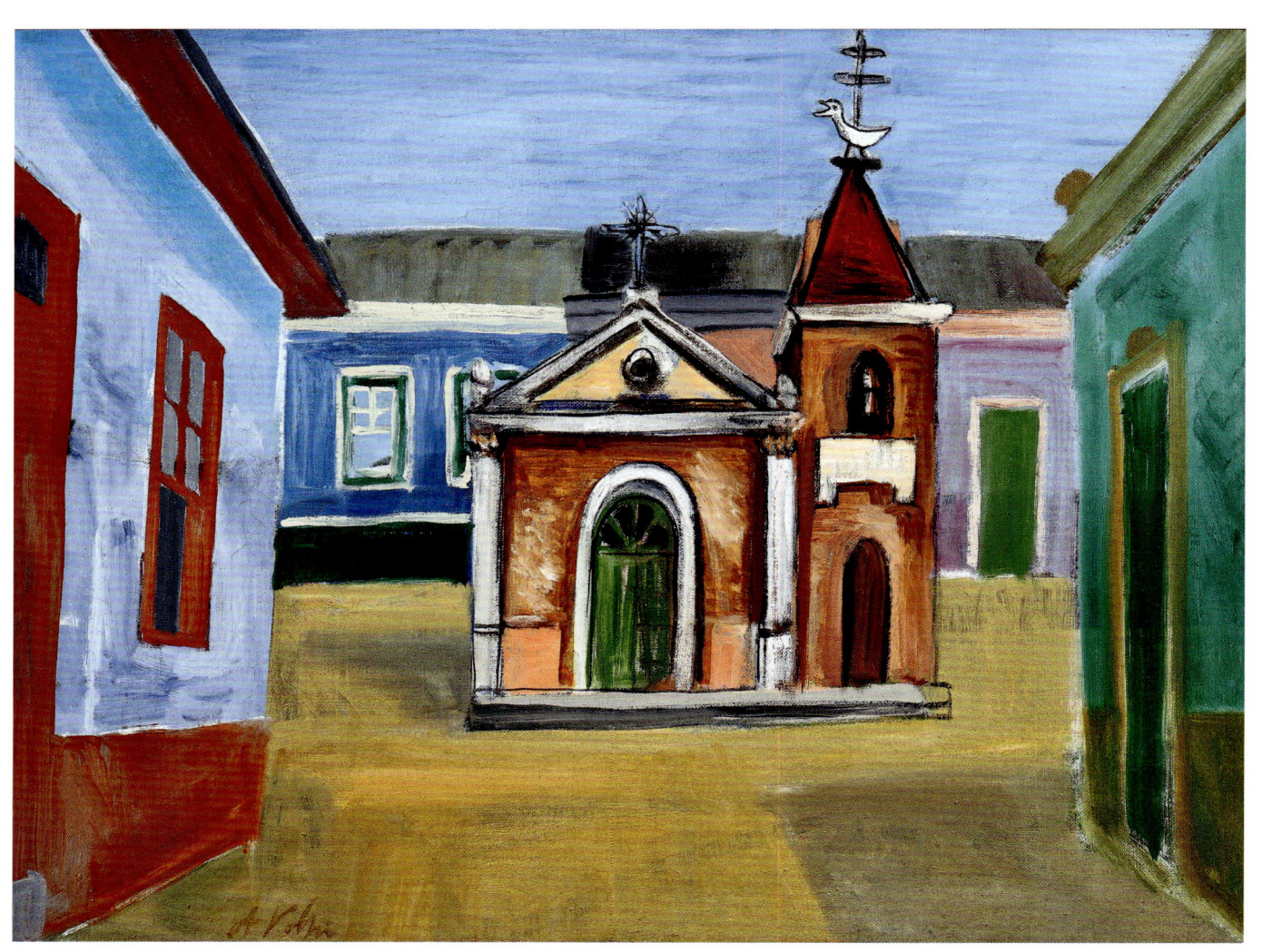

Capelinha (Little Chapel), 1940s

Untitled, 1945

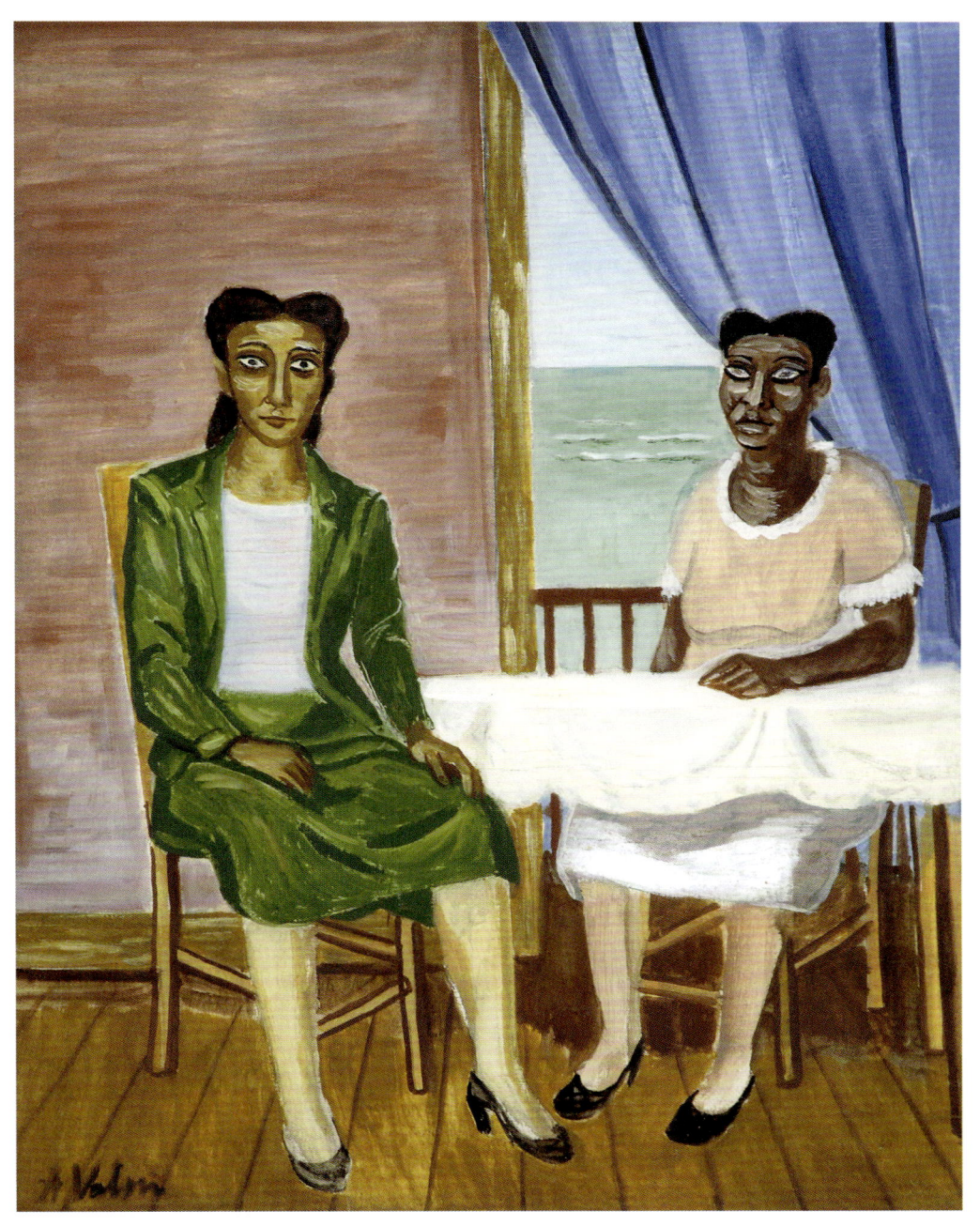

169   **Alfredo Volpi**

Brasil! Brasil!

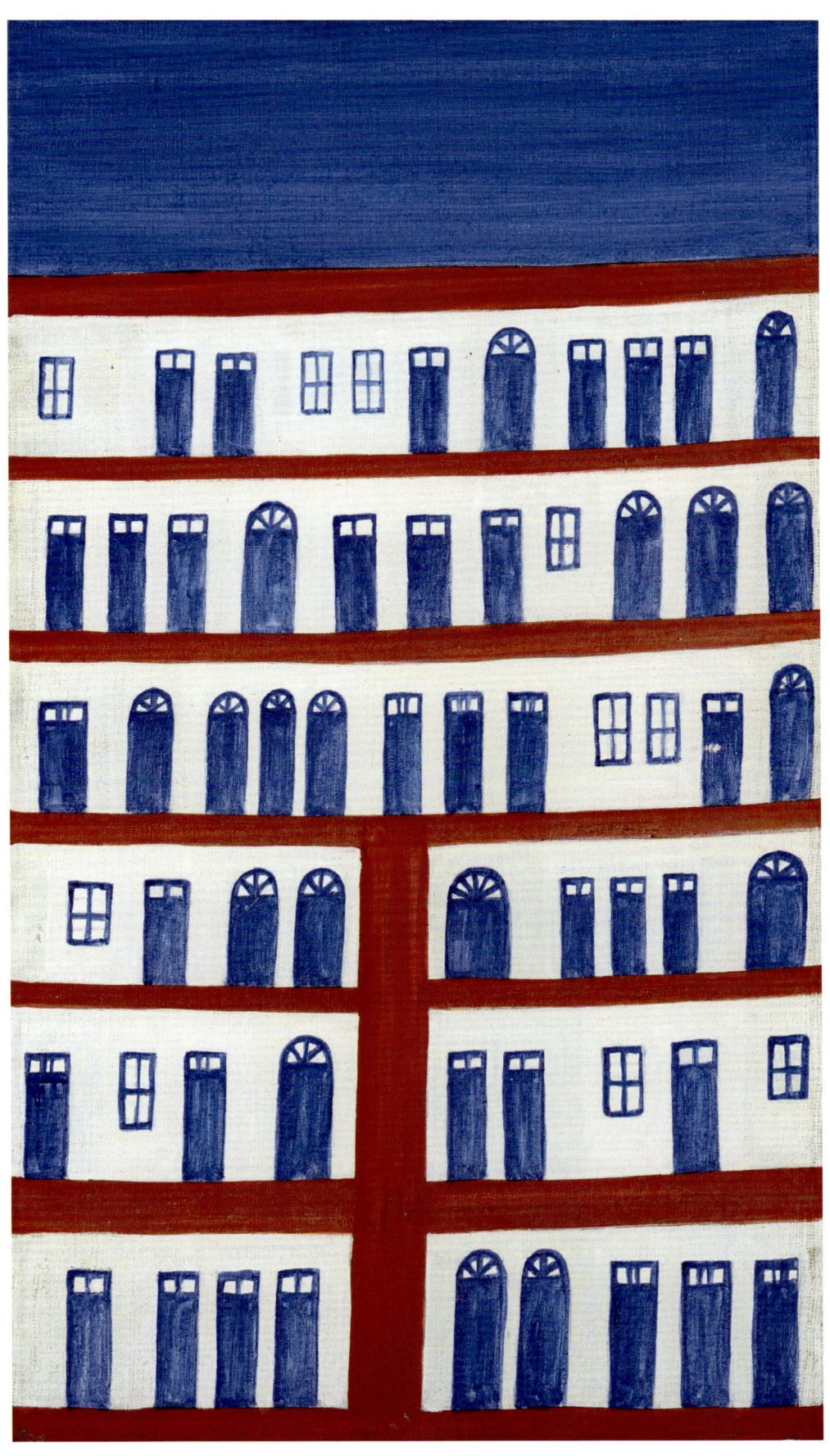

Alfredo Volpi

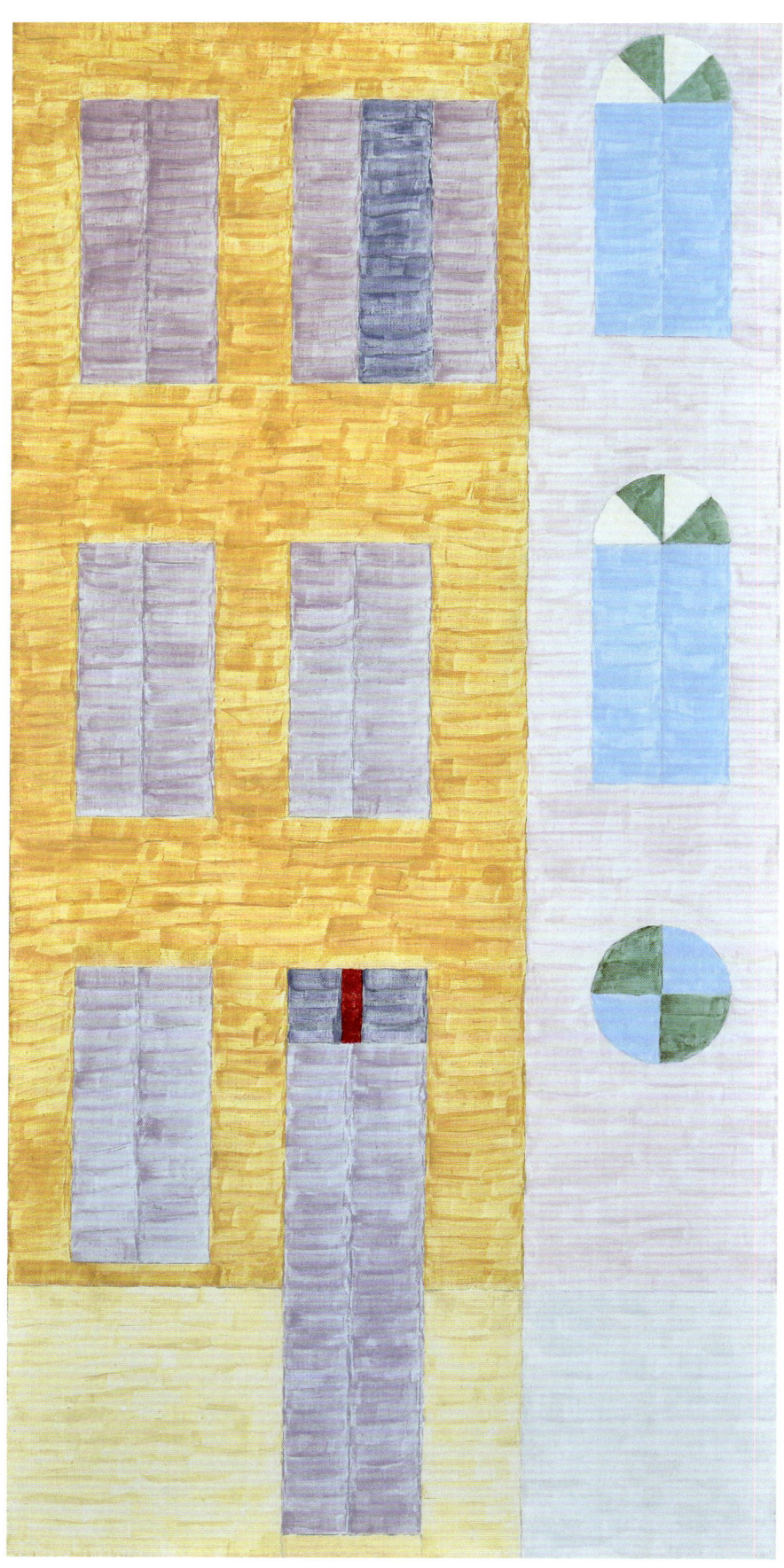

Brasil! Brasil!

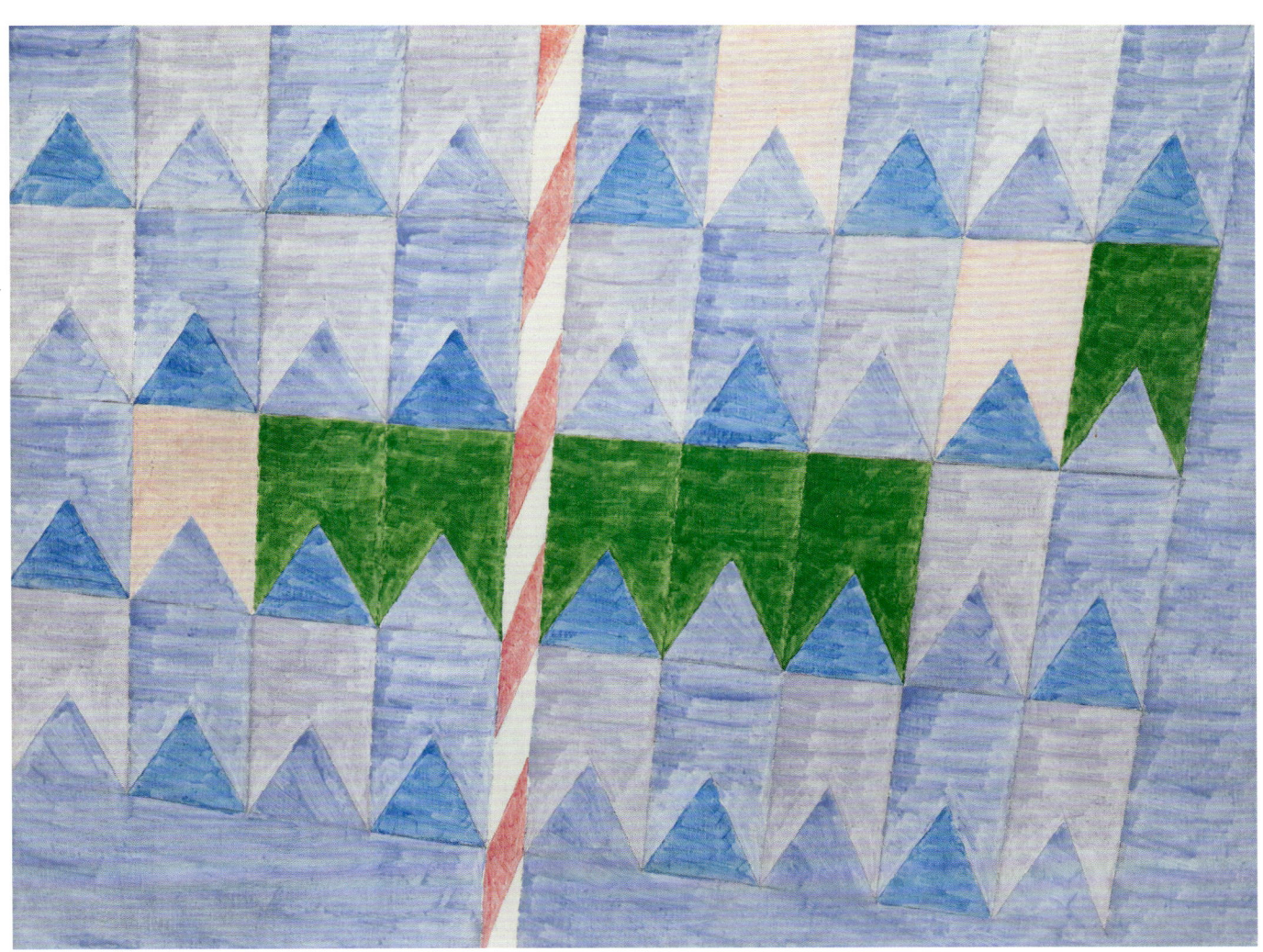

Untitled, 1980er

**Bandeiras e mastros
(Flags and Poles)**, 1970–1980

Alfredo Volpi

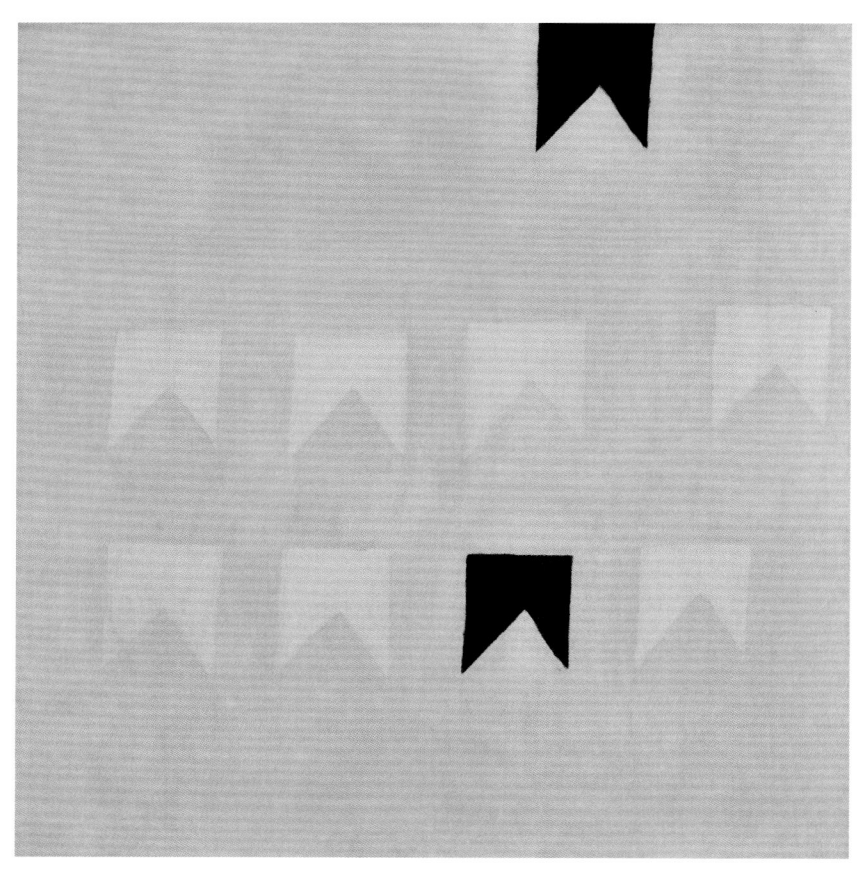

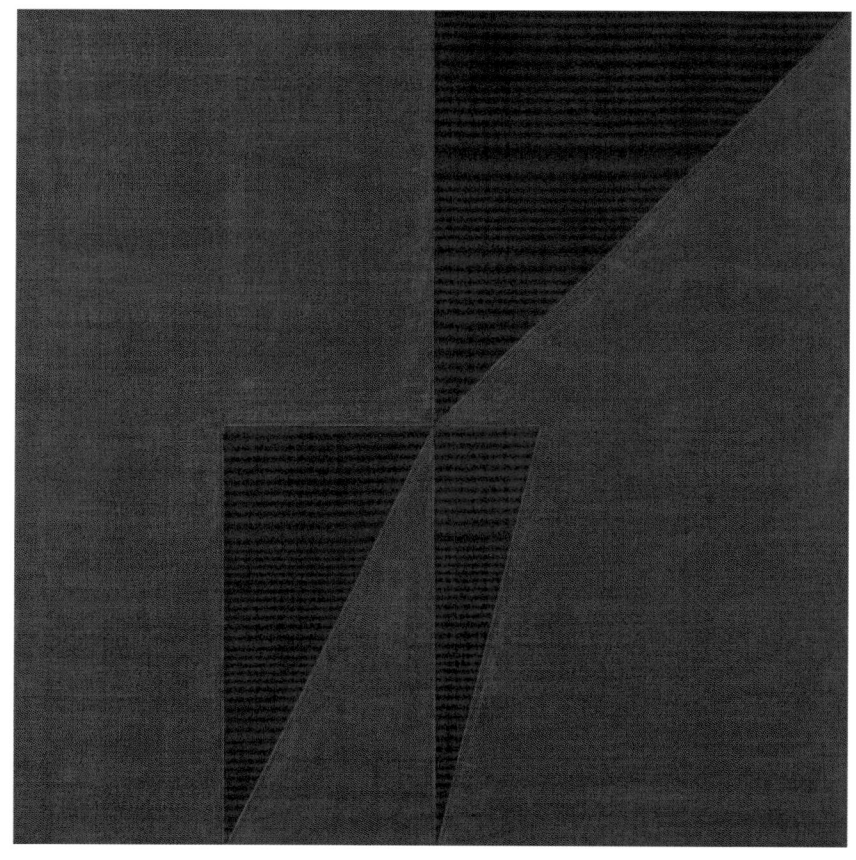

Brasil! Brasil!

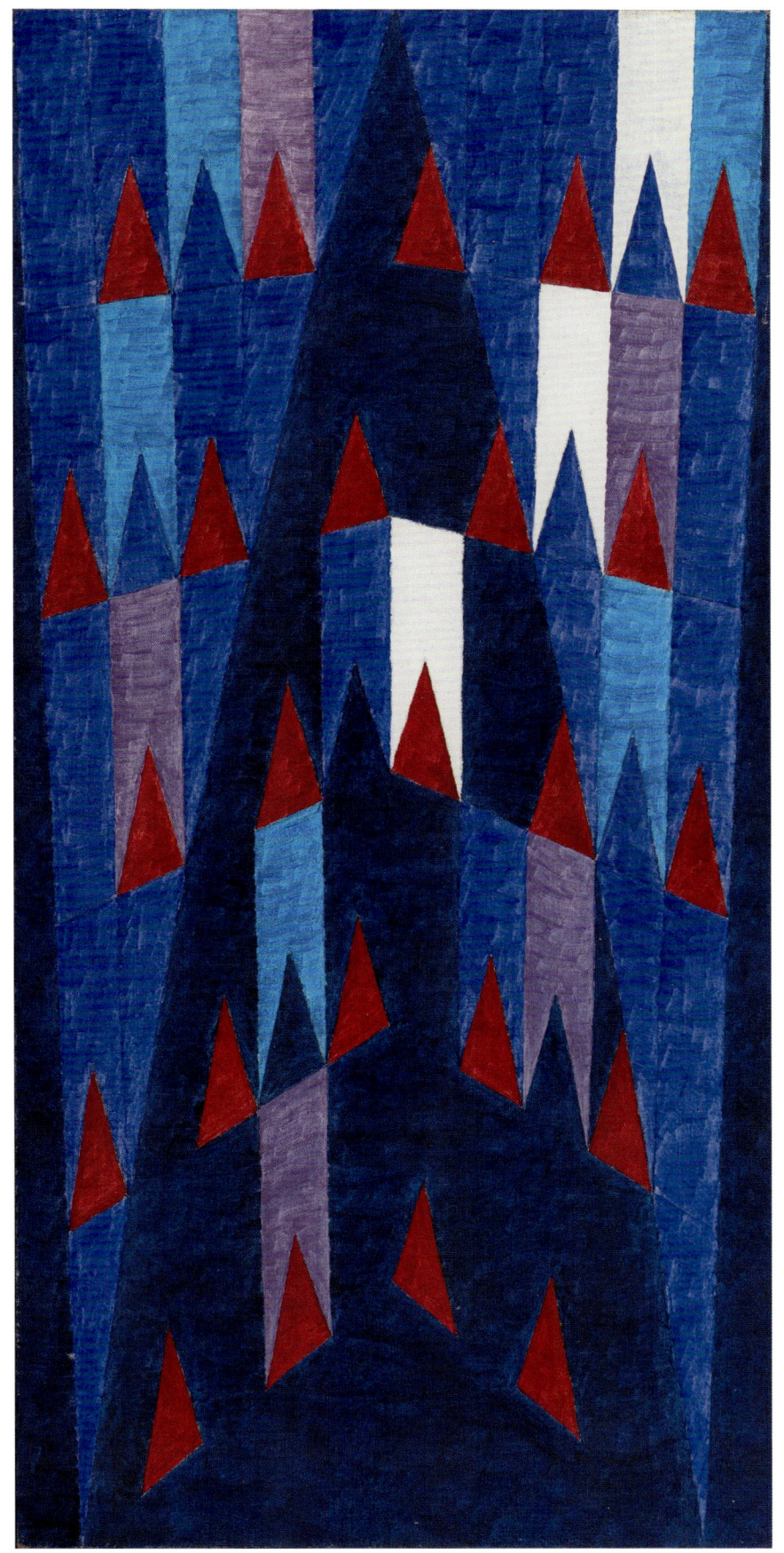

Alfredo Volpi

Untitled, late 1950s

**Composição concreta (0007)
(Concrete Composition,
0007)**, c. 1950s

Untitled, 1970

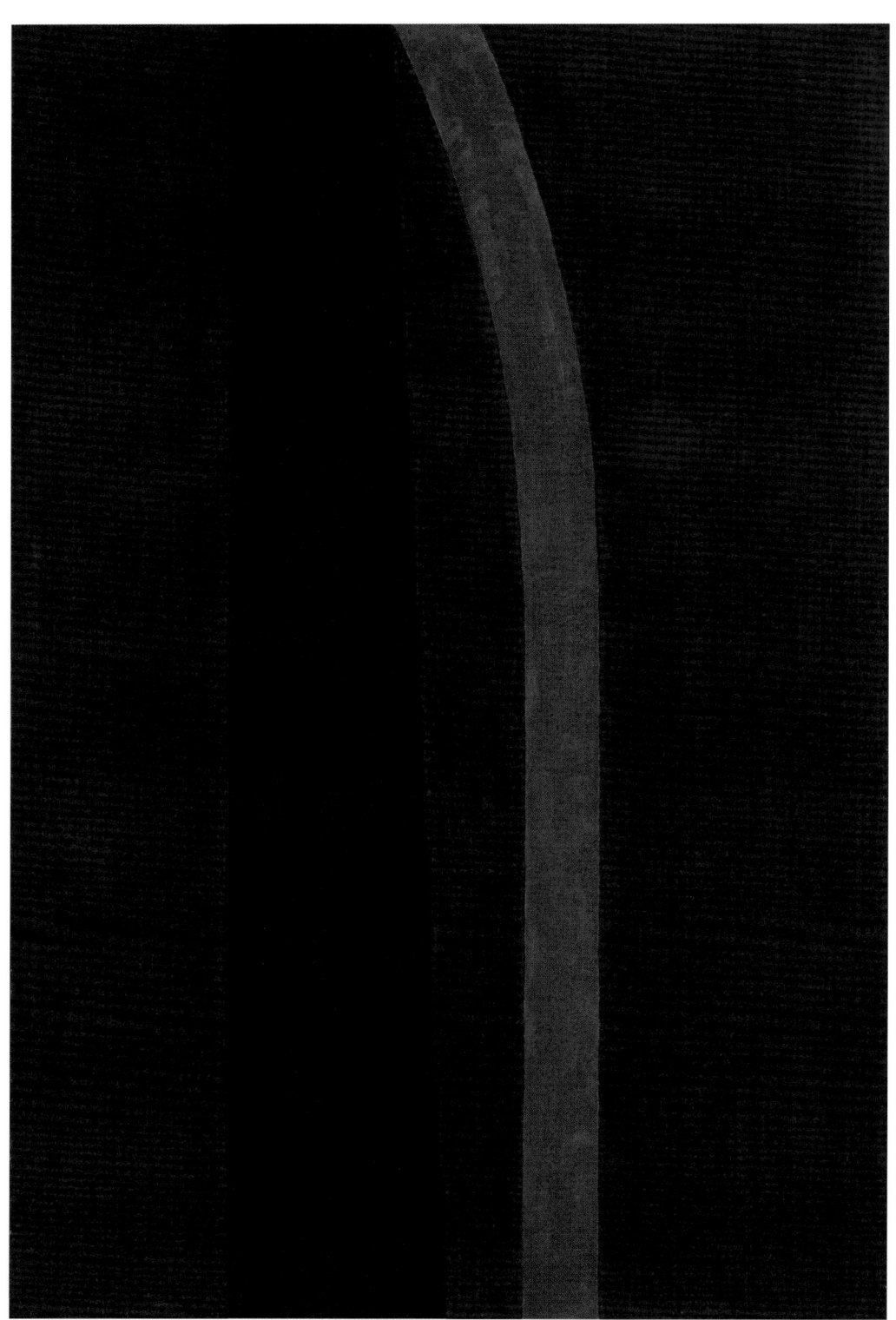

Brasil! Brasil!

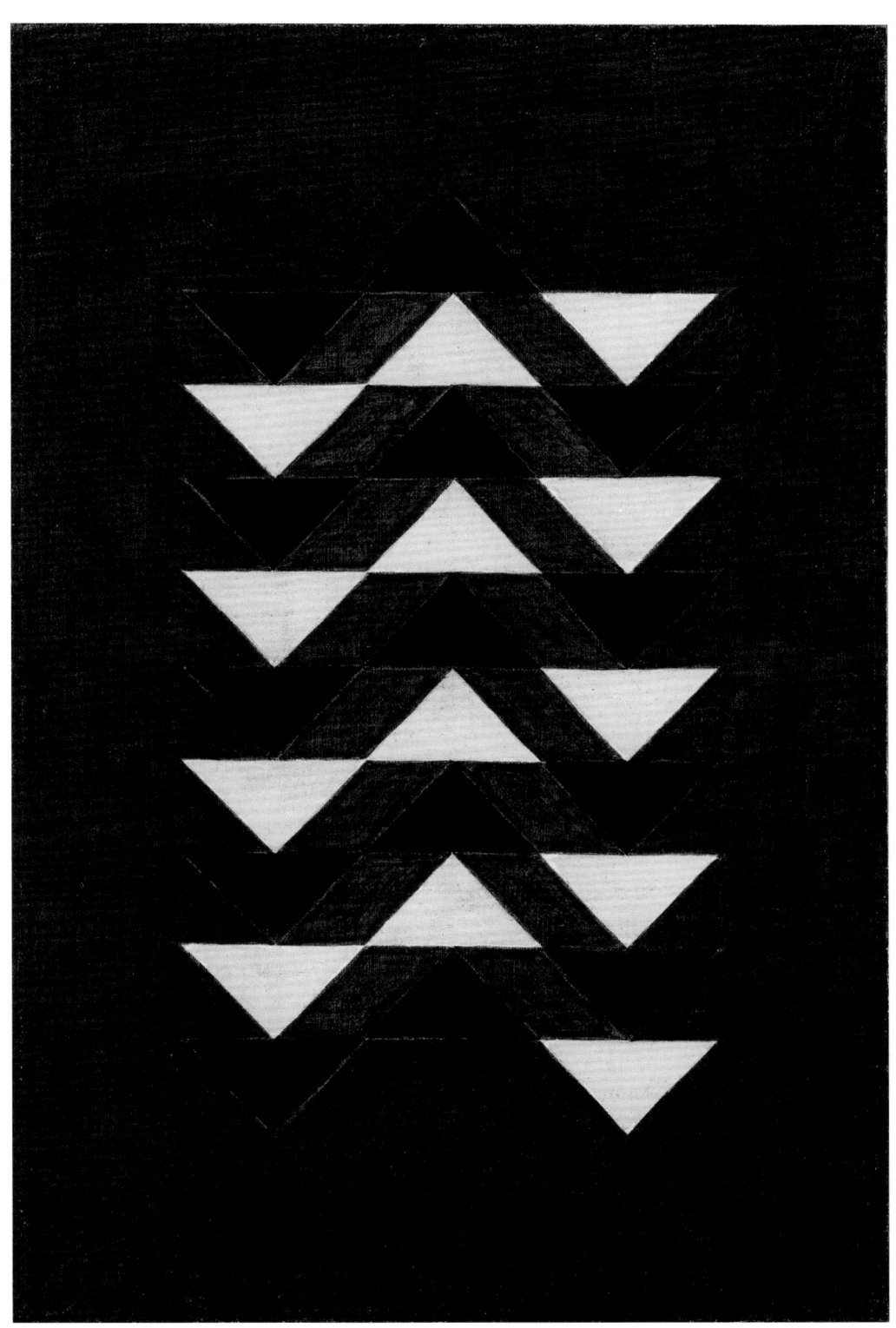

Untitled (Composição em azul) (Composition in Blue), c. 1959

Untitled, 1950

177   **Alfredo Volpi**

Djanira

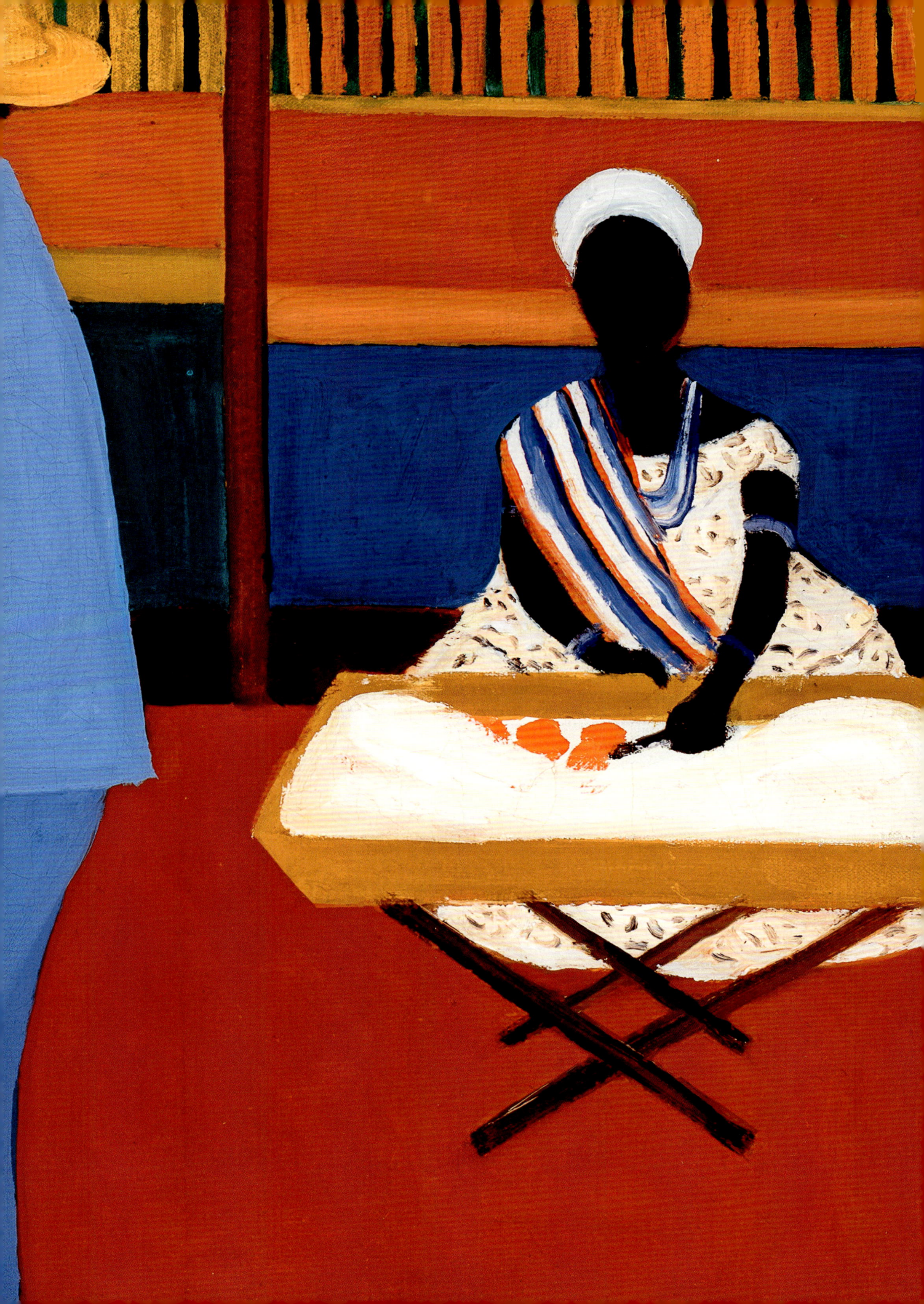

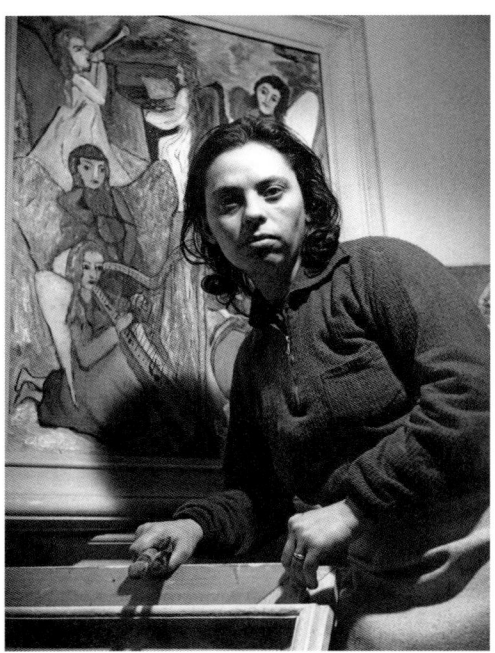

Djanira da Motta e Silva
1914, Avaré, Brazil –
1979, Rio de Janeiro, Brazil

The trajectory of Djanira da Motta e Silva, an artist who signed her work simply as Djanira, constitutes an interesting case of a largely self-taught artist who despite not having a significant formal training nevertheless intensely engaged with the artistic discussions of her time. Working in a moment when the antagonism between figuration and abstraction placed Brazilian artists in opposing artistic-ideological battlefields, as well as a time when so-called primitive artists were being seen and seriously discussed by critics and inserted into official instances of artistic dissemination, she matured her work in the course of the late 1940s and 1950s in an intermediate zone of stylistic sensibility: never abstract, but taking from abstraction the lessons she thought useful, nor in any way naive, a category into which she was inserted many a time by art critics, who besides naive also termed her work primitive. As she declared "I might be naive, but my painting is not."[1] Born in Avaré on June 20, 1914, in the hinterland of the state of São Paulo, she was of Indigenous heritage on her father's side, and a grandchild of Austro-Hungarian emigrants on her mother's. Living outside the artistic and cultural centres of Rio de Janeiro and São Paulo, she came in contact in her early years with popular manifestations of culture relatively untainted by European-based mores and customs, something she would use as nourishment for her practice throughout her career. Her peripatetic early years, which would be a great influence in her development, eventually took her to São Paulo and Santos, where she met, in 1932, her first husband, Bartolomeu Gomes Pereira, a machinist in the Merchant Navy. Diagnosed with tuberculosis she was advised to move to a sanatorium in São José dos Campos, where she miraculously recovered. It was during her convalescence that she first started to dabble in drawing. "I started painting by drawing the modest world around me: my animals, my balcony, the interior of the house, portraits of neighbours. A loving study of observation of the things I cherished."[2]

In 1939 we find Djanira in Rio de Janeiro, where she settled alongside her husband in the hilltop neighbourhood of Santa Teresa, an intellectual hub where artists congregated. There she worked as a seamstress, drawing in her free time, and soon established a boarding house, where she met the Romanian painter Emeric Marcier. He would teach her, according to Djanira herself, the basics of painting over a period of five months. For a couple of months she would also attend evening drawing classes at the Liceu de Artes e Ofícios, her formal training consisting solely of these two

Brasil! Brasil!

experiences. Her husband, never happy about her artistic endeavours, died during the war in November 1942, when his ship was torpedoed by Nazi Germany. Brazil's Estado Novo, despite its fascist inclinations, had joined the war on the side of the Allies sometime earlier. She would exhibit for the first time in that same year at the Salão Nacional de Belas Artes, showing once again in the next year's edition of the event, when she was awarded an honourable mention. Her first solo show took place in 1943 at the Associação Brasileira da Imprensa, following a trip to the historic colonial towns of Minas Gerais. Repositories of the eccentric and highly innovative Baroque style of art and architecture that the state saw flourish, they greatly influenced her work, as we can see in *Composição no. 1*. (fig. p. 185) Its hieratic figures in gloomy colours seem to perch in space in a manner akin to that of saints in a church retable. The show was well received by artists and critics. Lasar Segall was particularly effusive in his praises, going so far as to offer her financial aid if she ever needed it. It was also around this time that Djanira met the painter Milton Dacosta, an artist trained by the Escola Nacional de Belas Artes with whom she had a romantic relationship and who would exert some influence on her artistic progression, putting her in contact with more intellectualized aspects of artmaking, he himself being a deeply rational painter.

Djanira's second solo show was held in 1945 at Instituto dos Arquitetos do Brasil, and once again she was feted by critics and artists. One of the great examples of her style at the time is the oil *O circo* (fig. 1), from 1944. Exhibited at that year's Salão Nacional de Belas Artes it earned her a bronze medal. In one of the few works produced by the artist to don an ambitious collection of figures, Djanira usually limiting herself to single figures at the time, we see her personal style, blending the popular with the erudite, taking shape. The white seats of the circus on the bottom of the painting place a rooting crescent shaped basis, a resting point for our eyes, for the Baroque labyrinthine volute that begins in the right-hand side of the canvas on the musicians' platform, swirling vertiginously towards the centre of the arena, where the enchanting magic of the circus takes place. Blue poles counterbalance the painting's spiralling structure in vertical diagonals. Amid it all life makes itself felt in the numerous little moments depicted by the artist, the cigarette girl, the musicians,

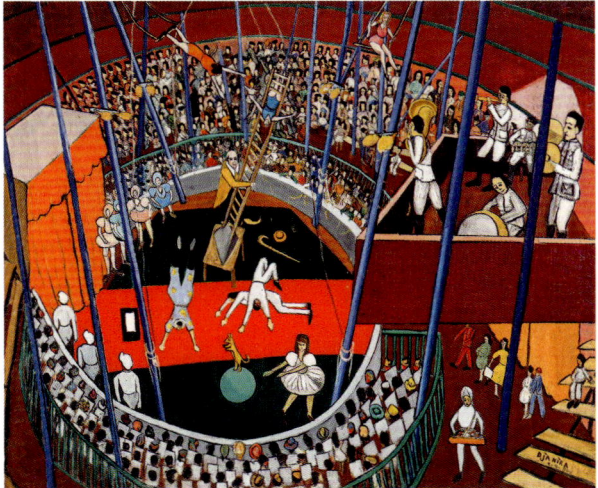

Fig. 1
Djanira, *O circo* (The Circus), 1944, oil on canvas, 97 × 117.2 cm, Museu Nacional de Belas Artes, Rio de Janeiro

Djanira

the public, all of whom are depicted without any individualizing features. Vividly flat, pure colours inhabit the painting, in which linear contours, almost always black, take on the value of decorative definition. Following her 1945 solo show, she moved to the United States. She would live in New York for the two following two years, during which she continued to produce paintings similar in style to *O circo*, such as *Central Park* (fig. 2), one of the highlights of her American period. During her time there she exhibited at the New School for Social Research, an exhibition that would not only be praised by former first lady Eleanor Roosevelt, but also earned her a celebratory reception at the Brazilian embassy in Washington D.C. organized by the wife of the ambassador, surrealist sculptress Maria Martins.

Djanira returned to Brazil in 1947. Upon her arrival she declared her artistic intents, a profession of faith that she would follow to the letter for the rest of her life: "Now that I am back home I intend to travel around Brazil, get to know it better, and as my destiny is to paint, I shall paint everything I find."[3] At this time her work developed in a different direction, adopting a modernist, geometricizing take on the popular sensibilities of her country, a combination hitherto unseen in Brazil. *Empinando pipa*, from 1950, is a good example of how she achieved this (fig. p. 187). On the outside the central rhombus, an enormous multicoloured kite, we see a continuation of her previous, head-on approach to figuration, characterized by her extensive use of lines as a defining element, inside this rhombus-cum-kite we perceive her distillation of the geometric and concrete musings that Brazil saw develop at the time. Both universes inhabit her work at once. In this context it is worth remembering her words "I believe with unshakable conviction in the beauty of both non-representational and figurative art. Art is one. We can coexist without mutual wars."[4] Her work itself constitutes a moment of concord of these mutually exclusive approaches, blending elements from one and the other.

The 1950s saw the continuation and stylistic progression of Djanira's concordant approach to the canvas, one in which the formal qualities of its construction were never undervalued. As she said, "I consider it important to be careful with the formal construction of a work of art. It is necessary to plasticize the subject with the maximum criteria of design, composition, and colouring. This is how I create my paintings."[5] As one can see from this statement, nothing could be less naive than her approach to the construction of a painting, even if the subject she treated was of a popular nature. At times she was strongly influenced by European

Fig. 2
Djanira, *Central Park / New York*, c. 1945, oil on canvas, 73 × 100 cm, Fundação José e Paulina Nemirovsky, on loan at Pinacoteca de São Paulo

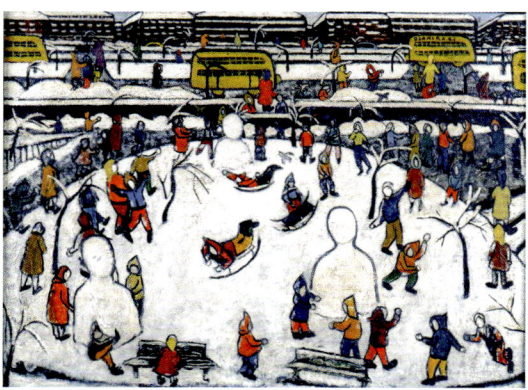

Brasil! Brasil!

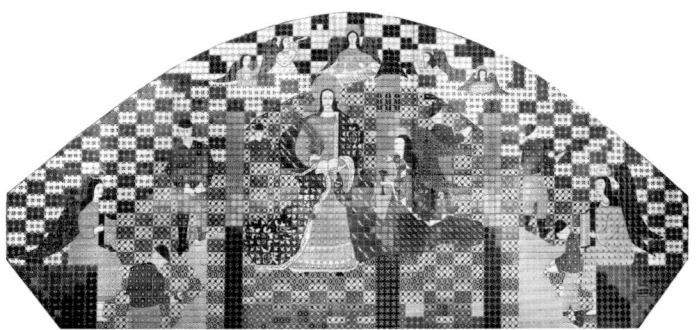

Fig. 3
Djanira, *Santa Bárbara e os operários* (Saint Barbara and the Workers), 1958, tile panel, Museu Nacional de Belas Artes, Rio de Janeiro

contemporaneous developments, such as in *Costureira* (fig. p. 194), in which the flowers of the wallpaper covering the walls of a seamstress's working room are reminiscent of the paintings produced by Henri Matisse in the late 1930s, whilst with others she was more inclined towards geometrical interpretations of Brazilian traditions, such as in *Caboclinhos* (fig. p. 192), a sophisticated exercise in the interplay of colourful diagonals and flat expanses of colour. She visited the state of Bahia for the first time in 1950, a place where she would return to time and again, keeping a studio there for a few months between 1954 and 1955. Her experiences there played a central role in the expansion of her subject matter, elements from Afro-Brazilian diasporic religions, such as Candomblé, and traditions, populating her work the 1950s onwards. Whilst in Bahia she met the poet and historian José Shaw da Motta e Silva, Mottinha as he was known. She would marry him in 1953.

Djanira not only visited many of her country's regions, but she also spent long stretches of time amongst the peoples that inhabited them, making the necessary effort to understand their specific regional cultures and ways of life to depict them more faithfully once back home. While it is true that artists before her, such as Tarsila do Amaral, had portrayed scenes of Brazilian themes and Candido Portinari had alluded to his Brodowski days, neither of them attempted to render into images other instances of the many Brazils existent in a country as continental in size and varied in cultural traditions as Brazil. Djanira, for her part, was the first one to search for the multivariate formal and cultural declensions of her country as an active participant, rather than predatorial observer. She would go so far as traveling to the northern state of Maranhão to live amongst the Canela Indigenous people. To quote her, "What is typical of Brazil is almost always forgotten (...) We have to look and see what is really ours."[6] Or in a more accusatory note, "We eat barbecue and vatapá[7], but insist in painting French still-lifes."[8] *Dança do Marrapaiá* (fig. p. 193) is a good example of Djanira's engagement with the myriad Brazilian traditions and their transmutation into geometric compositions of refined organization.

By the late 1950s and early 1960s Djanira's work was sufficiently inserted in Brazilian artistic circles for her to be commissioned to produce a vast, 130 square metre mural composed of 5,300 tiles for the Santa Bárbara tunnel in Rio de Janeiro. During the course of building works an accident had killed eighteen workers and it had been decided that a small chapel should be erected to honour their memory. Entitled *Santa Bárbara e os operários*, it was finished in 1963 (fig. 3). Taking Portinari's example at the Palácio

Gustavo Capanema as her starting point, she developed her composition in an entirely novel, even if profoundly tradition-based, manner. More fluent and less schematic than its predecessor it depicts in free-flowing, curvaceous forms the patron Saint of miners and protectress against thunderstorms side by side with workers and angels, against a geometric background made the more present by the many tiles from which the mural is made. A similar solution is found in the 1966 oil *Três orixás* (fig. p. 190), in which the triad of Afro-Brazilian deities composed of Yemanjá, Oxalá, and Oxum are placed against a rigidly geometric background of opposing colours, with two drum players behind them, essential elements of Candomblé. Despite their popular inspirations and the artist's deep understanding of the subjects depicted, these works are in no way primitive or naive. They come from the popular yet they become something else entirely at her hands. She would continue to develop this hybrid style, attaining heights of inspiration that still disconcert many of those who are confronted by works such as *Bananal* (fig. p. 195), where the leaves of a banana plantation dance around the background in swirling movements whilst the human figures they are juxtaposed with remain in a silent pose of strict rigidity, and *Barcos* (fig. p. 186), an exercise in quasi-abstraction.

In 1964, when on her way to Parati, a seaside town rich in colonial heritage and popular traditions where she kept a farmstead, Djanira was arrested under the accusation of subversive activities following the military coup that deposed president João Goulart and instated a repressive military dictatorship in Brazil. Despite the brevity of her incarceration, the experience deeply marked the artist. Following a second episode with the police in 1966 in which one of her dalmatians was shot in front of her, she left Parati for good. *Dança do Marrapaiá, Parati*, is the product of her experiences with the local traditions she encountered there. Her last decade of artistic activity was dedicated to the depiction of Brazilian workers of all sorts. Tea and coffee plantations, flour mills, sugar-cane fields, automobile factories, and iron and coal mines, become omnipresent in her work. She visited, as she had grown accustomed to, all these places, in spite of her always fragile and consistently deteriorating health. She also produced several depictions of saints, Djanira, as so many Brazilian artists, being a devout woman. Following a comprehensive exhibition of her work at the Museu Nacional de Belas Artes in 1976, she died from a heart attack in 1979. After her death, her widower donated more than 800 of her works to this institution, which has thus become the necessary go to point for anyone interested in the work of this popular-erudite, geometric-figurative artist of telluric force. One whose work continues to point to possible directions for the concord of the opposing, and at times contradictory, forces behind the constitutive principles of Brazilian modernist art.

Giancarlo Hannud

1   Xexéo, Barata and Abreu 2005, p. 47

2   Almeida 1967

3   Rio de Janeiro 1947

4   Apud Pedrosa, Rjeille and Moura 2019, pp. 268–269

5   Apud Pedrosa, Rjeille and Moura 2019, pp. 44–45

6   Apud Xexéo, Barata and Abreu 2005, p. 34

7   Afro-Brazilian dish typical of the state of Bahia made from bread, prawns, coconut milk, peanuts, and palm oil.

8   Apud Pedrosa, Rjeille and Moura 2019, pp. 56–57

Composição no. 1
(Composition No. 1), c. 1942

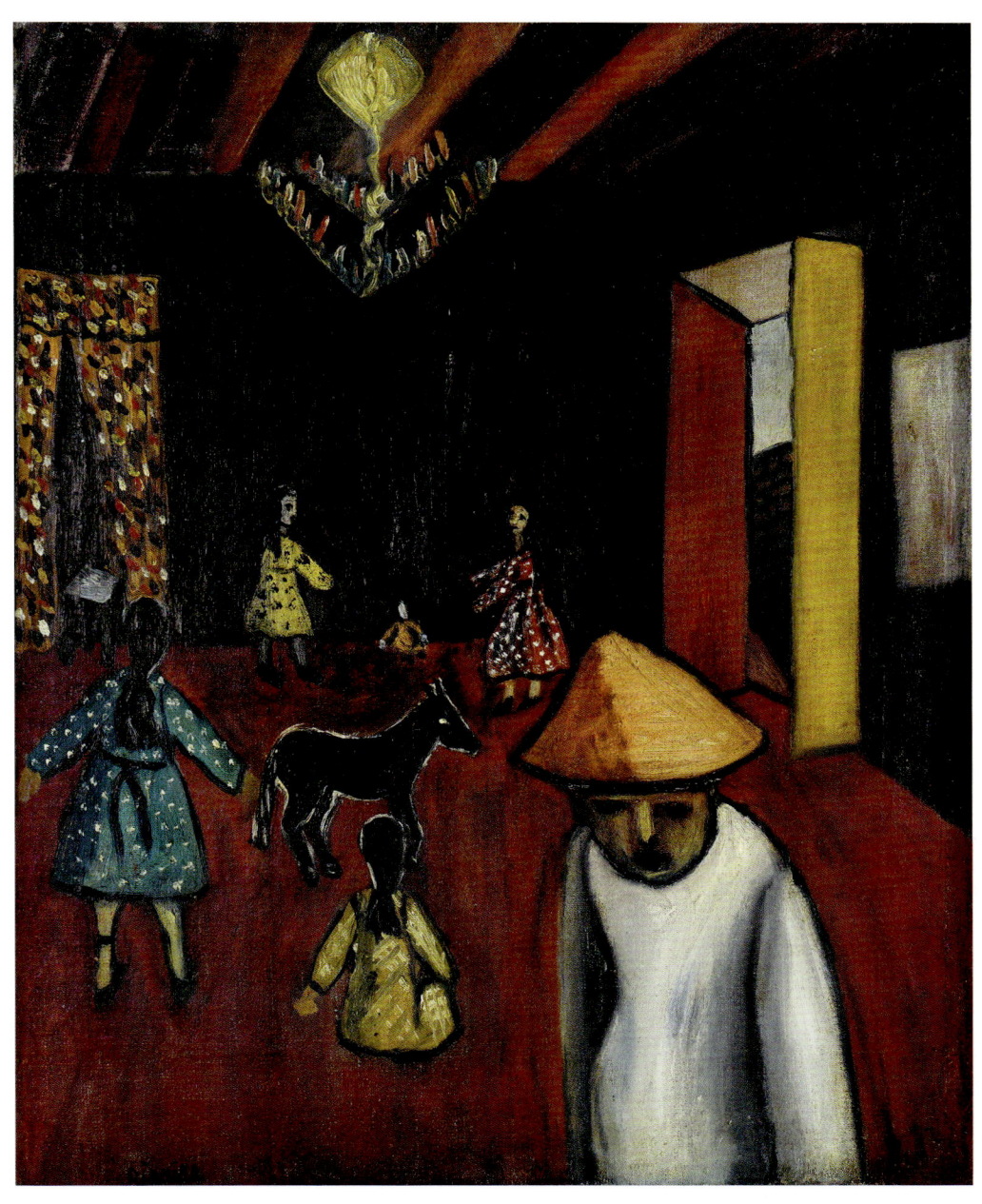

Djanira

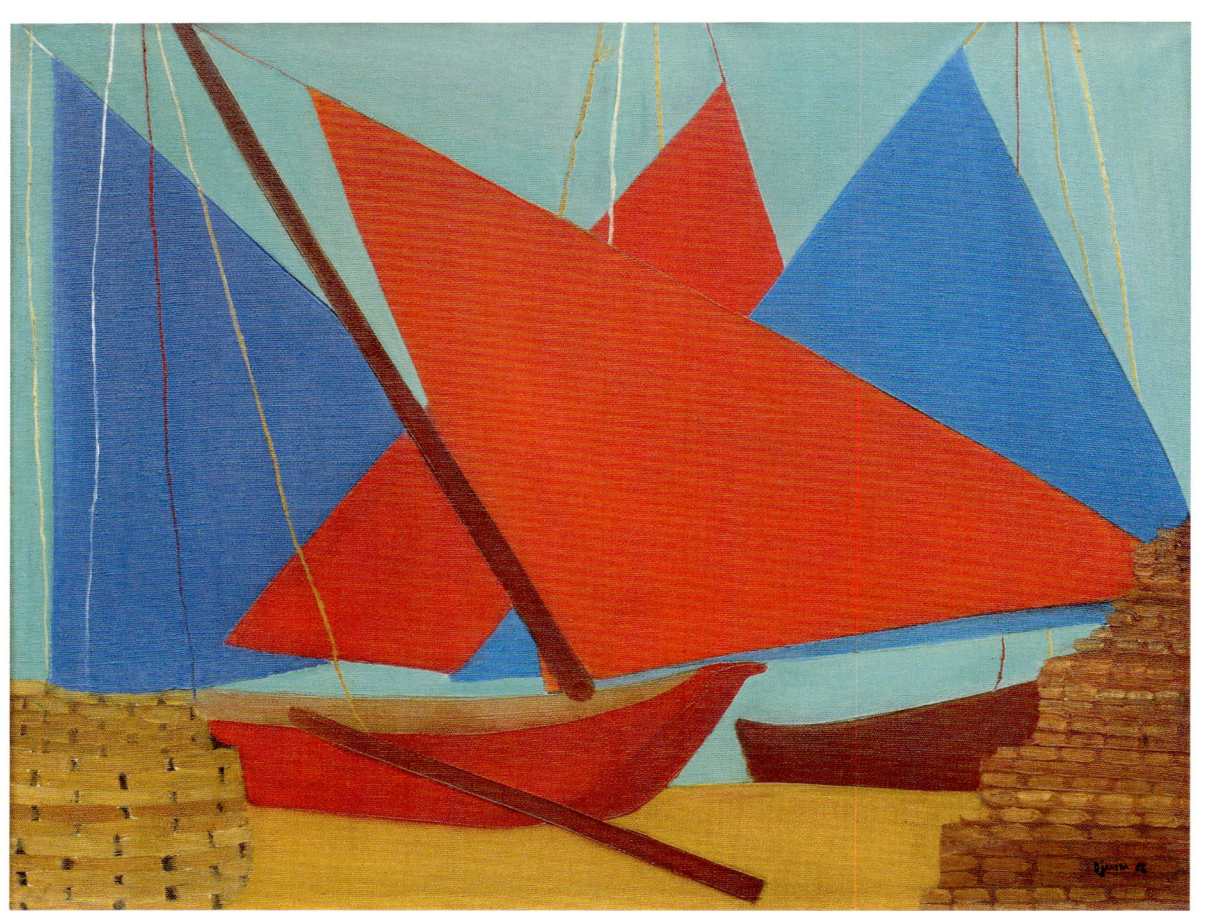

Brasil! Brasil!

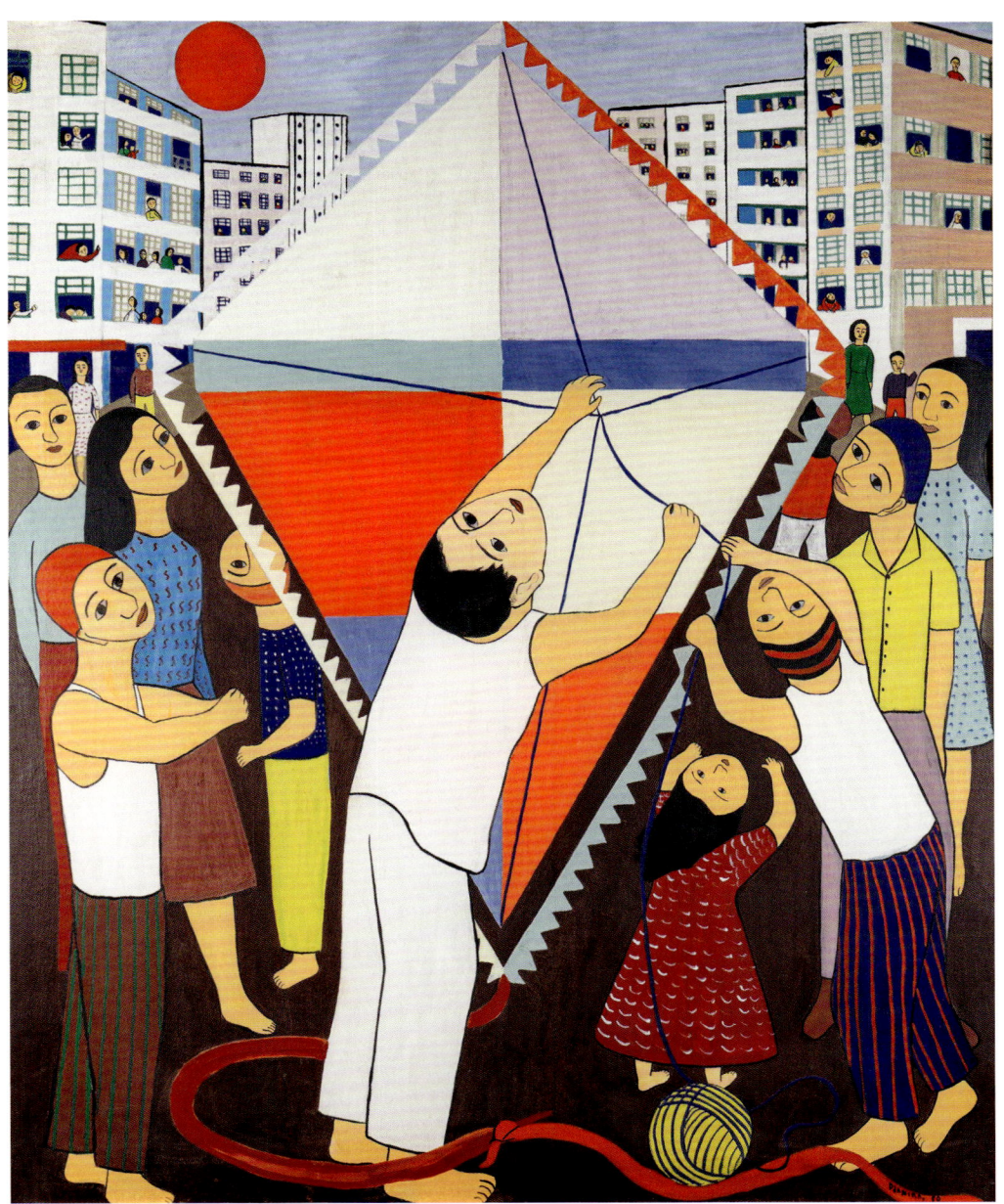

Barcos (Boats), 1962

**Empinando pipa
(Flying a Kite)**, 1950

187   **Djanira**

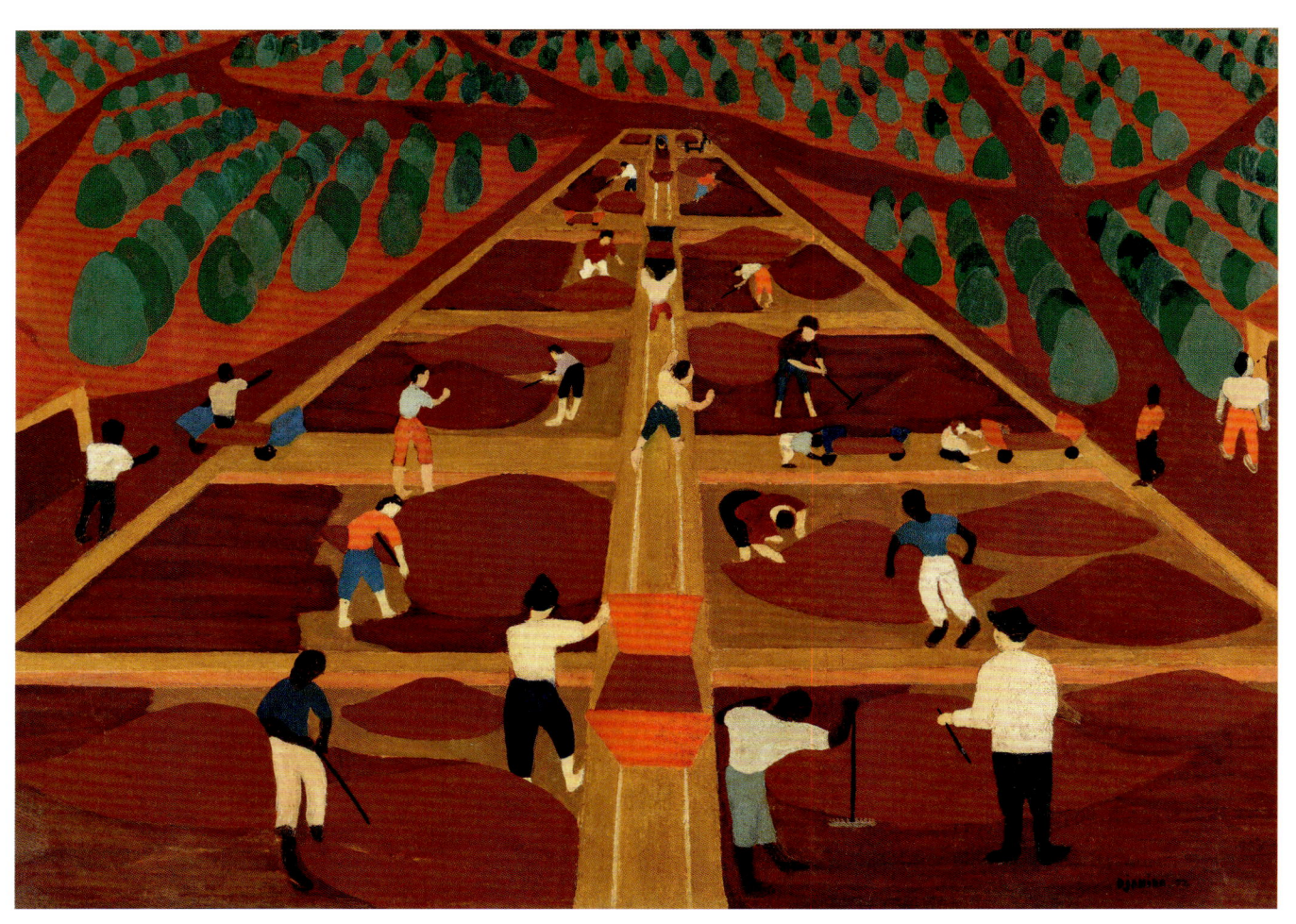

Brasil! Brasil!

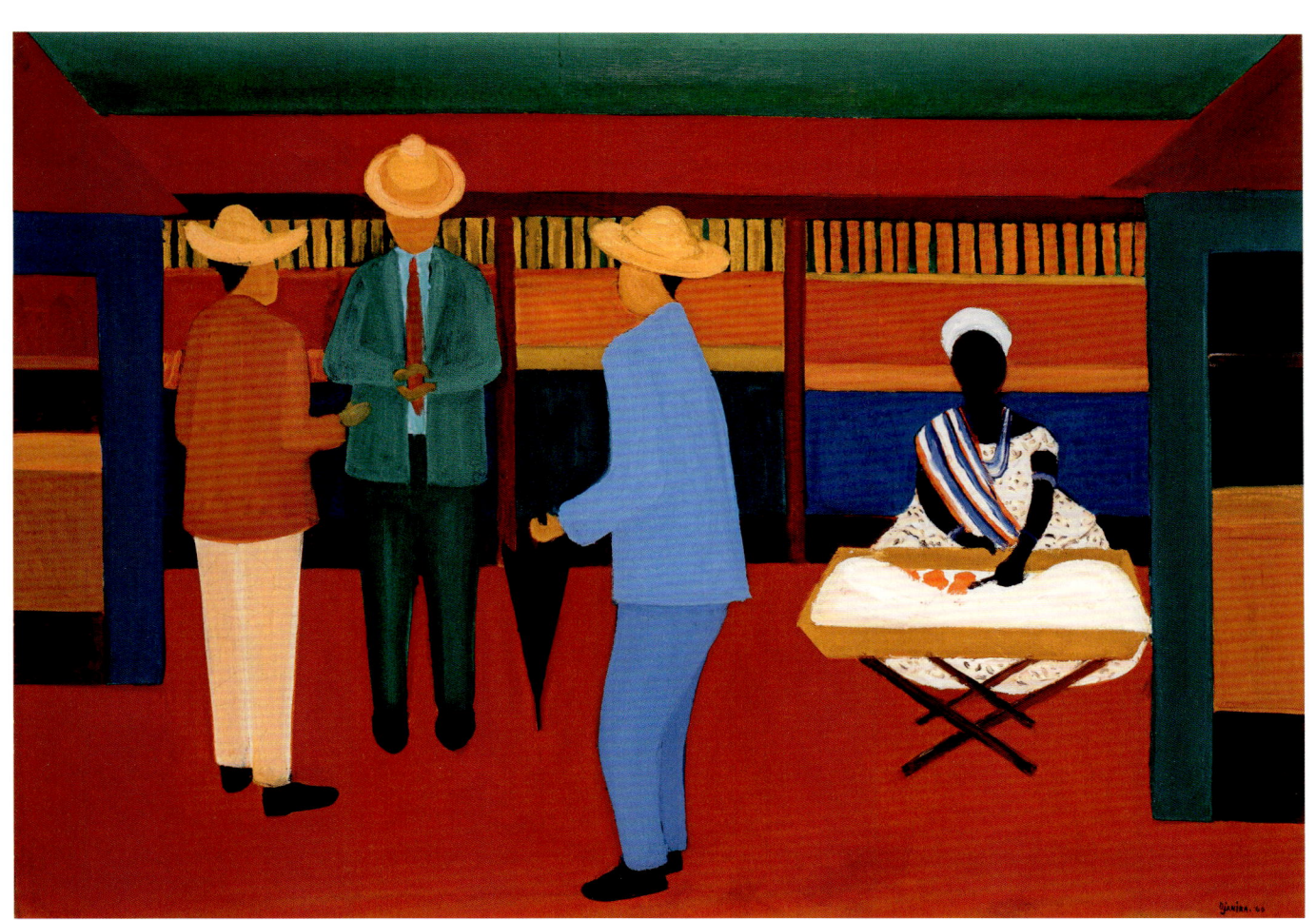

**Cafezal (Coffee
Plantation)**, 1952

**Cena de mercado
(Market Scene)**, 1960

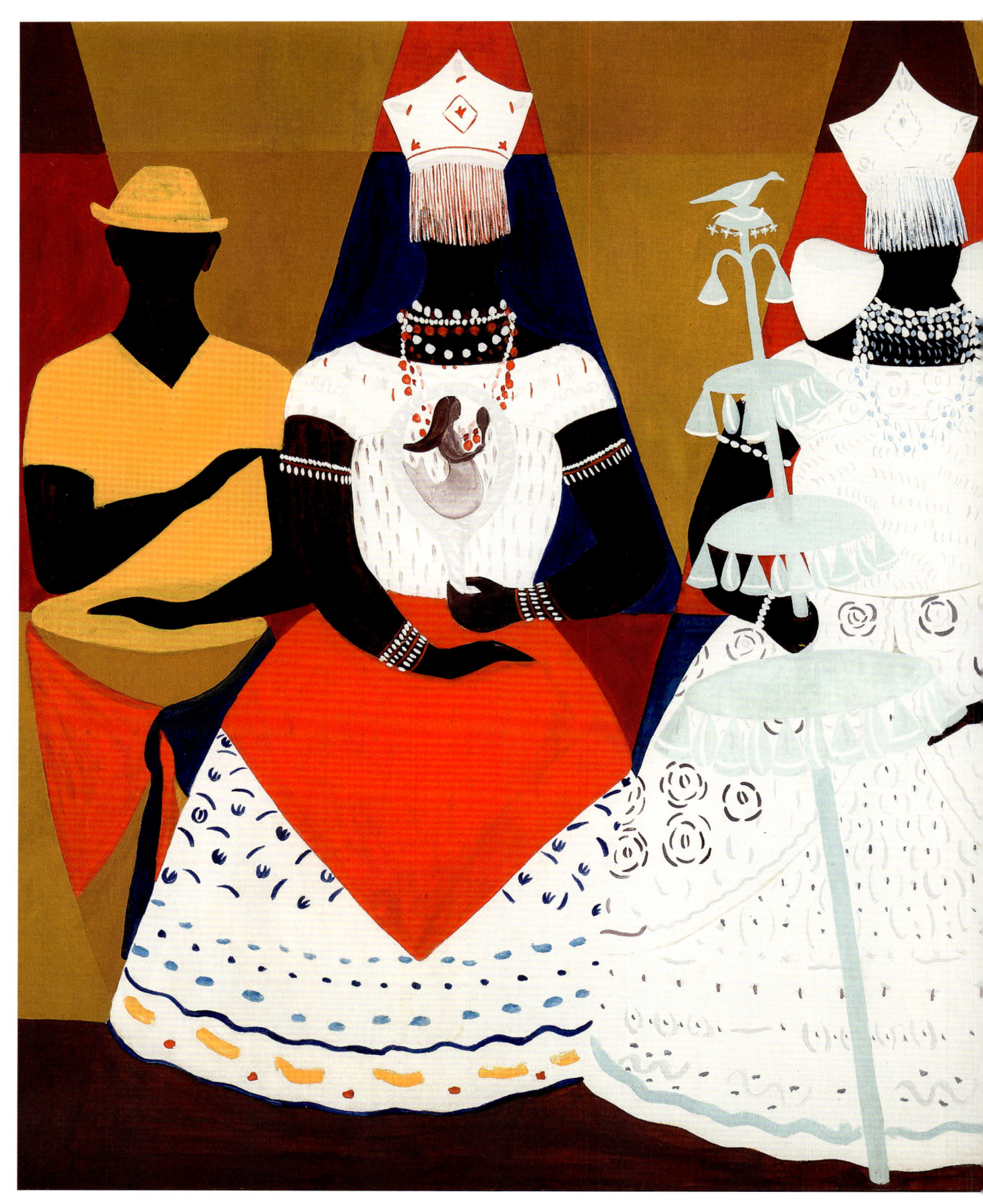

Brasil! Brasil!

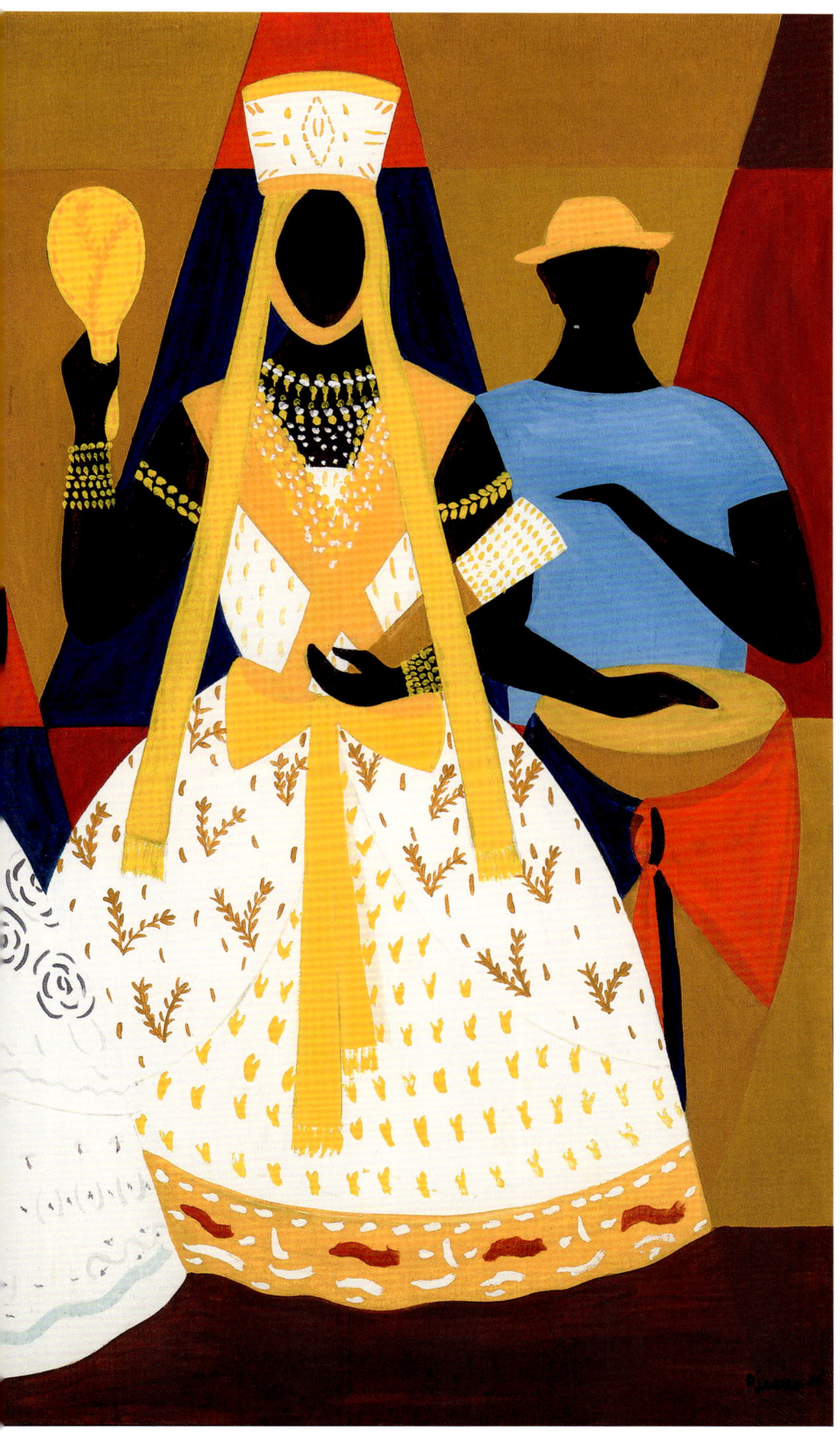

191   **Djanira**

Caboclinhos (Young
Caboclos), 1951

Dança do Marrapaiá, Parati
(Marrapaiá Dance, Parati), 1961

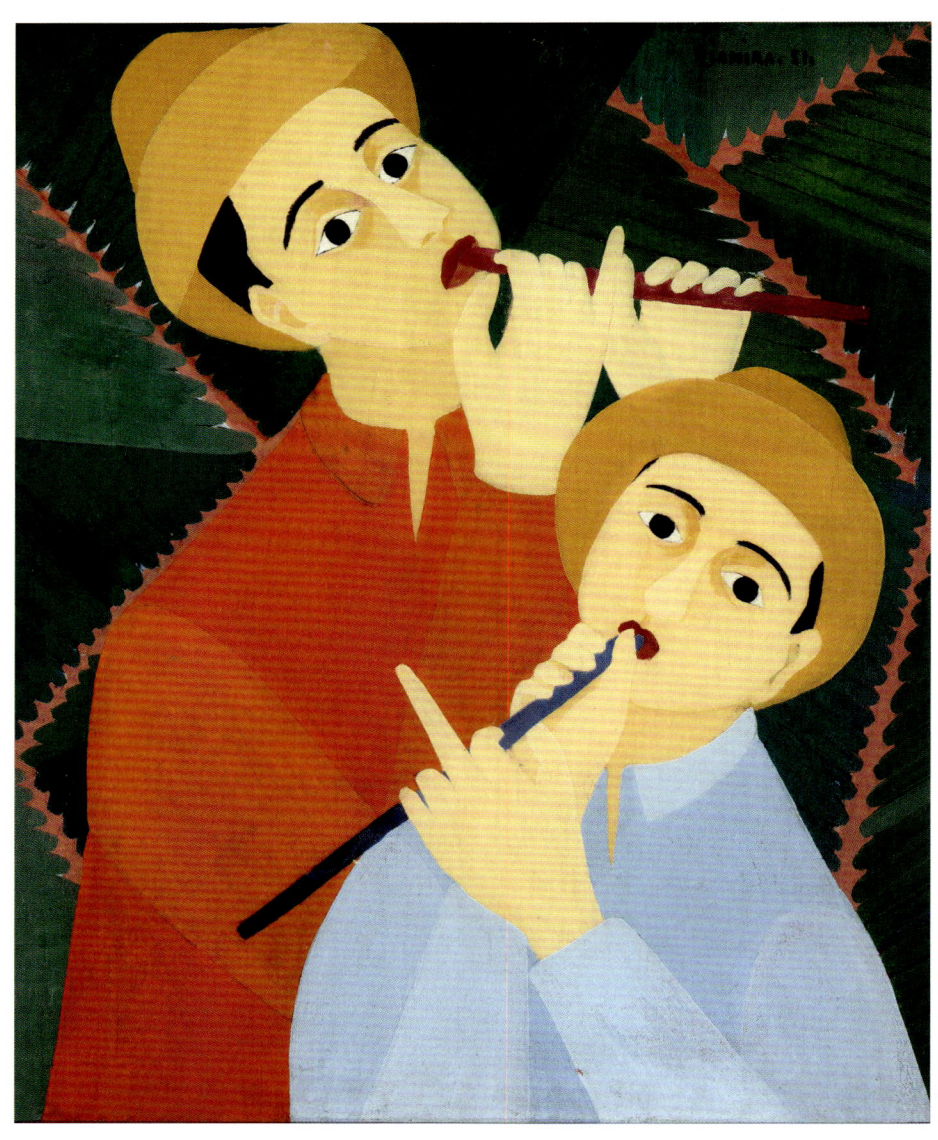

Brasil! Brasil!

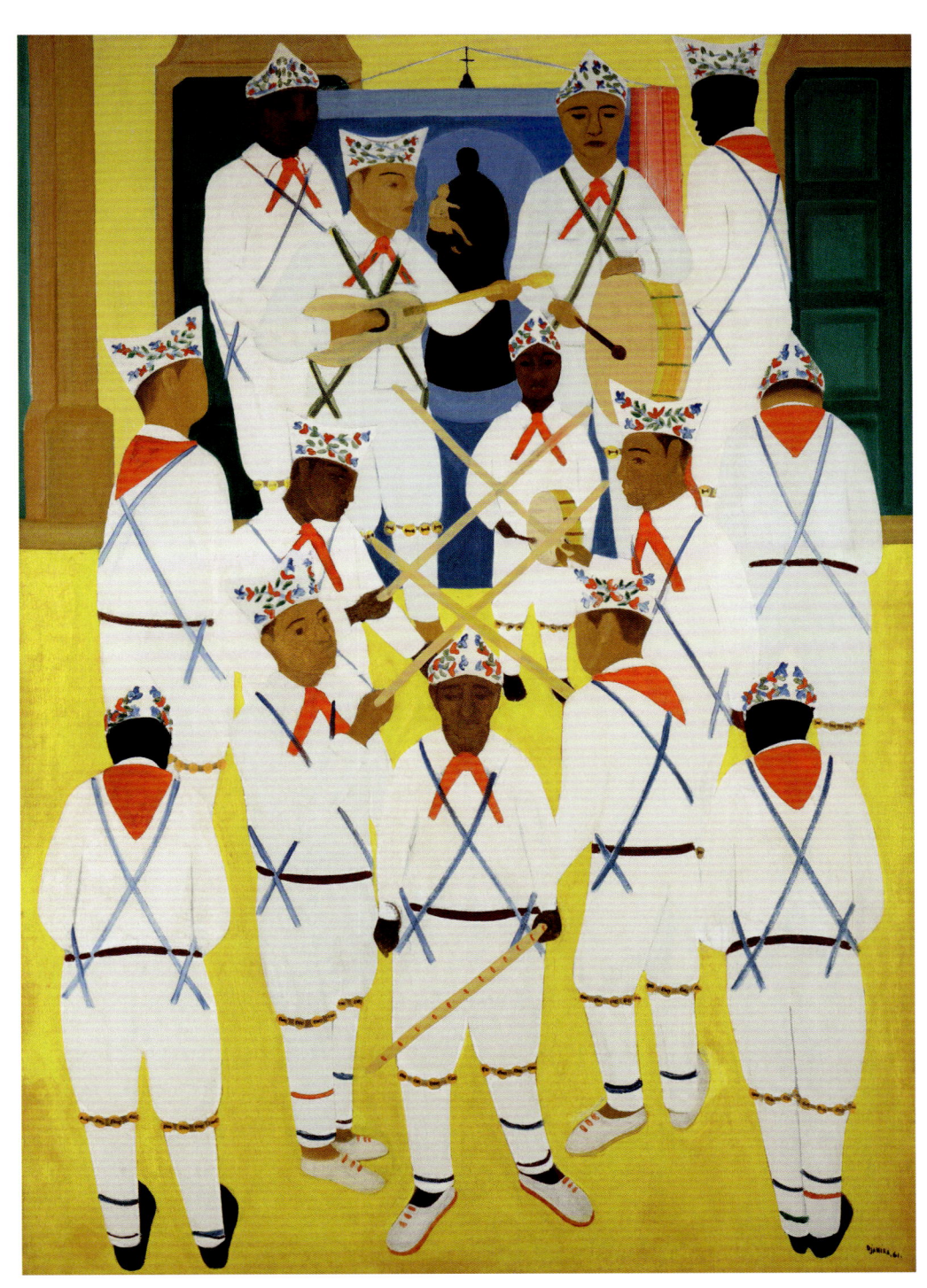

193 **Djanira**

Costureira (Seamstress), 1951

Bananal (Banana Grove), 1961

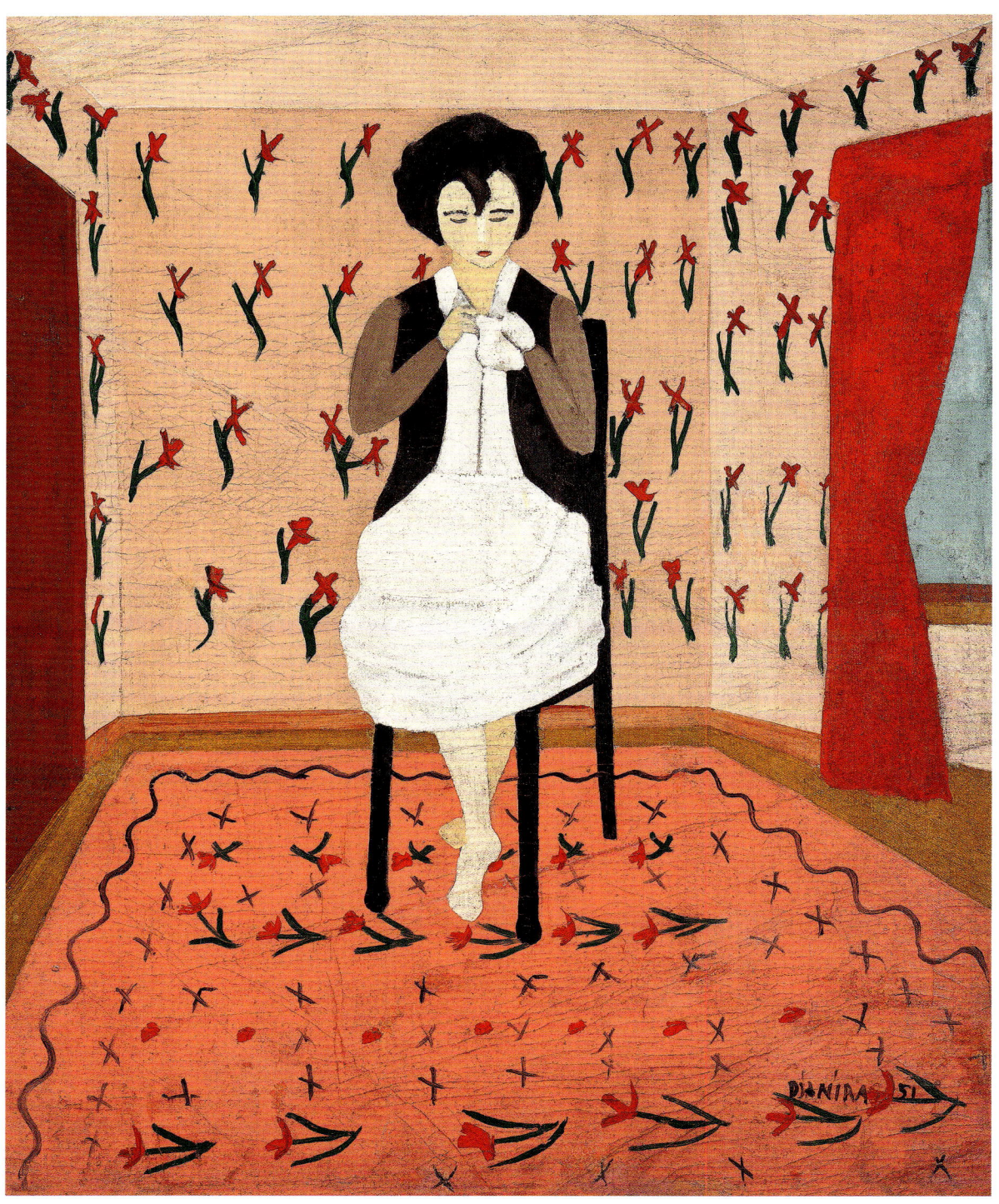

Brasil! Brasil!

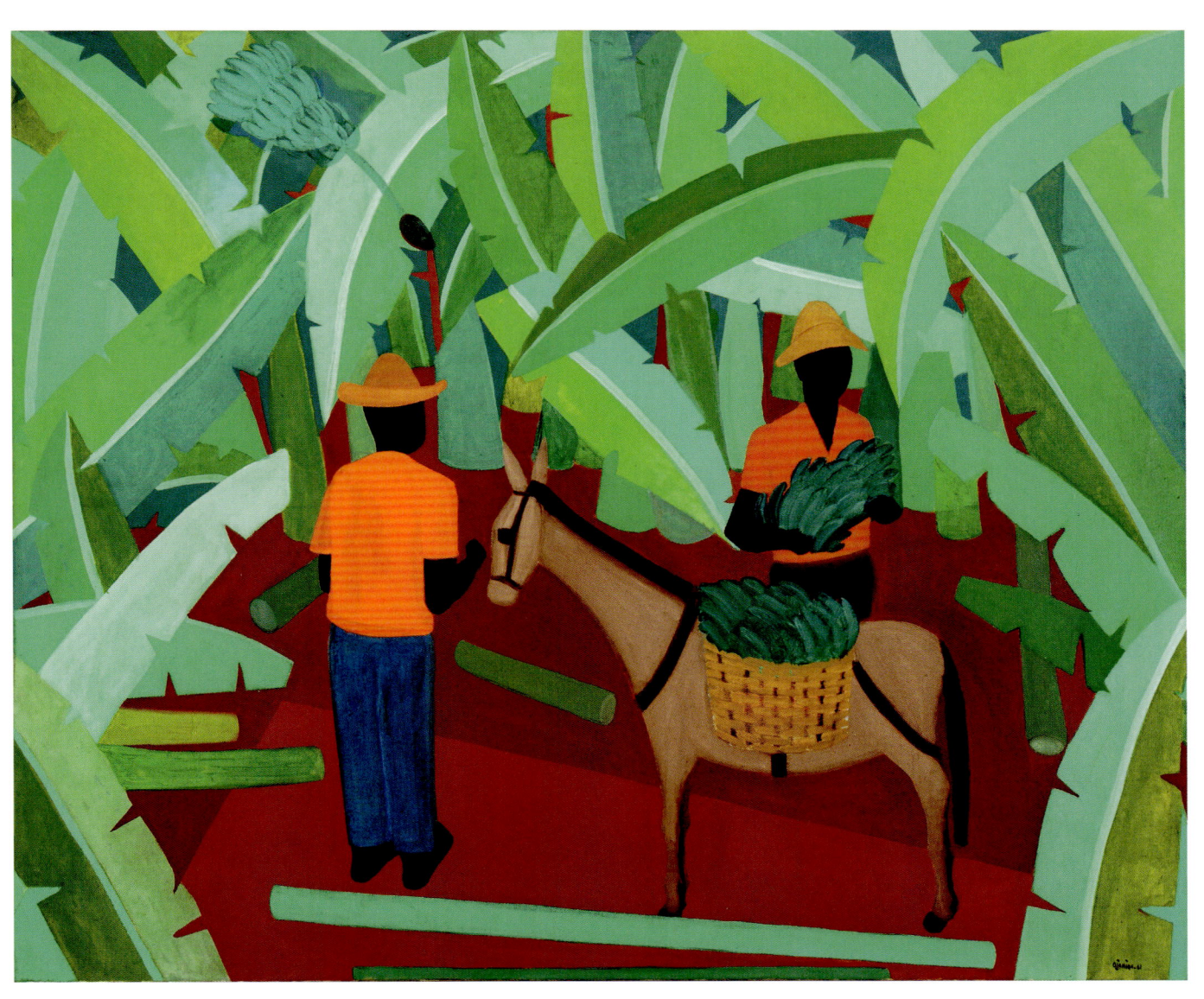

195   **Djanira**

Design

Design and Modernism in Brazil

Maria Alice Milliet

In Brazil, the modernisation process was delayed compared to Europe, with industrialisation and urbanisation only gaining momentum in the country from the 1930s onward. Until the 1929 crisis, Brazil was an agrarian economy, dominated by coffee exports. A significant portion of the population resided in rural areas, and societal attitudes toward housing and home life remained conservative, even in big cities like São Paulo and Rio de Janeiro. This provincialism was challenged during the *Semana de Arte Moderna* (Modern Art Week) in 1922 when, over three nights, the audience at the São Paulo Municipal Theatre reacted with indignation to avant-garde literary and musical performances and a modern art exhibition in the theatre's foyer. Thus, amidst booing and in a climate of defiance against prevailing aesthetic norms, Brazilian modernism was born.

The first expressions of modern architecture and design emerged during this period, a transitional time marked by a decline in international coffee prices following the Wall Street Crash, which led to the collapse of the Brazilian economy, and the increasing political turmoil that culminated in the Revolution of 1930. Despite the initial economic downturn, the Vargas era witnessed industrial growth and the emergence of a middle-class market. Design developed in Europe for mass consumer products remained largely the preserve of the cosmopolitan elite in Brazil until the middle of the twentieth century. Architects catered to this affluent clientele by designing modern residences and furniture for interior decoration. The production of utilitarian objects only gained momentum after World War II, driven by import substitution policies and the expansion of

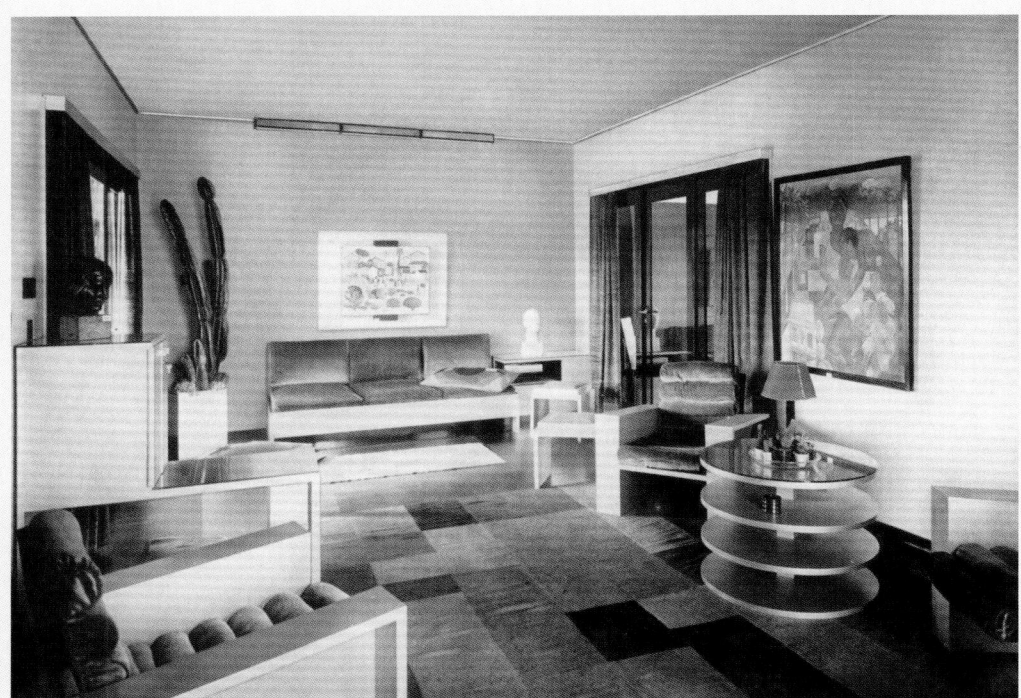

Fig. 1
Casa Modernista, Rua Itápolis, São Paulo. Living room with a painting by Tarsila do Amaral in the back, and by Lasar Segall on the right.

consumption. At this point, designers transitioned from commissioned work to industrial design.

The Brazilian pioneers adopted the modern design principles outlined by the Bauhaus and further developed by De Stijl, Le Corbusier, and the Ulm School of Design. Many of them were naturalised Brazilian immigrants, who were mostly architects trained in Europe. Few original objects designed by these pioneers have survived in collections. However, the recognition of the quality of their production has led to the reissue of many of these objects, particularly furniture, which are now highly valued and integrated into the history of international design.

Gregori Warchavchik, born in Odessa and trained as an architect in Rome, was the first to build works of modern architecture in Brazil. In 1928, he was unhappy with the prices and the scarcity of materials such as steel, glass, and cement to build his home. This same shortage extended to household items. Unable to find suitable industrial components, he took matters into his own hands, crafting the hardware and frames needed for his constructions. Setting up a workshop in the back of his house, he also began producing the furniture for his architectural designs. Landscaping was another area that required personal investment. His wife, Mina Klabin, undertook the task of landscaping the area surrounding the property. Her innovative approach included framing the architectural blocks with lush vegetation comprising cacti, dracaenas, and agaves, thus birthing the first tropical garden. By this time, the couple had seamlessly integrated into the modernist avant-garde, actively participating in the dissemination of modern art. Their residence in the Vila Mariana neighbourhood became a meeting point for illustrious visitors, including Le Corbusier when he travelled to São Paulo.

In 1930, Warchavchik made the decision to open Casa Modernista to the public in Pacaembu, a newly developed neighbourhood in São Paulo. His intention was to challenge biases against modernism and make this new style of living accessible to the public. Acting as a manifesto house, it featured a tropical garden designed by Mina Klabin Warchavchik, furniture and lighting fixtures designed by the architect himself, and high-quality modern art (fig. 1). The residence stood as a clear demonstration of the maturity modernist production had achieved just eight years after the *Semana de Arte Moderna*. Overall, the setting provided a powerful affirmation of modernist aesthetics. Among the highlights was the couple's bedroom, where the simplicity of Warchavchik's furniture contrasted with the vibrancy of the quilt created by Regina Gomide Graz and the equally striking painting by Tarsila do Amaral installed above the headboard. Both artists demonstrated full

mastery of their respective crafts: Gomide Graz combined fabrics of contrasting textures and sheens in an asymmetric composition reminiscent of art deco, while do Amaral harmonised elements from the pau-brasil and anthropophagic phases in an idyllic landscape titled *Cartão-postal* (Postcard, 1929).

While the visual arts demonstrated maturity at the Casa Modernista exhibition, architecture and interior design were only beginning to explore new avenues. In the field of design, Warchavchik and the Swiss-born John Graz were pioneers. Both arrived in São Paulo in the 1920s, marrying Brazilian women, Mina Klabin and Regina Gomide, respectively, who introduced them to the city's close-knit socio-cultural milieu. They benefitted from the professional collaboration with their wives, especially in the early years of their careers. Later, each pursued their own path – Warchavchik became renowned as an architect, while Graz excelled as an interior designer.

Warchavchik's primary interest had always been architecture. He worked as a designer only until he established himself as an architect, while Graz turned to interior design as soon as he realised he couldn't rely solely on painting. As designers, both aimed to adapt household items to modern life; however, they pursued different approaches. While Warchavchik prioritised functionality, simple forms, inexpensive materials, and low production costs, Graz focused on elaborate creations requiring expensive materials and highly specialised execution.

In 1930, the Swiss designer opened his own store, *John Graz Decorações*, expanding his clientele. For two decades, he was the preferred decorator (*artiste-décorateur*, as they said in France) among São Paulo's elite. For him, every project was a total work of art. From furniture to lighting, ceilings, floors, and walls, everything underwent rigorous planning. He entrusted the furniture to professionals from the Liceu de Artes e Ofícios, commissioned stained glasswork from Conrado Sorgenicht, and left the carpets, tapestries, screens, and cushions in the capable hands of his wife Regina. The Grazes, having

Fig. 2
Residence of Cunha Bueno, São Paulo. Living room with textiles by Regina Gomide Graz, furniture and doors by John Graz.

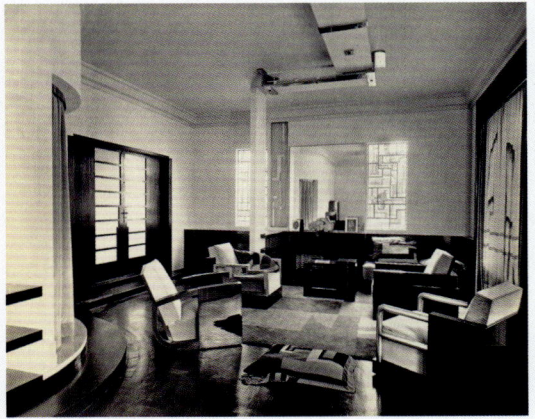

studied at the École Supérieure des Beaux-Arts in Geneva when they were young, always stayed up to date with the latest fashion. In 1925, they visited the *Exposition internationale des arts décoratifs et industriels modernes* in Paris, witnessing the triumph of Art Deco, an international style they would later introduce into the homes of São Paulo's haute bourgeoisie.

Once the trend faded, the old residences were demolished, and little remains today of the duo's accomplishments. Despite this loss, photographic evidence attests to the sophistication of the environments they created (fig. 2). John found in Regina a collaborator who shared his design vision. The Grazes' embrace of the prevailing trends in international modernism did not prevent them from seeking the Brazilian essence advocated by the Brazilian modernists. In his paintings, Graz expressed his fascination with tropical vegetation, Brazilian fauna, and themes from the national imagery, while many of the rugs and tapestries designed by Gomide Graz reflected her interest in the material culture of the native peoples of the Upper Amazon, as she advocated: "Since the motifs are Indigenous, the colours should be those used by our Indians: bright red, yellow, and black-blue, which correspond to the natural resources available to them: urucum, tabatinga, and jenipapo."[1]

Considering the challenges of the time, it can be said that Gomide Graz made significant efforts to integrate art and industry. In her collaboration with John Graz, she often remained in the background, similar to other female artists working alongside their husbands, such as Anni Albers, Sonia Delaunay, and Mina Warchavchik. Moreover, in a socio-cultural milieu resistant to female autonomy, it was uncommon for a woman to have her own business. Viewing design as a non-elitist endeavour, Regina Gomide Graz opened her studio to anyone interested in learning how to make rugs, quilts, and cushions. Later, she expanded this venture by establishing a small factory, *Tapetes Regina*, which boasted up to twenty looms. In her studio, she crafted felt panels inspired by classical and Amerindian myths. These were modestly sized, inexpensive pieces designed for the petite bourgeoisie. In her factory, which lasted until the 1940s, she produced both commissioned and mass-produced rugs. This represented modernity, shifting away from the exclusivity of mansions to reach the newly built smaller houses in São Paulo's burgeoning neighbourhoods. However, recognition of her work was slow to materialise. It was Pietro Maria Bardi, then director of Museu de Arte de São Paulo (MASP), with his international experience, who first called attention to her importance: "Regina, in the field of applied arts, holds the same value that we attributed to Tarsila. She was a woman who deeply grasped the evolving times; she possessed the strength of a European education infused with a distinctly national sentiment."[2]

Among the modernists, Flávio de Carvalho stands out as perhaps the most audacious. Trained in engineering in England, he joined the modernist group during the anthropophagic phase. His often performative actions never went unnoticed. Engaging in architecture, theatre, and writing for newspapers, he never ceased to draw and paint. This creative freedom led him to design bold buildings that, despite being submitted to competitions, were never actually built (fig. 1, p. 136). In 1938, following Warchavchik's example, Carvalho invited the public to experience a new way of living. The rental properties he designed, aimed at the middle class, brought surprising innovations, such as a living room with double-height ceilings and a sun deck with a shower. Despite providing a pamphlet with instructions on how to use the modernist houses, there was significant resistance to the innovations, and the residences remained unoccupied for a long time.

Transgression, coupled with irreverence, defined the life and work of this rebel. In São Paulo, he became known for his performances, often seen as provocations. Here, he drew close to Oswald de Andrade, sharing the notion of art as a form of psychic liberation and a penchant for the playful. These principles guided his early *Experiências*, social experiments, planned actions that directly challenged the conservative mindset that prevailed in São Paulo society during the 1930s. Later, Carvalho embarked on *Experiência N.3*, strolling the streets of São Paulo clad in a striking outfit of his own design, that he called "New Look" (fig. 3). It sparked a scandal. A man in a short skirt, sheer blouse, sandals, and stockings couldn't but shock the crowd, predominantly composed of men in suits and ties, who traversed the city centre daily. However, the artist, perceived by the public as an exhibitionist, infused the event with sociocultural significance. His aim was to promote a prototype garment meant to revolutionise fashion, freeing the tropical dweller from the constraints imposed by European civilisation. This celebration of a man liberated from Western taboos and open to all innovation was part of the anthropophagic utopia conceived by Oswald de Andrade – a movement he embraced. From architecture to fashion and furniture design, Flávio de Carvalho's journey was consistently original. He designed furniture and household items for his home, including the *FDC1* armchair and a pair of wooden chairs with high backs – one red, the other green – that resembled the thrones of African sovereigns.

The initial sense of strangeness evoked by these ground-breaking initiatives would gradually fade away. In 1945, the headquarters of the Ministry of Education and Health in Rio de Janeiro had just been inaugurated. Designed by Lúcio Costa and a team of young architects, including Oscar Niemeyer, the building, elevated on pilotis and featuring a rooftop garden in line with Le Corbusier's principles, soon garnered international attention. More than the beauty of the surrounding landscape, it was the architectural complex that captured Lina Bo Bardi's attention as the ship bringing her from Italy approached the port of Rio de Janeiro. Alongside her husband, the journalist and art connoisseur Pietro Maria Bardi, she had left war-torn Europe behind, determined to seek a fortune in Brazil – a country brimming with vitality and untapped potential. While still in Rio, the couple received an invitation from Assis Chateaubriand, owner of the country's largest newspaper chain, to establish an art museum in São Paulo. And so began the Bardis' journey on Brazilian soil.

Modernisation was at the forefront of their agenda. Bo Bardi collaborated with her husband overseeing the design of MASP's first headquarters, including all the furnishings. For the museum's auditorium, she designed a folding chair with a wooden frame and leather seat, drawing inspiration from stackable circus chairs. Noticing the absence of modern furniture available for purchase in the city, she co-founded Studio d'Arte Palma in 1948 with Giancarlo Palanti. The studio was dedicated to interior design and furniture projects, in conjunction with the Pau-Brasil factory, where the furniture designed by the studio was manufactured. Even then, her furniture already incorporated vernacular elements such as raw leather, fibres, and native woods. Her *Cadeira*

Fig. 3
Flávio de Carvalho,
Experiência N.3, 1956

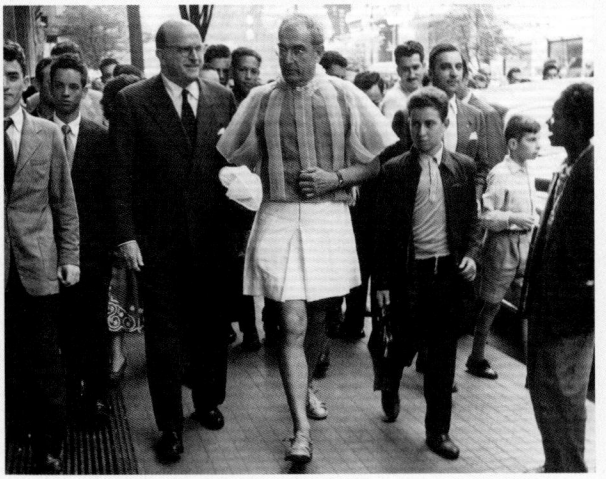

Design

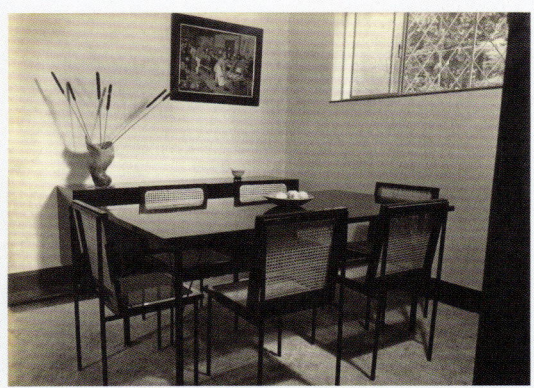

Fig. 4
Residence of Paulo Emílio
Salles Gomes with furniture
by Unilabor, designed by
Geraldo de Barros.

tripé (Tripod Chair), made of iron and leather, was inspired by hammocks – a cloth stretched between two stakes, accommodating the body in both sitting and lying positions – widely used by the Indigenous populations of Brazil. The attempt to industrialise the production of modern furniture lasted only two years before it faltered due to a limited consumer market.

From 1958 to 1964, the Lina Bo Bardi lived in Bahia. In Salvador, she came into contact with the African roots and *sertanejo* hinterland heritage of Brazilian people through figures like the photographer Pierre Verger, the sculptor Mário Cravo Júnior, and the young filmmaker Glauber Rocha, among other enthusiasts of popular culture. Venturing into the Sertão countryside, she sought clay pots, handwoven fabrics, lace, religious ex-votos carved in wood, and various handmade utensils. Her goal was to elevate these artefacts as the cornerstone of a truly Brazilian design,

rooted in the resourcefulness of the north-eastern people, whom she referred to as "this inventive people" – individuals who create out of necessity, often by repurposing industrial materials. However, when Lina Bo Bardi left the Bahian capital, stripped of her role as director of the Museu de Arte Moderna da Bahia (MAM-BA) by the newly established military regime, her project to transform popular craftsmanship into the foundation of national design was burried.

Another artist who took on the challenge of developing industrial design in Brazil was Geraldo de Barros. Invited by Max Bill, he attended the Hochschule für Gestaltung Ulm 1951 and, armed with this experience, collaborated with Waldemar Cordeiro on the creation of the manifesto *Ruptura*, a milestone in the introduction of Concrete Art in Brazil. For Geraldo, industrial design represented the radicalisation of the principles of modelling and serialisation proposed by the concretists. His first venture into the industrial sector was at Unilabor, a company he founded with the Dominican João Batista Pereira dos Santos (fig. 4). Inspired by Bill's concept of *Gute Form* – beautiful and functional form – he designed a modular system for home and office use. The furniture – chairs, tables, shelves – stood out for its essentiality. Barros's photographic essay on *Cadeira Unilabor* (Unilabor Chair, fig. 4, p. 210) illustrates the mathematical rationale behind the piece's design. With an iron structure and only the seat upholstered, the item is easy to manufacture and cost-efficient.

The factory operated on a communal production and management system for ten years, employing up to a hundred workers. It aimed to use design as a tool for social transformation, an aspiration that did not survive the pressures of capitalist market competition and the distrust of the military regime established in 1964. With the decline of the socialist vision, Geraldo de Barros returned to industrial design at Hobjeto, a company he founded with the carpenter Antonio Bione. By then, similar furniture factories were already thriving in the Rio de Janeiro/São Paulo region, led by designers like Joaquim Tenreiro, Michel

Arnoult, Zanine Caldas, Jorge Zalszupin, and others, in a favourable environment to the consolidation of the profession in Brazil.

Modernism thrived and solidified in the 1940s and 1950s with government backing. In Rio de Janeiro, the efforts of Lúcio Costa and the architects gathered around him, including Oscar Niemeyer, left a lasting impact on a generation that associated modernisation with improving the lives of the population. The inauguration of Brasília in 1960 represented the culmination of this project. Soon after, the aesthetic of the new capital gained widespread popularity, and the nation embraced the design of the Palácio da Alvorada columns as an icon of modernity.

The triumph of modern architecture paved the way for the expansion of the field of design. Anna Maria Niemeyer, daughter of Oscar Niemeyer, was tasked with equipping the Palácio da Alvorada, the official presidential residence, with all the comforts of modern life. Following her father's guidance, she designed furniture for a sober and functional environment, complemented by a few pieces of colonial art. Numerous designers were involved in the enormous task of furnishing the other government buildings. Today, in the halls, mezzanines, offices, and lobbies of these modernist monuments, one can find furniture designed by Sérgio Rodrigues, Bernardo de Figueiredo, Karl Heinz Bergmiller, and other contemporary designers. As a result, Brasília boasts one of the largest collections of modern and contemporary furniture, which is now part of the national heritage.

1   Revista *A Casa*, Rio de Janeiro, Feb. 1939, p. 16. In: São Paulo 2021, p. 54. Note: Urucum and jenipapo are Amazonian plant species used by Indigenous peoples of South America as dyes for textiles and body painting. Tabatinga, or white clay, extracted from the bottom of lakes and rivers, is used in traditional practices for pigmentation and wall coating.

2   Bardi 1978, p. 79

Geraldo de Barros

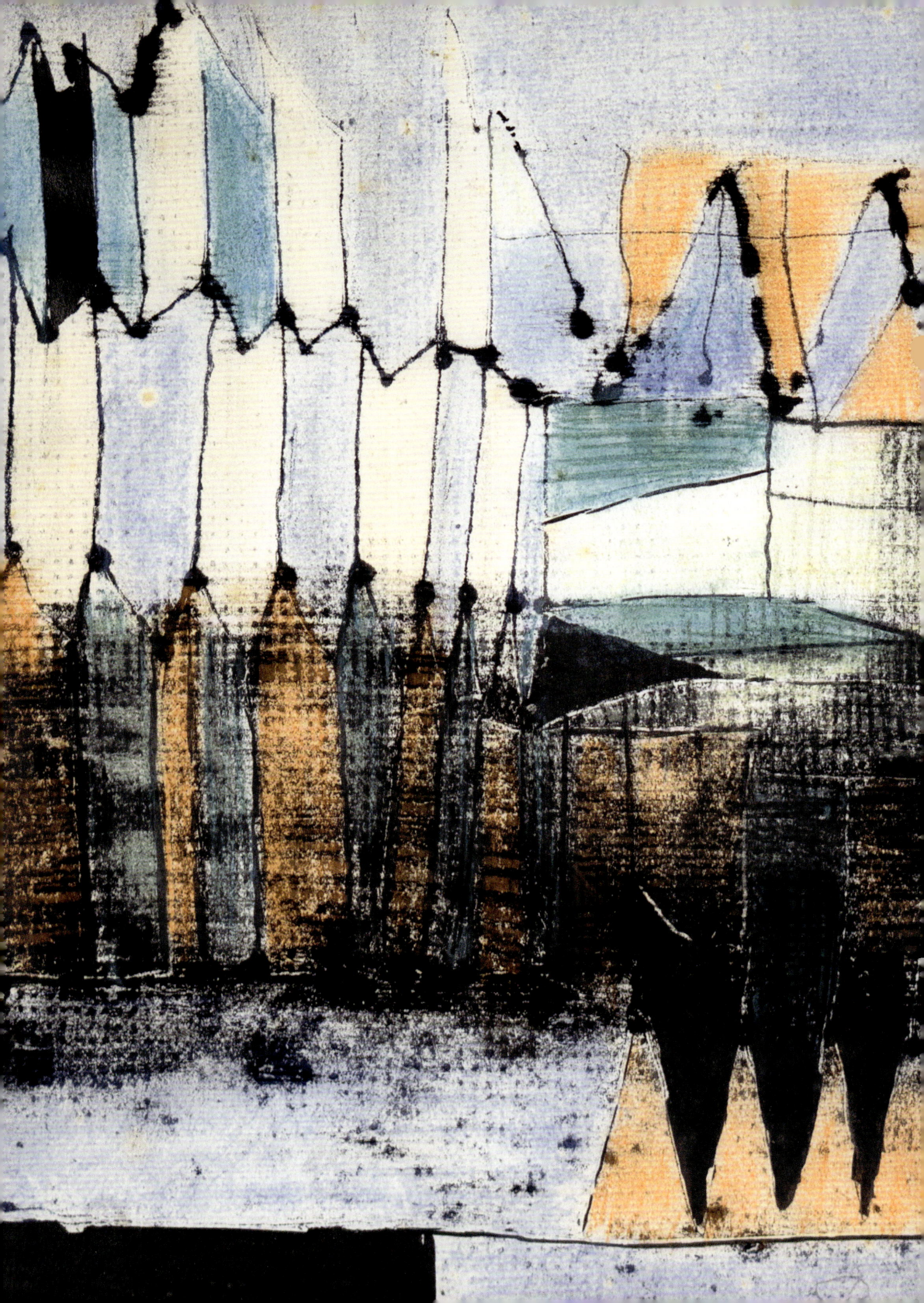

Born in the tiny town of Chavantes, located some 250 kilometres from the capital city of the state of São Paulo, on February 27, 1923, Geraldo de Barros was an artist unafraid to delve into all techniques and media available to him. He consistently changed styles and art-making methods throughout his long career, which spanned over more than five decades. He collaborated with other artists, designers, and intellectuals, aiming towards a liberty in the production of objects that sought to revolutionise the order of things. He produced photographs, paintings, drawings, prints, furniture, and commercial design without ever categorizing one above the other. All of them came together in an indefatigable investigation of the transformative possibilities of art. As a young boy de Barros moved with his family from Chavantes to São Paulo, where he would eventually study economic sciences, graduating in 1945. He started to seriously entertain the idea of being an artist in 1941, on the day following the death of his elder brother. Having to work to make a living, he obtained a part-time job at the Banco do Brasil, a position he would keep throughout his life. He worked a strenuous routine in these early years, working in the bank by day, studying art in the afternoons and attending university in the evenings. He attended lessons at the Associação Paulista de Belas Artes, an institution that catered little to his interests, stuck as it was in an uninspired method of artistic production that sought the complacent mimicry of reality. He studied with Colette Pujol and Clóvis Graciano, before becoming a student of Yoshiya Takaoka, a Japanese-born figurative artist part of the Grupo Santa Helena. Takaoka would exert some influence over de Barros, particularly in his self-portraits, adopting his schematic poses as guideposts for his own, such as in the oil *Autorretrato* (fig. 1), produced in Takaoka's studio, and the photograph of the same title from 1949 (fig. on the left), a numinous image of the artist as a young man.

The artistic scene of post-war Brazil was watching the unravelling of a violent debate that pitted abstraction and figuration against each other, with many of the first brazilian modernist artists firmly positioned in the former camp and others in favour of the latter. This confrontation took at times the most virulent of words, even if at times based on conceptually flimsy foundations. For if in Europe abstraction had been in the public's mind ever since the first decade of the twentieth century, in Brazil it had only taken short and hesitant steps, few artists delving into the expressive possibilities opened by the denial of a naturalistic approach to artmaking. It would only be with the inaugural

Geraldo de Barros
1923, Chavantes, Brazil –
1998, São Paulo, Brazil

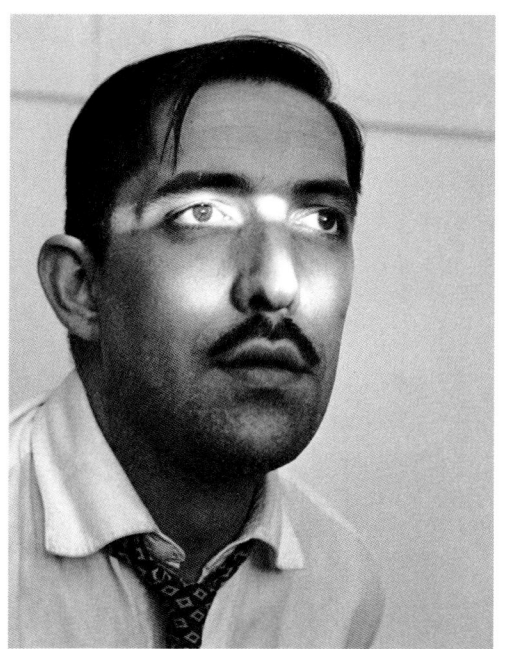

Brasil! Brasil!

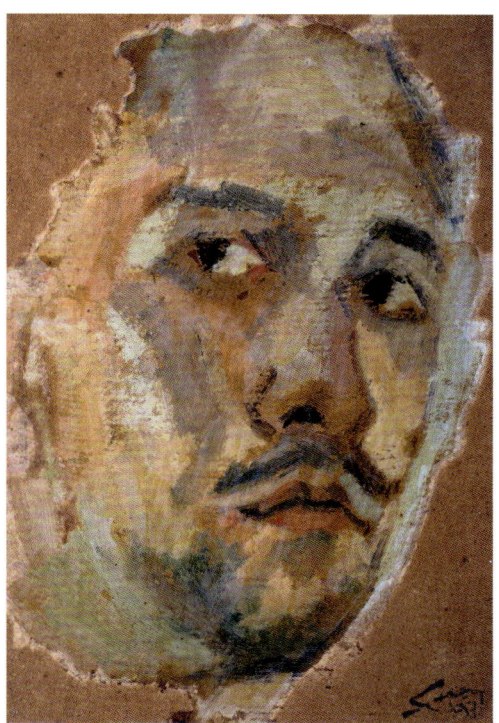

Fig. 1
Geraldo de Barros, *Autorretrato* (Self-portrait), 1947, oil on cardboard, 15 × 28 cm, Collection Lenora de Barros

exhibition of the Museu de Arte Moderna de São Paulo, an institution established in 1948 that took as its model New York's Museum of Modern Art, that a comprehensive view of abstraction and its many unravelling undercurrents would be available to the Brazilian public. De Barros's development as an artist was deeply marked by the blossoming of museums such as the Museu de Arte Moderna and the Museu de Arte de São Paulo, as well as the Bienal de São Paulo, and from the start he frequented the activities organised by them. He also regularly visited the Biblioteca Mário de Andrade, then run by Sérgio Milliet, which boasted a remarkable collection of books and magazines dealing with modernist art. His encounter with Paul Klee through reproductions in the reading rooms of the library was a particularly revealing moment for Barros, his work being deeply influenced by the encounter, as we can see in the painting *Grito na solidão* (fig. p. 211).

De Barros's interest in photography was first ignited around 1946, when he started taking pictures with an Agfa camera. But it was in 1948 that it took a more prominent role in his attentions. In that year he set up a photographic studio with one of his fellow students at Takaoka's studio, acquired a second-hand Rolleiflex camera, and a year later would for a period be part of the Foto Cine Clube Bandeirante, an association engaged with the dissemination of photography in São Paulo as an artistic medium. When working with photography he intentionally broke the rules of good image making, taking pictures against the light, playing around with negatives, taking multiple exposures, and so on. He would go so far as treating the negative as a matrix on which to engrave. As he wrote: "For me photography is a print-making process"[1]. Taking a dry point he engraved lines onto the negative. He would also scratch, cut, paint over, superimpose and blackout certain areas of the image to obtain a final photograph that enmeshed into its grains both the real world and the workings of the artist upon it (fig. p. 217). By doing so he incorporated the idea of error and chance, fundamental aspects of his practice, in the production of an artwork. In chance there was liberty, and in error new possibilities for making.

An apt example of de Barros's process is his *Homenagem a Paul Klee* (fig. p. 217). The primary photograph, taken of an old cemetery wall with its holes, abrasions, and scores, served as a starting point for the suggestion of a human face that was engraved and painted by de Barros onto the negative, holes serving as eyes, scarrings as nose. The photograph resulting from the worked-on negative is, as its title makes

Geraldo de Barros

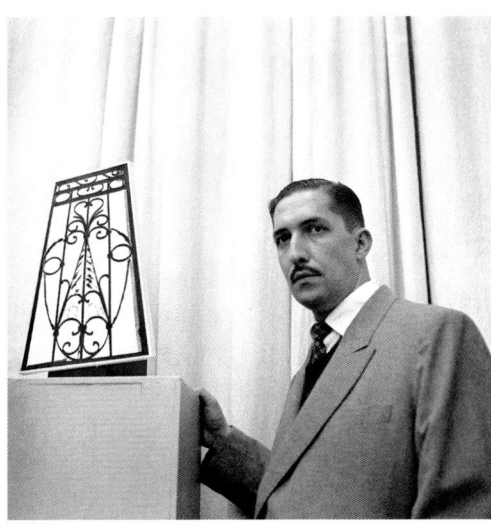

Fig. 2
Geraldo de Barros with the work *Máscara africana* (African mask) in the exhibition *Fotoforma*, Museu de Arte de São Paulo, 1951.

clear, reminiscent of Klee, even if technically miles away from him, and breathes an air of mysterious suggestion and the uncanny that is quite remarkable. His work baffled some of his colleagues, even if not all of them, some of whom could see the originality of his processes, but he was sufficiently well regarded to be entrusted with the task of setting up the photographic laboratory of MASP, alongside some of his colleagues from the Cine Club Bandeirantes, the same institution where he would present a one-man show two years later. It was in January 1951 that de Barros opened the exhibition, entitled *Fotoforma*, at MASP, a turning point for photography in Brazil. The show's expography was conceived by the Italian-born Brazilian architect Lina Bo Bardi who devised metal tubes onto which the photographs, sometimes in groups, sometimes in isolation, were directly placed. Some others were exhibited as objects, atop plinths in the gallery, lending them an object-like presence such as *Máscara africana*, a manipulated image of an iron grille made to resemble a mask (fig. 2). Later in the year de Barros was awarded a scholarship by the French Government, obtaining a year's leave from his part-time job at the Banco do Brasil to move to Europe.

Once in Paris de Barros attended painting and printmaking lessons at the École des Beaux-Arts, but more importantly visited Zurich, where he met, thanks to an introduction from MASP's director Pietro Maria Bardi, Max Bill, another profoundly influential figure in de Barros's development. Particularly interesting to him was Bill's notion that an artwork should be executed from a project, being thus the result of a pre-existent idea, and produced by means of a rational, preestablished, method. On his return to Brazil, he would concentrate on the production of paintings, leaving photography aside for a while, putting to good use his experiences in Europe. He produced deeply rational, geometric constructions of concrete character that optimistically engage with the sense of a universal language of colour and form, understandable to all. As he declared, "What I was trying to capture has a deeper meaning and escapes the visible and palpable materiality of the object, of the square or the painting. There's an organizing compulsion that is rooted within me, perhaps innate, that is to recognise the natural order of all things in the universe."[2] *Forma-objeto* (fig. p. 224) is a good example of his concrete period, and shows us the formal refinement of which he was capable.

Ever since the opening of the São Paulo institutions mentioned previously, a group of artists had congregated around them, forming bonds of artistic community in convivial gatherings where they discussed the paths open to abstraction in Brazil. A grouping of shared interests was thus formed that would eventually lead to the establishment of the Grupo Ruptura in 1952. The group, originally composed of seven artists, defended geometric abstraction as a means to the transformation of society, permeating the quotidian lives of people and organizing them in its many facets. Art, design, and architecture to them were fields that operated in unity. They also believed that abstraction, in its plain formal lexicon of lines, colours, and planes, was able to overcome the limits of language, geography, and nationality. Taking their cue from concrete rationales, they proposed a form of art based on logical principles, thus expunging the field of painting from any sense of individuality, which they considered inappropriate for their time. They produced the *Manifesto Ruptura*, in which we read a combative list of words of order, and whose essence was summed up in the adage "there is no longer any continuity in art". De Barros would develop his concrete language in the next couple of years, producing works of undeniable freshness such as *Arranjo de três formas semelhantes dentro de um círculo* (fig. p. 225).

Geraldo de Barros would not restrain himself for long to the field of painting. Upon his return from Europe he started to experiment with commercial design, submitting a design for the poster competition for the upcoming commemoration of São Paulo's 400th birthday in 1954, for which he was awarded first prize. His poster, based on a 1951 lithograph of his, *A City to Conquer* (fig. p. 212), depicts a Klee-like medieval walled city reduced to its most basic elements (fig. 3). It is a particularly noteworthy piece of de Barros for it signals his entrance into the more commercially oriented, but no less inventive, work he would do in the second half of the 1950s and into the 1960s, in particular his collaboration with the Dominican friar João Batista Pereira dos Santos in the setting up of Unilabor, a furniture production cooperative. Invited by the friar to visit the Capela do Cristo Operário, the chapel for which Alfredo Volpi had produced frescos in 1951 (fig. 2 p. 162) adjoining a Dominican complex composed of school, old people's home, and theatre. De Barros was overcome by the dormant possibilities offered by such a space. He quickly developed the idea of instituting a furniture manufactory, one which would produce high-quality designs, authored by him, of affordable modernist furniture. The Unilabor venture would bring together both friar João's ambitions of dignifying manual workers with the proceeds

Fig. 3
Geraldo de Barros, Poster for the 400th birthday of the city São Paulo, 1954, Collection Lenora de Barros

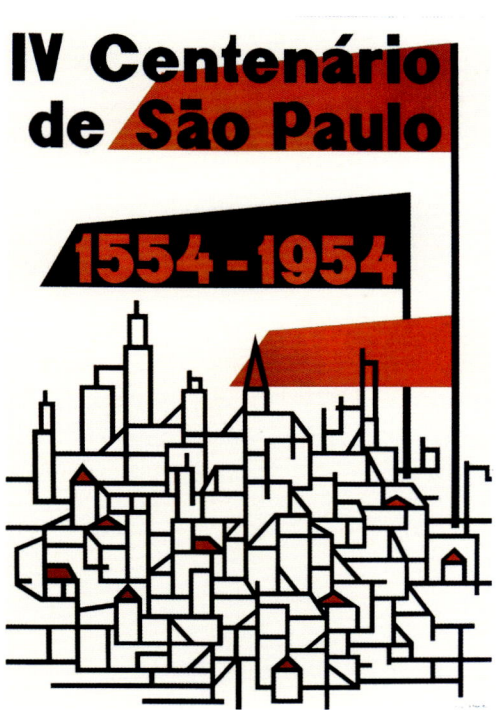

Geraldo de Barros

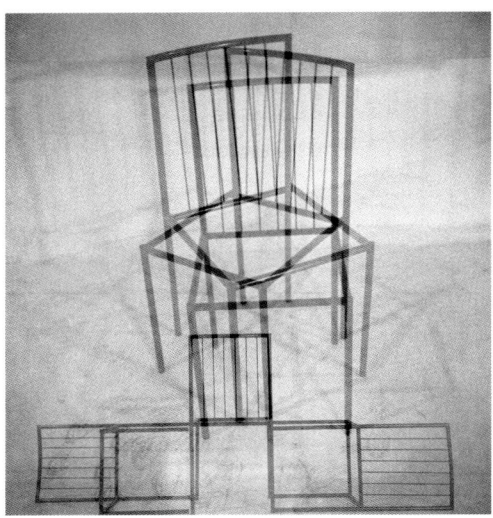

Fig. 4
Geraldo de Barros,
Fotoforma (Unilabor Chair),
photography, 1954–1955

from the profits and a release from capitalist production patterns and de Barros's own beliefs that through careful and attentive design art could be made available to all. He created the name and designed the manufactory's logotype, in addition to designing the furniture produced by it. One of Unilabor's most famous pieces, the *Cadeira Unilabor*, is an elegantly light structure of painted iron rods and brass tips that could accommodate a few options of upholstery. De Barros would use it as source for photographs in which the chair is playfully manipulated, creating abstract arrangements of lines (fig. 4).

The 1960s and 1970s saw de Barros's continuous explorations in all manner of media. He produced pop paintings, paintings over billboards, and a series of painting-like objects made from Formica. He also tried to create a painting that could be mass-produced, presenting in the fifteenth edition of the Bienal de São Paulo in 1979 a conceptual framework and schematic instructions for the production of five different pieces based on his work from the 1950s. As he had previously declared: "Objects obtained from a project are original and unique. The fact that they are equal between them is a consequence. If one copies an object made from a project, one isn't producing objects from projects. The difference resides in quality, not quantity. The project maintains its integrity, and the objects produced, in this case, remain unique, even though in enormous quantities, or en masse."[3] Following a stroke in the same year, de Barros started to experience problems with speech and mobility, but would continue to experiment with different ways of working, including producing in 1983 a series of nearly 200 pieces in Formica such as *Homenagem a Volpi* (fig. p. 223). His investigations with photography also continued. In his series *Sobras*, dated to the last two years of his life, he uses a series of discarded family negatives. Cut and mounted onto glass sheets the developed negatives result in strangely cryptic images, otherworldly realms of modified reality, and show us the inner workings of a consistently inquisitive creative sensibility unafraid to experiment with new possibilities. Following years of ill-health Geraldo de Barros died in São Paulo on April 17, 1998.

Giancarlo Hannud

1   Apud Barros 2013, p. 271

2   Apud Espada 2014, p. 27

3   Apud Rio de Janeiro/
São Paulo 1977, p. 208

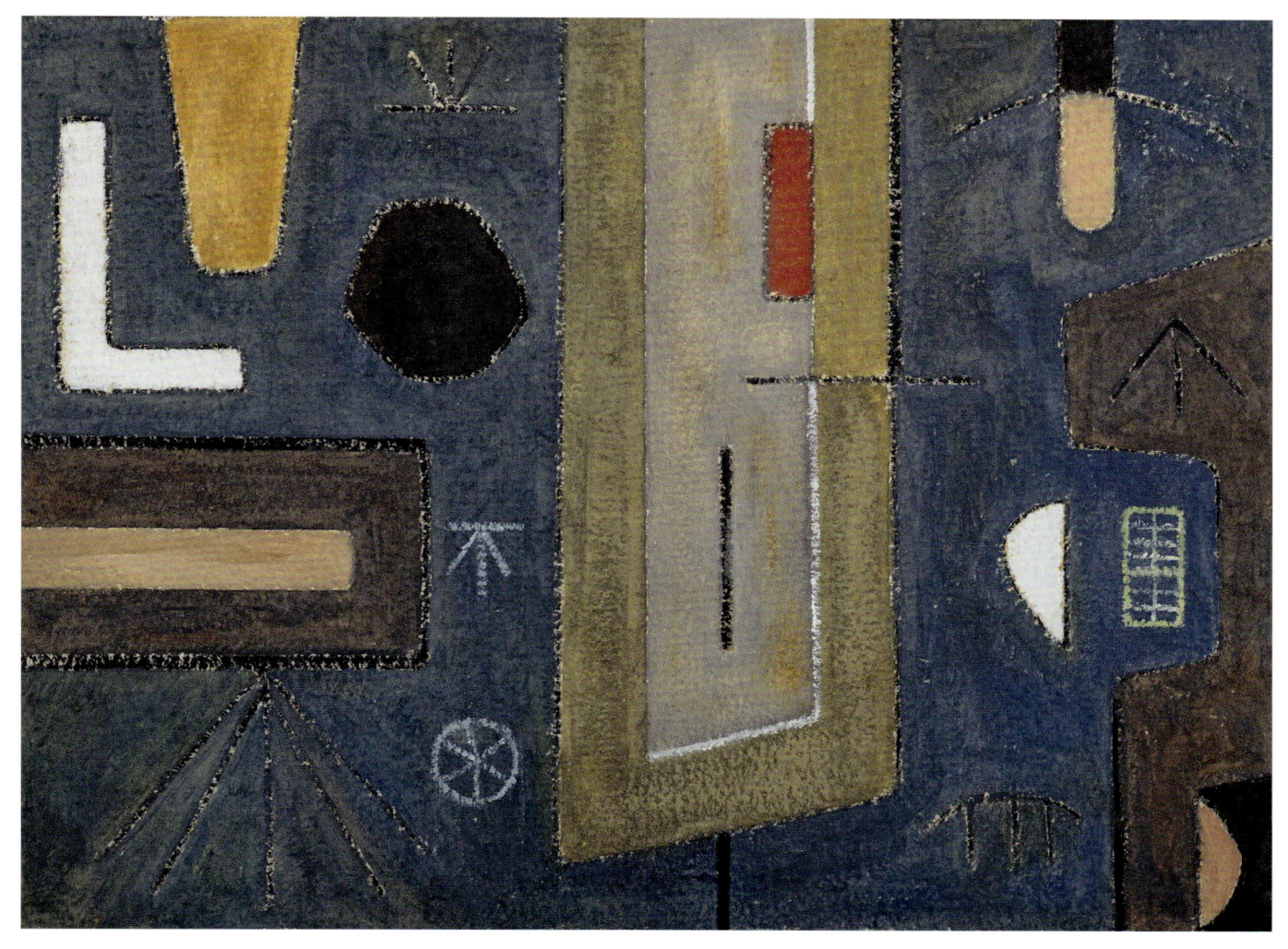

Geraldo de Barros

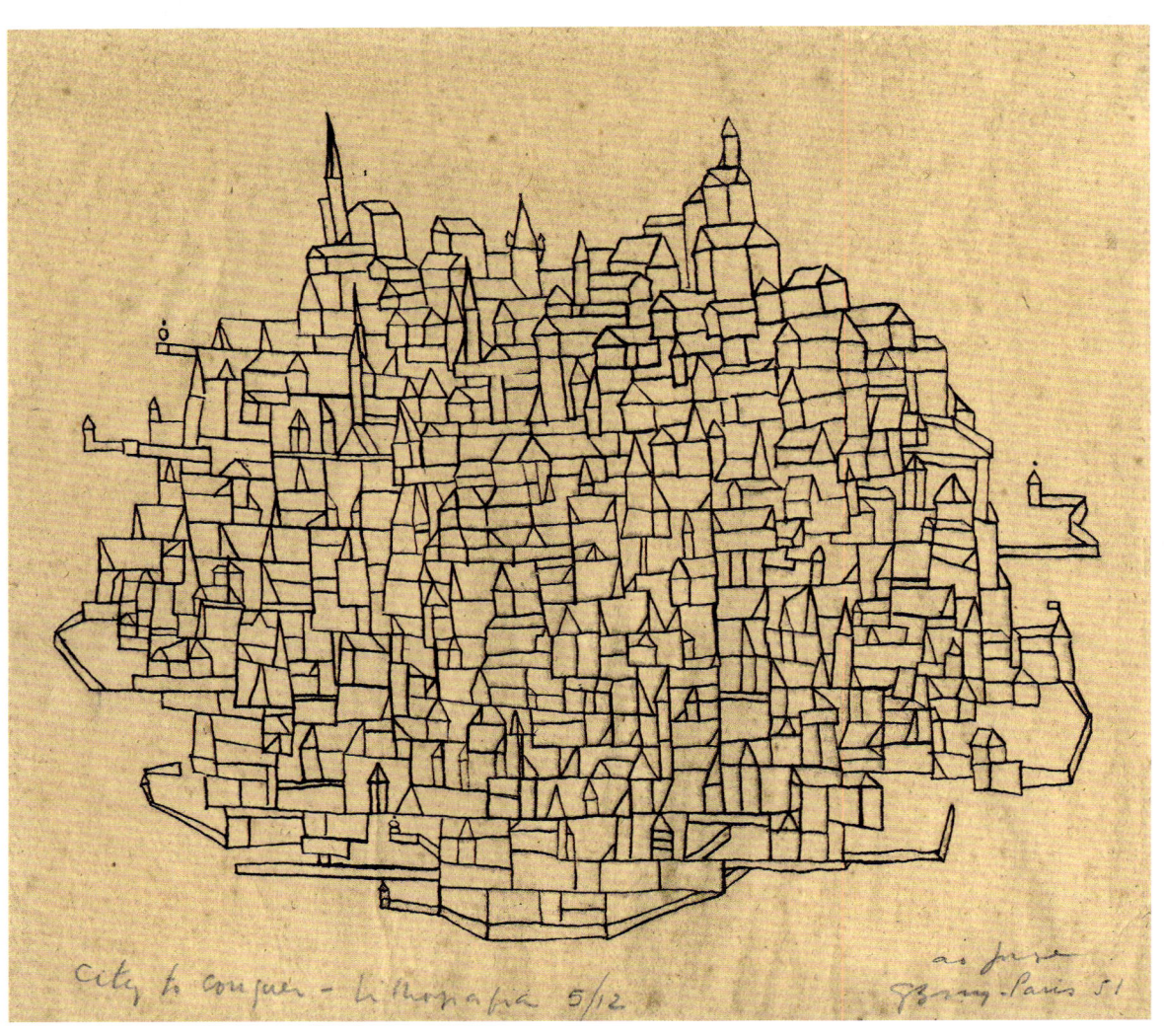

A City to Conquer, 1951

Vista de um porto
(Port View), 1951

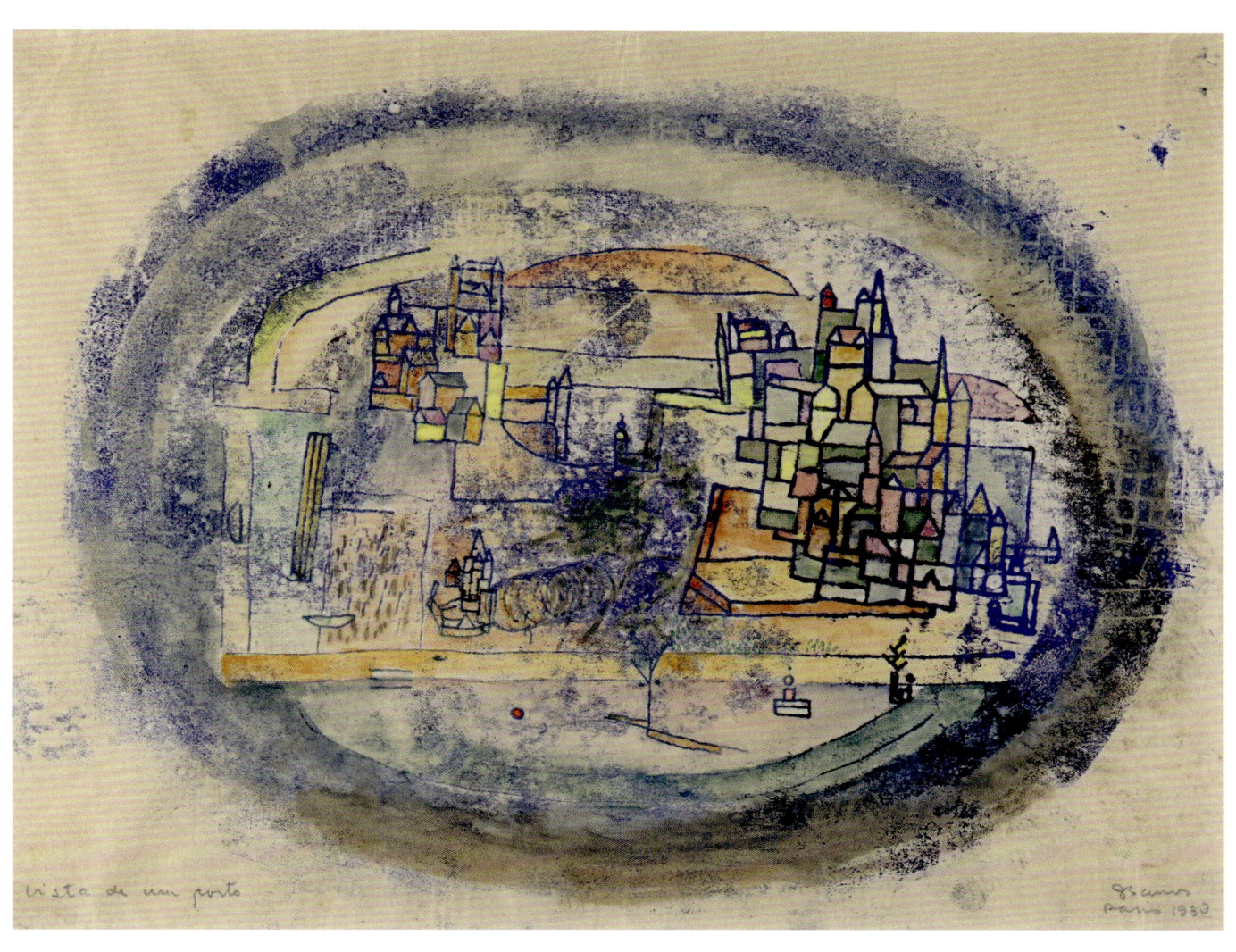

vista de um porto

Geraldo de Barros

Untitled, 1950

Untitled, 1951

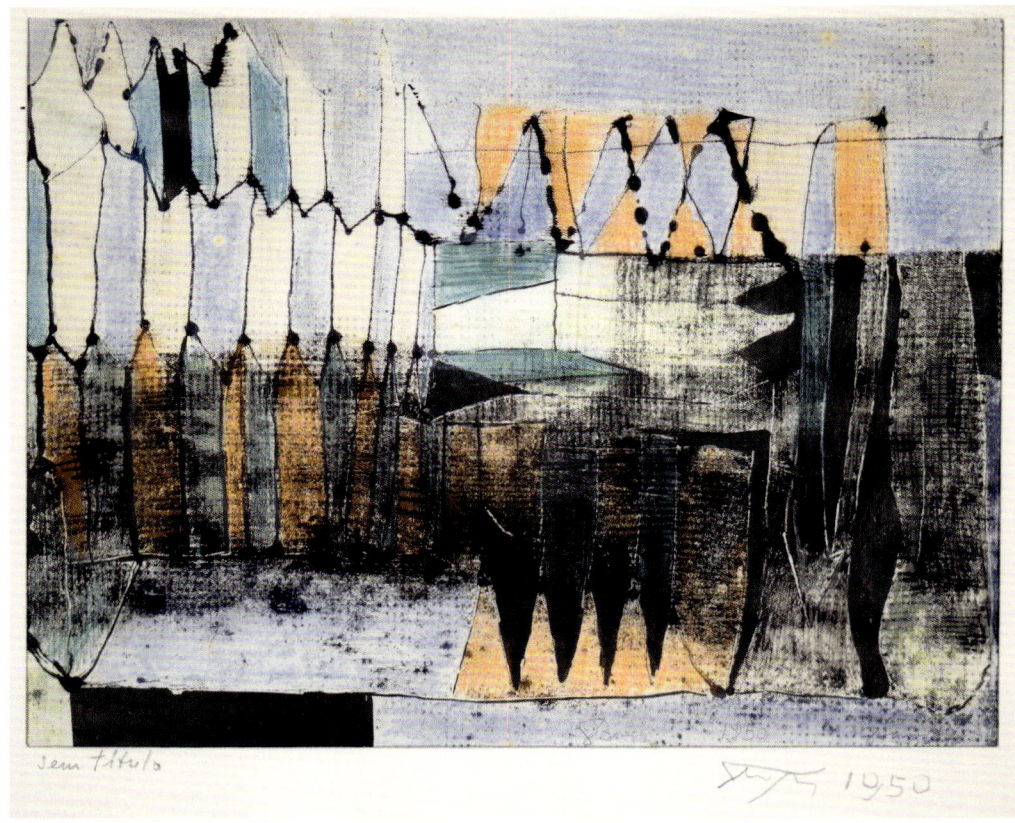

Brasil! Brasil!

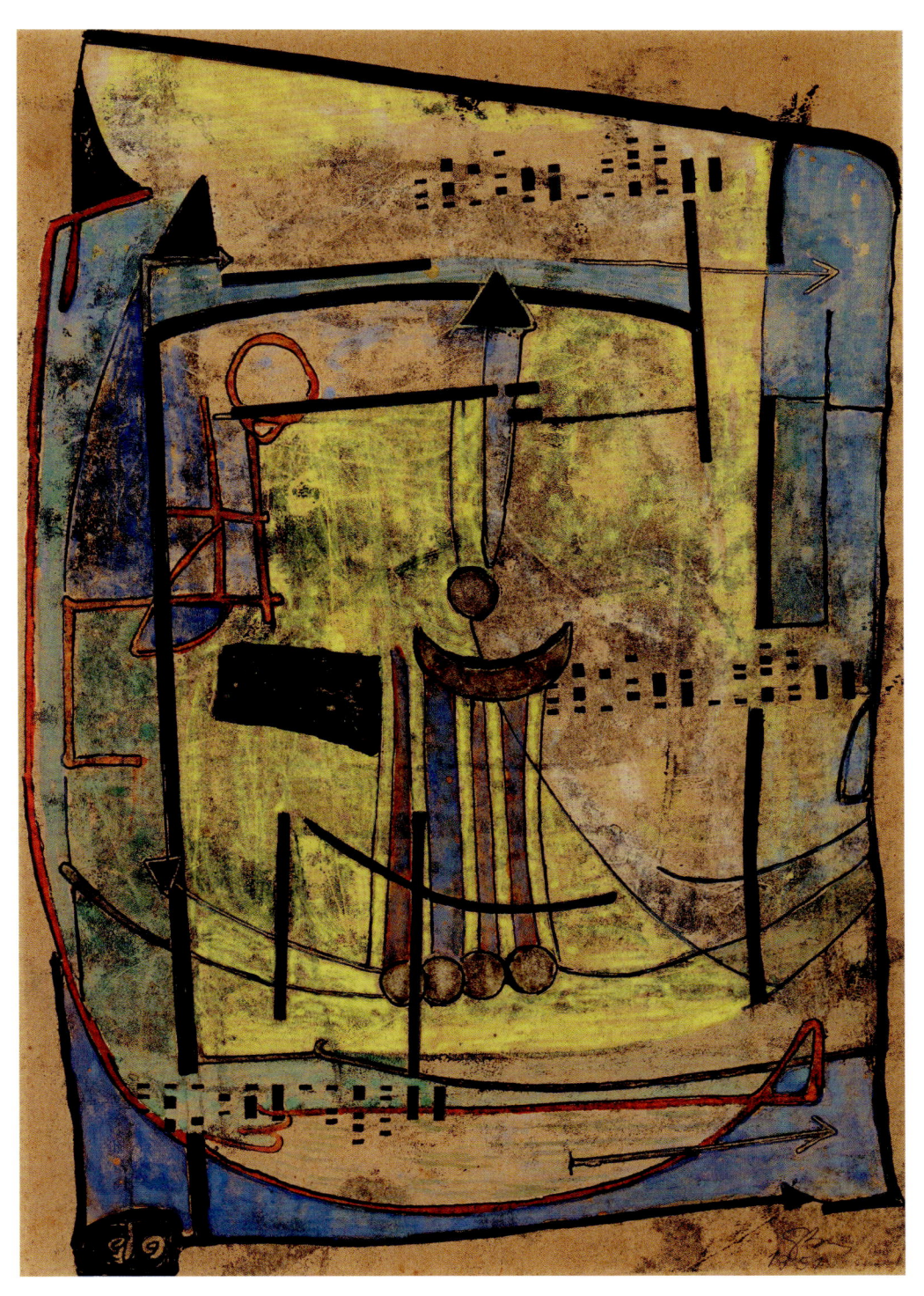

215   **Geraldo de Barros**

Máscara (Mask), 1950

Untitled, 1948/2014

**Homenagem a Paul Klee
(Homage to Paul Klee), Tatuapé,
São Paulo SP**, 1949 /2014

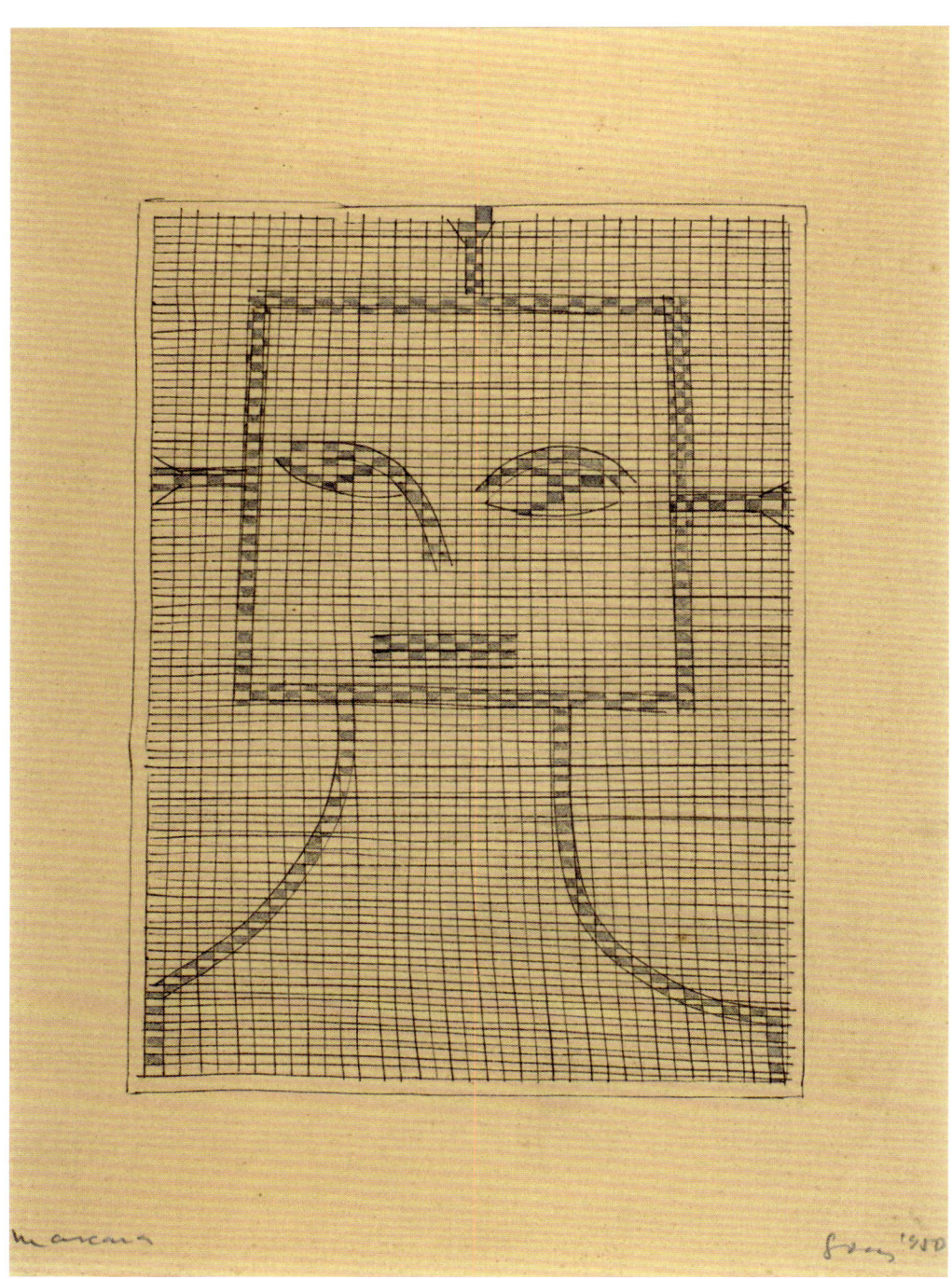

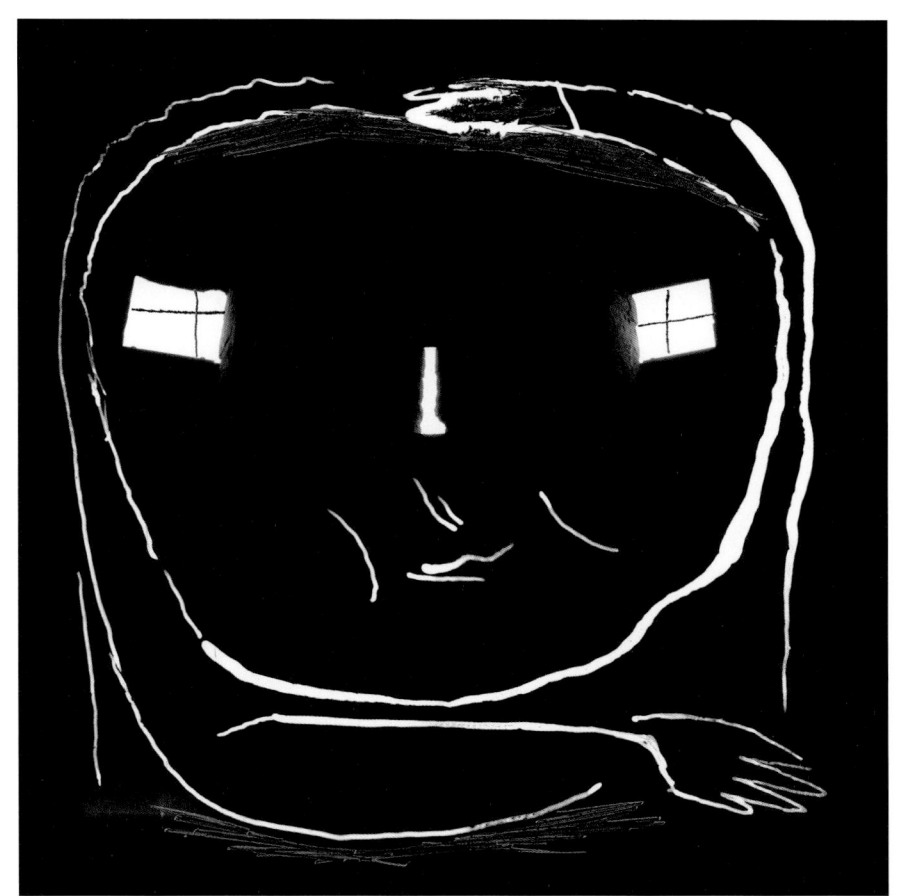

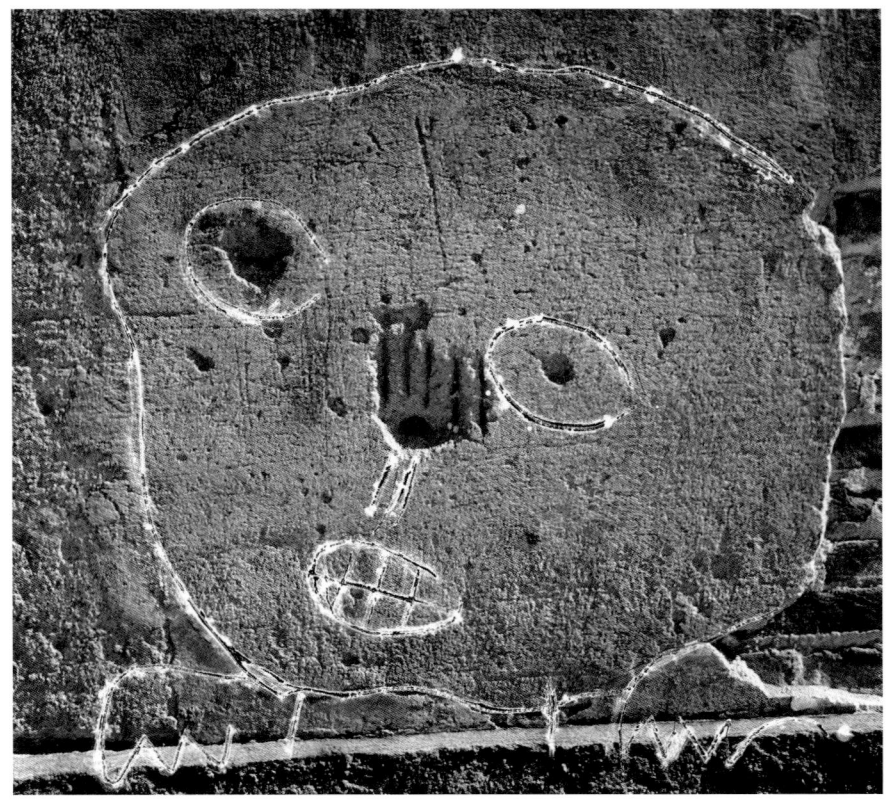

217   **Geraldo de Barros**

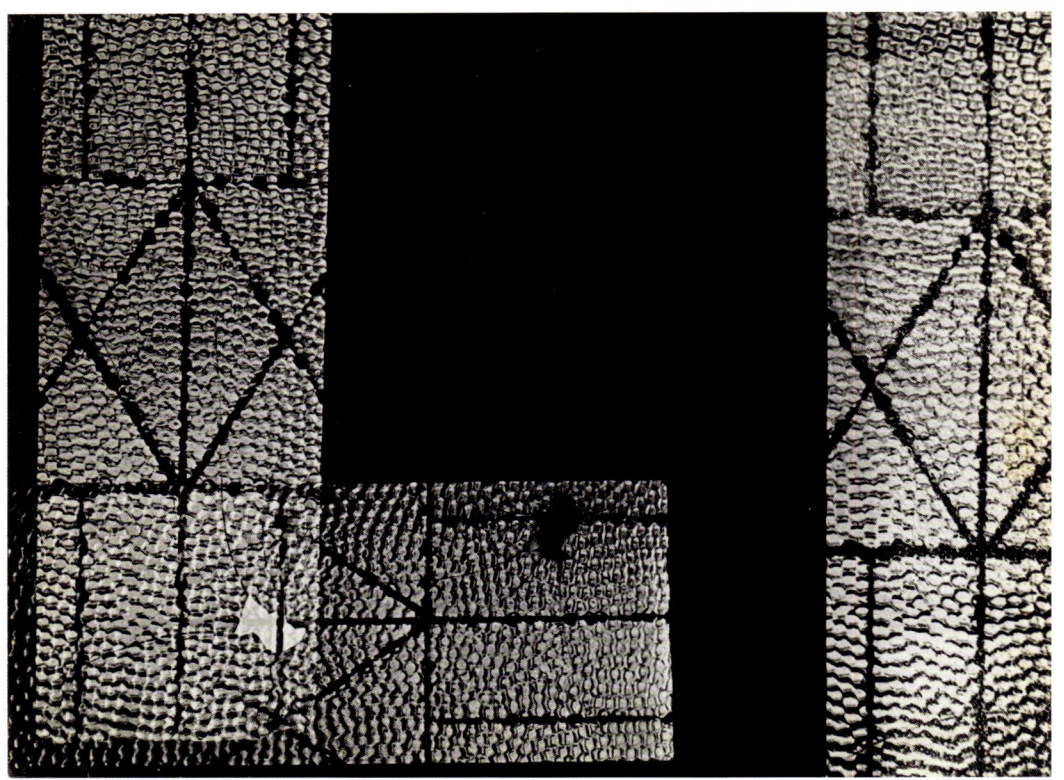

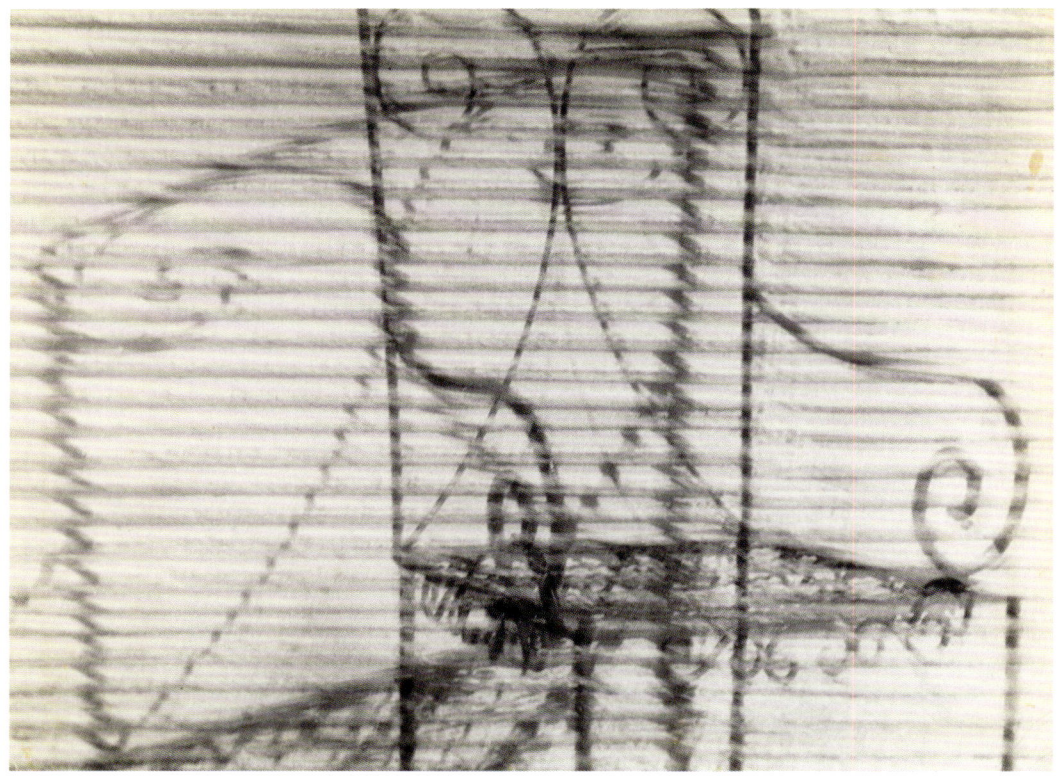

Abstração (São Paulo)
(Abstraction, São Paulo), 1949

Untitled (São Paulo)
Composição II
(Composition II), 1949

Untitled, Pampulha, Belo
Horizonte, 1951/2008

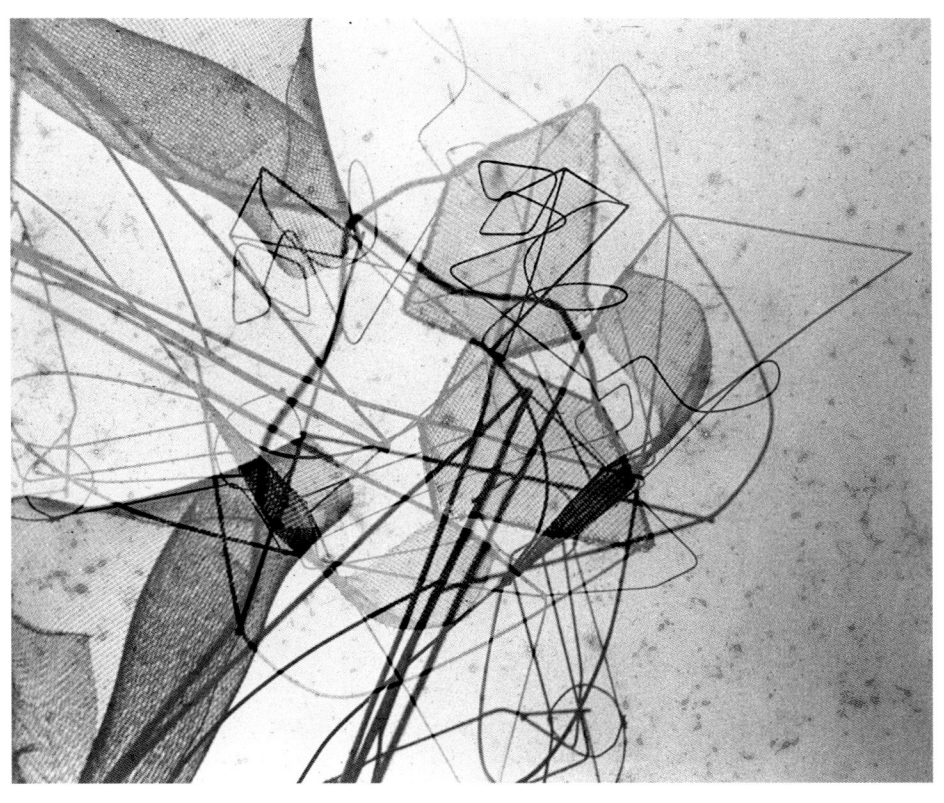

Geraldo de Barros

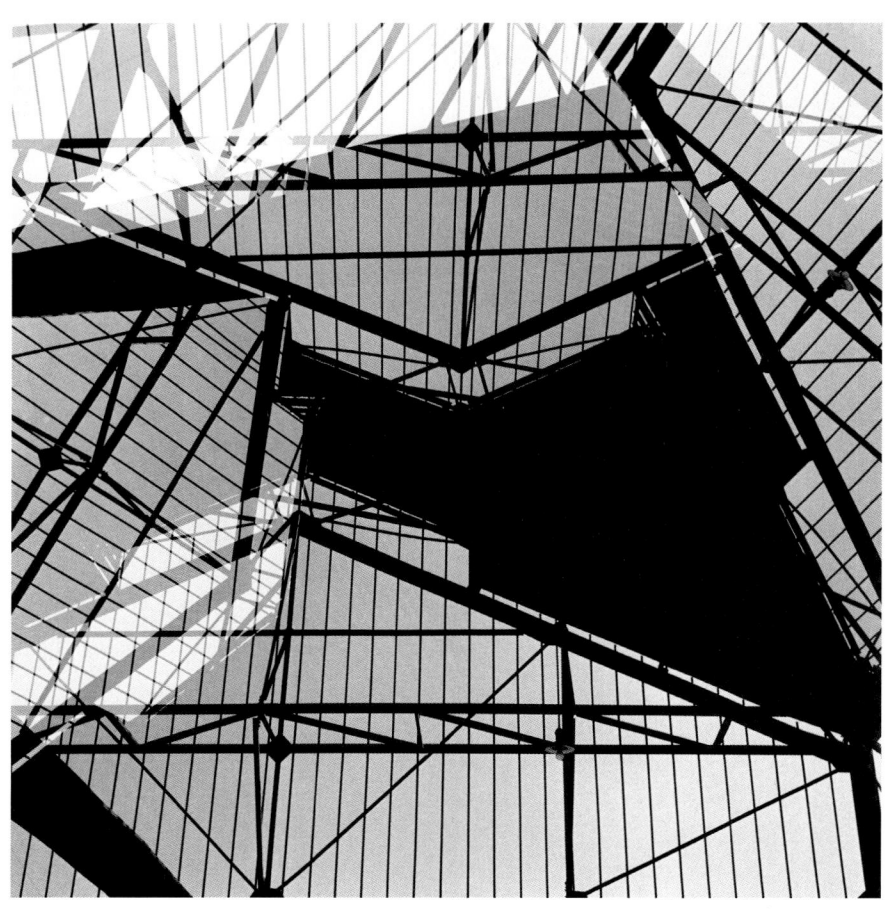

Abstrato, da série Fotoforma,
estação da Luz, São Paulo
(Abstract, from the
Fotoforma series, Estação da
Luz, São Paulo), 1949/2014

Fotoforma, 1952–1953/2014

Fotoforma, 1952–1953/2014

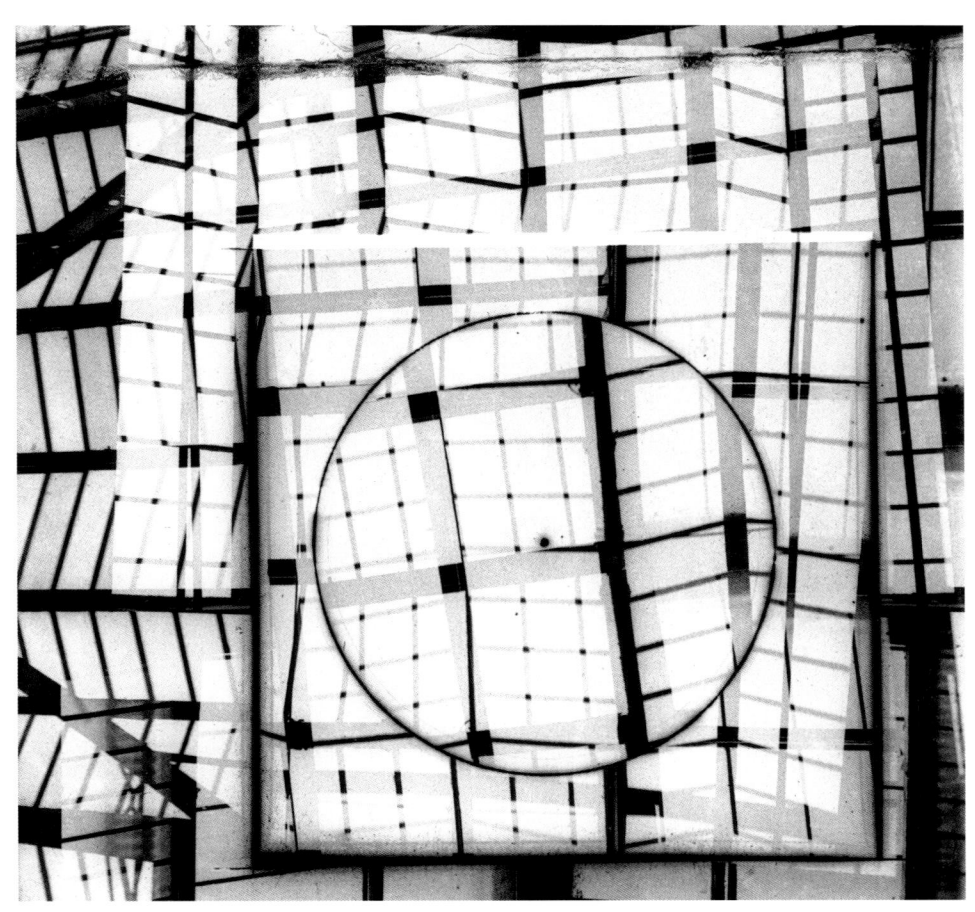

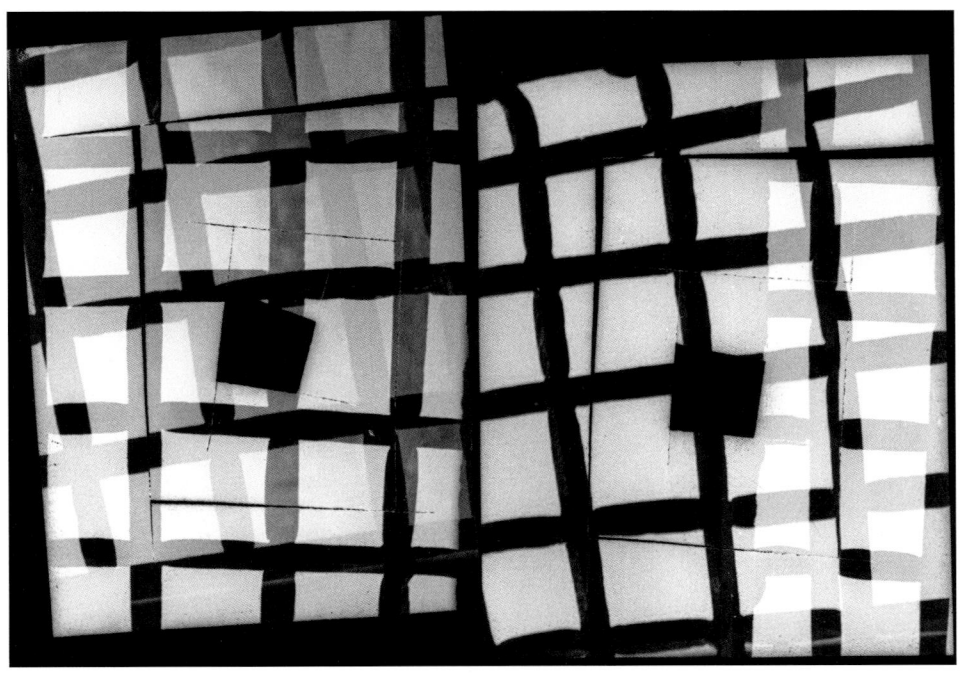

Geraldo de Barros

Fotoforma, 1949/2014

Homenagem a Volpi
(Homage to Volpi), 1983

Brasil! Brasil!

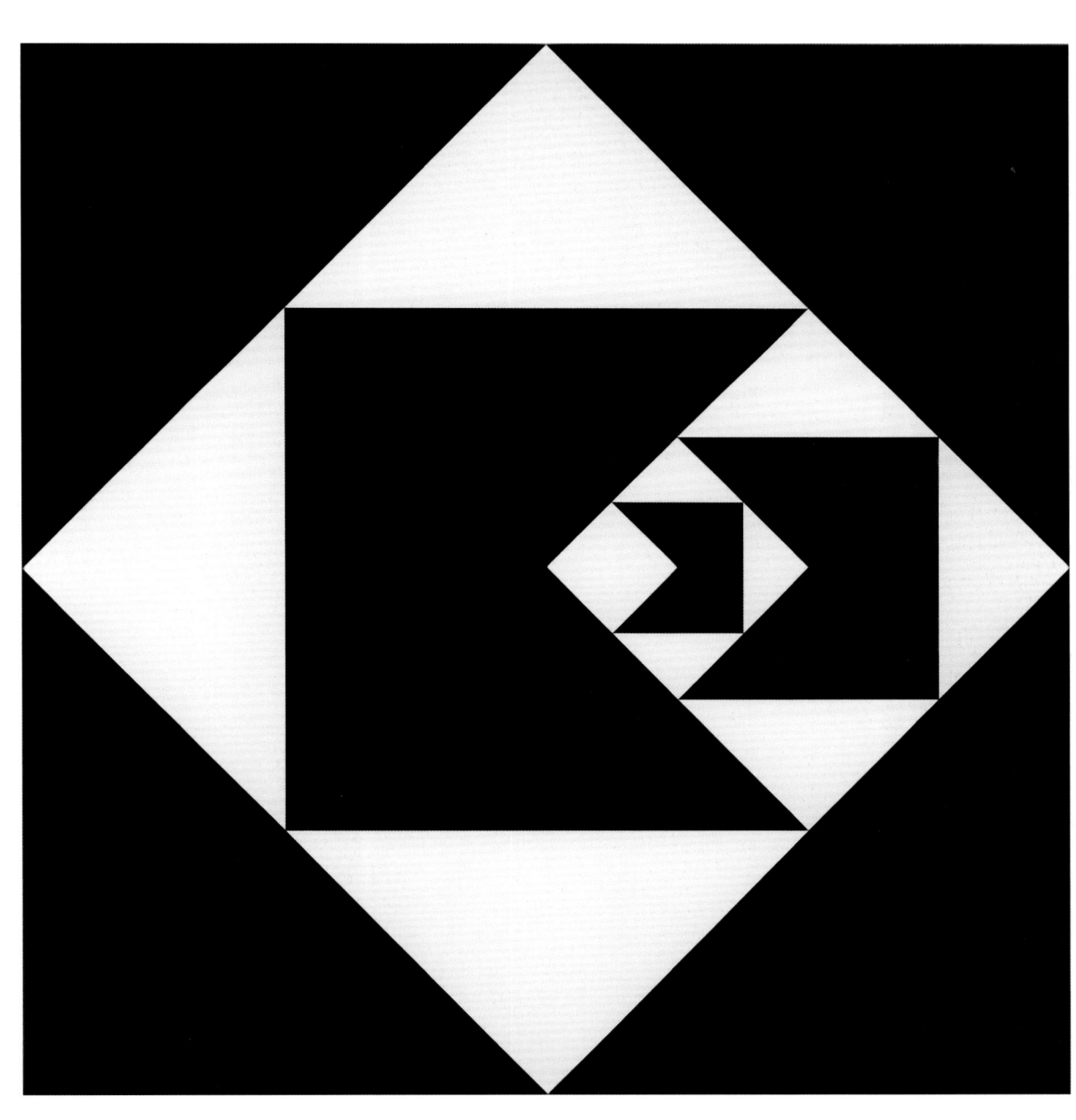

223   **Geraldo de Barros**

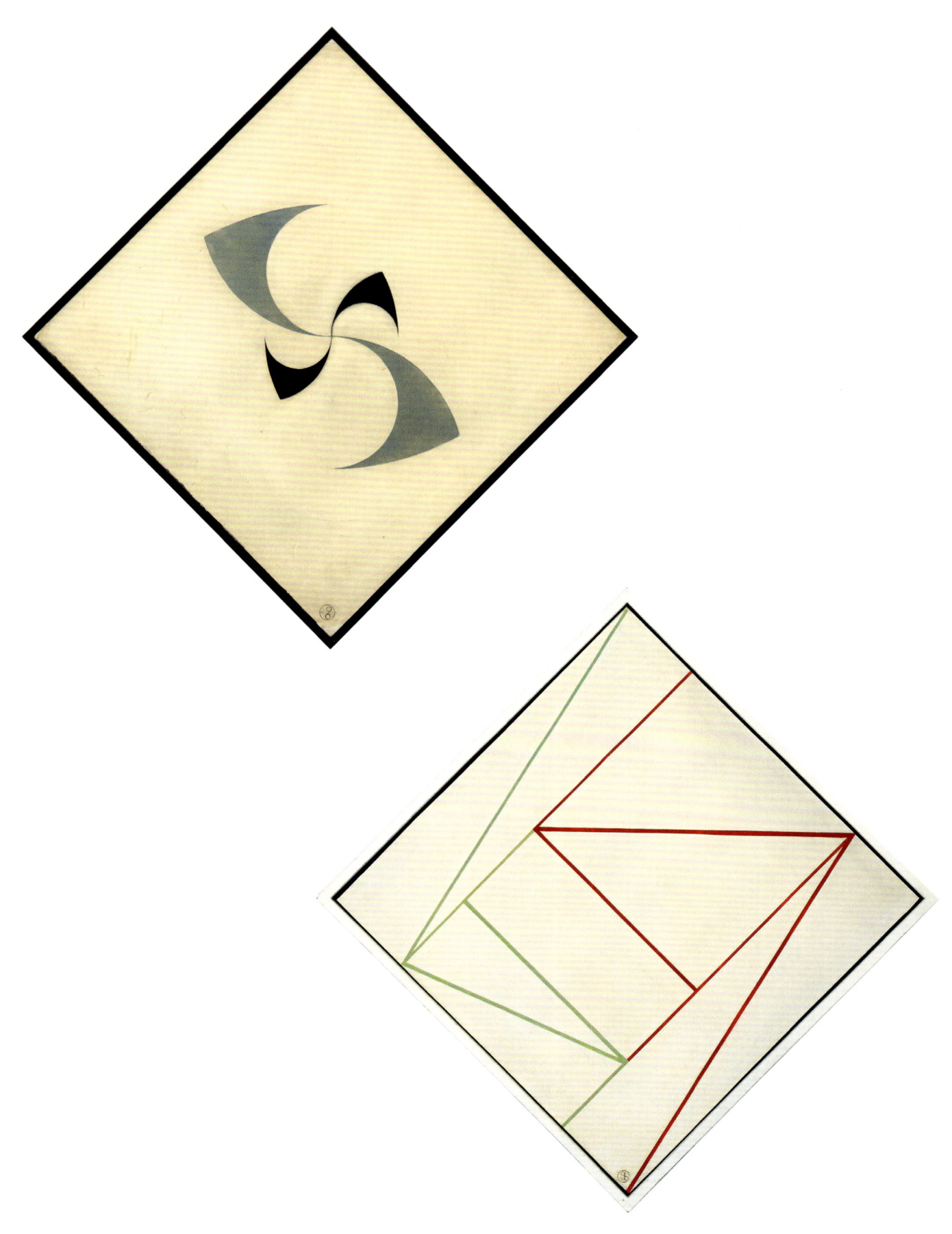

Brasil! Brasil!

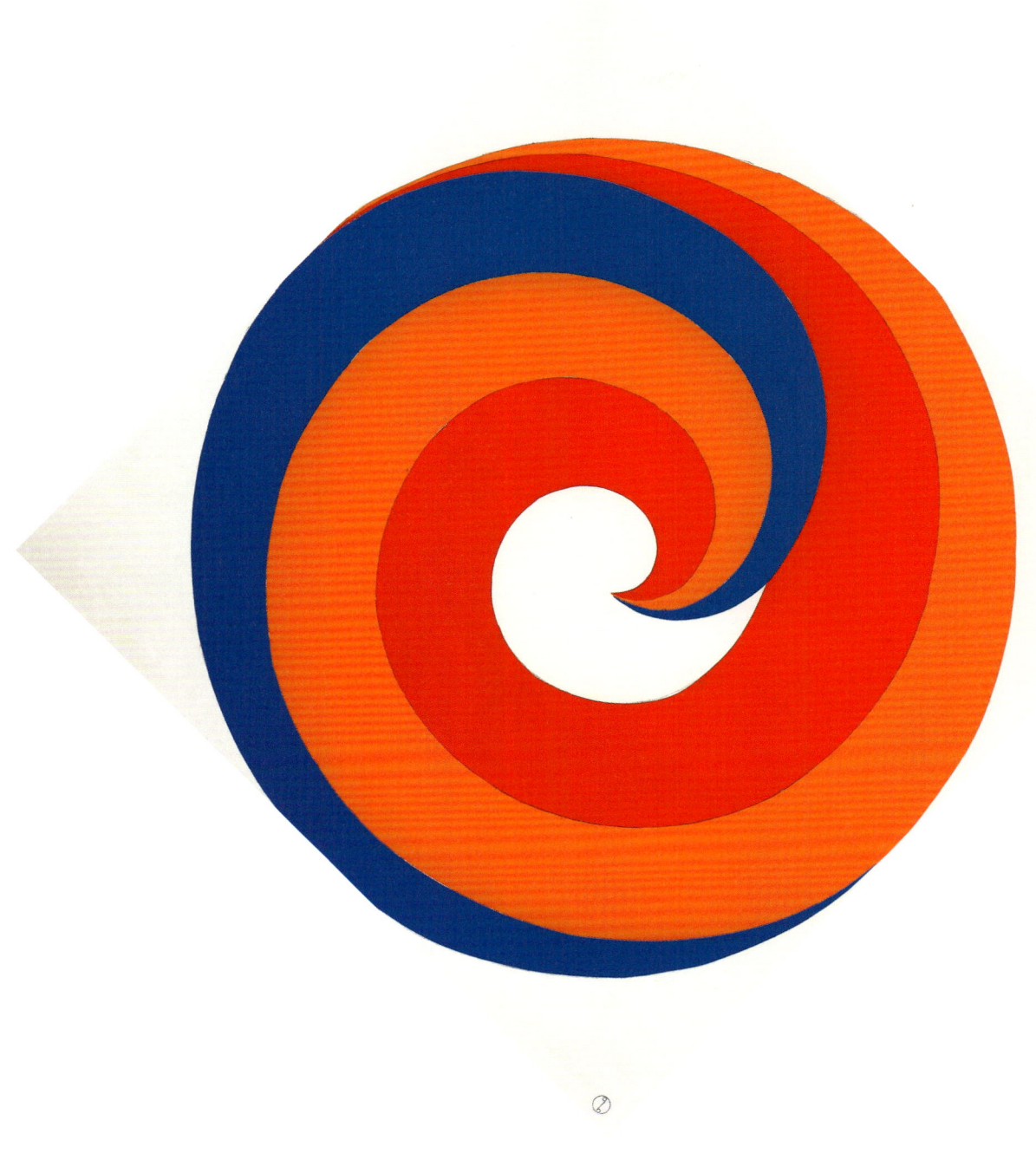

225   **Geraldo de Barros**

Ruben Valentim

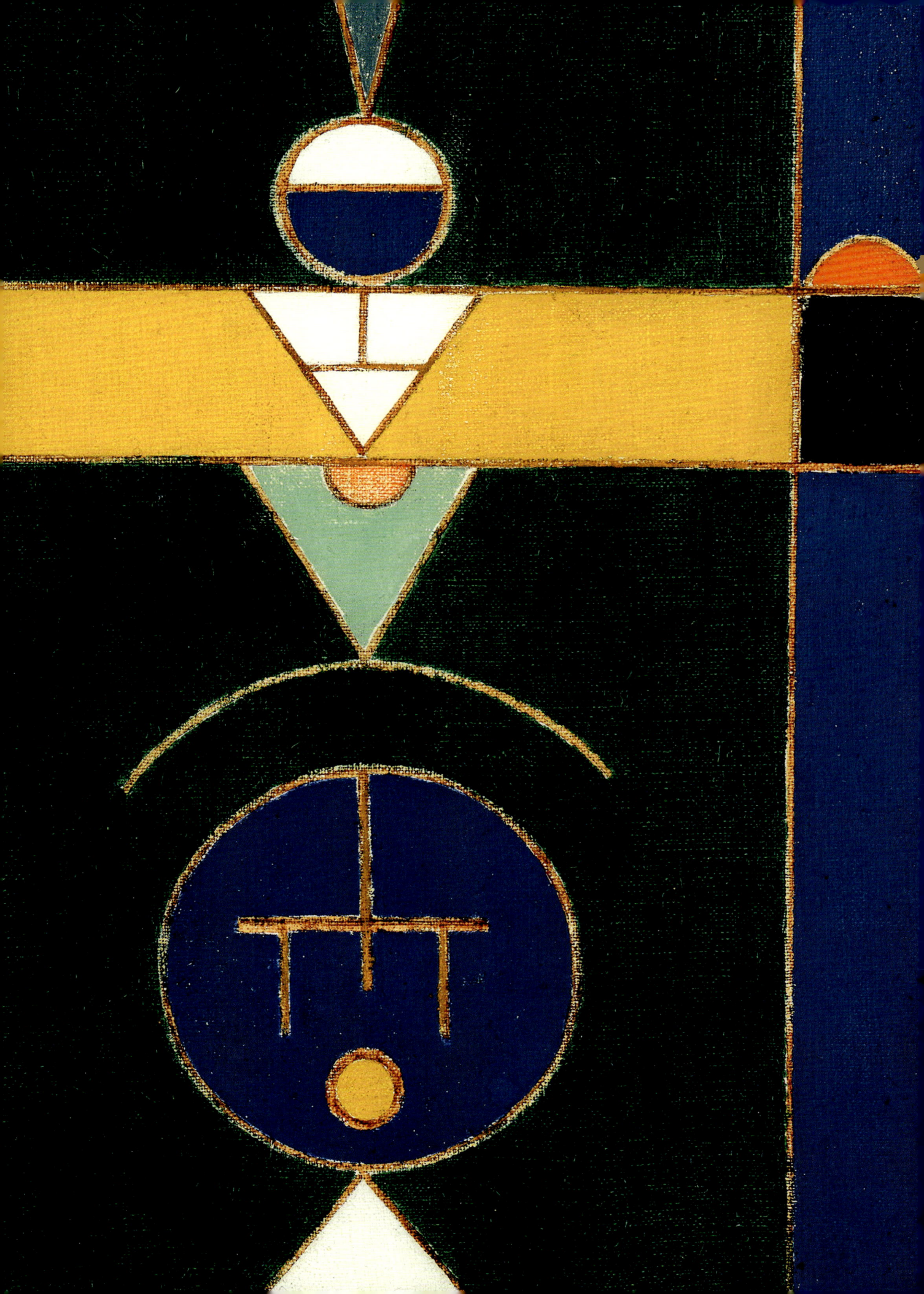

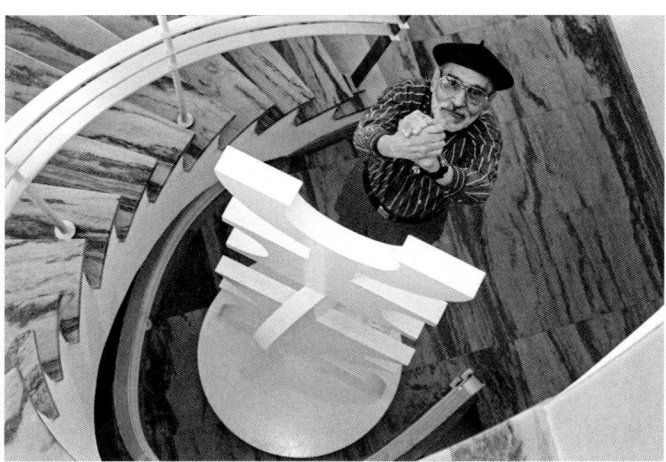

Rubem Valentim
1922, Salvador, Brazil –
1991, São Paulo, Brazil

Born in Salvador, the capital city of the north-eastern state of Bahia, on November 9, 1922, Rubem Valentim was the eldest child of an Afro-Brazilian family of humble origins. Growing up in the 1920s and 1930s in Salvador, a city that for nearly four centuries saw the influx of millions of enslaved African peoples, their myriad cultures, languages, religions, and traditions, and their consequent blending in with Portuguese and Indigenous elements, he was embedded in the magical world of a culture whose veneer was disguised as European, but in essence was in large part Black and African. As a child he helped his mother in the construction of popular nativity scenes and altars made from cardboard. He painted their backgrounds, cut out their figures and glued them onto board, creating a universe rooted in his background's syncretic traditions. His family, despite being Catholic, partook of the religious ceremonies of Candomblé, a typically Brazilian organisation of faith in which the pantheon and practices of afro-Brazilian diasporic religions are commingled with those of European Catholicism. Ferros de santo, religious artifacts that identify specific orishas made by authorised blacksmiths in the Candomblé tradition, and other Afro-Brazilian forms of material culture would be as influential to him in the development of his artistic language as the saints and altarpieces of the many Baroque churches that dot Salvador's panorama, not to mention the concrete investigations taking place in Brazil in the 1950s. He would also be deeply influenced by painter-decorator and popular artist Arthur Come-Só, Valentim's first initiator into the more formal world of artistic production, who taught him the basic techniques of painting. These formative experiences forged his sensibilities, taking the free-flowing magical world of syncretism and the universe of popular art as starting points to the development of a clean-cut lexicon of rigid geometric forms derived from the visual signs and emblems of Candomblé. He thus managed to create an original formal language, as rational as it is metaphysical, in which strong colours and manipulated forms attain a level of spiritual elevation entirely absent from the work of his contemporaries. A profoundly religious man who termed himself an "artist-priest"[1], his making of paintings, sculptures, and reliefs was the way through which his spirituality was transmuted into form, as he said, "There is no salvation outside of making."[2]

Brasil! Brasil!

As a child, Valentim studied at the Ginásio da Bahia, working diverse jobs from an early age to help his family. He would eventually study dentistry at the Universidade da Bahia, graduating in 1946. He worked for two years as a dentist before deciding, in 1948, and against his family's wishes, to devote himself solely to painting. An exhibition of reproductions of national and international modernist art held in Salvador's public library in the same year would open a world of possibilities to the artist. "I went to see it several times, dazzled, lost, shocked, by that fantastic world that was so new to me."[3] Amongst the artists of the exhibition were Paul Cézanne, a particular revelation to Valentim, who attributed his sense of composition to the Mont Sainte-Victoire painter, and Paul Klee, an important influence on him (fig. 1). "Through Klee I understood the freedom of visual expression and the fundamental value of the creative imagination."[4] He would also come in contact with a group of artists and intellectuals active in Salvador engaged in the updating of artistic production in Bahia, a place where the modernist artistic propositions of the south-east of Brazil of the past three decades knew little diffusion or acceptance. Valentim would exhibit his work in the first edition of the Salão Baiano de Belas Artes, in 1949, his inaugural inclusion in an exhibition, and at the 1950 show *Novos artistas baianos*, with one of his paintings reproduced in the exhibition's catalogue.

The oil *Casal popular* (fig. 2) of 1949 is an example of Valentim's early work. In it we find the depiction of the material culture of Bahia in a formal language influenced by Cézanne and Gauguin, as well as a tendency towards abstraction, with which he dabbled at the time, something that did not go down well with his artistic peers, some of whom upheld the Socialist Realism defended by the Communist party. An artistic crisis followed, Valentim destroying his drawings, studies, canvases, and materials in 1951. He would, however, soon be back at the easel, setting up a studio in the attic of the Galeria Oxumaré, an important space for the commercialisation and dissemination of modernist art in Salvador in the 1950s, where he would exhibit his work in the following years. The untitled work of 1953 (fig. p. 235) shows us his consistent efforts in the search for a language all his own, engaging with the many tendencies of abstraction available to him. In 1955 Valentim had his work included in the III Bienal de São Paulo, where he had the opportunity of seeing first-hand the work of Fernand Léger and Sophie Taeuber-Arp, artists who would give him clues on how to develop his investigations into abstraction. *Composição 3*, of 1955 (fig. p. 237), clearly reveals these influences.

Fig. 1
Rubem Valentim, Untitled, 1956, oil on chipboard, 24 × 35 cm, Private collection

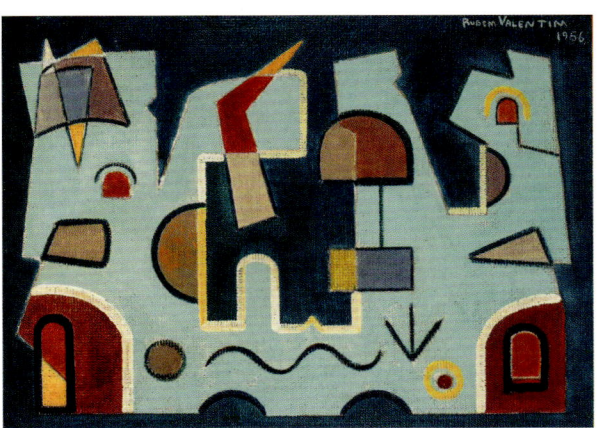

Rubem Valentim

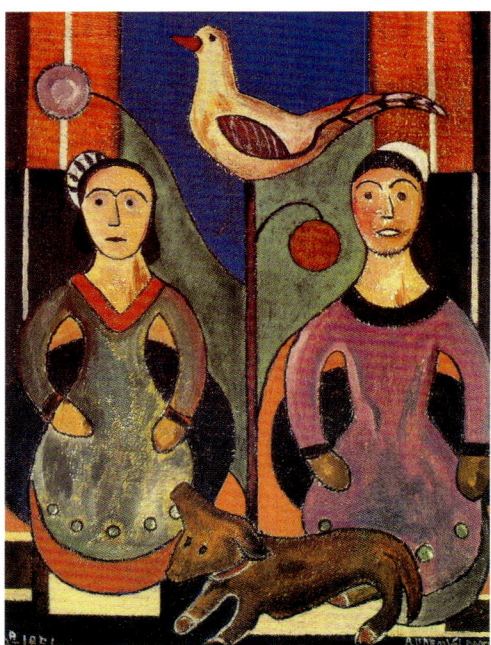

Fig. 2
Rubem Valentim, *Casal popular* (Traditional Couple), 1949, oil on canvas, 66 × 51cm, Private collection

In late 1957, following the production of his painting of 1956 (fig.1), where we see the slow synthetisation of his forms into the world of quasi-emblems, he decided to move to Rio de Janeiro, where he would live until 1963.

In the couple of years before his installation in Rio de Janeiro Valentim had been experimenting with the use of symbols and emblems of the deities of Candomblé, such as Xangô and his identifying double-edge axe, and Exu's trident. An example of this is the unfinished work of 1956 (fig. 3) in which we can see these investigations in embryonic form. Taken from their sacred contexts, they were translated, in his hands, into geometric forms. Manipulated and set down on canvas, they become sophisticated colouristic inventions of formal organisations of geometry. They are syncretic formal inventions that cannot be reduced to either the world of Concrete Art, or to the animistic universe of Candomblé, being something altogether different. Intimately enmeshed with the specificities of the space in which it was created, Valentim's work, however, did not isolate itself, nor did it ignore what was happening in the wider world. The artist himself would describe this process in his manifesto of faith and artistic beliefs *Manifesto ainda que tardio* of 1976. "Intuiting that my path lay between the popular and the erudite, the premordial and the refinement (...) I started to look at the symbolic implements, the tools of Candomblé, the *abebês*, the *paxorós*, the *oxés*, and saw therein a type of 'speech', a Brazilian visual poetic capable of properly configuring and synthesizing the entire core of my interest as an artist. What I wanted and continue to want is to establish a design (which I call RISCADURA BRASILEIRA (Brazilian tracing)), a structure capable of revealing our reality, or mine, at least, in terms of a sensitive order."[5] At times, his Brazilian tracing inventions can be reduced to their most basic elements, such as in *Composição* (fig. p. 245), likely due to his contact with artists working with concrete ideals, testimony to his engagement with contemporary artistic developments. Valentim was never part of their artistic consociation, however, keeping himself, like Volpi before him, at a distance from such consortiums.

During his years in Rio de Janeiro Valentim gained the acceptance of a variety of critics who celebrated the vitality of his work, even though a great many of them placed him in simplistic categories such as primitive and naive, thus limiting the extent of his expressive capabilities. He exhibited widely and taught art history at the Instituto de Belas Artes, the institutional heir to the Escola Nacional de Belas Artes. He also met Lúcia Alencastro, an art educator whom he would marry in March 1961 and who would play a major role in the development of his life and work. He held an exhibition at the Petite Galerie in the same year, his first solo show, for which the poet Ferreira Gullar wrote the introductory essay, in which we read, Valentim "is not a naive artist, from whose brush popular imagination flows spontaneously. On the contrary, his art feeds off a basic contradiction, expressed in each and every detail of his paintings: he is an artist who rationally constructs his work from magical elements (...); impregnated with the popular experience that is at the base of his cultural formation, he seeks the most elaborate and exact way to express it. But it is from this game of opposites that results the vitality of his art"[6]. Two untitled paintings from 1962 produced during his time in Rio show us what these precious, contradictory constructions were like (figs pp. 241 and 243). After having been awarded the travel grant at the XI Salão de Arte Moderna in 1962 and being included in the Brazilian representation at the XXXI Biennale di Venezia in the same year, Rubem Valentim moved to Europe in 1963. He would spend some time in London, but eventually moved to Rome, where he would live for the following two years, not without first visiting France, Holland, Belgium, Germany, Austria, Spain, and Portugal.

Once in Rome Valentim rapidly integrated into the local artistic circuit, exhibiting his work in the Palazzo Doria Pamphili, headquarters of the Brazilian Embassy in Rome. It was during the exhibition that he met the Italian art historian Giulio Carlo Argan, who, enchanted by his work, wrote a remarkably precise essay dealing with Valentim's artistic method. "The artist elaborates them (symbols and emblems) until the threatening obscurity of the fetish is made clear in the candid form of myth. He decomposes and geometrises them, tears them from their original iconographic seed; then reorganises them according to rigorous symmetries, reducing them to the essentiality of a primary geometry, made of verticals, horizontals, triangles, circles, squares, rectangles."[7] During this time his paintings gradually became more complex, incorporating a wide variety of emblems which are given, during this phase, an earthy naturalness due to his use of egg tempera, such as in *Composição Bahia 1* (fig. 4) from 1966. It was also in Rome that Valentim forged bonds of friendship and artistic collaboration with the African continent, particularly Senegal, where he took part in the inaugural edition of the World Festival of

Fig. 3
Rubem Valentim, Untitled, (unfinished), 1956, oil on canvas, 70 × 50 cm, Private collection

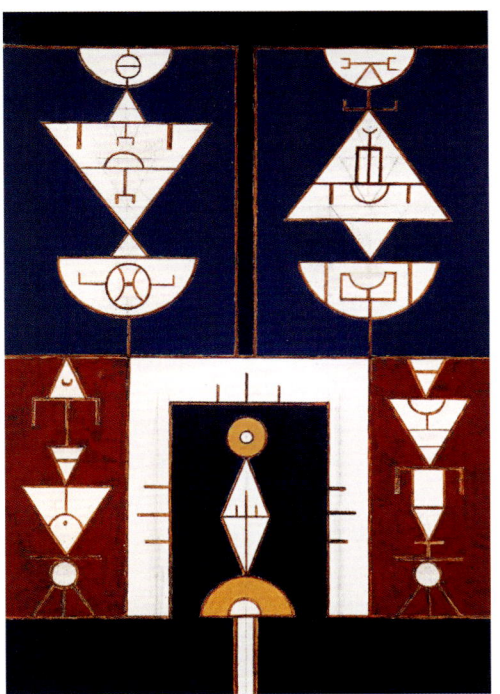

Rubem Valentim

Black Arts held in Dakar in 1966. He would return to Brazil later in the year, establishing himself at first in Rio de Janeiro. A year later he moved to the nation's new capital, Brasília.

Once in Brasília he started teaching painting at the Instituto Central de Arte da Universidade de Brasília. Working in a state university was no easy task during the leaden years of the Brazilian Military Dictatorship, one which amply used repressive censorship methods alongside arbitrary imprisonments and torture as a means of obtaining information and silencing any and all opposition. He gradually shied away from the post, eventually abandoning it altogether, but he remained in Brasília. The city, still a building site of concrete and red earth despite its official inauguration in 1960, afforded him not only the meditative beauty of its ample horizons and the vast wilderness of the Cerrado region, but also the opportunity, due to its colossal scale, to work in larger dimensions, taking the omnipresent, monumental quality of his work to different heights. He began an investigation of three-dimensionality that would lead him to produce a series of friezes, sculptures, and installations, as well as a series of commissions to produce works for public buildings, such as the 120 square meter marble mural enveloping the façade of the headquarters of Novacap. The *Objeto emblemático 1*, of 1969 (fig. p. 244), is a good example of the paths his works was taking, extracting the symbolic geometric emblems of his paintings, and placing them onto the physical world. They become altars of sorts, quasi-sacred constructions of geometric signs carrying within them the sacredness of their previous meanings. The 1970s would see the final consolidation of his work, Valentim experiencing a certain sense of officialisation of his practice in established artistic circles. Proof of that was his being commissioned to produce a mural for the Brasília headquarters of the Ministry of Foreign Relations in Brazil in 1977, and the production of a concrete sculpture over eight metres in height for São Paulo's Praça da Sé, the *Marco sincrético da cultura afro-brasileira*, installed in 1979 (fig. 5). A symbol of the syncretic qualities of Brazilian culture, it towers over the square that houses the institutionalised monuments of justice and religion, presenting a decided contrast with its celebration of freedom and the power of the comingling of diverse mores and cultures.

Valentim would continue to engage with the three-dimensional in the 1970s and 1980s, yet he never abandoned painting, moving from one to the other to refresh himself from their specificities.

Fig. 4
Rubem Valentim, *Composição Bahia 1* (Composition Bahia 1), 1966, oil on canvas, 100 × 73 cm, Private collection

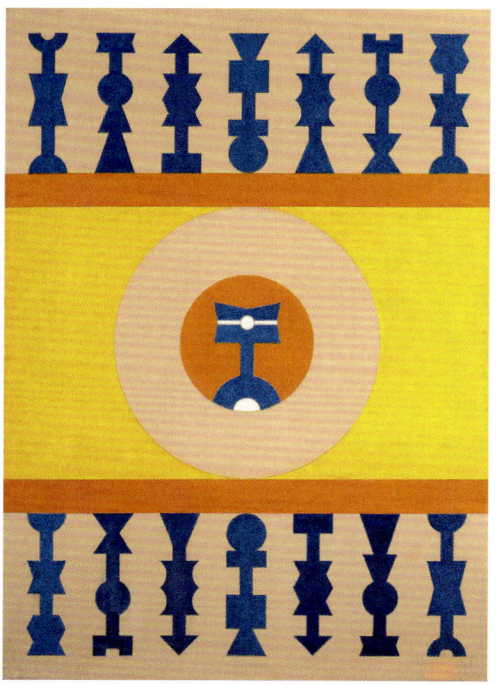

Brasil! Brasil!

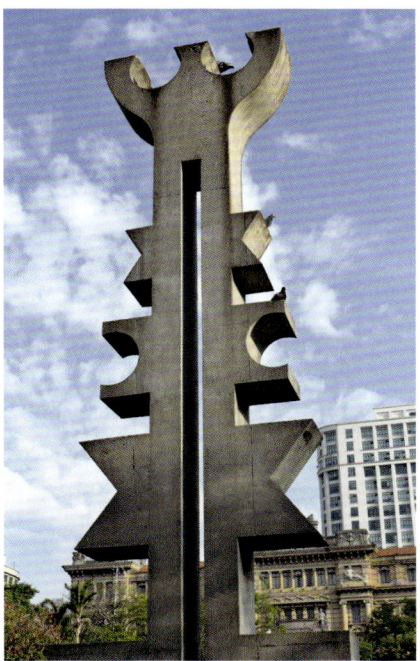

Fig. 5
Rubem Valentim, *Marco sincrético da cultura afro-brasileira* (Syncretic Monument for the Afro-Brazilian Culture), 1979, Praça da Sé, São Paulo

Works such as *Objeto emblemático* and *Conjunto altar sacral emblemático - E59* (figs pp. 242 and 238) are good examples of his later style, synthetic and of a remarkable economy of means, and demonstrate his spatial wisdom and the ingenuity of his constructions. The high point of his work with sculpture is undoubtedly the installation *Templo de Oxalá*, first exhibited at the Bienal de São Paulo in 1977, and once again in 2023, in which Oxalá, supreme deity and creator of mankind in the Candomblé tradition, is honoured by a group of twenty totem-like, all-white constructions, and a blue and white relief. The 1980s saw the artist dividing his time between Brasília and São Paulo, where he set up flat and studio in 1982. In the monastical silence of its interior he lived an austere, meditative lifestyle devoted to the production of his work and the development of his spiritual life. He read books dealing with spirituality and philosophy from which he took the fundamental principles of his artistic production, and listened to Gregorian Chants, Mozart and Bach. He also worked hard at the idea of establishing a space devoted to the study and display of his work. Unfortunately, his plans never got off the ground. He died in São Paulo, on November 30, 1991.

Giancarlo Hannud

1 Apud Fonteles 2022, p. 24, transl. Giancarlo Hannud

2 Apud Fonteles 2022, p. 17, transl. Giancarlo Hannud

3 Valentim 1967, pp. 24–26

4 Valentim 1967, pp. 24–26

5 Apud Fonteles 2022. pp. 80–81. Abebês (fan), paxorós (stick) and oxés (double axe) are objects used in Candomblé ceremonies.

6 Gullar 1961

7 Brasília/Rio de Janeiro 1970, n.p.

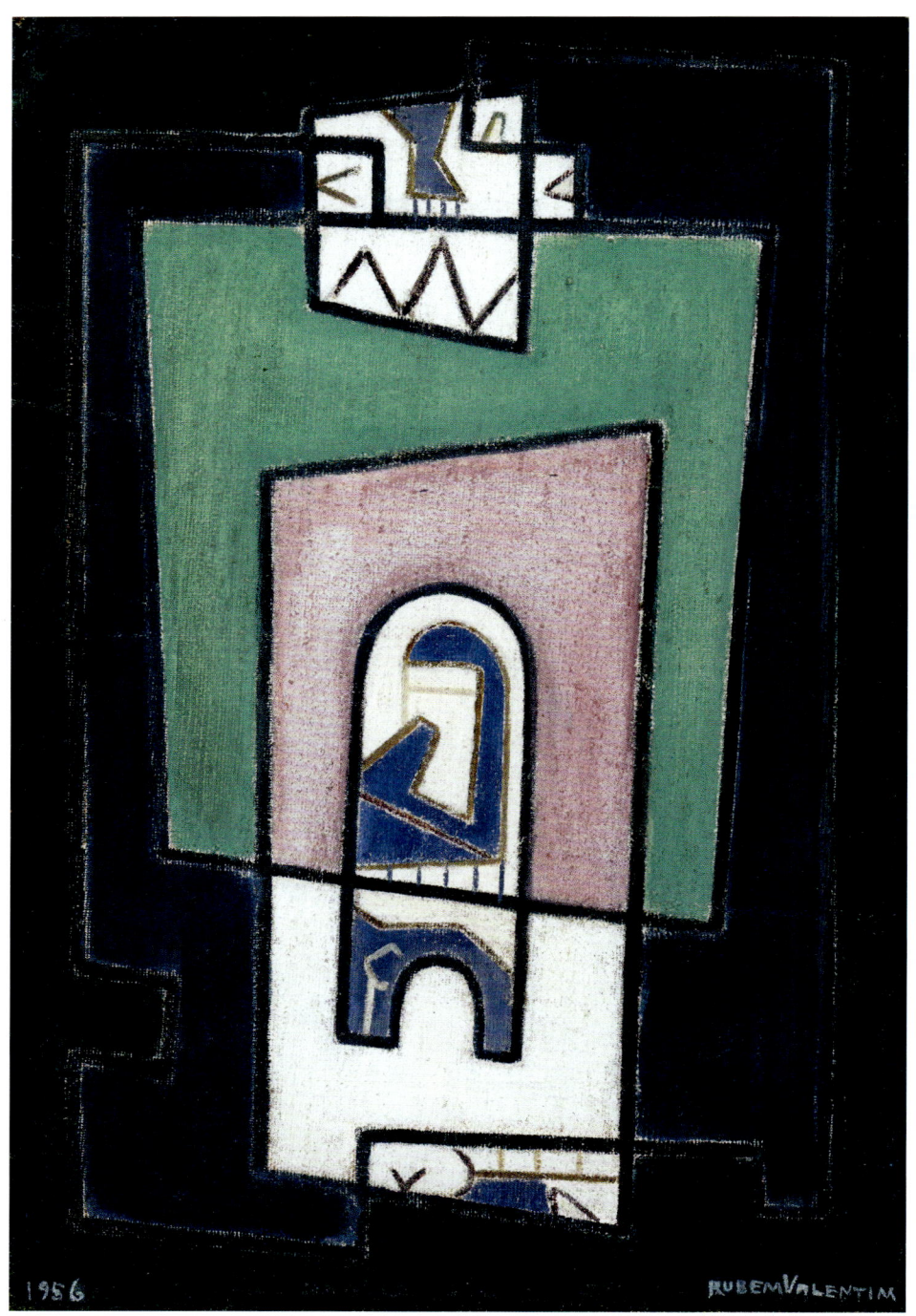

Untitled, 1956

Untitled, 1953

Brasil! Brasil!

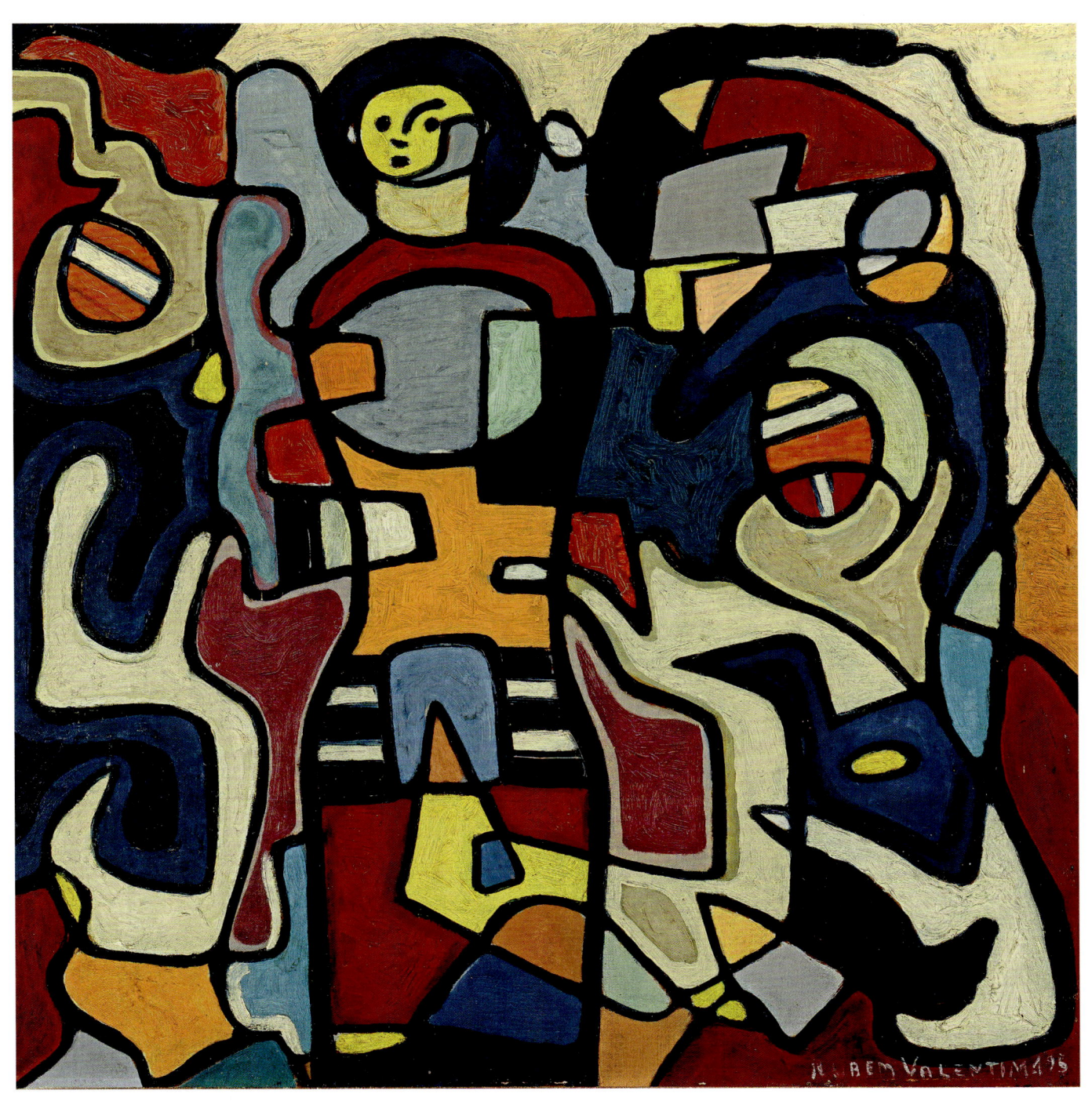

235   **Rubem Valentim**

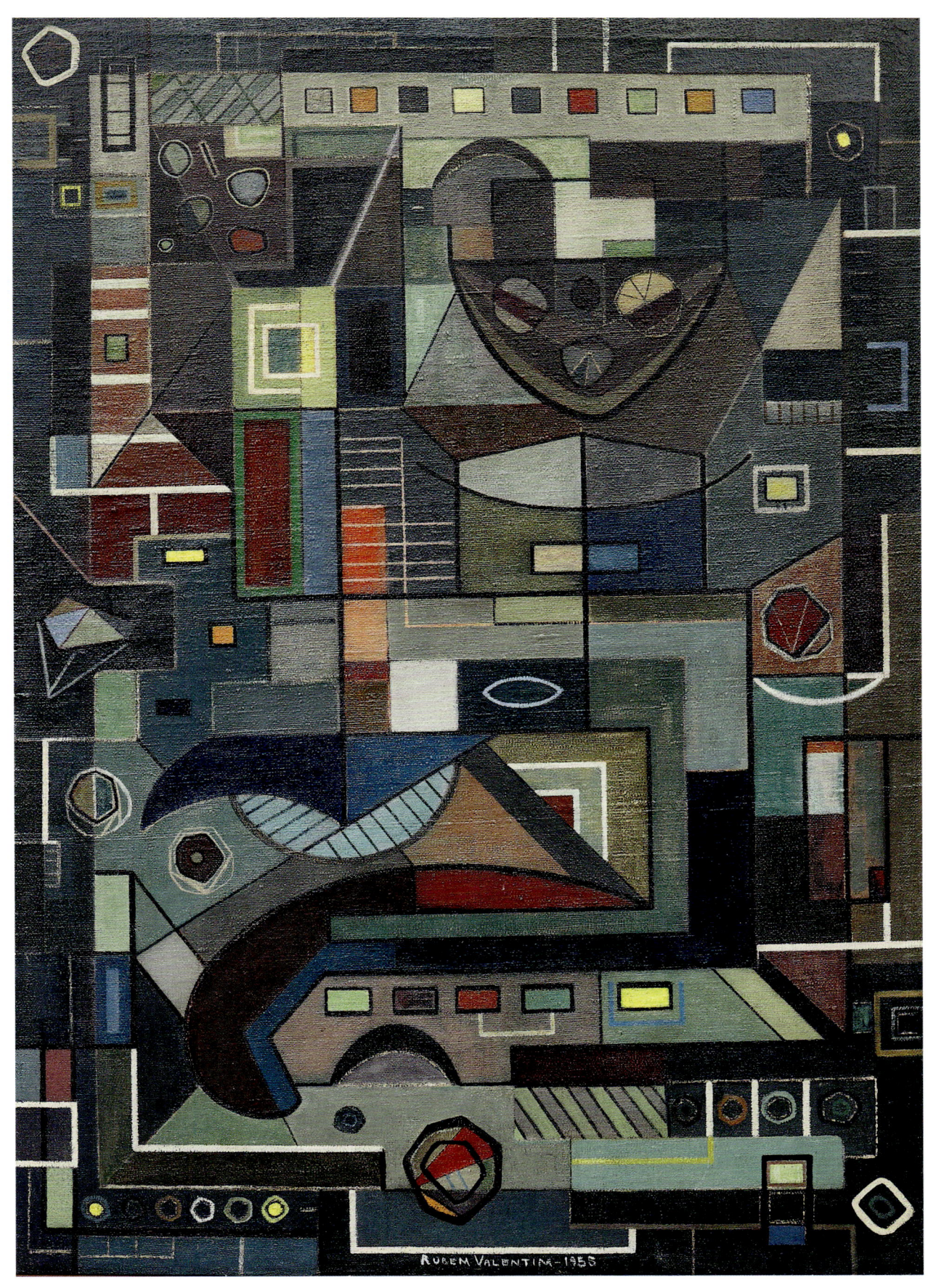

237   **Rubem Valentim**

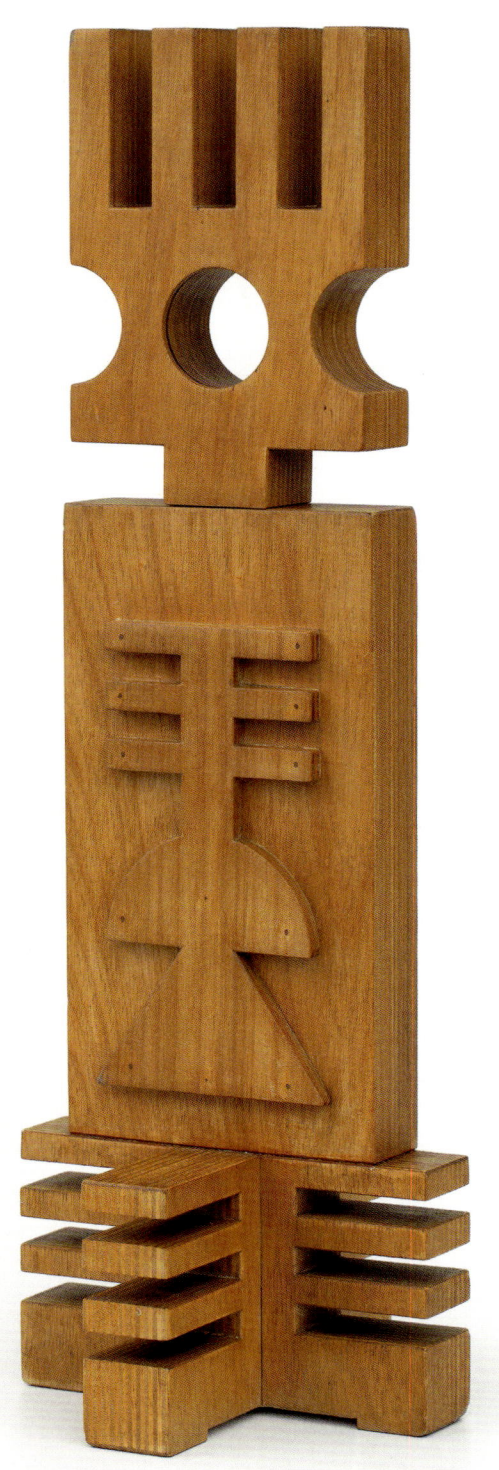

Brasil! Brasil!

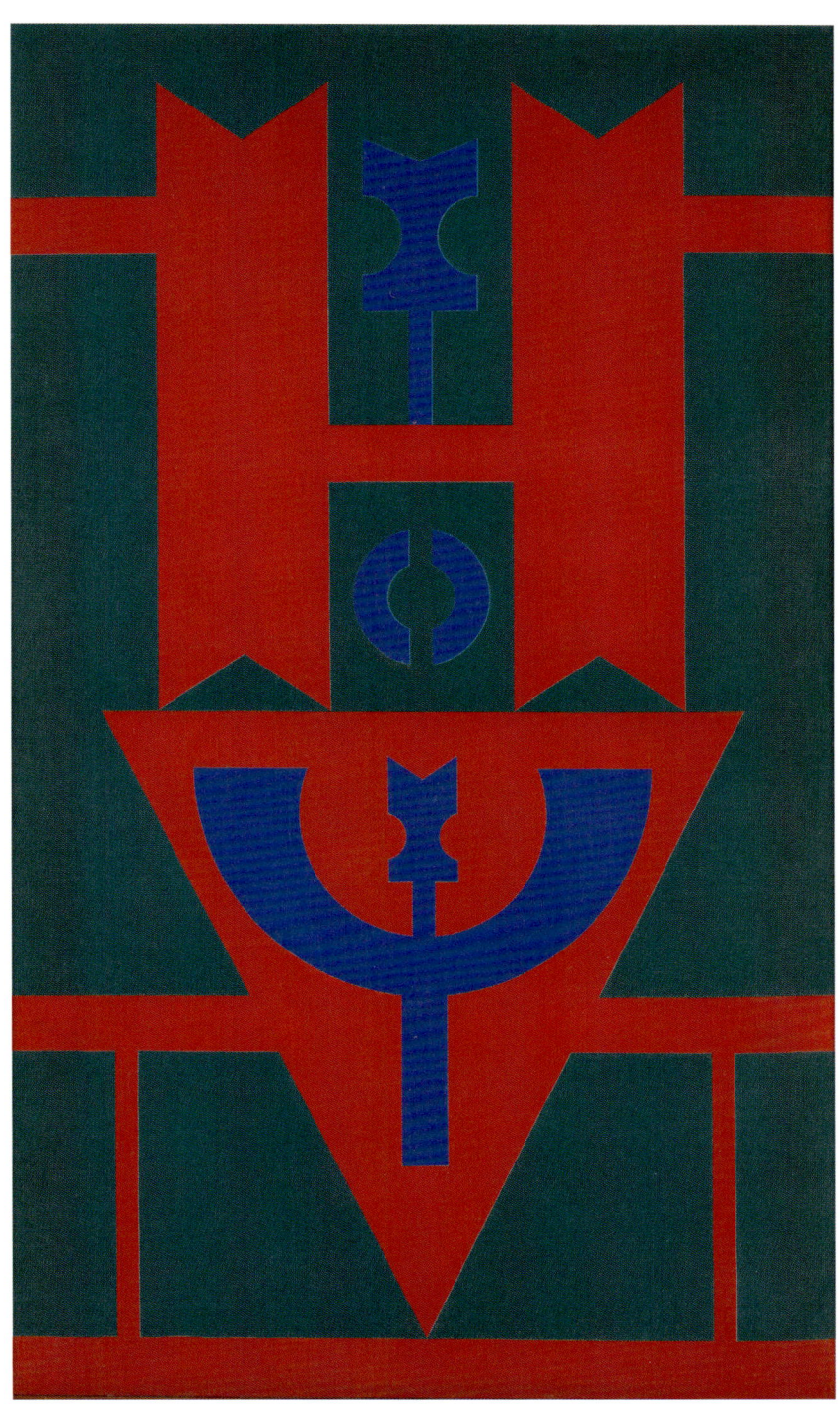

**Conjunto altar sacral
emblemático – E59
(Emblematic Sacral
Altar Set – E59)**, 1980

**Emblema 70 No. 2
(Emblem 70 No. 2)**, 1970

239   **Rubem Valentim**

Untitled, 1962

Brasil! Brasil!

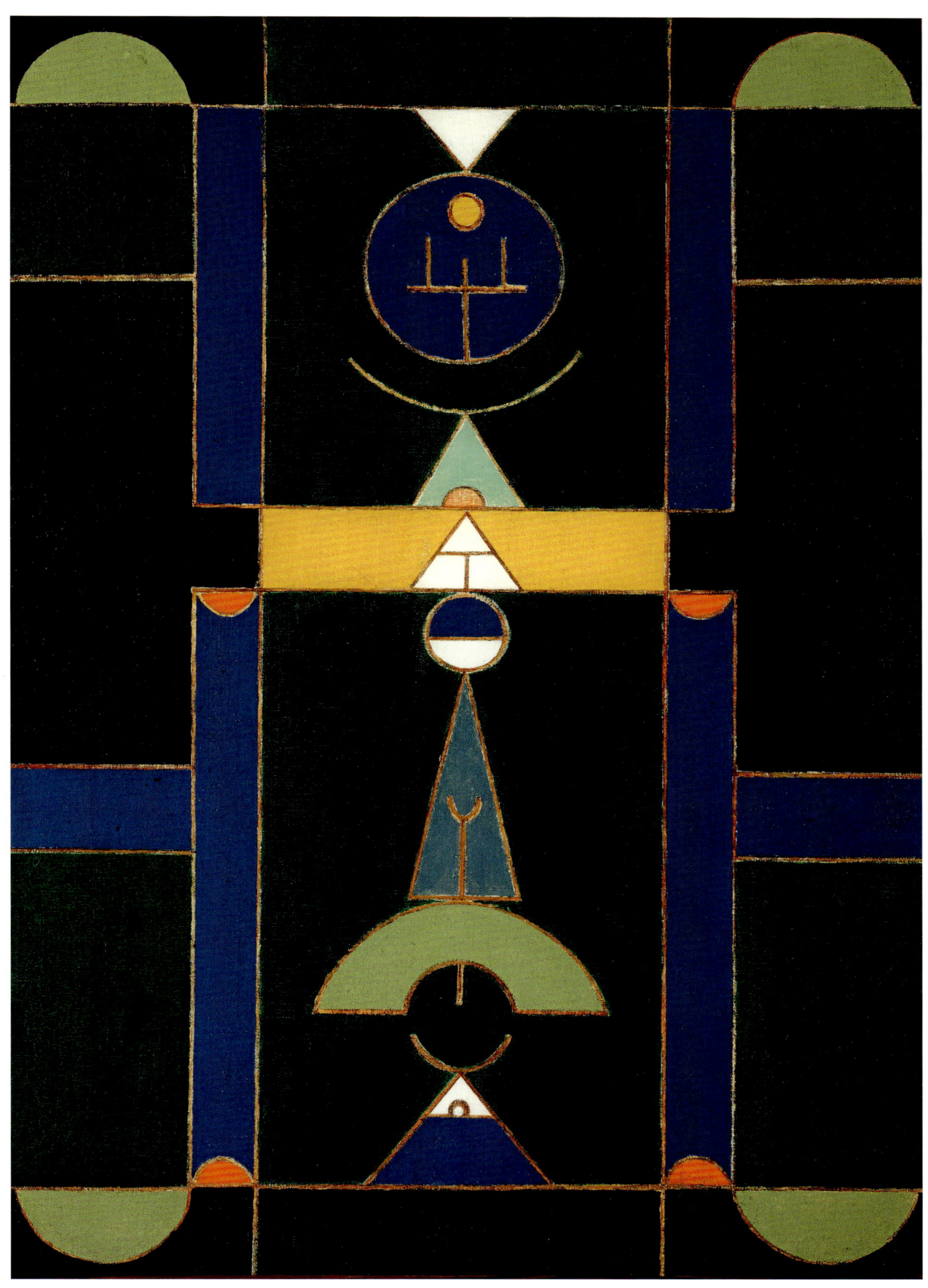

241   **Rubem Valentim**

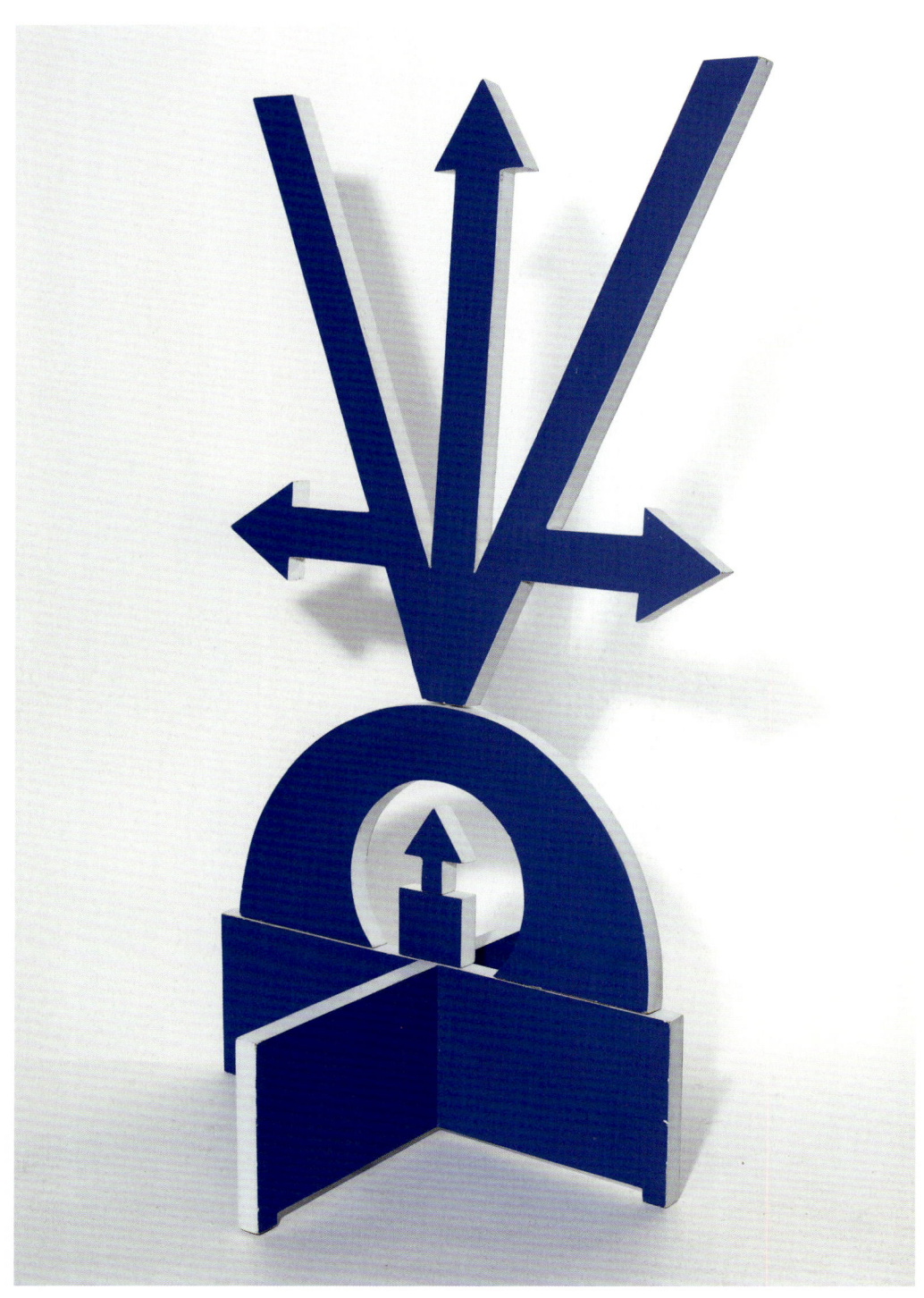

**Objeto emblemático
(Emblematic object)**, 1973

Untitled, 1962

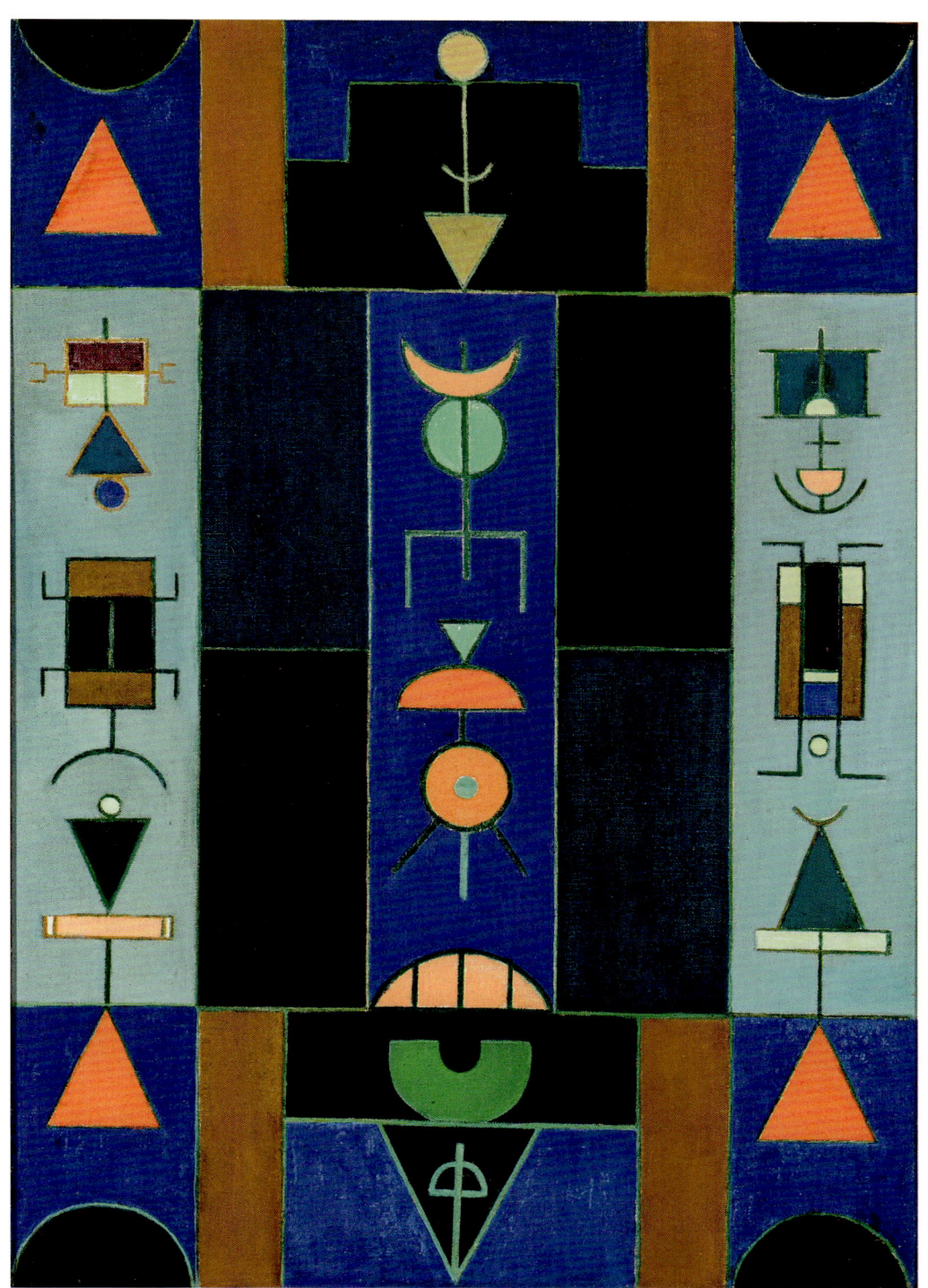

243   **Rubem Valentim**

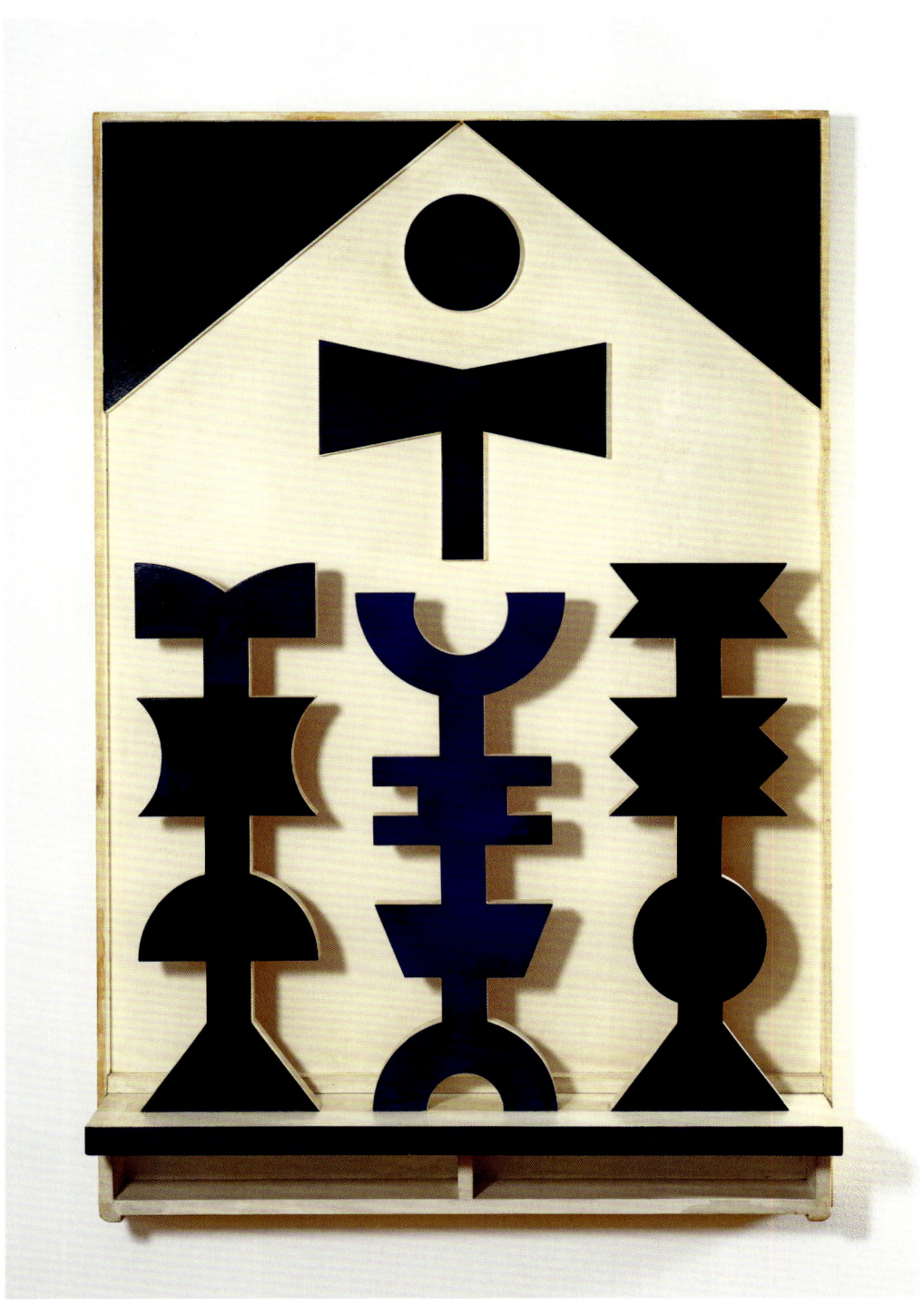

Objeto emblemático 1
(Emblematic Object 1), 1969

Composição (Composition), 1961

Brasil! Brasil!

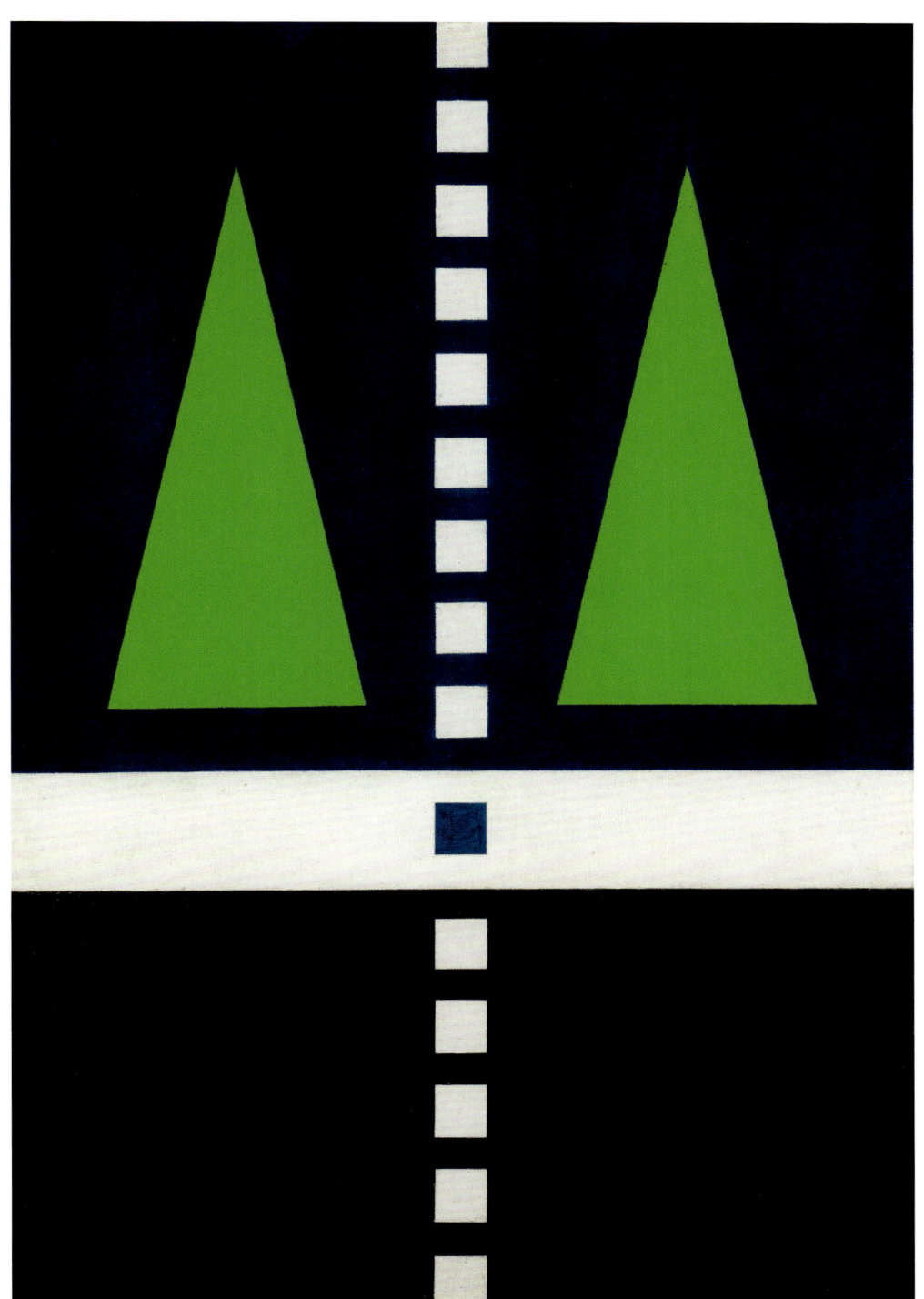

Rubem Valentim

Essays

Modernisms in Motion

Gênese Andrade

The impact of the 1920s Paris exhibitions, which featured paintings such as *Tropical* (c. 1916, fig. 2 p. 23) by Anita Malfatti; *Fim de combate* (End of Combat, 1923) by Vicente do Rego Monteiro; and *A negra* (1923, fig. 6 p. 264), and *Abaporu* (1928, fig. 1 p. 66) by Tarsila do Amaral, has not yet been fully assessed.[1] Did the reception of these paintings go beyond the exotic gaze? To what extent did they contribute to the dissemination, understanding, and appreciation (not in terms of the art market) of Brazilian culture at that time and thereafter?

What can be understood from a synchronic reading of paintings such as *Bananal* by Lasar Segall (1927, fig. p. 122) and *Bananal* by Djanira da Motta e Silva (1961, fig. p. 195) – which, despite sharing the same title, differ both chronologically and aesthetically, as well as in the way they depict a male versus female perspective and a national versus foreign perspective? What is the weight of the tension between representation and representativeness for the general viewer?

Can the works *Baiana* (1930, fig. p. 167) by Alfredo Volpi and *A colona* (1935, fig. p. 94) by Candido Portinari be read under the same concept of invisibilisation and erasure attributed to *A negra* by Tarsila do Amaral, considering that their titles generalise the subjects represented? How might the first two be interpreted when compared to self-portraits by the same painters, as is typically done in the case of do Amaral (see p. 277)? In Portinari's painting, is it possible to identity the caricature, the grotesque, and the deformation noted in do Amaral's work?

Does the fact that do Amaral, Segall, and Portinari were not personally affected by the social ills they denounce in their works –

Segunda classe (1933, fig. p. 85), *Pogrom* (1937, fig. p. 131), and *Retirantes* (1944, fig. p. 103), respectively – diminish their empathy towards the subject, turning their works into a form of "aestheticising poverty"? What are the criteria and parameters for evaluating the geometrisation of Indigenous motifs by Monteiro, Afro motifs by Valentim, Volpi's flag motifs, and Geraldo de Barros's photo-forms?

How does the belated appreciation of Afro-Brazilian and Indigenous artists impact the understanding of Brazilian culture, and how does this reflect on the contemporary national and international scene, beyond the art scene? Does it drive a reassessment of modernisms, and, if so, is it possible to determine whether the result is positive or negative?

These questions arise from the reinterpretation of modernist artists in the twenty-first century and the reassessment of the *Semana de Arte Moderna* (Modern Art Week) around its centenary in 2022. Held in São Paulo in February 1922, it is conventionally considered the starting point of modernisms in Brazil, encompassing various artistic languages throughout the twentieth century.

The choice of the adjective "modern" to describe the art featured in the exhibition is tied to the title *Exposição de pintura moderna Anita Malfatti*, which was held in December 1917 in São Paulo. It was this exhibition's reception (see p. 22), along with other cultural events, that led to the mobilisation that culminated in the 1922 event. Dismissing this process and labelling it as the outburst of inconsequential artists is biased. The negative reaction to Malfatti's 1917 exhibition, sparked by an article by Monteiro Lobato published in *O Estado de S. Paulo* on 20 December, served as a catalyst for artists influenced by the European avant-garde to seek greater visibility for their work, in opposition to academic or realistic art. On 11 January 1918, one day after the exhibition closed, Oswald de Andrade wrote a note in the newspaper *Jornal do Commercio* in defence of the artist, titled *Exposição Malfatti* (Malfatti Exhibition). On 27 May, he also published the

first article on emerging avant-garde poetry in the same newspaper, which opposed the then-prevailing Parnassian poetry and the absence of Brazilian colloquialism in literature. Titled *O meu poeta futurista* (My Futurist Poet), it reviewed Mário de Andrade's book *Paulicéia desvairada* (Hallucinated City), whose then-unpublished verses were recited at gatherings in his home and other meeting places. Another controversy surrounding "modern art" filled the newspapers. The word "futurism" extended beyond the artistic realm, and anything that deviated from political, social, and cultural norms – anything new, different, extravagant, or a reaction to academic art – was labelled as such, both in the press and in daily life, to express disagreement or ridicule. The term was not necessarily linked to the Italian Futurist movement, the best-known movement among the Brazilian public,[2] which had been discussed since 1909.[3]

Against a backdrop of contention surrounding the avant-gardes, the notion of staging a demonstration to promote new artistic ideas emerged. This moment coincided with preparations in Rio de Janeiro, then the capital of Brazil, to commemorate 100 years of Brazilian political independence. Writers and artists who defended works aligned with avant-garde trends sought the kind of art that could truly mirror this independence and the urban transformations unfolding in a city that was modernising but still provincial.[4] The art scene was confined to just a few museums, exhibition spaces within commercial venues, salons, and bookstores, along with modest sponsorship initiatives and gatherings in newspaper offices and the homes of the elite.

The São Paulo Municipal Theatre hosted the *Semana de Arte Moderna* – an exhibition of visual arts and architecture from 11 to 18 February 1922, accompanied by soirées featuring musical and dance performances, lectures, and literary readings on 13, 15, and 17 February. In the field of visual arts, many of the exhibited works dated before 1922. The catalogue lists twelve participants and 100 works on display, encompassing architecture as well. Malfatti presented twenty works, some previously shown in her controversial 1917 exhibition and others created afterward. Victor Brecheret, who was in Europe during the event, contributed twelve works produced before his departure. Monteiro contributed ten works; despite being in his second season in Paris during the event, he had left some works in Brazil. Other artists included Regina Gomide Graz, known for decorative arts, alongside John Graz, Ferrignac, Zina Aita, and others. Emiliano Di Cavalcanti, already acclaimed as an illustrator and caricaturist, displayed twelve works, and designed the cover of the event's catalogue and programme.[5]

Regarding the lectures, Graça Aranha presented "A emoção estética na arte moderna" (Aesthetic Emotion in Modern Art); and Ronald de Carvalho's was titled "A pintura e a escultura moderna do Brasil" (Modern Painting and Sculpture in Brazil). The use of the adjective "modern" in these titles is noteworthy. Mário de Andrade and Menotti Del Picchia also addressed the audience, and all the talks were accompanied or followed by musical performances and literary readings.

There were poetry recitations by Mário de Andrade, who read verses from *Pauliceia desvairada*, Guilherme de Almeida, and others; Oswald read excerpts from *Os condenados* (The Condemned); Del Picchia, from *O homem e a morte* (Man and Death); Ronald de Carvalho recited *Os sapos* (The Frogs) by Manuel Bandeira, who was absent. These are the only details available about the literary texts presented at the event.

One of the highlights was the musical contribution of Heitor Villa-Lobos, whose career had begun years earlier, alongside Guiomar Novaes, a pianist already renowned in Brazil and abroad. Also taking part were Ernâni Braga, Lucília Villa-Lobos, Paulina D'Ambrosio, Maria Ema, and others. Music dominated the programme, which also featured dance pieces by the dancer Yvonne Daumerie. Little is known to this day about her and the women musicians who participated, except for Novaes.

It is important to note that the *Semana* of 1922 did not aim to be all-encompassing. The choice of artists and artistic languages that comprised the event was related to social circles and the trends that interested its organisers, based on affinities and strategies. The absence of certain writers, artists, and artistic expressions – such as theatre, cinema, and photography – does not imply that these were unknown or overlooked. To consider absence as failure and choice as exclusion – as was the case during the event's centenary in 2022 – sparks controversy but does not broaden the reflection or reception of the event. On the contrary, it shifts the focus and leads to shallow and fleeting discussions.

The noted absence of Black artists, Indigenous culture, and popular culture, coupled with the minority (yet significant) female presence, along with the lack of information about certain female participants, has, in recent critiques, spurred the downplaying of the event, as well as distortions regarding aesthetic and ideological matters, and raised questions about its significance.

Some of the artworks exhibited featured representations of Black and Indigenous individuals: Malfatti presented *Baianas* (Women from Bahia), while Monteiro included *Cabeças de negras (afro-brasileiras)* (Heads of Black Women, Afro-Brazilian) and two works titled *Lenda brasileira (indígena)* (Brazilian Legend, Indigenous). Villa-Lobos presented his *Danças características africanas* (Characteristic African Dances), also known as *Danças indígenas 1, 2 e 3* (Indigenous Dances 1, 2, and 3) – *Farrapos* (Rags, 1914), *Kankukus*, and *Kankikis* (1915). Brecheret's sculpture *Cabeça de Cristo* (Head of Christ, 1920) is considered, due to the presence of braids, a portrayal of Jesus as mixed-race. Today, there is a deliberate effort to portray Di Cavalcanti and Mário de Andrade as mixed-race individuals (the latter also as homosexual), but neither they themselves nor literary and art critics did so at the time. Both, along with Malfatti and others, were not part of the elite – although some participants were and received support from patrons – which weakens the argument that the event was elitist. Social criticism, racial diversity, and the theme of sexuality are not absent from *Pauliceia desvairada*, but they were overshadowed by discussions that focused primarily on aesthetic matters.

The relationship between Brazilian modernists and Indigenous and African cultures was undoubtedly influenced by the interest of European artists, who regarded these cultures as exotic. The way our avant-garde artists dealt with the presence of Black people in Brazil, the legacy of slavery, miscegenation, and marginalisation are now being questioned. The fact that several artists, such as the Andrades, do Amaral, and Rego Monteiro, turned to Indigenous culture in the 1920s, despite not having direct contact with it, has been criticised by contemporary Indigenous artists. These critics question not only the legitimacy of the works but also the approach and its impact on the reception of Indigenous culture in Brazil over time.[6] Today, there is a demand for Black and Indigenous people to be present as subjects of and spokespersons for their own cultures, rather than resorting to the "outsider" approach used in the past. This has led to a discussion about the representation and representativeness of Black and Indigenous art[7] within modernism.

The issue of exoticism in the works of these artists, particularly those created after 1923 when they were all in Europe studying in Paris, fits into a broad and complex context. Do Amaral attended the ateliers of André Lhote, Albert Gleizes, and Fernand Léger, and studied cubism. In the second half of the year, she painted her iconic works *A negra, Caipirinha* (Countryside Woman), and *Autorretrato au manteau rouge* (fig. 4 p. 276). These works have always been celebrated, but they have recently become central to discussions around race, gender, representation, and self-representation.

Blaise Cendrars, who closely interacted with do Amaral, Oswald, Di Cavalcanti, and Paulo Prado in Paris, acted as a bridge between European and Brazilian artists. Invited to stay in Brazil, he arrived in February 1924 and remained until August.[8] In March, he, the Tarsiwald couple – as Mário de Andrade nicknamed Tarsila and Oswald – and Olívia Guedes Penteado went to Rio de Janeiro to spend Carnival. During this period, do Amaral created a series of drawings, some of which the poet requested as illustrations for *Feuilles de route* (Travel Notes), a book of poems documenting his journey from the Port of Le Havre to the Port of Santos and Estação da Luz in São Paulo (figs pp. 78 and 79). Cendrars chose a sketch of the painting *A negra* for the cover, thus introducing Brazilian modern art to Europe. Cendrars visited "fazendas" (farms) in the countryside of São Paulo and the historic towns of Minas Gerais, where he spent Holy Week. On this trip, other modernists, like Mário de Andrade, joined the group that had travelled to Rio de Janeiro. Cendrars was enchanted by the rural environment, the vivid "caipira colours"[9] of the buildings, the shapes and colours of tropical nature, the Gregorian chants of processions, the art of the baroque sculptor Aleijadinho, and the stories he collected along the way, which would later enrich his literature. He drew the attention of Brazilian artists to the richness of these elements, which were exotic to him but "native" and previously unappreciated by them.

While Oswald, influenced by their trip to Rio, wrote the *Manifesto da Poesia Pau-Brasil*, published in the Rio newspaper *Correio da Manhã* on 18 March 1924, Tarsila, through various drawings and sketches, introduced the themes of the paintings *Morro da favela* (fig. p. 75) and *Carnaval em Madureira* (Carnival in Madureira, 1924). This marked the beginning of the Pau-Brasil movement, which expanded into further paintings and the poems by Oswald, inspired by these journeys. These works would later form *Pau Brasil*, a book published in 1925, featuring illustrations by Tarsila. The close connection between the travels, Cendrars's presence, and the conception of the artworks that define the movement is evident. Some of do Amaral's paintings from this period were featured in her exhibition at Galerie Percier in Paris in 1926, including *A negra, Morro da favela*, and *Lagoa Santa* (fig. p. 81).

Works, showcasing a cubist aesthetic, represent a reinterpretation of Brazil inspired by European avant-garde movements. Also in 1924, the Lithuanian painter Lasar Segall settled in Brazil. While his expressive portrayal of Black people and Brazilian landscapes bears similarities to do Amaral's work, Segall's art already delved into social issues, a theme do Amaral would explore only later. The fact that white artists from privileged backgrounds – like Oswald, do Amaral, and Segall – addressed the Afro-Brazilian experience, marked by the legacies of slavery and socioeconomic disparities, has prompted critics to question the significance of their works and perceive them as embodying a purportedly aestheticised exoticism.

In 1928, inspired by do Amaral's painting *Abaporu* (fig. 1 p. 66), which acted as both a catalyst and a symbol of the Anthropophagic movement, Oswald wrote the *Manifesto Antropófago*, published in the first issue of *Revista de Antropofagia*. Rooted in the concept of devouring – "Abaporu" means "the one who eats human flesh" in Tupi language – the concept of anthropophagy aimed to tackle cultural dependency through transculturation. The assimilation of the other is selective, as in a cannibal ritual where the one who shows the most courage and bravery is devoured, even when defeated, so these qualities can be appropriated by the devourer. The original is then transformed through the reworking and merging of both elements.

The painting *Antropofagia* (fig. 2 p. 67) revisits *A negra*, overlaying it with the figure in *Abaporu*, embodying aspects of the native, the Black, and the Indigenous, in a cubist style. Do Amaral's paintings and the *Manifesto Antropófago* propelled the movement forward, finding literary expression in Mário de Andrade's *Macunaíma* (1928) and Raul Bopp's *Cobra Norato* (1931). However, Mário de Andrade's work, written in 1926 under the influence of *Von Roraima zum Orinoco* by the German researcher Koch-Grünberg, combined with his research into folklore and popular culture, preceded the manifesto.

Rego Monteiro studied Marajó Island ceramics at the Museu Nacional in Rio de Janeiro and delved into Indigenous art through books by Barbosa Rodrigues and Couto de Magalhães. He also drew inspiration from the works of Rugendas and Debret. Although he never visited the Amazon, Indigenous themes permeate his paintings exhibited in São Paulo, Rio de Janeiro, and Recife in 1920 and 1921, some of which were featured in the *Semana* of 1922. In 1921, he produced the drawing *Antropófago*. When invited by Oswald to join the movement initiated in 1928, he declined, asserting himself as its precursor. The matter can be clarified with Schwartz's statement: "What Rego Monteiro and Mário de Andrade intuit and anticipate, Oswald de Andrade provides theoretical support for, and Tarsila do Amaral offers extraordinary artistic form, and from this fortunate combination emerges a spirited rhetoric of cultural policy celebrated to this day."[10] These four artists brought visibility to Indigenous culture at a time when the art field did not. The current reception of these works, amidst narrative disputes, introduces new perspectives, whether in comparison to contemporary Indigenous art or when revisiting the works of European traveller-artists from the sixteenth and seventeenth centuries.

Some of Monteiro's mentioned works were used as illustrations for the book *Légendes, croyances et talismans des Indiens de l'Amazone*, published in France in 1923. He also published *Quelques visages de Paris* in France in 1925.[11] This book, featuring poems and illustrations by Monteiro himself, presents impressions of the city through the eyes of an Indigenous person, drawing comparisons between landmarks and elements of their own cultural universe. Before the manifesto and the Anthropophagic movement, these books already engage in a dialogue with them, much like Monteiro's paintings *Fim de combate* and *A caçada* (fig. 2 p. 43), both from 1923, and *O atirador de arco* (fig. p. 50), from 1925. Like do Amaral, he employs cubist aesthetics to address national themes. While aesthetics were once prioritised by art critics over subject matter, today, subject matter holds greater significance, often linked to the artist's identity, encompassing class, race, and gender, and historical discrimination.

While Indigenous motifs migrate from the jungles to the paintings and pages of books produced in France, one of the French postcards crosses the equator and lands in the suburbs of Rio de Janeiro. What do Amaral depicts in *Carnaval em Madureira* from 1924 is not a direct replica of the cosmopolitan monument she encountered the previous year. Instead, it is a carnival allegory created that year near the train station of Madureira – an "imitation of the Eiffel Tower":

This beautiful work of art features abundant electric lighting, with approximately 400 light bulbs. At the top, there is a lovely tribute to our illustrious compatriot Santos Dumont. The Demoiselle aircraft can be seen gracefully circling around the tower, showcasing beautiful movement. Also visible is the dome with its beautiful rotating beacon, adorned with the flags of Brazil, France, and Portugal. This is one of the three floors where, during Carnival, a trumpet band, dressed in full regalia, will perform.[12]

Therefore, she translated onto the canvas, with her strokes, the tower already integrated into the Rio de Janeiro carnival atmosphere. The same monument that the Indigenous character created by Monteiro in *Quelques visages de Paris* admires from his perspective:

une grande cheminée
où tour de combat :
il paraît qu'elle
n'est pas très solide

où, bien d'aplomb :
de peur qu'elle ne
tombe on l'a attachée
a terre de tous les
cotés par plusieurs
cordes bien tendues.
est-ce les débris de
la tour de Babel !

On 2 March, the Madureira Station issued 10,725 tickets, marking the start of Carnival.[13] This was followed by the arrival of the Paulistas (artists from São Paulo) and Cendrars on that day or the days that followed. On 4 March, amidst the festivities, the *Correio da Manhã* reported: "(Cendrars) is touring our country to create a book of poetry – *Douze poèmes de la faune carnavalesque.*"[14] Unfortunately, there are no traces of such verses. No one would have imagined that by bringing a foreigner to the country's most typical national event, the group would come across the "Eiffel Tower"! But it is likely that, confronted with the unusual replica of the Parisian tower, Cendrars would have appreciated the structure with less awe than the real thing. The amazement conveyed in the quote above likely reflects that of the locals upon seeing the tower. Similarly, during his time in the towns of Minas Gerais, Cendrars never tired of exclaiming "Quelle merveille!" (How wonderful!) at everything he saw, whether it was social inequality, religiosity, the landscape, the rustic charm of the houses and churches, or baroque art and architecture, and even tragic stories, which he found picturesque. Cendrars inspired Brazilian modernists to look at their own country in a different light. Is the "Eiffel Tower" in Madureira the counterpoint to the sketch of *A negra* on the cover of *Feuilles de route*? Can we consider it? the reversal of exoticism? Monteiro's Indigenous perspective on the tower and Paris in general is critical and, by extension, so is the artist's view of the Indigenous. The tower is associated with utilitarian elements (a chimney or watchtower) and is reduced to the ruins of the Tower of Babel, suggesting a broader understanding of diversity. Oswald, by applying the logic of Indigenous ritual to art theory, demonstrates an interpretation that is now supported by anthropology. Meanwhile, do Amaral relates the figures in her paintings from 1923 and 1928 to her memories and dreams, with critics often linking her work to surrealism due to its dreamlike quality. Reflecting on how they explored otherness is not straightforward and exceeds the scope of this text.

At that moment, avant-garde magazines were emerging across Brazil: *Klaxon* (São Paulo, 1922–1923), *Estética* (Rio de Janeiro, 1924–1925), *A Revista* (Belo Horizonte, 1925–1926), *Terra Roxa e Outras Terras* (São Paulo, 1926), *Madrugada* (Porto Alegre, 1926), *Verde* (Cataguases, 1927–1929), *Eléctrica* (Itanhandu, 1927), *Cigarra* (Natal, 1928–1929), amongst others.[15] With varying durations, though usually short, some had broader outreach and a wider array of collaborations, while others remained confined to their local contexts. What united them was the drive to spread new ideas, inspire new practices, and draw new adherents to their causes. This facilitated the establishment, intensification, and broadening of dialogues among artists and writers, although controversies and ruptures also ensued. Their most significant legacy was the dissemination of ideas across Brazil, expanding the production and reception of modernisms and refuting the notion of São Paulo-centrism within the movement.

Starting from the 1930s, there were several evaluations of modernisms, carried out by the writers who emerged in the 1920s, as well as those who appeared in the subsequent decades, along with literary critics.[16] The term "modernist movement" first appeared in the preface of Oswald's novel *Serafim Ponte Grande* in 1933 and in issue number 4 of the Rio de Janeiro magazine *Lanterna Verde* in 1936, which labelled the subsequent production as "post-modern". The term "pre-modernism" was coined by Tristão de Athayde in an article published in *O Jornal* in 1938. More than just a chronological demarcation, it was later interpreted by critics as an aesthetic valuation, with "pre" not only indicating something that comes before but also

implying inferiority in an evolutionary sense. This interpretation has been questioned due to its inclusion of literary works that are thematically and stylistically diverse.

In 1942, two decades after the 1922 *Semana*, Mário de Andrade delivered the lecture *O movimento modernista* (The Modernist Movement) in Rio de Janeiro.[17] He presented a panorama of its origins, causes, and consequences, ultimately offering a critical view of its political and social commitment, as well as its protagonists' relationship with their historical context. Critics of the lecture have noted its confessional and individualistic nature, focusing more on what it rejects and its pessimistic tone than on what it praises.[18] A more insightful reading should consider the lecture's erroneous or anachronistic approach to the past when viewed through present-day parameters.

In 1944, in Belo Horizonte, Oswald delivered the lecture *O caminho percorrido* (The Path Taken). In this reflection on the twenty-two years since the Week of Modern Art, he also celebrated the twentieth anniversary of the *Manifesto da Poesia Pau-Brasil* and the modernists' trip to the historic towns of Minas Gerais, known as the "rediscovery of Brazil".

The diversity of languages and artistic trends, along with the plurality of themes and forms, shaped the modernist movement in Brazil. Using "modernisms" in the plural, to acknowledge the heterogeneity, variations, and changes in its reception, aligns more closely with the fluidity that characterises it. The singular term has become associated with the production of the 1920s. It was after the Week of 1922 that the modernists expanded their repertoires, turned to other themes and issues, developed the aesthetics that would establish their legacy, and increased dialogues with both Brazilian and foreign artists, as well as the circulation of their works. The event has been consolidated from a retrospective perspective, as the works of its protagonists emerge, assert themselves, and endure,[19] while new artists broaden their agendas and introduce new themes and approaches to Brazilian art.

A more critical and comprehensive perspective on Brazilian modernisms expands the canon, highlighting artists whose works were rediscovered and appreciated by critics only later, reaching exhibition spaces and a broader audience only recently. This is the case with the works of Djanira da Motta e Silva and Rubem Valentim, among others, which invite new reflections on Afro-Brazilian and Indigenous art, representation, representativity, the art canon, and aesthetic value. However, asserting their importance and value should not imply the depreciation of their contemporaries. Whether or not artists and their works are recognised is not something that happens spontaneously or by imposition. It depends on various circumstances that change over time and across different contexts. As a result, artists and their works are critiqued, withstand controversies, are ignored, rediscovered, re-evaluated, and generate new questions. The answers to my initial questions are not straightforward. However, more important than definitive answers are the reflections raised by the works of art.

1   The paintings by Malfatti and Monteiro were showcased at the inaugural exhibition of the Maison de l'Amérique Latine in May 1923, under the titles *Femme aux fruits* and *Combat d'Indiens*, respectively. That same year, Monteiro's painting was also featured in the Salon des Indépendants. Amaral's works were exhibited at Galerie Percier in her solo shows in 1926 and 1928, titled *Negrèsse* and *Nu*, respectively.

2   Cf. Andrade 2022a, pp. 27–32

3   Published in *Le Figaro*, Paris, 20 February 1909, the *Futurist Manifesto* was disseminated in Brazil in the same year, translated by Almachio Diniz, in *Jornal de Notícias*, Salvador, 30 December 1909. Cf. Schwartz 2022a, p. 410

4   Cf. Andrade 2022a. See also articles by Oswald de Andrade in the same publication.

5   The Week of 1922 catalogue and programme are included, in facsimile, in Schwartz 2022b

6   Cf. Wapichana 2023

7   Cf. Santos 2022

8   Cf. Eulalio 2001

9   *Caipira* refers to the culture of the rural countryside or interior regions of Brazil.

10   Schwartz 2002, p. 146

11   Duchartre 1923; Rego Monteiro 2023

12   Rio de Janeiro 1924a, p. 6

13   Rio de Janeiro 1924b, p. 6

14   Rio de Janeiro 1924c, p. 4

15   Cf. Puntoni and Titan 2014; Trench 2022; Hermenegildo de Araújo 2022; Ruffato 2022

16   Cf. Andrade 2022c

17   Andrade 2022d

18   Cf. Andrade 2022e

19   Wisnik 2022

Modern Images, but not Afro-Indigenous: The Racial Issue in Brazilian Modernism

Alecsandra Matias de Oliveira

Brazil doesn't have citizens; it has spectators.
Lima Barreto, 1922[1]

On the margins of history, a large portion of Brazilians – including Black, Indigenous and mixed-race individuals (*mestiços*) – have long been denied adequate recognition of their memories and knowledge. The roots of this social exclusion lie primarily in the colonial system, fuelled by the exploitation of natural resources, slavery, and genocide of Indigenous people – factors that have become ingrained in the country's history, persisting well after independence in 1822 and the end of the slave regime (1888). The Brazilian state was founded on conservatism and violence, shaping social dynamics with an exclusionary and racist logic. In this context, history was primarily written by the "winners" – those with power and economic means, mostly intellectuals inspired by European ideals, who shaped narratives and interpretations of both nature and the "other".[2] Brazilian people, who were never given any historical agency, found themselves confined to the national iconography. From colonial times to the Empire, and later the Republic, the people of Brazil were depicted as passive observers, with social conflicts seldom represented in art or historical accounts. Black, Indigenous and mixed-race individuals were stereotyped according to European standards.

However, times change. Ways of being, seeing, and existing in the world have become more diverse. Discourses and events

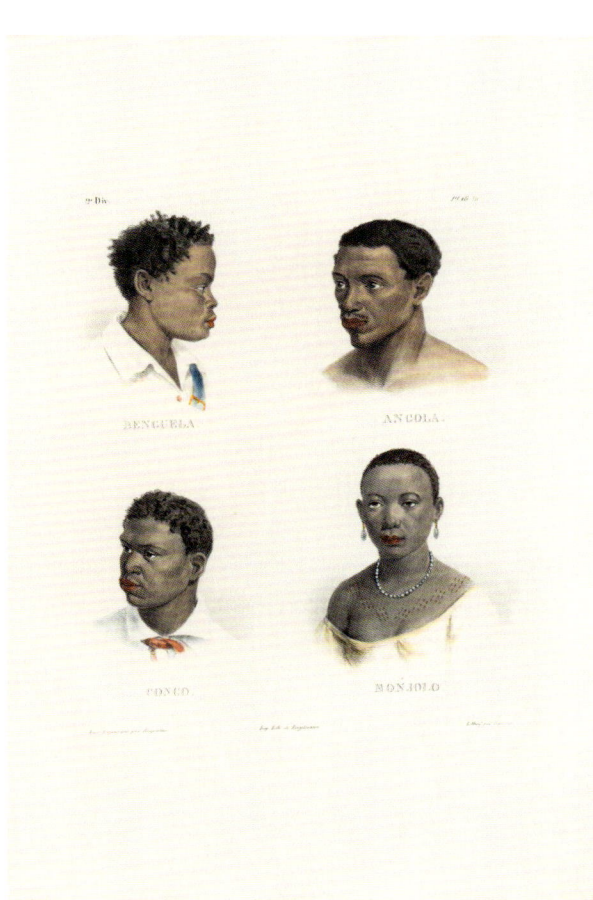

have altered the idea of a linear, progressive, and civilising history. Non-Western legacies and cultures have asserted their right to existence and preservation. New writers and artists have begun to express their experiences. And new approaches have led to concepts and pathways being revisited. The aim of many contemporary artists is to tell different stories; to bring to light discussions that had previously been silenced; to address themselves and their communities. This is evident, for example, in the valorisation of Afro-Indigenous heritage and ethno-racial issues. From this perspective, questions arise: what are the racial aspects of art, particularly in Brazilian modernism? How did the relationships unfold between those who represented and those who were represented? And how do these relationships fit into the contemporary debate? The responses to these questions must revisit the values "imported" from European avant-gardes and the concept of "Brazilianness".

Notably, Brazilian art history is marked by the embrace of modern art. In Brazil, the European avant-gardes became part of modernism – or, as some authors argue, modernisms.[3] The avant-gardes were integral to the notion of the new and the authentic in art. As an elastic concept (in terms of time and, in particular, language), its impact continues to resonate to this day. The *Semana de Arte Moderna* (Modern Art Week) in São Paulo in 1922, viewed as a historical landmark, has undergone significant re-evaluation in 2022. Debates, exhibitions and articles have explored the event's intentions and consequences. Under this renewed scrutiny, it is crucial to consider who writes and why, who portrays whom and even what is being portrayed. This is because the issue of race, both before and after modernism, is composed of intricate and complex elements. Black and Indigenous individuals have been depicted by representations – with all their possibilities and limitations – created through the lens of white artists.

Representation does not equate to representativeness. During that time, the agency of Black and Indigenous people, including their subjectivities and socio-political rights, was nearly non-existent. When Black or mixed-race artists and writers emerged as prominent figures, they were often either erased from, or whitewashed in, the historical record – such as Machado de Assis (1839–1908), one of the greatest Brazilian writers, and Chiquinha Gonzaga (1847–1935), a composer and conductor. Works by figures such as Lima Barreto (1881–1922) and painters Arthur Timótheo da Costa (1882–1922) and João Timótheo da Costa (1879–1930) were disregarded by their contemporary modernist critics. However, today they are recognised for their acts of resistance. Similarly, the works of modernists such as Tarsila do Amaral, Lasar Segall, Vicente do Rego Monteiro, Candido Portinari, Djanira da Motta e Silva, and Rubem Valentim are being re-examined. Each dealt with, in their own way, the representation of Black, mixed-race, and Indigenous people. Collectively, they played a role in shaping the national imaginary and identity. Their propositions combined local elements with European avant-gardes. Viewing and reviewing their works prompts reflection on the political, economic, and social realities that guided modernist production.

1922 is part of a broader process, symbolising the aspiration for a modern Brazil and an aesthetic renewal characterised by both rupture and continuity. Through the lens of modernism, there is no "real Brazil" but rather a historically constructed imaginary that delineates who belongs and who is excluded from its narrative. By grappling with the tensions and contradictions of Brazilian modernism, one can discern the appropriation of sources from Indigenous, popular, and African cultures – often perpetuating stereotypes and, most importantly, the ways in which these individuals were incorporated into Brazilian iconography. However, it also serves as a means of reflecting on the historical subjects who were kept outside the canon of modernism and are now reclaiming agency over their representation.

The Issue of National Identity

The paintings and drawings produced by travelling artists – a term employed to describe those who visited Brazil during the colonial and imperial periods – were creations guided by the colonising project and the artistic-scientific models that justified the dominance of the new lands. Drawing upon memory, fantasy and a desire to explore, classify and order the New World, these travellers were, in fact, foreigners who, in addition to exploring the lands, proved to be observers of nature and the "other". As a result, many illustrations created in the eighteenth and nineteenth centuries have become depictions of customs and rural and urban scenes in a neoclassical style, based on the concepts of the picturesque and the sublime. Their subjects are idealised, and their landscapes aim to capture beauty and evoke emotion, presenting various perspectives on Brazilian nature. Alongside depictions of landscapes, types and customs, these works also portray the punishment and trafficking of enslaved people. In the eyes of travellers, differences were prominent; the known and the unknown, and the relationships between the "self" and the "other". The image of the "other" became widely disseminated throughout the European world through iconography. For these foreign artists, what fascinated them most was the presence of slave labour in the countryside or cities, as well as the different customs, social structures, landscapes and the categorisation of human types. Black and Indigenous individuals, much like animal or botanical specimens, were depicted in ethnographic drawings; they were seen as "of the land", as picturesque as the light or lush nature (fig. 1).

The advent of photography in the nineteenth century enabled the technical documentation of people and landscapes – a departure from the methods of drawing and engraving. Marc Ferrez (1843–1923), a Brazilian photographer of French descent, captured landscapes, panoramic views and everyday scenes. His images have become a significant visual documentation of Brazil during that era. Yet, within these images resides a longing for modernity, a clear sign of societal evolution. However, one segment of society lacked ownership of their own image – the enslaved population. Photographs depicting Black individuals, particularly wet nurses and domestic slaves, reinforced the social hierarchy imposed by white masters or revealed the patriarchal system that governed Brazilian families (fig. 2). Photography often sought to comment on these individuals' exotic diversity, driven either by commercial reasons or anthropometric interests.

Alongside photographic records, Brazilian academic art – originating from the French Artistic Mission (1816)[4] and the establishment of the Academia Imperial de Belas Artes (1826)[5] – largely ignored the depiction of Black individuals but did prominently feature representations of Indigenous people, portraying them as inherently strong – a national symbol. In academic painting, the "Indian" embodied the ideal of the noble savage, depicted as a creature of nature seamlessly integrated into the idyllic landscape. While European artists and writers idealised the medieval knight, in Brazil, similar attributes were bestowed upon the natives. These artists aimed to forge a genuine national identity – an authentic culture. The novels by José de Alencar (1829–1877), the paintings by Victor Meirelles (1832–1903) and the sculptures by Rodolfo Bernardelli (1852–1931), all helped shape the image of Indigenous peoples as pure beings awaiting civilisation. This concept, known as "Indianism",[6] became an epic and lyrical expression of the nation's formation, suggesting

Fig. 2
João Ferreira Villela, *Augusto Gomes Leal com a Ama-de-Leite Mônica* (Augusto Gomes Leal with his wet nurse Mônica), 1860, Collection Francisco Rodrigues, Fundação Joaquim Nabuco, Recife, Pernambuco

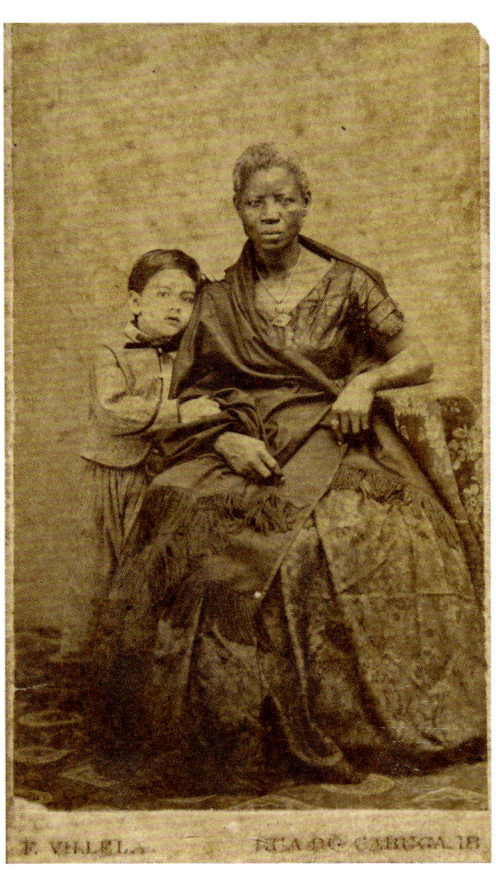

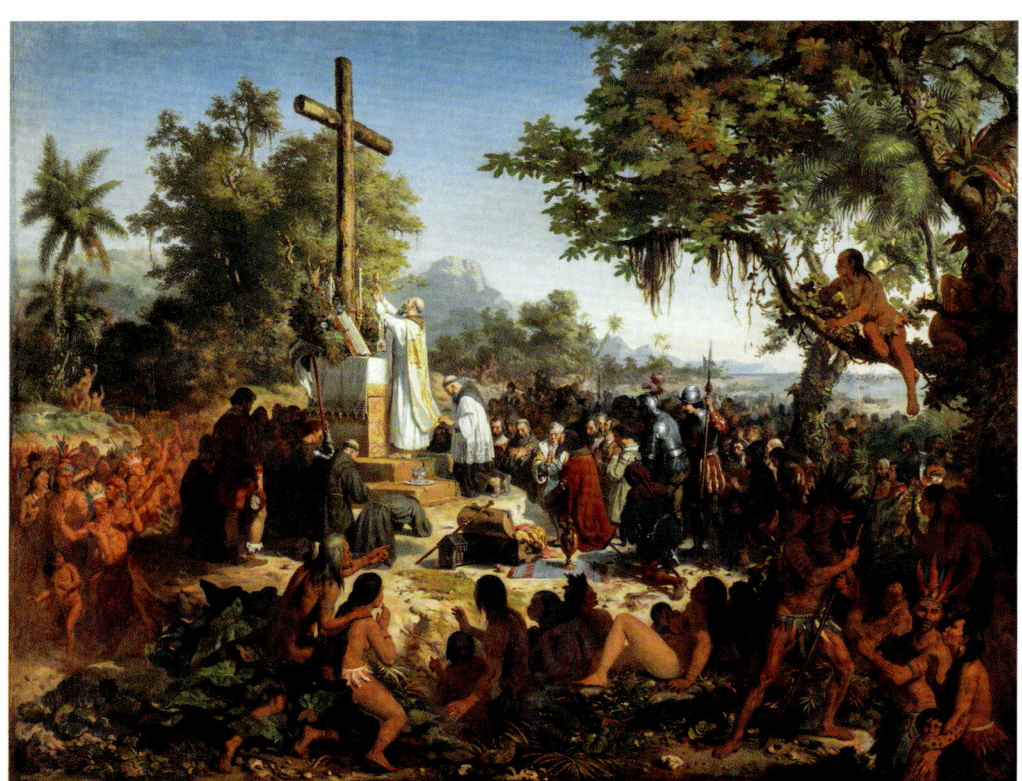

Fig. 3
Victor Meirelles, *A primeira
missa no Brasil* (The First
Service in Brazil), c. 1860,
Museu Nacional de Belas
Artes, Rio de Janeiro

Fig. 4
Almeida Junior, *Caipira picando
fumo* (Caipira cutting tabacco),
1893, Pinacoteca de São Paulo

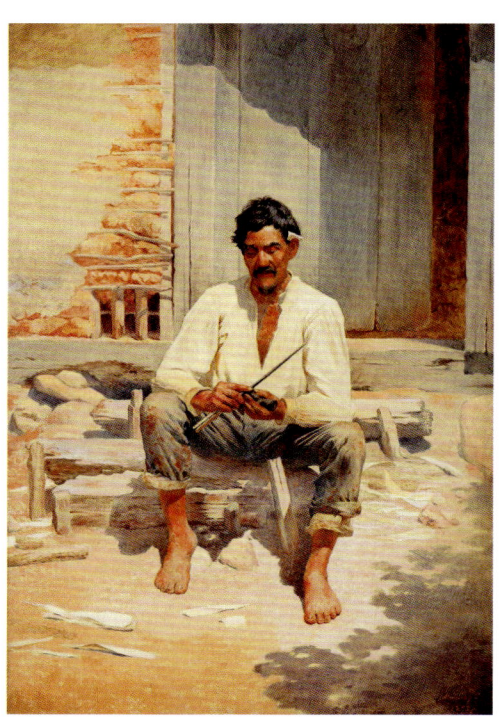

Brasil! Brasil!

that Brazilians were the result of the encounter between European pioneers and Indigenous people (fig. 3).

The identity of Brazilian people became a pressing issue – a constant quest in the history of national art. Initially, the figure of the Indigenous individual was exalted within the confines of the academy. However, shortly thereafter, the mixing of Indigenous peoples and colonisers emerged as the foundational myth. Take, for instance, Machado de Assis, who, in his essay *Instituto de Nacionalidade* (1873), discussed the risks of the picturesque in paintings of nature and customs. In this context, the academic trend emphasised the depiction of regional customs, colours and themes. Characters from the country's interior (the *caipira*, the *caboclo* and the *matuto*[7]) were prominently featured in the works of Almeida Júnior (1850–1899). This painter portrayed the lifestyles of Brazilians, showcasing their daily routines, work, homes, huts, and even poverty; his repertoire, according to some critics, laid the foundation for Brazilian identity, and the *caipira* became the symbol of "Brazilianness" (fig. 4).

At the turn of the twentieth century, following the end of the slave regime, the implementation of immigration laws, the rise of wage labour and the adoption of eugenicist policies, the Black population in Brazil was marginalised. The concept of racial improvement was embraced by doctors, engineers, journalists and other intellectuals, who viewed European descent as essential for the progress of the "nation of the future". Black and Indigenous peoples were perceived as hindrances to progress. Policies promoting "social hygiene" were enacted, which aimed to exclude Black and Asian immigrants, as well as the disabled, from society. The painting *A redenção de Cam* (1895)[8] by Modesto Brocos y Gomes (fig. 5) illustrates this ideal: a poor white man sits at the door of a hut, while a woman of mixed descent holds a child – noticeably lighter-skinned. The grandmother, a dark-skinned Black woman, possibly a former enslaved person, is thanking the heavens for her grandson's skin colour.

In essence, the ideas that shaped the Brazilian state found expression in art, which aimed to define identity – a process that oscillated between embracing or marginalising Black and Indigenous peoples. This phenomenon extends beyond the nineteenth century. Delving into the context preceding modernism is crucial for understanding both its continuities and ruptures. In the first two decades of the twentieth century, it became evident that Brazilian intellectuals were driven by another preoccupation: the aspiration for modernity.

On the brink of the centenary of independence in 1922, there were at least two visions of a "modern Brazil" – both conceived by the elites. Neither considered the suffering left by 300 years of slavery and the genocide of Indigenous peoples, nor envisioned policies for the social inclusion of Black, mixed-race and Indigenous individuals – those excluded from modernity. The disparities between the two projects were many, and during the celebrations of that year, they became irreconcilable.

The first project – an official initiative based in Rio de Janeiro (the Brazilian capital at the time) – had involved planning celebrations since 1916, and the commemorations aimed to portray a "civilised Brazil", one associated with industrialisation, republican ideals and a notion of an "improved race". The Centennial Exhibition, held between September 1922 and July 1923, showcased a "white and Europeanised Brazil". Officialdom, propelled by eugenicist rhetoric, saw Black, mixed-race, Indigenous and caboclo individuals as obstacles to "progress". A second project, based in São Paulo, sought to organise a modern cultural festival that challenged the official narrative behind the independence celebrations – the *Semana de Arte Moderna* of 1922. The event solidified the notion of "Brazilianness" through the portrayal of Indigenous, Black and mixed-race individuals. Influenced by the "primitivism" of European avant-gardes, the modernists were driven by a sense of nationalism, openly acknowledging the Afro-Indigenous roots of the Brazilian identity. Their aim was to discover "deep Brazil". In 1924, Mário de Andrade led a modernist caravan to Ouro Preto, into the hinterland of Minas Gerais, which took, among others, Blaise Cendrars on a journey in search of a national identity.

The Modernist Paradox

But who were the intellectuals behind the *Semana de Arte Moderna*? Most of its founders were young figures associated with the coffee bourgeoisie, industrialisation and international capitalism, that is, the social elite.[9] Many spent extended periods in Europe, notably in Paris, and maintained close ties with the European avant-gardes of the early twentieth century. Upon returning to Brazil, they rallied against the formalism that dominated academic art, advocating instead for the experimentation and audacity of the European avant-gardes. However, despite sharing common interests, the modernists were far from being a cohesive group, as their members disagreed on the motivations behind the movement:

> *Oswald (de Andrade), an internationalist, constantly travels abroad to satisfy his hunger for novelty. He has his eyes set on Marinetti's futurism, Picabia's cannibalism and Breton's surrealism. Mário (de Andrade), a nationalist, writes letters. He prefers to set out in search of Brazil, to explore the Amazonian myths and the Baroque of Minas Gerais.*[10]

For these and other reasons, it became more fitting to label them as "modernists". As such, Brazilian modernism entered history as the juxtaposition between European avant-gardes and Brazilian roots – which was, according to Ronaldo Brito, a paradox:

As European avant-gardes aimed to dissolve identities and dismantle traditional icons, the Brazilian avant-garde endeavoured to embrace local conditions, characterise them, and ultimately affirm them. This encapsulated our modern Being.[11]

After the *Semana de Arte Moderna*, albeit in a diverse and sometimes contradictory way, the movement remained active, and the boundaries of Brazilian modernism lay in the question of identity. "To rediscover, embrace, or even project Brazil, it was necessary, indispensable, to give it a face, a countenance."[12] And this countenance seems to have been instrumentalised by primitivism. Against the backdrop of all this, in the first two decades of the twentieth century in Europe, there emerged a quest for the "primitive" – anything associated with the original, the unconscious, "raw" emotions and formal simplicity. In this pursuit, African and other non-Western influences were paramount. It is worth noting that the concept of "primitive" became expansive, encompassing various meanings simultaneously: exoticism, African art, a "virgin" language, and even the reduction of art to its fundamental elements (including the geometric principles that cubism passed on to abstractionism).

Examples of the use of primitivism include the *Manifeste cannibale dans l'obscurité*, written and composed by Francis Picabia and recited by André Breton in a 1920 performance. Pablo Picasso and the Cubist artists also drew inspiration from statues and tribal masks from Africa and Oceania, which were exhibited at the Musée d'Ethnographie du Trocadéro in Paris. In 1921, the Franco-Swiss poet Blaise Cendrars released *Anthologie nègre*, and two years later, Fernand Léger staged the performance *La création du monde*, with a set inspired by African masks. Tarsila do Amaral assisted Léger in this production, and she had a close relationship with Cendrars.

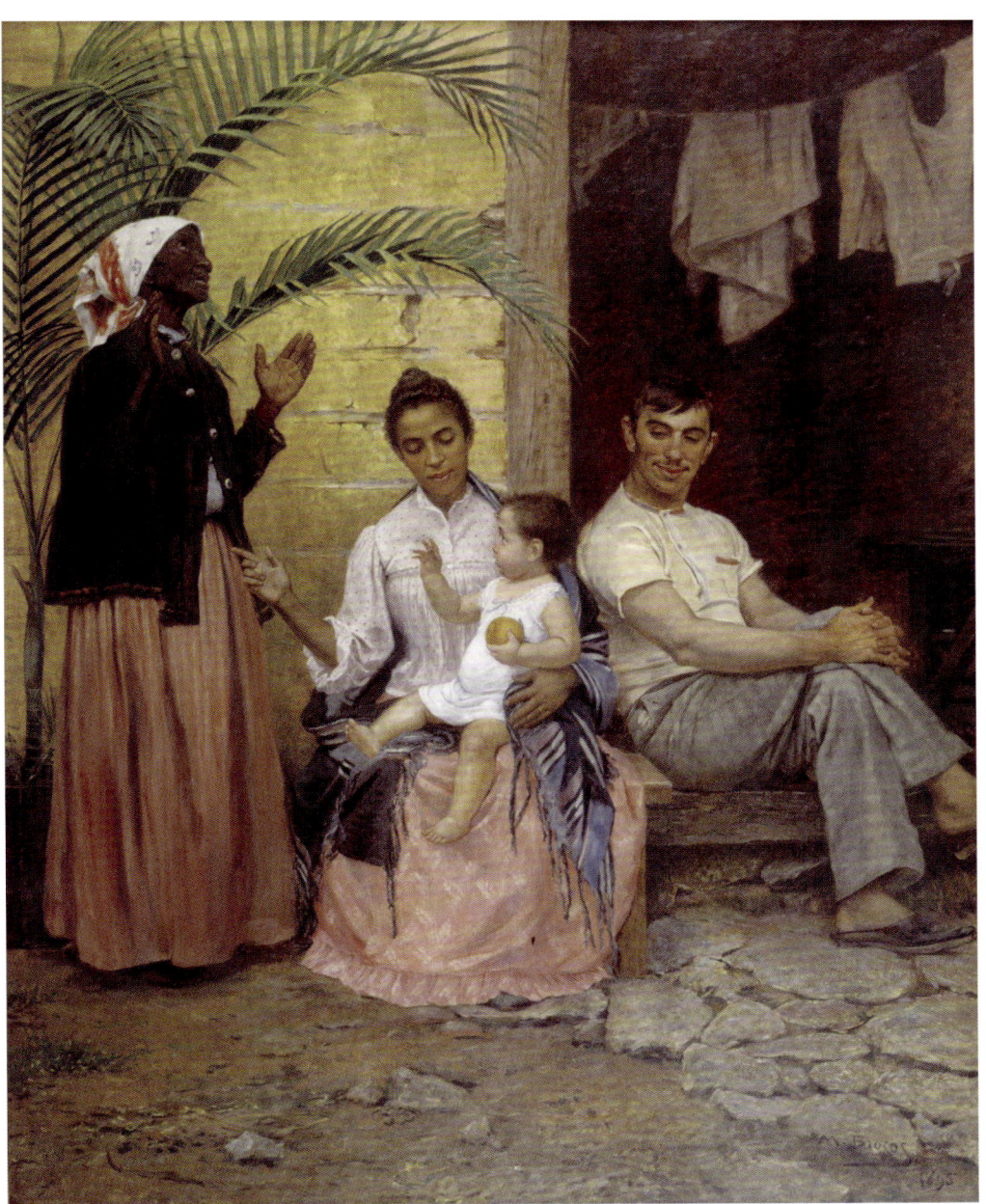

Fig. 5
Modesto Brocos y Gomes,
A redenção de Cam (Ham's
Redemption), 1895, Museu
Nacional de Belas Artes, Rio de
Janeiro

263   **Essays**

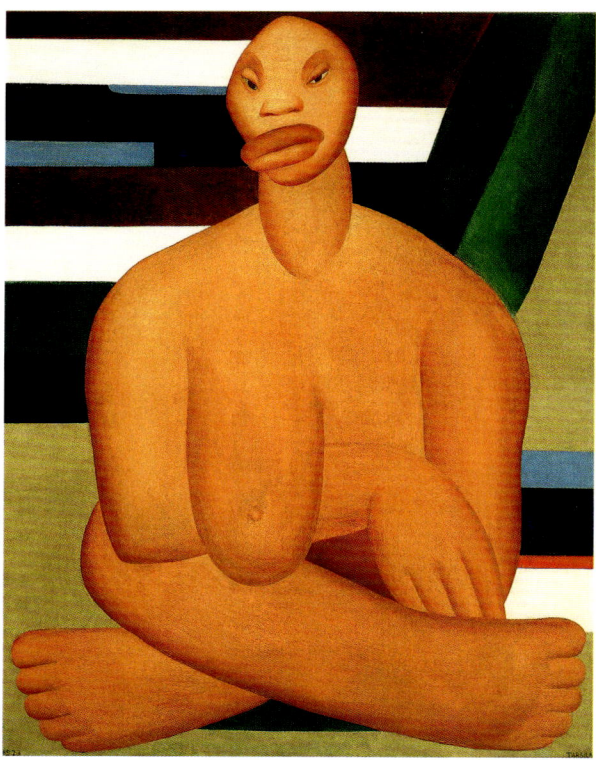

Fig. 6
Tarsila do Amaral, *A negra*
(Black Woman), 1923, Museu
de Arte Contemporânea da
Universidade de São Paulo

The sketch for *A negra* (1923, fig. p. 74) by do Amaral was created in this context, aiming to embody the ideals of modernism through the portrayal of a Black woman with a banana leaf in the background. It is worth noting that *A negra* has sparked debate in contemporary criticism (fig. 6) due to its incorporation of various elements that raise issues about race in Brazil. These include a portrayal that strips her of humanity and identity and accentuates attributes associated with labour, like the elongated breast symbolising her role as a wet nurse, reminiscent of motifs found in nineteenth-century photographs. Similarly, the painter emphasised the physical features of her model – a broad nose, large feet and hands, a small head, exaggerated lips, and the absence of hair – reinforcing her stigmatisation. The concept of the African mask suggests inspiration from primitivism. Who embodies the essence of Brazil? The Black person – recently freed from captivity, connected to the land and labour. By representing the "other", the painter objectifies them: the character has no name or history; they are merely a body exiled into servitude.

Themes and motifs from Indigenous culture also found their way into the new aesthetic. For example, Vicente do Rego Monteiro explored the legends and myths of the Amazon, immersing himself in the extensive collections of Indigenous ethnology at the Museu Nacional da Quinta da Boa Vista in Rio de Janeiro. Despite his in-depth research on the subject, there is no record of direct contact between the painter and Indigenous cultures. While living in Paris, the artist cultivated an artistic style that drew influences from art nouveau, symbolism and orientalism, blending elements of the national and the exotic, which were prevalent in the artistic scene of Paris between 1910 and 1920. Rego Monteiro employed formal stylisations and languid facial features in a mythical, mystical and metaphysical atmosphere. His repertoire ranged from figures of the American pantheon to biblical, classical and epic themes. Inspired by Marajoara pottery and Indigenous culture, he illustrated Pierre Louis Duchartre's book *Légendes, croyances* et talismans des Indiens de l'Amazone (1923). In his images, one can see the exploration of Marajoara and Tapajonic aesthetics, alongside the plasticity of European avant-gardes – an aspect that is evident in Menino nu e tartaruga (fig. p. 55) or O atirador de arco (fig. p. 50). According to Jorge Schwartz, these aspects highlight the pioneering spirit of his "avant-garde Indianism" at the height of the trends emerging from the School of Paris.[13]

In the process of encountering the "other", Lasar Segall stands out. His integration into the circle of modernists briefly changed his artistic approach – his cool, subdued colour palette was replaced with warm, vibrant hues. The fascination with colour found expression in works such as Mulata com criança and Paisagem brasileira (figs pp. 120 and 121). In Mulata com criança, the Black woman emerges as a part of the landscape – the vibrant colours adding to the sense of exoticism. However, his departure from cooler tones did not last long. In Bananal (fig. p. 122), the return to expressionist colours is executed with delicacy. The central presence of the Black man reaffirms the artist's marked aesthetic interest – as seen in earlier works such as Menino com lagartixas (fig. p. 125) and Mulata com criança. In Bananal, Segall's inspiration drawn from African masks blends with the Brazilian landscape, particularly the banana trees, resulting in a reflective exploration. Once again, the banana serves as a symbol of the local environment. Although some sources suggest that the man at the centre might be Olegário, a former enslaved man who lived on a farm belonging to friends of the painter, information beyond that is scarce. Overall, the composition introduces themes of otherness and national identity, imparting a sense of the exotic to the work. There is no doubt that the Black figure portrayed is a man "of the land".

In the 1920s, there was a somewhat "romanticised" notion of Brazil. While there was a desire for a "new independence", the models were still largely "imported". The effort to find expressions of national identity – explored through various channels, from the Semana de Arte Moderna in 1922 to the Manifesto da Poesia Pau-Brasil (1924)[14] and the Manifesto Antropófago (1928)[15] – already revealed the Modernist paradox that both reinforced stereotypes and fluctuated between continuities and ruptures.[16] Black and Indigenous people were not recognised as true agents of modernisation, yet their images were modern, shaped by European modernism.

In the 1930s, studies dedicated to the formation of the "Brazilian people" resumed, focusing on the construction of a collective identity. The prevailing founding myth regarded Brazil as the result of the amalgamation of three races[17] – Black, white and Indigenous. The pursuit of "Brazilianness" revived the celebration of this mixture, with the mestiço emerging as "the national". This marked a period when Indigenous and Black people were approached from an anthropological-cultural standpoint. There was a notable emphasis on systematically rehabilitating their image, although this did not translate into their political or social inclusion.

In 1933, Gilberto Freyre published Casa grande e senzala (The Masters and the Slaves), a study that portrayed miscegenation in a positive light. In 1937 and 1938, Mário de Andrade, then leading the Department of Culture, organised expeditions to the Brazilian northern and north-eastern regions to study folk culture. In this vision of a "racial paradise", not coincidentally, feijoada, known as "slave food", became the "national dish"; capoeira, once repressed by the police at the end of the nineteenth century, was recognised as a sport in 1937; likewise, samba emerged from marginalisation, and carnival parades began to receive official subsidies – all under the auspices of the state.

In the field of visual arts, modernists like Tarsila do Amaral and Candido Portinari depicted the "Brazilian people", addressing poverty, injustice and the world of the working classes – a social concern absent in earlier modernist works. In 1931, do Amaral held an exhibition in Moscow, and following this trip, she attended meetings of the Communist Party alongside her boyfriend, the doctor Osório César.

Stirred by the workers' cause, she painted works of denunciation, such as *Segunda classe* (fig. p. 85) and *Baile caipira* (fig. p. 84).

In turn, Candido Portinari, often referred to as the "portraitist of Blacks and mulattos", painted *O lavrador de café* (fig. p. 95), once again placing the Black man at the centre of the composition, with prominent hands and feet set against the backdrop of a coffee plantation. The bare and irregular feet of the coffee worker evoke Portinari's study of African statuary influenced by Cubism, likely conducted during his stay in Europe in 1928. The exaggeration of the feet and hands served as a metaphor for daily labour, becoming the hallmark of both the painter and those connected to nature.

The painter, born to Italian immigrants, is not strictly aligned with the historical modernist movement, as he was not directly involved in the pursuit of aesthetic renewal.[18] However, his work can be viewed as emblematic of an institutionalised modernism, in which the Brazilian state recognises itself in modern art. Portinari, along with other intellectuals like Mário de Andrade, saw art as a driver for social change. In his words: "We must put an end to the pride of creating art for a select few in Brazil. Artists must educate people by making themselves accessible to the public that fears art (...)". And he continued to urge artists: "Our artists must leave their ivory towers and engage in strong social action, taking an interest in the education of the Brazilian people".[19]

As the most renowned painter, particularly due to the display of his works in international exhibitions and institutions such as the United Nations (UN) and the Library of Congress in Washington D.C., Portinari represented Brazilian art on the global stage. In 1940, his work was featured in *Portinari of Brazil* at the Museum of Modern Art in New York. Effectively, he contributed to the perception of Brazil as a model society that valued its racial composition. By featuring Black and mixed-race individuals as central characters in his works, Portinari underscores the contradictions that existed between national themes, the artist's role and the treatment of avant-garde movements.

In this movement between modernist aesthetics and Afro-Indigenous representation, it becomes apparent that the modernists utilised Black and Indigenous themes and motifs as a pivotal element in their creative process, resulting in the creation of modern imagery. In their pursuit of a national identity, or "Brazilianness", they nurtured their mytho-poetic universe but failed to reflect on themselves and the ethno-racial issues surrounding them. Where were Black and Indigenous people in this modern Brazil? They appeared in modernist works but solely as images. The distinction between the "self" and the "other" persisted, alongside the notion of a "mixed-race" country – where the "other" was always the "Brazilian people."

Authorship and Themes

In the debate surrounding modern iconography and ethno-racial issues, reflecting on authorship and themes holds significant relevance. At the heart of this discussion lies the elite's narrative concerning "modern Brazil" and the portrayal of the "Brazilian people". The backstory of the country's entry into modernity reveals the trajectories of artists whose works were overlooked or even erased by elitist critiques – whether due to gender, ethnicity or social class. Today, the re-evaluation of Brazilian art history is turning to these artists, who are the subjects of new studies and interpretations.

Along this path, we encounter the art of Djanira da Motta e Silva. In her work, religiosity and a diverse range of Brazilian scenes and landscapes coexist. She delved into her subjects through drawings, paintings, and prints, immersing herself in their lives, occupations, and beliefs. She expressed her own convictions, stating, "My roots are firmly planted in the earth, and I do not shy away from my origins. I am not ashamed of being a native. I trust in the development of an art that is truly our own".[20] In the 1940s, Djanira's paintings had a sombre tone. Despite employing subdued colours like grey, brown, and black, she already displayed a penchant for geometric forms. Examples of this phase include *Composição no. 1* (fig. p. 185) and *Parque de diversões* (Amusement Park, c. 1944). During a trip to New York in 1945, she encountered the works of Pieter Bruegel (c. 1525/30–1569) and connected with Fernand Léger (1881–1955), Joan Miró (1893–1983) and Marc Chagall (1887–1985). However, her stay in Salvador in 1950 sparked a transformation in her palette, with the introduction of vibrant colours and themes linked to African ancestry, particularly the imagery of the *orixás*[21] in the religious practice of Candomblé. Here, *Três orixás* (fig. p. 190) stands out. It is a large-scale painting bursting with vibrant colours, featuring clean, harmonious shapes. Three *orixás* are depicted: Yemanjá in red, representing the sea and motherhood; Oxum in yellow, symbolising beauty, abundance and love, the deity of freshwater; and Oxalá in white, the highest deity of Candomblé, embodying purity. Two drum players accompany them.[22]

For a long time, Djanira's artistic journey was sidelined in the discussion of Brazilian art. She was often unfairly characterised as a "primitive artist" whose practice was deemed inferior or lacking erudition. In truth, her work did not neatly fit into the modernist aesthetic. Yet, over time, critics began to acknowledge her. As Mário Pedrosa pointed out, "Djanira is an artist who does not rely on improvisation, and who does not allow herself to be carried away. Her works may seem naive and instinctive, but they are the result of careful deliberation to achieve the outcome".[23]

Amongst those historically overlooked, there is a growing recognition of Black and Indigenous artists. Here, it is worth mentioning the work of Rubem Valentim, whose art, according to art critic Clarival Prado Valladares, is also rooted in the tradition of Western art, focusing on the exploration of geometric forms. However, Valentim himself affirmed, "I was never a Concrete artist", explaining that his use of geometry was

a tool like the rationalism of concretist artists. Geometric shapes dominate his works, highlighting the richness of his symbolic universe and ancestry, expressed not just aesthetically but also magically. His early experiences were abstract. However, soon after, he became interested in mystical symbolism – a defining feature of his work. Initially, Afro-Brazilian liturgical symbols appeared clustered on the canvas, arranged almost haphazardly, but, over time, a sort of "cleansing" took place, leading to a symmetrical organisation of these symbols on the canvas. There was also a transformation in colours: muted tones gave way to pure, vibrant hues. In the late 1960s, upon relocating to Brasília, Valentim shifted from two-dimensional to three-dimensional works, a natural progression given the clear distinction between figure and background in his early paintings. These objects evolved into "altars", exemplified by works such as *Objeto emblemático 1* (fig. p. 244), *Objeto emblemático* (fig. p. 242) and *Conjunto altar sacral emblemático – E59* (fig. p. 238). These altars evoke symbols from Afro-Brazilian religious practices, embodying what the artist termed his "plastic-visual-graphic language", deeply connected to the profound mythical values of Afro-Brazilian culture. This artistic direction aimed to transform objects into altars for Candomblé rituals.

Despite the broadening of the aesthetic landscape, the events surrounding and following the *Semana de Arte Moderna* depict a narrative intertwined with aspirations for progress and modernisation. However, it represents just one perspective among many. "Revisiting history" opens avenues for lesser-known narratives and figures, often overshadowed by mainstream portrayals. Moreover, it offers an opportunity to re-evaluate marginalised issues, including ethno-racial dynamics and the nuances between representation and representativeness.

In the field of art, reconsidering the paradigms surrounding the production, consumption and circulation of Brazilian modernism has become a challenging task due to the complexity of the symbolic systems that underlie social structures. Consequently, there is a growing body of studies and proposals that delve into the patterns influenced by the interactions of modernists with the European avant-gardes.

The portrayal of Black and Indigenous individuals was influenced by the viewpoint of the elite – and here, in a sense, there are both ruptures and continuities with the established norms of representing the "other" in academic art. The depictions of Black and mixed-raced individuals are modern, but not Afro-Indigenous. They lack representativeness. They were shaped through the lens of a white gaze on these cultures. Black artists and writers, such as Lima Barreto and many others who were overlooked, were never invited to the "modernist party". They created alternative narratives that are now being rediscovered. Meanwhile, artists like Rubem Valentim demonstrate the strength of Black authorship.

The modernist paradox, namely, the attempt to "discover Brazil" through European paradigms, prompted the quest for "Brazilianness" and the identity of the "Brazilian people". However, artists and writers resorted to "primitivism", popular within avant-garde circles, to assert that the original, the primitive and the "native" resided within Black and Indigenous populations. Furthermore, echoing the vanguard ethos, they positioned themselves as "cultural guides" for this "people".

1 Barreto 1922. As a Black and peripheral intellectual, Lima Barreto advocated for the inclusion of Black people in Brazilian society. He was the most incisive critic of the First Republic, breaking away from nationalist pride and exposing the privileges of aristocratic families.

2 This refers to an identity construct (the "self" versus the "other") or the notion of alterity, where "people" are the "other" in relation to the elites.

3 The use of *modernisms* in the plural helps us understand that there were multiple forms of renewal that displaced those attached to the past (which were also diverse).

4 In 1816, at the invitation of the Portuguese court, the French Artistic Mission arrived in Rio de Janeiro; it was led by Joaquim Lebreton (1760–1819) and comprised a group of artists including Jean-Baptiste Debret (1768–1848), Nicolas Antoine Taunay (1755–1830), Auguste Marie Taunay (1768–1824) and Grandjean de Montigny (1776–1850).

5 Formally opened in 1826, the Academy began regular operation in 1840 when Emperor D. Pedro II (1825–1891) increased financial support to the institution. Its aim was to provide artistic education, offering disciplines spanning drawing, painting, sculpture and architecture. Following the Proclamation of the Republic in 1889, it was renamed the National School of Fine Arts.

6 Before the proclamation of the Republic, Indianism was a prominent trend during the Romantic period in Brazilian arts and literature.

7 *Caipira* refers to a person from the rural countryside or interior regions of Brazil. Cabloco typically refers to a person of mixed Indigenous and European heritage in Brazil. Matuto typically refers to individuals from rural areas in Brazil, especially in the Northeast region.

8 The title of the work alludes to the first book of the Christian Bible, Genesis, chapter 9. In this episode, Ham exposes the nudity and drunkenness of his father, Noah, to his brothers, Shem and Japheth, and as a result, he is condemned by his father to be a slave. Noah prophesied that Ham would be "the last of his brothers' slaves". Ham is identified in the Bible as the supposed ancestor of African races. Ham's "redemption" lies in witnessing the "improvement of his grandson's race".

9 These individuals occupied a position in society from which power and control over politics and the economy emanated; they were the offspring of the "coffee barons", families of liberal professionals and military traditions. Artists and writers grouped themselves accordingly: in literature, Mário de Andrade (1893–1945), Oswald de Andrade (1890–1954), Sérgio Milliet (1898–1966), Menotti Del Picchia (1892–1988), Guilherme de Almeida (1890–1969), Paulo Prado (1869–1943), Ronald de Carvalho (1893–1935); in music, Heitor Villa-Lobos (1887–1959); in sculpture, Victor Brecheret (1894–1955); and in painting, Emiliano Di Cavalcanti (1897–1976), Zina Aita (1900–1967), Anita Malfatti (1889–1964), Vicente do Rego Monteiro (1899–1970), John Graz (1891–1980), and others. Tarsila do Amaral (1886–1973) did not partake in the Week, but she became a pivotal artist in the movement and its ramifications.

10 Morais 1994, p. 10

11 Brito 1983, p. 15

12 Brito 1983, p. 15

13 Schwartz 2013

14 Written by Oswald de Andrade, it championed naïve art (against pre-established rules), associated with surrealism (the desire to reveal the primitive in human beings). It found expression in cubism and expressionism and influenced poets such as Blaise Cendrars.

15 Also written by Oswald de Andrade, published in May 1928, and inspired by Tarsila's painting *Abaporu* (1928). Written in metaphorical language brimming with poetic aphorisms and humour, the Manifesto became the theoretical cornerstone of this movement seeking to re-evaluate Brazil's cultural dependence.

16 At this point, writer Mário de Andrade took a different approach from other modernists. He sought the roots of the Brazilian people not in the European model but in what he called "matavirginismo". In a letter to Tarsila do Amaral, he wrote: "Leave Paris! Tarsila! Tarsila! Come to the virgin forest, where there is no black art, where there are no gentle streams either. THERE IS VIRGIN FOREST. I have created matavirginismo. That is what the world, art, Brazil, and my dearest Tarsila need". Amaral 2001, p. 79

17 The German traveller and historian Carl Philipp von Martius (1794–1868) won a competition set up by the Brazilian Historical and Geographical Institute with the thesis *Como se deve escrever a história do Brasil* (How the history of Brazil should be written; 1844), proposing a tripartite division between Native Indians, European whites, and African Blacks.

18 As part of the historical modernists, we consider the works of artists who emerged in the 1920s, including Tarsila do Amaral, Lasar Segall, Vicente do Rego Monteiro, among others.

19 "(...) Brazilian art will only exist when our artists completely abandon useless traditions and devote themselves with all their soul to interpreting our surroundings." Portinari Apud Fabris 1996, p. 15

20 Apud Júnior 2004, p. 14

21 *Orixás* are deities of the Yoruba religion represented by forces of nature.

22 In recent Brazilian history, this painting has become a symbol of prejudice and religious intolerance. It was removed from display, at the Palácio da Alvorada, when an extreme-right government took power. Ironically, the painting was not vandalised during an attempted coup on January 8, 2022, when extremists sought to seize power during the transition between governments.

23 Apud Matias de Oliveira 2022

The Central Position of Women in Brazilian Modernism: A Historically Unique Case

Ana Paula Cavalcanti Simioni

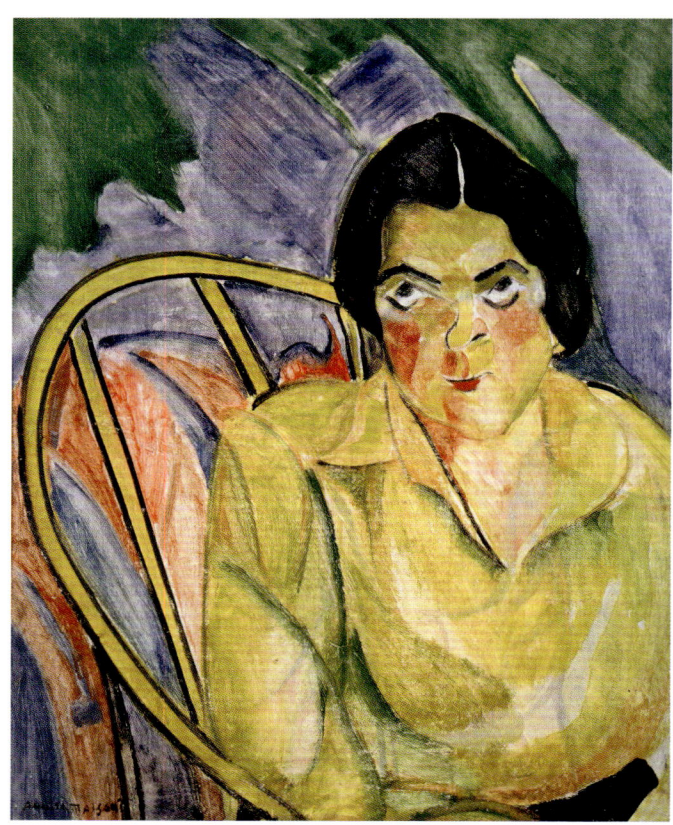

Fig. 1
Anita Malfatti, *A boba* (Silly Woman), 1915, oil on canvas, 61 × 50,6 cm, Museu de Arte Contemporânea, Universidade de São Paulo

In 1922, Brazil marked the centenary of its independence from Portugal. While official celebrations unfolded in Rio de Janeiro, the nation's capital, in São Paulo, a group of writers, intellectuals, and nonconformist artists, funded by the local elites, organised the *Semana de Arte Moderna* (Modern Art Week) at the Theatro Municipal.[1] The event plays a pivotal symbolic role in the country's modern art history, comparable in significance to the *Armory Show* in the United States.[2] While both exhibitions featured women artists, in the American show, the women artists, of which there were approximately fifty among the 300 exhibitors, have been largely forgotten.[3] In contrast, in Brazil, among the twelve visual artists showcased[4], of which three were women, at least one stands out: Anita Malfatti. The painter was prominently featured in the show, with twenty works, commanding a central position in the exhibition space. Although less recognised internationally than her contemporary and friend Tarsila do Amaral, Malfatti is acclaimed domestically as the trailblazer of modernism in Brazil, a distinction seldom bestowed upon a woman.

Anita Catarina Malfatti (1889–1964) received family support to pursue her studies abroad, initially in Germany, from 1910 to 1914.[5] Upon her return to Brazil in 1914, Malfatti had her first solo exhibition in her hometown São Paulo, showcasing paintings, drawings, and prints featuring innovative expressive deformations that were ground-breaking in the local art scene. Funded once again by her family, she travelled to New York, where she stayed from 1915 to 1917 and enrolled first in the Art Students League and then in the Independent School of Art. She regarded this period as "the greatest progress I made in my life (...)".[6] Under the guidance of Homer Boss, who encouraged students to seek their personal style through outdoor excursions, Malfatti experienced an environment of great freedom and artistic experimentation. During this period, she created some of her most highly valued works, such as *A boba* (fig. 1), *O homem amarelo* (fig. p. 27), and *A onda* (fig. p. 33). These paintings reveal an intense and vibrant chromaticism, devoid of any naturalistic appeal, coupled with expressive drawing. It is also worth noting her vigorous charcoal nude studies, many of them featuring male subjects, a bold move considering that, historically, women had been excluded from art academies due to the educational use of live models, which was considered an indecent activity for women (fig. 1 p. 22). In Brazil, it wasn't until 1892 that women were allowed to enrol at the Academy of Fine Arts in Rio de Janeiro, founded by a group of French artists in 1826.[7] These taboos persisted into the beginning of the twentieth century. Malfatti experienced an unusual period of effervescence and openness in New York following the Armory Show, which left a significant impact on several of her works.

In 1917, due to international political instability, the artist returned to Brazil and opened a new exhibition. However, this time the reception was different. The exhibition featured fifty-three works, including paintings, drawings, caricatures, and prints, some created in the United States and others more recently. Initially, everything went well, and some paintings even sold.[8] However, a few days after the opening, a highly critical text about the exhibition was published in the widely circulated newspaper *O Estado de S. Paulo*. Titled *A propósito da Exposição Malfatti* (Regarding the Malfatti Exhibition, later known as *Paranoia ou Mistificação*, Paranoia or Mystification), the review was signed by José Monteiro Lobato, a well-known writer, editor, and critic from São Paulo, who advocated for a "Brazilian" art with a realist/naturalist orientation.[9]

Anita Malfatti's works diverged from everything Lobato advocated. She employed colours independently, intentionally distorted models, and depicted human types overlooked by him, a notable advocate of the "caipira" as the epitome of the national image.[10] Malfatti, however, opted to depict immigrants (Japanese, Russian), or, as we see in *A boba*, a woman who deviated from the prevalent notion of "normality". The severity of Lobato's critique led to the return of some previously sold paintings, disappointing the family that had funded her studies, and deeply affecting the artist.[11] It should be noted however that, unlike most women artists who were often overlooked by critics or, as Lobato himself stated, received only "goody-goody" adjectives from them, he chose to take her seriously as a professional artist with whom he aesthetically disagreed yet recognised as relevant.[12]

Following the article's publication, Malfatti started receiving support in the press from several young writers and artists, including Oswald de Andrade, Menotti del Picchia, and Emiliano Di Cavalcanti, who defended her originality. This marked the beginning of the formation of the São Paulo modernist group, with the local press serving as its main platform for support and action. This initial group would later be joined by new members and supporters, culminating in the organisation of the *Semana de Arte Moderna* in 1922.

The artist's prominent role in the renowned exhibition is attributed to her peers' acknowledgment of her contribution to introducing new artistic languages to the country, as well as the obstacles she faced in gaining acceptance from the local audiences. As Annateresa Fabris aptly points out, the significance of the *Semana* lies only partially in the aesthetic character of the works presented, as many were not particularly daring formally. It is crucial to consider the reaction provoked by the event, which ignited debates around the concepts and ideas of modernism in the country. From a perspective that perceives that the history of art is not merely a history of forms but must also consider the context of reception, appropriation, and circulation of the artworks (and their authors), Anita Malfatti's 1917 exhibition was undoubtedly a watershed for Brazilian modernism.[14]

Such prominence for a woman artist, and her recognition as a pioneer of modern art, is uncommon in international modernist narratives. This acknowledgement is usually reserved for male figures like Matisse, Picasso, Duchamp, Marinetti, Malevich, Mondrian, Kandinsky, and Salvador Dalí in Europe, as well as Diego Rivera in Mexico, Pedro Figari in Uruguay, and Xul Solar and Emilio Pettoruti in Argentina. Griselda Pollock emphasises the patriarchal biases inherent in international modernist narratives. When examining the list of artists featured at MoMA's 1936 exhibition *Cubism and Abstract Art*,[15] Pollock raises the following questions:

Over each movement a named artist presides. All those canonized as the initiators of modern art are men. Is this because there were no women involved in early modern movements? No. Is it because those who were, were without significance in determining the shape and character of modern art? No. Or is it rather because what

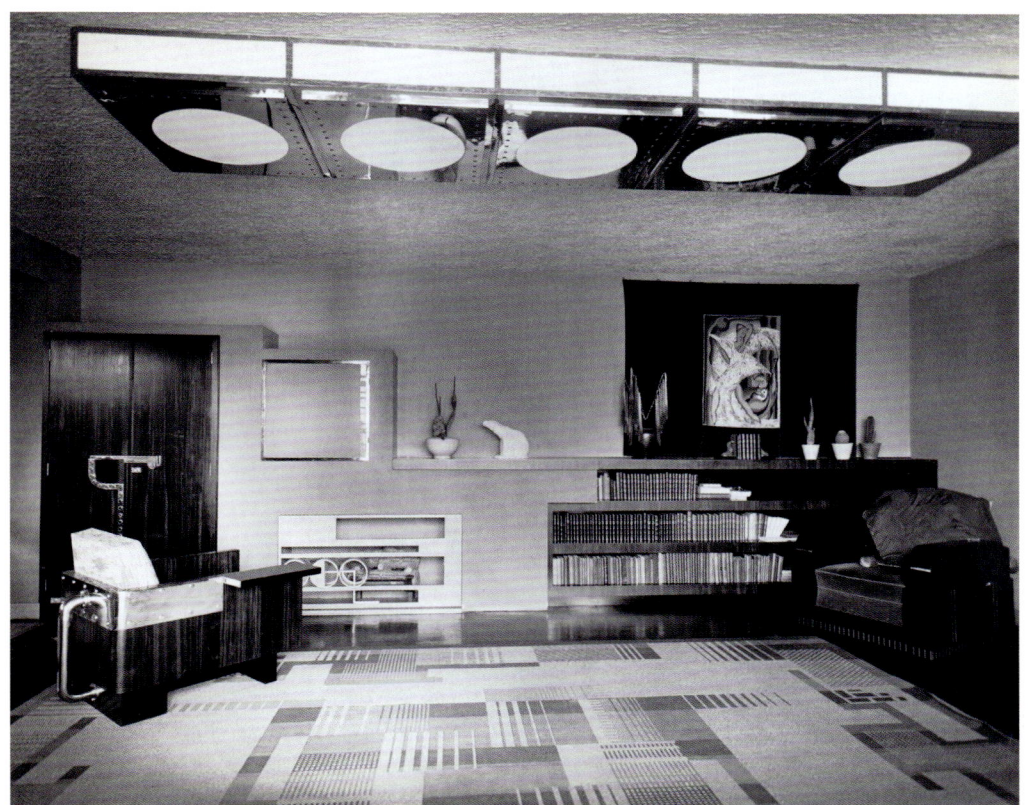

Fig. 2
Residence Roberto Simonsen, São Paulo.
Living room with a carpet by Regina
Gomide Graz and furniture by John Graz,
c. 1925, Instituto John Graz

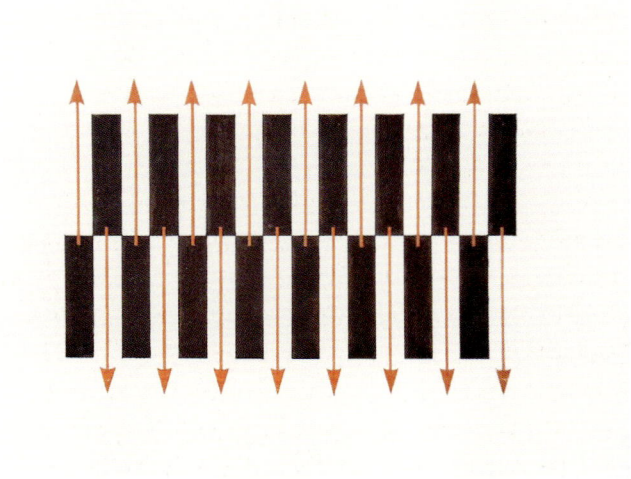

Fig. 3
Regina Gomide Graz, Drawing for a carpet,
c. 1930, ink on paper, Instituto John Graz

modernist art history celebrates is a selective tradition which normalizes, as the only modernism, a particular and gendered set or practices? I would argue for this explanation. As a result any attempt to deal with artists in the early history of modernism who are women necessitates a deconstruction of the masculinist myths of modernism.[16]

Pollock explains that the history of modern art does not constitute an objective or neutral discourse but rather a set of selective narratives that tend to prioritise practices and values associated with mythologies of masculinity. The prime example is the flâneur, the earliest depiction of the modern artist, which emerges in the writings of Charles Baudelaire in the nineteenth century. This privileged observer of modern life, who roams the streets of the metropolis seeing all yet remaining unseen, embodies a mobility privilege that only male bodies could enjoy in that context.[17] Which women would have been allowed the freedom to wander among the different spaces of modernity, from palaces to brothels? Expanding beyond her text, we might ask ourselves: which women could have left behind Western bourgeois life and settled in the Pacific islands to live "like savages" and be acclaimed for their daring, as Gauguin did?

These examples illustrate how the celebrated acts in modernist narratives often have an implicit male subject. While this observation holds true for central countries like France, England, and Germany, which were major stages for the emergence of modernist movements, what about peripheral countries where processes of modernisation—economic, social, political, and urban—were in their infancy and often characterised by an incomplete, fragmentary, and tumultuous nature? It is noteworthy that, despite this, it was precisely in one such country that a woman artist (from the middle classes and an immigrant) attained a unique position in terms of recognition.[18]

But not all participants in the *Semana* met the same fate. The case of Regina Gomide Graz (1897–1973) is both interesting and contrasting. To this day, there are doubts about her actual presence at the event, which has been extensively studied and debated in Brazil. On the one hand, the above mentioned sketch and testimonies from the time mention her among the exhibiting artists.[19] On the other hand, the absence of her name in the catalogue and her lack of recollection of participating, as mentioned in an interview given decades after the event, cast doubt on any certainty.[20] In my view, this uncertainty is indicative of how little interest the artist aroused throughout the twentieth century, leaving gaps in her career.[21] Most likely, this is due to her dedication to applied arts, which were traditionally looked down upon by the national art system, which favoured "pure" arts forms, such as painting, sculpture, printmaking, drawing, and so on.

Regina Gomide graduated from the École des Beaux Arts in Geneva (1913–1918), alongside her siblings Antonio Gomide, who would later become a renowned artist, and Maria, who did not pursue a professional career. Their studies were funded by their father.[22] At the school, after completing the preparatory course, Regina studied various subjects dedicated to ornament and perspective, indicating an education focused on the decorative arts, which were then prestigious in the Genevan context.[23] It was at this institution that she met John Graz, a young Swiss artist on the rise, who had won awards for posters and commissions for stained glass windows. In 1920, they married and moved to São Paulo, becoming involved in the city's cultural scene. This involvement earned them an invitation from the writer Oswald de Andrade to take part in the *Semana* 1922.

In 1925, inspired by their visit to the renowned *Exposition internationale des arts décoratifs et industriels modernes* (International Exhibition of Modern Decorative and Industrial Arts) in Paris and their previous training in

Switzerland, John and Regina Graz introduced something quite original to the Brazilian scene: modernist interior design. They were pioneers in embracing the concept of total art, seeking to achieve a synthesis of functional and modern aesthetics within homes. From the 1920s to the 1940s, they implemented these innovative designs in the homes of members of the local elite, including Roberto Simonsen, an influential industrialist, founder of the Federation of Industries of the State of São Paulo, and a prestigious intellectual (fig. 2).[24]

In these projects, there was a clear division of labour based on gender. John Graz handled the overall design, furniture, metals, doorknobs, stained glass, and sometimes paintings (in some cases, these were made by Antonio Gomide), while Regina Gomide Graz took charge of all the textile elements, such as rugs, cushions, and curtains. The delicate nature of these materials, coupled with their historical undervaluation (seen as artisanal, feminine, and subject to fashion fluctuations), resulted in few of the artist's works being preserved in private collections and museums.[25] Additionally, the projects were typically signed by John alone, leaving Regina in the role of her husband's collaborator without receiving authorship credit. In recent years, analyses informed by a gender perspective have challenged these assumptions. As some studies have revealed, even in the iconic Bauhaus modernist school, women were discouraged from enrolling in the architecture and painting studios, which were more prestigious, and were directed instead to the weaving studio, which was seen as less prestigious and thus became predominantly female.[26] The case of John and Regina appears to reflect this trend in Brazil, where international modernist projects often rely on a gender-based hierarchy of materials.

These considerations are crucial for redefining Gomide Graz's place in Brazilian art history, particularly her pioneering use of abstract languages. If these historically undervalued materials were elevated to the status of "art", akin to painting and sculpture in Brazil, this would prompt a revaluation of the timeline for the development of abstract art in the country. It is typically believed that it is only in the late 1940s, with the exhibition *Do figurativismo ao abstracionismo* (From Figuration to Abstraction), and throughout the 1950s, that abstraction truly gained recognition in Brazil. However, these languages were already present in tapestry studies in the 1930s, as well as in some works made in the following decades (fig. 3).

Unlike Regina Gomide Graz, whose work was featured at the *Semana* but who was largely side-lined in the history of modern art in Brazil, Tarsila do Amaral (1886–1973) did not participate in the event. However, this did not prevent her from becoming the most celebrated artist of the first Brazilian modernist generation, both nationally and internationally.[27] Born into a family of São Paulo landowners, do Amaral received a refined education abroad; she completed her studies in Barcelona, returned to São Paulo, and took private lessons with local painters. In 1920, she headed to Paris, funded by her family.[28] She enrolled at the Académie Julian, a renowned private academy that had gained international fame since the late nineteenth century, offering live classes for women artists. She only returned from this stay in June 1922. Upon her arrival, she was introduced to local circles by Anita Malfatti, who had been her acquaintance since the late 1910s. They quickly formed the "Group of Five", consisting of the two painters and the writers Mário de Andrade, Menotti del Picchia, and Oswald de Andrade, who would soon become her partner.

In late 1922, Tarsila and Oswald, who were then divorced from their previous partners, travelled together to Paris, where they remained until 1928, with occasional visits to Brazil. Like many other Brazilian artists, they were drawn to what was considered the "artistic capital of modernism".[29] However, few were able to integrate into Parisian circles as successfully as they did. Their financial, intellectual, and personal capital allowed them to mingle with emblematic figures of the French avant-garde, as do Amaral later reminisced:

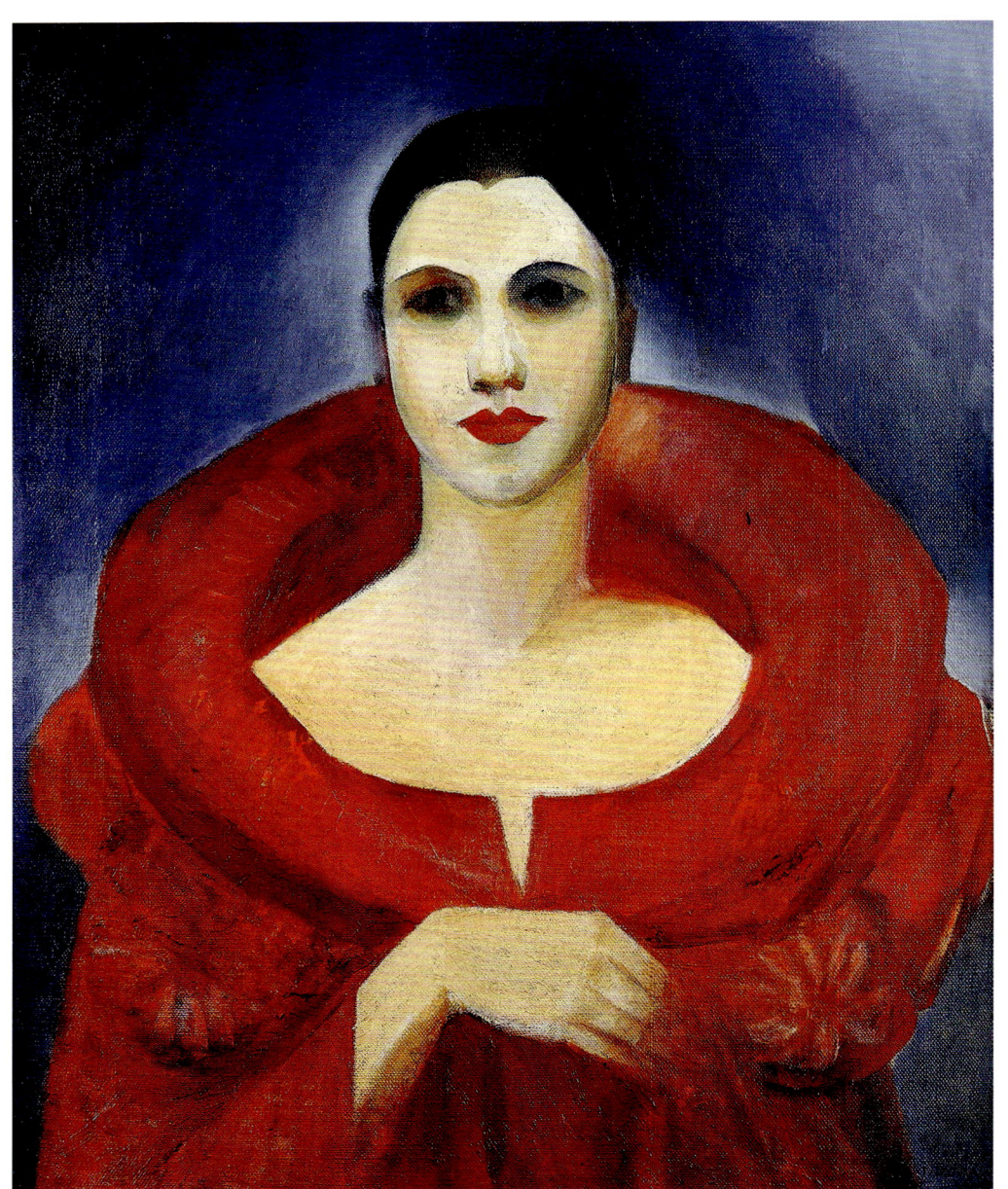

Fig. 4
Tarsila do Amaral. *Autorretrato au manteau
rouge* (Self-Portrait with Red Manteau),
1923, oil on canvas, 71.5 × 60 cm, Museu
Nacional de Belas Artes, Rio de Janeiro

In my studio on rue Hégésippe-Moreau in Montmartre, the entire artistic avant-garde of Paris would gather. Brazilian lunches were a regular occurrence there, complete with feijoada, bacuri compote, cachaça, and straw cigarettes, essential for adding an exotic touch. *My main concern was diplomatically forming homogeneous groups. The first team included Cendrars, Fernand Léger, Jules Supervielle, Brancusi, Robert Delaunay, Vollard, Rolf de Maré, Darius Milhaud, and the black prince Kojo Tovalu (Cendrars loved black people). Some of the aforementioned would move on to Jean Cocteau's group, which included Erik Satie, Albert Gleizes, André Lhote, and many other interesting individuals. Picasso, immersed in his work, rarely ventured out; Jules Romains and Valéry Larbaud were also good friends.*[30]

In this passage, do Amaral demonstrates her awareness of the strategies she and her partner employed to integrate themselves into Parisian circles. In their elegant and spacious studio, they meticulously and diplomatically invited groups of diverse writers and artists with similar interests. These guests were drawn to an intentionally exotic atmosphere created by the couple, stimulating their senses with food, drinks, tobacco, scents, music, and such, evoking their distant "tropical country". At a time when, as do Amaral notes, "Paris was tired of Parisian art", and cosmopolitanism was in vogue, the couple leveraged their "otherness" – highly valued in those modern circles – to their advantage. Additionally, they also enrolled as students in the studios of Gleizes, Lhote, and Léger, and acquired a significant collection of modernist works, including paintings by Delaunay, Léger, and Giorgio De Chirico.[31]

The couple's investment in shaping do Amaral's image as a beautiful, elegant, and cosmopolitan woman was also crucial. This was a project in which Oswald participated meticulously, as seen in the telegrams he sent her, one of which advised: "Display the paintings and keep abreast of the gallery scene, come very elegant, well-groomed, visit Patou, Poiret, etc., etc., hat too."[32] This image is captured in the painting *Autorretrato au manteau rouge*, from 1923 (fig. 4), where do Amaral, attired in Paul Poiret, stylises her (white) face to echo the sculptures of Brâncuşi, who featured in her personal collection. The pinned-up hair would become a kind of trademark, a visual identity, employed several times after this painting. Additionally, the self-portrait makes no reference to her work as a painter, a relatively common subject in this genre.

In my view, this painting acquires a clearer meaning when viewed alongside another work created in the same year: *A negra* (fig. 6 p. 264). I believe that both represent two sides of the same coin: they respond to do Amaral's quest to establish herself as an international, modern artist from the tropics in the cosmopolitan Paris of the 1920s.[33] *A negra* is undeniably one of the most significant, recognisable, and controversial images from the early years of Brazilian modernism.[34] An unnamed Black woman is portrayed through a body that rejects any erotic connotation associated with femininity, achieved by exaggerated features like breasts, feet, and lips, as well as the absence of hair. In this regard, the painting features a series of very bold elements. From a feminist perspective, it can be seen as part of a lineage of modernist works that rejected the representation of the female body as an object of contemplation for male viewers. This places her work alongside artists such as Paula Modersohn-Becker, Tamara de Lempicka, Émilie Charmy, and Frida Kahlo, among others.[35] Formally, its use of voluminous masses instead of detailed anatomy, as well as the tendency to blur the distinction between figure and background, reflects its dialogue with international cubist and post-cubist paradigms. However, it is also a particular and situated representation. Do Amaral's choice of theme alludes to a crucial and sensitive issue in Brazilian history: the enslavement of Black people. Brazil was economically, socially, and politically built on the labour of enslaved Africans and was one of the last countries in the Western world to abolish this system, as late as 1888.[36] When considering all aspects already mentioned, *A negra* represents a perfect synthesis of the modernist generation's desire for an "international-Brazilian" art, where elements of its specific history and culture were represented through universally modern languages.

However, this does not imply a "happy" synthesis.[37] On the contrary, it is a work infused with classist and racial tensions, which become even more explicit when juxtaposed with do Amaral's self-portrait. The paintings are contrasting facets of the same aesthetic pursuit. Through both, the painter asserts her identity as a modern artist, daring in the deconstruction of the female body and the representation of the "other" revered in France and Brazil. However, it is clear that the deconstructed body belongs to a generic "other", not her own. Thus, she keeps her privileges of class, race, and beauty intact, concepts aptly embodied in the muse-like image that accompanied her throughout her career.

As Rafael Cardoso noted, Tarsila do Amaral's painting functions as a "magical cloak", offering various interpretive possibilities.[38] These reveal the different readings that Brazilian modernism, along with its leading figures, has garnered over time. Despite being painted amidst cosmopolitan Paris, which esteemed exoticism and primitivism, *A negra* initially didn't receive significant acclaim in France. In do Amaral's exhibition at Galerie Percier in 1926, the painting *Morro de favela* (fig. p. 75) held more prominence in the catalogue. It is also worth noting that do Amaral selected *A cuca* (The creature, 1924) as the work to be donated to the French state, specifically to the Museum of Grenoble, the first institution in France to embrace modernist works. During the Vargas Era (1930–45), a period when the Brazilian government endorsed modernism (or some of its aspects) as official art, neither do Amaral nor Malfatti received any commissions. They were also overlooked for inclusion in the initial collection of Latin American art curated by MoMA in the 1940s.[39]

The prominence of both artists within Brazilian modernism was not acknowledged from the outset, nor was it a straightforward process. Recognition emerged gradually, especially from the 1950s onward, influenced by various factors. Notable events include Malfatti's retrospective at MASP in 1949[40] and do Amaral's exhibition at MAM São Paulo in 1951, curated by Sérgio Milliet.[41] Aracy Amaral notes that while the latter marked do Amaral's return to newspaper headlines and mass media, unanimous recognition was slow and only fully materialised with the retrospective organised by the Casa do Artista Plástico in 1961.[42]

In addition to these exhibitions, there was an emerging art historiography that established the prominence of São Paulo modernism, particularly focusing on figures like Anita Malfatti, Tarsila do Amaral, Mário and Oswald de Andrade, and others. This narrative solidified the discourse with institutional backing from the University of São Paulo, forming a "true" national canon.[43] It is also noteworthy to mention the acquisitions made by the State Government of São Paulo during the 1960s and 1970s, which included the personal collections (archives, libraries, and artworks) of Mário de Andrade, which were donated to University of São Paulo, and Guilherme de Almeida. Both were writers and collectors, known as prominent figures in São Paulo modernism, who received official recognition from the State. Other works were also acquired by the government for its collection, with a focus on São Paulo modernism, particularly Tarsila do Amaral.[44] Additionally, it is important to consider the role of the art market, which was firmly establishing itself in São Paulo and Rio de Janeiro during this period, particularly when it comes to the treatment of modernist works.[45] Many artists had recently passed away (among them Lasar Segall in 1957, Portinari and Guignard in 1962, Anita Malfatti in 1964, Vicente do Rego Monteiro in 1970, and

Tarsila do Amaral and Flávio de Carvalho in 1973), leaving behind estates with highly valued and sought-after artworks. This was especially significant given the emerging national canon, supported by universities, states, and the market.[46] It was no coincidence that during the 50th anniversary celebrations of the *Semana*, in 1972, Malfatti and particularly do Amaral were hailed as national stars.

Against this backdrop, a canon of Brazilian modernism emerged, incorporating female artists – a rarity in international modernist narratives, where women often occupy marginal or secondary roles. There are common threads in the trajectories of these artists; all three were affiliated with the artistic and intellectual circles of São Paulo. They all pursued their education abroad (in Germany, the USA, France, and Switzerland), underscoring that the endeavour to establish themselves as modern artists in early twentieth century Brazil was intertwined with specific privileges of class, origin, and region.

Finally, it is important to note that the recognition of these three artists was not despite their gender but rather through gendered narratives. Do Amaral was celebrated as the *muse* of modernism; Malfatti became a *martyr*, victimised by Lobato's criticism; and Gomide Graz was often seen as her husband's *collaborator*. The beautiful, the fragile, and the wife are tropes that reinforce traditional normative ideas of femininity, shedding light on yet another inherent (and intriguing) contradiction within Brazilian modernism.

1 Amaral 1970

2 Bastos 1991

3 Shircliff 2014

4 The remaining attendees included Zina Aita, a painter, draughtswoman, and illustrator who, after 1925, relocated to Naples where she worked as a ceramist until her death; and Regina Gomide Graz, an artist known for her contributions to decorative arts and for introducing Art Deco to Brazil.

5 Refer to the artist's entry in the catalogue. See also: Batista 2006, and the website: http://ver-anitamalfatti.ieb. usp.br/ (18 March 2024)

6 Batista 2006, p. 101

7 Despite being prohibited from attending the Imperial Academy of Fine Arts (renamed the National School of Fine Arts in 1890), women were permitted to take part in the general exhibitions held annually by the institution. Between 1846 (the inaugural year of the exhibition) and 1922, more than 200 female exhibitors were documented, with some receiving awards and recognition during their lifetimes. See: Simioni 2008

8 Anita Malfatti. *A chegada da arte moderna no Brasil*, typescript (C. PESP, 1951). Fundo AM. Arquivo, IEB-USP

9 Chiarelli 1995

10 *Caipira* is a Brazilian Portuguese term used to describe rural individuals who are often from mixed heritage (white and Indigenous).

11 Years later, Mário de Andrade claimed that after the review, Malfatti became less daring in her practice. This view must be challenged in light of local artistic disputes and the international artistic context, characterised by a "Return to Order". See: Chiarelli 2012a

12 Simioni 2008, pp. 78–84

13 Almeida 1976; Amaral 1970

14 Fabris 1994

15 In this exhibition, female participation was minimal. According to the catalogue, there are no women among the sixty-two exhibited painters, nor among the fifteen selected architects or ten interior designers. There were also no women filmmakers. In fact, only four women were mentioned, all in a specific category: "theatre/costumes/ set design", all from the Russian avant-garde: Natalia Goncharova, Liuba Popova, Alexandra Exter, and Varvara Stepanova. See: Simioni 2019

16 Pollock 1994, p. 50

17 Wolff 1985, pp. 37–46

18 I explore this uniqueness of the Brazilian case, specifically analysing the trajectories of Anita Malfatti, Regina Gomide Graz, and Tarsila do Amaral in Simioni 2022

19 The sketch is reproduced in Amaral 1970, p. 140. Regina Gomide Graz is mentioned among the painters who took part in the exhibition in an article published by the newspaper *A Gazeta*, titled "Futurismo. A Semana de Arte Moderna" (Futurism: The Week of Modern Art), São Paulo, 02/25/1922. She is also listed in an article titled "Semana de arte moderna", published by the newspaper *O Paiz* on 02/01/1922. See: https://memoria.bn.br/ DocReader/DocReader. aspx?bib=178691_05&pesq= %22Regina%20Graz%22&pasta= ano%20192&hf=memoria. bn.br&pagfis=8639 (18 March 2024)

20 Amaral 1968

21 See Simioni 2022, Chapter 4 "Gênero e Materialidade das Vanguardas: Regina Gomide Graz e a Experiência de uma Arte Decorativa Moderna"

22 Her father, a retired senior government official in Brazil, was then engaged in diplomatic activities in Geneva. He brought his five children to study in Switzerland, with the two eldest attending a school in Lausanne.

23 Pallini 2004; Fernandez 2005

24 Simioni 2016

25 For decades, the most comprehensive collection of the artist's works was owned by the collector couple Fulvia and Adolpho Leirner, who recently donated these works to the Museu de Arte Contemporânea (MAC), Universidade de São Paulo. For further details, refer to: Simioni and Migliaccio 2020. With regards to the donation, see: http://www.mac.usp.br/mac/ expos/2022/art-deco-leirner/ index.html (18 March 2024)

26 Droste 2004; Wortmann Weltge 1993

27 An example of this is the exhibition titled *Tarsila do Amaral: Inventing Modern Art* held at the MoMA in 2018. In 2024, the Musée du Luxembourg in Paris will dedicate a new solo exhibition to her. For further details, see: Lima 2020

28 With regards to the artist's career, see: Amaral 2003

29 Batista 2012; Greet 2018

30 Amaral 2008, p. 353. Author's highlights

31 With regards to the collection, see Amaral 2003, pp. 329–330

32 Telegram from Oswald de Andrade to Tarsila do Amaral, 31 October 1924. See also: Casarin 2022

33 Simioni 2022

34 To understand the significance of the painting and its underlying tensions, please refer to the text by Alecsandra Martins in this catalogue. See also: Cardoso 2019

35 Crippa 2003

36 A considerable bibliography on the subject exists in Brazil. Amongst others, I suggest: Pinsky 2018; Alencastro 2000; Almeida 2019

37 See Cardoso 2019

38 Cardoso 2019, pp. 152–53

39 On this topic, see Simioni 2022, Chapter 5 "Das Margens ao Centro: O Processo de Consagração das Artistas Modernistas"

40 MASP, founded in 1947, was the most important museum in São Paulo, with a universal and encyclopaedic character. It currently holds one of the most important collections in the Southern Hemisphere. The exhibition was titled *Anita Malfatti: exposição de sua obra 1918–1949*. In: Enciclopédia Itaú Cultural de Arte e Cultura Brasileira. São Paulo: Itaú Cultural, 2024. Available at: http://enciclopedia.itaucultural. org.br/evento238044/ malfatti-exposicao-de- sua-obra-1918-1949. (13 February 2024)

41 Established in 1948, the MAM was the city's first museum of modern art. Today, its original collection has been integrated into the MAC-USP. The exhibition in question was titled *Tarsila, 1918–1950*.

42 Amaral 2003, pp. 390–394

43 Coelho 2012; Cardoso 2022a

44 This refers to the collection owned by the Cultural Collection of the Government Palaces of the State of São Paulo, largely organised by GEAPAC during the aforementioned period. For further details, refer to Simioni 2022, Chapter 5. See: http://www.acervo. sp.gov.br/acervoColec.html (18 March 2024)

45 Durand 1989

46 Simioni 2013a

The *Exhibition of Modern Brazilian Paintings* at the Royal Academy of Arts in 1944

Adrian Locke

This was the grand conundrum for Latin American artists: to prove their modernity and universality at home they had to be conversant in European visual idioms, but in Europe evidence of this knowledge and training was judged somehow to impede the possibility of a unique or native perspective.[1]

Over the course of three weeks in the winter of 1944 the Royal Academy of Arts (RA) hosted the *Exhibition of Modern Brazilian Paintings* in its grand, neoclassical Main Galleries.[2] The show's title is somewhat misleading as it was, in effect, two distinct exhibitions rolled into one: the first, the *Exhibition of Modern Brazilian Paintings*, comprised 80 paintings and 86 works on paper displayed in two galleries; and the second, *Brazil Builds*, contained 192 photographs taken by the American architect G. E. Kidder Smith and occupied a single gallery. A rare, contemporary photograph (fig. 1) captures the dense salon hang of the *Exhibition of Modern Brazilian Paintings*, for which there was a brief catalogue with a preface by the aristocratic British art critic Sacheverell Sitwell and an introduction by the Brazilian art critic Ruben Navarra. The catalogue (fig. 2) included black-and-white photographs of twelve of the works. *Brazil Builds* was a pre-existing exhibition that had previously been shown at the Museum of Modern Art (MoMA) in New York and was transferred to the RA under the aegis of the Anglo-Brazilian Society of London.[3]

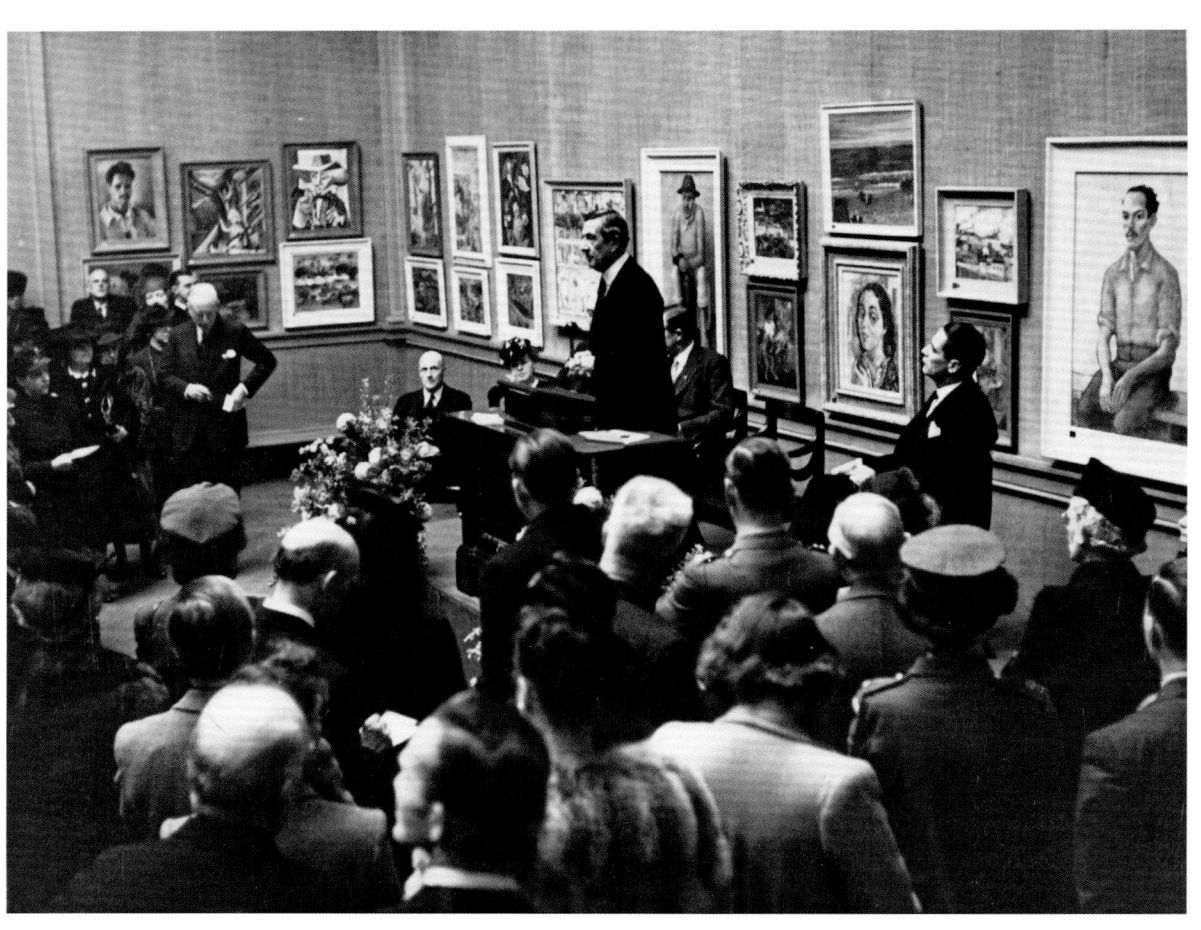

Fig. 1
Contemporary photograph
of the dense salon hang at
the opening reception of
the *Exhibition of Modern
Brazilian Paintings* at the
Royal Academy of Arts,
1944, The National Archives,
Gift of Brazilian paintings
in aid of war effort, 1944

Brasil! Brasil!

MoMA published *Brazil Builds: Architecture New and Old, 1652–1942*, a substantial and densely illustrated catalogue by the American architect Philip L. Goodwin, in New York in 1943 (fig. 3).

The *Exhibition of Modern Brazilian Paintings* was conceived as a gesture of solidarity following Brazil's formal entry into World War II in August 1942, two years before the exhibition opened in London. The Brazilian President Getúlio Vargas declared war against the Axis countries following a sustained campaign of harassment of Brazilian shipping by German and Italian submarines that began in January that year. Two years later, in November 1944, the Força Expedicionária Brasileira (FEB), the Brazilian Expeditionary Force, was sent to Italy. Following the two-year hiatus between Vargas's declaration of war and his sending troops to the European theatre, the Brazilian Expeditionary Force was known colloquially as the "Smoking Snakes", the suggestion being that one was more likely to see a snake smoke than to witness Brazil sending troops into battle. In fact, however, Brazil was the only Allied South American country to do so.

The arrival of Brazilian troops in Naples coincided with the arrival of artworks in London in November 1944. The impetus for the *Exhibition of Modern Brazilian Paintings* came from the statesman Oswaldo Aranha, formerly of the Brazilian Ministry of Foreign Affairs, and can be seen as a prime example of soft power, in this instance using culture to forge or strengthen diplomatic ties between nations.[4] Brazil's investment in cultural soft power continued with the building of three museums between 1947 and 1948: the Museu de Arte Moderna de São Paulo (MAM-SP), the Museu de Arte de São Paulo (MASP) and the Museu de Arte Moderna do Rio de Janeiro (MAM-RJ). The art critic Roberto Pontual referred to these initiatives as an "indication of the Brazilian desire to communicate with its own artists as well as associating with those international centres of artistic expression".[5] Not long afterwards, in 1951, Brazil inaugurated the Bienal de São Paulo: the first biannual exhibition anywhere in the world

after Venice, and a demonstration of the value Brazil placed on art and culture at that time, emphasising its determination to be part of the emerging post-war international art circuit.

In Brazil a call was put out to invite artists to gift examples of their work for the exhibition in London. These were to be sold for the benefit of the Royal Air Force Benevolent Fund. Seventy artists answered this call to donate their work to the cause; an expression of camaraderie that also reflected the attachment many of these artists felt for Europe, having previously lived, studied, worked and exhibited there, particularly in inter-war Paris. Their recently completed donations were exhibited in Rio de Janeiro (then the capital of Brazil), at the Palácio Itamaraty, the seat of the Foreign Ministry, before being packed and shipped to London (fig. 4).[6] Behind the scenes, Anthony Eden, the British Foreign Secretary, and Alfred Munnings, President of the RA, had held protracted discussions before the Royal Academy's Burlington House galleries were secured as the exhibition's venue. Several prominent London institutions had already turned down requests to host the show.[7] Eden was running out of options when eventually Munnings accepted, but not before expressing deep reservations in a letter to the Foreign Secretary: "The posters and catalogue will state clearly the provenance of the collection so that no responsibility will rest on the Royal Academy or the Government."[8]

The exhibition was well received: some 100,000 visitors saw it on its UK tour purchasing some 6,300 catalogues, with around half of the art works sold, and 1,200 pounds raised. It toured nationally to seven other venues,[9] before travelling to Amsterdam and ending up in Paris at the newly established UNESCO headquarters at the Hotel Majestic as part of UNESCO's inaugural exhibition *Exposition Internationale d'Art Moderne*. Among the works sold, twenty-three were purchased by, for example, the British Council as well as individuals such as the British architect Alfred, Lord Bossom, and donated to UK national and

283   **Essays**

regional museums.[10] Portinari's *Mulher e crianças* (fig. p. 104) was purchased by the Brazilian diplomat Hugo Gouthier and found its way back to Brazil. Of the seventy artists who donated works to the exhibition, six feature in the current exhibition and are represented by four works that were originally shown in 1944: Flávio de Carvalho; Djanira da Motta e Silva; Tarsila do Amaral (fig. p. 76); Candido Portinari (figs pp. 104 and 105); Lasar Segall (fig. p. 127); and Alfredo Volpi. Sitwell posited that Segall's *Lucy com flor* "may be the best painting in the exhibition".[11]

Although Navarro referred to the *Exhibition of Modern Brazilian Paintings* as "the first collective exhibition ever made by Brazilian Painters in Europe", numerous Brazilian artists had already exhibited in France and the US by this time.[12] Indeed, the novelty of exhibiting modern Brazilian art in London, which Sitwell captured in his preface to the catalogue, was countered by his somewhat patronising and dismissive tone. "The least we can do is to take their paintings seriously," he wrote, adding that it "would be tragically disappointing if the art of the South American tropics was in no way different from that of Czechoslovakia or Norway. As much as if the first returning cargoes of oranges and bananas were, in the end, but pears and apples."[13] By 1944, the tone of these comments was already out of touch, particularly compared to the reception these artists had received elsewhere and given that some were, by then, established and celebrated names both domestically and internationally.[14]

Since the early 1920s, artists including Tarsila do Amaral, Anita Malfatti and Vicente do Rego Monteiro had exhibited regularly at the Paris Salons.[15] The art historian Michele Greet has shown that, in 1923, Malfatti and do Amaral were the only women in an exhibition held at the Maison de l'Amérique Latine in Paris (location unknown), which displayed works by contemporary Latin American artists living in Paris as a unified group for the first time. In 1924 the *Exposition d'art américain-latin* included three paintings by Malfatti, as one of thirteen Brazilians.[16]

In 1930 the *Exhibition of the First Representative Collection of Paintings by Contemporary Brazilian Artists* took place in New York.[17] In 1939 MoMA had acquired Candido Portinari's *O morro* (The Hill, 1933), the first work by a South American artist to be added to their permanent collection. The following year, the Detroit Institute of Arts (DIA), which in 1932 had commissioned the Mexican artist Diego Rivera to paint a permanent mural cycle depicting the Ford Motor Company's plant in its Beaux-Arts building designed by Paul Cret, held a monographic exhibition on Portinari, which was later transferred to MoMA.[18] Portinari was only the second Latin American artist to have a monographic exhibition at MoMA, after Rivera.[19] That same year DIA also added *Gado* (Cattle, 1939), by Portinari, to its permanent collection. A monograph on the artist soon followed.[20] Portinari was subsequently commissioned to create four murals for the Hispanic Division Reading Room in the Thomas Jefferson Building at the Library of Congress, Washington DC, a task he completed in 1941.[21] By 1944 Portinari was already Brazil's most successful painter and an established star at home and in the US. Sitwell, comparing him to Rivera and the Brazilian composer Heitor Villa-Lobos, thought him too prolific, suffering from what he called "climatic fertility".[22]

Although not unlike the reception that Brazilian artists had initially received in Paris, Sitwell's criticism was twenty years out of date. By 1944, they had already weathered initial negative criticisms from the French critics and learned from them, an important experience that formed a crucial part of their artistic development. As Greet notes, "through the critical feedback Malfatti received for her submissions to the Salon d'Automne, she was able to refine her approach and find a voice as an artist that was both Brazilian and modern".[23] The implication is that Brazilian artists by this time had nothing new to learn from British critics, since they had already heard and responded to such comments from their French counterparts twenty years earlier.

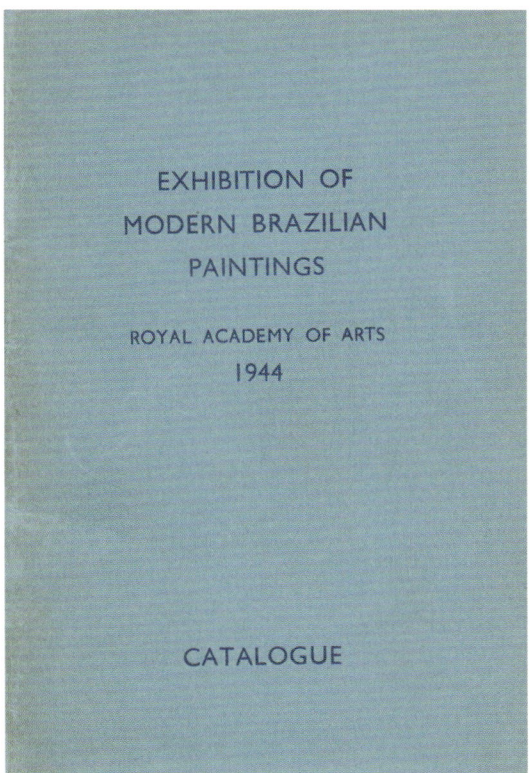

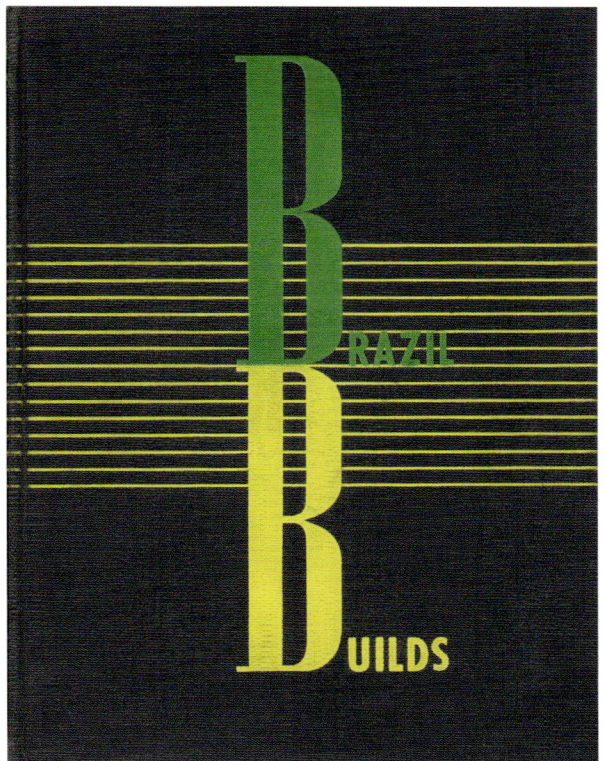

Fig. 2
The catalogue of the *Exhibition of Modern Brazilian Paintings*

Fig. 3
The American architect Philip L. Goodwin's 1943 catalogue of MoMA's exhibition *Brazil Builds*

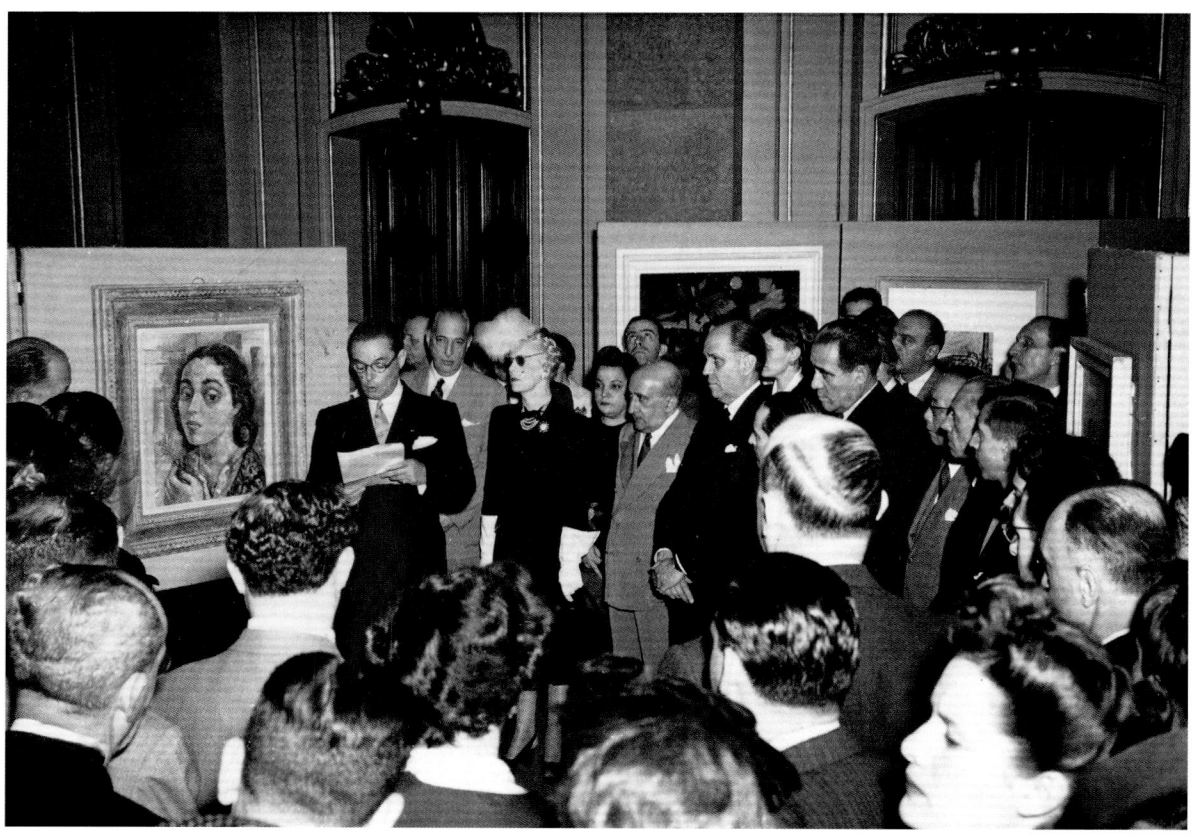

The art historian Dawn Ades notes that "almost all those (Latin American artists) who embraced Modernism did so from abroad".[24] In other words, the experience of living and working outside Latin America enabled artists to be part of a European avant-garde and, on their return, also to "set about creating in various ways specifically American forms of Modernism".[25] This was a natural and significant element in the evolution of Modernism across Latin America, as Greet argues, following the reception that artists exhibiting their art through the Paris Salons had experienced, which evolved from the hostile to the positive. By collecting the reviews many artists quoted or reprinted them in their home countries as a way to verify their success abroad, thereby demonstrating that the modernist approaches to creating art they had developed in Europe (and indeed the US) were legitimate.[26]

As Pontual stated, the ambitions of artists in Latin America to look to the latest European art and, at the same time, to seek a national identity "within the forms and words of a new-found collective unconscious", while apparently contradictory, were not mutually exclusive.[27] The *Exhibition of Modern Brazilian Paintings* at the RA reveals both that the UK was reluctant to receive the exhibition and that London was far behind such artistic centres as Paris and New York in embracing modern art from what was then considered to be the periphery. Unlike the comments French critics made much earlier, the reaction of art critics in Britain came too late to have any bearing on the work these artists were producing as they were by now already established and successful. This lack of curiosity about the "global south" meant that London was not to host another survey exhibition of Brazilian modernism for another forty years, when *Portraits of a Country: Brazilian Modern Art from the Gilberto Chateaubriand Collection* opened at the Barbican Art Gallery in 1984.

1 Greet 2018, p. 74

2 23 November to 13 December 1944. The three galleries allocated to the exhibition were, in sequence, the Lecture Room, Gallery Nine, and Gallery Eight.

3 MoMA, 13 January to 28 February 1943

4 For a comprehensive exploration of the diplomatic history behind the exhibition, see Gadelha 2023

5 Roberto Pontual, "Brazilian Modern Art from the Gilberto Chateaubriand Collection", in London 1984, pp. 7–67, here p. 48

6 The Palácio Itamaraty is now the Museu Histórico e Diplomático do Itamaraty.

7 These were the National Gallery, the National Portrait Gallery, the Tate Gallery, the Victoria and Albert Museum, and the Wallace Collection.

8 Letter dated 11 October 1944 from Alfred Munnings to Anthony Eden (AS 5149/698/6. TNA/FO)

9 The additional UK venues were the Castle Museum, Norwich; the National Gallery of Scotland, Edinburgh; Kelvingrove Gallery, Glasgow; the Victoria Gallery, Bath; Bristol Museum and Art Gallery; the Whitechapel Gallery, London; and Reading Museum and Art Gallery. Hayle Gadelha, "The Art of Diplomacy", in London 2018, pp. 47–49

10 For a full, illustrated list of these twenty-three works, see London 2018.

11 Sacheverell Sitwell, "Preface", in London 1944, pp. 3–7, here p. 4

12 Ruben Navarra, "Introduction", in London 1944, p. 8

13 London 1944, p. 3

14 For the reception the exhibition received in the British press see Gadelha 2023, pp. 106–124

15 Greet 2018 provides essential reading around the subject and provides a detailed account of the evolution of Latin American art exhibitions in Paris between the wars.

16 15 March to 15 April 1924 at the Musée Galliéra, Paris organised by the Maison de l'Amérique Latine et l'Académie internationale des Beaux-arts. A catalogue was produced to accompany the exhibition.

17 11 to 30 October 1930 at the International Art Center of Roerich Museum in co-operation with the Brazilian Society of Friends of Roerich Museum. A catalogue with a foreword by Christian Brinton was produced to accompany the exhibition.

18 16 August to 25 September 1940 at the Detroit Institute of Arts, and 9 October to 17 November 1940 at the Museum of Modern Art, New York. An illustrated catalogue with essays by Florence Horn and Michael C. Smith was produced to accompany the exhibition.

19 *Diego Rivera*, 22 December 1931 to 27 January 1932, Museum of Modern Art, New York. An illustrated catalogue written by Frances Flynn Paine and Jere Abbott was produced to accompany the exhibition.

20 Josias Leão and Rockwell Kent, *Portinari: His Life and Art*, Chicago, 1940

21 An illustrated booklet was subsequently produced, *Murals by Cândido Portinari in the Hispanic Foundation of the Library of Congress*, Washington DC, 1943, with a text by Robert C. Smith.

22 London 1944, p. 4

23 Greet 2018, pp. 86–87

24 Ades, in London/ Stockholm/Madrid 1989, p. 125

25 Ades, in London/ Stockholm/Madrid 1989, p. 125

26 Greet 2018, p. 92

27 London 1984, p. 22

Appendix

Chronology

1822

PROCLAMATION OF INDEPENDENCE. On 7 September, Dom Pedro I proclaims independence from Portugal and becomes emperor. The Empire of Brazil lasts until the proclamation of the First Republic in 1889. To this day, 7 September remains a national holiday.

1888

ABOLITION OF SLAVERY. Brazil is the last country in the Americas to formally abolish slavery. Although "freed", the formerly enslaved are disenfranchised. In search of work, many move to urban centres, where they continue to be exploited for cheap labour.

1889

PROCLAMATION OF THE REPUBLIC. A military coup leads to the proclamation of the republic. After the abolition of slavery, the monarchy lost the support of the elites, particularly the plantation owners. In the following years, the wealth of the coffee oligarchy is secured while workers remain oppressed.

1891

FIRST CONSTITUTION OF THE REPUBLIC. Inspired by the constitutions of Argentina, the United States, and Switzerland, Brazil's first constitution establishes a Federative Republic. Women and those who are illiterate, which includes most formerly enslaved people and Indigenous people, are denied the right to vote.

1900

MORRO DE FAVELA. The term "favela" is used for the first time to describe the Morro da Providência, a hill in Rio de Janeiro. After the demolition of cheap housing in the city for sanitary reasons, former soldiers and the previously enslaved construct makeshift homes without infrastructure.

1917

GENERAL STRIKE. The exploited plantation and factory workers – the formerly enslaved as well as immigrants from Europe and Japan – organise a general strike in São Paulo to implement basic labour rights. Numerous uprisings against the oligarchy follow. **ANITA MALFATTI'S EXHIBITION.** This show in São Paulo is a milestone in the history of modern Brazilian art. Although Anita Malfatti's expressionist paintings draw fierce criticism, modern writers and artists defend them. The modern artists Emiliano Di Cavalcanti and Vicente do Rego Monteiro have their first exhibitions in São Paulo and Recife, respectively. **SAMBA.** Donga releases the first samba song, "Pelo Telephone" (Over the Telephone). Samba emerged from dance rituals called *Roda de Samba* and *Batuque de Angola*. They were performed by formerly enslaved people in the Rio de Janeiro neighbourhood surrounding the Praça Onze square, which the painter and musician Heitor dos Prazeres referred to as "Pequenas Africas" (Little Africas). Candomblé, a religion combining several of West African and Christian rituals, was the crucible for samba. Since Afro-Brazilian traditions were often targeted by the police, they were performed in *terreiros* (private houses with yards). Tia Ciata, who hosted samba gatherings, and the musicians Sinhô, Pixinguinha, Donga, and João da Baiana are major figures in the development of samba.

1921

CHORO. Heitor Villa-Lobos composes his first choro. Choro is a popular musical style that combines European ballroom dances, such as the polka or waltz, with African rhythms. Villa-Lobos's aim was to achieve a synthesis of the stylistic elements and forms of Brazilian music.

1922

SEMANA DE ARTE MODERNA. With the financial support of the coffee oligarch Paulo Prado, a group of intellectuals organise the *Semana de Arte Moderna* (Modern Art Week) at the Municipal Theatre in São Paulo from 11 to 17 February. In addition to an exhibition with works by Anita Malfatti, Emiliano Di Cavalcanti, John Graz, Regina Gomide Graz, Vicente do Rego Monteiro, Zina Aita, Victor Brecheret, Martins Ribeiro, and others, there are concerts by Heitor Villa-Lobos, Ernani Braga, Guiomar Novaes, and Ronaldo de Carvalho; dance performances, including African dance; and lectures and readings of modern literature by Oswald de Andrade, Luís Aranha, Sérgio Milliet, Tácito de Almeida, Ribeiro Couto, Mário de Andrade, Plínio Salgado, Agenor Barbosa, and Yvonne Daumerie. The reactions were extremely mixed, ranging from outrage to enthusiasm. During a period of social and political instability, the *Semana de Arte Moderna* heralds new forms of Brazilian cultural expression that are not immediately embraced.

1923

MODERNISM BEYOND BORDERS. Tarsila do Amaral and Oswald de Andrade travel to Europe. Their work heightens the awareness of Brazilian culture among Parisian artistic and intellectual groups. Oswald delivers a lecture at the Sorbonne entitled "L'Effort intellectuel du Brésil contemporain" (Intellectual Effort in Contemporary Brazil). Vicente do Rego Monteiro prepares in Paris the publication *Légendes, croyances et talismans des indiens de l'Amazone* (Legends, Beliefs, and Talismans of the Amazon Indians). The Ukranian architect Gregori Warchavchik arrives in Brazil, where he designs the first modernist buildings. The artist Lasar Segall moves from Germany to São Paulo. The Swiss writer Blaise Cendrars meets Paulo Prado in Paris and is invited by him to Brazil.

1924

UPRISINGS. There is a series of uprisings against the oligarchy of the First Republic. Throughout the country, people demand improved social conditions. **PAU-BRASIL.** On March 18, Oswald de Andrade publishes the *Manifesto da Poesia Pau-Brasil* in the newspaper *Correio da Manhã*. Referring to the export good pau-brasil, or Brazilwood, he advocates for the export of Brazilian culture to counter the import of European artistic ideas. **DISCOVERING BRAZIL.** On the initiative of Blaise Cendrars, a group of friends, including the writers Mário de Andrade and Oswald de Andrade and the artist Tarsila do Amaral, travel to see the Carnival in Rio de Janeiro. Afterward, they visit baroque cities such as Ouro Preto in the federal district of Minas Gerais. Cendrars' fascination helps these Brazilian cultural figures to see Afro-Brazilian cultures anew, facilitating the development of their own vernacular.

1925

THE FIRST REGIONALIST CONGRESS. In response to the *Semana de Arte Moderna*, Gilberto Freyre holds a conference celebrating local Brazilian culture in Recife, in the northeastern state of Pernambuco. It highlights paintings by Cícero Dias and Vicente do Rego Monteiro. Freyre publishes the *Manifesto Regionalista* (Regionalist Manifest), in which he describes the traditional values of northeastern Brazilian culture as important to the formation of a Brazilian national identity.

1928

MANIFESTO ANTROPÓFAGO. Inspired by conversations with the writer Raul Bopp and his wife Tarsila do Amaral, who had painted *Abaporu* (which means in the Tupi-Guarani language "man who eats man"), Oswald de Andrade publishes the *Manifesto Antropófago* (Anthropophagic Manifesto). It calls for the consumption of European culture, for it to be digested in a sense, so that it may be transformed into an independent Brazilian art. The manifesto is de Andrade's response to the *Semana de Arte Moderna*, which he considered, from a distance, to be a manifestation of ideas imported from Europe. **MACUNAÍMA.** Inspired by his ethnographic travels to study the culture of Indigenous peoples, Mário de Andrade publishes the novel *Macunaíma: The Hero with No Character*. Born in the Amazonian rainforest, the protagonist has shapeshifting abilities that enable him to change his race. The same year, Mário de Andrade also publishes *Ensaio sobre a música brasileira* (Essay on Brazilian Music), the first study of popular Brazilian music from the country's many regions. **SAMBA SCHOOLS.** The Carnival in Rio de Janeiro was organised by Grandes Sociedades (Grand Societies), who hired artists to design their parade appearances. With the advent of samba schools, such as Deixa Falar (Let Them Talk, founded in 1928), the organisation of the Rio Carnival improved. Thereafter, it is more widely accepted as a form of cultural expression that combines music, dance, and design.

1929

BLACK TUESDAY. The crash of the New York stock market on 29 October unleashes a major crisis for the Brazilian coffee oligarchs and throughout the country; its economy depended heavily on the export of coffee and other raw materials. The economic crisis leads to new challenges for the republic. **VERDE-AMARELISMO.** As a reaction to the cosmopolitan and internationally connected Anthropophagic movement, the manifesto *Nhengaçu Verde-Amarelo* is published in the newspaper *Correio Paulistano* on 17 May. Named for the Brazilian green and yellow of Brazil's flags, the group advocated for a conservative and xenophobic form of nationalism.

1930

REVOLUTION. Supported by the military, Getúlio Vargas became the head of the provisional government and established the Second Republic. He served as president of Brazil from 1930 to 1945 and from 1951 until his suicide in 1954. During his first term, Vargas advances a nationalist ideology and advocates for labour rights and universal education. The Vargas Era ushers in a new phase of building the Brazilian nation, with forms of popular culture such as samba and carnival understood as the foundations of a Brazilian identity. Most modern artists begin to address social themes. Some artists align themselves with communists, which in some cases led to persecution while others worked with the government. **SPOKEN LANGUAGE AS LITERATURE.** Carlos Drummond de Andrade publishes his first book, *Alguma poesia* (Some Poetry). Manuel Bandeira's *Libertinagem* (Libertinism) comes out the same year. In 1922, Bandeira read his highly formalistic poem *Os sapos* (The Toads) at the *Semana de Arte Moderna*. Now, however, both writers

employ a more informal style emulating spoken language. **CASA MODERNISTA.** Gregori Warchavchik opens one of the first modernist houses to the São Paulo public. It includes furniture of his own design and modern art by Tarsila do Amaral, Anita Malfatti, and Lasar Segall as well as works by textile designer Regina Gomide Graz.

1931

NEW SOCIAL ORDER. The Brazilian state creates the Ministry of Labor, Industry, and Commerce, and declares the first social laws to protect the rights of workers. **PIONEER OF PERFORMANCE.** Flávio de Carvalho performs the *Experiência N.2*, donning a green cap and walking against the flow of a Corpus Christi procession. His act is considered an insult, and the crowd reacts violently. **SALÃO REVOLUCIONÁRIO.** During his short directorship of the Escola Nacional de Belas Artes in Rio de Janeiro, the architect Lúcio Costa modernises the traditional school. For the annual exhibition, he invites modern artists, including Manuel Bandeira, Anita Malfatti, and Candido Portinar, to serve on the jury. With more than 500 works by artists such as Tarsila do Amaral, Emiliano Di Cavalcanti, Victor Brecheret, Alberto Veiga Guignard, the exhibition gains renown as the *Salão Revolucionário* (Revolutionary Salon). Cícero Dias exhibits the large panel *Eu vi o mundo... e ele começava no Recife* (I Saw the World... and It Began in Recife), 1926–1929. He comments on the decentralisation of modernism, citing Recife as an important place for modern art beyond Rio de Janeiro and São Paulo.

1932

WOMEN'S RIGHTS. Women win the right to vote and run for office. **CONSTITUTIONALIST REVOLUTION.** From July 9 to October 2, there is an unsuccessful uprising in São Paulo against the Vargas regime. **MUSICAL EDUCATION.** After having visited more than fifty cities to introduce musical culture to remote regions in Brazil, Heitor Villa-Lobos is appointed as the director of the supervisory authority for musical and artistic education. During the Vargas Era, he primarily composes patriotic and educational music, with the exception of the "Bachianas brasileiras" (Bach-inspired Brazilian pieces). **MARCHINHA.** The first competition of samba schools with a parade in Rio de Janeiro takes place. With the carnival march *O teu cabelo não nega* (Your Hair Doesn't Deny It), the Valença brothers and Lamartine Babo originate a new musical genre. Called "marchinha", the diminutive form of march, its name satirises the solemnity of military marches. **CLUBE DOS ARTISTES MODERNOS.** In São Paulo, the multigenerational group of artists Antonio Gomide, Carlos Prado, Flávio de Carvalho, and Emiliano Di Cavalcanti found an independent club that aims to renew the anti-academic and experimental character of modern art. **SOCIAL ISSUES.** Literature and art increasingly address social issues, as in the books *Menino de engenho* (Plantation Boy) by José Lins do Rego with a cover by Manuel Bandeira and *Onde o proletariado dirige* (Where the Proletariat Leads) by Osório César with cover and images by Tarsila do Amaral. Murilo Mendes publishes *História do Brasil* (History of Brazil) with a cover designed by Emiliano Di Cavalcanti. **FASCISM.** Plínio Salgado establishes the *Ação Integralista Brasileira* (Brazilian Integralist Action), a nationwide Fascist movement inspired by Mussolini.

1933

MULTIETHNICITY. Gilberto Freyre publishes *Casa-grande e Senzala* (The Masters and the Slaves), with a cover designed by Cícero Dias. He presents a utopian vision of the early years of colonisation and offers the then-radical view that the very strength of modern Brazil resided in the mixing of races and cultures. His ideas oppose the prevalent concept of *Embranquiamento*, or "whitening" the Brazilian population through increased immigration from Europe. **TROPICAL ARCHITECTURE.** In April, young architects organise the *1° Salão Internacional de Arquitetura Tropical* (1st International Salon of Tropical Architecture), initiating the idea of modern Brazilian architecture. **EXPERIMENTAL THEATRE.** Flávio de Carvalho presents another unconventional performance: *Bailado do Deus Morto* (Dance of the Dead God). Wearing aluminum masks inspired by African cultures, the predominantly Black cast performs ritualistic dances. The piece is considered so scandalous and offensive that the police shut it down.

1934

CONSTITUTION OF THE SECOND REPUBLIC. The new constitution retains federalism with autonomous states, and confirms social and political reforms, granting rights to the middle class, workers, and industry as well as free education for all. Congress elects Getúlio Vargas as president for a four-year term. **INSTITUTIONALISING MODERNISM.** Gustavo Capanema becomes director of the Ministry of Education and Health. He hires the poet Carlos Drummond de Andrade as his chief of staff and surrounds himself with a diverse group of modern artists, writers, and architects. **1° CONGRESSO AFRO-BRASILEIRO.** Gilberto Freyre organises the *First Afro-Brazilian Congress*. This milestone in the analysis of Afro-Brazilian culture in Brazil is held in Recife.

1935

DEPARTAMENTO DE CULTURA DE SÃO PAULO. Mário de Andrade becomes director of the newly created Municipal Department of Culture in São Paulo. In numerous performances, lectures, and exhibitions, he presents the results of his research in ethnomusicology, which includes numerous recordings of popular and vernacular music throughout Brazil.

1936

PALÁCIO GUSTAVO CAPANEMA. In hiring Lúcio Costa to design a new building for the Ministry of Education and Health, Capanema demonstrates his support for modernism in Brazil. It is one of the first modernist public buildings in the Americas. Deeply impressed by Le Corbusier when he visited Brazil, Costa invites him to oversee the project. A collaborative effort between Costa, Affonso Eduardo Reidy, and many others, the building is enhanced by Candido Portinari's murals and gardens designed by Roberto Burle Marx. It is completed in 1943. Oscar Niemeyer, who would become one of the most famous Brazilian architects, is an intern in Costa's office.

1937

ESTADO NOVO. Getúlio Vargas leads a coup d'état to overthrow the National Congress and implements the Estado Novo. Afterward, he creates the National Councils of Petroleum, Labor, and Justice as well as the Press and Propaganda Department. Several regulations are implemented, including the nationalisation of production, taxing syndicates, and minimum salaries of workers. The republic becomes an oppressive dictatorship that emphasises the centralisation of power, nationalism, and anti-communism. **PROTECTION OF CULTURAL HERITAGE.** The Serviço do Patrimônio Histórico e Artístico Nacional (Service of National Historical and Artistic Heritage) is founded. Mário de Andrada designed the organisation dedicated to the protection of Brazil's cultural heritage at the request of Gustavo Capanema.

1938

BANANA BUSINESS. Wearing a basket on her head overflowing with bananas and other fruit, the actor and singer Carmen Miranda enjoys great success in the United States. Yet she also becomes an "exotic" stereotype of Latin America. As a white person who appropriates Afro-Brazilian culture, she becomes a symbol of national unity and a cultural asset in diplomacy. In 1939, she sings "O que é que a baiana tem?" (What Does the Woman from Bahia Have), composed by Dorival Caymmi. At almost the same time, Braguinha composes a Marchinha de Carnaval, "Yes, nós temos bananas" (Yes, We Have Bananas), referring to Carmen Miranda's statement "Bananas is my business." Criticised in Brazil for forgetting her Brazilian roots, she records the samba "Disseram que voltei americanizada" (They Said I've Come Back Americanised).

1940

PAMPULHA. Oscar Niemeyer designs his first major project: a garden city on the shores of Lake Pampulha, near Belo Horizonte in Minas Gerais. It symbolises the modernisation efforts of Belo Horizonte's mayor, Juscelino Kubitschek. Niemeyer collaborates with Burle Marx on the garden designs and Candido Portinari on the murals. The result is a perfect example of modern Brazilian architecture that fuses international modernism and local traditions.

1942

REVISITING THE SEMANA DE ARTE MODERNA. Twenty years after the event, Mário de Andrade delivers a lecture revisiting the *Semana de Arte Moderna*, increasing the acceptance of the modernist movement.

1943

NEW HEART BEATS. Clarice Lispector's *Perto do Coração Selvagem* (Near to the Wild Heart) marks the introduction of a new literary voice into the largely male literary intellectual scene. She gains international renown through her unconventional portrayal of affect and emotions.

1944

WORLD WAR II. The first contingent of the Força Expedicionária Brasileira (Brazilian Expeditionary Force) enters the war, joining the Allies to free Italy from German occupation. **EXHIBITION OF MODERN BRAZILIAN PAINTINGS.** On the initiative of the diplomat Oswaldo Aranha, seventy Brazilian artists agree to donate works to support the Royal Air Force Benevolent Fund. Their art is displayed at the Royal Academy in London along with the exhibition *Brazil Builds*. Through its use of culture to forge and strengthen diplomatic ties between nations, this exhibition is a prime example of soft power.

1945

FOURTH BRAZILIAN REPUBLIC. Forced out by the military, Getúlio Vargas renounces the presidency, ending the Estado Novo dictatorship. Eurico Dutra is elected president and opens the country to international investment.

1947

MASP. Having recently emigrated from Italy, the art historian Pietro Maria Bardi and his wife, the architect Lina Bo Bardi, open the Museu de Arte São Paulo (MASP) with the support of Assis Chateaubriand. **FAAP.** Armando Alvares Penteado founds an academic institution (Fundação Armando Alvares Penteado – FAAP) whose objective is to support, promote, teach, and advance modern art.

1948

MAM. Museums of modern art are founded in São Paulo and in Rio de Janeiro. **GRUPO XV.** Alongside Takaoka, Athayde de Barros, and Antonio Carelli, Geraldo de Barros creates the Grupo XV in São Paulo. Distrusting the binary of academic versus modern artist, they simply considered themselves to be "painters". Despite this emphasis on painting, de Barros begins to take photographs. Two years later, he shows his *Fotoformas* at MASP. **SOCIEDADE DE ARTE MODERNA.** In Recife, a society is founded to promote modern art. It holds exhibitions and courses in the state of Pernambuco.

1950

VARGAS'S SECOND TERM. Getúlio Vargas wins the presidential election. He protects the country's economy against foreign influence and creates Petrobras, the national petroleum company, in 1953.

1951

BIENAL DE SÃO PAULO. The first international biennial of São Paulo takes place. The international prize is awarded to Max Bill, whose solo show at MASP in the same year has a major impact on the younger generation of artists, including Geraldo de Barros, who eventually become known for advancing Concrete art.

1952

GRUPO RUPTURA. Alongside Lothar Charoux, Waldemar Cordeiro, and Luiz Sacilotto, Geraldo de Barros founds a new artist group to promote Concrete art in Brazil. The group's first show opens at MAM in São Paulo. **MUSEU DE IMAGENS DO INCONSCIENTE.** The psychiatrist Nise da Silveira, who transformed the treatment of people with mental illnesses by replacing lobotomies and electroshock treatments with art workshops, opens a museum dedicated to Outsider Art.

1953

LABOUR STRIKE. Due to high inflation, approximately 300,000 workers strike in São Paulo for better wages and working conditions. There is little improvement, and as many as 700,000 workers rally in 1957 and again in 1963.

1954

GRUPO FRENTE. In Rio de Janeiro, Ivan Serpa founds a group of Concrete artists together with Lygia Clark, Lygia Pape, and Hélio Oiticica. **UNILABOR.** Geraldo de Barros cofounds together with a Dominican priest the furniture factory Unilabor. Run by the workers themselves, it was intended to be more of a community than a company. De Barros designs furniture inspired by Concrete art.

1956

KUBITSCHEK ERA. After Vargas's suicide in 1954, Juscelino Kubitschek is elected Brazil's president on 3 October 1955 and inaugurated in 1956. Having run on the slogan "Fifty years progress in five", he advocated the diversification of Brazil's economy and opened it to foreign investment. **THE NEW LOOK.** Wearing a skirt, fishnet stockings, and sandals, Flávio de Carvalho launches the *New Look* and presents it as a performance in the streets of São Paulo. This new apparel liberates the "tropical man" from the discomfort of fashion imported from Europe.

1957

BRASÍLIA. Lúcio Costa wins the public competition for the urban planning of Brasília, the new seat of federal power. Many of the public buildings are designed by Oscar Niemeyer, and modern art plays an important role.

1958

BOSSA NOVA. With two songs, *Chega de Saudade* (Fly, My Heart) and *Bim Bom*, João Gilberto introduces the musical genre of bossa nova (the "new wave") to the world beyond Brazil. Its rhythms with delicate melodies and lush harmonies influence jazz and other musical genres in the United States and then around the globe. **CONCRETE POETRY.** Three young poets, Augusto de Campos, Haroldo de Campos, and Décio Pignatari, publish *Plano Piloto para a Poesia Concreta* (Pilot plan for Concrete Poetry) in *AD* (Magazine for Architecture). With the manifesto and their works, they proposed a poetry close to the new design of things, allying verbal with visual and sound.

1959

NEO-CONCRETE ART. At the Museu de Arte Moderna in Rio de Janeiro, the first exhibition of Neo-Concrete art is presented. The artists condemn the rationalist theories of geometric abstraction at the core of Concrete art and call instead for a return to a sensory dimension.

1960

NEW CAPITAL. Only three years after launching the project, Juscelino Kubitschek inaugurates Brasília, the new federal capital. Jânio Quadros and João Goulart are elected president and vice president of Brazil.

1964

MILITARY COUP. Following a coup d'état, the military takes power and imposes a military dictatorship until 1985. In 1964, the U.S. State Department provides military and logistical support to the coup. The first of a number of Institutional Acts (AI-1) is signed. These acts strengthen the military rulers' legal and political power while suspending the political rights of critics and other citizens.

1967

TROPICÁLIA. Hélio Oiticica exhibits a work entitled *Tropicália* in the exhibition *Nova objetividade brasileira* (New Brazilian Objectivity) at the Museu de Arte Moderna in Rio de Janeiro. Tropicália, also referred to as Tropicalismo, becomes a modern Brazilian artistic movement. Best known in music, it is characterised by the synthesis of Brazilian genres and popular traditions with international avant-garde styles. It is a reaction to the oppressive military dictatorship, which issues an oppressive constitution in 1967.

1968

MASP. The Museu of Arte inaugurates a new building designed by Lina Bo Bardi at Avenida Paulista. It features a large exhibition space where paintings are displayed on glass easels, with the information about the works on the back. Reacting against the hierarchical nature of chronological displays, she allows visitors discover individual works of art. **UPRISINGS.** The murder of the student Edson Luís de Lima Souto by the military police marks the beginning of a series of uprisings that culminate in the *Passeata dos Cem Mil* (One Hundred Thousand Person Rally) that takes place at Rio de Janeiro. The military's increased oppression following this event prompts many to go into exile.

1969

POPULAR ART. Lina Bo Bardi curates *A mão do povo brasileiro* (The Hand of the Brazilian People) at the MASP, an exhibition of everyday objects from Brazil's numerous regions. She thus highlights the sophisticated design of objects not typically exhibited in art museums. BIENNIAL OF THE BOYCOTT. As a reaction to the dictatorship, several Brazilian artists, including Lygia Clark and Hélio Oiticica, refuse to participate at the Bienal de São Paulo.

1970

WORLD CUP. The military dictatorship uses Miguel Gustavo's song *Pra frente Brasil* (Go ahead, Brazil), which was composed to cheer on the Brazilian soccer team during the World Cup in Mexico, as nationalist propaganda. When Brazil wins, Pelé becomes the country's most famous star.

1972

FIFTY YEARS AFTER THE SEMANA DE ARTE MODERNA. MASP organises the exhibition *A Semana de 22: antecedentes e consequências* (The Week of 22: Antecedents and consequences). Starting in the 1960s, the modern art promoted in 1922 is revaluated and acquired by museums and collectors. Women artists such as Tarsila do Amaral and Anita Malfatti are rediscovered.

1985

END OF THE MILITARY DICTATORSHIP. A slow process of re-democratisation takes place.

1988

NEW BRAZILIAN CONSTITUTION. Brazil passes one of the most progressive constitutions, replacing the autocratic constitution from 1967.

1998

BIENAL DA ANTROPOFAGIA. The theme of the 24th Bienal de São Paulo, curated by Paulo Herkenhoff and Adriano Pedrosa, stems from Oswald de Andrade's *Manifesto Antropófago*.

2022

CENTENARY OF THE SEMANA DE ARTE MODERNA. Numerous exhibitions, publications, and conferences take place throughout Brazil. Scholars question the canon of modern Brazilian art and advance new narratives of diverse modernisms.

**Fabienne Eggelhöfer und
Eduardo Jorge de Oliveira**

List of Works

ANITA MALFATTI

**Marinha, Monhegan
(Seascape, Monhegan)**, 1915
Oil on canvas, 35.5 × 46 cm
Luiz Carlos Ritter Collection,
Rio de Janeiro, Brazil
P. 33

O farol (Lighthouse), 1915
Oil on canvas, 46.3 × 61 cm
Gilberto Chateaubriand,
MAM Rio Collection
P. 34

**A estudante russa
(Russian Student)**, c. 1915
Oil on canvas, 76 × 61 cm
Universidade de São Paulo,
Instituto de Estudos Brasileiros,
Coleção Mário de Andrade –
Coleção de Artes Visuais
P. 28

**Homem de sete cores (Man
of Seven Colors)**, 1915–1916
Pastel and charcoal on
paper, 62 × 46 cm
Acervo Museu de Arte Brasileira
– MAB FAAP, São Paulo, Brazil
P. 31

**O homen amarelo
(Yellow Man)**, 1915–1916
Oil on canvas, 61 × 51 cm
Universidade de São Paulo,
Instituto de Estudos Brasileiros,
Coleção Mário de Andrade –
Coleção de Artes Visuais
P. 27

**O japonês (Japanese
Man)**, 1915–1916
Oil on canvas, 61 × 51 cm
Universidade de São Paulo,
Instituto de Estudos Brasileiros,
Coleção Mário de Andrade –
Coleção de Artes Visuais
P. 29

A onda (Wave), c. 1915–1917
Oil on wood, 26.7 × 36 cm
Hecilda e Sérgio Fadel
P. 33

**Marinha (Penhascos)
(Seascape, Cliffs)**
1915–1917
Oil on wood, 26 × 36 cm
Private collection
P. 32

**Primeiro nu cubista ou
O pequeno nu (First Cubist
Nude or The Little Nude)**, 1916
Oil on canvas, 51 × 39.5 cm
Luciana and Luis Antonio de
Almeida Braga Collection
P. 30

**A chinesa (Chinese
Woman)**, c. 1922
Oil on canvas, 100 × 77.3 cm
Luciana and Luis Antonio de
Almeida Braga Collection
P. 35

**Retrato de Mário de
Andrade (Portrait of Mário
de Andrade)**, c. 1923
Oil on canvas, 44 × 38 cm
Universidade de São Paulo,
Instituto de Estudos Brasileiros,
Coleção Mário de Andrade –
Coleção de Artes Visuais
P. 37

**Retrato de Oswald
(Portrait of Oswald)**, 1925
Oil on canvas, c. 47.5 × 41.5 cm
Hecilda e Sérgio Fadel
P. 36

VICENTE DO REGO MONTEIRO

**Composição indígena
(Indigenous Composition)**, 1922
Oil on wooden panel,
37.5 × 45.5 cm
Airton Queiroz Collection,
Fortaleza, CE
P. 46 (bottom)

**Composição indígena
(Indigenous Composition)**, 1922
Oil and ink on wooden
panel, 27.5 × 38 cm
Airton Queiroz Collection,
Fortaleza, CE
P. 46 (top)

**Composição indígena
(Indigenous Composition)**, 1922
Oil on wooden panel, 38 × 28 cm
Airton Queiroz Collection,
Fortaleza, CE
P. 47

Crucifixão (Crucifixion), 1922
Oil on canvas, 90 × 80 cm
Gilberto Chateaubriand/
ICGC Collection
P. 51

**Mulher diante do espelho
(Woman in Front of
the Mirror)**, 1922
Oil on canvas, 98 × 69 cm
Luciana and Luis Antonio de
Almeida Braga Collection
P. 45

**Menino nu e tartaruga
(Nude Boy and Turtle)**, 1923
Oil on canvas, 92 × 72 cm
Museu de Arte de São Paulo
Assis Chateaubriand, Gift of
the artist, 1962, MASP.00646
P. 55

Baigneuses (Bathers), 1924
Oil on canvas, 80 × 90 cm
Gilberto Chateaubriand,
MAM Rio Collection
P. 49

**Mulher sentada
(Seated Woman)**, 1924
Oil on canvas, 165 × 145 cm
Luciana and Luis Antonio de
Almeida Braga Collection
P. 48

Untitled, 1924
Oil on canvas, 45.7 × 37.7 cm
Luís Paulo Montenegro
Collection
P. 54

**Menino e ovelha
(Boy and Ewe)**, 1925
Oil on canvas, 38 × 46 cm
Igor Queiroz Collection,
Fortaleza, CE
P. 54

**O atirador de arco
(Archer)**, 1925
Oil on canvas, 108 × 137 cm
Private collection,
São Paulo, Brazil
P. 50

Tênis (Tennis), 1928
Oil on canvas, 99 × 80 cm
On Loan from Museum
& Art Swindon
P. 53

TARSILA DO AMARAL

**Autorretrato com vestido
laranja (Self-Portrait with
Orange Dress)**, 1921
Oil on canvas, 50 × 41 cm
Long-term loan MASP
Banco Central
P. 70

**Esboço para A negra (Sketch
for Black Woman)**, 1923
Pencil and watercolor on
paper, 23.4 × 18 cm
Universidade de São Paulo,
Instituto de Estudos Brasileiros,
Coleção Mário de Andrade –
Coleção de Artes Visuais
P. 74

O modelo (Model), 1923
Oil on canvas, 55 × 46 cm
Hecilda e Sérgio Fadel
P. 73

**Retrato azul (Sérgio Milliet)
(Blue Portrait, Sérgio
Milliet)**, 1923
Oil on canvas, 65 × 54 cm
Orandi Momesso Collection
P. 71

**Morro da favela
(Favela Hill)**, 1924
Oil on canvas, 64.5 × 76 cm
Hecilda e Sérgio Fadel
P. 75

A feira II (Market II), 1925
Oil on canvas, 45.3 × 54.5 cm
Private collection, São Paulo
P. 77

Lagoa Santa, 1925
Oil on canvas, 50.5 × 65 cm
Luciana and Luis Antonio de
Almeida Braga Collection
P. 81

**Untitled (Four Drawings
for Blaise Cendrars's
Feuilles de route)**, c. 1924
Indian ink on paper,
22.7 × 32 cm
Swiss National Library:
Swiss Literary Archives
(Fonds Blaise Cendrars)
PP. 78, 79

Untitled (Drawing for Blaise Cendrars's *Feuilles de route*), c. 1924
Indian ink on paper,
20.9 × 17.9 cm
Swiss National Library:
Swiss Literary Archives
(Fonds Blaise Cendrars)

O lago (Lake), 1928
Oil on canvas, 75.5 × 93 cm
Hecilda e Sérgio Fadel
P. 83

Paisagem com ponte (Landscape with Bridge), 1931
Oil on canvas, 39.5 × 46 cm
Private collection, São Paulo
P. 82

Segunda classe (Second Class), 1933
Oil on canvas, 112 × 150.5 cm
Private collection, Courtesy
Almeida & Dale Galeria de Arte
P. 85

Fazenda com sete porquinhos (Farm with Seven Piglets), 1943
Oil on canvas, 46 × 55 cm
Private collection, São Paulo
P. 76

Baile caipira (Country Dance), 1950–1961
Oil on canvas, 60 × 75 cm
Fundação Edson Queiroz
Collection, Fortaleza
P. 84

Povoação I (Settlement I), 1952
Oil on canvas, 72 × 98 cm
Airton Queiroz Collection,
Fortaleza, CE
P. 80

CANDIDO PORTINARI

Mestiça (Mixed-Race Woman), 1934
Oil on canvas, 46 × 38 cm
Acervo Museu de Arte Brasileira
– MAB FAAP, São Paulo, Brazil
P. 97

O lavrador de café (Coffee Agricultural Worker), 1934
Oil on canvas, 100 × 81 cm
Museu de Arte de São
Paulo Assis Chateaubriand,
Gift José Maria Whitaker,
1964, MASP.00519
P. 95

A colona (Settler), 1935
Tempera on canvas, 97 × 130 cm
Universidade de São Paulo,
Instituto de Estudos Brasileiros,
Coleção Mário de Andrade -
Coleção de Artes Visuais
P. 94

Retrato de Mário de Andrade (Portrait of Mário de Andrade), 1935
Oil on canvas, 73.5 × 61 cm
Universidade de São Paulo,
Instituto de Estudos Brasileiros,
Coleção Mário de Andrade –
Coleção de Artes Visuais
P. 96

Espantalho (Scarecrow), 1940
Oil on canvas, 99 × 83 cm
Mercer Art Gallery, Harrogate,
North Yorkshire Council
P. 105

Mulher e crianças (Woman and Children), 1940
Oil on canvas, 100 × 81 cm
Private collection
P. 104

Menino com carneiro (Boy with Ram), 1941
Tempera on canvas, 184 × 180 cm
Fundação Edson Queiroz
Collection, Fortaleza
P. 99

Retirantes (Migrants), 1944
Oil on canvas, 190 × 180 cm
Museu de Arte de São
Paulo Assis Chateaubriand,
Gift Assis Chateaubriand,
1948, MASP.00324
P. 103

Baiana (Woman from Bahia), 1947
Oil on canvas, 35 × 27 cm
Fundação Edson Queiroz
Collection, Fortaleza
P. 93

Bumba meu boi, 1956
Oil on cardboard, 34 × 26 cm
Fundação Edson Queiroz
Collection, Fortaleza
P. 101

Favela com músicos (Favela with Musicians), 1957
Oil on wood, 46 × 55 cm
Maria Luisa e Oscar Americano
Foundation Collection
P. 100

LASAR SEGALL

Menino com lagartixas (Boy with Geckos), 1924
Oil on canvas, 98 × 61 cm
Collection Museu Lasar
Segall/IBRAM/MinC
P. 125

Mulata com criança (Mixed-Race Woman with Child), 1924
Oil on canvas, 67 × 54.5 cm
Mauris Ilia Klabin
Warchavchik Collection
P. 120

Mulato II (Mixed-Race Boy II), c. 1924
Oil on canvas, 64.3 × 45.5 cm
Airton Queiroz Collection,
Fortaleza, CE
P. 120

Paisagem brasileira (Brazilian Landscape), 1925
Oil on canvas, 64 × 54 cm
Collection Museu Lasar
Segall/IBRAM/MinC
P. 121

Bananal (Banana Grove), 1927
Oil on canvas, 87 × 127 cm
Pinacoteca de São Paulo.
Purchased by the Governo do
Estado de São Paulo, 1928
P. 122

Retrato de Mário de Andrade (Portrait of Mário de Andrade), 1927
Oil on canvas, 73 × 60 cm
Universidade de São Paulo,
Instituto de Estudos Brasileiros,
Coleção Mário de Andrade -
Coleção de Artes Visuais
P. 126

Pogrom, 1937
Oil and sand on canvas,
184 × 150 cm
Collection Museu Lasar
Segall/IBRAM/MinC
P. 131

Lucy com flor (Lucy with Flower), 1939–1942
Oil on canvas, 56.2 × 47.4 cm
National Galleries of Scotland.
Presented by the British
Council in 1945, in recognition
of collaboration in a series
of exhibitions arranged
during the 1939-45 War
P. 127

Floresta fechada (Dense Forest), 1954
Oil on canvas, 65 × 46 cm
Paulo Segall Collection,
São Paulo
P. 129

Luz na floresta (Light Reflecting in the Forest), 1954
Oil on canvas, 130 × 114 cm
Maria Fernanda Vilela Collection
P. 128

Favela, 1954–1955
Oil and sand on
canvas, 65 × 50 cm
Collection Museu Lasar
Segall/IBRAM/MinC
P. 130

FLÁVIO DE CARVALHO

A inferioridade de Deus (Inferiority of God), 1931
Oil on canvas, 54 × 73.5 cm
Gilberto Chateaubriand,
MAM Rio Collection
P. 142

Anteprojeto para Miss Brasil (Study for Miss Brazil), 1931
Oil on canvas, 43 × 27 cm
Luciana e Luis Antonio de
Almeida Braga Collection
P. 148

Ascensão definitiva de Cristo (Christ's Final Ascension), 1932
Oil on canvas, 75.5 × 62 cm
Pinacoteca de São Paulo.
Purchased by the Governo do
Estado de São Paulo, 1969
P. 143

Casal (Couple), 1932
Oil on canvas, 59 × 55 cm
Orandi Momesso Collection
P. 147

Nu feminino deitado (Reclined Female Nude), 1932
Oil on canvas, 32 × 56.5 cm
Museu de Arte de São Paulo
Assis Chateaubriand, Gift of
the artist, 1948, MASP.00319
P. 146

Retrato ancestral (Ancestral Portrait), 1932
Oil on canvas, 81 × 60 cm
Hecilda e Sérgio Fadel
P. 145

Mário de Andrade, 1939
Oil on canvas, 110.6 × 79.2 cm
Coleção de Arte da Cidade/
Supervisão de Acervo/
CCSP/SMC/PMSP
P. 141

**Retrato de Ivone Levi
(Portrait of Ivone Levi)**, 1951
Oil on canvas, 100 × 70 cm
Acervo Museu de Arte Brasileira
– MAB FAAP, São Paulo, Brazil
P. 149

**Composição paisagem
interna (Interior Landscape
Composition)**, 1955
Oil on canvas, 55.4 × 66 cm
Acervo Museu de Arte Brasileira
– MAB FAAP, São Paulo, Brazil
P. 150

**Nossa Senhora do Desejo
(Our Lady of Desire)**, 1955
Oil on canvas, 92.3 × 73 cm
Acervo Museu de Arte Brasileira
– MAB FAAP, São Paulo, Brazil
P. 151

**Retrato de Niomar Moniz
Sodré Bittencourt (Portrait
of Niomar Moniz Sodré
Bittencourt)**, 1955
Oil on canvas, 93 × 72.5 cm
Acervo Museu de Arte Brasileira
– MAB FAAP, São Paulo, Brazil
P. 151

ALFREDO VOLPI

**Baiana (Woman
from Bahia)**, 1930
Oil on canvas, 44.3 × 31.6 cm
Acervo Museu de Arte Brasileira
– MAB FAAP, São Paulo, Brazil
P. 167

**Rua de Ouro Preto (Street
in Ouro Preto)**, c. 1935
Oil on canvas, 82 × 60 cm
Acervo Museu de Arte Brasileira
– MAB FAAP, São Paulo, Brazil
P. 166

Untitled, 1945
Oil on canvas, 81 × 65 cm
Orandi Momesso Collection
P. 169

**Capelinha (Little
Chapel)**, 1940s
Tempera on canvas, 60 × 80 cm
Ronaldo Cezar Coelho
Collection, Rio de Janeiro
P. 168

Untitled, 1950
Tempera on canvas, 73 × 49.5 cm
Daniela and Alfredo
Villela Collection
P. 177

**Composição concreta (0007)
(Concrete Composition,
0007)**, c. 1950s
Tempera on canvas, 70 × 70 cm
Private collection
P. 174

Untitled, 1955–1959
Tempera on canvas, 73 × 41 cm
Igor Queiroz Collection,
Fortaleza, CE
P. 171

Untitled, late 1950s
Tempera on canvas, 70 × 70 cm
Fundação Edson Queiroz
Collection, Fortaleza
P. 174

**Untitled (Composição
em azul) (Composition
in Blue)**, c. 1959
Tempera on canvas, 105 × 70 cm
Private collection, São Paulo
P. 176

Fachada (Façade), 1963
Tempera on canvas,
100.3 × 71.7 cm
Airton Queiroz Collection,
Fortaleza, CE
P. 165

Untitled, 1970
Tempera on canvas, 136 × 67.3 cm
Orandi Momesso Collection
P. 175

Fachada I (Façade I), 1970–1980
Tempera on canvas, 48 × 72.5 cm
Ana Eliza and Paulo
Setúbal Collection

Untitled, 1980s
Tempera on canvas,
135.5 × 68 cm
Fundação Edson Queiroz
Collection, Fortaleza
P. 172

**Bandeiras e mastros
(Flags and Poles)**, undated
Tempera on canvas, 86 × 111 cm
Long-term loan MASP
Banco Central
P. 173

DJANIRA DA MOTTA E SILVA

**Composição no. 1
(Composition No. 1)**, c. 1942
Oil on canvas, 73.5 × 60.5 cm
Airton Queiroz Collection,
Fortaleza, CE
P. 185

**Empinando pipa
(Flying a Kite)**, 1950
Oil on canvas, 113 × 94 cm
Banco Itaú Collection
P. 187

**Caboclinhos
(Young Caboclos)**, 1951
Oil on canvas, 63 × 53 cm
Leonel Kaz Collection,
Rio de Janeiro
P. 192

Costureira (Seamstress), 1951
Tempera on canvas, 54 × 46.1 cm
Museu Nacional de
Belas Artes/IBRAM
P. 194

**Cafezal (Coffee
Plantation)**, 1952
Oil on canvas, 63 × 90.5 cm
Gilberto Chateaubriand,
MAM Rio Collection
P. 188

**Cena de mercado
(Market Scene)**, 1960
Oil on canvas, 66 × 93.5 cm
Victor Adler Collection
P. 189

Bananal (Banana Grove), 1961
Oil on canvas, 131.5 × 162 cm
Leonel Kaz Collection,
Rio de Janeiro
P. 195

**Dança do Marrapaiá,
Parati (Marrapaiá
Dance, Parati)**, 1961
Oil on canvas, 162 × 113.5 cm
Victor Adler Collection,
Rio de Janeiro
P. 193

Barcos (Boats), 1962
Oil on canvas, 60.3 × 80 cm
Luiz Carlos Ritter Collection,
Rio de Janeiro, Brazil
P. 186

**Três orixás (Three
Orishas)**, 1966
Oil on canvas, 130.4 × 195.5 cm
Pinacoteca de São Paulo.
Purchased by the Governo do
Estado de São Paulo, 1969
P. 190

GERALDO DE BARROS

**Grito na solidão
(Lonely Cry)**, c. 1940
Watercolor and Indian ink
on paper, 24 × 32 cm
Carol & Flavio Veitzman
Collection
P. 211

Untitled, 1948/2014
Photograph, drawing on
photographic negative
with dry point and Indian
ink, 27.6 × 27.2 cm
Collection Fabiana de Barros
& Michel Favre, Geneva
P. 217

**Abstrato, da série Fotoforma,
estação da Luz, São Paulo
(Abstract, from the
Fotoforma Series, Estação da
Luz, São Paulo)**, 1949/2014
Photograph, multiple exposures
on the negative, 27.8 × 27.5 cm
Collection Fabiana de Barros
& Michel Favre, Geneva
P. 220

**Abstração (São Paulo)
(Abstraction, São Paulo)**, 1949
Silver gelatin print, 27.6 × 37.4 cm
Tate: Presented by the
American Fund for the Tate
Gallery, courtesy of the
Latin American Acquisitions
Committee and Susana and
Ricardo Steinbruch 2016
P. 218

Fotoforma, 1949/2014
Photograph, multiple exposures
on the negative, 26.7 × 30.6 cm
Collection Fabiana de Barros
& Michel Favre, Geneva
P. 222

**Homenagem a Paul Klee,
Tatuapé, São Paulo (Homage
to Paul Klee, Tatuapé,
São Paulo)**, 1949/2014
Photograph, drawing on
negative with dry point and
Indian ink, 26.7 × 29.5 cm
Collection Fabiana de Barros
& Michel Favre, Geneva
P. 217

**Untitled (São Paulo)
Composição II
(Composition II)**, 1949
Silver gelatin print, 27.6 × 38.2 cm
Tate: Presented by the
American Fund for the Tate
Gallery, courtesy of the
Latin American Acquisitions
Committee and Susana and
Ricardo Steinbruch 2016
P. 218

Máscara (Mask), 1950
Pencil and Indian ink on
paper, 26 × 19.3 cm
Collection Fabiana de Barros
& Michel Favre, Geneva
P. 216

List of Works

Untitled, 1950
Monotype, watercolor
and ink, 20 × 24 cm
Collection Fabiana de Barros
& Michel Favre, Geneva
P. 214

Untitled (Fios telegráficos)
(Telegraph Wires), c. 1950s
Silver gelatin print, 30 × 40 cm
Tate: Presented by the
American Fund for the Tate
Gallery, courtesy of the
Latin American Acquisitions
Committee 2016

A City to Conquer, 1951
Lithograph, 19.2 × 22.3 cm
Collection Fabiana de Barros
& Michel Favre, Geneva
P. 212

Forma-objeto
(Form-Object), 1952
Industrial paint on wooden
panel, 40 × 40 cm
Fábio Faisal Collection
P. 224

Granada, Spain, 1951
Silver gelatin print, 40 × 30 cm
Tate: Presented by the
American Fund for the Tate
Gallery, courtesy of the
Latin American Acquisitions
Committee 2016

Untitled, 1951
Multi-coloured monotype
on paper, 30 × 21 cm
Luís Paulo Montenegro
Collection
P. 215

Untitled, Pampulha,
Belo Horizonte, 1951/2008
Photograph, multiple exposures
on the negative, 28.2 × 34.1 cm
Collection Fabiana de Barros
& Michel Favre, Geneva
P. 219

Vista de um porto
(Port View), 1951
Multi-coloured monotype
on paper, 21 × 28 cm
Collection Fabiana de Barros
& Michel Favre, Geneva
P. 213

Fotoforma, 1952–1953/2014
Photograph, copy from a cut-
out negative pressed between
two glass plates, 25.4 × 37.4 cm
Collection Fabiana de Barros
& Michel Favre, Geneva
P. 221 (bottom)

Fotoforma, 1952–1953/2014
Photograph, copy from a cut-
out negative pressed between
two glass plates, 27.3 × 30.1 cm
Collection Fabiana de Barros
& Michel Favre, Geneva
P. 221 (top)

Arranjo de três formas
semelhantes dentro de
um círculo (Arrangement
of Three Similar Shapes
within a Circle), 1953
Enamel over kelmite on
eucatex, 59.5 × 59.5 cm
Collection Lenora and Fabiana
de Barros. Courtesy Luciana
Brito Galeria, São Paulo
P. 225

Movimento e contra
movimento (Motion and
Counter-Motion), 1953
Synthetic enamel on
kelmite, 50 × 50 cm
Private collection
P. 224

Homenagem a Volpi
(Homage to Volpi), 1983
Melamine laminate
glued to chipboard and
metal, 90.1 × 90.1 cm
Pinacoteca de São Paulo.
Donated by Associação
dos Amigos da Pinacoteca
do Estado, 1999
P. 223

RUBEM VALENTIM

Untitled, 1953
Oil on wood, 40 × 40 cm
Private collection
P. 235

Composição 3
(Composition 3), 1955
Oil on canvas, 100 × 73 cm
Private collection
P. 237

Untitled, 1956
Oil on canvas on wood,
55.5 × 38 cm
Private collection, Rio de Janeiro
P. 234

Composição
(Composition), 1961
Oil on canvas, 100 × 70 cm
Conrado Mesquita & Camila
Guarita, São Paulo
P. 245

Untitled, 1962
Oil on canvas, 70 × 50 cm
Hecilda e Sérgio Fadel
P. 243

Untitled, 1962
Oil on canvas, 70 × 50 cm
Luís Paulo Montenegro
Collection
P. 241

Objeto emblemático 1
(Emblematic Object 1), 1969
Oil on wood, 152 × 102.5 × 25 cm
Private collection, Rio de Janeiro
P. 244

Emblema 70 no. 2
(Emblem 70 No. 2), 1970
Acrylic on canvas, 123 × 73 cm
Lent by the Tate Americas
Foundation, courtesy of the
Latin American Acquisitions
Committee with support from
Almeida & Dale, Mendes Wood
DM, and Erica Roberts 2022
P. 239

Objeto emblemático
(Emblematic Object), 1973
Acrylic on wood,
123 × 69.5 × 65.5 cm
Private collection, Rio de Janeiro
P. 242

Conjunto altar sacral
emblemático – E59
(Emblematic Sacral
Altar Set – E59), 1980
Wood, 71 × 24 × 24 cm
Private collection, São Paulo
P. 238

Bibliography

AJZENBERG, HERKENHOFF
(ET. AL.) 2005
Elza Ajzenberg; Paulo
Herkenhoff (et. al.),
*Tarsila do Amaral; peintre
bréseliense à Paris 1923–1929*,
Rio de Janeiro, 2005

ALENCASTRO 2000
Luiz Felipe de Alencastro, *O
trato dos viventes. Formação
do Brasil no Atlântico
sul*, São Paulo, 2000

ALMEIDA 1967
Rodrigo Mello Franco
de Almeida, "Djanira",
Correio da Manhã, Rio de
Janeiro, 14 January 1967

ALMEIDA 1976
Paulo Mendes de Almeida, *De
Anita ao museu*, São Paulo, 1976

ALMEIDA 2019
Silvio Almeida, *Racismo
estrutural*, São Paulo, 2019

AMÂNCIO 2021
Kleber Amâncio, "Ensaio acerca
do entendimento negro: a
supressão de outros Brasis na
arte branco-brasileira", *MAC
USP processos curatoriais.
Curadoria crítica e estudos
decoloniais em artes visuais.
Diásporas africanas nas
Américas*, 2021, "https://
estudosdecoloniais.mac.
usp.br/palestras/kleber-
amancio/" (16 June 2023)

AMARAL 1939
Tarsila do Amaral, "Pintura
Pau-Brasil e antropofagia",
*RASM: Revista Anual do Salão
de Maio*, São Paulo, no. 1, 1939

AMARAL 1968
Aracy Amaral, "Às margens de
uma pesquisa: os artistas da
Semana de Arte Moderna",
Mirante das Artes, no. 8,
March–April 1968, pp. 11–12

AMARAL 1970
Aracy Amaral, *Artes Plásticas na
Semana de 22*, São Paulo, 1970

AMARAL 1984
Aracy Amaral, *Arte para
quê? A preocupação social
na arte brasileira, 1930–
1970*, São Paulo, 1984

AMARAL 2001
Aracy Amaral (ed.),
*Correspondência Mário de
Andrade e Tarsila do Amaral*,
São Paulo, 2001 (Coleção
de Correspondência de
Mário de Andrade, 2)

AMARAL 2003
Aracy Amaral, *Tarsila: sua
obra e seu tempo*, São
Paulo, 2003, 3rd ed.

AMARAL 2008
Tarsila do Amaral, "Blaise
Cendrars 'Diário de São Paulo',
19 de outubro de 1938", in
Laura Brandini (ed.), *Crônicas
e outros escritos de Tarsila do
Amaral*, Campinas, 2008

AMARAL 2010
Aracy Amaral, *Tarsila. Sua
obra e seu tempo*, São
Paulo, 2010, 4th ed.

ANDRADE 1930
Oswald de Andrade, "A
casa modernista, o pior
crítico do mundo e outras
considerações", *Diário da
Noite*, São Paulo, July 1930

ANDRADE 1991
Oswald de Andrade, "Aspectos
da pintura através de Marco
Zero", in Oswald de Andrade,
Ponta de lança, São Paulo, 1991

ANDRADE 2005A
Oswald de Andrade,
"Manifesto Antropófago",
in *Mestres do Modernismo*,
Maria Alice Milliet (ed.), São
Paulo, 2005, pp. 226-231

ANDRADE 2005B
Mário de Andrade, "O
movimento modernista",
in *Mestres do Modernismo*,
Maria Alice Milliet (ed.), São
Paulo, 2005. pp. 234-255

ANDRADE 2013
Mário de Andrade, *Poesias
completas*, edited, annotated,
and supplemented with
documents by Tatiana Longo
Figueiredo and Telê Ancona
Lopez, vol. 1, Rio de Janeiro. 2013

ANDRADE 2017
Mário de Andrade, *Macunaíma,
o herói sem nenhum caráter*,
edited by Telê Ancona
Lopez, Tatiana Longo
Figueiredo, São Paulo, 2017

ANDRADE 2022A
Gênese Andrade, "A ofensiva
nos jornais: Oswald de Andrade
e o momento artístico antes de
1922", in Oswald de Andrade,
*Arte do Centenário e outros
escritos*, Gênese Andrade (ed.),
São Paulo, 2022, pp. 11–53

ANDRADE 2022B
Gênese Andrade (ed.),
Modernismos 1922–2022,
São Paulo, 2022

ANDRADE 2022C
Gênese Andrade, "Memórias
do modernismo", in Andrade
2022b, pp. 596–642

ANDRADE 2022D
Mário de Andrade, *O
movimento modernista*, Rio
de Janeiro, 1942. Facsimile in *O
movimento modernista e outras
prosas afins*, Donny Correia
(ed.), São Paulo, 2022, pp. 21–102

ANDRADE 2022E
Gênese Andrade, "Entre o
entusiasmo e o desencanto:
Mário de Andrade e o
movimento modernista", in
*O movimento modernista
e outras prosas afins*,
Donny Correia (ed.), São
Paulo, 2022, pp. 191–223

ANDRADE 2022F
Oswald de Andrade, *Serafim
Ponte Grande*, São Paulo, 2022

ANDRADE 2023
Gênese Andrade (ed.), *A
Semana de 22 descentrada*,
Revista da Biblioteca
Municipal Mário de
Andrade, São Paulo, 2023

ARANTES 1997
Otília B. F. Arantes, "Lúcio Costa
e a 'boa causa' da arquitetura
moderna", in Otília B. F. and
Paulo E. Arantes, *Sentido
da formação: três estudos
sobre Antonio Candido, Gilda
de Mello e Souza e Lúcio
Costa*. São Paulo, 1997

ARAÚJO 1976
Olívio Araújo, "O mestre
de sua época", *Veja*, 398,
São Paulo, 21 April 1976

BANHAM 1962
Reyner Banham, *Guide
to Modern Architecture*,
London, 1962

BARDI 1978
Pietro Maria Bardi, *O
Modernismo no Brasil*,
São Paulo, 1978

BARRETO 1922
Lima Barreto, *Careta*, Rio
de Janeiro, 3 June 1922

BARROS 2005
Stella Teixeira de Barros (ed.),
*A Pinacoteca Municipal de
São Paulo*, São Paulo, 2005

BARROS 2011
J. D. Barros, "As influências da
arte africana na arte moderna",
Afro-Ásia, Salvador, no. 44,
2011, "https://periodicos.ufba.
br/index.php/afroasia/article/
view/21236" (16 June 2023)

BARROS 2013
Fabiana de Barros (ed.), *Geraldo
de Barros: Isso*, São Paulo, 2013

BASTOS 1991
Eliana Bastos, *Entre o Escândalo
e o Sucesso – A Semana de 22 e
o Armory Show*, Campinas, 1991

BATISTA 2006
Marta Rossetti Batista, *Anita
Malfatti no Tempo e no
Espaço*, São Paulo, 2006

BATISTA 2012
Marta Rossetti Batista,
*Os Artistas Brasileiros na
Escola de Paris – Anos
1920*, São Paulo, 2012

BATTELLA GOTLIB 2000
Nádia Battella Gotlib, *Tarsila
do Amaral: a modernista*,
São Paulo, 2000, 2. ed. rev.

BEAUFILS 1982
Marcel Beaufils, *Villa-Lobos,
musicien et poète du Bresil*,
Rio de Janeiro, 1982

BENSE 2009
Max Bense, *Inteligência brasileira: uma reflexão cartesiana*, translated by Tércio Redondo, São Paulo, 2009. English edition: Max Bense, *Brazilian Intelligence*, Georg Vrachliotis (ed.), Leipzig, 2018

BILL 1954
Max Bill, "The architect, the architecture, the society", *Architectural Review*, vol. 116, no. 694, October 1954 (lecture on June 9, 1953 at FAU – USP)

BRASÍLIA/RIO DE JANEIRO 1970
31 objetos emblemáticos e relevos-emblemas de Rubem Valentim, ed. by Giulio Carlo Argan, exh. cat. Fundação Cultural do Distrito Federal, Brasília, and Museu de Arte Moderna, Rio de Janeiro, 1970

BRITO 1974
Mário da Silva Brito, *História do modernismo brasileiro. Antecedentes da semana de arte moderna*, Rio de Janeiro, 1974

BRITO 1983
Ronaldo Brito, "O trauma do moderno", in *Sete ensaios sobre o modernismo*, Rio de Janeiro, 1983

CAMPELLO 2022
Felipe Campello, "Afinal o que é ser moderno no Brasil?" *Revista Continente*, 2022, "https://revistacontinente. com.br/secoes/artigo/afinal- -o-que-e-ser-moderno-no- brasil" (12 February 2024)

CANDIDO 1965
Antonio Candido, "Literatura e cultura de 1900 a 1945 (panorama para estrangeiros)", in *Literatura e sociedade – estudos de teoria e história literária*, São Paulo, 1965

CANDIDO 2000
Antonio Candido, *Formação da Literatura Brasileira: momentos decisivos*, Belo Horizonte 2000, 6th ed.

CANDIDO 2022
Antonio Candido, "Prefácio" in Paulo Duarte, *Mário de Andrade por ele mesmo*, São Paulo, 2022, 2nd ed.

CARDOSO 2019
Rafael Cardoso, "White skins, black masks: 'Antropofagia' and the reversal of primitivism", in Uwe Fleckner e Elena

Tolstichin (ed.): *Das verirrte Kunstwerk*, Hamburg, 2019

CARDOSO 2022A
Rafael Cardoso, "A reinvenção da Semana e o mito da descoberta do Brasil", *Estudos Avançados*, 36 (104), 2022, 14–34, "https://doi.org/10.1590/ s0103-4014.2022.36104.002" (18 March 2024)

CARDOSO 2022B
Rafael Cardoso, *Modernidade em preto e branco: Arte e imagem, raça e identidade no Brasil, 1890–1945*, São Paulo 2022

CARVALHO 1936
Flávio de Carvalho, *Diário de S. Paulo*, 24 September 1936

CARVALHO 2012
Ana Cristina Carvalho, *90 anos depois: a Semana de Arte Moderna*, São Paulo, 2012

CASARIN 2022
Carolina Casarin, *O guarda- roupa modernista: o casal Tarsila e Oswald e a moda*, São Paulo, 2022

CEPPAS AND PENNA 2021
Filipe Ceppas and João Camillo Penna, "Antropofagias futuras, seus tempos e textos", *Das Questões*, vol. 11, no. 1, 4 April 2021 "https://periodicos.unb.br/ index.php/dasquestoes/article/ view/37229" (28 March 2024)

CHIARELLI 1995
Tadeu Chiarelli, *Um Jeca nos Vernissages*, São Paulo, 1995

CHIARELLI 2012A
Tadeu Chiarelli, "Tropical, de Anita Malfatti: reorientando uma velha questão", in *Um modernismo que veio depois*, São Paulo, 2012

CHIARELLI 2012B
Tadeu Chiarelli, Um modernismo que veio depois, São Paulo, 2012

COELHO 2012
Frederico Coelho, *A semana sem fim: celebração e memória da Semana de Arte Moderna de 1922*, Rio de Janeiro, 2012

COSTA 1995
Lúcio Costa, "Depoimento", *Lúcio Costa: registro de uma vivência*. São Paulo, 1995

CRIPPA 2003
Giulia Crippa, "O grotesco como estratégia de afirmação da produção pictórica feminina",

Revista de Estudos Feministas, Florianópolis, vol. 1, no. 1, 2003

DELARUE-MARDRUS 1927
Lucie Delarue-Mardrus, "L'aventure d'un compositeur: musique cannibale", *L'Intransigeant*, 13 December 1927

DROSTE 2004
Magdalena Droste, *Bauhaus, 1919–1933*, Cologne, 2004

DUARTE 1998
Paulo Sergio Duarte, *Anos 60. Transformações da arte no Brasil*, Rio de Janeiro, 1998

DUCHARTRE 1923
Légendes, croyances et talismans des Indiens de l'Amazone, adapted by P. L. Duchartre; Illustrated by V. de Rego Monteiro, Paris, 1923

DURAND 1989
José Carlos Durand, *Arte, privilégio e distinção*, São Paulo, 1989

ESPADA 2014
Heloisa Espada (ed.), *Geraldo de Barros e a fotografia*, São Paulo, 2014

EULALIO 2001
Alexandre Eulalio, *A aventura brasileira de Blaise Cendrars*, São, Paulo 2001, 2. ed. (revised and updated by Carlos Augusto Calil)

FABRIS 1994
Annateresa Fabris, *Modernidade e modernismo no Brasil*, Campinas, 1994

FABRIS 1996
Annateresa Fabris, *Candido Portinari* (Artistas brasileiros, 4), São Paulo, 1996

FABRIS 2010
Annateresa Fabris, *Modernidade e modernismo no Brasil*, Porto Alegre, 2010, 2nd ed.

FERNANDEZ 2005
Nancy Fernandez, *Balade au coeur de la formation artistique à l'École Supérieure des Beaux- Arts de Genève*, Geneva, 2005

FERREIRA 2013
Glória Ferreira (ed.), *Brasil: Figuração × Abstração – no final dos anos 40*, São Paulo, 2013

FLECHET 2004
Anaïs Flechet, *Villa-Lobos à Paris – um écho musical du Brésil*, Paris, 2004

FONTELES 2022
Bené Fonteles, *Rubem Valentim: 1922–1991: Sagrada Geometria*, São Paulo, 2022

GADELHA 2023
Hayle Gadelha, *Public Diplomacy on the Front Line: The Exhibition of Modern Brazilian Paintings*, London, 2023

GÉO-CHARLES 1944
Géo-Charles, "Notas sobre a pintura de Monteiro", in *Vicente do Rego Monteiro – 42 reproduções em fotogravura*, Recife, 1944

GOMES CARDOSO 2016
Renata Gomes Cardoso, "A negra de Tarsila do Amaral: criação, recepção e circulação", *VIS Revista do Programa de Pós-graduação em Arte da UnB*, vol. 15, no. 2 (July– December), 2016, pp. 90–110, "https://periodicos.unb.br/ index.php/revistavis/article/ view/20394" (17 June 2023)

GREET 2018
Michele Greet, *Transatlantic Encounters: Latin American Artists in Paris between the Wars*, New Haven, 2018

GREMBECKI 1969
Maria Helena Grembecki, *Mário de Andrade e L'Ésprit Nouveau*, São Paulo, 1969

GREET 2018
Michele Greet, *Transatlantic Encounters: Latin American Artists in Paris Between the Wars*, New Haven, 2018

GUÉRIOS 2003
Paulo Renato Guérios, "Heitor Villa-Lobos e o ambiente artístico parisiense: convertendo-se em um músico brasileiro", in *MANA: Estudos de Antropologia Social*, vol. 9, no. 1, April 2003, Rio de Janeiro

GUIMARÃES 2021
Antonio Sérgio Alfredo Guimarães, *Modernidades negras. A formação racial brasileira (1930–1970)*, São Paulo, 2021

GULLAR 1961
Ferreira Gullar, "Rubem Valentim", *Diário de notícias*, Rio de Janeiro, 2 July 1961

HANNUD AND MONZANI 2019
Giancarlo Hannud and Marcelo Monzani (eds.), *70 documentos do acervo*, São Paulo, 2019

HERMENEGILDO DE
ARAÚJO 2022
Humberto Hermenegildo de
Araújo, "Vislumbres modernistas
no Nordeste dos anos 1920:
dos eventos às publicações", in
Andrade 2022b, pp. 380–404

JÚNIOR 2004
Geisel Júnior, *História
de Djanira: brasileira de
Avaré*, São Paulo, 2004

LAGO 2012
Manoel Aranha Corrêa do
Lago (ed.), *O boi no telhado:
Darius Milhaud e a música
brasileira no modernismo
francês*, Rio de Janeiro, 2012

LEITE 2008
Rui Moreira Leite, *Flávio
de Carvalho: o artista
total*, São Paulo, 2008

LIMA 2020
Nerian Teixeira de Macedo de
Lima, *Tarsila global: releituras
de sua obra*, electronic Diss.
Universidade Estadual de
Campinas 2020, "https://
repositorio.unicamp.br/
acervo/detalhe/1161687"
(18 March 2024)

LOBATO 1917
Monteiro Lobato, "A propósito
da exposição Malfatti",
O Estado de S. Paulo, São
Paulo, 20 December 1917

LONDON 1944
*Exhibition of Modern Brazilian
Paintings*, ed. by. Sacheverell
Sitwell and Ruben Navarra, exh.
cat. Royal Academy of Arts,
London, 1944, London, 1944

LONDON 1984
*Portraits of a Country:
Brazilian Modern Art from
the Gilberto Chateaubriand
Collection*, ed. by. John Hoole
and Roberto Pontual, exh.
cat. Barbican Art Gallery,
London, 1984, London, 1984

LONDON/STOCKHOLM/
MADRID 1989
*Art in Latin America: The
Modern Era, 1820–1980*, ed.
by Dawn Ades, exh. cat.
Hayward Gallery, London,
1989, Nationalmuseum and
Moderna Museet, Stockholm,
Palacio de Velázquez,
Madrid, New Haven, 1989

LONDON 2018
*The Art of Diplomacy: Brazilian
Modernism Painted for War*,
ed. by Michael Asbury,
Marcio Junji Sono and Hayle
Gadelha, exh. cat., Sala
Brasil (Embassy of Brazil),
London, 2018, London, 2018

MAIA AND REZENDE 2015
Ana Maria Maia and Renato
Rezende (eds.), *Flávio de
Carvalho*, Rio de Janeiro, 2015

MALFATTI 1951
Anita Malfatti, "A chegada
da arte moderna no
Brasil", in *Conferências de
1951*, São Paulo, 1951

MARIZ 2004
Vasco Mariz, *Villa Lobos:
compositor brasileiro*,
Rio de Janeiro, 2004

MATIAS DE OLIVEIRA 2018
Alecsandra Matias de Oliveira,
"A 'Onda negra': arte visual
afro-brasileira, legitimação
e circulação", *Jornal da USP*,
5 October 2018, "https://
jornal.usp.br/artigos/a-onda-
negra-arte-visual-afro-
brasileira-legitimacao-e-
circulacao/" (16 June 2023)

MATIAS DE OLIVEIRA 2022
Alecsandra Matias de
Oliveira, "Artistas de erudição
popular: primitivismo e
colonialidade", *Jornal da USP*.
17 November 2022, "https://
jornal.usp.br/?p=584224"
(13 February 2024)

MATIAS DE OLIVEIRA 2023A
Alecsandra Matias de Oliveira,
"O revide da mãe preta", *Jornal
da USP*. 20 June 2023, "https://
jornal.usp.br/articulistas/
alecsandra-matias-de-
oliveira/o-revide-da-mae-
preta/" (13 February 2023)

MATIAS DE OLIVEIRA 2023B
Alecsandra Matias de Oliveira,
"120 anos de Portinari,
'retratista de negros e mulatos'",
Jornal da USP, 23 October
2023, "https://jornal.usp.br/
articulistas/alecsandra-matias-
de-oliveira/120-anos-de-
portinari-retratista-de-negros-
e-mulatos/" (13 February 2023)

MILHAUD 1949
Darius Milhaud, *Notes sans
musique*, Paris 1949

MILLIET 1969
Sérgio Milliet, "Tarsila", *O Estado
de S. Paulo*, 12 April 1969

MORAIS 1994
Frederico Morais, "Prefácio",
in *Modernismo: anos
heróicos: marcos históricos*,
São Paulo, 1994, pp. 9–10

NAVES 1996
Rodrigo Naves, *A forma
difícil: ensaios sobre arte
brasileira*. São Paulo, 1996

NODARI 2020
Alexandre Nodari, "A
metamorfologia de Macunaíma.
Notas iniciais", *Crítica Cultural*,
Palhoça, Santa Catarina, vol. 15,
no. 1. January–June 2020

DE OLIVEIRA SOUZA
E SILVA 2015
Dalmo de Oliveira Souza e
Silva, "Tarsila do Amaral: a
construção de uma narrativa
sobre 'Brasilidade'", *Interthesis*,
vol. 12, no. 2, 2015 "https://
periodicos.ufsc.br/index.
php/interthesis/article/
view/1807-1384.2015v12n2p116"
(20 May 2017)

ORTIZ 2003
Renato Ortiz, *Cultura
brasileira e identidade
nacional*, São Paulo, 2003

PALLINI 2004
Stephanie Pallini, *Entre
modernisme et tradition:
la Suisse romande l'entre
deux-guerres faces aux
avant-gardes*, Bern, 2004

PEDROSA AND AMARAL 1981
Mário Pedrosa and Aracy
Amaral (ed.), *Dos murais
de Portinari aos espaços de
Brasília*, São Paulo, 1981

PEDROSA 2015
Mário Pedrosa, "A arquitetura
moderna no Brasil" (1953),
in Guilherme Wisnik (ed.).
*Arquitetura: ensaios críticos:
Mário Pedrosa*, São Paulo, 2015

PEDROSA, RJEILLE
AND MOURA 2019
Adriano Pedrosa, Isabella
Rjeille and Rodrigo Moura
(eds.), *Djanira: a memória do
seu povo*, São Paulo, 2019

PINSKY 2018
Jaime Pinsky, *A escravidão no
Brasil*, São Paulo, 2018, 21. ed.

POLLOCK 1994
Griselda Pollock, *Vision
and Difference. Feminity,
Feminism and the Histories
of Art*, London, 1994

PRADO VALLADARES 1968
Clarival do Prado Valladares,
"O Negro Brasileiro nas
Artes Plásticas", *Cadernos
Brasileiros*, no. 47, pp. 97–
109, May/June 1968

PUNTONI AND TITAN JR. 2014
*Revistas do modernismo, 1922–
1929*, Pedro Puntoni and Samuel
Titan Jr. (eds.), São Paulo, 2014

RAMOS 2010
Julio Ramos, *Papel Máquina:
Revista de Cultura II*, no. 4, 2010

REGO MONTEIRO 2023
Vicente do Rego Monteiro,
Quelques visages de Paris, Paris
1925. Facsimile in Vicente do
Rego Monteiro, *Do Amazonas
a Paris: as lendas indígenas
de Vicente do Rego Monteiro*,
Jorge Schwartz (ed.); translated
by Regina Salgado Campos,
São Paulo, 2023, 2. ed.

RIO DE JANEIRO 1924A
"A tradição de Madureira",
Correio da Manhã, Rio de
Janeiro, 2 March 1924, p. 6

RIO DE JANEIRO 1924B
"O Carnaval nos subúrbios",
A Noite, Rio de Janeiro,
3 March 1924, p. 6

RIO DE JANEIRO 1924C
"Tópicos e notícias", *Correio
da Manhã*, Rio de Janeiro,
4 March 1924, p. 4

RIO DE JANEIRO 1944
Revista Acadêmica, Rio de
Janeiro, no. 64, June 1944

RIO DE JANEIRO 1947
"Regresso de Djanira",
Diário de Notícias, Rio de
Janeiro, 16 November 1947

RIO DE JANEIRO 1952
"Trigésimo aniversário da
Semana de Arte Moderna. Anita
Malfatti: 'Foram as noitadas
mais tumultuosas a que assisti
na minha vida'", *Diário Carioca*,
Rio de Janeiro, 24 February 1952

RIO DE JANEIRO 1957
Volpi 1924-1957, exh. cat. Museu
de Arte Moderna do Rio de
Janeiro, 1957, Rio de Janeiro 1957

RIO DE JANEIRO/
SÃO PAULO 1977
*Projeto construtivo brasileiro na
arte: 1950–1962*, ed. by Aracy
Amaral, exh. cat. Museu de
Arte Moderna, Rio de Janeiro,
Pinacoteca do Estado de
São Paulo, São Paulo, 1977

RODRIGUES 2019
Pedro Henrique Belchior
Rodrigues, *O maestro do
mundo: Heitor Villa-Lobos
(1887–1959) e a diplomacia
cultural brasileira*, Rio de
Janeiro, 2019 (Dissertation
Rio de Janeiro 2019)

ROSSETTI BATISTA 1987
Marta Rossetti Batista, *Artistas brasileiros na escola de Paris, anos 20*, São Paulo, 1987 (Dissertation São Paulo 1987)

RUFFATO 2022
Luiz Ruffato, "No meio do caminho", in Andrade 2022b, pp. 348–379

SANTOS-DUMONT 1956
Alberto Santos-Dumont, *Os meus balões*, translated by A. de Miranda Bastos, Rio de Janeiro, 1956

SANTOS 2022
Renata A. F. dos Santos, "Representação, representatividade e necropolítica nas artes visuais", in *Modernismos 1922–2022*, Gênese Andrade (ed.), São Paulo, 2022, pp. 662–686

SÃO PAULO 1975A
"Saudades caipirinha", *Folha de S. Paulo*, 16 February 1975

SÃO PAULO 1975B
"Volpi, no limiar dos 80 anos", *Folha de S. Paulo*, 28 September 1975

SÃO PAULO 2006
Volpi: a música da cor, exh. cat. Museu de Arte Moderna de São Paulo, 2006, São Paulo, 2006

SÃO PAULO 2021
Desafios da modernidade: Família Gomide-Graz nas décadas de 1920 e 1930, ed. Maria Alice Milliet, exh. cat. Museu de Arte Moderna de São Paulo, 2021, São Paulo, 2021

SÃO PAULO 2022
Volpi Popular, ed. by Adriano Pedrosa and Tomás Toledo, exh. cat. Museu de Arte de São Paulo Assis Chateaubriand, 2022, São Paulo, 2022

SCHWARTZ 2002
Jorge Schwartz, "Tupi or not tupi: o grito de guerra na literatura do Brasil moderno", in *Da Antropofagia a Brasília: Brasil 1920–1950*, Jorge Schwartz (ed.), Valência, São Paulo, 2002, pp. 143–158

SCHWARTZ 2013
Jorge Schwartz, *Fervor das vanguardas. Arte e literatura na América Latina*, São Paulo, 2013

SCHWARTZ 2022A
Jorge Schwartz, *Vanguardas latino-americanas: polêmicas, manifestos e textos críticos*, São Paulo 2022, 2. ed. (revised and expanded)

SCHWARTZ 2022B
Caixa modernista, Jorge Schwartz (ed.), São Paulo, 2022, 2. ed. (revised)

SEGALL 1993
Lasar Segall, "Sobre arte", in *Lasar Segall: textos, depoimentos e exposições*, São Paulo, 1993

SEVCENKO 1992
Nicolau Sevcenko, *Orfeu extático na metrópole: São Paulo, sociedade e cultura nos frementes anos 20*, São Paulo, 1992

SHIRCLIFF 2014
Jennifer Pfeifer Shircliff, *Women of the 1913 Armory Show: their contributions to the development of American modern art*, electronic Diss. University of Louisville 2014, "https://doi.org/10.18297/etd/1322" (18 March 2024)

SIMIONI 2008
Ana Paula Cavalcanti Simioni, *Profissão artista: pintoras e escultoras acadêmicas brasileiras*, São Paulo, 2008

SIMIONI 2013A
Ana Paula Cavalcanti Simioni, "Le modernisme brèsilien, entre consécration et contestation", *Perspective*, vol. 2, 2013, pp. 325–342

SIMIONI 2013B
Ana Paula Cavalcanti Simioni, "Modernismo brasileiro: entre a consagração e a contestação", *Perspective. Perspective* "http://journals.openedition.org/perspective/5539" (30 April 2021)

SIMIONI 2016
Ana Paula Cavalcanti Simioni, "Les transferts de 'l'art total' de la Suisse au Brésil : une modernisation très particulière." *Artl@s Bulletin*, vol. 5, no. 1, 2016, "https://docs.lib.purdue.edu/artlas/vol5/iss1/5/" (18 February 2024)

SIMIONI 2019
Ana Paula Cavalcanti Simioni, "Modernas em Museus: a Consagração Tardia", in *História das mulheres, Histórias feministas: Antologia*, Adriano Pedrosa, Amanda Carneiro and André Mesquita (ed.), São Paulo, 2019, pp. 483–499

SIMIONI AND MIGLIACCIO 2020
Ana Paula Cavalcanti Simioni and Luciano Migliaccio, *Art déco no Brasil: coleção Fulvia e Adolpho Leirner*, São Paulo, 2020

SIMIONI 2022
Ana Paula Simioni, *Mulheres modernistas. Estratégias de consagração na arte brasileira*, São Paulo, 2022

SIMÕES 2021
Igor Simões, "Entre a raça e as constelações: uma abordagem curatorial sobre o acervo do MAC USP", MAC USP processos curatoriais. *Curadoria crítica e estudos decoloniais em artes visuais. Diásporas africanas nas Américas*, 2021, "https://estudosdecoloniais.mac.usp.br/palestras/kleber-amancio/" (16 June 2023)

SPERLING 2011
Katrin H. Sperling, *Nur der Kannibalismus eint uns. Die globale Kunstwelt im Zeichen kultureller Einverleibung: Brasilianische Kunst auf der documenta*, Bielefeld 2011

STERZI 2017
Eduardo Sterzi, "A irrupção das formas selvagens", in Andrade 2017, pp. 219–222

TINEM 2002
Nelci Tinem, *O alvo do olhar estrangeiro: o Brasil na historiografia da arquitetura moderna*, João Pessoa, 2002

TORELLY 2015
Luiz Philippe Peres Torelly, "O turista aprendiz e o patrimônio cultural", in Mário de Andrade, *O turista aprendiz*, Brasília, 2015

TRENCH 2022
Daniel Trench, "A forma inquieta: da Klaxon ao Suplemento Dominical do *Jornal do Brasil*", in Andrade 2022b, pp. 405–427

VALENTIM 1967
Rubem Valentim, "Oxé de Xangô na geometria revoltada de Rubem Valentim", *Revista Galeria de Arte Moderna*, Rio de Janeiro, 1967, pp. 23–26

VALENTINI 2013
Luisa Valentini, *Um laboratório de antropologia. O encontro entre Mário de Andrade, Dina Dreyfus e Claude Lévi-Strauss (1935–1938)*, São Paulo, 2013

WAPICHANA 2023
Cristino Wapichana, "A Antropofagia do absurdo", *Revista da Biblioteca Mário de Andrade*, n. 76, (Special number "A Semana de 22 descentrada", Gênese Andrade (ed.)), São Paulo, 2023, pp. 121–128

WARCHAVCHIK 1925
Gregori Warchavchik, "Acerca da arquitetura moderna", *Correio da Manhã*, Rio de Janeiro, 1 November 1925. Originally published in Italian under the title "Futurismo?", *Il Piccolo* newspaper, São Paulo, 14 June 1925

WARCHAVCHIK 1969
Gregori Warchavchik, "Homenagem a Walter Gropius", in Walter Gropius, *Bauhaus: novarquitetura*. São Paulo, 1969

WISNIK 2004
José Miguel Wisnik, "A Gaia Ciência: literatura e música popular no Brasil", in José Miguel Wisnik, *Sem receita*, São Paulo, 2004

WISNIK 2022
José Miguel Wisnik, "Semana de 22 ainda diz muito sobre a grandeza e a barbárie do Brasil de hoje", *Folha de São Paulo*, São Paulo, 13 February 2022

WOLFF 1985
Janet Wolff, "The Invisible Flâneuse. Women and the Literature of Modernity", *Theory, Culture & Society*, vol. 2, issue 3, November 1985

WORTMANN WELTGE 1993
Sigrid Wortmann Weltge, *Women's work. Textile art from the Bauhaus*, London, 1993

XEXÉO, BARATA AND ABREU 2005
Pedro Martins Caldas Xexéo, Mário Barata and Laura Maria Neves de Abreu, *A arte sob o olhar de Djanira*, Rio de Janeiro, 2005

ZANINI 1997
Apud Walter Zanini, *Vicente do Rego Monteiro: artista e poeta*, São Paulo, 1997

Photo Credits

© Alexandre Santos Silva: pp. 76, 174 (bottom)

Courtesy of Almeida & Dale Galeria de Arte, Photo: © Sergio Guerini: pp. 50, 82, 176, 238

Ares Soares: pp. 84, 93, 99, 101, 104, 172, 174 (top)

Bel Pedrosa: p. 228

Collection Bené Fonteles: pp. 230, 231

© Centre Pompidou, MNAM-CCI, Dist. GrandPalaisRmn. Photo: Philippe Migeat: p. 43

Coleção de Artes Visuais do Instituto de Estudos Brasileiros USP, Coleção Mário de Andrade: pp. 20, 27, 28, 29, 37, 74, 94, 96, 126

Daniel Cymbalista: p. 233

Djanira Instituto de Pesquisa e Ensino: p. 180

Eduardo Ortega: pp. 95, 146, 173

Falcão Junior: pp. 46 (top and bottom), 47, 54 (bottom), 80, 120 (right), 165, 185

FAUUSP Library Collection: pp. 154, 198

Fernando Silveira/MAB: pp. 31, 97, 149, 150, 151 (left and right), 166, 167

Fundo Flávio de Carvalho/Centro de Documentação Alexandre Eulálio-CEDAE/UNICAMP: pp. 134, 136, 137, 138, 139, 201

Gabriel Moreira: p. 128

© Gary Lawson Media: p. 105

Geraldo de Barros Archives: pp. 206, 208, 209, 210, 214, 217 (top and bottom), 219, 220, 221 (top and bottom) 222, 224 (bottom)

German Lorca: p. 202

Gustavo Scatena, Imagem Paulista: pp. 207, 225

Hildegard Rosenthal/Instituto Moreira Salles Collection: p. 114

Humberto Pimentel/Itaú Cultural: p. 187

IFUSP, Pedro Campos/Elizabeth Kajiya/Marcia Rizzuto: p. 103

Instituto John Graz: pp. 199, 273 (top and bottom)

Isabella Matheus: pp. 23, 58, 67, 122, 143, 190, 223

Ivan Shupikov: p. 162

Jaime Acioli: pp. 30, 32, 33 (top and bottom), 35, 36, 45, 48, 54 (top) 73, 75, 81, 83, 145, 148, 168, 171, 177, 183, 186, 188, 189, 192, 193, 194, 195, 229, 232, 234, 235, 241, 242, 243, 245

João Musa: p. 55

José Manuel Ballester, Col. Fundacion Juan March, Madrid: p. 157

Luiz Aureliano: p. 141

Madalena Schwartz/Instituto Moreira Salles Collection: p. 160

Museu de Arte Moderna do Rio de Janeiro: p. 142

Marcel Gautherot/Instituto Moreira Salles Collection: p. 155

Michel Favre: pp. 212, 213, 216, 224 (top)

Museu Lasar Segall: pp. 115, 116, 117, 118, 120 (left), 121, 125, 130, 131

Courtesy of Museum & Art Swindon: p. 53

The National Archives, ref. FO371/37862: pp. 282, 286

National Galleries of Scotland. Presented by the British Council in 1945, in recognition of collaboration in a series of exhibitions arranged during the 1939-45 War: p. 127

Projeto Portinari: pp. 88, 90, 91

Rafael Salim: p. 237

Romulo Fialdini/Tempo Composto: pp. 22, 24, 34, 42, 49, 64, 66, 68, 70, 71, 77, 85, 161, 163, 169, 181, 182, 264, 270, 276

Photo © Royal Academy of Arts, London, p. 285 (left and right)

Swiss National Library: pp. 78, 79

Sergio Guerini: pp. 129, 211

Photo: Tate: pp. 218 (top and bottom), 239

Thomaz Farkas/Instituto Moreira Salles Collection: p. 156

Vicente de Mello: p. 51

Zentralbibliothek Zürich: p. 111

Every effort has been made to contact the rightholders. In the event of an error or omission, we ask rightholders with legitimate claims to contact the editors.

This catalogue is published on the occasion of the exhibition
Brasil! Brasil! The Birth of Modernism

Exhibition organised by the Zentrum Paul Klee, Bern in collaboration with the Royal Academy of Arts, London.

Zentrum Paul Klee, Bern
7 September 2024 to 5 January 2025
Curated by Fabienne Eggelhöfer
and Roberta Saraiva Coutinho

Made possible through support from:

Royal Academy of Arts, London
28 January to 21 April 2025
Curated by Adrian Locke and
Rebecca Bray with Natasha Fyffe

Supported by:

Concept
Fabienne Eggelhöfer, Roberta Saraiva Coutinho

Editors
Fabienne Eggelhöfer, Nina Zimmer

Editing
Myriam Dössegger, Eduardo Jorge de Oliveira

Translation
Adriana Francisco, Sarah McGavran

Copy editing
Susie Hondl

Image rights clearance and image procurement
Andrea Bolanho

Graphic design
Flávia Nalon, Fábio Prata [ps.2]

© 2024 Zentrum Paul Klee, Bern and authors
Snoeck Verlagsgesellschaft mbH Cologne

Production
Snoeck Verlagsgesellschaft, Köln
Nievenheimer Str. 18
50739 Köln
www.snoeck.de

ISBN 978-3-86442-441-0

**Kanton Bern
Canton de Berne**

BATIA AND IDAN OFER

Schweizerische Eidgenossenschaft
Confédération suisse
Confederazione Svizzera
Confederaziun svizra

Swiss Confederation

Federal Department of Home Affairs FDHA
Federal Office of Culture FOC

SWISSLOS
Kultur Kanton Bern

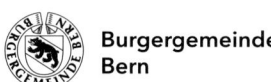

**Burgergemeinde
Bern**

RUTH & ARTHUR SCHERBARTH STIFTUNG

■■ URSULA WIRZ-STIFTUNG
■■